INSCRIPTIONS OF THE ŚARABHAPURĪYAS, PĀṆḌUVAṀŚINS AND SOMAVAṀŚINS

PART II

INSCRIPTIONS

Ajay Mitra Shastri

INDIAN COUNCIL OF HISTORICAL RESEARCH
NEW DELHI
AND
MOTILAL BANARSIDASS
DELHI

First published: 1995

Published on behalf of

INDIAN COUNCIL OF HISTORICAL RESEARCH
35, Ferozeshah Road, New Delhi 110 001

by

MOTILAL BANARSIDASS

Bungalow Road, Jawahar Nagar, Delhi 110 007

Branches:

120 Royapettah High Road, Mylapore, Madras 600 004
16 St. Mark's Road, Bangalore 560 001
Ashok Rajpath, Patna 800 004
Chowk, Varanasi 221 001

Part II ISBN: 81-208-0636-0
Set ISBN: 81-208-0637-9

PRINTED IN INDIA

BY JAINENDRA PRAKASH JAIN
AT SHRI JAINENDRA PRESS, A-45 NARAINA, PHASE I,
NEW DELHI 110 028

To
my wife
Dr Yogeshwari Shastri
who stood solidly by me
in all my undertakings

INSCRIPTIONS OF INDIA PROGRAMME

The value of inscriptions as a source of early Indian history has been widely recognised. In fact, the epigraphic records scattered all over India, Pakistan and Bangladesh form a very important source for the reconstruction of the political and cultural history of the Indian subcontinent from the third century B.C. to about the fourteenth century A.D. But for these records composed in Sanskritic and Dravidian languages and incised on a variety of materials—primarily lithic objects and copper-plates—our knowledge of the early history of India would have remained perfunctory. The number of inscriptions noticed till date far exceeds one hundred thousand, and a large majority of them offer valuable historical information not available from any other source. The mass of scattered epigraphical wealth noticed or published in numerous Indian and foreign, mostly occidental, periodicals devoted to orientology and other occasional publications, many of them long defunct or out of print, spread over nearly last two centuries, is not easily accessible to the students of Indian history. Therefore, the necessity of bringing out properly edited and handy compilations of chronologically, dynastically, regionally or otherwise allied inscriptions had been felt for a long time. As early as 1877, a volume of Aśokan edicts was published by the Archaeological Survey of India as the inaugural volume of its prestigious *Corpus Inscriptionum Indicarum* series. It was followed by a couple of other volumes comprising post-Aśokan Kharoṣṭhī (or Kharoṣṭī) and Gupta and allied epigraphs. In the last six decades or more only four more volumes including the inscriptions of the Vākāṭakas, Śilāhāras, Paramāras and Candellas and those dated in the Kalacuri-Cedi era have been brought out. In view of the urgency of the matter for historical studies and with a view to supplementing the *Corpus* series, the Indian Council of Historical Research has undertaken an ambitious programme of the publication of epigraphs dating from *circa* sixth to fourteenth century A.D., the chronological limits being flexible according to dynastic or regional requirements. Fortunately, despite certain difficulties the programme has recorded a steady progress and as many as four volumes covering the inscriptions of the Maukharis, Later Guptas, Puṣpabhūtis, Yaśovarman of Kanauj, Pallavas, Western Gaṅgas and Gajapatis of Orissa have already been published and a few more are in the pipeline. The volumes released so far have evoked welcome response.

The present volume deals with the inscriptions of the Śarabhapurīyas, Pāṇḍuvaṁśins and Somavaṁśins who played a major role in shaping the destinies of the Chhattisgarh region of Madhya Pradesh and Orissa from about the sixth to the early twelfth century A.D.

'Prachi', 23 Vidya Vihar
Rana Pratap Nagar
Nagpur-440 022
1 October 1992

AJAY MITRA SHASTRI
Co-ordinator
Inscriptions of India Programme
Indian Council of Historical Research, New Delhi

PREFACE

The present volume contains critically edited texts and detailed abstracts of the inscriptions of the Śarabhapurīyas, Pāṇḍuvaṁśins of Mekalā and South Kosalā and Somavaṁśins of Kosalā and Orissa. It is for the first time that all these historically allied important records have been brought together.

As regards the texts of the inscriptions, it must be pointed out that, unless otherwise stated, we have refrained from copying the published versions and have tried to verify them with the help of original or published facsimiles. In many a case this exercise has proved highly rewarding and it has been possible to improve upon the published readings.

No efforts have been spared to bring the present work up to date. After the volume was submitted to the Indian Council of Historical Research about seven years ago and even as the printing was in progress, several new inscriptions came to light. We have incorporated all of them either at the appropriate places in the body of the work or as a supplement. A few of these records are yet to be published. Special mention must in this connection be made of the recent discovery of as many as ten grants of the Pāṇḍuvaṁśin king Śivagupta Bālārjuna at Sirpur and Mallar, the two most important ancient sites connected with the dynasty, the salient features of which have been given in the Addenda at the end. The contents of three recently discovered copper-plate records of the Somavaṁśin king Mahābhavagupta I Janamejaya have also been noticed briefly in the same Addenda.

Two of the inscriptions incorporated in the present volume call for some remarks. It is now popularly believed that Amarāya-kula known from the Mallar plates of Vyāghrarāja was the real name of what is commonly known among historians as the Śarabhapurīya dynasty. We do not subscribe to this notion, and our reasons for it have been discussed in detail at the proper place. Therefore, the only known record of this family, *viz*., Mallar plates of Vyāghrarāja, has been included as an appendix to Section I comprising the inscriptions of the Śarabhapurīyas. The Malga plates of *Sāmanta* Indrarāja have been incorporated in an appendix to Section II devoted to the records of the Pāṇḍuvaṁśins of Mekalā, for there are cogent reasons to believe that he was closely connected with the Pāṇḍavas of Mekalā, though it is difficult to determine the exact nature of this relationship in the present state of our historical knowledge. This relationship has, for the first time, been established in these pages.

At the end photographic reproductions of practically all the epigraphs included in the present volume have been given with a view to enabling the discerning readers to check the readings. This was found advisable in view of the fact that our readings often differ from the published ones.

At the end it is our pleasant duty to acknowledge the valuable help and cooperation without which it would not have been possible to complete the present volume. I am grateful to Dr Snigdha Tripathy, Epigraphist, Orissa State Museum, Bhubaneswar, for supplying impressions of several inscriptions, both old and newly discovered, and her readings of some of the inscriptions; Professor K.S. Behera, Department of History, Utkal University, Bhubaneswar, who made available his edition of the highly valuable Banpur plates of Indraratha and the illustrative material; Dr Chandrashekhar Gupta, Senior Lecturer, Department of Ancient Indian History, Culture and Archaeology, Nagpur University, who has been of great help in the preparation of the press copy of the texts of inscriptions and the plates illustrating this work; Dr K.V. Ramesh, Director (Epigraphy), and Shri Madhava N. Katti, Chief Epigraphist of the Epigraphy Branch of the Archaeological Survey of India, for supplying some of the plates; and Shri Rahul Kumar Singh and Shri Ved Prakash Nagayach of the Archaeology Department, Government of Madhya Pradesh for supplying some of the valuable information about some recent epigraphic discoveries relating to the Pāṇḍuvaṁśins of South Kosalā. The proofs of this Part as of the first Part have been corrected by Professor K.M. Shrimali, Department of History, University of Delhi, and the Index and Errata have been done by Shri Devendra Handa, Chairman, Department of Ancient Indian History, Culture and Archaeology, Panjab University, Chandigarh. I am highly thankful to them for the great pains they have gone through in accomplishing the laborious task.

I am sincerely thankful to Dr V. Jha, Director (J P & L), and Dr B.K. Pandeya, Deputy Director (Research), Indian Council of Historical Research, New Delhi, for the keen interest they have taken in the publication of this volume.

We crave the indulgence of the discerning readers for the numerous misprints that have crept in despite careful proof-reading. Some of the more serious errors have been listed in the errata. Hyphens to mark the incompleteness of words at the end of lines in the texts of inscriptions have often been left out and letters of compounds have often been wrongly separated. The plates at the end leave much to be desired both as regards the quality of reproduction and the captions.

AJAY MITRA SHASTRI

'Prachi', 23 Vidya Vihar
Rana Pratap Nagar
Nagpur-440 022
1 October 1992

ABBREVIATIONS

ABORI	*Annals of the Bhandarkar Oriental Research Institute*
ARIE	*Annual Report on Indian Epigraphy*
ASI, AR	*Archaeological Survey of India, Annual Report*
BMC, AI	*Catalogue of Indian Coins in the British Museum* *Catalogue of the Coins of Ancient India*
BSS	Bombay Sanskrit Series
CASR	*Cunningham's Archaeological Survey Reports*
CII	*Corpus Inscriptionum Indicarum*
DMO	*Dynasties of Mediaeval Orissa* by Binayak Misra
DHNI	*Dynastic History of Northern India* by H.C. Ray
EI	*Epigraphia Indica*
HCIP	*History and Culture of the Indian People* edited by R.C. Majumdar *et al.*
HDS	*History of Dharmaśāstra* by P.V. Kane
HO	*History of Orissa* by R.D. Banerji
IA	*Indian Antiquary*
IC	*Indian Culture*
ICPB	*Inscriptions in the Central Provinces and Berar* by Hira Lal
IE	*Indian Epigraphy* by D.C. Sircar
IEG	*Indian Epigraphical Glossary* by D.C. Sircar
IHQ	*Indian Historical Quarterly*
INC	*Indian Numismatic Chronicle*
IO	*Inscriptions of Orissa*, iv, by S.N. Rajaguru
JAHRS	*Journal of the Andhra Historical Research Society*
JAIH	*Journal of Ancient Indian History*
JAOS	*Journal of the American Oriental Society*
JAS	*Journal of the Asiatic Society*, Calcutta
JAS, Letters	*Journal of the Asiatic Society, Letters*
JASB	*Journal of the Asiatic Society of Bengal*
JBBRAS	*Journal of the Bombay Branch of the Royal Asiatic Society*
JBORS	*Journal of the Bihar and Orissa Research Society*
JESI	*Journal of the Epigraphical Society of India*
JIH	*Journal of Indian History*
JKHRS	*Journal of the Kalinga Historical Research Society*
JNSI	*Journal of the Numismatic Society of India*
JOI	*Journal of the Oriental Institute*
JPASB	*Journal and Proceedings of the Asiatic Society of Bengal*

JRAS	*Journal of the Royal Asiatic Society*
JRASB, Letters	*Journal of the Royal Asiatic Society of Bengal, Letters*
NHIP	*New History of the Indian People*
NS	New Series
NS	*Numismatic Supplement of the JASB*
NSP	Nirnay Sagar Press
OHRJ	*Orissa Historical Research Journal*
PAIOC	*Proceedings of the All-India Oriental Conference*
PIHC	*Proceedings of the Indian History Congress*
SBE	Sacred Books of the East
SBH	Sacred Books of the Hindus
SIE	*Studies in Indian Epigraphy*
SII	*South Indian Inscriptions*
VIJ	*Vishveshvaranand Indological Journal*

CONTENTS

SUPPLEMENTARY INSCRIPTIONS

LIST OF ILLUSTRATIONS

IV: INSCRIPTIONS OF THE SOMAVAṀŚINS

SUPPLEMENTARY INSCRIPTIONS

PART II

INSCRIPTIONS

I

INSCRIPTIONS OF THE ŚARABHAPURĪYAS

I : I

PĪPARḌŪLĀ PLATES[1] OF NARENDRA, YEAR 3

Provenance: Pīparḍūlā, Raipur District, Madhya Pradesh.

References: D.C. Sircar and L.P. Pandeya Sarma, *IHQ*, xix, 139–46 and plates; S.P. Chaturvedi, *ibid.*, 358-59; D.C. Sircar, *ibid.*, xx, 82-83.

Language: Sanskrit. In prose except the usual benedictory and imprecatory stanzas at the end and the legend on the seal.

Metre: *Verses* 1–3: *Anuṣṭubh.*

Script: Box-headed variety of the Central Indian alphabet.

Date: Regnal Year 3, Mārgaśira 10. First half of the sixth century A.D.

TEXT[2]

First Plate

1 सिद्धम् [3][।*] स्वस्ति [।*] शरभपुरान्महाराजश्रीनरेन्द्रः
2 नन्दपुरभोगीयशर्करापद्रके ब्राह्मणा–
3 दीन्प्रतिवासिकुटुम्बिनो बोधयति [।*]
4 एष ग्रामो राहुदेवेन स्वपुण्याभिवृद्ध–
5 ये ब्राह्मणवाजसनेयभात्रेय[4] सगोत्र–

Second Plate : First Side

6 स्वामिप्पाय[5] ताम्र[6] (म्र)-शासनेनातिसृष्टो मया–
7 पि च भचाटभटप्रावेश्य इत्यनुमोदितो
8 यतो भवद्भिरस्य यथाकालं मेय–
9 हिरण्यादीनां प्रत्यायानामुपनयः
10 कर्त्तव्यः [।*] भविष्यतश्च भोगपतीनभिनन्दयति

1. 5¼″ long and 3½″ broad.
2. From plates in *IHQ*, xix, between pp. 145 and 146.
3. Expressed by a symbol.
4. Read °वाजसनेयात्रेय°
5. Sanskrit स्वाम्यात्मने
6. Sircar and Pandeya Sarma: ताम्र°

Second Plate : Second Side

11 पूर्वंदत्तेरनुपालनाच्छ्रेयस। सम्बन्धः ग्रा–
12 च्छेदाच्च प्रत्यपाय[7] इत्यनुप्रपश्यद्भिर्भवद्भि–
13 रस्य ग्रामस्यानुपालनं कर्त्तव्यम् [।*]
14 व्यासगीतावत्र श्लोकावुदाहरन्ति । पूर्व्वं–
15 दत्तां द्विजातिभ्यो यत्नाद्रक्ष युधिष्ठिर [।*]

Third Plate

16 मह्रीं मह्रीमतां श्रेष्ठ दानाच्छ्रयोनुपालनम् [॥१॥*]
17 षष्टिं वर्षसहस्राणि स्वर्ग्गे वसति भूमिदः [।*]
18 ग्राच्छेत्ता चानुमन्ता च तान्येव नरके
19 वसे [त् ॥२॥*][8]
प्रवर्द्धमानति (तृ) तीयवर्षस्य मार्ग्गशि–
20 **रमासदिवसे दशमे** [।*]
उत्कीर्ण्णा[9] श्रीदत्तेनेति ।[*]

Seal[10]

1 खड्गधाराजितभुवैः[11] **शर [भात्प्रा]** प्तजन्मनः [।*]
2 नृपतेश्श्री**नरेन्द्रस्य** शासनं रिपुशासिन [:] [॥३॥*]

ABSTRACT

The grant was issued from **Śarabhapura.**[12] It records that *Mahārāja* **Narendra** informed the agriculturist inhabitants including the Brāhmaṇas residing at

7. Read प्रत्यवाय
8. Sircar and Pandeya Sarma have shown it as the concluding part of line 18.
9. Sircar and Pandeya Sarma: उत्कीर्ण्णं. Read उत्कीर्ण्णं. The word *śāsanaṁ* has to be inserted after it.
10. The seal is circular with a diameter of about 2-4/5″. It is partitioned into two halves by a couple of horizontal lines in the middle. The upper half contains the representation of the motif of Abhiṣeka-Lakṣmī, with the goddess Lakṣmī standing in a frontal position, flanked by an elephant on each side pouring water over her from pitchers held in their trunks. The lower half contains the legend in the *Anuṣṭubh* metre. As the seal has not been reproduced by the original editors and I have not been able to see the original plates, the reading of the legend as given by Sircar and Pandeya Sarma is reproduced here. The description of the seal is also based on their account given by them.
11. Sircar and Pandeya Sarma suggest to amend भुवः to क्षितेः in order to meet the metrical requirements (*IHQ*, xix, 145, fn. 15). But *contra* S.P. Chaturvedi (*ibid.*, 358-59) who thinks that the remark of Sircar and Pandeya Sarma about the metrical defect and the suggested emendation both are uncalled for. For Sircar's rejoinder, see *ibid.*, xx, 82-83.
12. It has not been identified satisfactorily though several conjectures have been hazarded. For details, see introduction.

Śarkarāpadraka situated in the district (*bhoga*) of Nandapura[13] that the village (Śarkarāpadraka) had been granted, by a copper-plate charter, by Rāhudeva,[14] for the increase of his own religious merit, in favour of the Brāhmaṇa Svāmippa (Svāmyātman) belonging to the Vājasaneya (*caraṇa*) and Ātreya *gotra*, and that he approved the grant by making it free from the entry of the irregular (*cāṭa*) and regular (*bhaṭa*) soldiers. He further ordered the villagers to pay, in time, to the donee all the taxes (*pratyāya*) including the share of the agricultural produce (*meya*) and cash money (*hiraṇya*).

The future *bhoga-patis* (district officers) are requested to protect the grant of the village keeping in view the fact that by protecting the grant made previously (*i.e.*, by others) one gets prosperity and incurs sin by abrogating it. In support of it a couple of stanzas is quoted in the name of Vyāsa lauding the protection of a grant as more meritorious than making a new grant and setting out rewards and punishments in the other world accruing to the giver of the land and the violator of the grant respectively.

The grant was made on the **tenth day of the month of Mārgaśira in the prosperous third year (of Narendra's reign).**

It was engraved by Śrīdatta.

The legend on the seal states that the charter belongs to the illustrious king **Narendra,** son of Śarabha and chastiser of the enemies, who had conquered the earth by the edge of his sword.

13. The village Śarkarāpadraka and Nandapura, the headquarters of the district in which the donated village was situated, cannot be identified definitely. Neither of these is traceable in the proximity of Pīparḍūlā, the findspot of the charter. There is a Nandagaur on the Mahanadi in the former Sarangarh State (now incorporated in the Raigarh District) and nearby there exists a village called Sākarā which latter may perhaps be identical with Śarkarāpadraka. There still exist two adjoining villages named Nandaur big and Nandaur small in the Bilaspur District, some 40 miles from Sākarā, which contain some remains of antiquarian interest and may not improbably be identified with the headquarters of the district of Nandapura. Yet another village called Sākarā exists in the Raipur District; but Nandapura is not traceable in its vicinity. For details, see *ibid.*, xix, 144-45.
14. No information is supplied about Rāhudeva. It has been suggested by Sircar and Pandeya Sarma that he was probably a *bhogapati* of the Nandapura-*bhoga* forming part of the kingdom of Narendra with the limited right of alienation.

I : II

KURUD PLATES[1] OF NARENDRA, YEAR 24

Provenance: Kurud, Raipur District, Madhya Pradesh.

References: Moreshwar G. Dikshit, *EI*, xxxi, 263-66 and plates facing pp. 264 and 265; D.C. Sircar, *ibid.*, 267-68; Ajay Mitra Shastri, ***Studies in Indian Epigraphy*** (***Journal of the Epigraphical Society of India***), ii, 50–54.

Language: Sanskrit. In prose except the customary benedictive and imprecatory verses at the end and the legend on the seal.

Metre: Verses 1–4: ***Anuṣṭubh.***

Script: Box-headed variety of the Central Indian alphabet.

Date: Regnal Year 24, Vaiśākha 4. First half of the sixth century A.D.

TEXT[2]

First Plate

1 सिद्धम्[3] [।*] स्वस्ति । [।*] विजयस्कन्धावारात्**तिलकेश्वरवासका**त्परमभाग–

2 वतो मातापितृपादानुद्ध्यातः श्रीमहाराज**नरेन्द्रः चुल्लाड**–

3 **सीम (मा)**[4] भोगीयकेशवके ब्राह्मणपुरस्सरान्प्रतिवासि–

4 कुटुम्बिनस्समाज्ञापयति [।*] विदितमस्तु वः यथाय (यं) ग्राम [ः*]

5 परमभट्टारकपादै [ः*] भश्रुतस्वामिने[5] धारणिसगोत्राय

Second Plate : First Side

6 गङ्गाय (यां) मज्जन (नं) कुर्व्वद्भि [ः*] तालपत्रशासनेन स्वपुण्याभिवृ[6]–

7 द्धये दत्तकः [।*] तच्च तालपत्रशासन (नं) ग्रिहदाधे[7] दग्धमित्यधि–

8 करणावधारणया प्राक्प्रभ्रि (भृ)त्यव्यवच्छेदभोगेनाय (यं) ग्रा–

1. 5.9″ long and 3.2″ broad.
2. From plates in *EI*, xxxi, opposite pp. 264 and 265.
3. Expressed by a symbol.
4. Dikshit: °सीमा°
5. In line 9 below the name is spelt as Bhāśrutasvāmin.
6. The medial sign for *ṛ* is detached from *v* and is open to right. It differs from the same medial sign in *tṛ* in line 2 above where it is formed by elongating the vertical of *t* and making a strong curve as its lower end.
7. Read गृहदाहे

9 मो भुज्यत इति ।।[8] अधुना भाश्रुतस्वामिपुत्रशङ्खस्वामिने

10 परमभट्टारकपादाना (नां) पुण्याप्यायनादे (यै) व ताम्रशास–

Second Plate : Second Side

11 नेनानुमोदितः इत्येवमुपलभ्यास्याज्ञाश्रवण–विधेया

12 भूत्वा यथो (था) कालमुचितभोगभाग–धान्यहिरण्यादोरुप–

13 नयं कर्ष्यथेति[9] ।। भविष्यतश्च भूपा [न्*] कुशलोपेतमनु–

14 दर्शयति ।[10] दूतकमधिकरण [म्*] ।। व्यासगीता (तां) श्चक श्लोकानुदाह–

15 रन्ति ।। बहुभिर्व्वसुधा दत्ता राजभिस्सगरादिभि [:*] । यस्य यस्य

Third Plate

16 यदा भूमिस्तस्य तस्य तदा फल[म्*] ।।[१।।*] पूर्व्वदत्तां द्विजातिभ्यो य–

17 त्नाद्रक्ष युधिष्ठिर[।*] महीं महिमतां[11] श्रेष्ठ दानाच्छ्रयोनुपाल–

18 न [म्*] ।।[२।।*] षष्टिवर्षसहस्राणि स्वर्गे मो[12]दति भूमिदः [।*] आच्छे–

19 त्ता चानुमन्ता च्च (च) तान्येव नरके वसेत् [।।३।।*] **प्रवर्द्धमानविज–**

20 **यराज्यसम्व (संव) त्सरे चतुर्व्विङश (र्व्विंश) तिमे २० ४ वैशाखदि ४**

21 [13]उत्कि (त्की) र्ण्णं श्रीदत्तेनेति ।।[14]

Seal[15]

1 खड्गधाराजितभुव [:*] **शरभात्**प्राप्तजन्मनः ।

2 नृपते [श्श्री] **नरेन्द्र**स्य शासनं रिपुशासन [म् ।।४।।*][16]

8. These *daṇḍas* (punctuation marks) are not required.
9. Read करिष्यथेति
10. Dikshit gives two *daṇḍas*, but the facsimile shows only a single *daṇḍa*.
11. Read महीमतां
12. Part of the medial sign for *o* is attached to the top and part to the lower part of the right vertical of *m*.
13. This line is engraved in the middle, the space on its two sides being left blank.
14. The conclusion of the epigraph is indicated by two vertical lines showing leftward curve on top.
15. The seal is circular, its diameter being about 2·8″. It is divided into two equal compartments by a couple of horizontal lines in the middle. In the upper half we have the figure of goddess Lakṣmī, standing on a lotus facing full front, being anointed by an elephant on either side pouring water over her from a jar held in its uplifted trunk. The topmost part of the seal bears the representation of the sun and the moon in the form of a small pellet and a crescent respectively. The lower half is occupied by the two-line legend in the *Anuṣṭubh* metre.
16. In the legend on the seal attached to the Pīparḍūlā plates of Narendra we have रिपुशासिनः. See *supra* No. I:I.

ABSTRACT

The charter was issued from the camp of victory at **Tilakeśvara.**[17] by *Mahārāja* **Narendra** who is described as a devout worshipper of Bhagavat (*i.e.*, Viṣṇu) and as meditating upon the feet of his parents.[18] He commands the agriculturist inhabitants including the Brāhmaṇas living at the village Keśavaka[19] situated in the district (*bhoga*) of Cullāḍasīmā[20] that the village (Keśavaka) was (originally) given away by the *Paramabhaṭṭāraka-pāda*,[21] while taking bath in the Gaṅgā,[22] in favour of the Brāhmaṇa Bhaśrutasvāmin (or Bhāśrutasvāmin)[23] belonging to the Dhāraṇi *gotra* for the increase of his own religious merit, by means of a charter written on palm leaves (*tālapatraśāsana*).[24] That palm-leaf charter was burnt in a conflagration in the donee's house and, therefore, King **Narendra**, after ascertaining by official investigation that the village was in continuous enjoyment (*i.e.*, possession) by the donee, confirmed the grant by means of a copper-plate charter in favour of Śaṅkhasvāmin, son of Bhaśrutasvāmin, for the religious merit of the *Parambhaṭṭāraka-pāda*. The villagers were asked to obey the donee and pay him, in time, all the dues including periodical offerings (*bhoga*), share of the produce (*bhāga*), grains (*dhānya*) and cash money (*hiraṇya*).[25]

The *dūtaka*[26] of this grant was the secretariat (*adhikaraṇa*) itself.[27]

17. It cannot be identified. But judging from the name-ending *īśvara*, it appears to have denoted a Śiva temple and the king might have encamped in its vicinity.
18. It will be noticed that the allusion to the king's religious leanings and his devotion to parents, which is conspicuous by its absence in the same king's Pīparḍūlā plates, has been added here for the first time and is hereafter met with in practically all the records of the dynasty.
19. Keśavaka is probably represented by the modern village of Keshwa on the bank of a nullah known as Keshwanala, some 5½ miles to the south-east of Mahasamund, the head-quarters of the tahsil of the same name in the Raipur District.
20. The *bhoga* may have been so called because it probably bordered on a place called Cullāḍa, which has been tentatively identified with the modern village of Charoda, about 7 miles due east of Keshwa. For another possible reference to the village Keśavaka and the district Cullāḍasīmā see No. I:VIII below. Also *vide Studies in Indian Epigraphy*, ii, 50-54.
21. Dikshit takes this expression to refer to Narendra's father. But as pointed out by Sircar, in all probability the allusion is to the Gupta overlord.
22. According to Dikshit, the river Gaṅgā mentioned here can only be the Mahanadi. But there is nothing to show that the Mahanadi was ever known as Gaṅgā, and in view of the mention of the Gupta overlord, the Gaṅgā cannot be identified with any river except the well-known river of that name.
23. The name is spelt in both ways.
24. Reference to a charter written on palm-leaves is extremely rare.
25. The Pīparḍūlā grant specifies only *meya* and *hiraṇya*; the expressions *bhoga* and *bhāga* as revenue terms are met with here for the first time in so far as the Śarabhapurīya records are concerned.
26. *I.e.*, executor or the conveyor of the royal order in respect of the grant to the concerned officers.
27. The mention of the secretariat (*adhikaraṇa*) itself functioning as the *dūtaka* of a grant is of rare occurrence in inscriptions.

The future kings are exhorted to protect the grant, and three usual benedictive and imprecatory stanzas, attributed to Vyāsa, describing the merit arising from making and protecting land-grants and the sin accruing from their violation, are quoted.

The grant was issued on the **fourth day of the month of Vaiśākha in the twenty-fourth year[27a] of the prosperous and victorious reign (of Narenda).** It was engraved by Śrīdatta.[28]

The metrical legend on the seal describes King Narendra almost in the same manner as that on the seal of No. I above.

27*a*. The year is indicated both in words and figures, but the day only in figures.

28. The Pipardūlā plates were also engraved by Śrīdatta.

I : III

RAWAN PLATE[1] OF NARENDRA

Provenance: Rawan,[2] Raipur District, Madhya Pradesh.

References: S. Bajpai, *Prāchya Pratibhā*, v (i), 182-183 and plate facing p. 182; Usha Jain, *JESI*, vi, 44-45 and plate facing p. 46.

Language: Sanskrit. In prose.[3]

Script: Box-headed variety of Central Indian alphabet.

Date: Beginning of the sixth century A.D.

TEXT[4]

सिद्धम्[5] [।*] स्वस्ति [।*] **शरभपुरात्परम**–भागवतो मातापितृपादानुद्धयात–
श्श्रीमहाराज**नरेन्द्र** [:*] मण्टराजभुक्तौ तोरामके ब्राह्मणादी [न्*] प्रति
वासिकुटुम्बिनस्समाज्ञापयति [।*] विदितमस्तु वो यथास्माभिर्व्वं–
टपद्रकीयकारितकदेवकुले भगवते श्रीधरस्वामिने मातृ(तृ)रा–
जकुलाना (नां) पुण्याभिवृद्धये खण्डस्फुटित—संस्कार्बलिचरु–
सतृ(त्र)

ABSTRACT

Beginning with the *siddham* symbol and *svasti* and issued from **Śarabhapura,** the charter records that King **Narendra,** who is described as in earlier records, granted the village Torāmaka[6] situated in the Maṇṭarāja *bhukti*[7] to the temple

1. Rectangular in shape, the plate is 9 cms. in breadth and 19 cms. in length. Its ends are rounded and there is a hole about the middle of the left margin for the passage of the ring.
2. The plate was found in possession of a resident of the village Rawan, but according to his information the plate was actually discovered at Mallar. If this information is correct, the plate should be called 'Mallar Plate'.
3. The plates containing imprecatory stanzas and the seal bearing an eulogistic verse are missing.
4. From plate in *Prāchya Pratibhā*, v (i) and *JESI*, vi.
5. Expressed by a symbol.
6. Both Bajpai and Jain took the name of the village to be Ārāmaka; but it is clearly Torāmaka. It has not been identified.
7. Both Bajpai and Jain relate it to king Maṇṭarāja of Kurāla in Dakṣiṇāpatha defeated by Samudragupta and suggest that his kingdom was situated in the Chattisgarh region of Madhya Pradesh. But as the ruler of Kosala, which covered the Chhattisgarh region

of God Śrīdharasvāmin at Vaṭapadra[8] for meeting the expenditure on its repairs, the *bali caru* offerings and the free feeding house which was evidently attached to the temple. The merit from the gift was to accrue to the family of Mātṛrāja.[9]

---

and the adjoining area of Orissa is mentioned separately, this identification is unlikely to be correct. The identity of the name of the chief in question and of that of the *bhukti* appears to be accidental

8. A village named Vaṭapadra is mentioned in no. III:VI, text-lines 5-6 as situated in the Kośīranandapura *viṣaya*. Evidently our Vaṭapadra has nothing to do with it unless it is supposed that the area in which the village was situated was reorganised under the Pāṇḍuvaṁśins. As there are numerous villages named after the banyan tree, the village cannot be identified satisfactorily.
9. No information is forthcoming about this Mātṛrāja and the position he occupied. But he must have been an influential personage. The use of plural (*kulānām*) is rather strange. Alternatively, it may refer to the regal family (*rāja-kula*) of the mother (*mātṛ*) of Narendra. If this interpretation is accepted, one will have to believe that Narendra's mother hailed from a royal family. But the relevant expression may also be taken to mean 'of the mother and members of the royal family.' The last explanation will explain the employment of the plural number.

I : IV

AMGURA PLATES[1] OF JAYARĀJA, YEAR 3

Provenance: Amgura, Kalahandi District, Orissa.

Reference: Snigdha Tripathy, *JESI*, iv, 70–75 with illustrations on pp. 72–74, D.C. Sircar and Jitamitra Prasad Singh Deo, *Indian Museum Bulletin* XI, part 1, pp. 57-59.

Language: Sanskrit. In prose except for the benedictory and imprecatory stanzas and the inscription on the seal.

Metres: Verses 1–3, 5: *Anuṣṭubh*; Verse 4: *Indravajrā*.

Script: Box-headed variety of the Central Indian alphabet.

Date: Regnal year 3, Māgha 7. About the middle of the sixth century A.D.

TEXT[2]

First Plate

1 सिद्धम्[3] ।[3a] स्वस्ति [।*] **शरभपुरा**त्परमभागवतो मातापितृपादानु–

2 द्ध्यातश्श्री**महाजयराज** [:*] साम्पराजभुक्तीयराज्यग्रामे प्र–

3 तिवासिनस्समाज्ञापयति [।*] विदितमस्तु वो यथास्मा–

4 भिरयं ग्रामो वाजसनेयकौशिकसगोत्रब्राह्मणविष्णुस्वा–

5 मिने मातापित्रोरात्मनश्च पुण्याभिवृद्धये उदकपूर्व्वं [ँ] ताम्र–

Second Plate : First Side

6 शासनेनातिसृष्टस्ते यूयमेवोपलभ्यास्याज्ञाश्रवणविधेया[4] भू–

7 त्वा यथोचितं भोगभागमुपनेष्यथ[5] [।*] भविष्यतश्च भूमिपाला–

8 न्बोधयति[6] [।*] भवद्भिरप्यस्या दत्ते [:*] प्रतिपालनं कर्त्तव्य–

9 मतश्च व्यासगीतानपि श्लोकानुदाहरंत्ति (रन्ति) । बहुभिर्व्वसुधा

10 दत्ता राजभिस्सगरादिभिः [।*] यस्य यस्य यदा भूमिस्तस्य तस्य

1. Each plate measures 5·9/10″ in length and 3·2/10″ in breadth.
2. From plates in the *Journal of the Epigraphical Society of India*, iv.
3. Expressed by a very cursive symbol.

3a. This mark of punctuation, which is joined to the *siddham* symbol, has not been noticed by Tripathy who supplies it on her own.

4. Read यूयमेवमुपलभ्यास्या°
5. In other plates of this ruler we have ०मूपनयन्तः सुखं प्रतिवत्स्यथ.
6. Other records of this king generally have भूमिपाननुदर्शयति.

Second Plate : Second Side

11 तदा फलं (लम्) [।।१।।*] स्वदत्ता (त्तां) परदत्तां वा यत्नाद्रक्ष युधिष्ठिर [।*]म–

12 ही (हीं) महीमता (तां) श्रेष्ठ दानाच्छ्रेयोनुपालनं (नम्)। [।२।।*] षष्ठिम्वर्षं[7]–

13 सहस्राणि स्वर्ग्गे वसति भूमिद[:] [।*] आच्छेप्ता[8] चा–

14 नुमन्ताच तात्येव नरके वसे [त्।।] [३।।*] अग्नेरपत्यं प्रथमं

15 सुवर्ण्णं भूर्व्वैष्णवी सूर्य्यसुताश्च गाव [:।*] लोकास्त्रय–

Third Plate

16 स्तेन भवंत्ति[9] दत्ताः ।।[10] य X काञ्चनं[11] गाञ्च महीञ्च दद्या–

17 दिति [।।४।।*] दूतकमधिकरण [म्।*] स्वमुखाज्ञया च[12] **प्रवर्द्धमानवि–**

18 **जयसाम्वत्सार[13] ३ माघ** ७ उक्ति (क्ती) र्ण्णं [ँ] सुवर्ण्णा–

19 काराचलसिङ्घेन[14] ।।

Seal[15]

1 प्रसन्न (हृ) दयस्यैव विक्क्रमाक्क्रा[ँ]तविद्विषः [१]

2 श्रीमतो **जयराजस्य** शासन[ँ] रिपुशासन[ँ] [।।५।।*]

ABSTRACT

Issued from **Śarabhapura,** the charter registers the order of the King **Mahā-Jayarāja,** described simply as a devout devotee of Bhagavat (Viṣṇu) and as meditating upon the feet of his parents, to the inhabitants of the village called Rājyagrāma situated in the Sāmparāja *bhukti*[16] that he had granted the village, by means of a copper-plate charter, in favour of the Brāhmaṇa Viṣṇusvāmin, who was a student of the Vājasaneyi Saṁhitā (of the *Yajurveda*), for the in-

7. Read षष्टिं वष° or षष्टिवर्षं°
8. Read आच्छेत्ता as in other plates of the dynasty.
9. Tripathy: भवान्ति. Read भवन्ति
10. These marks of punctuation are superfluous.
11. Read कांचनं or काञ्चनं
12. This letter, which is clear in the facsimile, has escaped the notice of Tripathy.
13. Read संवत्सर
14. Read °सिंहेन
15. The seal has a diameter of 3·4/10″ Its surface is divided into two parts by a couple of horizontal lines drawn across it. The upper part contains the representation, in relief on a countersunk surface, of the goddess Lakṣmī standing to full front being bathed by an elephant on her either side standing on a lotus flower by the trunk raised above her head. A full blown lotus is to be seen in the right corner and a conch shell on the proper left. The lower half is occupied by a stanza in the *Anuṣṭubh* metre incised in two lines.
16. Neither the donated village nor the chief place of the *bhukti* wherein it was included has been identified.

crease of the religious merit of his parents as well as of his own self and that knowing this they should be obedient to the donee and pay him the usual periodical offerings (*bhoga*) and the royal share of produce (*bhāga*).

Next follows the exhortation to the future rulers of the land to maintain the grant, and this request is sought to be supported by citing four benedictory and imprecatory stanzas in the name of the sage Vyāsa highlighting the merit accruing from making or protecting a grant and the sin following its violation.

The *adhikaraṇa* (secretariat) acted as the *dūtaka*[17] of the grant, and the order concerning the grant was issued by the king himself by the word of his own mouth.

The charter was issued on the **seventh day of the month of Māgha in the third year of the increasingly victorious reign (of Mahā-Jayarāja).**

The record was incised by the goldsmith Acalasiṁha.[18]

The verse on the seal refers the charter, styled chastiser of the enemies, to the illustrious *Jayarāja*, who is described as the son of Prasanna (*i.e.*, Prasannamātra) and as annihilator of his enemies by his own prowess.

17. The *dūtaka* either conveyed a request or message for grant (as in the Khalimpur plates of Dharmapāla, *EI*, iv, 250) or, according to some scholars, carried the royal order about land-grant to the local officers who then drew up the charter and delivered it to the donee/donees. But the present inscription seems to indicate that the *dūtaka* was responsible for the execution of the charter. In the Kurud plates of Narendra (above, No. I:II) also the *adhikaraṇa* is said to have acted as *dūtaka*.
18. Acalasiṁha is mentioned as the engraver in other records of Jayarāja also. But it is only in the present epigraph that he is called a goldsmith.

I : V

MALLAR PLATES[1] OF MAHĀ-JAYARĀJA, YEAR 5

Provenance: Mallar, Bilaspur District, Madhya Pradesh.
Reference: D.C. Sircar, *EI*, xxxiii, 155–58 and plates facing pp. 156 and 157.
Language: Sanskrit. In prose but for the usual benedictive and imprecatory verses at the end.
Metres: Verse 1: *Vasantatilakā*; Verse 2: *Indravajrā*; Verses 3-4: *Anuṣṭubh*.
Script: Box-headed variety of the Central Indian alphabet.
Date: Regnal Year 5, Kārttika 5. About the middle of the sixth century A.D.

TEXT[2]

First Plate

1 स्वस्ति [।*] **शरभपुरात्** द्वि(वि)-क्क्रमोपनतसामंत्त(त) चूडामणि-प्रभाप्रसेकाम्बु–
2 भिधौँतपादयुगलो रिपुविलासिनीसीमत्तो(न्तो)द्धरणहेतुर्व्वसुवसुधा–
3 गोप्रद परमभागवतो मातापित्रि(तृ)पादानुद्ध्यातः[3] **श्रीमहाजयराजः**
4 श्रंत्त(त) रनालकीयकदं(द) म्बपद्रुल्लके प्रतिवासिकुटुम्बिनः[4](न) स्समा–
5 ज्ञापयति ।[5] विदितमस्तु वो यथास्माभिरयं ग्रामस्त्रिदशपति–
6 सदनसुखप्रतिष्ठाकरो यावद्रविशशिताराकिरणप्रतिहत–

Second Plate : First Side

7 घोराद्ध(न्ध) कार(रं) जगदवतिष्ठते तावदुपभोज्य(ग्य) [:*]
सनिधिस्सोपनिधि[6]—
8 रचाटभटप्रावै(वे)श्य [:*] सर्व्वंकरविसर्ज्जित × कौत्ससगोत्रब्राह्मणकप–

1. Measuring about 5·4" long and 2·95" broad, these plates have rounded corners. The central plate is thicker (about 1/8") than the other two plates (1/16").
2. From plates in *EI*, xxxiii, opposite pp. 156 and 157.
3. The *visarga* here as well in lines 4 and 11 and once in line 17 below is indicated by two horizontal strokes. Elsewhere it is expressed by a couple of dots placed one above the other as at present.
4. The *visarga*, which is indicated by two minute horizontal strokes placed one above the other, has escaped Sircar's notice. It is, however, unnecessary. Alternatively, the reduplication of the letters that follows would be superfluous.
5. The mark of punctuation is indicated by two dots placed one above the other.
6. Originally the *akṣara dhī* was engraved, but later the dot inside the circle indicating the length of the medial was cancelled.

9 द्दिस्वामिनस्सोभोपरागे[7] मातापित्रोरात्मनश्च पुण्याभिव्र (वृ) द्ध–

10 ये उदकपूर्व्वं ताम्ब्र (म्र) शासनेनातिसृष्टः[8] स्ते[9] यूयमेवमुपल–

11 भ्यास्याज्ञाश्रवणविधेया भूत्वा यथोचितं भोगभागमुपनयंत्तः (यन्तः) सुखं

12 प्रतिवस्य (त्स्य) थ ।[10] भविष्यतश्च भूमिपानानुदर्शयति ।[10]
दानाद्विशि[ष्ट]–

Second Plate : Second Side

13 मनुपालनजं पुराणात्[11] धर्म्मेषु निश्चितधिय ⌒ प्रवदंत्ति (दन्ति)[12] धर्म्मं[13] [।*]

14 तस्मा[द्*] द्विजाय सुविशुद्धकुलश्रुताय दत्तां भुवं भवतु वो मति–

15 रेव गोप्तुं[14] (प्तुम्) [।।१।।*] भवद्भिरप्येषा दत्तिरनुपाल–

16 यितव्या ।[15] व्यासगीतांश्चात्र श्लोकानुदाहंरत्ति (रन्ति) ।[16] अग्नेरपत्यं

17 प्रथमं सुवर्णं ।[17] भूर्व्वैष्णवी सूर्य्यंसुताश्च गांवः[18] [।*]दत्तास्त्रय–

18 स्तेन भवंत्ति (वन्ति) लोका ।[19] य X काञ्चनं गां (गा) ञ्च महीञ्च दद्या [त्][।।२।।X]

Third Plate

19 षं (ष) ष्टिवर्षसहस्राणि स्वर्ग्गे मोदति भूमिदः [।*] आच्छेत्ता चानुमं–

20 त्ता (मन्ता) च तां (ता) न्येव नरके वसेत् [।।३।।*] बहुभिर्व्वसुधा दत्ता राजः (ज) भिस्स

21 गरादिभिः [।*] यस्य यस्य यदा भूमिस्तस्य तस्य तदा

22 फलं (ल) मिति [।।४।।*][20] स्वमुखाज्ञया ।[21] उक्ती (क्तौ) र्ण्णं अचलसिङ्घेन[22][।*]

7. Read. °स्वामिने सोमोपरागे. Sircar, however, indicates the possibility that the sixth case ending may have been employed here for the Brāhmaṇa having paid some money for the purchase of the village. See *EI*, xxxiii, 157, fn. 5.
8. The *visarga* is redundant.
9. Read °सृष्टस्ते. Alternatively °सृष्टः ते. As suggested by Sircar (*ibid.*, 157, fn. 7), in such contexts in this as well as other records *tad* would be a better expression than *te* which is used wrongly.
10. This mark of punctuation consists of a horizontal stroke with one dot above and one below it.
11. Read पुराणा
12. Sircar: प्रवदन्ति
13. Read धर्म्मम्
14. After this the words मतिरेव गोप्तुं were engraved for the second time and were, on realising the redundance, rubbed off.
15. The punctuation mark is composed of a horizontal stroke with one dot above and one below it.
16. The mark of punctuation is here indicated by a couple of horizontal strokes placed one above the other.
17. The punctuation mark, indicated by a couple of horizontal strokes, is superfluous.
18. The *visarga* here consists of two horizontal strokes.
19. The mark of punctuation, consisting of a couple of horizontal strokes, which has escaped the notice of Sircar, is superfluous.
20. Better read फलम् [।।४।।*] इति
21. The mark of punctuation here consists of a horizontal stroke with one stroke above and one below it.
22. Read अचलसिंहेन

23 प्रवर्द्धमानविजयसंव्वत्सर पं(प)ञ्च[23] ५ कार्त्तिकदिसो[24] ५ [।।*]

ABSTRACT

After mentioning the place of issue, *Śarabhapura,* the preamble introduces king *Mahā-Jayarāja* who is described as one whose pair of feet is washed by the waters in the form of the flowing forth of the radiance of the crest-jewels of the feudatory chiefs, bowing down before him, subdued by his prowess, and as the cause of the tearing out of the parted hair of the women of his enemies, the giver of wealth, land and cows, the devout worshipper of Bhagavat (Viṣṇu), and meditating upon the feet of his parents.[25]

Next is recorded the King's order to the agriculturist house-holders residing at Kadambadrupallaka[26] situated in Antaranālaka[27] to the effect that he had given away, by means of a copper-plate charter, this village (Kadambadrupallaka), for the increase of the religious merit of his parents and of his own self, to the Brāhmaṇa Kaparddisvāmin of the Kautsa *gotra,* on the occasion of a lunar eclipse. The grant, which was intended to last as long as the darkness is removed by the rays of the sun, the moon and the stars (i.e.., for ever), was exempted from all the taxes and the entry of both the irregular (*cāṭa*) and regular (*bhaṭa*) soldiers and carried with it right to major and minor treasures (*nidhi* and *upanidhi*). The villagers are asked to live in the village happily by obeying the donee and paying him the royal share of the produce (*bhāga*) and the periodical offerings (*bhoga*).

The future rulers are then requested to protect the grant, and four customary verses, three of them in the name of Vyāsa, setting out the merit accruing from land-grants and their protection and sins consequent upon their violation, are quoted.

The charter was incised by Acalasiṁha. It was issued on the **fifth day of the month of Kārttika in the fifth year of the increasingly victorious reign (of Mahā-Jayarāja)**.

23. Read संवत्सर: पञ्चम:. Sircar suggests to correct it to संवत्सरा:.
24. Read °दिवस: Sircar suggests दिवसा:.
25. This description of the ruling chief became stereotyped and is met with in almost all the later records of the Śarabhapurīyas.
26. Sircar suggests that the name of the gift village Kadambapadraullaka seems to be a combination of the names of two contiguous localities called Kadambapadraka and Ullaka. It cannot be identified.
27. Antaranālaka, which was evidently the name of the district, has not been identified.

I : VI

ARANG PLATES[1] OF MAHĀ-JAYARĀJA, YEAR 5

Provenance: Arang, Raipur District, Madhya Pradesh.
References: A. Cunningham, *ASIR*, xvii, 15 ff. and pls. xxiv-xxv; J.F. Fleet, *Inscriptions of the Early Gupta Kings and their Successors, CII*, iii, 193-94, pl. xxvi; Hira Lal, *ICPB*, 105, No. 175; Bhandarkar's List, No. 1878.
Language: Sanskrit. In prose with the exception of customary benedictory and imprecatory verses at the end and the legend on the seal.
Metres: Verse 1: *Vasantatilakā*; Verse 2: *Indravajrā*; Verses 3–6: *Anuṣṭubh*.
Script: Box-headed variety of the Central Indian alphabet.
Date: Regnal Year 5, Mārgaśira 25. About the middle of the sixth century A.D.

TEXT[2]

First Plate

1 स्वस्ति [।*] **शरभपुरात्** द्विक्क्रमो[3]पनतसामं(म)त्त(न्त)–चूडामणिप्रभाप्रसेकां(का)–
2 म्बुभिर्धो(र्धौ) तपादयुगलो रिपुविलासिनीसीमंत्तो[4]द्धरणहेतु––
3 र्व्वसुवसुधागोप्रदः⌣परमभागवतो[5] [6]मातापितृपा––
4 दानुद्धयातः श्श्री[7]**महाजयराजः** पूर्व्वराष्ट्रीय पम्वां[8] प्रति––
5 वासिकुटुं(टु)म्बिनः[9] स्समाज्ञापयति ।[10] विदितमस्तु वो यथा––

Second Plate : First Side

6 स्माभिरयं ग्राम ।[11] स्त्रिदशपतिसदनसुखप्रतिष्ठाकरो याव–

1. The plates are about $5\frac{3}{8}$" long and $2\frac{3}{4}$" broad at the ends and a little less in the middle.
2. From pl. xxvi facing p. 194 in *CII*, iii.
3. Read °राद्विक्क्रमो°
4. Read °सीमन्तो°
5. Read °प्रद⌣ परमभागवतो
6. The sign for medial *ā* is attached to the right lower limb of *m* here as well as at other places.
7. Read °द्ध्यातश्श्री°
8. As suggested by Fleet (*CII*, iii, 193, fn. 9), the intended reading probably is पम्वायां
9. The *visarga* is superfluous.
10. This mark of punctuation is indicated by a short horizontal line.
11. The mark of punctuation isunnecessary.

7 द्रविशशितारा किरणप्रतिहतघोराद्ध (न्ध) कारं[12] जग[द*] वतिष्ठत

8 तावदुपभोग्यस्सन (नि) -धि[13]स्सोपनिधिरचाटभटप्रावेश्यस्स–

9 व्वंकरविर्सज्जितः वाजि (ज) सनेयकौण्डिन्य सगोत्रः (त्र) ब्रह्मदेव–

10 स्वामिने ।।[14] मातापित्रोरात्मनश्च पुण्ये (ण्या) भिव्रिधये[15] ।। उदकपूर्व्वं (व्वं)

Second Plate : Second Side

11 ताम्र (म्र) शासनेनातिसृष्टः [।*] ते यूयमेवमुपलभ्यास्याज्णा (ज्ञा)[16] श्रवण–

12 विधेया[17] भूत्वा यथोचितं भोगभागमुपनयंत्ता (यन्तः) सुखं प्रतिवस्य (त्स्य)—

13 थ[18][।*] भविष्यतश्च भूमिपाननुदर्शयति ।। दानाद्विशिष्टम—

14 नुपालनजं पुराणा[19] ।।[19a] धर्म्मेषु निश्चितधिय ⌒ प्रवदं (द) न्ति धम्मं (र्म्मम्) ।

15 तस्मा [द्*] द्विजाय सुविशुद्धकुलश्रुताय ।।[19a] दत्ता (त्तां) भुवं भवतु वा मं [ति*] रे–

Third Plate : First Side

16 व गोप्तु[म्*] ।। [१।।*] तद्भवद्भिरप्येषा दत्तिरनुपालयितव्या ।। व्यासगीतांश्चात्र

17 श्लोकानुदाहंरत्ति[20] ।। अग्नेरपत्यं प्रथमं सुवर्ण्णं (र्ण्णं) भूर्व्वैष्णवी सू—

18 र्य्यसुत (ता) श्च गावः [।*] दत्तास्त्रयस्तेन भवंत्ति[21] लोकाः य × [22] काञ्चनं गा (गां)

19 च मही (हीं) च दद्या [त्*] ।।[२।।*] षष्टि वर्षसहस्राणि स्वर्ग्गे वसति भूमिदः [।*]

20 आच्छेत्ता चानुमत्ता (न्ता) च तान्येव नरके वसे [त्*] ।। [३।।*] स्वदत्ता (त्तां) परदत्ता (त्तां) वा य–

Third Plate : Second Side

21 त्ना[द्र]क्ष युधिष्ठिर ।। (१) महीत्महिमतां[23] च्छ्रे (श्रे) ष्ठ दानाच्छ्रेयोनुपालनं (नम्) [।।४।।*]

12. Fleet: °रान्धकारं°
13. Fleet: °स्सनिधि°
14. The punctuation mark is quite clear. But it does not resemble *visarga* as stated by Fleet (*ibid*., iii, p. 193, fn. 14). It looks like a semi-square open to left. This as well as the next mark of punctuation is, however, superfluous.
15. Fleet reads वृधये. However, the medial sign for *i* over *vr* is quite clear while the subscribed sign is undoubtedly *r* which bears close resemblance to that in *tro* earlier in the same line. Read °वृद्धये.

    The punctuation mark found here consists of a couple of horizontal strokes exactly as in the case of *visarga* in the previous line. As noted above, this mark is unnecessary.
16. Fleet reads °स्याज्ञा. But the subscript attached to *j* is clearly *n* and is identical with the sign for *ṇa* at the end of this line.
17. Fleet: °वीधेया
18. Fleet gives double punctuation mark after this word, but his facsimile does not warrant it.
19. Fleet: पुराणे

19*a*. These *daṇḍas* one superfluous.

20. Read °हरन्ति
21. Read भवन्ति
22. The sign for *jihvāmūlīya* bears very close resemblance to *m* with the medial sign for *ā* attached to the right lower limb exactly as in *mātā*° in line 2 and *samājñāpayati* in line 5 above.
23. Read महीं महीमतां

22 बहुभिर्व्वसुधा दत्ता राजिभिस्सगरादिभि: [:*] । यस्य [यस्य*] यदा भूमिस्त—
23 स्य तस्य तदा फलमिति [॥५॥*] स्वमुखाज्ञया उक्ती(त्की)र्ण्णं[24] अच-
24 लसिङ्घेन[25] **प्रवर्द्धमानविजयसंव्वत्सर**[26] **५ मार्गशिर २० ५** [॥*]

The Seal[27]

1 प्रसं(स)न्नहृ[द] यस्यैव विक्क्रमाक्क्रां(क्रा)त्त(न्त) विद्विष [:] [।*]
2 श्रीमतो **जयराजस्य** शाम्म [नं] रिपुशासनं (नम्) [॥६॥*]

ABSTRACT

Issued from *Śarabhapura,* the charter introduce king *Jayarāja* who is described almost exactly in the same manner as No. I: V above. It then records the order of the King to the agriculturist house-holders residing at Pamvā[28] sitated in Pūrvarāṣṭra[29] to the effect that he had given away this village (Pamvā) to Brahmadevasvāmin belonging to the Vājasaneya *Śākhā* and the Kauṇḍinya *gotra* for the religious merit of his parents and of his own self. The grant carried the same privileges and exemptions as those recorded in No. I: V above.

The future kings are then exhorted to protect the grant, and five stanzas, extolling the land-grants and their maintenance and condemning their violation, are quoted, four of them in the name of Vyāsa.[30]

The order in respect of the grant was given by the King himself (literally, by his own mouth).

The grant was engraved by Acalasiṁha.[31] It was issued on the **twenty-fifth**

24. As suggested by Fleet (*CII*, iii, 194, fn. 7), the word *śāsanaṁ* should be supplied here.
25. Read °सिंहेन
26. Read संवत्सर
27. The diameter of the seal, which is circular, is about 3¦". The upper half, divided from the lower half by a couple of horizontal lines in the middle, bears the representation of the goddess Lakṣmī, facing full front, being bathed by an elephant standing on a water-lily on either side and an expanded water-lily on its stalk in the left corner and a conch-shell in the right corner. The lower half contains a two-line legend in the *Anuṣṭubh* metre and probably a floral device below it.
28. According to B.C. Jain, Paṁvā is probably represented by modern Pamgarh, about 32 kms. to the east of Bilaspur.
29. Fleet observes that it was perhaps so called because of its lying on the east of the Mekala range of mountains (*CII*, iii, 192, fn. 1). Jain thinks that it probably denoted the region round Bilaspur. It was known by this name evidently because it comprised the eastern part of the Śarabhapurīya kingdom.
30. Hereafter these five stanzas are found quoted in almost all the records of the Śarabhapurīya kings.
31. Acalasiṁha also figures as the scribe in the Amgura plates of the third (No. I:IV) and Mallar plates of the third (*supra*, No. I:V) and ninth (*infra*, No. I:VII) years of Jayarāja.

day of the month of Mārgaśira in the fifth year of the King's increasingly victorious reign.

The stanza on the seal avers that the charter belongs to the illustrious *Jayarāja*, son of Prasanna,[32] who had assailed the enemies with his own prowess.

32. The full name was Prasannamātra as we know from his coins.

MALLAR PLATES[1] OF JAYARĀJA, YEAR 9

Provenance: Mallar, Bilaspur District, Madhya Pradesh.
References: G. Bhattacharya and M. Sivappa, *EI*, xxxiv, 28–31 and plates opposite pp. 30 and 31.
Language: Sanskrit. In prose except the customary benedictory and imprecatory stanzas at the end and the legend on the seal.
Metres: Verse 1: *Vasantatilakā*; Verse 2: *Indravajrā*; Verses 3–6: *Anuṣṭubh*.
Script: Box-headed variety of the Central Indian alphabet.
Date: Regnal Year 9, Jyeṣṭha 5. About the middle of the sixth century A.D.

TEXT[2]

First Plate

1 स्वस्ति [।*] **शरभपुरात्** द्वि(वि)क्क्रमोपनतसामं(म) न्तमकुटचूडामणि प्रभा–
2 प्रसेकाम्बुधौतपादयुगलो रिपुविला[3]सिनीसीमं(म)न्तोद्धरणहेतु—
3 र्व्वसुवसुधागोप्रद ͜ परमभागवतो मातपितृपादानुद्ध्यातः(त)—
4 श्श्री**महाजयराजः**[4] नगरोत्तरपट्टि (ट्टी)-यमोक्केप्पिकायां प्रतिवासिकुटुम्बि—
5 नस्समाज्ञापयत्यस्तु[5] वो विदितं [6] यथास्माभिरयं ग्रामस्त्(स्त्रि)दशय(प)ति—
6 सदनसुख प्रतिष्ठाकरो यावद्रविशशिताराकिरणप्रतिहतघोरां (रा)न्ध–

Second Plate : First Side

7 कारं जगदवतिष्ठते तावदुपभोग्यस्सनिधिस्सोपनिधिरचाटभट प्रावेश्य [:*]
8 सव्व(र्व्वं) करविसर्ज्जितो[7] मातापित्रोरात्मनश्च पुण्याभिवृध्य (द्धय)र्त्थं(त्थं)[8] हडप्पग्राह[9]
[व]–

1. Having rounded corners, the plates measure approximately 6" by 3·2".
2. From plates in *EI*, xxxiv, between pp. 30 and 31.
3. The medial sign for *ā* is attached to the right lower part of the letter *l*.
4. Bhattacharya and Sivappa place *visarga* in the square bracket, but it is quite clear in the facsimile accompanying their article.
5. The engraver first incised समाज्ञापति following the usual phraseology of the other records of Jayarāja but later corrected it to समाज्ञापयत्य°
6. The mark of punctuation is superfluous.
7. In some other records of Jayarāja this is followed by the name and description of the donee.
8. In other charters of Jayarāja we have पुण्याभिवृद्धये
9. Read हृतप्रग्राह

9 [10]त्सेन बह्वृच[11] भार्ग्गवसगोत्रमहेश्वरस्वामि[12] । [13]एव(वं) शबरभोगिक[14]—

10 बव्रि[15](ह्वृ) च भार्ग्गवरुद्रस्वामि[16] . . . .
. . . .

11 . . . . .नामि(म)–[17]तिसृष्टको

12 भूत्वा ताम्ब्र(म्र) शासनेनास्माभिरन(नु)मोदितः(त) स्ते यूयमेवमुपल–

Second Plate : Second Side

13 भ्यैषामाज्ञाश्रवणविधेया भूत्वा यथोचित भोगमागमुपनय

14 त्ते[18](न्त)स्सुखं प्रतिवत्स्यथ [।*] भविष्यतश्च भूमिपाननुदर्शयति [।*]

15 दानाद्विशिष्टमनुपालनजं पुराणा ।[19] धर्म्मेषु निश्चितधिय॒प्रवदं(द)[20]—

16 न्ति धर्म्मं(र्म्मम्) । तस्मा [द्*] द्विजाय सुविशुद्धकुलश्रुताय[21] दत्ता(त्तां) भुवं भ–

17 वतु वो मतिरेव गोप्तु [म्] । [।१।।*] तद्भूवद्भिरप्येषा द [त्ति*] रनुपालयितव्या । व्यास–

18 गीता(तां) श्चात्र श्लोकानुदाहरन्ति[22] [।*] अग्नेरपत्यं प्रथमं सुवर्णं भूर्व्वै–

Third Plate : First Side

19 ष्णवी सु(सू)र्य्यसुताश्च गावः [।*] दत्तास्त्रयस्तेन भवं(व)न्ति लोकाः[23]

20 य × काञ्चनं गां च मही (हीं) च दद्या [त्*] ।। [२।।*] षष्टिवर्षसहस्राणि स्वर्गे मोद–

21 ति भूमिदः [।*] आच्छेत्ता चानुमंत्ता[24] च तान्येव नरके वसे [त्*] ।। [३।।*] बहुभि—

22 र्व्वसुधा दत्ता राजाभिस्सगरादिभिः [।*] यस्य यस्य यदा भूमि—

23 त (स्त) स्य तस्य तदा फलं (लम्) ।। [४।।*] स्वदत्तां परदत्तां वा यत्नाद्रक्ष युधिष्ठिर ।

10. The entire text from here to line 23 is incised on an erasure.
11. Some space after the *akṣara hvṛ* being occupied by the square hole for the ring, the letter *ca* is engraved slightly above the line.
12. Read स्वामी
13. The mark of punctuation is superfluous.
14. After this Bhattacharya and Sivappa read the *akṣaras bavṛ* as forming part of this line, whereas these letters actually belong to the following line.
15. Bhattacharya and Sivappa: °बवृ°
16. Hereafter the remaining space of this and a considerable space in the beginning of the next line is blank with traces of earlier writing.
17. The use of plural suggests that the blank space preceding it was intended to contain the name of a third donee. Otherwise the employment of plural will have to be regarded as an error for the dual.
18. Bhattacharya and Sivappa: °न्ते°
19. The mark of punctuation is superfluous.
20. Partially beaten in subscript *ya*, which undoubtedly belonged to the original writing, being visible, the *akṣara* looks like *dyam.*
21. The mark of punctuation is unnecessary.
22. The sign following it, visible in the plate, undoubtedly belongs to the original writing.
23. Read लोका. Hereafter there are traces of two letters which undoubtedly belonged to the original writing.
24. Read चानुमन्ता

24 मही (हीं) त्महिमताछ्रेष्ठ[25]दानाच्छ्रेयोनुपालनमिति ॥ [५॥*]

Third Plate : Second Side

25 स्वमुखाज्ञया उत्कीर्ण्णं **अचलसिङ्घेन**[26] । **प्रवर्द्धमानविजय–**

26 **संव्वत्सर ७ ज्येष्ठ दि ५** [॥*][27]

The Seal[28]

1 **प्रसं (स)** न्नतनयस्येदं विक्क्रमोत्खात्तविद्विषः [।*]

2 श्रीमतो **जयराजस्य** शासन (नं) रिपुशासनं (नम्) [॥६॥*]

ABSTRACT

After mentioning the place of issue, *Śarabhapura*, and describing king *Jayarāja* in almost the same words as in Nos. I:V and VI[29] the charter records that Vatsa, who held the office of *Haḍappagrāha*,[30] had given away the village of Mokkeppikā[31] situated in Nagarottarapaṭṭa[32] to Maheśvarasvāmin and *Śabarabhogika*[33] Rudrasvāmin, both belonging to the Bahvṛca *śākhā* and the Bhārgava *gotra*,[34] and that the grant was endorsed by issuing a copper-plate charter by the King. The grant carried with it the same privileges and exemptions as enumerated in No. I:V above.

25. Read महीमताञ्छ्रेष्ठ
26. Read अचलसिंहेन
27. As a mark of the conclusion of the record we find here six vertical lines, each following one being smaller than the preceding one, followed by a horizontal line.
28. The seal is similar to that affixed to the Arang plates of Jayarāja. Vide No. I:VI above.
29. The only difference is that the crest-jewel is here described as worn on the crown (*makuṭa*).
30. *Haḍappagrāha* is evidently the same as *Hadappaggāhamatya* (Sanskrit *Hṛtapragrahāmātya*) mentioned in the Kanukollu plates of the Śālaṅkāyana king Nandivarman (vide *EI*, xxxi, 6, text-line 40, fn. 9) and was evidently in charge of tracing stolen goods. As pointed out by D.C. Sircar (*ibid.*), it reminds one of the officer (*Yukta*) in charge of *pranaṣṭ-ādhigata-dravya* mentioned in the *Manusmṛti* (viii. 34) and *Cauroddharaṇika* referred to in some later inscriptions (N.G. Majumdar, *Inscriptions of Bengal*, iii, 184).
31. Probably identical with Mopka, about 10 miles from Bilaspur, the headquarters of the district of the same name.
32. It was probably the name of a district situated to the north of the capital city Śarabhapura. It may be identified with Nargoda, about 10 miles from Bilaspur.
33. Bhattacharya and Sivappa think that the adjective *Śabarabhogika* may indicate either that Rudrasvāmin hailed from an administrative division (*bhoga*) called Śabara or that he was the *jagirdar* enjoying a locality called Śabara. They propose to identify Śabarabhoga with Seorinarayan or Śavarīnārāyaṇa (*EI*, xxxiv, 29). We feel that the expression should be taken to mean that Rudrasvāmin acted as a priest of the Śabaras.
34. The use of the plural number probably indicates that there was a third donee in addition to the two whose names are mentioned. Alternatively, it may be regarded as a grammatical mistake.

The future rulers are exhorted to maintain the grant, and to strengthen this request are quoted five imprecatory and benedictive stanzas, four of them in the name of Vyāsa, which are the same as those found in No. I:VI above.

The order in respect of the grant was issued by the King himself.

The charter was engraved by Acalasiṁha and issued on the **ninth day of the month of Jyeṣṭha in the ninth year of the increasingly victorious reign.**

The verse on the seal states that this charter belongs to the illustrious *Jayarāja*, son of Prasanna, who had extirpated his enemies by his own prowess.

I: VIII

NAIINA[1] PLATES [1a] OF SUDEVARĀJA, YEAR 2

Provenance: Nahna or Naina, Kalahandi District, Orissa.

References: Sten Konow, *EI*, ix, 170–73 and plates; Hira Lal, *ICPB*, 106, no. 177; B.C. Jain, *Catalogue of the Antiquities preserved in the Archaeological Section of the M.G.M. Museum, Raipur*, vi, 16–8, pls. x–xii.

Language: Sanskrit. In prose except the usual imprecatory and benedictory verses at the end and the legend on the seal.

Metres: Verse 1: *Vasantatilakā*; Verse 2: *Indravajrā*; Verses 3–6: *Anuṣṭubh*.

Script: Box-headed variety of the Central Indian alphabet.

Date: Regnal Year 2, Śrāvaṇa 29. Latter half of the sixth century A.D.

TEXT[2]

First Plate

1 स्वस्ति [।*] शरभपुराद्विक्क्रमो[3]पनतसामन्तमकुटचूडामणि–
2 प्रभाप्रसेकाम्बुधौ [4]तपादयुगलो रिपुविलासिनी[5]सीमन्तोद्धरण–
3 हेतुर्व्वसुवसुधागोप्रद ‿ परमभागवतो माता[6]पितृ[7] (तृ) पादानुद्धया–

1. On the basis of erroneous information originally available to him, Sten Konow had mentioned the village of Khariar as the findspot of this grant which he accordingly christened as Khariar plates. But as pointed out by him in a footnote (*EI*, ix, 172, fn. 7), the plates were actually found at Nahna or Naina, about 5 kms. south of Khariar, which was anciently known as Navannaka as would be evident from line 4 of the record. This observation of Konow has escaped the notice of all the later writers who continue, though erroneously, to refer to these plates as Khariar plates. We have, however, preferred to rechristen them as Nahna plates after their actual provenance and thereby correct an error prevalent for several decades.

1*a*. 14 cms. long and 8 cms. broad.

2. From plates in *EI*, ix.
3. The *ā*-stroke of medial *o* is attached to the lower end of the right stroke of the letter *m* and the *e*-stroke on its top.
4. In some early records of Jayarāja (I: V-VI) we have °म्बुभिर्धौत°. But all the records of Jayarāja have °म्बुधौत°.
5. The length of the medial *i* is indicated by a small vertical stroke attached to the base of the circle denoting medial *i*.
6. The *ā* sign is appended to the lower end of the right vertical of *m*.
7. Jain: °पितृ°

4 तश्श्रीमहासुदेवराजः[8] क्षितिमण्ड.हारीयनवन्नक[9]एतत्प्रावेश्य[10]

5 शाम्बिलकयो॒प्रतिवासिकुटुम्बिनस्समाज्ञापयति ॥[11] विदितमस्तु

Second Plate: First Side

6 वो यथास्माभिरेतदाग्राम[12]द्वयं तृ(त्रि) दशपतिसदनसुखप्रतिष्ठाकरो याव–

7 द्रविशशितााकिरणप्रतिहतघोरान्धकारं[13] जगदवतिष्ठते तावदुप–

8 भोग्यस्सनिधिस्सोपनिधिरचाटभटप्रावेश्यस्सर्व्वकरविसर्ज्जि–

9 तो मातापित्रोरात्मनश्च पुण्याभिवृद्धये वाजि (ज) सनेयकौशिकसगोत्र—

10 विष्णुस्वामिनस्ताम्र (म्र) शासनेनातिसृष्टः [।*] ते यूयमेवमु[14]पलभ्यास्या—

Second Plate: Second Side

11 ज्ञाश्रवणविधेया भूत्वा यथोचितं भोगभागमुपनयन्तस्सुखं प्रति—

12 वत्स्यथ [।*] भविष्यतश्च भूमिपाननुदर्शयति [।*] दानाद्विशिष्टमनुपा–

13 लनजं[15] पुराणा धर्म्मेषु निश्चितधिय॒ प्रवदन्ति धर्म्म[म्*][16] ॥ (।) तस्मा [द्*] द्विजा–

14 य सुविशुद्धकुलश्रुताय दत्तां भुवं भवतु वो मतिरेव गोप्तु [म्*]॥ [१॥*]

15 तद्भवद्भिरप्येषा दत्तिरनुपालयितव्या [।*] व्यासगीतांश्चात्र श्लोकानु—

Third Plate : First Side

16 दाहरन्ति ॥ अग्नेरपत्य (त्यं) प्रथमं सुवर्णं भूर्व्वैष्णवी[17] सूर्य्य–

17 सुताश्च गावः [।*] दत्तास्त्रयस्तेन भवन्ति[18] लोकाय ×काञ्चनं[19] गां च महीं च द–

18 द्यात् [॥ 2॥*] षष्टिवर्षसहस्राणि स्वर्ग्गे मोदति भूमिदः [।*] आच्छेत्ता

19 चानुमन्ता च तान्येव नरके वसेत् [॥ ३॥*] बहुभिर्व्वसुधा दत्ता राजभि–

20 स्सगरादिभिः [।*] यस्य यस्य यदा भूमिः तस्य[20] तस्य तदा फलं (लम्) ॥ [४॥*]

8. The *visarga* is indicated by a couple of horizontal strokes.
9. Jain: °नवन्नके°
10. Jain: च तत्प्रा°
11. The mark of punctuation is indicated by two horizontal strokes exactly similar to those indicating *visarga*.
12. Jain: °स्माभिरेतत्ग्राम°: The engraver had originally inscribed °स्माभिरय° but later corrected it into °स्माभिरेत°
13. Jain: °रांधकारं°
14. There is a superfluous *e*-stroke attached to the *akṣara mu*.
15. The letter *na*, which had been left out due to inadvertence, is engraved below the line.
16. Jain: धर्म्मम्
17. Jain: भूर्व्वैष्णवी
18. There is a superfluous dot in the circle indicating the medial *i*.
19. Jain: यम्काञ्चनं
20. Read °भूमिस्तस्य°

Third Plate : Second side

21 स्वदत्तां परदत्तां वा यत्नाद्रक्ष युधिष्ठिर [।*] महीम्महीमता[21]ञ्छ्रेष्ठ

22 दानाच्छ्रेयोऽनुपालनमिति [।।५।।*][22] स्वमुखाज्ञया **सम्वत्सर**[22a] २ **श्रावण वि** २०६

23 उत्कीर्ण्णं ताम्ब्र (म्र) शासनं द्रोणसीङ्घेण[23] [।*]

Seal[24]

प्रसन्नार्ण्णवसम्भूत[25]—

मानमात्वेन्दुजन्मन[26] [:।*]

श्रीम[त्सुदेव] राजस्य

स्थिरं जगति [शासनम्] [।।*]

ABSTRACT

The charter was issued from *Śarabhapura* by king *Sudevarāja* who is described exactly in the same manner as Jayarāja in the preceding grant. It aims at recording the king's order addressed to the agriculturist householders residing in the villages Navannaka[27] and Śāmbilaka[28] situated in the district (*āhāra*) of Kṣitimaṇḍa[29] that he had donated these two villages to the Brāhmaṇa Viṣṇusvāmin who was a student of the Vājasaneyi *śākhā* of the *Yajurveda* and belonged to the Kauśika *gotra* by means of a copper-plate charter for the increase of the religious merit of his parents as well as of his own self and to last as long as the rays of the sun, the moon and the stars continue to remove the darkness in this world. The grant was accompanied by the same usual privileges and exemptions as named in the previous record and the villagers were asked to obey the grantee and pay him the royal share

21. Jain: म्महिमता:
22. Better read °नुपालनम् [।।५।।*] इति [।*]
22.a Read संवत्सर
23. Konow and Jain: द्रोणसिङ्घेन. Read द्रोणसिंहेन
24. Slightly damaged and 7·5 cms. in diameter, the seal is divided into two parts by two horizontal lines in the middle. In the upper part is depicted the AbhiṣekaLakṣmī motif with the goddess Lakṣmī, standing to full front, flanked by an elephant on her either side standing on an expanded water-lily and bathing her with water poured from a pitcher held in its uplifted trunk. The lower part contains an *Anuṣṭubh* stanza in two lines below which there is a floral device.
25. Jain: °संभूत°
26. Jain: °जन्मनः°
27. Now represented by Nahnā or Nainā, the findspot of the plates, three miles south of Khariar.
28. Said to have been attached to or included in (*etat-prāveśya*), Śāmbilaka has yet to be identified. It is quite possible that it has lost its separate existence and merged itself in the village of Nahnā.
29. It has not been identified.

of the agricultural produce (*bhāga*) and the periodical offerings (*bhoga*) as due and thereby live happily in the village.

The future rulers are entreated to protect the grant, and five imprecatory and benedictory verses, four of them attributed to Vyāsa, are extracted in support of the exhortation.

The royal order about the donation was given by the king himself by the word of his own mouth.

The charter is dated on the **twenty-ninth day of the month of Śrāvaṇa in the second year**[30] and was incised by Droṇasiṁha.

The stanza on the seal avers that this permanent charter belongs to the illustrious Sudevarāja, son of Mānamātra who was born in the family of Prasanna.[31]

30. Though not specifically so described, the year has evidently to be referred to the regnal period of the issuing chief. In other records of the family the mention of the year is generally preceded by the expression *pravarddhamāna-vijaya-rājya* in full or partially.
31. Mānamātra is figuratively described as the moon born from the ocean of Prasanna. The allusion is evidently to the legend of the churning of the ocean by gods and demons which resulted, *inter alia*, in the origin of the moon.

I : IX

DHAMATARI PLATES[1] OF SUDEVARAJA, YEAR 3

Provenance: Dhamatari, Raipur District, Madhya Pradesh.

References: Balchandra Jain, *JESI*, v, 93–97 and plates between pp. 96 and 97.

Language: Sanskrit. In prose with the exception of imprecatory and benedictory verses at the end and the legend on the seal.

Metres: Verse 1: *Vasantatilakā*; Verse 2: *Indravajrā*; Verses 3–6: *Anuṣṭubh*.

Script: Box-headed variety of the Central Indian alphabet.

Date: Regnal Year 3, Kārttika 9. Latter half of the sixth century A.D.

TEXT[2]

First Plate

1 सिद्धम्[3] [।*] स्वस्ति [।*] **श्रीपुराद्विक्रमोपनतसामन्तमकुटचूडामणिप्र–**
2 भाप्रसेक(का)म्ब[4](म्बु) धौतपादयुगलो रिपुविलासिनीसीम(मं) तोध (द्ध)र–
3 णहेतुर्व्वसुवसुधागोप्रद [:*] परमभागवतो मातापितृपादा–
4 नुद्ध्यातः श्रीमहादुर्ग[5]राजः (ज) पुत्रश्रि[6] (श्री) **मा(म)[7]हासुदेवराज** [:*]
5 डकरीभोगि(गी) यखलपद्रके प्रतिवासिनस्समाज्ञाप–
6 यति [।*] विदितमस्तु वो यथास्माभिरयं ग्रामत्र (स्त्रि) दस(श) पति–
7 सदनसुखप्रतिष्टा(ष्ठा) करो यावद्रविशशिताराकिरण

Second Plate: First Side

8 प्रतिहतघोरान्धकारं जगदवतिष्ट (ष्ठ) ते तावदुपभोग्यः

1. The plates are rectangular, measuring 9" in length and 7·5" in breadth. They have a square hole, about 1", about the middle of the proper right margin for the passage of the copper ring which holds them in position.
   Jain calls the grant 'Mahasamund plates' after the tahsil in which the findspot of the record is situated. But we prefer to call it 'Dhamatari plates' following the usual practice to name inscriptions after the provenance.
2. From photographs supplied by Shri B.C. Jain.
3. Expressed by a symbol.
4. Jain: °पादाम्बु°
5. *G* is without a box.
6. Jain: श्री
7. Jain: म°

9 सनिधिसो (स्सो) पनिधिरचाटभटप्रावेश्यस (स्स) र्व्वकराविसर्ज्जि–

10 त (तो) मातापित्रोरात्मनश्च पुण्याभिवृद्धये कास्य (श्य) प [स*] गोत्र–

11 वाजसनेयिमाधवचतुर्व्वेदस्वामिने ताम्ब्र (म्र) शासने–

12 नातिस्त्रि (सृ) ष्ठः (ष्टः) [।*] ते यु (यू) य[8]–मेवमुपलभ्य आज्ञाश्रवणविधेय (या)

13 भूत्वा यथोच (चि) तं भोगभागमुपनयं (य) न्त [:*] सुखं प्रतिवत्स (त्स्य) थ [।*]

14 भविश्य (ष्य) तश्च[9] भूमिपालाननुदर्शयति [।*] दानाद्विशिष्टमनुपा–

Second Plate: Second Side

15 लनज (जं) पुर (रा) णा धर्म्मेसु (षु) निश्चितधिय [:*] प्रवदन्ति धर्म्मं (र्म्मम्) [।*]
तस्मा [द्*] द्विजा–

16 य सुविसु (शु) ध (द्ध) कुलश्रुताय दता (त्तां) भुव (वं) भवतु वो मतिरेव गो–

17 स्तु (प्तु) [म् ॥१॥*] तद्भवद्भिरप्येशा (षा) दत्तिग्नुपालयितव्याः (व्या,) [।*] व्यासगीत
(तां)–

18 श्चात्र श्लो [का*] नुदाहरन्ति [।*] अग्नेग्पत्यं प्रथमं सु–

19 वर्ण्णं (र्ण्णं) भूव्वै (र्व्वै) ष्णवी सूर्य्यसुताश्च गावा (वः) [।*] दत्तास्त्रयस्तेन

20 भवन्ति लोक (का) य×काञ्चन (नं) गाञ्च महीञ्च दद्यात् ॥ [२॥*]

Third Plate: First Side

21 (ष) ष्टिं वर्षसहस्त्र (स्रा) णि[10] स्वर्गे मोदति भूमिदः [।*] आच्छे–

22 त्ता ञ्चा (चा) नुमन्ता ञ्च (च) त (ता) न्येव नरके वसेत् ॥ [३॥*] बहुभिर्व्वसु–

23 धा दत्ता राजभिस्सगरादिभिः [।*] यस्य यस्य यदा भूमिस्त–

24 स्य तस्य तदा फलं (लम्) [॥४॥*] स्वदत्तां परदत्ताम्वा (त्तां वा) यत्नाद्रक्ष यु–

25 धिष्ठिर [।*] मही (हीं) महि (ही) मतां श्रेष्ठ दानाच्छ्रेयोनुप (पा) लनमिति ॥ [५॥*]

26 सर्व्व (र्व्वा) धिकाराधिकृतश्रीमहा (सा) मन्त इन्द्रबलराज [:*] ॥

Third Plate: Second Side

27 य (प्र) वर्द्धमानविजय राज्ये (ज्य) सम्व (संव) त्सरू[11] (र) 3 कार्त्तिकदिन 9

28 शाश (स) नं (न) मुत्कीर्ण्णं अक्क (क्ष) शालिकगोल (सिं) ह्ने (हे) न ।

Seal[12]

क्रमाधिगतराज्यस्य द्वि (वि) क्रमोत्खातविद्विष [:।*]
श्रीम [त्सुदेव] राजस्य स्थिरं जगति शासनं (नम्) [॥६॥*]

8. Jain: यूय°
9. Jain: भविष्यतश्च
10. Jain: सहस्राणि
11. Jain: सम्वत्सर
12. The seal, which is circular with a diameter of 7·5 cm., bears, in the upper part, in relief on a countersunk surface the figure of goddess Lakṣmī standing on lotus and flanked by an elephant on either side pouring water over her. On her proper right and left sides are a wheel and a conch shell. In the lower part is a two-line legend below which is perhaps the representation of a pitcher.

ABSTRACT

The plates were issued from **Śrīpura**[13] by King **Sudevarāja** who is spoken of in a conventional manner as in the preceding grant except that here he is described as son of the illustrious Mahā-Durgarāja. It records the king's order to the inhabitants of the village Khalapadraka[14] situated in the Ḍakarī *bhoga*[15] that he had given away the village by means of a copper-plate charter in favour of a *caturvedin*[16] Brāhmaṇa named Mādhavasvāmin[17] who belonged to the Kāśyapa *gotra*[18] and was a student of the Vājasaneya *śākhā* (of the *Yajurveda*) for the augmentation of the religious merit of his parents as well as of his own self. The grant was intended to last as long as the rays of the sun, the moon and the stars continue to remove the darkness of the universe and carried with it the right to receive the *bhoga* and *bhāga* as due from the villagers who were asked to offer the same to the donee and to obey him.

Next the king exhorts the future kings to maintain the grant and five benedictive and imprecatory verses, four of which are attributed to Vyāsa, have been quoted in order to strengthen the request.

The record next refers to the illustrious *Mahāsāmanta* Indrabalarāja, who enjoyed the office of the *Sarvādhikārādhikṛta* or Chief Minister.[19]

The record is dated on the **ninth day of the month of Kārttika in the third year of the increasingly victorious reign** and was incised by the goldsmith (*akṣaśālika*) Golasiṁha.[20]

The stanza on the seal avers that the charter belongs to the illustrious **Sudevarāja** who had obtained the kingdom in the proper order of succession and had destroyed enemies by his prowess.

13. Modern Sirpur in the Raipur District of Madhya Pradesh.
14. Jain proposes to identify it with modern Khalari in the Raipur District which is found mentioned by the name Khalvāṭikā or Khalavāṭikā in an inscription of Hari-Brahma-deva, dated V.S. 1470, found at this place. See *CII*, iv, 575ff.
15. Ḍakarī, the chief place of the *bhoga*, has not been identified.
16. Meaning 'learned in the four Vedas', this title is not met with in any other record of the dynasty.
17. The name is mentioned in a rather unusual manner inasmuch as the word *caturvveda* is inserted between the first and the second parts of the name.
18. Brāhmaṇas of this *gotra* are not referred to in any other Śarabhapurīya epigraph.
19. Although Indrabalarāja is spoken of as occupying the same office in Kauvatal plates also, there he is mentioned as *dūtaka* whereas the reason of his mention in the present record is left unspecified. But it will not be wrong to conjecture that he acted as *dūtaka* of this charter also.
20. Golasiṁha figures in the same capacity in the Kauvatal plates of Sudevarāja and both the known grants of his successor Pravararāja all of which were issued from Śrīpura. But the epithet *akṣaśālika* is employed for him only in this record.

I : X

SIRPUR PLATES[1] OF MAHĀ-SUDEVARĀJA, YEAR 7

Provenance: Sirpur, Raipur District, Madhya Pradesh.

References: Hira Lal, *ICPB*, 106-A, No. 177(b); Lochan Prasad Pandeya, *Mahakoshal Historical Society's Papers*, ii (1937), 42-43; *ARIE*, 1945-46, 12, No. 52; S. L. Katare, *EI*, xxxi, 103-08 and plates facing pp. 106 and 107; Ajay Mitra Shastri, *Studies in Indian Epigraphy*, ii, 50–54.

Language: Sanskrit. In prose but for the customary imprecatory and benedictory stanzas at the end and the legend on the seal.

Metres: Verse 1: *Vasantatilakā*; Verse 2: *Indravajrā*; Verses 3–6: *Anuṣṭubh*.

Script: Box-headed variety of the Central Indian alphabet.

Date: Regnal Year 7, second (intercalary) Bhādrapada 10. Latter half of the sixth century A.D.

TEXT[2]

First Plate

1 सिद्धम्[2a] [।*] स्वस्ति [।*] शरभपुराद्विक्क्रमोपनतसामन्तमकु [टचूडामणि *][3]–
2 प्रभाप्रसेकाम्बुधौतपादयुगलो रिपुविलासि [नीसीमन्तोद्धरण*]–
3 हेतुर्व्वसुवसुधागोप्रद⁀परमभागव [तो मातापितृपादा*]–
4 नुद्धयातश्श्रीमहासुदेवराजः चु[4] [. . . . .][5]–

1. The plates are 5·5″ long and 3·3″ broad.
2. From plates in *EI*, xxxi, facing pp. 106 and 107.

2*a*. Expressed by a symbol. Katare: ओं.

3. A portion of the first plate on its proper left having been broken off, some letters at the end of all the six lines on this plate are lost. However, except in line 4, the lost portion can be restored with certitude with the help of other records of Mahā-Sudeva rāja. The same has been included in square brackets with asterisk marks in this as well as in the following lines.
4. Katare reads it as *vu*; but a close look at the letter *v* in other lines of this record shows that its lower part is a more or less perfect square, whereas the lower part of the *akṣara* in question is a rectangle which is characteristic of the letter *c*. We, therefore, prefer to read it as *cu*.
5. This lost portion contained part of the name of the donated village and that of the district in which it was situated as in other records of the dynasty. The name of the district began with the *akṣara cu* which is the last preserved letter of this line. In view of the sameness of the opening and concluding letters of the compound and the number of the lost letters (*i.e.* 9) the missing *akṣaras* may, with much probability, be

5 वके[6] प्रतिवासिकुटुम्बिनस्समा[7]ज्ञा [पयति । विदितमस्तु वो*]
6 यथास्माभिरयं ग्रामस्तृ (स्त्रि) दशपतिस [दनसुखप्रतिष्ठाकरो*]

Second Plate : First Side

7 यावद्रविशशिताराकिरणप्रतिहतघोरान्धकारं जगदवतिष्ठ–
8 ते तावदुपभोग्यस्सनिधिस्सोपनिधरचाटभटप्रावेश्यस्सर्व्वक–
9 रविसर्ज्जित [:*] पूर्व्वं नन्नपादैस्तैत्तिरीयपाराशरसगोत्रब्राह्म–
10 णकारणिककन्सिप्पस्वामिनो (ने) दत्त इदानीमप्यस्माभिरपि
11 महादेवीराजकुलानां वीज्ञाप्या[8]स्ताम्ब्रशासनीकृतः ते यूयमे—
12 वमुपलभ्यास्याज्ञाश्रवणविधेया भूत्वा यथोचितं भोगभाग–

Second Plate : Second Side

13 मुपनयन्तस्सुखं प्रतिवत्स्यथ [।*] भविष्यतश्च भूमिपाननु–
14 दर्शयति । दानाद्विशिष्टमनुपालनजं पुराणा धर्म्मेषु निश्चित–
15 धिय‿प्रवदन्ति धर्म्मं (र्म्मम्) [।*] तस्माद् [द्*] द्विजाय सुविशुद्धकुलश्रुताय दत्तां
16 भुवं भवतु वो मतिरेव गोप्तु [म्*] ।। [१।।*] तद्भवद्भिरप्येषा दत्तिरनु–
17 पालयी (यि) तव्या[9] [।*] व्यासगीतांश्चात्र श्लोकानुदाहरन्ति [।*] अग्नेरपत्यं प्र–
18 थमं सुवर्णं भूर्व्वैष्णवी सूर्य्यसुताश्च गावः [।*] दत्तास्त्रयस्ते—

Third Plate : First Side

19 न भवन्ति लोकाः (का) य × का[10]ञ्चनं गां च मही (हीं) च दद्यात् [।।२।।*] षष्टिवर्षस–
20 हस्राणि स्वर्ग्गे मोदति भूमिदः [।*] आच्छेत्ता चानुमन्ता च तान्ये–
21 व नरके वसेत् [।।३।।*] बहुभिर्व्वसुधा दत्ता राजभिस्सगरादिभिः [।*] यस्य
22 यस्य यदा भूमिः (मि) त (स्त) स्य तस्य तदा फलं (लम्) [।।४।।*] स्वदत्तां परदत्तां वा
23 यत्नाद्रक्ष युधिष्ठिर [।*] महीत्म (म्म) हि मताञ्छ्रेष्ठ दानाच्छ्रेयोनुपाल–
24 नमिति [।।५।।*] स्वमुखाज्ञया **प्रवर्द्धमानवी (वि) जय[11] सम्व (संव) ७ द्विमाद्रवि १०**

---

restored as °*llāḍasīmābhogīyaKeśa*° with the help of the Kurud plates of Narendra, *vide* No. I: II above. Thus, *Cullāḍasīmā* and Keśavaka appear to have been the names of the district and the donated village respectively. For a detailed discussion of this question see *Studies in Indian Epigraphy*, ii, 50ff.

6. The name of the donated village ended with *vaka*; but the earlier part of the name, which formed the concluding portion of the last line, is lost. However, as stated above, the name of the village seems to have been Keśavaka.
7. The medial *ā* is indicated by the downward elongation of the right vertical of the letter *m*.
8. Katare: विज्ञाप्यास्ता°. Read विज्ञाप्य ताम्र°
9. Katare: पालयितव्या
10. The sign of *jihvāmūlīya* is exactly identical in shape with *m* and the medial *ā* is attached to the lower end of its right vertical exactly as in *mā* in line 24.
11. Katare: °विजव°

Third Plate : Second Side

25 उक्ती (त्की) ण्णं द्रोणसि(सिं)(ङ्घे)(घे) न[12]

Seal[13]

1 प्रसन्नतनयस्येदं विक्क्रमोत्खातविद्विष [:।*]
2 श्रीमतोजयराजस्य शासनं रिपुशासन [ं] (नम्) [॥६॥*]

ABSTRACT

Issued from **Śarabhapura,** the charter belongs to King **Sudevarāja** who is described in the conventional manner as in the previous record. Its object is to record that the grant of a village formerly made by one Nanna[14] in favour of the *Karaṇika*[15] Brāhmaṇa Kansippasvāmin, a student of the Taittirīya *śākhā* of the *Yajurveda* and belonging to the Pārāśara *gotra*, was confirmed by Sudevarāja by issuing a copper-plate charter. The royal order in confirmation of the grant was addressed to the agriculturist householders inhabiting the village and was issued after duly informing the chief queen and the members of the royal household.[16] The grant, which was intended to endure as long as the universe illumined by the rays of the sun, the moon and the stars lasts, carried with it the same privileges and exemptions as mentioned in the preceding record. The villagers were, as usual, asked to be obedient to the donee and pay him the periodical offerings (*bhoga*) and

12. This line is engraved in the middle of the plate. The record was evidently intended to be completed on the inner side of the third plate, but the engraver could not carry out this intention.
13. The seal is similar to those attached to the charters of Mahā-Jayarāja, described above *vide* Nos IV-VII above. This is as it should be; for the seal actually belongs to him as indicated by the two-line *Anuṣṭubh* legend which refers to Jayarāja, son of Prasanna, and not to Sudevarāja, as one would normally expect. Katare, therefore, thinks that the plates were "taken out from their original ring bearing the seal of Mahā-Sudevarāja and were misjoined to a seal which must have originally belonged to some charter of Mahā-Jayarāja (*EI*, xxxi, 103). This was also the view of Hira Lal (*ICPB*, 106-A, No. 177-b). However, as pointed out by D.C. Sircar (62, 103, fn. 4), there are several instances of royal charters to which the seal of the predecessor of the issuing chief is attached. But we are of the opinion that the seal which originally belonged to charter of Jayarāja, was attached to this charter by mistake.
14. The employment of the word *pāda* and the plural number seems to indicate that Nanna was held in great esteem.
15. A scribe or a writer of legal documents. *Karaṇika-Brāhmaṇa* would denote a *Karaṇika* belonging to the Brāhmaṇa community. See *IEG* 146. According to Kane, however, *Karaṇika* was an officer in charge of a State Department or an office. See *HDS*, iii, 979.
16. *Rāja-kula* in the original literally denotes royal family. By implication it came to denote a member of the royal household or a royal officer. For some other references to this expression, see *CII*, iii, 31, text-line 5; 180, text-line 76; *EI*, xxv, 156.

royal share of agricultural produce (*bhāga*) as due and live happily in the village.

The name of the village donated and that of the administrative division in which it was situated cannot be made out as the portion of the record containing the same is broken away. But the preceding and following letters indicate that the district had a name beginning with the *akṣara cu* whereas the concluding portion of the name of the village was *vaka.*[17]

The future kings are exhorted to uphold the grant, and five imprecatory and benedictive stanzas, four of them in the name of Vyāsa, are quoted.

The order about the grant was issued by the king himself.

The charter, which was issued on the **tenth day of the second Bhādrapada**[18] **in the seventh year of the increasingly victorious reign,** was engraved by Droṇasiṃha.[19]

The seal attached to the record belongs to Jayarāja and the inscription on it refers to him as the son of Prasanna and as one who had destroyed his enemies by the prowess of his arms and describes his charter as the chastiser of the enemies.

17. We have suggested elsewhere that Cullāḍasīmā and Keśavaka were probably the names of the district and the village respectively.
18. This shows that there were two Bhādrapadas in that year and the charter was issued in the second month.
19. He is evidently the same as the homonymous engraver of the earliest grant of Sudevarāja (No. I: VIII).

I : XI

ARANG PLATES[1] OF SUDEVARĀJA, YEAR 7

Provenance: Arang,[2] Raipur District, Madhya Pradesh.

References: Hira Lal, *ICPB*, 106-A, No. 177-a; L.P. Pandeya, *EI*, xxiii, 18–22 and plate between pp. 20 and 21; B.C. Jain, *Catalogue of the Antiquities preserved in the Archaeological Section of the M.G.M. Museum, Raipur*, vi, 18-22 and pls. xiii-xv.

Language: Sanskrit. In prose with the exception of the customary benedictive and imprecatory verses at the end and the legend on the seal.

Metres: Verse 1: *Vasantatilakā*; Verse 2: *Indravajrā*, Verses 3-6: *Anuṣṭubh*.

Script: Box-headed variety of the Central Indian alphabet.

Date: Regnal Year 7, Vaiśākha 29. Latter half of the sixth century A.D.

TEXT[3]

First Plate

1 सिद्धम् [।*][4] स्वस्ति [।*] **शरभपुराद्विक्क्रमो**[5]पनतसामन्तमकुटचूडामणिप्रभाप्र–

2 सेकाम्बुधौ तपादयुगलो रिपुविलासिनीसीमन्तोद्धरणहेतु–

3 र्व्वसुवसुधागोप्रद⁀पर[6]मभागवतो मातापितृपादानुद्धयात–

4 श्श्री[7]**महासुदेवराजः** तोसट्ड (ड्ड) भुक्तीयशिविलिङ्गके प्रतिवासि–

5 कुटुम्बिनस्समाज्ञापयति ।।[8] विदितमस्तु वो यथायं ग्राम–

Second Plate : First Side

6 स्तृ (स्त्रि) दशपतिसदनसुखप्रतिष्ठा [क*] रो यावद्रविशशिताराकिरणप्रति–

7 हतघोरान्धकारं[9] [10]जगदवतिष्ठते तावदुपभोग्यस्सनिधिस्सोपनिधि–

1. The plates are 3. 2″ broad and 6. 4″ long.
2. Although nothing definite is known about the findspot of the charter, it was in the possession of a cultivator of Arang and is reported to have been lying in his house for well over half a century since the time of his father.
3. From plates in *EI*, xxiii.
4. Expressed by a symbol. Pandeya:
5. One part of the medial *o* is attached to the top of *m* and the other part is formed by the elongation to the right of the horizontal line of *m*.
6. The engraver had begun to inscribe *ma* after *pa*, but later corrected it to *ra*.
7. The subscript *r* closely resembles medial *r*.
8. Pandeya transcribes this mark of punctuation, which consists of a couple of strokes, by a single *daṇḍa*.
9. *Ra*, which was at first omitted by oversight, is written below *ja* with a *kākapada* mark (+) and the *anusvāra*, which should have been placed over *ra*, is placed over *kā*.
10. There is a *kākapada* over *ja* indicating that something has to be inserted here. Actually its proper place was over *kā*.

8 रचाटभट[11]प्रावेश्यस्सर्व्वकरविसर्ज्जितः प्रतिहार भोगिल्लेन माता–

9 पित्रोरात्मनश्च पुण्याभिवृद्धये कात्यायनसगोत्रमाध्यन्दिनवाज–

10 सनेययज्ञस्वामिनः (ने) अध्यर्द्धाङ्शेन[12] भारद्वाजकुमारवत्स आत्रे–

Second Plate : Second Side

11 य[13]काण्ववाजसनेययज्ञस्वामिने प्रत्यङ्शेन[14] कात्यायनविशाख[15]–

12 स्वामिकौशिकमाध्यन्दिन[16]गोलस्वामि (मी) एवं[16a] दामोदरस्वामिदासस्वामि

13 भारद्वाजपञ्चालिस्वामिदीक्षितायनीका [न्*] प्रत्यर्द्धाङ्शेन[17] ताम्ब्र (म्र) शास–

14 नेनातिसृष्टो भूत्वास्माभिरनुमोदितः[18] [।*] यूयमेवमुपलभ्यैषा–

15 माज्ञाश्रवणविधेया भूत्वा यथोचितं भोगभागमुपनयन्तस्सुखं

16 प्रतिवत्स्यथ [।*] भविष्यतश्च भूमिपाननुदर्शयति [।*] दानाद्विशिष्ट[19]–

Third Plate : First Side

17 मनुपालनज (जं) पुराणा धम्मे (र्म्मे)षु निश्चितधिय प्रवदन्ति धर्म्मं (र्म्मम्) ॥ (।)
तस्मा [द्*] द्वि–

18 जाय सुविशुद्धकुलश्रुताय दत्तां भुवं भवतु वो मतिरेव गोप्तु [म्*] ॥ [१॥*]

19 तद्भवद्भिरप्येषा दति (त्ति) रनुपालयितव्या [।*] व्यासगीता (तां) श्चात्र श्लोकानु–

20 दाहरन्ति [।*] अग्नेरपत्य (त्यं) प्रथमं सुवर्ण्णं ॥[20] भूर्व्वैष्णवी सूर्य्यसु–

21 ताश्च गाव [ः।*] दत्तास्त्रयस्तेन भवं (व) न्ति लोका य × काञ्चनं गां च मही (हीं) च दद्यात्
[॥२॥*]

22 षष्टिं वर्षसहस्राणि स्वर्ग्गे मोदति भूमिद [ः।*] आच्छेत्ता चानुमं (म) न्ता च ता–

Third Plate : Second Side

23 न्येव नरके वसे [त् ॥३॥*] बहुभिर्व्वसुधा दत्ता राजभिस्सगरादिभि [ः।*]

24 यस्य यस्य यदा भूमित (स्त) स्य तस्य तदा फलं (लम्) [॥४॥*] स्वदन्ता (त्तां) परदन्ता (त्तां)
वा यत्ना–

25 द्रक्ष युधिष्ठिर [।*] महीम्महि (ही) मताञ्छ्रे ष्ठ दाना[21]च्छ्रे योनुपालनमिति [॥५॥*] स्वमु–

11. The letter *ta*, which was first omitted, is written below the line.
12. Read अध्यर्द्धांशेन
13. Read °वत्सात्रे°
14. Read प्रत्यंशेन
15. *Kha*, which is faint in the facsimile accompanying Pandeya's article, is quite clear in the facsimile given by B.C. Jain.
16. Pandeya reads °मध्यन्दिन. But the medial *ā* is clearly indicated by the downward elongation of the right vertical of *m*.

16a This word is unnecessary.

17. Read प्रत्यर्घांशेन
18. The medial sign for *i*, which was first engraved on *t* by oversight, was later cancelled.
19. There is full mark of punctuation here which is unnecessary.
20. The punctuation mark is uncalled for.
21. The letters *dānā*, which were omitted here, have been engraved below the line with a *kākapada* mark. There is a *kākapada* sign before *ṣṭha* also. Its proper place was after *ṣṭha*.

26 [खा]म्न (ज्ञ)या संव्व (वत्) ७[22] वैशाख दि २० ६ उक्ती (क्ती) र्ण्णं द्रोणसिंघे(हे)न॥

Seal[23]

1 प्रस [न्नार्ण्णं] वसम्भू[त] मा [न]मात्वेन्दुजन्मन [:।*]
2 श्रीमत्सु.........[शा] सनं (नम्) [॥६॥*][24]

ABSTRACT

The grant was issued from **Śarabhapura** *by* King **Sudevarāja** who is introduced in the same stereotyped manner as in most of the earlier records. It records that he confirmed the grant of a village called Śivaliṅgaka[25] situated in the Tosaḍḍa *bhukti*[26] made by the *Pratihāra* Bhogilla by issuing a copper-plate charter in favour of certain Brāhmaṇas. The village was divided into 6½ shares for the purpose of this grant. The details of the grantees and the shares allotted to them are as under:—

Particulars of the Grantees	*Shares*
1. Yajñasvāmin of Kātyāyana *gotra* and a student of the Mādhyandina *śākhā* of the Vājasaneyi Saṁhitā of the *Śukla Yajurveda*	1½
2. Kumāravatsa of Bhāradvāja *gotra*	1
3. Yajñasvāmin of Ātreya *gotra* and a student of the Kāṇva *śākhā* of the Vājasaneyi Saṁhitā of *Śukla Yajurveda* . .	1
4. Viśākhasvāmin of Kātyāyana *gotra*	½
5. Golasvāmin of Kauśika *gotra* and a student of the Mādhyandina *śākhā*	½
6. Dāmodarasvāmin, same as above	½
7. Dāmasvāmin, same as above	½
8. Pañcālisvāmin of Bhāradvāja *gotra*	½
9. Dīkṣita Āyanīka, same as above	½

22. Pandeya reads the figure as 8, but we feel inclined to agree with N.P. Chakravarti in taking it as 7. See *EI*, xxiii, 22, fn. 4.
23. The seal is similar to those attached to the other charters of Sudevarāja.
24. Following the other plates of Sudevarāja, Pandeya proposes to restore the second half of the *Anuṣṭubh* stanza as श्रीमत्सुदेवराजस्य स्थिरं जगति शासनम्. But the seal attached to some plates of this king has शासनं रिपु° in place of स्थिरं जगति. Thus it can also be restored as श्रीमत्सुदेवराजस्य शासनं रिपुशासनम्.
25. It has not been located.
26. According to Pandeya, the headquarters of the *bhukti*, Tosaḍḍa, is probably represented by the modern village of Tosarā in the erstwhile Patna State, E.S.A. V. V. Mirashi's identification of it with Tusdā near Dumarpalli about thirty miles to the south-east of Arang, the provenance of the plates, appears more probable.

The addressees of the royal order were the agriculturist householders living in the village who were asked to obey the donees and pay them the due *bhoga* and *bhāga*. The grant was intended to be as durable as the world with its darkness removed by the rays of the sun, the moon and the stars and bestowed on the grantees the same privileges and exemptions as enumerated in the preceding record.

The future rulers are exhorted to uphold the grant, and this request is sought to be strengthened by quoting five imprecatory and benedictory stanzas, four of which are ascribed to Vyāsa.

The order was issued by the king by the word of his own mouth.

The grant is dated on the **twenty-ninth day of the month of Vaiśākha in the seventh year, evidently of the reign of Sudevarāja**

It was engraved by Droṇasiṁha.

The inscription on the seal is literally the same as that on the seal of the Nahna plates of the second year of the reign of **Sudevarāja** who is described as born of the moon that was Mānamātra who emerged from the ocean in the form of Prasanna.

I : XII

KAUVATAL PLATES[1] OF SUDEVARĀJA, YEAR 7

Provenance: Kauvatal, Raigadh District, Madhya Pradesh.

References: L.P. Pandeya, *IHQ*, xxi, 294-95; D.C. Sircar, *ibid.*, xxii, 62-63; *Ancient India,* No. 5, 49; *ARIE*, 1945-46, 12, App. A, No. 53 and plate facing p. 12; A.N. Lahiri, *EI*, xxxi, 314-16; Ajay Mitra Shastri, *Studies in Indian Epigraphy*, iii, 152-53.

Language: Sanskrit. In prose with the exception of a few imprecatory and benedictory verses and the legend on the seal.

Metres: Verse 1: *Vasantatilakā*; Verse 2: *Indravajrā*; Verses 3–6: *Anuṣṭubh*.

Script: Box-headed variety of the Central Indian alphabet.

Date: Regnal Year 7, Mārgaśīrṣa 10. Latter half of the sixth century A.D.

TEXT[2]

First Plate

1 सिद्धम्[3] [।*] स्वस्ति [।*] **श्रीपुराद्विक्रमोपनतसामं** (म)न्तमकुटचूडामणिप्रभाप्रसेका–

2 म्बुधौतपादयुगलो रिपुविलासिनीसीमं (म)न्तोद्धरणहेतुर्व्वसुवसुधा–

3 गोप्रदः परमभागवतो मातापितृपादानुद्धयातः श्रीमहादुर्ग्गराजपुत्र–

4 श्री**महासुदेवराजः** हकिरीभोगीयसुनिकायां[4] प्रतिवासि–

5 नस्समाज्ञापयति । विदितमस्तु वो यथास्माभिरयं ग्रामः तृ (मस्त्रि) दश–

6 पतिसदनसुखप्रतिष्ठाकरो यावद्रविशशिताराकिरणप्रतिहत–

Second Plate : First Side

7 घोरान्धकारं जगदवतिष्ठते तावदुपभोग्यः सनिधिःस्सो (धिस्सो) पनिधि–

8 रचाटभटप्रवेश्यः सर्व्वंकरविसर्ज्जं (र्ज्जि)तः मातापित्रोरात्मनश्च

9 पुण्याभिवृद्धये पारास (श)रगोत्राय[5] वाजसनेयिने भट्टपुर–

10 द (न्द)रस्वामिने[6] ताम्ब्र (म्र) शासनेनातिसृष्टः [।*] ते यूयमेवमुप–

11 लभ्या (भ्य) श्राज्ञाश्रवणविधेया[7] भूत्वा यथोचितं भोगभागमुपनय–

1. The plates are 7·4″ long and 4·2″ broad.
2. From plate in *ARIE*, 1945-46.
3. Expressed by a symbol.
4. This phrase is engraved on an erasure.
5. The word *Pārāsara* is engraved on an erasure. The *anusvāra* above, first engraved by oversight, was later cancelled.
6. The letters *dara* are written on an erasure.
7. The original intention seems to have been to write °लभ्यास्याज्ञा° as in most other records of the family.

12 न्तः सुख(खं) प्रतिवत्स्यथ [।*] भविश्य(ष्य)तश्च[8] भूमिपालाननुदर्शयति [।*]

Second Plate : Second Side

13 दानाद्विशिष्टमनुपालनजं पुराणा धर्म्मेषु निश्चितधिय [:*]
14 प्रवदन्ति धर्म्मं(र्म्मम्) [।*] तस्मा [द्*] द्विजाय सुविषु(शु)द्धकुलश्रुताय दत्ता(त्तां)
15 भुवं भवतु वो मतिरेव गोप्तुं(प्तुम्) [।।१।।*] तद्भवद्भिरप्येशा(षा) दत्तिरनुपालयि—
16 तव्या [।*] व्यासगीतांश्चास्त्र(त्र) श्लोकानुदाहरन्ति [।*] अग्नेरपत्यं
17 प्रथमं सुवर्ण्णं भूर्व्वैष्णवी सूर्य्यसुताश्च गावः [।*] दत्तास्त्रयस्ते–
18 न भवं (व)न्ति लोका यष्का (य×का)ञ्चना(नं) गाञ्च महीञ्च दद्यात् [।।२।।*] षष्ठी (ष्टि) वर्ष–

Third Plate : First Side

19 सहस्राणि स्वर्ग्गे मोदति भूमिदः [।*] आच्छेत्ता चानुमन्ता च तान्येव
20 नरके वसेत् [।। ३।।*] बहुभिर्व्वसुधा दत्ता राजभिः सगरादिभि [:।*] यस्य य–
21 स्य यदा भूमिस्तस्य तस्य तदा फलं (लम्) [।।४।।*] स्वदत्ता (त्तां) परदत्ता (त्तां) वा यत्ना–
22 द्रक्ष युधिष्ठिर [।*] मही (हीं) महि (ही) मतां श्रेष्ठ दानाच्छ्रेयोनुपालन–
23 मिति (म् ।।५।। इति) । सर्व्वाधिकाराधिकृत–श्रीमहासामं(म)न्त इन्द्रबलराज– ।[9]
24 श्चात्र दूतकः [।*] **प्रवर्द्धमानविजयस(सं)व्व(व)त्सर ७ माग(र्ग) शीर्ष दि १०**

Third Plate : Second Side

25 उकि(त्की)र्ण्णं गोलसिङ्घेन[10] [।*]

Seal[11]

1 क्रमाधिगतराज्यस्य विक्रमोत्खातविद्विषः [।*]
2 **श्रीमत्सुदेवराजस्य** स्थिरं जगति शासनं(नम्) [।।६।।*]

ABSTRACT

The charter was issued from **Śrīpura**[12] by King **Sudevarāja** who is described exactly in the same manner as in the previous record except that here he is

8. Lahiri: भवि[ष्य]तश्च.
9. The mark of punctuation is unnecessary.
10. Read गोलसिंहेन.
11. The seal is circular, its diameter being 3″. Having a circular border, it is divided into two parts by a couple of horizontal lines in the middle. In the upper half we have the figure of Gaja-Lakṣmī as described above, and a wheel (*cakra)* and a conch-shell (*śaṅkha*) in the left and right fields respectively. The lower half has an *Anuṣṭubh* stanza in two lines and below it what looks like a *pūrṇa-kumbha.*
12. Modern Sirpur, Raipur District, Madhya Pradesh.

referred to as the son of the illustrious Mahā Durggarāja.[13] It registers the grant by the king of the village of Sunikā situated in the Hakirī *bhoga*[14] in favour of *Bhaṭṭa* Purandarasvāmin who belonged to the Pārāśara *gotra* and was a student of the Vājasaneyi *śākhā* of the *Yajurveda*. The royal order concerning the grant was addressed to the residents of the donated village. The grant, which was made by means of a copper-plate charter and intended to last till the rays of the sun, the moon and the stars continue to illumine the world, carried with it the usual privileges and exemptions enumerated in the preceding inscription. The villagers were called upon to render obedience and make over to the donee due periodical offerings (*bhoga*) and the royal share of the agricultural produce (bhāga) and thereby live happily in the village.

Then follows exhortation to the future rulers to maintain the grant, and five imprecatory and benedictory verses, four of them said to have been extracted from Vyāsa, are cited in support of this entreaty.

The illustrious *Mahāsāmanta* Indrabalarāja,[15] who occupied the office of the *Sarvādhikārādhikṛta* (Chief Minister), acted as the *dūtaka* of the grant.

The record is dated on the **tenth day of the month of Mārgaśīrṣa in the seventh year of the increasingly victorious reign.**

The charter was engraved by Golasiṁha.

The verse on the seal refers this permanent charter to the illustrious **Sudevarāja** who had obtained his kingdom in the proper order and had uprooted his enemies by prowess.[16]

The fact that the names of the donated village and the district in which it was situated, part of the name of the donee and the donee's *gotra* are incised on erasures gives rise to some doubts regarding the genuineness of the charter and it is clear that the most vital portions of the grant were tampered with.[17]

13. As in the case of Sudevarāja, the actual name must have been onlyDurggarāja. The reference to the donor king as the son of a particular person is extremely rare in the Śarabhapurīya records. In fact, this is a solitary instance. In other records this information is given only in the seal inscription.
14. Sunikā and Hakirī, the chief place of the *bhoga* designated after it, have yet to be identified.
15. He is generally identified with the Pāṇḍuvaṁśin chief Indrabala, son of Udayana and grandfather of Tīvaradeva. See *IHQ*, xxi, 275; xxii, 63. But it cannot be regarded as certain.
16. The first half of the inscription on this seal is different from that of the stanza found on the seals attached to the other known charters of Sudevarāja.
17. See *Studies in Indian Epigraphy* iii, 152-53.

I : XIII

RAIPUR PLATES[1] OF SUDEVARĀJA, YEAR 10

Provenance: Raipur, Raipur District, Madhya Pradesh.
References: Cunningham, *ASR*, xvii, 55ff., pls. xxvi-xxvii; J.F. Fleet, *CII*, iii, 196-200, pl. xxvii; Hira Lal, *ICPB*, 106, No. 176.
Language: Sanskrit. In prose but for the usual benedictive and imprecatory verses at the end and the legend on the seal.
Metres: Verse 1: *Vasantatilakā*; Verse 2: *Indravajrā*; Verses 3–6: *Anuṣṭubh*.
Script: Box-headed variety of the Central Indian alphabet.
Date: Regnal Year 10, Māgha 9. Latter half of the sixth century A.D.

TEXT[2]

First Plate

1 सिद्धम्[3] [।*] स्वस्ति [।*] शरभपुराद्विक्क्रमोपनतसामन्तमकुट चूडामणि–
2 प्रभाप्रसेकाम्बुधौ तपादयुगलो रिपुविलासिनीसीमन्तोद्ध–
3 रणहेतुर्व्वसुवसुधागोप्रद ⌣[4]परमभागवतो मातापितृ–
4 पादानुद्ध्यातश्श्रीमहासुदेवराजः पूर्व्वराष्ट्रीयश्रीसाहि–
5 कायां प्रतिवासिकुटुम्बिनस्समा[5]ज्ञापयति ।।[6] (।) विदितमस्तु वो
6 यथास्माभिरयं ग्रामस्तृ (स्त्रि) दशपतिसदनसुखप्रतिष्ठाक—

Second Plate : First Side

7 रो यावद्रविशशिताराकिरणप्रतिहतघोरान्धकारं जगदव–
8 तिष्ठते तावदुपभोग्यस्सनिधिस्सोपनिधिरचाटभटप्रावेश्य [:*]
9 सर्व्वकरविसर्ज्जित ×को (कौ) ण्डिन्यसगोत्र[7]वाजसनेयसवित्त (तृ)–

1. About 6″ long and 3¼″ broad at the ends and a little less in the middle.
2. From *CII*, iii, pl. xxvii.
3. Fleet: ओं Expressed by a symbol.
4. The sign of *upadhmānīya*, which is not clearly formed, is indicated by very faintly engraved stroke in the middle of the square top of the following letter *pa*.
5. The long medial *ā* is here formed by a downward elongation of the right vertical of *m*.
6. It is not half mark of punctuation as understood by Fleet (*CII*, iii, 198, 1.5. *Vide* also *ibid*., 193, fn. 14), but full mark consisting of a couple of strokes.
7. Fleet: °सगोत्त°. But the subscribed *t* is quite clear. *Contra tra* at the end of this line.

10 स्वामिने [आ*] त्मीयकन्याप्रदाने [न*] औपमन्यव [व*] त्ससगोत्र[8] [9]यामा–
11 [10]त्रो [:*] नागवत्सस्वामिबन्धुवत्सस्वामिनोस्ताम्ब्र (म्र) शासनेनाति–
12 स्तृ (सृ)ष्टको भूत्वास्माभिरप्युत्तरायणे मातापित्रो[11]रात्मनश्च

Second Plate : Second Side

13 पुण्ये (ण्या) भिवृद्धयेनुमोदितः[12] [।*] ते यूयमेवमुपलभ्यास्याज्ञाश्र[13]–
14 वणविधेया भूत्वा यथोचित (तं) भोगभागमुपमुपनयन्त[14]स्सु–
15 ख (खं) प्रतिवत्स्यथ [।*] भविष्यतश्च भूमिपा [न*]नुदर्शयति । दानाद्विशिष्ट–
16 मनुपालनजं पुराणे (णा) द्ध (ध) र्म्मेषु निश्चितधिय ‿ प्रवदं (द)न्ति धर्म्मं (र्म्मम्) । तस्मा [द्*]
17 द्विजाय सु[15]विशुद्धकुलश्रुताय दत्ता (त्तां)[16] भुव (वं)[17]भवतु वो मतिरेव गोप्तु[18] [म् ॥१॥*]त–
18 द्भवद्भिरप्येषा दत्तिरनुपालयितव्या [।*] व्यासगीता (तां) श्चात्र श्लोकानुदाहरन्ति[।*]

Third Plate : First Side

19 अग्नेरपत्यं प्रथमं सुवर्ण्णं (र्ण्णं) भूर्व्वैष्णवी सूर्य्यसुताश्च गाव [:।*] दत्ता–
20 स्त्रयस्तेन भवन्ति लोका य×काञ्चनं गाञ्च महीञ्च दद्यात् [॥२॥*] षष्टिव–
21 र्षसहस्राणि स्वर्गे मो[19]दति भूमिदः [।*] आच्छेत्ता चानुमन्ता च तान्ये–
22 व न [र*]के वसेत् [॥३॥*] बहुभिर्व्वसुधा दत्ता राजभि [:*] सगरादिभिः [।*] यस्य
23 यस्य यदा भूमिस्तस्य तस्य तदा फलं (लम्) [॥४॥*] स्वदत्ता (त्तां) परदत्ता (त्तां) [वा*] य–

8. Fleet: °सगोत्र°
9. Before this word, above the line, we have a cross (*kākapada*) which indicates that this is not its proper place. As suggested by Fleet (*ibid.*, 198, fn. 1), the intended reading was as follows:
सवितृस्वामिन आत्मीयकन्याप्रदानेन यामात्रोरौपमन्यवत्ससगोत्रनागवत्सस्वामिबन्धुवत्सस्वामिनो°
10. Before *tro*, *mi* was engraved and then cancelled. And after it *ba* was probably engraved and cancelled and in its place *tro* was engraved.
11. Fleet: °पित्रो°
12. There is a cross above *visarga* indicating that something, not engraved here, has to be inserted. According to Fleet, the passage commencing with अस्मिन्नेव ग्रामे in lines 25 and 26 below should be inserted here.
13. Read °भ्यैतयोराज्ञा°
14. Read °भागमुपनयन्त°
15. By oversight at first *si* was engraved; later the medial *u* was added, but the engraver forgot to cancel the medial *i*.
16. Fleet: दत्तां
17. Fleet: भुवं.
18. Fleet: गोप्तुम्. There is a *svastika* symbol after प्तु which has escaped Fleet's notice.
19. Of the medial *o*, one part is attached on the top while the other is formed by the downward elongation of the right vertical of *m*.

24 त्वाद्रक्ष युधिष्ठिर [।*] महि महिमता[20] श्रेष्ठ दानाच्छ्रेयोनुपा[21]–

Third Plate : Second Side

25 अस्मिने (न्ने) व ग्रामे पूर्व्वतटाकस्य पर्य्यंत्त (न्त) भूमिवप्रबद्धा श्री–

26 [22]वापिका पत्था (न्था) नं[23] यावज्जा (ज्ज्ये)ष्ठ इति कृत्वा नाग [व*] त्तस्वामिने ग्रामर्द्ध-स्याधि[24] का दत्ता

27 लनमिति[25] [।।५।।*] स्वमुखाज्ञया **प्रवर्द्धमानविजयसंव्व (व)त्सर १०[26] माघ ९[27]**

28 [28]उक्ती (त्की)र्ण्ण (र्ण्णं) द्रोणसिङ्घेन[29] [।*]

The Seal[30]

1 प्रसन्नहृदयस्वयं विक्क्रमाक्क्रान्तविद्विषः [।*]

2 श्रीमत्सुदेवराजस्य[31] शासनं रिपुशासनं (नम्) [।।६।।*][32]

ABSTRACT

The auspicious words *siddham*, indicated by a symbol, and *svasti*, are followed by the mention of **Śarabhapura,** whence the plates were issued by

20. Read महीमतां
21. Fleet reads °नुपाल but the last letter of the line is clearly *pā* and there is no room for another letter. The remaining part of this passage, °लनमिति, is engraved in the beginning of line 27.
22. Before *vāpikā* there is a cross indicating that something has to be added here, viz. ग्रामार्द्धस्याधिका found at the end of the line. As suggested by Fleet (*ibid.*, 199, fn. 1), this should actually be inserted before श्री in the previous line. The intended arrangement of these two lines is अस्मिन्नेव ग्रामे पूर्व्वतटाकस्य पर्य्यन्तभूमिवप्रबद्धा ग्रामार्द्धस्याधिका श्रीवापिका पन्थानं यावज्ज्येष्ठ इति कृत्वा नागवत्तस्वामिने दत्ता which has to be inserted after अनुमोदित: in line 13 where also we have a cross.
23. Fleet: पन्थानं.
24. There is a cross over *dhi* indicating that something has to be added here, viz. °का दत्ता, which has been engraved in the space intervening between lines 26 and 27.
25. This is the remainder of °नुपा° at the end of line 24.
26. Cunningham proposed to read the symbol as 80.
27. Fleet points out the possibility of the symbol being interpreted as 30, but rejects it in favour of 9.
28. This line is engraved on the proper left side of the plate and the space on the proper right is left blank.
29. Read द्रोणसिंहेन.
30. The seal is circular, its diameter being about 3-5/8". The upper surface has been almost completely destroyed owing to the action of fire to which it was subjected at some time or other. But faint traces of the two-line *Anuṣṭubh* stanza are visible.
31. The lithograph in *ASR*, xvii, pl. xxvi, shows श्रीमहासुदेव,, but it does not suit the metre.
32. The legend, which, with the exception of the word *Prasanna* at the beginning of the first line, is entirely obliterated, has been restored by Fleet with the faint traces here and there and the legend on the seal of the Arang plates of Mahā-Jayarāja. See No. I: V above.

King **Sudevarāja** who is described in conventional terms as in the earlier records. The object of the inscription is to register the king's order to the agriculturist householders inhabiting the village of Śrīsāhika[33] situated in the Pūrvarāṣṭra[34] to the effect that he had given his assent, on the occasion of *Uttarāyaṇa*, to the grant of this village made by means of a copper-plate charter in favour of the Brāhmaṇas Nāgavatsasvāmin and Bandhuvatsa-svāmin[35] students of the Aupamanyava *śākhā* and belonging to the Vatsa *gotra*, who, by the gift of his daughters in marriage, had become the sons-in-law of Savitṛsvāmin, who belonged to the Kauṇḍinya *gotra* and was a student of the Vājasaneyi *śākhā* of the *Yajurveda*. Both the donees received half of the village. But being older of the two, Nāgavatsasvāmin was also given a stepped well called Śrīvāpikā,[36] constructed within the same village on the land bordering on the eastern tank,[37] and extending up to the road, in addition to the common share of half the village.[38] The grant carried with it the same exemptions and privileges as enumerated in the earlier records and the villagers were ordered to obey the donees and to pay them *bhoga* and *bhāga* as due.

Five imprecatory and benedictory stanzas, four of them said to be of Vyāsa, are quoted in support of the request to the future rulers to maintain the grant.

The order recorded in the inscription was given by the king himself by the word of his mouth.

The charter was issued on the **ninth day of the month of Māgha in the tenth year of the increasingly victorious reign** and was engraved, like the preceding records, by Droṇasiṁha.

The verse on the seal states that this charter, which is the chastiser of the enemies, belonged to the illustrious **Sudevarāja**, the very heart (of the family) of Prasanna,[39] who had assailed his enemies by his prowess.[40]

33. According to Hira Lal (*EI*, ix, 283) it is represented by the modern Sirsāhī in the Baloda Bazar, Tahsil of the Bilaspur District.
34. Evidently the eastern part of the Śarabhapurīya kingdom. The mention of the Pūrvarāṣṭra shows that the territory under the Śarabhapura chiefs was divided, for administrative purposes into two *rāṣṭras*, eastern and western.
35. They were evidently brothers, Nāgavatsasvāmin being elder, as subsequently stated in the record itself.
36. Fleet refers to Śrīvāpikā as an irrigation well while we have taken it to be a step well on the basis of the common connotation of the word *vāpī* or *vāpikā*. It may have, of course, served the purpose of irrigation.
37. The reference to the eastern tank indicates that there must have been more than one tanks in the donated village.
38. It appears that Savitṛsvāmin, who was something like a *jāgīrdār*, made a gift of the village from his own landholding with the approval of the ruling Śarabhapurīya monarch.
39. *Prasanna-hṛdaya* in the original is rendered by Fleet by 'who verily has a gracious heart'. He evidently missed the reference to Prasanna-mātra to whose family Sudevarāja belonged.
40. The first quarter of this stanza is not found in the inscription on the seal attached to any other charter of Sudevarāja.

I : XIV

SARANGARH PLATES[1] OF SUDEVARĀJA[2]

Provenance: Sarangarh, Raigarh District, Madhya Pradesh.

References: R.L. Mitra, *JASB*, xxxv, 195ff.; Fleet, *CII*, iii, 193, fn. 2; Hira Lal, *EI*, ix, 281-85 and plate facing p. 283; *ICPB*, 181, No. 310.

Language: Sanskrit. In prose except the usual benedictory and imprecatory verses at the end.

Metres: Verse 1: *Vasantatilakā*; Verse 2 (incomplete): *Indravajrā*

Script: Box-headed variety of the Central Indian alphabet.

Date: Details lost in the missing plate. Latter half of the sixth century A.D.

TEXT[3]

First Plate

1 सिद्धम्[4] [।*] स्वस्ति [।*] **शरभपुराद्विक्क्रमोपनतसामन्तमकुटचूडामणिप्रभाप्र**—

2 सेकाम्बुधौ तपादयुगलो रिपुविलासिनीसीमन्तोद्धरणहेतुर्व्वसु–

3 वसुधागोप्रद ‿ परमभागवतो मातापितृ[5]पादानुद्धयातश्श्री**महासुदे**–

4 **वराज**[6]: तुण्डरकभुक्तीयचुल्लण्डरके प्रतिवासिकुटुम्बिनस्स–

5 माज्ञापयाति [।*] विदितमस्तु वो यथायं ग्रामः[7] त्रिदशपतिसदनसुख–

6 प्रतिष्ठाकरो यावद्रविशशिताराकिरणप्रतिहतधोरान्धकारं ज–

Second Plate : First Side

7 गदवतिष्ठते तावदुपभोग्यस्सनिधिस्सोपनिधिरचाटभटप्रावेश्य [:*]

8 सर्व्वंकरविसर्ज्जितः राज्यमहादेवीरो(रा)जकुलैः[8] मातापित्रोरात्मनं(न)श्च पु–

1. The plates are 6½″ long and 3½″ broad. The hole about the middle of the left margin is roundish on one side and squarish on the other, the diameter being 7/16″.
2. The third plate having been lost, the record is incomplete. The lost portion of the text included, besides some of the imprecatory verses, the date and the name of the engraver. The seal is also not forthcoming.
3. From plates in *EI*, ix.
4. Expressed by a symbol.
5. The medial i, which was first engraved by oversight, was later cancelled. Hira Lal: °पित्रि°.

6-7. *Sandhi* has not been observed here as well as at several other places.

8. The sign of *visarga* is rather unusual, consisting as it does of a somewhat irregular square above and a short horizontal stroke below. Elsewhere in this record, as in several others, it is indicated by a couple of horizontal strokes one above the other. *Sandhi* has not been observed here.

9 ण्याभिवृद्धये उदकपूर्व्वं को (कौ) शिकसगो[9]त्रत्रिसहस्त्रविद्यभास्करस्वामि–..
10 प्रभाकरस्वामिबर्ब्बरिस्वामि-बोटस्वामि-दत्तस्वामि-विष्णुस्वामि– ।।[10]
11 फल्गुस्वामि-स्वामि-कीर्त्तिस्वामिशं (श) ङ्करस्वामिना (नां)[11] ताम्ब्र (म्र) शासनेनातिसृ–
12 ष्टो भूत्वास्माभिरनुमोदितः [।*] ते यूयमेवमुपलं (ल) भ्यैषा[12]माज्ञाश्रव–

Second Plate : Second Side

13 णविधेया भूत्वा यथोचितं भोगभागमुपनयन्तस्सुख (खं) प्रतिवत्स्यथ [।*]
14 भविष्यतश्च भूमिपाननुदर्शयति । दानाद्विशिष्टमनुपालनज (जं) पु–
15 राणां (णा) ।।[13]धर्म्मेषु निश्चितधियऽप्रवदन्ति धर्म्मं (म्मर्म्) ।। (।) तस्मा [द्*] द्विजाय सुवि–
16 शुद्धकुलश्रुताय दत्तां भुवं भवतु वो मतिरेव गोप्तुं (प्तुम्) ।।[१।।*] तद्भवद्भि–
17 रप्येषा दत्तिरनुपालयितव्या [।*] व्यासगीतांश्चात्र श्लोकानुदाहर–
18 न्ति ।। अग्नेरपत्यं प्रथमं सुवर्ण्णं ।।[14] भूर्व्वैष्णवी सूर्य्यसुता[15]–

ABSTRACT

Inaugurated by the auspicious words *siddham* and *svasti,* the former expressed symbolically, the charter was issued from **Śarabhapura** by King **Sudevarāja** who is described in exactly the same fashion as in the earlier records. It records the confirmation by the king of the grant of the village of Cullaṇḍaraka[16] included in the Tuṇḍaraka *bhukti*[17] made by the chief queen[18]

9. Oversight the subscript *r* is formed like medial *r*.
10. The mark of punctuation, which is left out unnoticed by Hira Lal, is superfluous.
11. Hira Lal: शङ्कर°
12. Hira Lal: °मुपलभ्यै°
13. Hira Lal takes the two horizontal strokes following *nāṁ* as standing for *visarga.* It would, however, be more reasonable to regard them as a mark of punctuation. It may be noted that in the Śarabhapurīya records we often come across a may punctuation mark after the word *purāṇā*. It is, however, unnecessary.
14. Hira Lal puts the mark of punctuation within a round bracket, but it is quite clear in the facsimile accompanying his paper. It is, however, superfluous.
15. The remaining portion of this stanza, some other imprecatory and benedictive verses, the date and the name of the engraver were inscribed on the third plate which is not traceable.
16. It cannot be identified. But it must have been situated close to the modern village of Tūṇḍrā, which represents the *bhuki* in which it was situated. Hira Lal observes that if the village exists, we would now find the name in a form like Culāndur, a characteristic Chhattisgarhi name. Mirashi proposes to identify the village with the modern Childa, 82°31′ and 21°31′. See *EI*, xxii, 22.
17. The chief place of the *bhukti*, Tuṇḍaraka, is now represented by the village of Tūṇḍrā, about six miles south of Sheorinarayan on the Mahanadi and about thirty-five miles west of Sarangarh, the findspot of the plates. It is now included in the Baloda Bazar Tahsil of the Raipur District. We do not know if this *bhukti* was in any way connected with the Tuṇḍa *rāṣṭra* mentioned in the Thakurdiya plates of Pravararāja. See *infra,* I: XV.
18. It is interesting to note that she is styled the chief queen of the state (*rājya-mahādevī*).

and other members of the royal family[19] by means of a copper-plate charter in favour of the Brāhmaṇas Bhāskarasvāmin, Prabhākarasvāmin, Barbbarisvāmin, Boṭasvāmin, Dattasvāmin, Viṣṇusvāmin,[20] Phalgusvāmin, Svāmin,[20a] Kīrttisvāmin and Śaṅkarasvāmin accompanied by the usual privileges and exemptions[21] for the increase of their own religious merit as well as that of their parents. The king's order was, as usual, addressed to the agriculturist householders of the granted village who were exhorted to obey the donees and offer them due *bhoga* and *bhāga* and thereby live happily.

Next followed the usual request to the future rulers to maintain the grant and a few imprecatory and benedictory verses, at least three of which are attributed to Vyāsa, were cited.[22]

Other details cannot be made out as the last plate is not forthcoming.

19. *Rājakula* in the original.
20. As suggested by Hira Lal, one of the grantees, Viṣṇusvāmin, is perhaps the same as the donee of the Nahna plates.
20*a*. Hira Lal clubs the word *svāmin* with the following name Kīrttisvāmin, whose full name would then be Svāmikīrttisvāmin, which is rather unusual.
21. These include right to the *nidhis* and the *upanidhis* and freedom from the entry of the *cāṭas* and the *bhaṭas* and exemption from all the taxes.
22. One full verse and part of only a single stanza said to be of Vyāsa are accommodated on the second side of the second plate. As the third plate is lost, it is dificult to say exactly as to how many verses were actually quoted. That there must have been at least three verses can be inferred from the use of the plural *Vyāsagītān*. In all likelihood four verses were quoted in the name of Vyāsa as in most other records of the family.

I : XV

THAKURDIYA PLATES[1] OF PRAVARARĀJA, YEAR 3

Provenance: Thakurdiya, Raigarh District, Madhya Pradesh.

References: Hira Lal, *ICPB*, errata, p. 1; V.V. Mirashi, *EI*, xxii, 15-23 and plates opposite pp. 22 and 23.

Language: Sanskrit. In prose but for the customary benedictory and imprecatory verses at the end and the legend on the seal.

Metres: Verse 1: *Vasantatilakā*; Verse 2: *Indravajrā*; Verses 3–6: *Anuṣṭubh*.

Script: Box-headed variety of the Central Indian alphabet.

Date: Regnal Year 3, Mārgaśirṣa 2. Latter half of the sixth century A.D.

TEXT[2]

First Plate

1 सिद्धम्[3] [।*] स्वस्ति [।*] श्रीपुराद्विक्रमोपनतसामं(म)न्तमकुटचूडा[4]मणिप्रभाप्र–

2 सेकां(का)म्बुधौतपादयुगलो रिपुविलासिनीसीमं(म)न्तोद्धरणहेतु[5]—

3 र्व्वंसुवसुधागोप्रदः[6] परमभागवतो मां(मा)तापितृपादानुद्ध्यातः

4 श्रीमहाप्रवरराजः तुण्ड[7]राष्ट्रियाषाढके प्रतिवासिनः समाज्ञा–

5 पयति [।*] विदितमस्तु वो यथास्माभिरयं ग्रामः (म) स्त्रिदशपतिसदन–

6 सुखप्रतिष्ठाकरो यावद्रविशसि(शि)ताराकिरणप्रतिहतघोरान्धका–

Second Plate : First Side

7 र(रं)जगदवति[8]ष्ठते तावदुपभोग्यः सनिधिः सोपनिधिरचाटभटप्रावे—

8 श्यः सर्व्वंकरविसर्ज्जितः मातापित्रोरात्मनश्च पुन्या(ण्या)भिवृद्धये पराश–

9 रसगोत्राय वाजसनेयी(यि) ने भट्टकपुरन्दरस्वामिने ताम्त्र(म्र)शा–

10 सनेनातिसिस्त्र(सृ)ष्ट [:।*] ते यूयमेवमुपलभ्य आज्ञाश्रवणविधेया

1. The plates are 7·1″ long and 3·6″ broad.
2. From plates in *EI*, xxii, opposite pp. 22 and 23.
3. Mirashi: ओं. Expressed by a symbol.
4. The engraver first engraved *dhā* but later corrected it to *ḍā*.
5. There is a superfluous dot at the end of the line.
6. *Daḥ* was at first omitted by oversight but was later inscribed at its proper place below the line.
7. Mirashi: तुण्ड°
8. *Ṣ* is without a cross-bar which is left out inadvertently.

11 भूत्वा यथोचितं भोगभागमुपन्त[9]सुखं प्रतिवत्स्यथ [।*] भविष्यतश्च भू-
12 मिपालाननुदरीशयती[10] [।*] दानाद्वीशि[11]ष्टमनुपालनजं पुराणा

Second Plate : Second Side

13 धर्म्मं (र्म्मे) षु[12] निश्चितधियः प्रवदन्ति धर्म्मं[13] [म् ।*] तस्मा [द्*] द्विजाय सुविशुद्धकु-
14 लश्रुताय दत्तां भुवं भवतु वो मतिरेव गोप्तुं (प्तुम्) [॥१॥*] तद्भवद्भिरप्येषा दत्ति-
15 रनुपालयितव्या [।*] व्यासगीतांश्च श्लोकानुदाहरन्ति [।*] अग्नेरपत्यं प्र-
16 थमं सुवर्ण्णं भूर्व्वैष्णवी सूर्य्यसुताश्च गावः [।*] दत्तास्त्रयस्ते--
17 न भवं (व) न्ति लोकायः काञ्चनं गाश्च महीञ्च दद्यात् [॥२॥*] शष्टी[14] वरिशस[15]-
18 हस्राणि स्वर्ग्गे मोदति भूमिदः [।*] आच्छेत्ता चानुमं (म) न्ता च तान्येव नर-

Third Plate : First Side

19 के वसेत् [॥३॥*] बहुभिर्व्वसुधा दत्ता राजभि [:*] सगरादिभिः [।*] यस्य य-
20 स्य यदा भूमित (स्त) स्य तस्य तदा फलं (लम्) [॥४॥*] स्वदत्तां परदत्ताव्वां[16] यत्ना-
21 द्रक्ष युधिष्ठिर [।*] मही (हीं) महि (ही) मतां श्रेष्ठ दानाच्छ्रेयोनुपाल-
22 नमिति [॥५॥*][17] स (स्व) मुखाज्ञया **प्रवर्द्धमानविजयसंव्व (व) त्सर ३ मार्ग्ग**
23 **शीर्ष दि** २ उकि (त्की) र्ण्णं गोलसिङ्घेन[18] ॥[18a]

Seal[19]

1 मानमात्र[सु]त[स्ये]दं स्वभुजोपार्ज्जितक्षितेः [।*]
2 [श्री] **मत्प्रवरराजस्य** शासन (नं) शत्रु-शासन (नम्) [॥६॥*]

9. Read °मुपनयन्तः
10. Mirashi: दरिशयति. Read दर्शयति
11. Mirashi: दानाद्वि°. Read °दानाद्विशिष्ट°.
12. Mirashi: धर्म्मेषु.
13. Mirashi: धर्म्मं.
14. Read षष्टि.
15. Read वर्ष°.
16. Read परदत्तां वा.
17. Better read °पालनम् [॥५॥*] इति.
18. Mirashi: शील°. Read गोलसिंहेन°
18*a*. This mark of punctuation consists of a vertical stroke with its top curved to left followed by another straight vertical line.
19. Lower portion of the bronze seal, which is circular, is broken. The surface of the seal, as of other seals of the dynasty, is divided into two equal halves by a couple of horizontal lines in the middle. The upper half contains the figure of Lakṣmī with a halo around her face, standing on a lotus and facing full front. Holding lotus in her upraised right hand and an uncertain round object in her left hand which is held akimbo, she is being bathed by an elephant standing on a lotus on her either side with the water poured from a pot held in its uplifted trunk. In both the left and right corners there is a waterlily. There seems to be a crescent, indicated by scaloping a portion of the double line border on left and the solar disc on right above the neck of the elephant. The lower half contains an *Anuṣṭubh* verse in two lines. The device, if any, below the legend cannot be ascertained as the lower portion is broken

ABSTRACT

The charter was issued from **Śrīpura** by King **Pravararāja,** who, like his predecessors, is eulogised as one with his feet washed by the waters that is the flowing forth of the effulgence of the crest-jewels of the feudatory chiefs subdued by his prowess and as the cause of the tearing out of the parted hair of the ladies of his enemies, the giver of the wealth, earth and cattle, the devout devotee of *Bhagavat, i.e.,* Viṣṇu, and the meditator upon the feet of his parents. It aims at registering the grant by him of the village of Āṣāḍhaka[20] included in the Tuṇḍa *rāṣṭra*[21] in favour of the *Bhaṭṭaka*[22] Purandarasvāmin,[23] who belonged to the Parāśara *gotra* and was a student of the Vājasaneyī Saṁhitā (of the *Śukla Yajurveda*). The grant, which was made by issuing a copper-plate charter, bestowed on the donee the same privileges and exemptions as enumerated in the earlier records. The royal command in respect of the grant was addressed to the inhabitants of the donated village who were asked to be obedient to the donee and offer him the usual *bhoga* and *bhāga*.

The usual request to the future kings to uphold the grant is sought to be supported by five imprecatory and benedictory stanzas four of which are said to belong to Vyāsa.

The order concerning the grant was given by the king by the word of his own mouth.

The charter was issued on the **second day of the month of Mārgaśirṣa in the third year of the increasingly victorious reign, evidently of Pravararāja,** and it was incised by Golasiṁha.[24]

The seal-inscription avers that this enemy-chastising charter is of the illustrious **Pravararāja,** son of Mānamātra, who had acquired the earth by (the valour of) his own arms.

20. It is probably represented by the modern village of Asoṇḍ, 82°54′ and 21°45′, about two miles to the north of Mahanadi.
21. Tuṇḍa, the headquarters of the *rāṣṭra* christened after it, may be identified with one of the villages named Tuṇḍa, Tuṇḍra, Tuṇḍrī or Tuṇḍragaon near Sheorinarayan, some 25 to 30 miles from Thakurdiya, the findspot of the record. The identification with the first named villages seems more probable.
22. The same as *Bhaṭṭa*, a title of the learned Brāhmaṇas.
23. It will follow from the sameness of the names, the *gotras* and the Vedic *śākhās* that the donee of this charter is the same as that of the Kauvatal plates of Sudevarāja. It is also noteworthy in this connection that both the grants were issued from the same place, *viz.*, Śrīpura.
24. He is evidently the same as the homonymous engraver of the Dhamatari and Kauvatal plates of Sudevarāja issued from Śrīpura in the third and seventh years respectively of his reign. See above I: IX and XII.

I : XVI

MALLAR PLATES[1] PRAVARARĀJA, YEAR 3

Provenance: Mallar, Bilaspur District, Madhya Pradesh.

References: *ARIE*, 1958-59, 2 and 26, No. A-7; G. Bhattacharya, *EI*, xxxiv, 51-52 and plates between pp. 52 and 53.

Language: Sanskrit. In prose with the exception of the customary benedictive and imprecatory verses at the end and the legend on the seal.

Metres: Verse 1: *Vasantatilakā*; Verse 2: *Indravajrā*; Verses 3–6: *Anuṣṭubh.*

Script: Box-headed variety of the Central Indian alphabet.

Date: Regnal Year 3, Pauṣa 2. Later half of the sixth century A.D.

TEXT[2]

First Plate

1 सिद्धम्[3] [।*] स्वस्ति [।*] श्रीपुराद्वी (द्वि)क्रमोपनतसामं(म)न्तमकुटचूडामणिप्रभा–
2 प्रसेकाम्बुधौतपादयुगलो रिपुविलासिनीसीमं (म) न्तोद्धरणहे—
3 तुवसुर्व्वसुधागोप्रद:[4] परमभागवतो मातापितृपादानु–
4 द्धयातश्श्रीमहाप्रवरराजः शङ्खचक्राभोगि(गी)यमित्रग्रामके प्र–
5 तिवासिन: समाज्ञापयति [।*] विदितमस्तु वो यथास्माभिरयं ग्रा–
6 म:[4a] तृ(त्रि) दशपतिसदनसुखप्रतिष्ठाकरो यावद्रविशशितारा–

Second Plate : First Side

7 किरणप्रतिहतघोरान्धकारं जगदवतिष्ठते तावदुपभोग्य:
8 सनिधिस्सोपनिधिरचाटभटप्रावेश्य: सर्व्वंकरविसर्ज्जित: मा–
9 तापित्रोरात्म[5]नश्च पुण्याभिवृद्धये भारद्वाजसगोत्रव(ब) हृ्वृचदामोद–
10 रगणपुत्रशुभचन्द्रस्वामिने ताम्ब्र(म्र)शासनेनातिस्त्री (सृ)ष्ट:[6] [।*]
11 ते यूयमेवमुपलभ्याज्ञा[6a]श्रवणविधेया भूत्वा यथोचित (तं)भोग[7]–

1. About 6·9″ long and 3·5″ broad. The holes for the passage of the ring in the margin on the left are square. The rims of the plates are thickened and slightly raised.
2. From plates in *EI*, xxxiv, between pp. 52 and 53.
3. Expressed by a symbol.
4. Read °तुर्व्वसुवसुधा°
4a. *Sandhi* has not been observed here.
5. The subscript *m* is cut off by the hole made for the passage of the ring.
6. Bhattacharya: °स्त्रिष्ट:
6a. Better read °भ्यास्याज्ञा° as in most other records of the family.
7. Bhattacharya reads; भाग° but the stroke for *e* (turning to left) is also quite clear in the facsimile published with his paper. The opening word of the following line should accordingly be read as °भाग°

12 भागमुपनयनास्स (स्सु))ख(खं) प्रतिवत्स्यथ [।*] भविष्यतश्च भू–

Second Plate : Second Side

13 मिपालाननुदर्शयति [।*] दानाद्विशिष्टमनुपालनजं षु(पु)राणा

14 धर्म्मेषु निश्चितधिय प्रवदंत्ति[8] धर्म्मं(र्म्मम्) [।*] तस्मा[द्*] द्विजाय शु(सु) विषु(शु) द्धकुल–

15 श्रुताय दत्तां भुवं भवतु वो मतिरेव गोप्तु [म्*] ।। [१।।*] तद्भवद्भिरप्ये [षा]

16 दत्तिरनुपालयितव्या [।*] व्यासगीतांश्च श्लोकानुदाहरं(र)न्ति[9] [।*] अ–

17 ग्नेरपत्यं (प्र)थमं सुवर्ण्णं(र्ण्णं)भूर्व्वैष्णवी सूर्य्यसुताश्च गाव [:।*] [दत्ता]–

Third Plate : First Side

18 [स्त्र] यस्तेन भवं(व) न्ति लोका य: काञ्चनं गाञ्च महीञ्च दद्यात् [।।२।।*] सष्टी–[10]

19 वर्षसं (स) हस्त्राणि स्वर्ग्गे मोदति भूमिद: [।*] आच्छेत्ता चानुमन्ता च ता–

20 न्येव नरके वसेत् [।।३।।*] बहुभिर्व्वसुधा दत्ता राजभिस्सगरादि–

21 भि: [।*] यस्य यस्य यदा भूमित(स्त)स्य तस्य तदा फलं (लम्) [।।४।।*] स्वदत्तां प–

22 र[दत्तां] वा यत्नाद्रक्ष युधिष्ठिर [।*] मही(हीं) महि हि मतां[11] श्रेष्ठ दानाच्छ्रेयो–

23 नुपालनमिति ।।[५।।*][12] **प्रवर्द्धमानविजयसं(व) तु (त्) ३ पौषदिन २**

Third Plate : Second Side

24 [13]उत्कीर्ण्णं गोलसिङ्घेन[14] [।*]

Seal[15]

1 मानमात्रसुतस्येदं स्वभुजोपार्ज्जित[क्षि]ते [:] [।*]

2 श्रीमत्**प्रवरराजस्य** शासनं शत्रुशा [स]न (नम्) [।।६।।*]

ABSTRACT

Issued from **Śrīpura,** the charter belongs to King **Pravararāja** who is described in a fashion exactly identical with that of the preceding record. It records his order to the inhabitants of the village Mitragrāmaka situated in

8. Read प्रवदन्ति.
9. Bhattacharya: °नुदाहरन्ति.
10. Read षष्टि°.
11. Bhattacharya: मह [ी] मतां.
12. Better read°पालनम् [।।५।।] इति.
13. This line is written in the middle of the plate.
14. Read गोलसिङ्हेन.
15. The circular seal attached to the ring holding the plates together, which is broken in the upper left portion, bears a close resemblance to the one affixed to the Thakurdiya plates of the donor of the present charter. However, the portion below the legend, which is intact, bears the representation of a rose planted by a floral device on either side.

the Śaṅkhacakrā *bhoga*[16] to the effect that he had given away the village to the Brāhmaṇa Śubhacandrasvāmin, son of Dāmodaragaṇa, belonging to the Bhāradvāja *gotra* and a student of the *Ṛgveda*, by means of a copper-plate charter and that knowing this fact they should pay the grantee the *bhoga* and *bhāga* as due and thereby live happily in the village. The donee was granted the usual privileges listed in the earlier records.

The future kings are exhorted to protect the grant, and five imprecatory and benedictive verses, which are also met with in the previous record, are cited in order to strengthen this request.

The charter was issued on the **second day of the month of Pauṣa in the third year of the increasingly victorious reign (of Pravararāja)** and was engraved by Golasiṁha.[17]

The inscription on the seal is literally the same as that found on the seal attached to the previous grant.

16. The chief plase of the *bhoga*, Śaṅkhacakrā, as well as the donated village, Mitragrāmaka, has not been identified.
17. Golasimha figures in the same capacity in the Dhamatari and Kauvatal plates of Sudevarāja and the Thakurdiya plates of Pravararāja, all the three issued from Śrīpura.

APPENDIX I

A STRAY ŚARABHAPURĪYA PLATE

A single plate of copper was found in possession of Shri Shivajirao Mahadik of Raksha, Rajim, in the Raipur District of Madhya Pradesh. It was reported that originally a complete set of three copper-plates together with its ring was found while digging a plot of land near Pokhra. But a dispute arose among the diggers about the ownership of the set and it was decided to divide the plates equally. Two of the plates and the ring were melted before the information about the discovery of the record reached Moreshwar G. Dikshit, who published the portion of the record inscribed on this plate in *IHQ*, xxxiii, 84-85.

The plate (about 6″ in length and 3″ in breadth) bears writing on both the sides. There are altogether twelve lines of writing, each side bearing six lines. The characters belong to the box-headed variety of the Central Indian alphabet, and the language is Sanskrit. The format, general tenor, the provenance and palaeographic considerations leave no room for doubt that this is the second or middle plate of a three-plate Śarabhapurīya charter. As in other charters of the dynasty, the name and description of the issuing chief must have been given on the inner side of the first plate and that of the engraver and the details of date on the third plate. And as both these plates are lost, we have no knowledge as to who made the grant recorded in this inscription. The seal, the legend on which could have supplied this information, is also not forthcoming. From the mode of drafting we can only conclude that the record cannot be placed earlier than the Mallar plates of Jayarāja dated in the fifth year of his reign (*vide* No. I: V above). However, Moreshwar G. Dikshit suggested, on the basis of the tenor of the inscription that the plate in question belonged to Sudevarāja, son of Mānamātra-Durgarāja. The name of the donated village and the administrative division in which it was situated also cannot be made out as they were given on the first plate which is lost.

The portion of the inscription inscribed on this plate records that a certain Daṇḍacakra[1] gave away a village to *Dīkṣita* Anantasvāmin of the Vājasaneya *śākhā* (of the *Yajurveda*) and the Bhāradvāja *gotra* with all the usual privileges and exemptions and that this grant was approved by the king by means of a copper-plate charter.[2] The villagers were exhorted to pay to the donee

1. The expression *sa-bāla-vṛddha-Daṇḍacakkreṇa* seems to indicate that the children and elderly members of his family were also associated with Daṇḍacakra in making the grant.
2. Dikshit wrongly states that the grant was made for the religious merit of Daṇḍacakra.

periodical offerings and the royal share of agricultural produce regularly. The future rulers were then entreated to protect the grant and a few customary imprecatory and benedictive stanzas (at least four), at least three of them attributed to Vyāsa, were quoted. Only one of these stanzas is fully accommodated and the second partially on the available plate, the first being in the *Vasantatilakā* and the second in *Indravajrā* metres. Both these stanzas are already familiar from the Śarabhapurīya charters.

The inscription is edited here from the facsimile accompanying Dikshit's article.[2a]

TEXT[3]

Second Plate : First Side

1 शिताराकिरणप्रतिहतघोरान्धकारं[4] जगदवतिष्ठा (ष्ठ)ते[5]ता [व*] दुपभोग्य–

2 [6]स्सनिधिस्सोपनिधिरचाटभटप्रावेश्यस्सर्व्वंकरविसर्ज्जितः सबा–

3 लवृद्धदण्डचक्रेण[7] पुण्याभिवृद्धये वाजसनेयभरद्वाजस–

4 गोत्रदि (दी)क्षिता[8]नन्तस्वामिनः श्रतिसृष्टका (को)[9] भूत्वा ताम्ब्र (म्र) शासने–[9a]

5 नास्माभिरनुमोदितः ते यूयमेवमुपलभ्यास्याज्ञा[10]श्रवणविधे[11]–

6 या भूत्वा[12] यथोचितं भोगभागमुपनयन्तस्सुखं प्रतिवि (व) त्स्यथ[13] [।*]

---

the fact is that the grant was made by Daṇḍacakra himself with the approval of his master. Unfortunately we have no information about the position occupied by Daṇḍacakra. Among the Śarabhapurīya records we have several instances of the kings endorsing the grants made by his subordinates or members of the royal family. See above, I: I, VII, XIII, etc.

2a. The plate has been edited by the present author in *JAIH*, xi, 13-17.

3. From plate in *IHQ*, xxxiii.

4. *The anusvāra* is misplaced, being engraved on the left of the *akṣara ra* and not above it as usual.

5. Dikshit: °दवतिष्ठते.

6. Dikshit: °स्मनिधि°.

7. Dikshit: °बृद्धदण्डचक्रेण. The expression *sa-bāla-vṛddha*, probably employed to indicate the involvement of some other younger and elderly members of the family in the grant, is not met with in any other Śarabhapurīya record.

8. Dikshitş दीक्षिता°.

9. Dikshit: अतिसृष्ट को.

9a. Dikshit: ताम्म्रशासने°.

10. Dikshit proposes to correct it to °ष्येषामाज्ञा° which is wrong and unwarranted. The donee being only a single individual, *asya*, used in the charter, and not *eṣāṁ*, suggested by Dikshit, would be the correct expression.

11. Dikshit has left out the letter *dhe* in his transcript though the same is quite clear in the facsimile and is required.

12. Dikshit: भूत्वा.

13. Dikshit: प्रतिवत्स्यथ:

Second Plate : Second Side

7 भविष्यतश्च भूमिपाननुदर्शयति[14] ।।(।) दो(दा) ना[15]द्विशिष्टमनुपाल–

8 नजं पुराणा धर्म्मेषु निश्चितधि[16]य ⁀ प्रवदन्ति धर्म्मं (र्म्मम्) [17] ।।(।)तस्मा [द्*] द्विजाय: (य)

9 सुविशुद्धकुलश्रुताय दत्तां भुवं भवतु वो मती(ति)रेव[18] गोप्त (प्तु) [म्*] ।।[19]

10 तद्भवद्भिर्प्य(प्ये)षा[20] दत्तिरनुपालयितव्या [।*] व्यासगी[21]तांश्चात्र[22] श्लोकानुदा[23]–

11 हरन्ति [।*] अग्नेरपत्यं प्रथमं सुवर्ण्णं(र्णं) [24] ।। भूर्व्वैष्णवी[25] सूर्य्यसुता–

12 श्च[26] गाव: [।*] दत्तास्त्रयस्तेन भवन्ति लोका:(का) य × काञ्चनं [27]गां च मही(हीं) च[28]

14. Dikshit: °ननुदर्शयति°
15. Dikshit: दाना°.
16. There is a superfluous stroke attached to the base of the circle indicating medial *i* in the *akṣaras ści* and *dhi*. Superfluous strokes, sometimes dots, are found at the bottom of a few other letters also.
17. Dikshit reads; धर्म्मं: but the two horizontal strokes after *rmmaṁ* actually indicate the mark of punctuation.
18. Dikshit: मतिरेव.
19. Dikshit reads गोप्त: and suggests to correct it to गोप्तम्.
20. Dikshit: °रप्येषा.
21. The box-head of *g* is left out unengraved.
22. There is a superfluous stroke before *tra*.
23. There is superfluous appendage below the letter *dā*.
24. Dikshit: सुवर्ण्णं:. But the two short horizontal strokes are actually intended to indicate a mark of punctuation which is, however, superfluous.
25. Dikshit: भुर्व्वैष्णवे.
26. Dikshit: °सुताश्च.
27. There is an unnecessary stroke to the left of the letter *gā*.
28. The verse is incomplete. At least two more stanzas must have followed it as indicated by the employment of the plural number.

APPENDIX II

MALLAR PLATES OF VYĀGHRARĀJA

The plates bearing this record were found in 1958 at the historically renowned village of Mallar, some sixteen miles from Bilaspur in the Bilaspur District of Madhya Pradesh.[1] The place, it may be added, has yielded a large number of early epigraphic records, some of which are incorporated in the present volume, and other antiquities and has recently been subjected to large-scale archaeological operations which have thrown welcome light on its early history.[1a] The inscription was originally edited by D.C. Sircar and G. Bhattacharya in *EI*, xxxiv, 45-50 and plates between pp. 48 and 49.[2]

The **charter** is incised on a set of three rectangular plates of copper with their corners rounded off. The **plates** measure about 7″ long and 3.5″ broad, the middle or second plate being somewhat thicker than the other two plates. They are held together by a ring, 1.3″ thick and about 11.4″ in diameter, passing through a round hole bored about the middle of the left margin of each plate. The surface of the circular **seal** (1.9″ in diameter), attached to the ring, is considerably corroded, making it difficult to recognise the devices on it definitely. It is divided into two parts by a thick horizontal line running across it in the middle. The upper portion bears the representation of the side-view of a wheel, the head of an animal or bird (probably Garuḍa)[3] and a conch-shell in a row from left to right while the lower half contains a single-line legend giving the name of the issuing chief, preceded by the honorific *śrī*, in nominative singular, and an indistinct device, which looks like a lotus flower,[4] below it. The first and third plates bear writing only on the inner side whereas the second plate is engraved on both the sides. The inscription contains in all twenty-four lines of writing of which the first and the last plates bear six lines each while the first and second sides of the middle plate have seven and five lines respectively.

The **characters** belong to the South Indian alphabet and are of the nail-headed variety with the tops of letters being formed by hollow or linear triangular marks.[5] Palaeographically, the record may be placed in the late

1. *ARIE*, 1958-59, App. A, No. 6.
1a. For details, see K.D. Bajpai and S.K. Pandey, *Malhar* (Sagar 1978).
2. See also B.C. Jain in *Navabhārata* (Hindi Daily, Nagpur), Dīpāvalī Special, 1960, and *Catalogue of the Antiquities preserved in the M.G.M. Museum*, Raipur (Hindi), vi, 174-76, pls. lv-lvi.
3. According to Sircar and Bhattacharya, it is probably lion's head.
4. Sircar and Bhattacharya think that it may be the head of an elephant to front.
5. The characters have been compared to those of the Hingniberdi plates of Vibhurāja (*EI*, xxix, pl. opp. p. 176), the Khanapur plates of Mādhavavarman (*ibid.*, xxvii, pls. between pp. 316 and 317) and the Arga plates of Kāpālivarman (*ibid.*, xxxi, pl. facing p. 232), etc.

sixth or early seventh century A.D.[6] The **language** is Sanskrit and the inscription is composed in prose but for the four conventional imprecatory and benedictive stanzas at the end.

The inscription belongs to a chief named **Vyāghrarāja** who is described as younger brother of king Pravara-bhaṭṭāraka who was himself son of Jaya-bhaṭṭāraka. Pravara-bhaṭṭāraka is described as the very moon on the firmament that is the family known as Amarārya-kula. Its **object** is to register the grant by Vyāghrarāja of the village Kunturapadraka situated in Pūrva-*rāṣṭra* in favour of the Brāhmaṇa *Dīkṣita* Agnicandrasvāmin, son of *Dīkṣita* Durggasvāmin, who was a student of the *Ṛgveda* and belonged to the Kāpy-Āṅgirasa *gotra*.

The inscription opens with the auspicious word *svasti* followed by the mention of **Prasannapura** whence the charter was issued. The town is said to have been sanctified by the river Niḍilā (*i.e.*, the city was situated on its bank) and adorned by the rows of gardens and forests and to have surpassed the fame of the city of the gods, *i.e.*, Amarāvatī. Next follows a somewhat detailed description of Jaya-bhaṭṭāraka's son Pravara-bhaṭṭāraka who, in addition to the reference to his family, is compared to Pṛthu and Manu and said to have been an abode of the multitude of all the arts and a very festival to the eyes of the people and a dispeller of darkness. He is further said to have conquered the entire circle of the earth by the prowess of his supple arms. Vyāghrarāja is described simply as younger brother of Pravara-bhaṭṭāraka and his order in respect of the grant, which is addressed to the high (literally, respectable) officers of the king, was issued after worshipping the present and future Brāhmaṇas. The grant was made for the augmentation of the religious merit of his parents and of himself and the officers were ordered to endorse and maintain it. Next are quoted four imprecatory and benedictory stanzas followed by the mention of the date which is the **twenty-seventh day of the month Pauṣa in the forty-first year**[7] of the increasingly

---

Nail-heads are noticed on the first plate of Vibhurāja's grant, the Shorkot inscription of 402 A.D. (*ibid.*, xvi, pl. opp. p. 15), the Malga plates of Indrarāja assigned to *circa* seventh century A.D. (see *infra*, II: Appendix), etc.

6. Sircar and Bhattacharya place it in the sixth century A.D. But this view is evidently based on the assumption that Vyāghrarāja belonged to the Śarabhapurīya dynasty for which, as will be shown in the sequel, there is no definite evidence.

7. As horizontal stroke also stood for punctuation mark, Sircar and Bhattachrya (*EI*, xxxiv, 50, fn. 2) hint at the possibility of the preceding symbol standing for 4 also though they prefer to read the date as 41. B.C. Jain and V.V. Mirashi (*Studies in Indology*, i,260, fn.4) are inclined to read the figure for the year as 4. But as the punctuation mark is generally not found after the figure indicating the year in copper-plate grants (numerous examples can be seen in the present volume), we read the date as 41. Sircar and Bhattacharya take the figure preceding that for 1 to stand for 40. However, it may as well be taken as 4 and in that case the year will have to be taken as indicated according to the new or decimal system of numeral notation. It may be pointed out in this connection that exactly the same form of 4 (except for the notch in the lower left portion which is a South Indian characteristic and the

victorious reign. The inscription concludes with a reference to Jyeṣṭhasiṁha who was responsible for the execution of the charter.

It is not stated clearly as to whose reign, *viz.*, Pravarabhaṭṭāraka's or Vyāghrarāja's, the date has to be referred. The facts that the legend on the seal refers to Vyāghrarāja and that while making the grant in question Vyāghrarāja does not make any specific reference to his securing the permission of his elder brother for this purpose[8] leave the impression that the grant was made by Vyāghrarāja in his own right and that the date has to be taken as referring to his own reign and not to that of his elder brother Pravarabhaṭṭāraka. However, we have some strong grounds against such a hypothesis. While Pravarabhaṭṭāraka is described so very eloquently and styled *manuja-pati*, *i.e.*, king, no regal title is employed for Vyāghrarāja and there is no other indication that he was on the throne at the time of making the grant. The non-employment of the word *bhaṭṭāraka* for him also is a pointer in the same direction. The mode of address in respect of the order concerning the grant is particularly instructive in this connection. The royal officers to whom the order is addressed are referred to as 'respectable officers of the king' (*rājñaḥ sumānya-rājapuruṣān*) which conclusively shows that he was not on the throne at the time of making the grant, and that the date must be referred to the reign of his elder brother Pravarabhaṭṭāraka. But in that case one will have to explain as to how his younger brother Vyāghrarāja issued the charter under his own seal and made the grant in his own name without making any reference to the reigning king's permission.[8] It is not improbable, as pointed out by Sircar and Bhattacharya, that Vyāghrarāja was 'ruling the kingdom on behalf of his brother when the latter was temporarily incapacitated to bear the burden of the state owing to illness or any other cause'[9] or that he 'was the governor of Pūrva- *rāṣṭra* with his headquarters at Prasannapura and that his brother empowered him to issue the charter in respect of the grant he was permitted to make'.

As stated above, Pravara-bhaṭṭāraka is said to have belonged to the Amarārya-kula. It is generally held that Vyāghrarāja, and for that matter, his elder brother Pravarabhaṭṭāraka and father Jayabhaṭṭāraka belonged

box-head which is due to the employment of the box-headed variety) it is met with in numerous epigraphic and numismatic records dating from the early centuries A.D. and in the Bower manuscript dating from *circa* sixth century A.D. (See G.H. Ojha, *Bhāratīya Prācīna Lipimālā*, pls. lxxi-lxxii). The employment of the decimal notation side by side with the old system of expressing numbers involved in the mention of the day (20 7, *viz.*, 27) need not cause any surprise as we come across similar instances of the use of both the methods in the Lodhia plates of Śivagupta Bālārjuna (*infra*, no. III: VIII) and a stray plate from Burhikhar (Mallar), attributable to the same king (*infra*, III: Appendix II).

8. For instances of grants made by private individuals or members of the royal family with the approval of the king, see *supra*, nos. I: I, IX, XII, XIII. The grant recorded in the last-mentioned charter was made by the queen and other members of the royal family and approved by the king.
9. In that case, Prasannapura was in all probability the capital of Pravara-bhaṭṭāraka.

to what is popularly known as the Śarabhapurīya dynasty. And as Pravara-bhaṭṭāraka is explicitly described as a member of the Amarārya-kula, the latter is believed to have been the real name of the Śarabhapurīya family.[10] This view is based on the following considerations:—

(i) Prasannapura, wherefrom the charter was issued, is reminiscent of the Śarabhapurīya king Prasanna or Prasannamātra, the father of Jayarāja and Mānamātra-Durgarāja. The city was evidently named after him.

(ii) The names Jaya-bhaṭṭāraka and Pravara-bhaṭṭāraka, borne by Vyāghra-rāja's father and elder brother respectively, remind one of the Śarabha-purīya rulers Jayarāja and Pravararāja. And as kings bearing such names and belonging to any other family are not known to have flourished in South Kosala during the period represented by the record under consideration, these kings appear to have belonged to the Śarabhapurīya dynasty.

(iii) The village granted by Vyāghrarāja by means of the present charter is said to have been situated in the district known as Pūrva-rāṣṭra in which were also included the villages granted by the Arang plates of Jayarāja[11] and the Raipur plates of Sudevarāja[12] both of whom are known to have belonged to the Śarabhapurīya dynasty.

However, these arguments are far from convincing. Even if Prasannapura was founded by or named after the Śarabhapurīya chief Prasannamātra, which is quite likely, this by itself does not prove anything. There are instances of copper-plate charters issued from localities established by members of other or even alien dynasties.[13]

The similarity between the names Jayabhaṭṭāraka and Pravarabhaṭṭāraka known from this record on the one hand and those of the Śarabhapurīya kings Jayarāja and Pravararāja respectively on the other is only apparent, not real. In the inscriptions of the Śarabhapurīyas themselves Jayarāja and Pravararāja are never called Jayabhaṭṭāraka and Pravarabhaṭṭāraka. Secondly, the word *mahat*, which is invariably prefixed to the names of the Śarabhapurīya chiefs in the body of the text of their copper-plate charters,[13a] is conspicuous by its absence in the case of Jayabhaṭṭāraka and Pravarabhaṭṭāraka. We have a solitary case of the mention of the ruling chief's father's name in a couple of Śarabhapurīya records

10. *EI*, xxxiv, 48; B.C. Jain, *Navabhārata*, Dīpāvalī Number, 1960; *Catalogue of the Antiquities preserved in the M.G.M. Museum*, Raipur, vi, Introduction, six-eight; V.V. Mirashi, *Studies in Indology*, i, 249 (genealogy, where Vyāghrarāja and his elder brother Pravara-bhaṭṭāraka are mentioned as Śarabhapurīya kings).
11. Above, no. I: VI.
12. Above, no. I: XIII.
13. The Riddhapur plates of Nala Bhavadattavarman were issued from Nandivardhana, the capital of the Vākāṭakas who were enemies of the Nalas, and the Pāṇḍuvaṁśins of South Kosala issued their charters from Śrīpura which is known to have been the capital of some later members of the Śarabhapurīya dynasty.

13*a*. From the time of Jayarāja.

and the word *mahat* is attached to his name also.[14] If the record under review also belonged to the Śarabhapurīya dynasty it is inexplicable as to why this eye-catching feature is conspicuously absent in it. Thirdly, the title *bhaṭṭāraka*, which is applied to Jaya and Pravara in our record, is not met with in any Śarabhapurīya record. Fourthly, the relationship between Jayabhaṭṭāraka and Pravarabhaṭṭāraka as indicated in this inscription is different from that known to be existing between the Śarabhapura chiefs Jayarāja and Pravararāja.[15]

It is true that the Pūrva-rāṣṭra was an administrative division under the Śarabhapurīyas as well as under Pravarabhaṭṭāraka. But administrative divisions often remained unaffected by the change of rulers. There is consequently nothing surprising if Pravarabhaṭṭāraka, even if he belonged to a different dynasty, continued the administrative system of the Śarabhapurīyas unaltered.

And lastly, if the Śarabhapura kings really belonged to the Amarāryakula they would not have remained reticent on this point in their other records which are quite numerous.

We may now refer to certain points which seem to positively negative the attribution of the present grant to the Śarabhapurīyas. As admitted by Sircar and Bhattacharya, the characters, style and seal of the present record are quite dissimilar to those of the known Śarabhapurīya charters. Thus, while all the Śarabhapurīya inscriptions are written in the box-headed variety of the Central Indian alphabet the charter of Vyāghrarāja is written in characters belonging to the South Indian alphabet showing nail-heads. If Vyāghrarāja and his predecessors on the throne are regarded as members of the Śarabhapurīya dynasty, it will have to be explained as to why the nail-headed variety of the South Indian alphabet was chosen for use in a solitary record as against the box-headed variety of the Central Indian alphabet employed in all the other records. The attempt of Sircar and Bhattacharya to explain it away by conjecturing that the donee of this charter hailed from the South is hardly convincing. Stylistically this record is miles apart from all the other records of the dynasty to which it is sought to be assigned. The Śarabhapurīya charters contain nothing like the ornate description of the place of issue as found in the present record and refer to the place of issue without even a single adjective. The description met with in this grant reminds one of classical Sanskrit literature which abounds in such narratives. Likewise, the description of Pravara-bhaṭṭāraka is entirely different from that of the acknowledgedly

14. In the Dhamatari and Kauvatal plates of Mahā-Sudevarāja the latter is described as the son of Mahā-Durgarāja. See above, I: IX and XII.

15. According to the Śarabhapurīya records, Pravararāja was the son of Mānamātra-Durgarāja, and not of Jayarāja, B.C. Jain tries to overcome this difficulty by speculating that Mānamātra-Durgarāja was the same as Jayarāja. If this view is accepted, we shall have to believe that Jayarāja was known by as many as three different names which is unlikely.

Śarabhapurīya rulers. Besides the conventional description the Śarabhapurīya inscriptions makes a pointed reference to the issuing chief's religious inclinations and devotion to his parents which are conspicuous by their absence in Vyāghrarāja's record. The grant portion including the notification noticed in this epigraph also bears no resemblance whatsoever to that of the known Śarabhapura records. The latter contain no reference to worshipping the present and future Brāhmaṇas whereas the present charter is silent about the privileges and exemptions attached to the grant. All the Standard Śarabhapurīya records from the time of Jayarāja contain five imprecatory and benedictive stanzas the last four of which are ascribed to Vyāsa. Vyāghrarāja's charter, on the other hand, has only four such stanzas which again are not referred to Vyāsa and the wording of even these verses differs considerably from that of the corresponding stanzas of the Śarabhapurīya grants. There is also some difference between the two sets of records in regard to the manner of referring to the engraver. As regards the seals, there is absolutely no similarity between this and the Śarabhapurīya grants. The upper half of the seals affixed to the latter shows the Abhiṣeka-Lakṣmī motif conspicuously absent on that attached to the former which contains three Vaiṣṇavite symbols in a row. While Vyāghrarāja's seal contains a small prose legend in its lower portion that of the Śarabhapurīyas contains a two-line metrical legend referring to the father and martial qualities of the donor. It will thus be seen that there is no strong ground to treat Vyāghrarāja and other members of his family referred to in the former's solitary record as Śarabhapurīya kings. The differences between the two sets of records are too vital to be ignored in any discussion on the lineage of Vyāghrarāja, his brother Pravarabhaṭṭāraka and father Jayabhaṭṭāraka. Accordingly, there remains no basis to regard the Śarabhapura chiefs as belonging to the Amarārya-kula.

As regards **place-names** met with in the record, Pūrva-rāṣṭra has already been dealt with in connection with the Arang plates of Jayarāja and the Raipur plates of Sudevarāja which also record grants of villages included in the same district. Prasannapura cannot be located. But according to Sircar and Bhattacharya, it is not improbable that Prasannapura was situated in the neighbourhood of Śrīpura. The river Niḍilā, on the bank of which Prasannapura is said to have been situated, and the donated village Kunturapadraka have not been identified.

TEXT[16]

First Plate

1 स्वस्ति [।*] प्रसन्नपुरादुपवनवनराजिराजितादप(म)रपुर—

2 कीर्त्तिविजयिनः प्रवरकामिनी नितम्बवि(बि)म्बाभिधात—

16. From plates in *EI*, xxxiv.

3 भिन्नाम्भसा च स्रोतस्वत्या निडिलया पवित्रीकृतादम–
4 रार्य्यकुलाम्बरशशिनः सकलकलाकलापनिलय–
5 स्य जिततमसो जननयनोत्सवस्य श्रीजयभट्टारकसू–
6 नोः श्रीप्रवरभट्टारकस्य प्रि(पृ)थोरिव पृथुनु(भु)ज–

Second Plate : First Side

7 युगलबलाज्जितोजित[17]सकलमहीमण्डलमण्डन–
8 यशसो मनोरिव मनुजपतेरनुजः श्रीव्याघ्रराजदेवो
9 वर्त्तमानां[18] भविष्यतश्च ब्राह्मणां[19] सम्पूज्य राज्ञः सुमान्य–
10 राजपुरुषां[20]समाज्ञापयति [।*] विदिमस्तु वो यथास्माभि–
11 रयं पूर्व्वराष्ट्रीयकुन्तुरपद्रकग्रामो मातापित्रोरात्मन–
12 श्च पुन्या(ण्या) भिव्रि(वृ)द्धये बहवृचकाप्याङ्गिरसगोत्रदीक्षितदु–
13 र्गस्वामिसूनवे दीक्षिताग्निचन्द्रस्वामिने दत्त इत्यु–

Second Plate : Second Side

14 पलभ्य भवद्भिरप्यनुमन्तव्यः पालयितव्यश्चेति[21] ।
15 बहुभिर्व्वसुधा दत्ता राजभिः [।*] सगरादिभिः [:।*] यस्य
16 यस्य यदा भूमिस्तस्य तस्य तदा फलं (लम्) ॥[22] [१॥*] मा भू–
17 दफलस(श)ङ्का वः परदत्तेति पार्थिवाः [।*] स्वदाना–
18 त्परदानस्य तस्माच्छ्रेयोनुपालनं (नम्)।[23] [।२॥*][24]

Third Plate

19 षष्टिवर्षसहस्राणि स्वर्गे मोदति भूमि–
20 दः [।*] आछे(च्छे)त्ता चानुमन्ता च तान्येव नरके वसे[त्] [॥३॥*]
21 स्वदत्तां परदत्तां वा यो हरेत वसुन्धरां (राम्) [।*] स्ववि–
22 ष्ठायाङ्कमिभू (र्भू) त्वा पितृभिस्स [ह*] मज्यत[25] [॥४॥*] इति प्रवद्ध(र्द्ध)–

17. Read °बलार्ज्जितोर्जित°.
18. Read वर्त्तमानान्.
19. Read ब्राह्मणान्.
20. Read पुरुषान्.
21. The mark of punctuation is indicated by a couple of horizontal strokes placed one above the other.
22. The punctuation mark appears to be indicated by two sets of a couple of horizontal strokes.
23. The mark of punctuation is constituted by a single horizontal stroke which is quite clear in the plate though it has escaped the attention of Sircar and Bhattacharya.
24. Note that this verse is not met with in any Śarabhapurīya record.
25. Read मज्जति.

23 मानविजय राज्यसंव्वत् ४० १[26] पो(पौ) षवि २० ७ जे (ज्ये) ष्ठसि

24 ह्णेन[27] कर्म्मं सृ (कृ)त[म्*] [।*]

Seal

श्रीव्याघ्रराजः[28]

26. Sircar and Bhattacharya point out that if the second symbol is taken to be a mark of punctuation, the preceding symbol may stand for 4 also. They, however, prefer to read both the symbols together as 41. It is likely that the year is indicated in accordance with the decimal notation involving the invention of zero, the first symbol standing for 4 and the second for 1. Some others are inclined to read the year as 4.
27. Read ज्येष्ठसिंहेन.
28. For discussion on certain problems connected with this record, see Ajay Mitra Shastri, "Mallar Plates of Vyāghrarāja: A Re-appraisal," *JESI*, ix, 40-47.

II

INSCRIPTIONS OF THE PĀṆḌUVAṀŚINS OF MEKALĀ

II : I

BAMHANI PLATES[1] OF UDĪRṆAVAIRA,[2] YEAR 2

Provenance: Bamhani, Rewa District, Madhya Pradesh.

References: B.Ch. Chhabra, *Bhārata-kaumudī* (R.K. Mookerjee Volume), i, 215-19; *EI*, xxvii, 132-45 and plates opposite pp. 140 and 141; V.V. Mirashi, *Indica* (The Indian Historical Research Institute Silver Jubilee Commemoration Volume), 288ff.; *Studies in Indology,* i, 230-36. *Inscriptions of the Vākāṭakas, CII,* V, 82-88 and pl. xix; Ajay Mitra Shastri, *Bhāratī-Bhānam K.V. Sarma Felicitation* Volume, 439-43.

Language: Sanskrit. In a mixture of verse and prose.

Metres: Verses 1, 10 and 11: *Sragdharā*; Verse 2: *Vasantatilakā*; Verse 3: *Upajāti*; Verses 4 and 9: *Mālinī*; Verse 5: *Indravajrā*; Verses 6-7: *Śārdūlavikrīḍita*; Verse 8: *Āryā*; Verses 12-14: *Anuṣṭubh.*

Script: Southern class of Central Indian alphabet.

Date: Bhādrapada kṛṣṇa 13, Puṣya nakṣatra, regnal year 2. Early seventh century A.D.

TEXT[3]

1 सिद्धम्[4] [।*] स्वस्ति ।।[5] आसीद्यः[6] पाण्डवानां सुविमलयशसामन्वये भूरिधाम्ना (म्नां) रा–

1. The plates measure roughly $7\frac{3}{4}''$ long and $4\frac{1}{2}''$ broad. They are held together by a copper-ring, about $\frac{1}{4}''$ thick, which passes through a hole, $\frac{3}{4}''$ in diameter, cut in the centre at the top. Its ends are secured under a small seal, measuring $\frac{3}{4}''$ in diameter, which does not appear to bear any writing or device. The seal attached to the Mallar plates of the same ruler, however, bears representation of a couchant bull to left in the upper part and the one-line legend *Śrīpuruṣaḥ* in the lower part, the two being divided by horizontal line in the middle. It is not impossible that the seal of the present charter also originally bore the same device and legend which have now disappeared.
2. Chhabra, who published this charter originally, attributed it to Bharatabala. A comparison with the Mallar plates (*infra,* II: II), however, reveals that the record actually belongs to Udīrṇavaira, son and successor of Bharatabala, who is mentioned in verse 11. The erroneous attribution was due to the inadvertent omission of a prose passage referring to Bharatabala's son Śūrabala, also known as Udīrṇavaira.
3. From plates in *EI*, xxvii.
4. Chhabra: *Om.* Expressed by a symbol. There is a superfluous dot to the left at the bottom and another dot to the right at the top of the symbol. Such superfluous dots are noticed at several places on these plates and should better be ignored.
5. The punctuation mark is here indicated by two dots placed one above the other which also denotes *visarga*. We find the mark of punctuation indicated similarly in some other early records also. Elsewhere in this record a single mark of punctuation (*daṇḍa*) consists of a small curved horizontal stroke and the double mark of a couple of such strokes.
6. The construction is rather uncommon; the verb *āsīt* alone forms the principal clause, the subject (*saḥ*) being understood.

2 जाभूत्मे (न्मे) कलायां क्षितिपतितिलकः संप्रसूतोरुकीर्त्तिः [।*] श्रीमां (मान्) श्रीसं-

3 विधा[ता*] जयबल इति यः ख्याप्यते स्वैर्य्यशोभिः (भि) लो (र्लो) केस्मि[7] (स्मिन्) सर्व्वदे (दै) [व*]

4 प्रवरगुणगणालङ्कृतश्चार (रु) मूर्त्ति (र्त्तिः) [॥१॥*] तस्याहवाहृतजयः प्रथि [तो दया? *]

5 वां (वान्) वत्सेवरः (र) प्रतिसमो गुणवान्विधिज्ञः [।*] पुत्रोभवद्रिपुग्र (गृ) होप-

6 वनानि येन वन्यैर्मृ गैः प्रचुरतामुपपादितानि । [॥२॥*] महानुभाव [:*]

7 सुकृतप्रशंन्सी[7a] (शंसी) गुणान्तरज्ञः पुरुषोपभोग्यः [।*] सद्धर्म्म[8]शोलो (लः) सुनय[प्र]-

8 धानः श्रीवत्सराज (जौ) नृपतिर्व्वं (र्ब्बं)- भूव ॥[३॥*] तस्य पुत्र[8a]स्तपादानुध्यातः प-

9 रममाहेश्वरः परमब्रह्मण्यः परमगुरुदेवताधिदैवतविशेष [:*]

10 श्रीमां (मान्) श्रीमत्यां देव्यां द्रोणभट्टारि-कायमुत्पन्नः श्रीमहाराजना-

11 गबलः [।*] तुग्गखुरनिपात क्षुण्णमार्ग्गा[8b] धरी (रि) त्री (त्त्री)[8c] मलिनयति दिगन्तां[9]- (न्तान्)

12 पा (पां) सुरूक्षाकुलान्तां (न्तान्) [।*] मदमलिनकपोला वारणा यस्य

Second Plate : First Side

13 य (या) तः प्रशममुपनयन्ते शीकरार्द्रा (द्रान्) क्षणेन । [।४॥*] ततस्तस्य पुत्रस्तपादा-

14 नुध्यातः परममाहेश्वरः परमब्रम (ह्म) ण्यः परमगुरुदेवताधिदैवत-

15 विशेषः श्रीमत्यां देव्यामिन्द्रभट्टारिकायाम (मु) त्पन्नः[9a] श्रीमहाराजभरत [:।*]

16 इन्द्रो दयाशीलगुणान्विताया औदार्य्यचातुर्य्यसमं (म) न्विताया [:।*] पु-

17 त्त्र [:*] प्रसूतोमलचारुकान्तिः शैलेन्द्रपुत्र्या[9b] इव कार्त्तिकेयः [॥५॥*] इन्द्रो दा-

18 रणिसंभवेथ[10] हुतभुक्तत्तेजोज्वल[11] स्नेहवां (वान्) त्स (स) द्वृत्तस्थितिविप्रमन्द्र-

19 विधृतप्र (प्रा) प्तप्रमाणोन्नति [:*]। दृष्टः साधुसुखोदयाय हि नृणां ध-

20 र्म्मार्थसंपादकः (को) वेद्यामध्वरसंस्थिते वसुहुतः पूज्यः सतां सर्व्व-

21 दा। [॥६॥*] येनोत्तुङ्गरिपुद्रुमैरविरलैर्म्भं (र्भं) ग्नैः समस्ता दिशच्छ (श्छ) न्ना दिश्व (ग्व) र-

22 दन्तिनेव गुरुणा व्यक्रि (क्र) ष्य विफूर्ज्जिता [:*]। यस्यैव (वं) विधचेष्ट (ष्टि) तस्य नृ-

23 पतेः कृत्स्ने महीमण्डल (ले) सौराज्यश्री (श्रि) यमादधातु विपुला धर्म्मार्थकाम-

7. The *anusvāra* is placed a little away from *smi* to the left at the bottom of the letter *māṁ* in the upper line.

7*a*. Mirashi: °प्रशंन्सि.

8. There is a superfluous dot or *anusvāra* over the superscript *r*.

8*a*. Mirashi: पुत्र°.

8*b*. Mirashi: मार्ग्ग.

8c. Mirashi: धरित्रि.

9. The *anusvāra* touches the bottom of *nā* in the previous line.

9*a*. Chhabra: मुत्पुन्नः.

9*b*. Mirashi: °पुत्र्या.

10. The reading of this portion is beyond doubt, but the sense is not clear.

11. हुतमुक्तेजोज्ज्वलः seems to be the intended reading.

24 प्रदा:[12] [।।७।।*] श्रीभरत: क्षितिनाथ: क्षितिपतितिलक: सुरेन्द्रसमवि (वी) र्य्य: [।*]
25 विनिहतरिपुगणलक्ष्मि (क्ष्मीं) दधार य: संशृ (श्र) तां स्वभुजो:[13] [।।८।।*][14] एकैव[14a]

Second Plate : Second Side

26 स्फटिकविमलशुभ्रं वि (बि) भ्रति (ती) शीलतोयन[15] ।[16] यमनियतु (म) तटान्तप्रान्तशु–
27 द्धप्रवहं[16a] (वाहम्) [।*] प्रशमगुणगणोमि (र्मि) या (र्या) जनं पावयंन्ति (यन्ती) स्वयमिह सुर–
28 लोकादगता जाह्नवीव ।।[९।।*] श्रीमच्चा (च्च) न्द्रा (न्द्रां) शुकि (की) र्तेर्भरतव (ब) लनृप–स्योत्तम (मा) र (रा) ज–
29 पत्नि (त्नी) ।[16b] जाता य (या) कौ (को) सलायाममरजकुलजां (जा) कितिमच्चै[17]र्दधाता (ना) ।। (।) शश्वद्धर्मार–
30 कार प्रतिविहिततमातीव[18] लोकप्रकाशा याता र (पौ) त्रैः पु (प्र) पौत्रै[18a]र्न [य] विनयर–
31 तै राजसि (सिं) घै (है) : प्रतिष्ठा[म्*] ।।[१०।।*] योसौ संपूर्णशक्तित्रयविनिपतितानेक–सामन्त–
32 मूर्द्धप्रोद्धृष्टोत्फुल्लपपर्दति[19] चलनयगा[20]क्रान्तदिक्र (क्च) क्रवाल: [।*] सौम्य: सो–
33 यश्च[20a] वंश: प्रभव इति जने (नै:) का (की) र्त्ये (र्त्यं) ते यस्य चोच्चै: स श्रीमां (मान्) सवभुवास्र–

12. The construction of the second half of the stanza is defective. In order to make it yield a coherent sense Chhabra proposes to reconstruct it as follows:—
यस्यैवंविधचेष्टितं स नृपति: कृत्स्ने महीमण्डले
सौराज्यश्रियमादधाति विपुलां धर्म्मार्थकामप्रदाम् ।।
13. As pointed out by Chhabra, this usage implies the existence of the word *bhuj* synonyous with *bhuja* or *bhujā* even as *pad* is used as an equivalent of *pada* or *pāda*. Mirashi suggests to correct it to भुजे.
14. The composer or the engraver appears to have left out by inadvertence a prose passage referring to Bharatabala's son and successor, Śūrabala, between verse 8, which is the last of the stanzas describing Bharatabala, and 9 with which the description of Bharatabala's queen and Śūrabala's mother begins. On the basis of the Mallar plates this passage may be restored as follows:
तस्य पुत्रस्तत्पादानुध्यात: परममाहेश्वर: परमब्रह्मण्य: परमगुरुदेवताधिदैवतविशेष: श्रीमान श्रीमत्यां महादेव्यामुत्पन्न: श्रीमहाराजशूरबल:.
14*a*. एकैव has nothing to do with verse 9 and has reference to the mother of Śūrabala described in verse 10.
15. Read °तोयं.
16. This mark of punctuation is superfluous.
16*a*. Mirashi: प्रवाहं.
16*b*. This punctuation mark is not required.
17. Read कीर्तिमुच्चै.°
18. Judging from the Mallar plates, the intended reading appears to be °द्धर्म्माधिकारप्रति-विहिततया°.
18*a*. Mirashi: प्रपौत्रै°.
19. The intended reading is पद्मद्युति°, which is found in the Mallar plates.
20. The intended reading seems to be °चरणयुगा°.
20*a*. Mirashi: यण्य.

34 तिर्यं[21] गुणा(ण) **गणोदि(दी) र्णवैरो** ने(न)रेन्द्रः [॥११॥*] ततः मेकलायं (याम्) उत्तर राष्ट्रे पाञ्चग–

35 र्त्ताविषये वर्द्धमानके ।[22] ग्रामकूटद्रोणाग्रक-नायकदेववारिकगण्डक–

36 प्रमुखां (खान्) सर्वां (र्वा)नेव यथाप्रतिवासिनः समाज्ञापयति [।*] विदितमस्तु

37 महैय[23] पादैरय ग्रासा(मः) सा(सो) द्रगा(ङ्ग): सोपरिकरः अचाटभटप्रवेशीं(श्यः) सनि–

38 धिः सोपनिधि: (धि)श्चोरदण्डवर्जतं चतुः[24] सि(सी)मापर्य्यन्त आचन्द्रार्कक्षित(ति)–

Third Plate

39 तारकानिरोधेन मात(ता)पित्रोरात्मनश्च पुण्याभिवृध(द्ध)ये वत्ससगोत्रश्रीमा–

40 द्धिय(द्धय)न्दिनलोहितसरस्व(स्वा)मिनः(ने) प्रतिपादितेत्यवगम्य[25] यथोचितभागभो–

41 गेनाज्ञाश्रवणविधेयैर्भवितव्यमिति [।*] स्वयमाज्ञापना [।*] ये चास्मद्व(द्वं) ङशे(शे) समुत्प–

42 द्यन्ते राजानः(न)स्तैरपीयं दत्तिरनुमोदनीयानुपालनीया च [।*] यः (य) श्चैमां(तां) दत्ति(त्तिं) विलोपमा–

43 प(पा) दयिष्यति स पञ्चभिर्महा [पा*]तकैः संयुक्त [:*] स्य(स्या)दिति [।*] बहुभिर्वसुधा भुक्ता(दत्ता) राज–

44 भिस्सगरादिभिः [।*] यस्य यस्य यदा भूमिस्तस्य तस्य तदा फलं(लम्) [॥१२॥*] षष्टि वर्षस–

45 हस्त्राणि स्वर्ग (र्गे) मोदति भूमिद [:।*] आच्छेत्ता चानुमन्ता च तान्येव नरके वसेत् [॥१३॥*] स्व–

46 दत्ता(त्तां) परदत्ता(त्तां) बा(वा) यत्नाद्रक्ष नराध(धि)प [।*] मही(हीं) महि(हीं) मतां श्रेष्ठ दानाच्छ्रेयोनुपालन [म्*] [।१४॥*]

47 समाप्तं चेदं शासनं(नम्) [॥*] प्रवर्द्धमान ।[26] **विजयराज्यसंवत्सरे २ भ(भा)द्रपद(कृ)ष्णत्र**

48 **योदश्यां पुष्यनक्षत्रेण**[26a] [॥*] लिखितं (त)ञ्चेदं शासनं राहसिकेशानपुत्रेण शिवेनो–

49 त्कीर्णञ्च सुवर्ण्णकारेश्वरपुत्रेण मिहिरकेने (णे)ति ॥

ABSTRACT

After the auspicious formulae *siddham*, expressed symbolically, and *svasti*, the charter, in its preamble, gives an account of the history of the Pāṇḍava dynasty of Mekalā[27] to which the issuer of the grant, **Udīrṇavaira**, belonged. The first member of the dynasty mentioned in the record was Jayabala, whose description is purely conventional (v. 1). He was followed by his son,

21. Chhabra proposes to restore these seven syllables as **सार्वभौमः प्रथित°** But on the basis of the Mallar plates the relevant portion can be restored as **संबभूवाप्रतिम**.
22. The mark of punctuation is unnecessary.
23. Read **मह्य°** as suggested by Chhabra. Mirashi thinks that perhaps **मदीयपादैः** is intended, though it would look queer in the donor's mouth.
24. Read **°वर्जितश्च°**. Mirashi reads it as **°वर्जंतं** and suggests to correct it as **चोरदण्डवर्जम**.
25. Read **प्रतिपादित इत्य°**.
26. This *daṇḍa* is superfluous.

26*a*. Mirashi: **नक्षत्रेण**.

27. It is represented by the Maikal range stretching from Khairagarh to the Rewa region in Madhya Pradesh including the Amarkantak hills. Vide D.C. Sircar, *Studies in the Geography of Ancient and Medieval India* (2nd ed., Delhi, 1971), 42, fn. 9. Chhabra defines it more precisely as comprising the south-eastern part of the

Vatsārāja by name, who is compared to the well-known Vatsa king Udayana.[28] His valour and virtue are eulogised in a general manner and there are vague references to his successes against his enemies in battles (vv. 2-3). His son and successor, begotten on his queen Droṇabhaṭṭārikā, was Nāgabala, who is styled *Mahārāja* (*ll.* 8-11). He is described as a devout worshipper of Maheśvara, highly devoted to the Brāhmaṇas (*parama-brahmaṇya*), teachers, various gods and the supreme divinity (*parama-guru-devat-ādhidaivata-viśeṣaḥ*).[29] Verse 4 describes his military exploits in a conventional manner, referring as it does to the movements of his horses and elephants. Nāgabala was succeeded by his son, born of queen Indrabhaṭṭārikā, named Bharata, whose full name is given as Bharatabala in v. 10. Like his father, he is also said to have meditated upon the feet of his father and to have been a devout devotee of Maheśvara and highly devoted to the Brāhmaṇas, teachers, various gods and the supreme divinity (*ll.* 13-15). He had Indra for his second name and his birth from Indrabhaṭṭārikā is compared to that of Kārttikeya from the daughter of the lord of mountains, *i.e.*, Pārvatī (v. 5). He is further compared to god Indra in prowess (v. 8) and in causing rift in enemy ranks and is said to have received gifts of gold at the time of his sacrifices (v. 6). Next two stanzas contain vague allusions to his military exploits.[29a] Verses 9-10 are devoted to the description of Bharatabala's queen who was born in the Amaraj family[30] in the Kosalā[31] country. She is compared to the

---

(former) Rewa State, portions in the north of the Bilaspur District and some area in the east of the Mandla District. See *EI*, xxvii, 138. Also see my *India as seen in the Bṛhatsaṁhitā of Varāhamihira*, 54.

28. Chhabra took Vatseśvara mentioned in verse 2 and Vatsarāja spoken of in the following stanza as the same person, Vatsarāja being the proper name and the use of the form *Vatśesvara* being due to the exigency of the metre (*EI*, xxvii, 143, fn. 4). N.P. Chakravarti, on the other hand, suggested that the *visarga* after the name Vatseśvara should be regarded as an error and omitted. We shall consequently get *Vatseśvara-pratisamo* which would mean that Vatsarāja was equal to the king of the Vatsa country, viz. Udayana, who also belonged to the lineage of the Pāṇḍavas. Chhabra termed this suggestion 'very happy' but pointed out that in that case verses 2 and 3 will have to be regarded as a *yamaka* and one of the verbs, *abhavat* and *babhūva*, will become superfluous. A comparison with verse 2 of the Mallar plates, however, leaves no doubt that a comparison between the Pāṇḍava king Vatsarāja and the traditional Vatsa king Udayana is intended.

29. Chhabra, however, renders this expression as 'distinguished as a highly venerable personage, a deity and a supreme divinity' (*ibid.*, 136), and D.C. Sircar as 'one who is a great teacher to his subjects and is devoted to the various gods and of (*sic*) the supreme divinity' (*IEG*, 236). Cf. the expressions like *parama-guru*, *parama-brahmaṇya*, *parama-daivata* and *parama-daivat-ādhidaivata* often met with in inscriptions.

29*a*. As stated earlier, hereafter there must have been a reference to his son and successor Śūrabala which is left out by inadvertence.

30. Chhabra, however, takes the expression *amaraja-kulajā* in the literal sense, *i.e.*., 'of a divine origin' (*EI*, xxvii, 144). Mirashi also takes it to mean 'born in a family of the gods.'

31. It evidently refers to South Kosala which comprised the Chhattisgarh region of Madhya Pradesh and the Sambalpur region of Orissa.

holy river Jāhnavī, *i.e.*, Gaṅgā, descended from heaven and purifying the people inasmuch as she possessed water in the form of pure and crystal-like brilliant character with its flow bounded by the twin banks of self-restraint (*yama*) and self-discipline (*niyama*) and is said to have attained worldwide renown by performing religious duties and risen to a high status by virtue of her having grandsons and great-grandsons.[31a] In verse 11 is described a king called Udīrṇavaira[32] whose lotus-feet were rubbed by many a feudatory chief humbled by his perfect triple power and who was born in the lunar lineage.[32a]

The inscription next proceeds to record the donation, evidently by king Udīrṇavaira, of the village Varddhamānaka,[33] included in the Pañcagarttā *viṣaya*[34] (district) of the Uttara-rāṣṭra[35] (Northern Province) in Mekalā, in favour of the Brāhmaṇa Lohitasarasvāmin, belonging to the Vatsa *gotra* and a student of the Mādhyandina *śākhā* of the Śukla *Yajurveda,* for the increase of the religious merit of his parents and of his own self. The order in respect of the grant, which was issued by the king himself (*svayam-ājñāpanā*), was addressed to all the inhabitants of the village, the chief among them

31*a*. Chhabra and Mirashi took Lokaprakāśā in verse 10 to be the name of Bharatabala's queen. But the restoration of the reading of the preceding portion here suggested on the basis of the corresponding verse of the Mallar plates clearly indicates that like some other expressions in this and the preceding stanzas this word has also to be taken as an adjective.

32. Chhabra separated the relevant portion of the verse into *guṇa-gaṇo* and *dīrṇavairo* and took both the expressions to be adjectives describing Bharatabala. Mirashi follows Chhabra. The Mallar plates, however, show that Udīrṇavaira has to be taken here as the name (or title) of the issuing king.

32*a*. Chhabra, followed by Mirashi, thought that this verse described Bharatabala. But the Mallar plates leave no doubt that it describes not Bharatabala, but his son Udīrṇavaira. Chhabra and, following him, Mirashi further found in this stanza a veiled allusion to Bharabala's acceptance of the suzerainty of the Vākāṭaka king Narendrasena. This suggestion is mainly promted by the occurrence of the word *narendra* at the end of this stanza and the statement in the Balaghat plates of the Vākāṭaka king Pṛthiviṣeṇa II that Narendrasen's commands were obeyed, among others, by the lord of Mekalā (*CII*, v, 81, text-lines 27-28; also see Mahurjhari plates of Pṛthiviṣeṇa II, *Vidarbha Saṁśodhana Maṇḍala Vārṣika*, 1971, 75, text-line 22). But this suggestion does not go well with the description of the *Pāṇḍava* king in the same verse.

33. Probably the same as Bamhani, the findspot of the record, which is possibly a contraction of the original form.

34. Probably the region round Bamhani watered by five rivers or rivulets which, in the present case, seem to refer to the five tributaries of the river Son. *Cf.* Trigarta denoting the territory round Kangra watered by the three rivers, *viz.*, the Ravi, the Beas and the Sutlej. The village Panchgaon, some three miles south of Shahdol, is probably the modern representative of the headquarters of the district of Pañcagartā.

35. It shows that the Pāṇḍava kingdom of Mekalā was divided into at least two provinces, *viz.*, Uttara-rāṣṭra and Dakṣina-rāṣṭra. The latter is mentioned in the Mallar plates.

being the officials *Grāmakūṭa,*[36] *Droṇāgraka,*[37] *Nāyaka,*[38] *Devavārika*[39] and *Gaṇḍaka.*[40] The grant, which was intended to last as long as the moon, the sun, the earth and the stars endure, carried with it the right to the *udraṅga,* the *uparikara,* the *nidhis* and the *upanidhis* and was exempted from the entry of the *cāṭas* and the *bhaṭas,* with the exception of the fines imposed on thieves (*cora-daṇḍa*). The villagers were asked to pay the *bhāga* and the *bhoga* to and obey the orders of the grantee.

The future kings of the family are then exhorted to maintain the grant, and three conventional benedictive and admonitory stanzas are quoted.

The charter was issued on the **thirteenth day of the dark fortnight of the month of Bhādrapada, when the nakṣatra was Puṣya, in the second year of the increasingly victorious reign.**

The inscription was written by Śiva, son of the *Rāhasika*[41] Īśāna,[42] and engraved by Mihiraka, son of the goldsmith Īśvara.[43]

36. *I.e.*, village-headman. For some other epigraphical references to the office of *Grāmakūṭa*, see *IEG*. 120-21.
37. According to Kauṭilya (*Arthaśāstra*, ii. 1.4), *droṇamukha* denotes the headquarters of a group of four hundred villages. *Droṇāgraka* may, therefore, be taken to refer to the officer in charge of *droṇamukha* or *droṇāgra* and may be compared to the modern tahsildar. The *Divyāvadāna* (ed. Cowell and Neil, 620) mentions the terms *droṇamukha* and *droṇamukhya*. D.C. Sircar (*IEG*, 101) takes it in the sense of 'the king's grain-share fixed per *droṇa* measure'.
38. This office is found mentioned in the *Arthaśāstra* (i.12.6) and the *Śukranītisāra* (i. 192) and is taken by Kane (*HDS*, iii, 990) in the sense of the 'head of ten villages'. Chhabra takes it to mean 'a leader' or 'a military commander' (*EI*, xxvii, 139) and D.C. Sircar, in the present context, 'a royal officer or a ruling chief' (*IEG*, 214). For some other references, see *ibid.*
39. It probably denotes the 'superintendent of a temple' comparable to the modern Paṇḍā. See *ibid.*, s.v. *devavārika* and *vārika*. According to Chhabra (*EI*, xxvii, 139), it means 'a superintendent of temples and holy places'.
40. Chhabra thinks that in the present context it possibly means 'a warrior' (*ibid.*). But as *gaṇḍaka* also means coins, can it refer to an officer associated with coining or minting activity?
41. It has been taken in the sense of a 'privy councillor', a 'private secretary' or an 'adviser' (*IEG*, 269). Cf. *Rahasya*, *Rahasika*, *Rahasādhikṛta*, *Rahasyādhikṛta* and *Rahasiniyukta*, etc., occurring in numerous inscriptions. See *ibid.*,; *EI*, xxvii, 139.
42. According to Chhabra (*ibid.*, 139, fn. 8), the composer probably intended to state that 'this charter has been written by *Rāhasika* Śiva, son of Iśāna!.
43. Chhabra thinks it possible that the intention of the composer was to state that the charter was 'engraved by the goldsmith Mihiraka, son of Iśvara'.

II : II

MALLAR PLATES[1] OF ŚŪRABALA UDĪRṆAVAIRA, YEAR 8

Provenance: Mallar, Bilaspur District, Madhya Pradesh.

Reference: B. Sitaraman and M.J. Sharma, *Studies in Indian Epigraphy* (Journal of the Epigraphical Society of India), iii, 183-93 and plates; Ajay Mitra Shastri, *Bhāratī Bhānam, K. V. Sarma Felicitation Volume*, 435-443.

Language: Sanskrit. In a mixture of prose and verse.

Metres: Verses 1-2, 6 and 7: *Sragdharā*; Verse 3: *Upajāti*; Verse 4: *Indravajrā*; Verse 5: *Mālinī*; Verses 8 and 9: *Anuṣṭubh*.

Script: Southern class of Central Indian alphabet.

Date: Regnal Year 8, Kārttika kṛṣṇa 11, nakṣatra Pūrvaphālgunī Early seventh century A.D.

TEXT[2]

First Plate

1 श्रोम्[3] [*] स्वस्त्यपरिमितगुणसमुदयस्य भगवतस्तृ(स्त्रि)शूलपाणेर्व्व–
2 रवृषभवाहनस्य स्फुरद्भुजगपरिकरस्यानङ्गाङ्गविध्वत्सिन:[4]
3 तृ (त्रि) दशपतिनुतचरणां(णा)ब्ज[4a]युगलस्य श्रीजयेश्वरभट्टारकस्ये–
4 वं(दं) शासनं:(नं) लिख्यते श्री **उदीर्ण्णवैरा**नुमत्यया[5] ॥[5a]। ततः (त) श्रा-
5 सीद्यः पाण्डवानाः (नां) सुविमि(म) लय[6]शसामन्वये भूरिधाम्नां
6 राजाभूत्मे (न्मे) कलायां: (यां) क्षितिपतितिलकः संप्रसूतोरुकी–
7 र्त्तिः [।*] श्रीमां(मांन्) श्रीसंविधाता जयबल इति यः ख्याप्यते स्य (स्वै)र्य्यं–
8 शोभिल्लो (ल्लो) केस्मि[7](स्मिन्) सर्व्वंदैव प्रवरगुणगणालं(ल)ङ्कृ[7a]तश्चारुमूत्ति(र्त्ति) [:॥१॥*][8]

1. The plates measure about 18·5 cms. in length and 10·6 cms. in breadth and are about 0·2 cm. thick. They have a hole in the middle at the top for the passage of the ring, 0·8 cm. in diameter, the ends of which are soldered to the seal.
2. From photographs supplied by Dr. K.V. Ramesh.
3. Expressed by a symbol.
4. Read विध्वंसिन:.

4*a*. Probably the original intention was to write चरणांबुज.

5. Read °नुमत्या.

5*a*. This mark of punctuation has escaped the notice of Sitaraman and Sharma who supply it on their own.

6. The scribe had originally engraved *śā*, but later cancelled the medial *a* sign for *ā*.
7. Sitaraman and Sharma: °श्मिं.

7*a*. Sitaraman and Sharma: °लङ्कृत°.

8. Sitaraman and Sharma: मूर्त्ति. This stanza is also found in the Bamhani plates.

9 तस्यासीद्वत्सराजः स्वभुजबलगुणाक्क्रान्तशत्नु[8a]प्रताप [:*]

10 श्रीमा[न्*] वत्साधिपेव[8b] क्षितिपतितिलको वत्सराजः[9] क्षितीश [:।*]

11 पुत्त[9a][:*] सद्वङ्श[10]केतुर्म्मणिरिव सुमहानुन्नतः श्रीनिकेत [:]

Second Plate : First Side

12 केयूरोद्भासितात्सः स्फुरितमणिरुचा चारुपि(पी) नोरुबाहुः [।।२।।*][11]

13 तस्य पुत्त[11a]स्तत्पादानुध्यात्त(त): परममाहेश्वरः परमब्रह्मण्य [:*]

14 परमगुरुदेवताधिदैवतविशेषः[12] श्रीमां(मान्) श्रीमत्यां देव्या (व्यां) द्रोणभ–

15 ट्टारिकायामुत्पन्नः श्रीमहाराजा(ज)नागबलः [।।*] नागैः क्षरत्प्र–

16 स्तुतदानगण्डैः (ण्डै) भ्र (भ्रं) मत्पताकाकुलितान्तरालः [।*] सैन्य–

17 स्फुरः(र) च्छस्त्ररुचा[13] परि(री)तं(तो)विराजते यस्य रणाग्य(ग्र) भूमौ [।।३।।*][14]

18 तत [:] (त)स्तस्य पुत्त[14a]स्तत्प(त्पा)दानुध्य(ध्या)तः परममाहेश्वरः

19 परमब्रह्मण्यः परमगुरुदेवताधिदैवतविशेष [:*]

20 श्रीमां[15](मान्) श्रीमत्यां देव्यामिन्द्राभट्टारिकायामुत्पन्नः श्री–

21 महाराजभरतः [।*] इन्द्रो दयाशीलगुणान्विता–

22 [16]या श्रौदार्य्यंचातुर्य्यंसमन्वितायाः [।*] पुत्त[16a] [:*]

Second Plate : Second Side

23 प्रसूतोमलचारुकान्तिः शि(शै)लेन्द्रपुत्र्या[16b] इव कात्ति(र्त्ति) केय [:।।४।।*][17] दशर–

24 थकुलजत्मा(न्मा)द्रा(रा)घवस्यानुजोभूद्भरत इति समन्तादिग(द्गी)यते य [:*]

25 क्षितीशैः [।*] तदनु गुणगणोपि प्रश्रयानम्रमूर्त्तिर्भरतनृपते (ति)–

8*a*. Sitaraman and Sharma: शत्रुः.

8*b*. This is an example of wrong *sandhi*.

9. Sitaraman and Sharma overlook the *visarga* in the original and supply the same on their own.

9*a*. Sitaraman and Sharma: पुत्र.

10. Read सद्वंश°.

11. This stanza is not found in the Bamhani plates which contain two verses descriptive of Vatsarāja.

11*a*. Sitaraman and Sharma: पुत्र.

12. Sitaraman and Sharma: विशेषं.

13. The reading of this portion proposed by Sitaraman and Sharma (°च्[छ]स्त्रचा) is somewhat confusing.

14. This stanza replaces verse 4 of the Bamhani plates.

14*a*. Sitaraman and Sharma: पुत्र°.

15. This word is conspicuous by its absence in the Bamhani plates. The *anusvāra* over *mā* is very faint.

16. Space sufficient for one letter on left has been left out unengraved.

16*a*. Sitaraman and Sharma: पुत्र.

16*b*. Sitaraman and Sharma: पुत्र्या.

17. This verse occurs as no. 5 in the Bamhani plates.

26 रस्मिम्भूतल[18](ले)न्दु[19]प्रकाशः [।।५।।*][20] तस्य पुत्त[20a]स्तत्पादानुध्यातः परममाहेश्व–
27 रः परमब्रह्मण्यः परमगुर(रु)देवताधिदेवतविशेषः श्रीमां(मान्)श्री–
28 मत्यां महादेव्यामुत्पन्न [:*] श्रीमहाराजशूरबलः [।*] श्रीमच्चन्द्राङ्शु[21]–
29 कीर्त्तेर्भरतबलनृपस्योत्तमा राजपत्नी जाता या कोसलाया[22]–
30 ममरजाकुलजा कीर्त्तिमुच्चैर्द्दधाना। शश्वद्धर्म्माधिकारप्रतिवि–
31 हिततयातीव लोका(क) प्रकाशा याताः[23](ता)पुत्तै[23a] [:*] प्रपौत्रै[23b]र्न्नयविन–
32 यरतै राजसिङ्घैः[24] प्रतिष्टां(ष्ठाम्) [।।६।।*][25] योसौ संपूर्ण्णशक्तित्वय[25a]विनि–
33 पतितानेकसामन्तमूर्द्धप्रोङ्घ(द्घृ)ष्टोत्फुल(ल्ल)पद्मद्युति चलनयता[26]–
34 क्क्रान्तदिक्चक्रवालः [।*] सौम्यः सोमस्य वङ्शः[27] प्रभव इति जने (नै)[28] [:*]
35 [29]कीर्त्यते यस्य

Third Plate : First Side

36 चोचै(च्चै) [:*] सः श्रीमां(मान्) संव(ब)भूव(वा) प्रतिमगुणगण(णो)दीर्ण्णवैरो नरेन्द्रः [।।७।।*][30] ततः मे–
37 कलायां दक्षिणराष्ट्रे सं (स)ङ्गमग्रामके ग्रामकूटप्रमुखां (खान्) नायक–
38 प्रमुखां [श्*][31]च ग्रामं[32] समाज्ञापयति विदितमत्सु(स्तु) वोम्सा(स्मा)भिर[33]य(यं) ग्रामः
39 सोद्रङ्गः सोपरिकरः श्रा(अ) चाटभटप्रवेशी(श्यः) सनिधि [:*] सोपनिधिः चोर–
40 दण्डवर्ज्जितः चतुःसि(सी)मापर्य्यन्तः आचन्द्रार्कक्षितितारकानिरोधेन मा–

18. Read °स्मिन् भू°.
19. Sitaraman and Sharma: °भूतलेन्दु°.
20. This verse is not met with in the Bamhani plates.
20*a*. Sitaraman and Sharma: पुत्र.
21. Read °द्रांशु°.
22. In the Bamhani plates we have Kausalāyā°.
23. Sitaraman and Sharma: यातः.
23*a*. Sitaraman and Sharma: पुत्रै°.
23*b*. Sitaraman and Sharma: प्रपौत्रै°.
24. Read °सिंहैः.
25. This is the same as the 10th verse of the Bamhani plates.
25*a*. Sitaraman and Sharma: °त्रय°.
26. Read चरणयुगा°. Sitaraman and Sharma: °लनपताका°.
27. Read वंशः.
28. Sitaraman and Sharma: जनी.
29. Space enough to accommodate three letters on the left and a considerable space on the right has been left unengraved.
30. This is identical with verse 11 of the Bamhani plates.
31. The list of officers to whom the order in respect of the grant is addressed in the Bamhani plates is comparatively larger. In addition to the two officers specified in the present grant, it includes *Droṇāgraka*, *Devavārika* and *Gaṇḍaka*.
32. In view of the employment of the plural in the adjectives one would expect the substantive also to be in plural. In the Bamhani plates we have सर्व्वानेव यथाप्रतिवासिनः in place of ग्रामं of the present record. The same words appear to be intended here also.
33. In the Bamhani plates we have *mahaiya-pādai*° in place of *vo-smābhir* of the present grant.

41 तापित्रा[33a] (त्रो)रात्मनश्च पुण्याभिवृद्धये यत्र[33b] वणिकमनोरथपौत्रस्य[33c] बो–

42 टपुत्रस्य[33d] नरसिङ्घस्य[34] प्रसादीकृतस्तदनेनाप्यस्मदनुमत्या भ–

43 गवतः श्रीजयेश्वरभट्टारकस्य प्रतिपादितेत्यवगम्य[35] यदुचितमुपनयन–

44 सुखं प्रतिवत्स्यथेति[36] [।*] स्वयमाज्ञापन (ना) [।*] ये चास्मद्वङ्गे[37] समुप (त्प)द्यन्ते राजान-
स्तैरपी–

45 यं दत्तिरनुमोदनीयानुत्पा (पा) लनीया च [।*] यश्चै (श्चे)मां दत्ति विलोपमा[37a] पादयिष्य–

46 ति स पञ्चभिर्म्महापातकैः स(सं)युक्त [:*]स्य (स्या)त् [।*] बहुभिर्व्वसुध (धा) भुक्ता
(दत्ता) राजभिस(स्स)–

47 गरादिदिः(भिः)[।*] यस्य यस्य यदा भूमिस्तस्य तस्य तदाफल [म् ॥८॥*]षष्टि—

48 वर्षसहस्राणि स्वर्ग्गे मोदति भूमो (मि)दः [।*] आच्छेत्ता चानुमन्ता च ता–

49 [38]न्येव नरके वसेदिदि (त् [॥९॥*] इति) [।*] समाप्तञ्चेदं शासन [म् ॥*]

Third Plate : Second Side[39]

50 **प्रवर्द्धमाना(न) विजयराज्यस(सं)वत्सरेष्टमेकार्त्तिकक्ृ**

51 **ष्णपक्षे(क्षै)कादश्या (श्यां) पूर्व्वं(र्व्वं)फाल्गुण्यां(न्यां) बुधदिनेनेति** [।*] लिखित

52 ञ्चेदं शासनं शिवेनोत्कि (त्की)र्ण्णंञ्च महिरकेनेति। [*]

Seal[40]

श्रीपुरुषः [।*]

ABSTRACT

Following the auspicious words, *om,* expressed by a symbol, and *svasti,* it is averred that this charter belonging to the illustrious lord Jayeśvara-bhaṭṭāraka (god Śiva called Jayeśvara), who is described as carrying a trident in his hand, having an excellent bull (Nandin) for his mount and snakes for his retinue and as one who put Anaṅga (god of love) ablaze and whose lotus-feet are adored by the lord of gods, *i.e.* Indra, is written with the permission

33*a*. Sitaraman and Sharma: °पित्रा°.
33*b*. Sitaraman and Sharma: यत्र.
33*c*. Sitaraman and Sharma: पौत्रस्य.
33*d*. Sitaraman and Sharma: पुत्रस्य.
34. Read सिहस्य.
35. प्रतिपादित इत्यवगम्य would be the grammatically correct expression.
36. In the Bamhani plates we have at this place यथोचितभागभोगाज्ञाश्रवणविधेयैर्भवितव्यमिति.
37. Read °द्वंशे.
37*a*. Sitaraman and Sharma: विलोपेना°.
38. Some space on left is left blank.
39. The letters on this plate are much larger in size than those on the other plates.
40. It is roundish with a diameter of 2·3 cms. Its surface is divided into two almost equal parts by a horizontal line in the middle. The upper part is occupied by the figure of a bull couchant to left in relief and the lower portion by a one-word legend.

of the illustrious **Udīrṇavaira.**[41] Next follows the description of the Pāṇḍava dynasty of Mekalā. Jayabala, the first member of the family referred to in the present record, is described in a purely conventional manner as in the preceding charter. His son Vatsarāja is compared to the traditional Vatsa monarch Udayana and is said to have assailed his enemies by the prowess of his own arms and virtues (v. 2). He was followed by his son *Mahārāja* Nāgabala, who was begotten on queen Droṇabhaṭṭārikā. He is said to have meditated upon the feet of his father and to have been a devout worshipper of Maheśvara and highly devoted to the Brāhmaṇas, teachers, various divinities and the supreme divinity. Verse 3 alludes to his warfare in conventional terms. His son and successor, begotten on his queen Indrabhaṭṭārikā, was Bharata, also called Bharatabala, who is also described, like his father, as meditating upon the feet of his father and as a great devotee of Maheśvara and as highly adoring the Brāhmaṇas, teachers, various gods and the supreme divinity. Verse 5 of the preceding inscription informing us that he was also known as Indra and comparing his birth from Indrabhaṭṭārikā to that of god Kārttikeya from Pārvatī is repeated in this record also (v. 4). In a stanza not met with in the previous inscription he is further compared to king Bharata, younger brother of Rāghava (Rāma) and born in the family of Daśaratha.[42] After Bharatabala came his son *Mahārāja* **Śūrabala** who was begotten on queen Mahādevī.[43] He, too, is said to have been a devout adorer of god Maheśvara, the Brāhmaṇas, teachers, various gods and the supreme divinity and to have meditated upon the feet of his father.[44] Next are described Bharatabala's queen and king Udīrṇavaira in a couple of stanzas (vv. 6-7) which are repeated from the previous record (vv. 10-11).

The epigraph next records that the king (Udīrṇavaira) was pleased to make over the village of Saṅgama,[45] situated in the Dakṣiṇa-rāṣṭra[46] (Southern Province) in Mekalā to one Narasiṁha, son of Boṭa and grandson of the

41. From the sequel it would appear that Śūrabala was his name, Udīrṇavaira, here used as a name, being his *viruda*. It seems, however, that the latter became more popular than the former.
42. The description of Bharata, who was the son of Daśaratha, as one born in the family of Daraśaratha looks somewhat strange.
43. Unless Mahādevī is taken to be the personal name and the word *mahādevyām* is regarded as serving the dual purpose of the title and the name, it will have to be assumed that the name of Śūrabala's mother has been left out by inadvertence.
44. This description of Śūrabala appears to have been left out inadvertently in the Bamhani plates.
45. It has been identified with the modern village of Tālā (also known as Saṅgama) near the confluence of the rivers Maniārī and Śivanātha in the Bilaspur District. K.D. Bajpai (*ABORI*, Diamond Jubilee Volume, 435) points out that near the confluence there were two early Śiva temples and that the main temple may have been that of Jayeśvara-bhaṭṭāraka.
46. The mention of Dakṣiṇa-rāṣṭra in this inscription proves that the Pāṇḍava kingdom of Mekalā was divided into at least two provinces, a fact earlier deducted from the mention of the Uttara-rāṣṭra in the Bamhani plates.

merchant (*vaṇik*) Manoratha, who, with the permission of the king, gave it away to the illustrious god Jayeśvara bhaṭṭāraka. The grant was endowed with the same privileges and exemptions as enumerated in the previous charter. The order about the grant, which was issued by the king himself, was addressed to the royal officers led by the *Grāmakūṭa* and the *Nāyaka*. The villagers were advised to live happily in the village offering the donee his dues.

The kings to be born in future in the dynasty are requested to protect the grant and anyone revoking it is threatened with the five great sins. Two imprecatory verses are quoted.

The charter is dated **Wednesday,[47] the eleventh day of the dark fortnight of the month of Kārttika, when the nakṣatra was Pūrva-Phālgunī, in the eighth year of the increasingly victorious reign.**

The record was written by Śiva and inscribed by Māhiraka.[48]

The seal contains the word *śrī-puruṣa*.

47. This is one of the early epigraphical reference to a weekday. So far the antiquity of the practice of specifying the weekday in inscriptions has been traced to the Eran inscription of the time of Budhagupta, dated 484 A.D.

48. The correct form of the name was evidently Mihiraka which is mentioned in the Bamhani plates. The writer and the engraver of this as well as Bamhani plates were thus identical. The information about the names and occupations of the fathers of these persons given in the previous record is missing in this inscription.

APPENDIX

MALGA PLATES OF SĀMANTA INDRARĀJA

The record was found in possession of a person at the village of Dhobahar in the Bilaspur District of Madhya Pradesh and is stated to have been owned by a resident of Malga, P.O. Kotma, Shahdol District, Madhya Pradesh. It was edited by D.C. Sircar and S. Sankaranarayanan in *EI*, xxxiii, 209-14 and plates between pp. 212 and 213. The present author also contributed a paper on this record in *Sri Venkateswara University Oriental Journal,* xxi-xii, 19-25.

The charter is engraved on a set of three **copper-plates,** each measuring about 4″ broad and 9½″ long. The plates are held together by a ring, some 2-¾″ in diameter and about ¼″ in thickness. The hole for the passage of the ring is bored about the middle of the upper portion of each of the plates. The joints of the ring are soldered under a rectangular **seal** which bears a short prose legend giving the name of the issuing chief, preceded by the honorific *śrī* in nominative singular. The first plate bears **writing** only on the inner side while the remaining two plates are engraved on both sides. The inscription consists of thirty lines of writing which are distributed as follows: seven lines on the inscribed sides of the first and second plates and the inner side of the third plate and a couple of lines on the second side of the third plate.

The inscription is written in a variety of early Nāgarī **characters** with hollow triangular marks (nail-heads) on top and on palaeographical grounds it has been placed in the first half of the seventh century A.D.[1] The **language** is Sanskrit, and the record is composed in a mixture of prose and verse.

The epigraph refers itself to the reign of **Indrarāja** who is styled *Sāmanta* or a feudatory chief though there is no mention of the overlord whom he owed allegiance. It aims at registering his grant of a village in favour of a Brāhmaṇa and is dated the **eleventh day of the first fortnight of the month of Jyeṣṭha in the year which can be read variously as 1 or 11[2] of the increasingly**

1. D.C. Sircar and S. Sankaranarayanan place it roughly between the Bodhgaya inscription of Mahānāman, *c.* 580 A.D. and the Aphsad inscription of Ādityasena, *c.* 670 A.D. and thinks that Indrarāja may have originally owed allegiance to the Maukharis and ruled semi-independently for some time between the death of Maukhari Grahavarman and the establishment of Harṣavardhan's power over the former Maukhari dominions. They also entertain the possibility of assigning the period of Indrarāja's rule to a date subsequent to Harṣavardhana's death in 647 A.D. We are of the opinion that the latter dating is too late.
2. We have a couple of slightly curved horizontal strokes one after the other which taken together, according to the decimal system of numeral notation, appear to stand for 11. If, however, the second strokes is taken as a mark of punctuation, which is not unlikely, the reference will be to the first regnal year.

victorious reign, evidently of Indrarāja himself the week-day being Tuesday and the nakṣatra Uttarabhādrapada. As the date is not given in any well-known reckoning, it has been dated roughly in the first half of the seventh century A.D.

The inscription opens with the auspicious words *siddham*, expressed symbolically, and *svasti* followed by a couple of verses describing a ruling chief, probably named Kṣitipati,[3] and his son and successor, Indrarāja, in a purely conventional manner. Next follows a prose passage recording an order issued from Maṇḍaka by the *Sāmanta* Indrarāja, styled *Paramamāheśvara* (a devout worshipper of Maheśvara) and described as meditating upon the feet of his parents, to the effect that he had donated the village of Sālagrāmāmantamaraka (or Sālagrāmamantamaraka) included within Gulagrāmaka[4] situated in the Ākāśa *rāṣṭra* which formed a part of the Cheṇḍaparaṅga *viṣaya* to the Brāhmaṇa Bhavasvāmin, son of Nāgasvāmin,[5] who belonged to the Śāṇḍilya *gotra* and was a student of the Vājasaneya-Mādhyandina *śākhā* (of the *Yajurveda*). The royal order about the grant was addressed to the officers including the *Grāmakūṭa*,[6] *Droṇāgrika*,[7] *Gaṇḍakānāyaka*[8] and *Devavārika*[9] and all the chief persons and residents of the village. The grant, which was made for the increase of the religious merit of the king's parents and of his own self and was intended to last as long as the moon, the sun, the earth and the stars endure, is said to have carried with it right to the *udraṅga*,[10] *parikara*,[11] *nidhis* and *upanidhis* and exemption from the entry of the *cāṭas* and *bhaṭas* and the *cora-daṇḍa*.[12] The villagers were ordered to be obedient to the donee and offer him *bhoga* as due and thereby live happily. The future rulers of the family are then exhorted to maintain and endorse the grant and those obstructing it are threatened with the five great sins. As many as seven imprecatory and benedictive stanzas are cited in support of this exhortation. Some of these verses, it may be noted, are not found in

3. In case it is not taken as a proper name, we shall have to concede that Indrarājā's father is left unnamed.
4. The reference actually appears to be to two hamlets called Sālagrāma and Mantamaraka or Amantamaraka which formed part of the village Gulagrāmaka. See below.
5. Sircar and Sankaranarayanan take Nāgasvāmiśarman to be the name of the donee's father. The name-ending *śarman* is, however, not attached to his name in the text.
6. *I.e.*, the village headman.
7. Sircar and Sankaranarayanan observe that this official designation is not met with in any other record and hint at the possibility of ist being a mistake for *Drāṅgika*. But actually it is an error, for *Droṇāgraka* is mentioned in the Bamhani plates of Śūrabala.
8. This expression, according to Sircar and Sankaranarayanan, is not known from any other epigraph. But it is found mentioned in the aforementioned Bamhani plates and has been discussed in connection with that record.
9. Also referred to in the Bamhani grant, he was an officer connected with the supervision of temples.
10. It is mentioned in Śūrabala's Bamhani and Mallar grants also.
11. Probably an error for *uparikara* referred to in the two charters of Śūrabala.
12. All these exemptions are specified in Śūrabala's records also.

any other record included in this volume. The charter was written by the *Rājaputra*[13] Deva and incised by one Droṇāka, son of the goldsmith Īśvara. The record ends with the specification of the details of the date which have been indicated above.

As for the **localities** specified in the record, the place of issue, Maṇḍaka, was probably the capital of Indrarāja. This seems to find some support from the absence of any word like *vāsaka* or *skandhāvāra* suffixed to the name which is generally the case when a grant is issued from a place other than the capital. It has not been identified, though the possibility of the name Malga being a modified form of the ancient Maṇḍaka cannot be altogether ruled out. The name of the granted village, Sālagrāmāmantamaraka or Sālagrāmamantamaraka, seems to consist of the names of two localities, *i.e.*, Sālagrāma and Amantamaraka or Mantamaraka, which, forming a single unit, were apparently a part of the village Gula-grāmaka.[14] These, as well as the subdivision called Ākāśa and the locality named Cheṇḍaparaṅga, which lent its name to the *viṣaya*, cannot be identified.

There is no information forthcoming about the family to which Indrarāja belonged. But we find considerable similarity between this record on the one hand and the Bamhani[15] and Mallar[16] plates of Śūrabala *alias* Udīrṇavaira, the Pāṇḍava king of Mekalā, on the other. Thus, all the three records are written in the nail-headed alphabet, the nail-heads or triangular tops being hollow, and are composed in a mixture of prose and verse. Grant portions of the three charters are also composed in an almost similar style, and in many cases exactly the same expressions are met with. The addressees of the royal command concerning the grant[17] and the privileges and exemptions transferred to the respective donees[18] are also practically similar. Close similarity is also observed in the exhortation to future rulers[19] and the manner of mentioning the date.[20] All the three inscriptions specifically refer to their completion. The seals of these records are also similar inasmuch as their

13. This is a title of nobility.
14. It is somewhat strange that a settlement comprising two hamlets and large enough to be designated as a village (*grāma*) is said to have formed part of another village.
15. *Supra,* II: I.
16. See above, II: II.
17. The Bahmani plates mention all the addressees referred to in the present grant while the Mallar charter specifies only the *Grāmakūṭa* and *Nāyaka* but implies other officers by the word *pramukha.*
18. What is most interesting, the privileges and remissions are specified exactly in the same order in all the three grants in question.
19. In all the three charters the exhortation is addressed to the future kings of the issuing chief's family and the violators of the grants are cursed with the five great sins in almost the same words.
20. All the three records specify the year, month, fortnight and *nakṣatra* in exactly the same manner. The present grant and the Mallar plates refer to the weekday also which is conspicuously absent in the Bahmani charter.

legend consists of a single word.[21] The ring-hole on the plates of all the three charters is bored about the middle at the top. And, what is most interesting, both Mihiraka,[22] the engraver of the Bamhani and Mallar plates, and Droṇaka, who incised the present charter, are described as sons of goldsmith Īśvara, showing thereby that they were related to one another as brothers. And lastly, the area over which our Indrarāja ruled is not far removed from that under the Pāṇḍuvaṁśins of Mekalā. In view of these overriding considerations it is very likely, nay almost certain, that *Sāmanta* Indrarāja was connected with Śūrabala's family, although the exact nature of this relationship cannot be determined in the present state of inadequate information.

The close affinity verging on identity in respect of formal matters between the Pāṇḍava records on the one hand and the only known inscription of Indrarāja on the other and the fact that the engravers of all these records were brothers point to the chronological closeness of Śūrabala *alias* Udīrṇavaira and Indrarāja. And, as shown above, there was also spatial closeness between the regions under them. The use of the title *Sāmanta* by Indrarāja may be justifiably taken to indicate that he owed allegiance to the Pāṇḍuvaṁśins of Mekalā. But as Indrarāja did not feel the necessity of referring to his overlord even once and as the engraver of his only extant epigraph was a brother of the scribe responsible for incising both the complete records of the last known Mekalā Pāṇḍava chief, Śūrabala *alias* Udīrṇavaira, it is almost certain that he flourished in a period of political confusion following the termination of Śūrabala's reign when he was not yet in a position to renounce the suzerainty of his Pāṇḍava overlord but was all the same strong enough not to find it necessary to mention him by name [22a]

TEXT[23]

[*Metres:* Verse 1: *Śārdūlavikrīḍita*; Verse 2: *Sragdharā*; Verses 3–9: *Anuṣṭubh.*]

First Plate

1 सिद्धम्[24] [।*] स्वस्ति [।*] श्रासि (सी) दिन्द्रसमः क्षितौक्षित (ति) पति [:*] शक्त्या क्वि (क्रि) याभिर्गुणैरु–

2 त्फुल्लामलचारुविम्व[25]वदना य (यं) श्री [:*] सदा सेवते । यो देवद्विजसाधुप–

21. The seal attached to the Bahmani plates does not bear any device or legend. If there was any originally, it has altogether disappeared leaving absolutely no trace.
22. In the Mallar plates his name is erroneously spelt as Mahiraka.
22*a*. For a detailed discussion, see my paper in *Sri Venkateswara University Oriental Journal*, xxi-xxii, 19-25.
23. From plates in *EI*, xxxiii.
24. Expressed by a symbol.
25. Read बिम्ब.

3 ण्डितजनस्याधा[26]रभूतो ह्वा[27] सिद्धाध्यासितहेमतुङ्गशिखरः शैलै (ले) न्द्रराजो यथा [॥१॥*]

4 जात[स्त*] स्यात्मजा (जो) पि प्रकटघ (ग) जघट (टा) घट्टनः (न) श्चारुमूर्त्ति (र्त्ति) नि (र्नि) त्य (त्यं) दाताभिमा–

5 नी रणचपलपटु:[28] (टु) भ्रा (भ्रा) न्तपर्यन्त[की]र्तिं [:।*] निर्जित्वारातिपक्ष:[29] प्रसभमपहि (ह)–

6 तो (त:) येच (न) लक्ष्मी विशाला स श्रीमा [न्*][30] श्रीनिकेतः प्रतिमतिसुचिरः **इन्द्र**[31]–

7 **राजा (जो)** नरेन्द्रः [॥२॥*] **मण्डकात्पर** [म*] माहेश्वरा (रो) मातापितृपादानुध्यातः श्री–

Second Plate : First Side

8 सामा (म) न्त **इन्द्रराजः** च्छे (छे) ण्डपरङ्गविषयप्रतिवद्धः[32] आकाशराष्ट्रे गुल–

9 ग्रामके ।[33] सालग्रामामन्तमरके[34] ग्रामकु (कू) टद्रोणागी (ग्रि) क–

10 गण्डकानायक देववारिक (का) [न्*] सर्व्वामि (ने) व प्रमुखा [न्*] यथा प्रतिवासिनं (नः) समाज्ञा–

11 पयति [।*] विदिमस्तु भवता (तां) यथास्माभिरय (यं) ग्राम [:*] सोद्रङ्गः सपरिकरः

12 अचाटभटप्रवेशी[35] (शः) सनिधिः सोपनिधिः (धि) श्चोरदण्डवलितः[36] चतुःशी (सी)–

13 माधानपर्यन्त आचन्द्र (न्द्रा) र्कक्षितितारकानिरोधेन[37] मातापित्रोरात्मनश्च पुन्या (ण्या)–

14 भिवृद्धये ।[38] श (शा) ण्डिल्यगोत्रवाजसनेयमाध्यन्दिननागस्वामिपुव (त्र)–

Second Plate : Second Side

15 भवस्वामिनस्य[39] प्रतिपादितेत्यवगम्य[40] ।[41] यथोचितभोगमुपन–

26. The letter *dhā*, which was left out by oversight, is engraved above the line.
27. As suggested by Sircar and Sankaranarayanan, °भूतोभवत् would be a better reading.
28. Originally *dā* seems to have been engraved in place of *ṭu*. Sircar and Sankaranarayanan hint at the possibility of the reading of the word as *manaḥ* which, it may be pointed out, would give a better meaning.
29. Read निर्जित्यारातिपक्षं.
30. Sircar and Sankaranarayanan restore the missing letter as *ñ*; but rules of grammar would require either *śrīmān śrī-niketaḥ* or *śrīmāñ-cchrī-niketaḥ*.
31. Better read सुचिरश्चेन्द्र°.
32. Read °बद्ध (if *sandhi* is observed) or °बद्धे.
33. The mark of punctuation is superfluous.
34. Originally the letters *lekhyā* were written which were later erased and replaced by °*lagrāma*. The letters *buḍayyake*, which had been engraved between °*maraka* and *grāmakuṭa*, were later erased. In case the *ā* sign of *mā* is taken to be a part of an erased letter, the reading would be सालग्राममन्तमरके.
35. Sircar and Sankaranarayanan: °प्रवेशा.
36. Read °वर्जितः.
37. Read °निरोधं.
38. The mark of punctuation is unnecessary.
39. Read भवस्वामिने.
40. Read प्रतिपादित इत्यवगम्य.
41. The punctuation mark is uncalled for.

16 यन्तः[42] आज्ञाश्रवणविधेयैर्भूत्वा सुखं प्रतिवा(व)स्तव्यमिति स्वयमा

17 ज्ञापना। ये चास्मद्व(द्वं)ङशे(शे)समू(मु)त्पद्य(त्स्य)न्ते राजानः (न) स्तैरपनीय[43] दत्तिरनु–

18 पालनीयातु (नु) मोदनीया च। यश्चेमो(मां) दत्ति(त्तिं) विलोपमापादयिष्यति स

19 पञ्चभिर्महापातकैः सह संयुक्तं(क्तः) स्य (स्या)त् [।*] [ब*] हुभिर्वसुधा भूत्वा राजने[44]

20 सगराजि(दि)भिः [:।*] यस्य यस्य यदा भूमित(स्त)स्य तस्य तदा फलं(लम्)॥ [३॥*] षष्टि–

21 वरिष[45] सहस्राणि स्वर्गे मोदति भूमिदः। आछे(च्छे)त्ता चानुमन्ता

Third Plate : First Side

22 च त्ता (ता)न्येव नरके[46] वसे [त् ।।४।।*] स्वदत्तां परदत्ताम्वा[47] यो हरेति(त) वसुन्धरा [म् ।*] कपिलाशतघा–

23 तीनामेनसा प्रतिपद्यते [।।५।।*] खिलभुग्ना तु या भूमिया(र्या) च भुक्ता दशापरे[48] (रा) [।*] शत(तं) या–

24 [व] न्तु(त्तु) या भुक्ता न राजा हन्तुमरहति[49] ।।६।।*] आस्फोटयन्ति पितर [:*] प्रवल्गन्त (न्ति) पितामहा [:।*]

25 त्वमेकोस्मि(स्म) त्कुले जाता(तः)स मत्रा भविष्यति[50] [।।७।।*] प्राप्स्यसे विपुला[न्*] भोगा [न्*] पूर्व्वंदत्ते (त्त)स्य तत्फ–

26 लं (लम्) [।*] पुनर्देहीति दानाभि(द्धि) पुनर्भोगी भविष्यसि [।।८।।*] इह लोककृतं कर्मं तत्प[र*] त्रोपि (प)–

27 भुज्यति(ते)। तलसिक्तस्य वृक्षस्य फलं शाखासु दृश्यति(ते)। [।९।।*] लिखितञ्च राजपुत्ता (त्र) देवे [न ।*]

28 उत्कीर्ण(र्णं) सुवर्णकरइस्वर[51]पुत्रेण[52] द्रोणाकेन [।*] समाप्तञ्च(ञ्चे) द(दं)शासन(नं) ज्य(ज्ये)ष्ठप्रथ[53]

Third Plate : Second Side

29 मपक्ष उरत्तर[54] भाद्रपद (दे)।[55] अङ्गारा(र)वार (रे) द्दि (दि) वस एकादश (०शे)। प्रवद्ध(र्द्धं) मान

42. Read °यद्भिः.
43. Read तैरपीयं.
44. Read दत्ता राजभिः.
45. Read वर्षं.
46. The letter *ra* is written below the line.
47. Read परदत्तां वा.
48. Originally °पुरे was engraved.
49. Read हतुं मर्हति.
50. Read स नस्त्राता भविष्यति or त्वं नस्त्राता भविष्यसि, preferably the latter.
51. Read सुवर्णकारेश्वर°.
52. The letter *ṇā* is written below the line.
53. The *akṣara tha* is incised below *rṇa*, the third letter of the line.
54. Read उत्तर°.
55. The mark of punctuation is not required.

30 विजयराज्यसम्वत्परः [56] १।[57]

Seal

श्रीइन्द्रराजः[58]

56. Read संवत्सरः.
57. The mark of punctuation, if the same is intended, is indicated by a slightly curved horizontal line very similar to the preceding sign for 1. In case the former also stands for 1, the date will actually be 11.
58. Observance of *sandhi* rules would require श्रीन्द्रराजः.

III

INSCRIPTIONS OF THE PĀṆḌUVAMŚINS OF SOUTH KOSALA

III : I

ARANG STONE[1] INSCRIPTION OF BHAVADEVA RAṆAKESARIN AND NANNARĀJA[2]

Provenance: Arang, Raipur District, Madhya Pradesh.[3]

References: Stevenson, *JBBRAS*, i, 148ff.; A. Cunningham, *ASR*, ix, 127; F. Kielhorn, *JRAS*, 1905, 617-33 and plate facing p. 628; Hira Lal, *ICPB*, 13, No. 14; Bhandarkar's List, No. 1650; V.V. Mirashi, *EI*, xxiii, 116-17; xxvi, 227; xxxiii, 252-54; Moreshwar G. Dikshit and D.C. Sircar, *ibid.*, xxxi, 34; D.C. Sircar, *ibid.*, xxxiii, 256; D.C. Jain, *Catalogue of Antiquities in the M.G.M. Museum,* Raipur (Hindi), vi, 28-36 and pl. xix, S.N. Rajguru, *IO*, iv, 287-95.

Language: Sanskrit. In verse except the introductory auspicious formula *siddhaṁ namaḥ*.

Metres: Verses 1, 4, 6, 8, 11-12, 20, 22, 27, 29, 35 and 38: *Anuṣṭubh*; Verses 2, 7, 18, 25, 30 and 33: *Śārdūlavikrīḍita;* Verses 3, 9, 21, 31, 34, 40-42: *Sragdharā*; Verse 5: *Vasantatilakā*; Verses 10 and 37: *Vaṁśastha*; Verse 13: *Hariṇī*; Verse 15: *Rathoddhatā*; Verses 16, 23 and 32: *Āryā*; Verse 19: *Mālinī*; Verse 28: *Upajāti*; Verse 36: *Śālinī*(?); Verse 39: *Puṣpitāgrā*

1. The inscription is incised on red sandstone with a yellowish tinge and covers a space between 4′ 4″ and 4′ 10″ long and about 1′ 11″ broad. But it is only a remainder of a larger stone of which a portion on the proper left is broken as a result of which about 28 to 35 letters are missing at the end of all the lines. Originally the stone appears to have measured about 6′ long and 1′ 11″ broad.
2. Kielhorn captioned this record as 'Nagpur Museum Buddhist Inscription of Bhavadeva Raṇakesarin' (*JRAS*, 1905, 617) because the inscription was then preserved in the Central Museum, Nagpur. Another reason behind such a caption may have been uncertainty about its findspot. The inscription is now deposited in the Mahant Ghasidas Memorial Museum, Raipur, where it was shifted after the reorganisation of States as a result of which Nagpur, the capital of the erstwhile Central Provinces, came to be included in the Bombay State and later in Maharashtra.
3. There has been some unnecessary controversy about the actual findspot of this inscription. Rev. Dr. Stevenson, who first published this record, mentioned Bhandak (now called Bhadrāvatī) as its provenance (*JBBRAS*, i, 148ff.). Cunningham also did the same in *ASR*, ix, 127. But in the Central Museum, Nagpur, this inscription somehow came to be connected with Ratanpur in the Bilaspur District of Madhya Pradesh, and Kielhorn, while publishing it in *JRAS*, 1905, 617ff., stated that it was 'reported to have been brought from Ratanpur' (*ibid.*, 618). Hira Lal, after necessary investigation, concluded that it was found at Bhandak and accordingly summarised it under the caption 'Bhandak Buddhist Inscription' (*IA*, xxxvii, 208, fn. 20; lxii, 163; *ICPB*, 13, No. 14). D.R. Bhandarkar did the same (Bhandarkar's *List*, No. 1650). Later, V.V. Mirashi and Y.K. Deshpande invited attention to important evidence and pointed out that the inscription came neither from Bhandak nor

Script: Early Nāgarī.[4]
Date: About the middle of the Seventh century A.D.

TEXT[5]

1 सिद्धं[6] [।*] नमः ।। अनुत्तरज्ञानचापयुक्तमैत्रीशिलीमुखः । जयत्यजय्याजानीकजयी जिन-
धनुर्द्धरः ।। [१।।*] स्त्रीसङ्गाद्विरतोसिचेत्कथमियं मुक्तिः सदा प्रेयसी सत्व [।](त्त्वा)र्थैं?]
करसा तथा च करुणा त्वच्चेतसि स्थापिता । दुःखा[नन्त?] रदु ⏑ — ⏑ ⏑ ⏑ — — — ⏑
— — ⏑ — — — — ⏑ ⏑ — ⏑ — ⏑ ⏑ ⏑ — — — ⏑

2 नः पातु वः ।। [२।।*] निर्जीवश्चेतनावान्हृतसकलगतिर्लोकधात्वन्तगामी स[7]र्व्वंम्पश्यत्य
दृष्टिः[8] कृतजगदभयो भीतिहेतुः स्मरस्य[9] । दीप्तो निर्व्वाण [वा] ही सुरनरलपितै[र्लं]ब्ध
(ब्ध)मानोप्यमेय पश्चात्तायी चिरम्वः[10][स विरचि?]तमहाधर्म्मं[व?]— ⏑ — —[।।३।।*]

. . . .

. . . .

3 [वर्षं ?][11] रक्षतु सर्व्वदा ।। [४।।*] आसीत्क्षितौ क्षितिपतिनृंपमौलिमालामाणिक्यभृङ्ग-
परिचुम्वि (म्बि) तपादपद्मः । श्रीसूर्य्यघोष इति सूर्य्यं इवैकचक्रयान प्रसाधितजगत्प्रथितो
[रुधा]मा ।।[५।।*] खङ्गय[ष्ट] यां श्रितो यस्य भ्रमन्नुर्व्वीं न रोचते । अतिवृद्धो रिपुस्त्रीभ्यः [प्र]
तापो. ⏑ — ⏑ — [।।६।।*] — — — ⏑ ⏑ — ⏑ —
⏑ ⏑ ⏑ — — — ⏑ — — ⏑ — — — —

4 [न] मयूरवराजितदिशि स्फारस्फुरत्तेजसि । छायाकम्पितभीरुचेतसि जयैर्भीमे महासाविव
द्राघीयानुपलक्षितः[स] विमलो वङशोत्र[12] लव्धो(ब्धो)न्नतिः [।।७।।*] [अदुर्गा] श्रयिणा

---

from Ratanpur, but from Arang in the Raipur District of Madhya Pradesh (*EI*, xxiii, 116-17; xxvi, 227, fn. 2; xxxiii, 252-54; A.J. Rajurkar, *Candrapūraca Itihāsa*, Introduction, 4-5). This suggestion is based on the testimony of Vinayakarao Aurangabadkar who was deputed by Jenkins, Resident at Nagpur, to search for and report on the inscriptions in Chattisgarh. Moreshwar G. Dikshit and D.C. Sircar, while publishing the Senkapat inscription of the time of Śivagupta, rejected Mirashi's view and reiterated the stand that the record belonged to Bhandak (*ibid.*, xxxi, 34; also see Sircar, *ibid.*, xxxiii 256). We believe that the evidence in favour of Arang is much stronger than that in favour of either Bhandak or Ratanpur. See Introduction.

4. The script is variously known as 'Early Nāgarī', 'Kuṭila', 'Northern class of alphabets', 'acute-angled alphabet' and 'nail-headed characters'. The possibility of its Indian name being Siddhamātṛkā was hinted at by Bühler on the authority of a statement of Al-Biruni who says that the 'most generally known alphabet' in his time was called by this name (E. Sachau, *Alberuni's India*, i, 173). D.C. Sircar has recently argued in favour of adopting this name (*JAIH*, iv, 116).
5. From facsimile in *JRAS*, 1950, opposite p. 628.
6. Expressed by a symbol.
7. Better read सर्व्वं पश्य°.
8. Kielhorn suggests to correct it to °न्नदृष्टिः.
9. Jain reads स्मारस्य and then proposes to correct it to स्मरस्य.
10. Better read चिरंवः.
11. As pointed out by Kielhorn, the reading is very doubtful.
12. Read वंशोत्र.

येन पादसे[वि]कलावता । अभूतिपरु [रु] षा लोके धृतान्यैवेश्वरस्थितिः ॥ [८॥*] खङ्गात्क
—⏑——⏑⏑⏑ ⏑⏑⏑———⏑——⏑————⏑——⏑⏑⏑⏑
⏑ ——⏑—

5 त्यं पुरस्तात् । मत्तोपीयं तथेष्टा निवसित हृदये भूभृदीशस्य लक्ष्मीरित्येवं यस्य शुद्धा जलनिधि-
मविशत्कीर्त्तिरीर्ष्या[त][13] एव [॥९॥*] उद्वृत्तमत्तद्विपकुम्भभेदि[ना] ——— सरक्तमुक्ता
[फल] दन्त [धा?][14][रि]णा । रणे कृपाणेन निशातकोटिना मृगद्विषो यस्य नखाङ्कुरायितम्
॥[१०॥*] [श?]क्तिर्भ्रमति . . . .
. . . . [॥११॥*] . . . .

6 वीर्य्येण धीरा वीरकुटुम्वि(म्बि) नी । नोपसर्पति संरक्ता पद्मा पद्माकरानपि ॥ [१२*]
भवनशिखरात्तुङ्गात्पुत्रे निपत्य मृते प्रिये गुरुतरशुचा संमग्नोभूत्स भूमिपतिस्तदा । प्रव(ब)
लमथवा जन्माभ्यस्तं जग [त्सु] कृतास्पदं वु(बु)धमपि जनं कर्तुं प्रेम प्रय(या) स्यति वा(बा)
लिशं (शम्) [॥१३॥*] . . . .
. . . .

7 . .[15] [॥१४॥*] तेन वीक्ष्य फणिभोगभंगुरं जीवितं भवसमुद्रलंघिना । धाम कारितमिदं
मुनेर्महत्कान्तिनिर्जिताहिमाचलद्युति ॥[१५॥*] गच्छति भूयसि काले भूमिपतिः क्षपित-
सकलरिपुपक्षः ।पा[ण्ड] ववंशादगुणवानुदयननामा समुत्पन्नः ॥[१६॥*] . . . .
. . . .[16]

8 स्य तनूजन्मा अक्रूरे कृतसंगमेन दधता चक्रं द्विषां भीतिदं दूरोत्सारितरौद्रनारकभयेनात्मा-
नमुत्कर्षता । ज्येष्ठं चानुयता व (ब) लं सुव (ब) हुशः शत्रुक्षयं कुर्व्वता कृष्णेनेव नृपेण
येन [16a][ध] रणेर्भारावतारः कृतः ॥[१८॥*] सुविहितवृष———⏑——⏑——
⏑⏑⏑⏑⏑⏑———⏑——⏑——
⏑⏑⏑⏑⏑⏑———⏑

9 लोकोपकारी भव इव **भवदेव**स्तस्य पुत्रस्तुरीयः [१९॥*] कृपाणनरवरेणाशु विक्रम्य दल-
यन्रणे । अभवद्वैरिमत्तेभान्स एको **रणकेसरी** ॥[२०॥*] शेषः क्लेशेन मूर्ध्ना कथमपि धरणीं
धारयन्भारगुर्व्वीशक्त[ः] कम्पान्न पातुं न च कुलगिरयो निश्चलत्वे स——[।]————⏑
— — ⏑⏑⏑⏑⏑⏑——⏑——⏑————⏑——⏑⏑⏑

10 इव नृपो योष्टमोन्यः कुलाद्रिः ॥[२१॥*] करग्रहमकृत्वापि मण्डलभ्रमणाद्विना । अपूर्व्वो यः
क्षितेर्भर्त्ता जातो लक्ष्मीपतिर्भवन् ॥[२२॥*] स्वीकृतशिलीमुखेन प्रियेण हृदयस्य सुरभिणा
शाश्वत् । मधुनेव येन लोको नवकुसुमे . . . .[17][॥२३॥*] . . . .
. . . .

11 लोकस्य स्वा[मितां] [स्थि]रः ॥[२४॥*]सद्वृत्तोपि धृतायतिर्गुरुपि प्रारव्ध (ब्ध) शिक्षोधमो
दोषोन्मूलन तत्पर⁐प्रतिदिनं पूर्णः कलावानपि । दृष्टः काञ्चनपुञ्जपिञ्जरतनुर्य्यो रक्त-
वर्णोपि सन्निर्दग्धद्वि[ष]दिन्धनोपि नितरां दीप्तो नृणां भूतये ॥[२५॥*] येन . . . .
. . . . [॥२६॥*]

13. Jain: °गतेव.
14. The reading is doubtful. The syllable *dhā* appears to have been originally left out and engraved above the line.
15. Kielhorn: °वत्.
16. The verse being in the *Āryā* metre, the exact number of the missing syllables cannot be determined.
16*a*. The use of the word *dharaṇī* as an *i*-ending masculine is noteworthy.
17. The metre being *Āryā*, the exact number of the lost syllables cannot be ascertained.

12 पूरिताशं समुन्नम्य [ये] न सर्व्वत्र वर्षता। न क्वचिद्दर्शित⌣पङ्क इति कस्य न विस्मयः
।। [२७।।*] जनाभिरामो नयनाभिनन्दी दानेन कर्ण्णं धिषणं धिया च। जयन्स शत्रावपि
सान्त्ववादी गीतो ज [ग] **त्यप्रियवैशिका**ख्यः ।।[२८।।*] येन नग्नग[ले१]. . . . . .
. . . . [।।२९।।*]
—— ⌣ ⌣ — ⌣

13 यस्य सततं माधुर्य्यमेवाधिकं वृद्धिर्नक्षयमेति नापि च जलैरात्मा भृतः सर्व्वदा। नित्यं नाग-
सनाथतामुपगतो यो न द्विजिह्वाश्रयः स श्रीमान्**रणकेसरी** विजयतां रत्नाकर⌣पञ्चमः
।।[३०।।*][गाम्भी]र्य्यं वारिराशेः स्थितिमवनिभृतां सप्त [सं]—⌣——————⌣——
⌣⌣⌣⌣ ⌣⌣——⌣———⌣————⌣——⌣⌣

14 हृतवपुषः सूर्य्यपुत्रस्य दानम् (नं) यः स्वैरेतैरजस्रं लघयति रघुना (णा) तुल्यकीर्त्तिप्रभावः
[।।३१।।*] जनयति शत्रुषु चिन्तां योधैर्दुर्गैश्च संगरे यस्मात् [।*] येन रणघस्मरोसौ **चि**
[न्तादु]र्गाख्यतामगमत् ।।[३२।।*] भू मिर्य्यास्य य --⌣—⌣⌣⌣———⌣———⌣—
———⌣⌣—⌣—⌣⌣⌣———⌣——⌣————

15 सुगतस्य सद्म कृतिना धीरात्म [ना] पालितं धर्म्मे वा सुरलोकसङ्गसुमुखे को न त्वरावान्भवेत्
।।[३३।।*] तस्य प्रेमाधिवासः श्रुतसुगतवचा वैद्यके चाभियुक्तः शान्तः शिक्षापदी स्यात्सकल-
जनहि[ता]भ्युद्यतो योग्रजन्मा। तेनालं जीर्ण्ण———⌣⌣⌣⌣⌣———⌣——⌣——
————⌣———⌣⌣⌣⌣⌣⌣———⌣——
⌣——[।।३४।।*]

16 व्र (ब्र)ह्मचारी नमोवु (बु)द्धो जीर्ण्णमेतत्तदाश्रयात् [।*] पुनर्नवत्वमनयद्वो (द्बो) धिसत्व
(त्त्व) समः कृती ।।[३५।।*] वापीकूपोद्यानसा (शा) लाट्ट चैत्यैर्नेत्रानन्दैर्भूषितो भूरिभूषः।
जित्वा कान्त्या सर्व्वशोभां [वि]हारो हासोन्मिश्रोभूदिवायं सुधा[क्तः] [।।३६।।*]
———⌣———⌣——⌣———
———⌣——⌣⌣——⌣———
———⌣———⌣⌣——⌣—

17 वदास्तामिदं वेश्म महज्जिनस्य ।।[३७।।*] सद्वर्ण्णा जातिसुभगा विद्वन्मधुकरप्रिया। कृता
भास्करभट्टेन प्रशस्तिः स्रगिवोज्व (ज्ज्व)ला ।।)[18] ।।[३८।।*] इति कमलदलाम्वु
(म्बु) वि (बि) न्दुलोलं श्रि[य]मनुचिन्त्य मनुष्यजीवितञ्च। सकलमणि⌣⌣—⌣—⌣——
⌣⌣⌣⌣—⌣⌣—⌣—⌣——— [।।३९।।*][19]
. . . .[20]

18. This is evidently an auspicious mark and is met with in a slightly different form, on the punch-marked, uninscribed cast copper and local coins. See Allan, *CICBM*, *AI*, xxxv, xxxviii, xl, xli, xlii, lxxv, lxxxvii, xcv, xcvi, xcix, 32, 35, 41, 56, 68, 86-87, 129, 148-49. The only difference is that the pellet in the centre is solid on coins. The occurrence of this device in this record, which is chronologically separated from the coins in question by a few centuries, is very interesting.

19. As this stanza is often met with in copper-plate inscriptions, the missing portion can be easily restored as °दमुदाहृतं च बुद्ध्वा नहि पुरुषैः परकीर्त्तयो विलोप्याः.

20. As pointed out by Kielhorn, it is difficult to say if, after verse 39, there was any writing at the end of line 17, and to ascertain the exact number of syllables, if any. On the analogy of the original portion of the Pathari pillar inscription it has been suggested that the inscription originally ended here with a date, for which there could have been just suffii- cient space after the verse.

18 ताक्ष्र्याक्षाक्षो[भ्य]–[ङ्ग]क्ष‿‿फणिफणारत्नगोगुप्त——प्रोत्तुङ्गाम्भस्त [र[ङ्गस्फुट‿‿
‿‿भुजालिङ्गिताङ्गा[मि] मांङ्गा (ङ्गाम्) [।*] [प्रा ?]——सङ्ग[ग?] ङ्गासलिलक-
लकल[क्षे]पदक्ष [:?] क्षिती [श?] श्राजावजित्य गोप्ताजनि जगति [ज]यी **नम्नरा**
[जाधि]——[21] [।।४०।।*] ———‿——‿‿‿‿‿——‿——‿
————‿——‿‿‿‿‿‿—

19 [स्या?] रव्य [या?] ख्यातकी [र्त्तिर्मीमान्सा ?[22]]द्—‿ पक्षे ललदमलशिखा [शेख]रः
कल्पवह्निः सांख्याख्याख्या[न] [मत्त?] द्विपदलनपटुः केसरी [चि] त्रमत्र ।।[४१।।*]
———‿——स्फुट[कु] मुदरुचेस्तण्डुलस्याष्टभागै [श्च?] क्रेसौ वायसा[नां]
स्फुरदुरुकरुणः सत्र (त्र) मेकेन — —[। *] ———‿——‿‿‿‿‿
‿——‿—————‿—— ‿‿‿‿‿‿——‿

20 –[चन्द्र?] [भा] भिः[23] [।।४२।।*][24]

ABSTRACT

The inscription opens with the *siddham* symbol and salutation (*namaḥ*), evidently to the Buddha. They are followed by four stanzas which praise, and invoke the protective blessings of the Buddha, who is mentioned by the names Jina (v. 1) and Tāyin(v. 3)[25]. The first verse describes him as a bow-bearer who, with the arrow in the form of benevolence (*maitrī*) fixed on the bow which is unsurpassed knowledge (*anuttara-jñāna*), conquers the invincible hosts of the Unborn, *i.e.*, Kāma or Māra. The next verse states that liberation (*mukti*) is very dear to him and that compassion (*karuṇā*) is firmly established in his mind. The third stanza avers that he freed the whole world from fear except only the god of love (*Smara*) who is afraid of him. Next eleven verses (5-15) are devoted to the description of king Sūrya-ghoṣa who appears to have been an independent ruler.[26] He was plunged in deep grief when his dear son died by falling from the top of the palace and, realising the ephemeral nature of life, built a magnificent temple of the Muni (Buddha) which, we are told, surpassed by its loveliness, the splendour of the mountain of snow, *i.e.*, Himācala (v. 15).

After a long time there flourished another king, Udayana by name,[27] who

21. The missing syllables may be conjecturally but reasonably restored as °राजः.
22. Read मीमांसा (?)
23. This is extremely doubtful.
24. After this stanza another verse in the *Sragdharā* metre is engraved; but so much of this stanza is effaced or doubtful that the few letters that can be deciphered with certainty are of no use and as such need not be transcribed.
25. For the occurrence of this name in inscriptions and literature, see *IA*, xiv, 46, textlines 6 and 11; *Mahāvastu* (edited by M. Senart), ii, 543.
26. His successes in war are alluded to in vv. 5-7 and 10. Otherwise the description is conventional. In v. 5 he is compared to the sun who has a single-wheeled chariot, whereas verse 8 draws contrast between him and god Śiva as the former does not seek the shelter of a fortress (*adurga*), homage is paid to his feet by men well-versed in arts (*kalāvat*) and his sternness brings misfortune (*abhūti-paruṣa*) while the latter is attached to his consort Durgā, his head is adorned by the moon and his body is stained with ashes.
27. He has been identified with the homonymous Pāṇḍava king mentioned in a Kalanjar inscription. See *JRAS*, 1905, 621, where the relevant stanza from this inscription is quoted.

was born from the Pāṇḍava family (v. 16). His son, whose name is lost in the missing portion of verse 17, is described in the next two verses (17-18), the last of which compares him to Kṛṣṇa.[28] Next is mentioned his[29] fourth son, king **Bhavadeva**, whose description claims as many as fifteen stanzas (19-33) which inform us that he was also known as Raṇakesarin[30] (v. 20), Apriya-vaiśika[31] (v. 28) and Cintādurga[32] (v. 32).[33] He gave protection to the abode of Sugata (v. 33) which, when it had fallen into decay, was repaired by a Brāhmaṇa, whose name has disappeared but who is described as a favourite of king Bhavadeva, well-versed in the words (teachings) of Sugata and the science of medicine, and a *śikṣāpadin* (one who observes the ten precepts of religious life prescribed by Buddhism), and a *brahmacārin* named Namo-buddha,[34] who is compared to a Bodhisattva (vv. 34-35). Verse 36 refers to this restored structure as a monastery, whereas in the following stanza, three-fourth of which is lost, customary wish for the preservation of this great abode of Jina is expressed. This eulogy (*praśasti*), we are told in verse 38,

28. It is said that by associating himself with the gentle (*akrūra*), possessing an army that frightened enemies, raising himself after dispelling the terrible fear of hell (*narakabhaya*), and frequently causing the annihilation of the adversaries while attending upon his elder brother Bala (Indrabala according to Kielhorn) he looked like Kṛṣṇa who was associated with Akrūra, carried a wheel (*cakra*) inspiring fear in the minds of the adversaries, raised himself up after putting an end to the fear from the demon Naraka and attended upon his elder brother Balarāma.
29. It is not quite clear from the inscription whether Udayana's or of his son (described in vv. 17-18) whose name is lost, though the latter interpretation is more likely if the word *bala* actually refers to Indrabala who is known from some other records (no III: XIII) to have been a son of Udayana.
30. We are told that by slaying the rutting elephants of the enemies with his claw-like sword he became a unique Raṇakesarin, *i.e.*, a lion in the battle.
31. *i.e.*, not fond of harlotry, is a rather strange appellation.
32. Bhavadeva is said to have earned this name by causing anxiety (*cintā*) to his adversaries and himself being difficult to assail (*durga*) by warriors in combat.
33. In the course of general description there are some interesting references which may be outlined here. In verse 21 he is said to have surpassed the serpent Śeṣa who somehow bears the heavy earth on his head and is described as the eighth Kulādri. The seven Kulaparvatas are Vindhya, Pāriyātra, Śuktimat, Ṛkṣa, Mahendra, Sahya and Malaya. *Vide Kāvya-mīmāṁsā*, 92. Another stanza (22) says that he became a unique lord of the earth even without grasping her hand and walking round (the fire). The uniqueness lies in not being required to grasp the hand of the bride and walk round the fire which constitute essential rites of marriage. The other sense of the relevant expressions is 'without levying taxes (*kara-graham* = *akṛtv-āpi*) and without any commotion of the realm (*maṇḍalabhramaṇād* = *vinā*). In other verses he is compared to Karṇa (v. 28), son of Sūrya (v. 31), in liberality, Dhiṣaṇa, *i.e.*, Bṛhaspati, in intelligence (v. 28) and Raghu in fame (v. 31). In yet another verse (30) he is spoken of as the fifth ocean, *i.e.*, he surpassed the four oceans by his qualities.
34. It is comparable to words like *yadbhaviṣya* (one habitually saying *yad bhaviṣyati bhaviṣyati*—whatever is to happen will happen) and would primarily denote a person habitually using the expression *namo Buddhāya* = salutation to the Buddha. Similar formulae of a religious or sectarian character are still in popular use in India by way of greeting or salutation.

was composed by the poet Bhāskarabhaṭṭa. Next comes an imprecatory stanza (v. 39). The original record seems to end here, and the following four verses, none of which is intact, appear to have been added at a slightly later date.

Verse 40 refers to king **Nannarāja** who is probably styled *adhirāja* and is reported to have gained victories in battle-field. The following stanza describes learning, whether of the king or of someone else is not clear.[35] In verse 42 there seems to be an allusion to the creation of a *sattra* (free feeding house) for crows. The few letters of verse 43 that can be deciphered refuse to yield any sense.

35. The person concerned was hostile to the Sāṅkhya system. There is also a reference to Mīmāṁsā, but his attitude towards it cannot be ascertained because of the loss of a portion of the verse.

III : II

BONDA PLATES[1] OF TĪVARADEVA, YEAR 5

Provenance: Bonda, Raigarh District, Madhya Pradesh.

References: *ARIE*, 1959-60, 15, App. A-56; D.C. Sircar, *EI*, xxxiv, 111-16 and plates between pp. 114 and 115; S.N. Rajaguru, *IO*, iv, 18-23.

Language: Sanskrit with certain Prakritisms.[2] In a mixture of prose and verse.

Metres: Verse 1: *Āryā*; Verse 2: *Vasantatilakā*; Verses 3, 5-8: *Anuṣṭubh*; Verse 4: *Indravajrā*.

Script: Box-headed variety of the Central Indian alphabet.

Date: Regnal Year 5, Mārgaśīrṣa 1. Latter half of the seventh century A.D.

TEXT[3]

First Plate

1 सिद्धम्[4] [।*] जयति जगत्र (त्त्र) यतिलकः क्षितिभृत्कुलभवनमङ्गल[स्त*]म्भः [।*] श्रि (श्री) **मति(त्ती)वरदेवो** [धौ]-

2 रेय [:*] सकलपुण्यकृताम् ।।[5] [१।।*] स्वस्ति **श्रीपुरा**त्समधिगतपञ्चमहाशब्दानेकनतनृ-

3 पतिकिरीटकोटिघृष्टचरणनखदर्प्पणोम्भा (द्भा)सितोपकण्ठदिङमुखः प्रकटरि-

4 पुराजलक्ष्मीः (क्ष्मी) केशपाशाकर्षणदुर्ल्ललितपाणिप[6]ल्लवः निशितनिस्त्रि(स्त्रिं)ङश(श) घन

5 घातपातितारिद्व (द्वि)रदकुम्भमण्डलगलद्व(द्ब) हलगो (शो)णितसदासिक्तमुक्ताफल-

6 प्रकरमुण्डितरणाङ्गणः विविधरत्नसंभारला[7]भा(भ)लोभविजृम्भमाणारिक्षा-

7 खारिवाडवानलश्चन्द्रोदय इवाकृतकरोद्वेगः क्षीरोद इवाविर्भूतानेक(का) तिशा-

1. Measuring 8·95" in length and 5·42" in breadth in the middle, the plates are slightly less in length and breadth at the ends and their corners are slightly rounded off. The copper ring, which holds the plates together, is about ·4" thick and about 4·5" in diameter. There is a circular hole about the middle of the left margin in each plate for the passage of the ring.
2. *Cf. Phāliha* = Sanskrit *sphaṭika* in the name of one of the donees, *viz.*, Lāṭa-Phāliha svāmin. Also *cf. sāppū* in the name Sāppūpakṣa, the exact meaning of which cannot be made out.
3. From plates in *EI*, xxxiv, opposite pp. 114 and 115.
4. Expressed by a symbol.
5. The mark of punctuation is indicated by a couple of curved vertical strokes, the first one having a hook towards left on the top.
6. Originally *pā* had been written, but later medial *ā* was cancelled.
7. Originally *lo* had been engraved, but later the *e*-stroke of medial *o* was cancelled.

8 यिरत्नसम्पत् गरुत्मानिव भुज[8]ङ्गोद्धारचतुरः परामृष्टशत्रुकलत्रनेत्राञ्जनो(न)कमल[8a]–

9 कपोलकुङ्कुमपत्रभङ्गः शिष्टाचारव्यवस्थ(स्था) परिपालने(नै) कदत्तः(त्त) चित्तः [।*] अपि च प्रा–

10 क्तने तपसि यशसि रहसि चेतसि चक्षुसि (षि) वपुषि च पूजितो जनेनाक्लिष्टतया नि[9]–

Second Plate : First Side

11 तान्तमवितृप्तो गु(गू)ढो गाढं स्वच्छः प्रसन्नो यौवनेन च(चा)लङ्कृतः स्वामीभवन(न्न) प्यबहुलप–

12 नोनुज्झितकुतृष्टो(ष्णो)पि नितान्तत्यागी रिपुजनप्रचण्डोपि सो(सौ)म्यदर्शनो भूतिविभूष–

13 णोप्यपरुषस्वभावः [।*] किञ्चासन्तुष्टो धर्म्मार्जने न सम्पल्ल(ल्ला)भे स्वल्प [:*] क्रोधे न प्रभावे लु–

14 ब्धो यशसि न परवित्तापहारेः (रे) सक्तः सुभाषितेषु न कामिनीक्रीडासु प्रतापानलदग्धाशेष–

15 रिपुकुलतूलराशिस्तुहिनशिलाशैलधवलयशोराशिप्रा(प्र)काशितदिगन्तः क(का)न्तः प्रकृ–

16 त्या श्रीमदिन्द्रबलसूनोरलङ्कृतपाण्डव (वं)ङ्ग(श)स्य श्रीन (न्न) देवस्य तनय [:*] प्र(प्रा)–

17 प्त सकलको [स*] लाधिपत्यः स्वपुण्यसम्भारप्रशमिताशेषजगदुपद्रवः स्वप्रज्ञा–

18 सु(सू) चीसमुद्धृताखिलकण्टकः परमवैष्णवो मातापितृपादानुद्धचातः **श्रीमा(म)हा–**

19 **शिवतीवरराजः** पिहराजभुक्तीप (य) बोन्दकअवडिकसहित[10]प्रतिवासिनः समाज्ञा–

20 पयति विदि [त*] मस्तु भवतां यथास्माभिरयं ग्रामो यावद्रविशशितारा किरण–

21 प्रतिहतघोरान्धकारं जगदवतिष्ठते तावदुपभोग्यः सनिधिसो(स्सो)प–

Second Plate : Second Side

22 निधिरचाटभटप्रावेश्यः सर्व्वकरसमवेतः[11] सदाशापराधः सापुत्रिकवेणी–

23 भोज्यः यजुर्व्वेदा(द) सामवेदचरकाद्ध्वर्य्यं (र्य्यु) मैत्रायनि(णी)य[12]भट्टमधुसूदनोपाद्धचा–

24 य ।।[13] एवत्रिपाद्धया(न्त्रि) विक्रमोपाद्धयाय[14] ।।देवसोमोपाद्धचाय ।। स्वामिदत्तोपाद्धचाय ।। विष्णुघो–

25 षोपाद्धचाय ।। स्थावरोपाद्धचाय ।। भट्टकमलपक्षस्वामि ।। भट्टरविणा(ना)गस्वामि । [।*]

26 शम्भुभवस्वामि ।। ब(बं)धुदेवयोरङ्गविष्णुभवस्वामि ।। लाटफलिहस्वामि ।।

27 अशोकस्वामि ।। श्रीधरभू[15]तिस्वामि ।। शीलपक्षस्वामि ।। साप्पूपक्षस्वामि । [।*]

8. Originally *jo* had been incised, but later medial *o* was struck off.

8*a*. Read कोमल as in the Rajim plates of the same ruler.

9. Sircar: °नी°.

10. As suggested by Sircar, °भुक्तीयावडिकसहितबोन्दक° or बोन्दके अवडिकसहिते would be a better reading. The non-observance of *sandhi* has enabled us to know the correct form of the name of the village Avaḍika. Otherwise it would have been difficult to decide whether the correct form was Avaḍika or Āvaḍika.

11. As suggested by Sircar, समेतः would be a better reading.

12. Sircar: मैत्रायनीय°

13. This and other marks of punctuation up to line 29 are superfluous.

14. Sircar: र(अ) वन्तिविक्रमो°

15. At first *bhā* had been incised, but later the sign for medial *ā* was cancelled.

28 वामनस्वामि ।। नागशर्म्मस्वामि ।। गोल [च*]न्द्रस्वामि ।। भद्रस्वामि ।। छान्दोगच—
29 रणि(णी)यगोपेन्द्रस्वामि एवं[16] वामन[17]स्वामि ।। सोमस्वामि ।। यज्ञस्वामि ।।
30 उन्नतमेघस्वामिभ्यः पञ्चवि(विं)ऋश(श)तिभ्यः मातापित्रोरात्मनश्च पुण्याभि–
31 वृद्धये उदकपूर्व्वम्प्रतिपादित इत्युपलभ्य यथोचितं भोगभाग–

Third Plate

32 मुपनयन्तः सुखं प्रतिवत्स्यथेति ।। भाविनश्च भूमिपालनानुदि्द–
33 श्येदमि(म)भिधीयते [।*] भूमिप्रदा दिवि ललन्ति पति(त)न्ति हन्त हृत्वा मही(हीं) नृपत–
34 यो नरके नृश(शं) त्सा (सा) [:।*] एता(त)द्वं (द्व)यं परिकलय्य चल(ला)ञ्च लक्ष्मी-मायुस्तथा(था) कुरुत य–
35 द्भवत(ता) मभि (भी)ष्ट [म्*] ।। [२।।*] अपि च [।*] रक्षापालनयोस्त(स्ता)वत्फल (लं) सुगतिदुर्ग्गती [।*] को नाम स्वर्ग्ग[18]–
36 मुत्सृज्य नरक(कं) प्रतिपाद्यते ।। [३।।*] व्यासगीता(तां)श्चात्र श्लोकानुदाहरन्ति [।*] अग्नेरपत्यं प्र–
37 थम(मं) सुवर्ण्णं (र्ण्णं) भूर्व्वैष्णवी सूर्य्यसुताश्च गावः [।*] दत्तास्त्रयस्तेन भवन्ति लोका
38 य⁀काञ्चनं गाञ्च महीञ्च दद्यात् ।। [४।।*] षष्टिवर्षसहस्र(स्रा)णि स्वर्ग्गे मोदति भूमिदः
39 अ(आ)च्छेत्ता च्चा(चा) नुमन्ता च्च(च) तान्येव नरके वसेत् ।।[५।।*] बहुभिर्व्वसुधा दत्ता राजभिस्स–
40 गरादिभिः [।*] यस्य यस्य यद(दा)भूमिस्तस्य तस्य तदा फलं(लम्)[।।६।।*] स्वदत्ता(त्तां) परदत्तां(त्तां) म्वा(वा) यत्नाद्र–
41 क्ष युधिष्ठिर [।*] महीन्म(म्म)हि(ही)मतां श्रेष्ठ दानाच्छ्रेयोनुपालनमिति ।।[७।।*] **प्रवर्द्धमानविजयरा–**
42 **ज्ये स (सं) म्व(व) त् ५ मार्ग्गदि** उक्ती (त्की) र्ण(र्णं)अ(म) क्षसा(शा)लिकयोत्र-नागसूनुना बोप्पनागेन ।।

Seal[19]

1 श्रीमत्तीवरदेवस्य कोसलाधिपतेरिदं (दम्) [।*]
2 शासनं धर्म्मवृद्धयत्थँ स्थिरमाचन्द्रतारकं (कम्) [।।८।।*]

16. *Evam* should better be omitted, for all the names of the donees have to be treated as forming a single compound.
17. *Vomana* had been originally incised, but the *e-stroke* was probably cancelled.
18. The scribe had originally engraved *svārgga*, but later cancelled the medial *ā*.
19. The bronze seal, affixed to the joint of the ring, is circular, its diameter being 3·2". The countersunk surface, with a circular border, is divided into two parts by a couple of horizontal lines, the upper part being smaller than the lower one. The upper part bears, in the centre, the figure of Garuḍa, seated facing full front, depicted with human head and the body of a bird, with expanded wings, and holding a serpent with raised hood in each of his two hands. On the proper right of Garuḍa there is a *cakra* (wheel) and on the proper left a *śaṅkha* (conch-shell), both being emblems of god Viṣṇu. In the lower part we have a two-line legend in the *Anuṣṭubh* metre and a floral device below it.

ABSTRACT

The inscription opens with the auspicious word *siddham*, expressed symbolically, which is followed by a stanza in praise of the reigning king **Tīvaradeva** who is described as an ornament of the three worlds, an auspicious column supporting the mansion that is the family of the kings and the foremost of all the performers of meritorious deeds. Next is mentioned the place of issue, **Śrīpura**. Then follows a long prose passage describing king **Mahāśiva Tīvararāja**, son of Nannadeva of the Pāṇḍu-vaṁśa and grandson of Indrabala, in a hyperbolic manner. He is said, *inter alia*, to have obtained lordship over the whole of the Kosala[20] country, and meditated upon the feet of his parents and to have been a devout worshipper of god Viṣṇu. It is said that a number of chiefs who had acquired the five *mahāśabdas*[20a] had the ends of their crowns rubbed at his feet.

He informed the inhabitants of the villages Bondaka[21] together with another place called Avaḍika[22] situated in the district (*bhukti*) of Piharāja[23] that he had donated this village, for the increase of the religious merit of his parents and of his own self, to the twenty-five Brāhmaṇas (enumerated below) and ordered them to pay the *bhāga* (royal share of the produce) and *bhoga* (periodical offerings) to the donees regularly. The grant, which was intended to last for ever, carried with it right to the *nidhi* (hidden treasure),

20. Kosala denoted the Raipur-Bilaspur-Raigarh region of Madhya Pradesh and the Sambalpur-Balangir region of Orissa.

20*a*. The correct interpretation of the expression *pañcamahāśabda*, generally met with in inscriptions in connection with feudatory chiefs, has eluded epigraphists for long. Monier Monier-Williams (*A Sanskrit-English Dictionary*, 801) took it in the sense of, *inter alia*, 'any official title beginning with the word *mahā*, and *pañca-mahāśabda* should accordingly mean five titles beginning with the word *mahat*'. The expression was, therefore, taken to refer to the titles *Mahāsāmanta, Mahāpratīhāra, Mahādaṇḍanāyaka, Maha-kārtākṛtika* and *Mahārāja*. Later, on the basis of some references in Chandbardāi's *Pṛthvīrājarāso*, Tulsīdāsa's *Rāmacaritamānasa* and other medieval writings, it was rendered as 'the five great sounds (producedby five kinds of musical instruments). For a detailed summary of these views, see Fleet, *CII*, iii, 296-97, note 9). But we feel inclined to take it to mean 'five titles beginning with *mahat*', the term *śabda* being often used in the sense of 'title'. See Junagadh inscription of Rudradāman I, *EI*, viii, 44, text-line 12. This finds support from Kalhaṇa who informs us that the Karkoṭa monarch Lalitāditya Muktāpīḍa granted five great titles (*pañca-mahāśabdas*) to his minister of peace and war, Mitraśarman, in recognition of his services, and hat the five offices (*karma-sthānas*) created by him (Lalitāditya), *viz.*, *Mahāpratihārāpīḍ Mahāsandhivigraha, Mahāśvaśālā, Mahābhāṇḍāgāra* and *Mahāsādhanabhāga*, got precedence over the well-known eighteen *tīrthas* (administrative departments) introduced earlier by Jalauka. See *Rāja-taraṅgiṇī*, iv. 140-43. Also see *ibid.*, iv. 512.

21. It is represented by modern Bondā, the findspot of the plates, in the Sarangarh Tahsil of the Raigarh District. It lies anout two miles from the bank of the Mahānadī near Balpur.

22. It appears to have been a locality adjoining Bondaka.

23. Piharāja, the headquarters of the *bhukti* of that name, is represented by modern Piharā, aoout a mile to the south-east of Bonda.

upanidhi (minor underground deposits), all the taxes, *daś-āparādha* (fines for the ten offences), *aputrika-veṇī* (property of persons dying without leaving heirs) and exemption from the entry of the *cāṭas* (irregular soldiers) and *bhaṭas* (regular soldiers).

The grantees are mentioned in two groups, one belonging to the Maitrāyanīya *śākhā* of the *Yajurveda* and the other to Chandoga *caraṇa* of the *Sāmaveda*. The Brāhmaṇas are further stated to have been priests of the Caraka section of the *Yajurveda* and the *Sāmaveda*.[24] The donees of the first group included (i) *Bhaṭṭa* Madhusūdanopādhyāya, (ii) Trivikramōpādhyāya,[25] (iii) Devasomopādhyāya, (iv) Svāmidattopādhyāya, (v) Viṣṇughoṣopādhyāya, (vi) Sthāvaropādhyāya, (vii) *Bhaṭṭa* Kamalapakṣasvāmin, (viii) *Bhaṭṭa* Ravināgasvāmin, (ix) Śambhubhavasvāmin, (x) Bandhudeva, (xi) Yoraṅgaviṣṇubhavasvāmin,[25a] (xii) Lāṭa-Phalihasvāmin,[26] (xiii) Aśokasvāmin, (xiv) Śrīdharabhūtisvāmin, (xv) Śīlapakṣasvāmin, (xvi) Sāppūpakṣasvāmin,[27] (xvii) Vāmanasvāmin, (xviii) Nāgaśarmmasvāmin, (xix) Golacandrasvāmin, and (xx) Bhadrasvāmin. The second group comprised (i) Gopendrasvāmin, (ii) Vāmanasvāmin, (iii) Somasvāmin, (iv) Yajñasvāmin, and (v) Unnatameghasvāmin.[28]

The future kings are exhorted to protect the grant and six imprecatory stanzas, four of them in the name of Vyāsa, describing the merit accruing from making and maintaining land-grants and the sufferings resulting from their violation, are quoted in support of this exhortation.

The grant was made on the **first day of the month of Mārgaśīrṣa in tne fifth year of the increasingly victorious reign, evidently of Māhāśiva Tīvaradeva.**

The inscription was incised by Boppanāga, son of *akṣaśālika* (goldsmith) Gotranāga.

The legend on the seal mentions the permanent charter, apparently meaning the order in respect of the grant engraved on these plates, of the illustrious **Tīvaradeva,** the lord of Kosala.

24. It has to be noted that the Carakas were actually affiliated to the Kṛṣṇa (Black) *Yajurveda*.
25. Sircar reads the name as Ra (A) vantivikram-opādhyāya and thinks that he belonged to a family which originally hailed from Avanti (West Malwa).
25*a*. The initial portion of the name looks somewhat strange.
26. The family of Phalihasvāmin appears to have originally belonged to Lāṭa (Central and Southern Gujarat).
27. The meaning of the word *sāppū* is obscure.
28. It will be noticed that some of these names are uncommon.

III : III

RAJIM PLATES[1] OF TĪVARADEVA, YEAR 7

Provenance: Rajim, Raipur District, Madhya Pradesh.

References: Srivarmasuri and H.H. Wilson, *Asiatic Researches,* xv, 499 ff., pl. xiv; A. Cunningham, *ASR*, xvii, 17, pls. vi-viii; J.F. Fleet, *Inscriptions of the Early Gupta Kings and their Successors, CII*, iii, 291-99, pl. xlv; Hira Lal, *ICPB*, 97, No. 172; Bhandarkar's *List*, No. 1652; V.V. Mirashi and L.P. Pandeya, *EI*, xxiii, p. 116; S.N. Rajaguru, *IO*, iv, 24-31.

Language: Sanskrit. In a mixture of prose and verse.

Metres: Verse 1: *Āryā*; Verse 2: *Vasantatilakā*; Verses 3, 5-8: *Anuṣṭubh*; Verse 4: *Indravajrā*.

Script: Box-headed variety of the Central Indian alphabet.

Date: Regnal Year 7, Kārttika 8. Second half of the seventh century A.D.

TEXT[2]

First Plate

1 सिद्धम्[3] [।*] जयति जगत्र (त्त्र) य तिलक [:*] क्षितिभृत्कुलभवनमङ्गलस्त भ(म्भ)[4] [:।*][5] श्रि (श्री)मत्ति(त्ती)वरदेवो धौरेय [:*]स-

2 कलपुण्यकृता[6] [म्॥१॥*] स्वस्ति श्रि (श्री)पुरा[7]त्समधिगतपञ्चमहाशब्दानेकनतनृपतिकिरि (री)ट-

3 कोटिघृप्ट[8](ष्ट) चरणनखदर्पणोद्भासितोपि(प)कण्ठदु(दि)न्मु (ङ्मु)ख[9][:*] प्रकटरिपु राजलक्ष्मि(क्ष्मी)-

1. The plates measure about 8-1/8" long and 5-7/8" broad. The ring, which is circular, is about 7/16" thick and 4-1/2" in diameter. About the middle of the left margin of the plates there is a circular hole for the passage of the ring.
2. From pl. xlv in *CII*, iii.
3. Fleet: ओम्. Expressed by a symbol
4. Fleet: °सूत्र. But the first letter is clearly *sta* and the second *bha*, the intervening *anusvāra* or *m* being omitted due to oversight. Other plates of Tīvaradeva also have *stambhaḥ* in the corresponding verse.
5. Fleet: श्रृमत्°. However, the subscribed letter is clearly *r* which closely resembles that in °*traya*° earlier in this line. But it should be pointed out that the scribe has not maintained a clear distinction between subscribed *ṛ* and *r*.
6. Fleet: पुण्यकृतां.
7. Fleet: श्रृपुरा°.
8. Fleet: °घृप्त°.
9. Fleet: °तोपि कन्धदुन्मुख°. However, the letter following *ka* is clearly *ṇṭha* and not *ntha*. Our suggestion regarding the intended reading is based on the reading of the corresponding portion of the other two records of Tīvaradeva.

4 केशपाशाकर्षणदुर्ललितपाणिपल्ल[वो*]निशितनिस्तृ[10] (स्त्रि)ङ्श (श) घनघातपातितारि-
द्विरदकु–

5 म्भमण्डलगलद्व (द्ब) हलशोणितसदासिक्तमुक्ताफलप्रकरमण्डितरणाङ्गण–

6 द्वि (वि) विधरत्नसंभारलाभलोपविजृम्भमाणारिक्षाखारिवाडवानलश्चन्द्रोदय इवाकृत–

7 करोद्वेगः क्षि (क्षी) रोद इवाद्वि (वि) र्भूतानेकातिशायिरत्नसम्पत् गरुत्मानिव भुजङ्गोद्धार-
चतुर [:*]

8 परामृष्टग (श) त्रुकलत्रनेत्रांजनकोमलकपोलकुङ्कुमपत्रभङ्गत् (ङ्गः) शिष्टाचारब्य (व्य)
वस्था–

9 परिपालनैकदत्तचित्त [:।*] अपि च प्राक्तने तपसि यशसि रहसि चेतसि चक्षुषि ब (व) [पु]–

Second Plate : First Side

10 षि च पूजितो जनेनाक्लिष्टतया नितान्तमवितृप्तो गूडो (ढो) गाडं (ढं)[11] स्वच्छ[:*]
प्रसन्नो य (यौ) व–

11 नेन[12] चाप्लङ्कृत [:*] स्वामि (मी) भवन (न्न) प्यबहुलपनोनु[13]ज्झितकुतृष्णोपि नितान्तत्या–

12 गि (गी) रिपुजनप्रचण्डोपि सो (सौ) म्यदर्शनो भूतिविभूषणोप्यपरुषः (ष) स्वभाव [:।*][14]कि–

13 ञ्चासन्तुष्टो धर्मार्जनेन सम्पल्लाभे स्वल्प [:*] क्रोधे न प्रभावे लुब्धोयशसि न प–

14 रवित्तापहारे स[क्त]:[15] सुभासि (षि) तेषु न कामिनि (नी) क्रि (क्री) डासु प्रतापान-
लदग्धाशेष–

15 रिपुकुलतूलराशिस्तुहिनशिलाशैलधवलयशोराशिप्रकाशितदिगन्त [:*] कान्त [:*] प्रकृत्या

16 श्रि (श्री) मदिन्द्रबलसूनोरलङ्कृतपाण्डुव (वं) ङ्श (श) स्य श्रि (श्री) नन्नदेवस्य तनय [:*]
प्राप्तः[15a] स्वपुन्य (ण्य)–

17 संभारप्रस (श) मिताशेषजगदुपद्रवः स्वप्रज्ञाशू (सू) चि (ची) समुद्धृताखिलकण्टकः पर–

18 मवैष्णवो मातापितृपादानुध्यातः श्री **महाशिवति (ती) [व*]रराजः**[16] कुशली ।।[17]पेण्ठाम-
भुक्ति (क्ती) य[18]–

10. The subscript *r*, which turns to right, is rather unusual.
11. Fleet: गाड(ढ)°. However, the *anusvāra* is quite clear.
12. Fleet: गाड(ढ)स्वच्छप्रसन्नय(व)दनेन. However, the corresponding portion of the other plates of Tīvaradeva reads गाढं स्वच्छः प्रसन्नो यौवनेन and the same appears to be intended here.
13. Fleet: स्वामिभवन [ी *] प्यबहुलपनो°. However, the reading of the corresponding portion of Tīvraeva's other grants is स्वामीभवन्नप्यबहुलपनो.
14. Fleet: °प्यपरुषः स्वभाव [तः *].
15. Fleet: स (श) क [ल]:
15*a*. The intended reading is प्राप्तसकलकोसलाधिपत्यः which is met with in the other grants of Tīvaradeva. The omission of सकलकोसलाधिपत्य is obviously due to oversight.
16. As pointed out by Fleet (*CII*, iii, 295, fn. 1), the engraver first incised *rā* of *rājaḥ* omitting both *va* and *ra*; and later realising the error, he partially cancelled the medial *ā* but again forgot to insert *va*.
17. The mark of punctuation, which is indicated by a couple of vertical lines the first of which shows a hook in the upper part, is superfluous.
18. Fleet: भुक्तीय°

Second Plate : Second Side

19 पिम्परिपद्रके ब्राह्मणां (णान्) संपूज्य प्रतिवासिनः समाज्ञापयति [।*] विदि [त*] मस्तु
20 भवतां यथास्माभिरयं ग्रामो यावद्रविशशिताराकिरणप्रतिहतघोरान्धकारं ज-
21 गदवतिष्ठते तावदुपभोग्य [:*] सनिधिः सोपनिधिः (धि) रचाट[19]भटप्रवेश (श्यः)[20] दा-
22 रद्रणकसर्वकरादानसमेतो माता[21]पित्रोरात्मनश्च पुण्याभिबृ[22](वृ)द्धये भा-
23 रद्वाजसगोत्र वाजसनेयमाध्यन्दिनभट्टगौरि(री)दत्तपुत्र[23]भट्ट-
24 भवदत्तभट्टहर[24]दत्ताभ्यां ज्येष्ठद्वादश्यामुदकपूर्वं प्रतिपादित इ-
25 त्यवगम्य भवद्भिर्यथोचितमस्मै[25] भोगभागमुपनयद्भिः सुखम्प्रति-
26 वस्तब्य[26] (व्य) मिति ॥ भाविनश्च भूमिपालानुद्दिश्येदमभिधीयते [।*]भूमिप्र-
27 दा दिवि ललन्ति पतन्ति हृ(ह)न्त हृत्वा महि(हीं) नृपतयो नरके नृश(शं)ऽसा(सा):[।*]

Third Plate

28 एत[द्*] द्वय(ठ) परिकलय्य चलाञ्च लक्ष्मि (क्ष्मी) मायुस्तथा कुरुत यद्भवताम भि(भी) ष्ट[म्॥२॥*]
29 अपि च [।*] [26a]रक्षापालनयोस्तावत्फलं सुगतिदुर्गति(ती) [।*]को नाम स्वर्गमुच्छृ (त्सृ)ज्य
30 नरकं प्रतिपाद्यते [॥३॥*] ब्या (व्या) सगि(गी)तांश्चात्र श्लोकानुदाहरन्ति [।*] अग्नेर [प*]त्यं प्रथमं
31 सुवर्णं भूर्व्वैष्णवि (वी) सूर्य्यसुताश्च गावः [।*] दत्तात्र (स्त्र) यस्तेन भवन्ति लोका यः काञ्चनं गा-
32 ञ्च महि (ही) ञ्च[27] दधा [त्॥४॥*] षष्टिवर्षसहस्राणि स्वर्गे मोदति भूमिदः [।*] आक्षेप्ता
33 चानुमन्ता च तान्येव नरके वसेत् [॥५॥*] बहुभिर्वसुधा दत्ता राजभिः सगरादिभिः [।*]
34 यस्य यस्य यदा भूमित(स्त) स्य तस्य तदा फलं(लम्) [॥६॥*। स्वदत्तां परदत्तां बा (वा) यत्नाद्रक्ष
35 युधिष्ठिरः (र) [।*] महि(हीं)महि (ही) मतां श्रेष्ठ दाना श्रेयो[28]नुपालनमिति ॥ [6॥*] प्रवर्द्धमान-

19. The engraver first wrote *va* and then, realising his mistake, he struck off part of the vertical, thereby correcting it into *ṭa*.
20. Fleet: °प्रवेश [ो*].
21. The scribe first began to incise *pitro*; and then realising the omission, he corrected it into *mātā*.
22. At first *bṛi* was incised, and then medial *i* was partially struck off.
23. Fleet: °पुत्र°
24. Originally *rā* was engraved, and then the superscript *ā* was cancelled.
25. Read °तमाभ्यां.
26. First *bye* was engraved, and then medial *e* was cancelled.
26*a*. The hook attached to the middle of the vertical is superfluous.
27. The lower part of *ñca* being incomplete, it was engraved again and formed correctly; but the major portion of this second *ñca* has been lost due to the ring-hole and only its portion on the right is now visible.
28. Read दानाच्छ्रेयो°

36 विजयराज्यसम्व (संव) त्सरु ७ कार्त्तिक दिवसु अष्ठ (ष्ट) मु[29] ८ [।।*]

Seal[30]

1 श्रीमत्ति (त्ती) वरदेवस्य कोसलाधिपतेरिदं (दम्) [।*]

2 शासनं धर्म्मवृद्धयर्त्थं स्थिरमाचन्द्रतारकं (कम्) [।।८।।*]

ABSTRACT

After opening with the *siddham* symbol, the charter contains a stanza introducing king **Tīvaradeva**, the issuer of the grant, which is identical with that met with in No. III : III above. It is followed by the mention of **Śrīpura** whence the grant was issued. Then comes a long prose passage describing Tīvaradeva which is identical with that found in No. III: II above with the only difference that here there is no reference to his obtaining lordship of the entire Kosala country, the omission being evidently due to oversight.

After worshipping the Brāhmaṇas he informed the inhabitants of the village Pimparipadraka[30a] situated in the Peṇṭhāma *bhukti*[31] that he had given away the village in favour of the Brāhmaṇas *Bhaṭṭa* Bhavadatta and *Bhaṭṭa* Haradatta, sons of *Bhaṭṭa* Gaurīdatta, belonging to the Bhāradvāja *gotra* and the Vājasaneya-Mādhyandina *śākhā* (of the *Yajurveda*) on the twelfth day of the month of Jyeṣṭha[32] for the increase of the religious merit of his parents and of his own self and asked them to live happily by paying the *bhoga* and *bhāga* to the grantees regularly. The privileges attached to the grant included the right to the *nidhis,* the *upanidhis,* the *dāradraṇaka*[33] and to levy all the taxes and the exemption from the entry of the *cāṭas* and the *bhaṭas*.

Future rulers are then requested to maintain the grant and six benedictive and imprecatory stanzas, the same as those met with in the Bonda plates (III : II above), four of them in the name of Vyāsa, are quoted.

29. The *u*-ending in the words *samvatsaru*, *divasu* and *aṣṭamu* which is now in vogue in Telugu, is noteworthy.

30. The seal, which is about $3\frac{3}{16}$" in diameter, is similar to that attached to the Bonda plates of Tīvaradeva.

30*a* It has not been identified satisfactorily. It is not impossible that the ancient name is now represented by the modern village of Piparaud, about three miles north-west of Rajim, the findspot of the plates. See *EI*, xxiii, 116, fn. 5.

31. Peṇṭhāma cannot be identified. But it may be modern Pāṇḍukā near Rajim. Alternatively it may be represented by Pondh, about six miles north of Rajim. See *ibid.*

32. The 11th (*ekādaśī*) of Jyeṣṭha is regarded as specially sacred by the Hindus and the grant was probably made on the occasion of the *pāraṇā* on the following day.

33. *Dāradraṇaka*, which is a fiscal term of uncertain import, is met with here for the first time. According to Fleet (*CII*, iii, 299, fn. 1), it may refer either to some agricultural cess or to a marriage tax. Also see U.N. Ghoshal, *Contributions to the History of the Hindu Revenue System*, 2nd edition (Calcutta, 1972), 398, *IEG*, 83.

The charter was issued on the **eighth day of the month of Kārttika in the seventh year of the increasingly victorious reign.**[34]

The legend on the seal is identical with that found on the seal of the Bonda plates.

34. It may be noted that the charter was issued several months after the date when the grant recorded in it was actually made.

III : IV

BALODA PLATES[1] OF TĪVARADEVA, YEAR 9

Provenance: Baloda, Raipur District, Madhya Pradesh.

References: E. Hultsch, *EI*, vii, 102-7 and plates facing pp. 104 and 105; Hira Lal, *ICPB*, 96-97, No. 171; Bhandarkar's *List*, No. 1653; S.N. Rajaguru, *IO*, iv, 32-38.

Language: Sanskrit. In a mixture of prose and verse.

Metres: Verse 1: *Āryā*; Verse 2: *Vasantatilakā*; Verses 3, 5-8; *Anuṣṭubh*; Verse 4: *Indravajrā*.

Script: Box-headed variety of the Central Indian alphabet.

Date: Regnal Year 9, Jyeṣṭha 27. Second half of the seventh century A.D.

TEXT[2]

First Plate

1 सिद्धम्[3] [।*] जयति जगत्र(त्रा) यतिलक [:*] क्षितिभृत्कुलभवनमङ्गलस्तम्भः[4] [।*] श्रि(श्री) मत्ति(त्ती)वरदेवो[5]

2 धौरेय[:*] सकलपुण्यकृताम् ।।[6][१।।*]स्वस्ति श्रि(श्री)पुरात[7]समधिगतपञ्चमहाशब्दानेकन-

3 तनृपतिकिरीटकोटिघृष्टचरणनखदर्प्पणोद्भासितोपकण्ठदिङमुखः प्र-

4 कटरिपुराजलक्ष्मीः (क्ष्मी) केशपाशाकर्षणदुर्ल्ललितपाणिपल्लवः निशितनि-

5 स्त्रि(स्त्रिं)ङश(श)घनघ(घा)तपातितारिद्विरदकुम्भमण्डलगलद्व(द्ब)हलशोणित-

6 सटासिक्तमुक्ताफलप्रकरमण्डितरणाङ्गणः विविधरत्नसंभारला-

7 भलोभविजृम्भमाणारिक्षारवारिवाडवानलश्चन्द्रोदय इवाकृतकरोद्वे-

8 गः क्षि(क्षी)रोद[8] इवाविर्भूतानेकातिशायिरत्नसम्पत् ।।[9] गरुत्मानिव भुजङ्गोद्धा-

9 रचतुर [:*] परामृष्टशत्रुकलत्रनेत्राञ्जनकोमलकपोलकुङ्कुम[10]पत्र-

1. The plates measure about 9½" in length and about 5⅜" in width in the middle and a little less at the ends. About the middle of the left margin there is a square hole for the passage of the ring which is about 4½" in diameter and about 3/8" in thickness.
2. From facsimile in *EI* vii, opposite pp. 104 and 105.
3. Hultzsch: ओं. Expresed by a symbol.
4. Here and in lines 3, 4, 6, 10, 21, 22, 24, 27, 33, 37 and 38 the *visarga* is indicated by two circles placed one above the other. Elsewhere it consists of two similarly placed points.
5. Hultzsch: श्रीमत्तीवरदेवो.
6. The mark of punctuation is indicated by two somewhat curved vertical lines, the first one having a hook in its upper part.
7. Hultzsch: श्रीपुरा°
8. Hultzsch: क्षीरोद.
9. The mark of punctuation is indicated by a couple of slightly curved vertical lines.
10. Hultzsch: °कुङ्कुम°.

10 भङ्गः शिष्टाचारव्यवस्थापरिपालनैक[11]दत्तचित्तः [।*] अपि च प्राक्तने तप–

Second Plate : First Side

11 सि यशसि रहसि चेतसि चक्षुषि ब(व)पुषि च पूजितो जनेनाक्लिष्टतया नि–
12 तान्तमवितृप्तो गूढो गाढं स्वच्छः प्रसन्नो यौवनेन चालं (ल)ङ्कृतः स्वामी भ–
13 वन(न्न) प्यबहुलपनोनुज्झितकुतृष्णोपि नितान्तत्यागी रिपुजनप्रच–
14 ण्डोपि सो (सौ)म्य[12]दर्शनो भूतिविभूषणोप्यपरुषस्वभावः [।*]किञ्चासन्तुष्टो
15 धर्म्माज(र्ज) नेन सम्पल्लाभे स्वल्पः क्रोध (धे) न प्रभावे लुब्धो यशसि न प–
16 रवित्तापहारे सक्त [:*] सुभाषित (ते) षु न कामिनीक्रीडासु प्रतापानल—
17 दग्धाशेषरिपुकुलतूलराशिस्तुहिनशिलाशैलधवलयशोराशिप्र—
18 काशितदिगन्तः कान्तः प्रकृत्या श्रीमदिन्द्रव(ब) लसूनोरलङ्कृतपाण्डुव(वं)–
19 ङश(श) स्य श्रीनन्नदेवस्य तनय [:*] प्राप्तसकलकोसलाधिपत्यः स्वपुण्य–
20 सम्भारप्रशमिताशेषजगदुपद्रवः स्वप्रज्ञासूचीसमुद्धृताखि–

Second Plate: Second Side

21 लकण्टकः परमवैष्णवो मातापितृपादानुद्धयातः **श्रीमहाशिवत्ती(ती) वरराजः**
22 सुन्दरिकामार्ग्गि (र्गी)य[13]मोङ्किड्डुके प्रतिवासिनः समाज्ञापयाति [।*] विदितमस्तु
23 भवता(तां) यथायं ग्रामो यावद्रविशशिताराकिरणप्रतिहतघोरान्धकारं[14]
24 जगदवतिष्ठते तावदुपभोग्यस्सनिधिस्सोपनिधिरचाटभटप्रवेश्यः
25 सर्व्वकरसमेतः समधिगतपञ्चमहाशब्दप्रियजामातृश्रि(श्री)[15]
26 नन्नराजविज्ञा(ज्ञ)प्त्या[16] बिल्वपद्रके परिकल्पि [तसत्त्र] भोक्तृ (क्तृ)णां[17] यथ(था)प्रा–
27 प्तब्राह्म[णा*] दिजनाना (नां) त्रि (त्रि)ङश(श)तः प्रत्यहमुपभोगाय अधिष्ठानेन च
28 प्रतिपालना कार्य्यँ(र्य्यें)त्यनया व्यवस्थयास्माभिर्म (र्मा)तापित्रोरात्मनश्च पुण्याभि–
29 बृ(वृ)द्धये प्रतिपादित इत्युप [ल*] भ्य यथोचितभोगभागमुपनयन्त [:*] सु–
30 खं प्रतिवत्स्यथेति ।। भाविनश्च भूमिपालानुदि (द्दि)श्येदमभिधि(धी) यते[18] [।*] भू–

Third Plate : First Side

31 मिप्रदा दिवि ललन्ति पतन्ति हन्त हृत्वा महि[19] नृपतयो नरके
32 नृश(शं)ङशा(सा) [:।*] एत[द्*] द्वयं परिकलय्य चलाञ्च लक्ष्मीमायुस्तथा कुरुत यद्भ–

11. In the syllable *nai* a square hole was cut into the plate and a fresh piece of coppes inserted into the hole, probably for correcting *nai* which might have been spoiled accidentally in the original engraving. Vide *EI*, vii, p. 103.
12. Hultzsch: सौम्य°.
13. Hultzsch: °मार्ग्गीय°.
14. The *anusvāra* is indicated here by a circle. Elsewhere it consists of a point.
15. Hultzsch: °श्री°.
16. Hultzsch: °विज्ञ (1) प्त्या.
17. Hultzsch: °भोक्तृणां.
18. Hultzsch: °भिधीयते.
19. Hultzsch: मही. Read महीं.

33 व (ता) मभिष्टः[20] [।।२।।*] अपि च [।*] रक्षापालनयोस्तावत्फल(लं) सुगतिदुर्ग्गति (ती)[21] [।*] को नाम

34 स्वर्ग्गमुत्सृज्य नरक(कं) प्रतिपद्यते ।।[३।।*] व्यासगि(गी)ता(तां)श्चात्र[22] श्लोकानुदाह-[र*]न्ति [।*] अग्ने-

35 रपत्य (त्यं) प्रथम(मं) सुवर्ण्ण(र्ण्णं) भूर्व्व(र्व्वै)ष्णवि(वी)[23]सूर्य्यसु[ताश्च] गाव [:।*] दत्त (।)स[त्र]यस्तेन

36 भवन्ति लोका य ×क(का)ञ्चन(नं) गाञ्च महि(ही) ञ्च[24] दद्य (द्या) त्[25] ।। [४।।*] षष्टिवर्षसहस्राणि

37 स्वर्ग्गे मोदति भूमिदः [।*] अ (आ)च्छेत्ता च्चा(चा)नुमन्ता च तान्येव नरके वसेत् ।। [५।।*] बहु-

38 भिर्व्वसुधा दत्ता र(रा) जभिस्सगरादिभिः [।*] यस्य यस्य यदा भूमित (स्त) स्य तस्य तदा

39 फलं (लम्)।। [६।।*] स्वदत्ता(त्तां) परदत्ताम्वा[26] यत्नाद्रक्ष युधिष्ठिर [।*] महि(ही)न्म (म्म) हि (ही) मता(तां)[27] श्रेष्ठ

40 दानाच्छ्र्योनुपालनमिति ।।[७।।*] **प्रवर्द्धमान विजयराज्ये सम्वत्सरु**[28] **९ ज्येष्ठादि २० ७**

Third Plate : Second Side[29]

41 उत्कीर्ण्ण आ(मा) क्ष्कशालिकसोत्रणागसूनुना बोप्पणागेन[30] ।[31]

Seal[32]

1 **श्रीमत्तीवरदेवस्य** कोसल(ा)धिपतेरि[दं] (दम्) [।*]

2 शास [नं] ध [र्म्म]वृ[द्धचर्त्थं] स्थितमाचन्द्रत(ा)र[कं] [कम] [।।८।।*]

20. Hultzsch: °मभीष्ट. Read °मभीष्टम्.
21. Hultzsch: °दुर्गती.
22. Hultzsch: °गीता°.
23. Hultzsch: °र्व्वैष्णवी.
24. Hultzsch: महीञ्च.
25. Hultzsch: दद्यात्.
26. Better read परदत्तां वा.
27. Hultzsch: महीन्महीमता.
28. Read संवत्सरु. As pointed out by Hultzsch (*ibid.*, vii, 106, fn. 4), *ru* of सम्वत्सरु seems to have been engraved on an erasure and differs from the same syllable occurring elsewhere in this record. The *u*-ending is interesting and is also met with in the Rajim plates.
29. As Hultzsch has not illustrated this side of the plate, the reading of the last line incised on this side is that given by him.
30. As the scribe of the present record, Boppanāga, is the same as that of the Bonda plates (III: II above) of the fifth regnal year of the same king, the intended reading of this line, on the analogy of the corresponding portion of the Bonda plates, seems to be उत्कीर्णमक्षशालिकयोत्रनागसूनुना बोप्पनागेन.
31. Hultzsch points out that the mark of punctuation is here represented by a *visarga.* We have already seen that in many records the punctuation mark is indicated by a couple of dots or circles which also stand for *visarga.*
32. Hultzsch states that the seal of this charter is similar to that of the Rajim plates. It measures 3¼" in diameter and bears in relief on a deep countersunk surface across the centre a two-line legend in the *Anuṣṭubh* metre with a floral device below it and the figure of Garuḍa flanked by a discus on left and a conch-shell on right.

ABSTRACT

After opening with the auspicious *siddham* symbol, the inscription, in the preamble, introduces king **Tīvaradeva** in an *Āryā* verse, mentions the place of issue, **Śrīpura**, and describes, in a long prose passage, the qualities of **Tīvaradeva**, called **Mahāśiva Tīvararāja**. This portion is literally identical with that found in the Bonda and Rajim plates (Nos. III : II and III above).

He informed the inhabitants of Meṅkiḍḍaka[33] situated in Sundarikā-*mārga*[34] that he had granted the village (Meṅkiḍḍaka) at the request of his dear son-in-law, the illustrious Nannarāja, who had acquired the five *mahā-śabdas*,[35] in order to feed daily thirty Brāhmaṇas or other persons who happen to come over to the free feeding house (*sattra*) established at the village of Bilvapadraka[36] with the condition that it has to be maintained by the local body (*adhiṣṭhāna*) for the religious merit of his (Tīvaradeva's) parents and of his own self. The grant, which was intended to last for ever, was endowed with the right to the *nidhis*, the *upanidhis* and all the taxes as well as the exemption from the entry of the *cāṭas* and the *bhaṭas*. The villagers were ordered to pay the periodical offerings and the royal share of produce to the grantee regularly and thereby live happily in the gift village.

Then follows the request to the future rulers to protect the grant, and six customary imprecatory and benedictive stanzas, four of them attributed to Vyāsa, are cited.

The charter was issued on the **twenty-seventh day of the month of Jyeṣṭha in the ninth year of the increasingly victorious reign, obviously of Mahāśiva Tīvara.**

The inscription was engraved by Boppanāga,[37] son of the goldsmith Sotranāga[38], who is described as *Ārkaśālika*.[39]

The legend on the seal is the same as that met with on the seals of the Bonda and Rajim plates.

33. It cannot be identified.
34. Sundarikā has not been identified. The word *mārga* is found suffixed to place-names in several inscriptions and has been generally taken in the sense of a territorial division. Vide V.V. Mirashi, *Inscriptions of the Vākāṭakas*, *CII*, v, 19, text-line 13; 36, text-line 12; 40, text-line 8; 60, text-line 20; 71, text-lines 2-3; 96, text-line 5. Also see *ibid.*, introduction, xxxv, fn. 3. But it may also denote 'way' or 'road'. Accordingly, Sundarikā-*mārga* may also be taken to mean Sundarikā road (*i.e.*, road or way leading to Sundarikā).
35. For the expression *samadhigata-pañca-mahāśabda*, see *supra* No. III: II, note 20*a*.
36. It has not been identified.
37. Boppanāga figures as an engraver in *supra*, No. III: II also.
38. As pointed out above, it is an error for Yotranāga.
39. As stated above, the intended word is *akṣaśālika*, *i.e.*, goldsmith.

III : V

AḌHABHĀRA PLATES[1] OF NANNARĀJA[2]

Provenance: Aḍhabhāra,[3] Sakti Tahsil, Bilaspur District, Madhya Pradesh.

References: B. C. Jain, *EI*, xxxi, 219-22 and plates facing pp, 220 and 221; *Catalogue of the Antiquities in the M. G. M. Museum, Raipur*, vi 176-78; Ajay Mitra Shastri, *JOI*, xxv 67-69.

Language: Sanskrit. In prose except the usual benedictory and imprecatory verses at the end.

Metres: Verse 1: *Vasantatilakā*; Verse 2: *Anuṣṭubh;* Verse 3 (incomplete): *Indravajrā*.

Script: Box-headed variety of the Central Indian alphabet.

Date: Bhādrapada kṛṣṇa 12.[4] Latter half of the seventh century A.D.

TEXT[5]

First Plate

1 सिद्धम्[6] [।*] स्वस्ति [।*] श्रि (श्री) पुरादनेकजन्मान्तराराधितभगवन्नाराय–

2 णभट्टारकपादप्रसादासादितनयविनयसत्यत्याग–

3 शौर्य्यादिगुणसम्पत्सं (त्स) म्पादितप्रथमपृथ्वीपतिप्र[भा]वप–

4 रिभाविसम्भावनस्य भावनाभ्यास प्रकाशीभूतनिर्म्मं–

5 लज्ञेयशशिनः शशिव (वं) ङश (श) संभूतेः स्वभुजपराक्रमो–

6 पार्जितसकलकोसलोत्कलादिमण्डलाधिपत्यप्राप्तमाहा–

7 त्म्यस्य श्रि (श्री) महाशिवतीवरराजस्य प्रद्युम्ना (म्न)[7] इव कैटभारेरात्म–

8 ज[स्त]च्चरितानुकरणपरायणः प्राप्तसकल[क]ोसलाम–

Second Plate : First Side

9 ण्डलाधिपत्यः परमवैष्णवो मातापितृपादानुध्यातः श्रि (श्री) म–

10 हानन्नराजः [:*] कुशलि (ली)॥[8] अष्टद्वारविषये कोन्तिणीकग्रामे ब्रा–

1. The plates measure 8" in length and 4·95" in width. About the middle of the left margin there is a circular hole for the passage of the ring. The ring and the seal are lost.
2. The record is incomplete although there is sufficient space left blank on the inner side of the third plate.
3. The name is also spelt as Aḍbhār or Arbhār.
4. This is the date on which the grant was made. The record being incomplete, the regnal year, normally found at the end of the copper-plate charters of the Pāṇḍuvaṁśin kings of South Kosala, is not available.
5. From plates in *EI*, xxxi, facing pp. 220 and 221.
6. Jain: ओं. Expressed by a symbol.
7. Jain: प्रद्युम्न.
8. The mark of punctuation, which is indicated by a couple of vertical lines the first of which shows a leftward curve on top, is superfluous.

11 ह्मणां (णान्) सम्पूज्य प्रतिवासिनः समाज्ञापयति विदितमस्तु

12 वो यथास्माभिरयं ग्राम (मो) यावद्रविशशिताराकिरणप्र–

13 तिहतघोरान्धकारं जगदवतिष्ठते तावदुपभोग्यः स–

14 निधि [:*] सोपनिधिरः (र) चाटभटः (ट) प्रावेश्य [:*] सर्व्वंकरादानसमेत [:*]

15 सर्व्वंपीडावर्जितो मातापित्रोरात्मनश्चपुन्या (ण्या) भिबृ (वृ) द्धयेः (ये)[9][कौ]–

16 ण्डिन्यसगोत्राय वाजसनेयमाध्यदि (न्दि) नभागवतब्राह्मण–

Second Plate : Second Side

17 नारायणोपाध्याय मातापित्रोरात्मनश्च पुण्यभिबृ (वृ) द्धये[10]

18 भाद्रपदकृष्णद्वादश्या (श्यां) संक्रान्तौ उदकपूर्व्वं (र्व्वं) शासनेन प्र–

19 तिपादित इत्यवगम्य विधेयैर्भूत्वा समुचितं भोगभाग–

20 मुपनयद्भि [:*] सुखं प्रतिवस्तब्य (व्य) मिति ॥ भाविनश्च भूमि–

21 पालानुदि (द्दि) श्येदमभिधि (धी) यते [।*] भूमिप्रदा दिवि ललं (ल)–

22 न्ति पतं (त) न्ति हन्त हृत्वा मर्हि (हीं) नृपतयो नरके नृश (शं) न्सा (साः) ॥ (।)

23 एत [द्*] द्वय (यं) परिकलय्य चलाञ्च लक्ष्मीमायुस्तथा कुरुथ

Third Plate

24 यद्भवतामभि (भी) ष्टं (ष्ट) म् । [।१॥*] अपि च [।*]दाना (न) त्या (पा) लनयोस्ताव-
त्फल (लं)

25 सुग [ति]दुर्गति [।*] को नाम स्वर्गमुत्सृज्य नरकं प्रतिप–

26 द्यते ॥ [२॥*] ब्या (व्या) सगि (गी) ता (तां) श्चात्र श्लोकानुदाहरान्ति ॥ अग्नेरपत्यं

27 प्रथमं सुवर्णं भूर्व्वैष्णवी सूर्य्यंसुताश्च गावः [।*][11]

ABSTRACT

The record opens with the *siddham* symbol followed by the word *svasti* and the mention of **Śrīpura** whence the charter was issued. Then comes a long prose passage introducing Mahāśiva Tīvararāja (Tīvaradeva) and his son king **Mahā-Nannarāja,** the issuer of the present grant.[12] The former is said to have been born in the lunar family (*śaśi-vaṁśa*) and to have excelled the lustre of the first lord of the earth (*i.e.,* Pṛthu) by the perfection of qualities like statesmanship, humility, truthfulness, liberality, bravery and the

9. This expression beginning with माता° is unnecessarily repeated in line 17 below.
10. The expression मातापित्रोरात्मनश्च पुण्याभिवृद्धये has already come in line 15 above and is consequently redundant.
11. The second part of this stanza, which is well-known from other records, and at least two more verses and the remainder of the formal portion of the grant two more verses. including the date and probably the name of the scribe have been left out even though there was much blank space available in the lower part of the plate. Obviously for some reason not known at present the charter was left incomplete and the grant recorded on these plates was actually never made. For a full discussion of this point, see *JOI.*
12. The relationship between Mahā-Nannarāja and Mahāśiva Tīvara is compared to that between Pradyumna and his father Kṛṣṇa, the enemy of the demon Kaiṭabha.

like which were acquired by the grace of god Nārāyaṇa pleased with the adoration in several births. He is futher represented to have obtained the lordship of the whole of Kosala, Utkala and other regions (*maṇḍalas*) by dint of the prowess of his own arms.[13] Mahā-Nannarāja, who was a devout worshipper of god Viṣṇu, was intent on emulating the deeds of his father and acquired mastery of the entire Kosalā country.

After worshipping the Brāhmaṇas Mahā-Nannarāja informed the inhabitants of Kontiṇīka[14] situated in the district (*viṣaya*) named Aṣṭadvāra[15] that he had donated the village, for the increase of the religious merit of his parents and of his own self, to a Bhāgavata (devotee of Bhagavat, *i.e.*, Viṣṇu) Brāhmaṇa named Nārāyaṇopādhyāya, belonging to the Kauṇḍinya *gotra* and the Vājasaneya-Mādhyandina *śākhā* (of the *Yajurveda*), on the occasion of a **saṅkrānti, on the twelfth day of the dark half of the month of Bhādrapada.** The villagers were ordered to pay the *bhoga* and *bhāga* to the donee regularly and thereby live happily. The grant was accompanied by the right to the *nidhis,* the *upanidhis* and to levy all the taxes and exemption from the entry of the *cāṭas* and the *bhaṭas* as well as all the oppressions and was intended to last for ever.

Next follows the request to the future rulers to protect the grant, and the record ends with a few imprecatory and benedictive stanzas extolling the gift of the land as well as its maintenance and threatening with dire consequences those obstructing the enjoyment of the grant.[16]

13. It is interesting to note that Tivaradeva's own inscriptions, three of which are known (Nos. III: II-IV above), describe him only as the master of the entire Kosala country.
14. As suggested by Jain, Kontiṇīka may be identified with either of the modern villages Kāthākonī and Kotmī, both about twelve miles from Aḍhabhāra, the findspot of the record.
15. It is evidently identical with Aḍhabhāra, the provenance of the present inscription, in the Sakti Tahsil of the Bilaspur District of Madhya Pradesh.
16. As we have shown elsewhere, this charter is incomplete and was never granted. Vide *JOI,* xxv, 67-69.

III : VI

BARDULA PLATES[1] OF ŚIVAGUPTA, YEAR 9

Provenance: Bardula, Raigarh District, Madhya Pradesh.
References: P.B. Desai, *EI*, xxvii, 287-91 and plates facing pp. 290 and 291; S.N. Rajaguru, *IO*, iv, 55-59.
Language: Sanskrit. In prose with the exception of a few customary benedictive and imprecatory stanzas at the end and the legend on the seal.
Metres: Verse 1: *Vasantatilakā*; Verse 2, 5-7: *Anuṣṭubh*; Verse 3: *Indravajrā*.
Script: Box-headed variety of the Central Indian alphabet.
Date: Regnal Year 9, Kārttika śukla 12. About the middle of the eighth century A.D.

TEXT[2]

First Plate

1 सिद्धम्[3] [।*] स्वस्त्यशेषक्षिति (ती) शविद्याभ्यासविशेषासादितमहनीयविनयस–
2 म्पत्सं (स)म्पादितसकलविजिगीषुगुणो गुणव:(व)त्समाश्रयप्रकृष्टत–
3 रशौर्य्यप्रज्ञाप्रभावसम्भावितमहाभ्युदय: कार्ति (र्त्ति)केय इव कृत्तिवा–
4 ससो र[ाज्ञ] [:*] [शि] (श्री) हर्प(र्ष)देवस्य[4] सुनु: सोमव(वं)ङ्श (श) सम्भव [:*] परममाहेश्वरो मा–
5 तापितृपादानुध्यात: शृी (श्री) **महाशिवगुप्तराज:** कुशली ॥[5] कोशीरनन्द–
6 पुरविषयीयवटपद्रके ब्राह्मणां (णान्) सम्पून्य सप्रधानां (नान्) प्रतिवासिनो
7 यथाकालाध्यासिनस्समाहर्तृं सन्निधातृप्रमुखानधिकारिणस्स–
8 करणानन्या(न्यां)ङश्चा[6] (श्चा) स्मत्पादोपजीविन: (न)[6a]स्सर्व्वराजपुरुषां (षान्) समाज्ञा–

Second Plate : First Side

9 पयति [।*] विदितमस्तु भवतां यथास्माभिरयं ग्रामस्सनिधि: सोपनिधि:
10 सदशापराध: सर्व्वकरसमेत: सर्व्वपि(पी)डावर्ज्जित: प्रतिषिद्ध–

1. 9" long and 6" broad and about ·1" thick. About the middle of the left margin of the plates there is a circular hole, ·6" in diameter, for the passage of the ring.
2. From plates in *EI*, xxvii, opposite pp. 290 and 291.
3. Desai: *Om*. Expressed by a symbol.
4. Desai reads. **हर्षदेवस्य**. But the cross-bar, which distinguishes *ṣ* from *p*, is absent.
5. The mark of punctuation, indicated by a vertical line with its top bent to left followed by another vertical line, is superfluous.
6. Desai: °**न्यांङश्च**°.
6a. Better read **स्वपादोपजीवि**°.

11 चाटभटप्रवेशः(श)च्छा(श्छा)त्रनाटासीमनी(नि)वी (वि) ष्टच्छान्दोगच्छात्रनारायणो

12 पाध्याय।[7] त्रैलोक्यहन्सो (हंसो)पाध्याय। विद्याधरह(हं)ङसो (सो) पाध्याय। परम–

13 ह(हं)ङसो (सो)पाध्याय।[8] नक्षत्ररूप।[8] सलोणविद्याधर।[9] विदग्धासुर।पृ–

14 थिवि(वी)रूप। दुर्गकलश। पोदवराह[10]। तालरूग। मध्याह्नरूपेभ्यो द्वा–

15 दशे(श)भ्यस्तथार्द्धा(र्द्धा)ङश (श) भाजस्त्र (जे त्र) योदशमविग्रहचरिताय च कार्त्तिक-शुक्ल–

16 द्वादश्यां मातापित्रोरात्मनश्च पुण्याभिबृ(वृ)द्धये ताम्ब्र(म्र) शासनेनाचन्द्रा–

Second Plate : Second Side

17 र्कसमकालोपभोगार्थं (र्थं) मुदकपूर्व्वं प्रतिपादित इत्यतो विधेय–

18 तया एभ्यः समुचितं भोगभागादिकमुपनयद्भि(र्भ)व[द्भिः] सुखं प्र–

19 तिवस्तब्य(व्य)मिति ॥ भाविनश्च भूमिपालानुद्दिश्येदमभिधीयते [।*] भू–

20 मिप्रदा दिवि ललन्ति पतन्ति हन्त हृत्वा महीं नृपत[यो]नर–

21 के नृश(शं)ङसात् (साः)। एत [द्*]द्वयं [ं] परिकलय्य चलाञ्च लक्ष्मि[11] (क्ष्मी) मायुस्तथा कु–

22 रुत यद्भव(ता)मभि(भी)ष्ट[ं](ष्टम्) [॥१॥*]अपि च [।*] रक्षापालनयोस्तावत्फल [ं] सुगति-दुर्गती [।*] को

23 नाम स्वर्ग्गमुच्छि(त्सृ)ज्य नरक [ं] प्रतिपद्यते ॥[२॥*] व्यासगीता(तां)श्चात्र[12] श्लो[का]नुदाह[र]न्तिः(न्ति) [।*]

24 अग्नेरपत्य [ं] प्रथमं सुवर्ण्णं भूर्व्वैष्णवी सूर्य्यसुताश्च गावः[।*]दत्तात्र (स्त्र)यस्ते–

Third Plate

25 न भवन्ति लोकाय [ः*] काञ्चनं गाञ्च महीं[च][13] (श्च) दद्यात्।[14] [।३॥*] षष्टी(ष्टि) वर्षसह–

26 स्राणि स्वर्ग्गे मोदति भूमिद [ः] [।*] आक्षेत्पा (प्ता)च [।]नुमन्ता च तान्येव नरके

27 वसेत्। [।४॥*] व(ब) हुभिर्व्वसुधा दत्तां राजभिः [ः*] सगरादिभिः [ः।*] यस्य यस्य यदा भूमि–

28 स्तस्य तस्य तदा फलं (लम्) [॥५॥*] स्वदत्ता(त्तां) परदत्ताम्वा(त्तां वा) यत्नाद्रक्ष युधी(धि)ष्ठिरः[15](र) [।*] मही(हीं)

7. The mark of punctuation consists of a single *daṇḍa* curved to left at its top. This and the following *daṇḍas* up to line 14 are superfluous, for the entire portion from *Cchātranāṭā* in line 11 to *Madhyāhnarupebhyo* in line 14 forms a single compound.
8. This *daṇḍa* is straight.
9. The top of this as well as of the following *daṇḍas* is curved to left.
10. Originally *Podevarāha* had been engraved and then the superscript *e* of *de* was cancelled.
11. Desai: लक्ष्मी°.
12. Desai: °श्चात्र.
13. This letter is engraved below the line between *hī* and *da*.
14. The presence of this *daṇḍa* has escaped the notice of Desai.
15. Desai: युधिष्ठिर. *Ṣṭhi* is written below the line between *dhi* and *ra*.

29 महीमता(तां)[16] श्रेष्ठ दानाच्छ्रेयोनुपालनमिति ।।[६।।*][17] प्रवर्द्धमानविजयराज्य-
30 सम्व(संव)त्स [र*] ६ । कार्तिक-शुक्लादि १० २ [।।*]

Seal[18]

1 राज्ञ [:*] श्रीहर्षगुप्तस्य सूनो [:]सद्गुणशालिन [:] [।*]
2 शासन शिवगुप्तस्य [स्थि]तमा[भु]व[न]स्थिते [:] [।।७।।*]

ABSTRACT

After the auspicious *siddham* symbol the inscription introducing the king **Śivagupta** (called **Mahā-Śivagupta)** who is described as one who had acquired all the qualities of a conqueror by means of the perfection of commendable discipline attained by a special study of all the kingly lores, who has attained great prosperity by the patronage of accomplished persons, exceedingly great valour, intelligence and majesty, who is son of the king, illustrious Harṣadeva even as Kārttikeya is of the wearer of the skin (i.e. god Śiva), who is born of the lunar family, most devout worshipper of Maheśvara and meditates on the feet of his mother and father and is in good health.

After honouring the Brāhmaṇas in the village Vaṭapadaka[19] situated in the district (*viṣaya*) of Kośīranandapura[20] Śivagupta informed the inhabitants of the village together with their *Pradhāna*[20a], *Samāhartṛ*[20b],

16. The correction of महीमतां into महिमतां suggested by Desai is unwarranted and wrong.
17. Better read °नुपालनम् [।।६।।*] इति.
18. The surface of the circular seal, 3.2" in diameter, is divided into two parts by a couple of horizontal lines, the lower part being almost twice in size than the upper portion. The upper part contains the representation, in relief, of the figure of a humped bull (Nandin) couchant to left with a *triśūla* in front and a *pūrṇa-kumbha* behind. Below this in the lower portion we have a two-line legend giving a verse in the *Anuṣṭubh* metre and below it a large full-blown lotus flanked by a leaf with stalk on either side. As the seal has not been illustrated, we have quoted the legend as given by Desai.
19. It now appears to be represented by the village Baṭapadaka, about four miles from Bardula, the findspot of the charter.
20. This district may be identical with the Nandapura *bhoga* referred to in the Pipardula plates of the Śarabhapurīya chief, Mahārāja Narendra. *Vide ante* No. I: I. As suggested by Desai, the word *kośīra* is probably a derivative from *kuśara* and used in the sense of 'scrubby' and has been employed to qualify the name of the head-quarters of the Nandapura *viṣaya* in order to distinguish it from other places of the same name. It is probably identical with the site of the two adjoining villages Nandapura large and Nandapura small, in the Bilaspur District, close to Sakti, the headquarters of the tahsil of the same name in the Bilaspur District.

20*a*. Though sometimes used as an official designation denoting the chief minister or administrator (Sircar, *IEG*, 254; Kane, *HDS*, iii, 992), in the present context it seems to refer to the village headman. This view finds support from its use (*sa-pradhānān*) as an adjective of *prativāsinaḥ*, 'inhabitants'.

20*b*. Generally rendered as Collector-General, *Samāhartṛ* was an official entrusted with the duty of collecting revenue from various sources. His duties are described in detail in Kauṭilya's *Arthaśāstra*, ii. vi. Hereafter he is generally referred to in copper-plate

Sannidhātṛ[20c] and other officers together with their subordinates[20d] who may be posted there from time to time as well as all the other royal officers who may be dependent on him (lit. on feet) that he had granted the village to the twelve Brāhmaṇas (i) Nāryāṇopādhyāya, (ii) Trailokyahaṁsopādhyāya, (iii) Vidyādharahaṁsopādhyāya, (iv) Paramahaṁsopādhyāya, (v) Nakṣatrarūpa,[21] (vi) Saloṇavidyādhara, (vii) Vidagdhāsura, (viii) Pṛthivīrūpa, (ix) Durgakalaśa, (x) Podavarāha, (xi) Tālarūpa, and (xii) Madhyāhnarūpa, who had settled at the place called Chāttranāṭāsīman[22] or on the borders of Chātranāṭā) and were students of the *Chandoga caraṇa*,[22a] and the thirteenth part to one Avigrahacarita,[23] who received half portion,[24] on the twelfth day of the bright half of the month of Kārttika[25] for the increase of the religious merit of his parents and of his own self. The grant was endowed with the right to the *nidhis*, the *upanidhis*, the *daś-āparādhas*[25a] and all the taxes and freed

---

charters in connection with land-grants. For other references, see Kane, *HDS*, iii, 143 and 1006; Sircar, *IEG*, 288. U.N. Ghoshal (*Contributions to the History of the Hindu Revenue System*, 52), compares him to the *Qānungo* of the Mughal period.

20*c*. Frequently mentioned along with the *Samāhartṛ* in copper-plate charters in connection with land-grants, it has been variously taken to refer to an official in charge of the receipt of various articles into the royal treasury or the superintendent of the construction of the royal treasury, store houses, etc. See Kane, *HDS*, 143 and 1006; Ghoshal, *op. cit.*, Sircar, *IEG*, 298. A perusal of the *Arthaśāstra* ii.v, shows, however, that the *Sannidhātṛ* combined both these functions.

20*d*. *Karaṇa* in the original has been taken to mean a clerk, a scribe or an accountant. See Kane, *HDS*, iii, 979; Sircar, *IEG*, 145.

21. This and many of the following names are strange and are not met with elsewhere.

22. It has not been identified; but as pointed out by Desai, it reminds one of Dravidian territorial names like Punnāṭa and Karṇāṭa.

22*a*. It is also possible that the adjective *Chātrānāṭā-sīmāniviṣṭa-cchāndoga-cchātra* qualifies only the first-mentioned Brāhmaṇa, *viz.*, Nārāyaṇopādhyāya.

23. Desai takes *avigrahacarita* as an adjective meaning one of unimpeachable character and as referring to one of the above-mentioned twelve Brāhmaṇas as a recipient of the additional half portion.

24. The donated village was obviously divided into thirteen shares, twelve of which were full and one half. The names of the twelve Brāhmaṇas, each of whom was to receive one full share, and of the thirteen one who was to get half share, are clearly specified. The suggestion of Desai that the name of the thirteenth donee entitled to receive the half share is not mentioned and that his selection was to be made later on the condition that his character should be above suspicion (*EI*, xxvii, 291, note 1) is not borne out by the text. In fact, no condition appears to have been laid down for the selection of the thirteenth donee whose name is clearly given as Avigrahacarita.

25. The grant was evidently made on the occasion of the *pāraṇā* following the fast on the *devotthāna ekādaśī* which is regarded as very sacred.

25*a*. Literally meaning 'ten offences', the expression was apparently intended to convey to the beneficiary of land-grant the right to fines levied for the ten offences which, according to Nārada, included disobedience of the king's order, murder of a woman, confusion of Varṇas, adultery, theft, pregnancy from one other than the husband, abuse and defamation, obscenity, assault and abortion. According to Kane, the fines levied on these offences were made over to the donee as and when received by the king. See *HDS*, iii, 264-65.

from all the oppressions and the entry of the *cāṭas* and the *bhaṭas*. The villagers were asked to pay the *bhoga*, *bhāga*, etc. to the donees in time and thereby live happily in the village.

The future kings are requested to protect the grant and six customary benedictory and imprecatory stanzas, three of them in the name of Vyāsa, are quoted.

The charter was issued on the **twelfth day of the bright half of the month of Kārttika in the ninth year of the increasingly victorious reign.**

The stanza on the seal states that this charter belongs to king **Śivagupta,** son of the illustrious Harṣagupta.

III: VII

BONDA PLATES[1] OF ŚIVAGUPTA BĀLĀRJUNA, YEAR 22

Provenance: Bonda, Sarangarh Tahsil, Raigarh District, Madhya Pradesh.

References: V.V. Mirashi and L.P. Pandeya, *EI*, xxxv, 60-65 and plates between pp. 64 and 65; *ARIE*, 1959-60, 43, Appendix A, No. 57; S.N. Rajaguru, *IO*, iv, 81-85.

Language: Sanskrit. In prose except a few imprecatory and benedictive stanzas at the end and the legend on the seal.

Metres: Verse 1: *Vasantatilakā*; Verses 2, 4-7: *Anuṣṭubh*: Verse 3: *Indravajrā*.

Script: Box-headed variety of the Central Indian alphabet.

Date: Regnal Year 22, Pauṣa Kṛṣṇa 6.[2] Second half of the eighth century A.D.

TEXT[2a]

First Plate

1 सिद्धम्[3] [।*] स्वस्त्यशेषक्षी (क्षि)ति(ती)ष(श)[वी] (वि)द्याभ्यास[4]विशेषासादितमह-
नीयविन-

2 यसम्पत्संपादितसकलवी(वि)जिगि(गी)षु[5]गुणो गुणवत्समाश्रय:

3 प्रकृष्टतरशौर्य्यप्रज्ञाप्रभावसंभावितमहाभ्युदय: कार्त्तिके-

4 य इव कृत्तिवाससो राज्ञ: श्रि[6](श्री)हर्षदेवस्य सूनु [:*] सोम-

5 वङ्श(वंश)सं (स)म्भव:[7] परममाहेश्वरो मातापित्तृ[8]पादानुध्यात [:*] श्रि(श्री) **महाशो
(शि) व-**

6 **गुप्तराज** [:*] कुशलि(ली)।।[9] लायोड्डकवैषयिकशर्क्करापाटके व्रा-

7 ह्मणां (णान्) संपु(पू)ज्य सप्रधाना [न्*] प्रतिवासिनो यथाकालाध्यासिन [:*]

1. The size of the plates is not given by the original editors. There is a circular hole, .7″ in diameter, about the middle of the left margin for the passage of the ring, about .4″ in thickness.
2. This is based on the assumption that in this record as in other records of the dynasty, the pūrṇimānta month is intended.

2*a*. From plates in *EI*, xxxv, between pp. 64 and 65.

3. Expressed by a symbol.
4. Mirashi and Pandeya: °क्षीतिराविद्याभ्यास°
5. Mirashi and Pandeya: °विजिगिषु°
6. The subscript *r* here and in line 5 closely resembles the medial sign for *ṛ*.
7. Mirashi and Pandeya: °सम्भव:
8. Mirashi and Pandeya: °पितृ°
9. The *daṇḍas*, the first of which has a hook on its top, are superfluous.

Second Plate : First Side

8 समाहर्त्तृ सं(स)न्निधात्तृ[10] (तृ) प्रमुखानन्याङश्चा[11]स्मत्पादोपजीवी (वि)न [:][12]
9 सर्व्वराजपुरुषान्समाज्ञापयति [।*] विदितमस्तु भवतां यथा–
10 स्माभिरयङग्रामः सनिधिः सोपनिधिः सदशापराधः सर्व्वक–
11 रादानसमेतः सर्व्वपि(पी)डावर्ज्जितः प्रतिषिद्धचाटभटप्रवे–
12 शो च्छान्दोग[13]भरद्वाजसगोत्रभट्टत्(त्रि)विक्रमस्वामिने पौषसंक्रान्त्या–
13 मुदकपूर्व्वं मातापित्रोरात्मनश्च पुण्याभिबृ(वृ)द्धये ताम्ब्र[14]शासनेना–
14 चन्द्रार्कसमकालोपभोगार्थं प्रतिपादित इत्यवगत्यास्य विधे–

Second Plate : Second Side

15 यतया समुचितं भोगभागादिकमुपनयद्भिर्भवद्भि [:*] सुखं[15] प्रति–
16 वस्तब्य (व्य)मिति ॥ भाविनश्च भूमिपालानुद्दिश्येदमभिधि(धी) यते [।*] भूमी(मि)[16]–
17 प्रदा दिवि ललन्ति पतन्ति हन्त हृत्वा महिं (हीं) नृपतयो नरके नृशङसा–
18 त्[17] [।*] एत [द्*] द्वयं परिकलय्य चलाञ्च लक्ष्मि (क्ष्मी) मा [यु*] स्तथा कुरुत य–
19 द्भवतामभि(भी)ष्ट [म् ॥१॥*] अपि च [।*] रक्षापालनयोस्तावत्फं (त्फ)लं[18] सुगती (ति)[19]–
20 दुर्ग्गति(ती) [।*] को नाम स्वर्ग्गमुच्छि्(त्सृ) ज्य नरकं प्रतिपद्यते। [॥२॥*] ब्या (व्या) सगी–
21 तांश्चात्र श्लोकानुदाहरन्ति [।*] अग्नेरपत्यं प्रथमं सुवर्णं

Third Plate : First Side

22 भूर्व्वैष्णवि(वी) सूर्य्यसुता गावः [।*] दत्त(त्ता) स्त्रयस्तेन भवन्ति लोका य [:*]
23 क (का)ञ्चनं गाञ्च महिं (ही) ञ्च दद्यात् [॥३॥*] षष्टिवर्षसहस्राणि स्वर्ग्गे मो–
24 दति भूमिदः [।*] आच्छेत्ता चानुमन्ता च तान्येव नरके वसेत् [॥४॥*]ब–
25 हुभिर्वसुधा दत्ता राजभिः सागरादिभिः [।*] यस्य यस्य यदा भूमि–
26 त (स्त) स्य तस्य तदा फलं(लम्)[॥५॥*] स्वदत्तां परदत्ताम्बा[20] यत्नाद्रक्ष युधिष्ठिर [।*] महि (हीं)
27 महि (ही) मतां श्रेष्ठ दाना श्रेयो[21]नुपालनमिति[22] ॥ [६॥*] **प्रवर्द्धमानविजयराज्ये**

10. Mirashi and Pandeya: °सन्निधात्तृ°
11. Read°न्यांश्चा.° The words *adhikāriṇaḥ sa-karaṇān* found between *pramukhān* and *anyāṁ-śca* in the previous record are omitted here.
12. स्वपादोपजीविनः would be the correct expression.
13. Read प्रवेशश्छन्दोग°
14. Read ताम्र°
15. The curve attached to its vertical on right is superfluous.
16. Mirashi and Pandeya: भूमि°
17. Read नृशंसाः
18. Mirashi and Pandeya: °त्फलं.
19. Mirashi and Pandeya: सुगति.
20. Read परदत्तां वा.
21. Read दानाच्छ्रेयो.°
22. Better read °नुपालनम् [॥६॥*] इति.

28 सम्वत्सरे[23] द्वाविङ्शे[24] पौषप्रथमपक्षषष्ठ्यामङ्केनापि संव (व)त् २० २ पुष्य

Third Plate : Second Side

29 दिन ६ ।[25]

Seal[26]

राज्ञ [:*] श्री [ह] र्षगुप्तस्य
सूनो [:*] सद्‌गुणशालिन [:।*]
शासनं [शि]वगुप्तस्य
स्थितमाभुवनस्थितेः [।।७।।*]

ABSTRACT

The charter opens with the auspicious *siddham* symbol and then introduces the donor, king **Śivagupta** (called **Mahā-Śivaguptarāja**), who is described in exactly the same words as in the previous inscription.

After honouring the Brāhmaṇas in the village Śarkarāpāṭaka[27] situated in the district (*viṣaya*) of Lāyoḍḍaka[28] the king informed the residents of the village together with their *Pradhāna, Samāhartṛ, Sannidhātṛ* as well as all the other royal officials dependent on him[29] that he had given away, by means of a copper-plate charter, the village to the *Bhaṭṭa* Trivikramasvāmin, who was a student of the Chandogya (*Sāmaveda*) and belonged to the Bhāradvāja *gotra*, on the occasion of the Pauṣa *saṅkrānti* for the increase of the religious merit of his parents and of his own self. The grant carried with it the same privileges and exemptions as specified in *ante*, III: VI. The villagers were ordered to offer to the donee the *bhoga, bhāga* and other dues regularly and thereby live happily in the village.

Next follows the usual exhortation to the future rulers to protect the grant and six customary benedictive and imprecatory stanzas, four of them attributed to Vyāsa, are cited.

The charter was issued on the **sixth day of the first fortnight of the month of Pauṣa**[30] **in the twenty-second year of the increasingly victorious reign.**

23. Read संवत्सरे.
24. Read द्वाविंशे.
25. This mark of punctuation is indicated by a slightly curved vertical line.
26. The circular seal is exactly similar to that attached to the previous charter. Its diameter is, however, 3.7".
27. It has not been identified.
28. It is possibly represented by the village Lārā lying about 10 miles north by east of Bonda, the findspot of this inscription.
29. The reference to the subordinates (*Karaṇas*) met with in the previous charter is conspicuous by its absence here.
30. As regards the Pāṇḍuvaṁśin records, mention of fortnights is made only in the solitary incomplete grant of Mahā-Nannarāja and a few records of Mahā-Śivagupta. But

III:VIII

LODHIA PLATES[1] OF ŚIVAGUPTA BĀLĀRJUNA, YEAR 57

Provenance: Lodhia, Raigarh District, Madhya Pradesh.

References: L.P. Pandeya, *Quarterly Journal of the Mythic Society,* xxxvi, 1-4; *Proceedings of All-India Oriental Conference,* 12th session, iii, 595-96; *Journal of the Kalinga Historical Research Society,* ii, 121-24; *EI,* xxvii, 319-25 and plates facing pp. 324 and 325, S.N. Rajaguru, *IO,* iv 86-90.

Language: Sanskrit. In prose with the exception of a few benedictory and imprecatory verses at the end and the legend on the seal.

Metres: Verse 1: *Vasantatilakā*; Verses 2, 4-7 and 9: *Anuṣṭubh*; Verse 3: *Indravajrā.*

Script: Box-headed variety of the Central Indian alphabet.

Date: Regnal Year 57, Kārttika 30. Second half of the eighth century A.D.

TEXT[2]

First Plate

1 सिद्धम्[3] [।*] स्वस्त्यशेषक्षितीशविद्याभ्यासविशेषासादि[4]तः (त) महनीयः (य) नयवि–
2 नयसम्पस (त्स) म्पादितसकलवी (वि) जी (जि) गीषुगुणो गुणवत्समाश्रयः प्रकृष्ट–
3 तरशो (शौ) र्यः (र्य) प्रज्ञाप्रभावसम्भावितमहाभ्युदयः कार्त्तिकेय इव कृत्ति[5]–
4 वाससो राज्ञः[6] श्री (श्री) हर्षदेवस्य सु (सू) नुः सोमवङ्श (वंश) सम्भव [।*] परम–
5 माहेश्वरो म (मा) तापितृपादानुध्यातः श्री (श्री) **मा (म) हशिवगुप्तराजदेव** [:*]कुशली
6 श्रोणिभोगि (गी) यग्रामवैद्यपद्रके ।[8] ब्राह्मणा [न्*] सम्पु (म्पू) ज्य तत्प्रतिनिवासिकुटुम्बि–

1. Details about the size of the plates are not given.
2. From plates in *EI*, xxvii, opposite pp. 324 and 325.
3. Pandeya: *Om.* Expressed by a symbol.
4. As pointed out by Pandit Pandeya, this letter looks like *dī* in the impression. He informs us that the original shows it correctly *di* and that the dot seen within the circle indicating the length of the medial *i* in the impression is due to a natural depression on the plate.
5. Pandeya: कृति°
6. The subscript *ñ* is formed incompletely and the downward stroke attached to the right of its vertical is missing.
7. The letter *ś* of *śi* shows a superfluous cross-bar which, as pointed out by Pandeya, is due to a flaw in the plate.
8. The mark of punctuation, which is indicated by a straight vertical line, is superfluous.

The stanza on the seal is the same as that on the seal attached to the previous record.

---

in all these records except the present one, they are specified as *śukla* or *kṛṣṇa pakṣa*. It isonly in this record that the fortnight is styled *prathama* or first. However, as both the *pūrṇimānta* and *amānta* systems of lunar months were in vogue in those days, both the *kṛṣṇa* and the *śukla pakṣas* could be designated as the first fortnight according to the *pūrṇimānta* and *amānta* schemes respectively. But there is sufficient evidence to show that during the time of the Pāṇḍuvaṁśins the *pūrṇimānta* scheme was in common use in South Kosala. As such, the first fortnight should normally be taken to refer to the dark fortnight. Mirashi and Pandeya, however, think that the Pauṣa *saṅkrānti* on which the grant recorded in the present charter is said to have been made was the same as the Makara *saṅkrānti* and that the *tithi* on which it occurred, which is not specified in the charter, was identical with that on which the grant was recorded, *i.e.*, the sixth *tithi* of the first fortnight of Pauṣa. Now, if it is held that the *pūrṇimānta* scheme is intended here as in other records of the dynasty, it will have to be supposed that the Makara *saṅkrānti* occurred in the dark half of the *amānta* Mārgaśirṣa; for, the dark fortnight of the *pūrṇimānta* Pauṣa corresponds to the dark fortnight of the *amānta* Mārgaśīrṣa. And this is impossible, as the *saṅkrānti* occurring in the *amānta* Mārgaśīrṣa must be Dhanus, not Makara. According to Mirashi and Pandeya, the only way of solving this difficulty is to hold that the word *prathama-pakṣa* in this record refers to the bright fortnight and that the *amānta* Pauṣa is intended here.

However, the above arguments are far from convincing. First, it is not necessary to equate the Pauṣa *saṅkrānti* mentioned in the inscription with the Makara *saṅkrānti*; it could have been Dhanus *saṅkrānti*. Had Makara *saṅkrānti* been intended, it would have been specifically mentioned by this name. And even if the Makara *saṅkrānti* was intended, it is not necessary to assume that the record was incised on the same date on which the grant was made. For, as pointed out by Mirashi and Pandeya themselves, often there was an interval of several months between the date of the grant and that of recording the same. The Mandhal plates of Vākāṭaka Pravarasena II were written exactly one year after the grant recorded on them was made. See Ajay Mitra Shastri, *Vidarbha Saṁśodhana Maṇḍala Vārṣika, 1977*, 153-57. We, therefore, feel that *Pauṣa-prathama-pakṣa-ṣaṣṭhī* in our record refers to the sixth *tithi* of the dark fortnight of the month of Pauṣa.

7 नो[9] यथाकालाध्यासिनः समाहर्तृ[10] सन्निधात्तृ[11]प्रभृतीनस्मत्पादोपजीविन [:*][12]

8 सर्ब्वं[13](र्व्वं) राजपुरुषा [न्*] समाज्ञापयति[14]। विदितमस्तु भवतां यथा ग्रामोयमस्मा–

Second Plate : First Side

9 भिः[15] सम्प्रति सनिध (धा) नः स (सो) पन (नि) ध (धा) नः[16] सर्ब्वं[17](र्व्वं) कर (रा)-
द (दा) नसम (मे) तः[18]सर्ब्वं[19] (र्व्वं) प (पी) डाव (वि) व–

10 जि (र्जि) तः[20] सदशापराधः[21] प्रतिषिद्धचाटभटप्रवेशः अस्यां कार्त्तिकयो (पौ) र्ण्णमा–

11 स्यां पत्तनखदिरपद्रतलप्रतिष्ठितश्री (श्री) मदीशानेश्वरभट्टारकार ।[22] ब–

12 ली (लि) चरुनि (नै) वेद्यसत्रनृत्तवादित्रखण्डस्फुटितस (सं) स्कारार्थं[23] द्वैतवनी–

13 य[24] श्रिृ[25] (श्री) मत्पञ्चयज्ञ[26] तपोवनविनिर्गतश्चपलगोचरिणः[27] भगवच्छ्रि[28] (च्छ्री)–

9. In other plates of Śivagupta we have सप्रधानान् प्रतिवासिनो in place of तत्प्रतिनिवासिकुटु-म्बिनो of the present grant.
10. Pandeya: समाहर्त्तृ°
11. Pandeya: सन्निधातृ°
12. स्वपादोपजीविनः would be a better expression. In the Bardula (*ante*, III:VI) and Mallar plates (*infra*, III: IX) we have सन्निधातृप्रमुखानधिकारिगणस्सकरणानन्यांश्च and in the Bonda plates (*ante*, III:VII) सन्निधातृप्रमुखानन्यांश्च in place of सन्निधात्तृप्रभृतीन् found in the present plates.
13. Pandeya : सर्ब्बं°
14. Pandeya states that this *daṇḍa* is not necessary. It is, however, very much required by the syntax.
15. Pandeya: °मस्माभि. In other grants of the same king we have यथास्माभिरयं ग्रामः in place of यथा ग्रामोयमस्माभिः of the present charter.
16. Pandeya: स्म्प्रतिसनिधानः सोपनिधानः. Other grants of Śivagupta have सनिधिः सोपनिधिः in place of सम्प्रति सनिधानः सोपनिधानः of the present grant.
17. Pandeya: सर्ब्बं°
18. The Bardula (*ante*, III:VI) and Mallar plates (*infra*, III:IX) have सर्व्वंकरसमेतः in place of सर्व्वंकरादानसमेतः of this as well as the Bonda grant (*ante* III : VII).
19. Pandeya : सर्ब्बं°
20. Pandeya: [पी] डाविवजि (र्जि) तः. It is quite possible that the medial signs in this as well as in two preceding expressions in line 9 may be clear in the plate and Pandit Pandeya's readings may be correct in so far as the medial signs are concerned; they are, however, not visible in the plate.
21. In other plates of Śivagupta this expression comes before सर्व्वंकरसमेतः (*ante*, III: VI; *infra*, III:IX) सर्व्वंकरादानसमेतः (*ante*, III:VII).
22. This mark of punctuation is superfluous.
23. The *anusvāra*, which should have been placed over *tha*, is placed away from it and very close to *dvai*.
24. The slightly curved vertical stroke appended to the left lower end of the box is superfluous.
25. Pandeya: श्रृी
26. The subscript *ñ* is imperfectly formed as the stroke to the right of its vertical is missing. *Cf. rājñaḥ* in line 4 above.
27. Pandeya suggests °विनिर्गतिच (?) पलगोचरिणः though somewhat doubtfully. Grammatically, however, गोचरि not गोचरिणः is expected.
28. Pandeya: भगवच्छि°

14 प्रमथाचार्यशिष्यश्री (श्री) शूलपाणिभ[29]गवत्पादप्रार्थनं (न) या[30] मातापित्रो–

15 र (रा)त्मनश्च पुण्याभिबृ (वृ)द्धये समक (का)लोपभोगार्थमाचन्द्रतारकार्कं[31] पय [:*]–

16 पु (पू) र्व्व (र्व्व)कं[32] ताम्ब्र (म्र)शासनेन[33] प्रतिपादितो यतोवगत्य[34] समुचितभोगभागादिक-

Second Plate : Second Side

17 मुपनयन्तो भवन्तः सुखं प्रतिवसन्तु ।।[35] भाविनश्च भूमिपाला[36]नुदि (द्दि)–

18 श्येदमभिधी[37]यते [।*] भूमिप्रदा दिवि ललन्ति पतन्ति हन्त हृत्वा महि (हीं)

19 नृपतयो नरके नृत्सा[37a] (नृशंसाः)[।*] एत[द्*] द्वयं परिकलय्य चलाञ्च ल्लक्ष्मि (लक्ष्मी) मायुस्त–

20 था कुरुत यद्भवतामभि (भी)ष्ट [म्*] ।[38] [।१।।*] अपि च [।*] रक्षापालनत्यवत्फलं[39] सुग–

21 तिदुर्गती[40] [।*] को न (ना)म स्वर्गमुत्सृज्य नरकं प्रतिपद्यते ।।[41] [२।।*] व्या (व्या) सगि (गी)–

22 ताश्चा[42] (तांश्चा)त्र श्लोकानुदाहरन्ति ।[43] अग्नेरपत्य (त्यं) प्रथम (मं) सुवर्ण्णं भूर्व्वै[44] (र्व्वै)–

29. The left limb and the lower portion of the letter *bh* are inadvertently joined resulting in a peculiar shape.
30. Pandeya: प्रार्थनया.
31. आचन्द्रतारकार्कसमकालोपभोगार्थम् would be a better expression. In the Bardula (*ante*, III:VI) and Bonda plates (*ante*, III:VII) we find आचन्द्रार्कसमकालोप भोगार्थम् and in the Mallar plates (*infra*, III:IX) आचन्द्रार्क्कसमकालम् instead of समकालोपभोगार्थमाचन्द्रतारकार्क्क of the present record.
32. Pandeya: पुब्बंकं. In other grants of Śivagupta we have उदकपूर्वम् in place of पयः पूर्व्वकं met with in the present charter.
33. In other plates of Śivagupta the expression ताम्रशासनेन comes before आचन्द्रार्कसमकालोपभोगार्थम् or आचन्द्रार्कसमकालम्.
34. In place of यतोवगत्य of the present plates we find इत्यतः in the Bardula (*ante*, III:VI) and Mallar (*infra*, III:IX) plates and इत्यवगत्य in the Bonda plates (*ante*, III:VII) of Śivagupta. In other plates this expression is followed by विधेयतया which is missing in the present charter.
35. In other plates of Śivagupta this sentence is found employed in the passive voice, viz. उपनयद्भिर्भवद्भिः सुखं प्रतिवस्तव्यम्. In the Bonda and Baloda plates of Tīvaradeva (*ante*, III:II and IV) also we find the use of active voice: but the verbal form employed there is प्रतिवत्स्यथ. प्रतिवसन्तु is met with only in this grant.
36. Pandit Pandeya points out that the medial sign for *ā* in *lā*, which is evidently present in the plate, has not come out in the impression.
37. The plate does not show the dot of the *ī* sign in *dhi*; but Pandit Pandeya informs us that the original contains it, though it is very shallow.

37a. The *visarga* following नृत्सा in Pandeya's transcript is not seen in the facsimile.

38. The *daṇḍa* indicating the mark of punctuation is straight.
39. Read रक्षापालनयोस्तावत्फलं.
40. Pandeya: दुर्गति.
41. The first *daṇḍa* shows a leftward hook on the top.
42. Pandeya reads ताञ्च. But the *ā* sign of *cā* is clearly visible in the facsimile.
43. The *daṇḍa* is straight.
44. Pandeya: भूर्व्वै°.

23 ष्णवि(वी) सु(सू)य(र्य) सुताश्च गावः [।*] दत्तास्त्रयस्तेन भवन्ति लोक[45] (का) यः काञ्चनं गाञ्च म-

24 हीञ्च[46] दद्यात् । [।३।।*] षष्टिर्ब्व[46a] (व)र्षसहस्त्राणि स्वर्ग्गे मोदति भु(भू) मिदः [।*] ग्र(ग्रा)च्छेत्ता चा-

Third Plate

25 नुमन्ता च तान्येव नरके वसेत् । [।४।।*] बहुभिर्ब्व (र्व्व)सुधा[47] दत्ता[48] राजभि [ः*] सगरादि-

26 भि[49] [ः।*] यस्य यस्य यदा भूमिस्तस्य तस्य तदा फलं (लम्) । [।५।।*] स्वदत्ता(त्तां) परदत्ताम्बा(त्तां वा) य-

27 त्नाद्रक्ष युधिष्टि (ष्ठि)र [।*] महि (हीं) महि (ही)भृतां श्रेष्ठः(ष्ठ)[50] दानाश्रे(च्छे)-योनुपालनं(नम्) ।। [६।।*] ग्रस्मा-

28 कमुपरोधेन नित्यं धर्म्मस्य गो (गौ) खादस्मद (द्ध) त्ति [ः*] स्वकि (की) येव पाल्या भा-

29 वि[51]क्षिति(ती) श्वरैं [ः*] ।। [७।।*] इति कमलदलाम्बुबिन्दुलोला (लां) श्रि (श्रि) यमनुची (चि)-

30 न्त्य मनुष्याजि(जी) वितं(त) ञ्च [।*] सकलमिदमुदाहृतञ्च बु [द्*] ध्वा न हि पुर(रु)[52]

31 षैः परि(र) कि(की)र्त्तयो विलोप्या [ः*] ।। [८।।*][53] **प्रवर्द्धमानविजयराज्ये (ज्य) सम्ब (संव)त्सरे सप्त-**

32 **पञ्चाशत्तमे कार्त्तिकपो(पौ) र्ण्णन(मा) स्यां अङ्केन सम्ब(संव)त् ।[54] ५० ७ कार्त्तिक दिन ३०** [।।*].

Seal[55]

राज्ञः[56] श्रृी (श्री) हर्षगुप्तस्य

सूनोः सद्गुणशालिनः [।*]

शासनं[57] **शिवगुप्तस्य**

स्थितमाभुवनास्थितेः [।।६।।*]

45. Pandeya reads लोका. The *ā* sign of *kā* is, however, not seen in the facsimile.
46. Pandeya: महिञ्च 46a. Pandeya: °ष्टिब्बर्ब°
47. Pandeya ब्बंसुधा
48. Pandit Pandeya informs us that the medial sign for *ā* in *ttā* and *rā*, though visible in the original, has not come out in the impression.
49. In the facsimile it looks like *bhī*. Pandit Pandeya, however, tells us that the dot in the circle indicating the length of the medial *ī* is not to be found in the original.
50. Pandit Pandeya suggests a punctuation mark (*daṇḍa*) within a square parenthesis with an asterisk. This is, however, not required.
51. Pandeya: भा [क] . *Vi* is, however, quite clear in the accompanying plate.
52. Pandeya: पुरु°. The *u* sign of *ru* is, however, not to be seen in the facsimile.
53. Stanzas 7 and 8 are not to be found in any other copper-plate inscription of the Pāṇḍavavaṁśins of South Kosala.
54. This *daṇḍa* is unnecessary.
55. The devices and the two-line legend in the *Anuṣṭubh* metre on the seal are exactly the same as those found on the seals affixed to the other copper-plate grants of Śivagupta.
56. This letter is not visible in the plate.
57. The *akṣara śā* is not to be seen in the facsimile.

ABSTRACT

After the auspicious *siddham* symbol is introduced king **Śivagupta** (called **Mahā-Śivaguptarājadeva**) who is described exactly in the same words as in the last two inscriptions.

After honouring the Brāhmaṇas at the village Vaidyapadraka[58] situated in the Oṇi *bhoga*[59] the king informed the agriculturist householders living in the village together with all the royal officials dependent upon him including the *Samāhartṛ*, *Sannidhātṛ* and other officers posted there from time to time[60] that he had granted the village, by means of a copper-plate charter, to god Īśāneśvara Śiva enshrined in the temple[61] at Pattana Khadirapadra-tala[62] for the offerings of *bali, caru* and *naivedya,* the maintenance of feeding house (*sattra*), dance and instrumental music as well as the repairs and maintenance of the temple, at the request of the holy illustrious Śūlapāṇi, the disciple of the holy illustrious Pramathācārya who hailed from the celebrated penance-grove called Pañcayajña-tapovana situated in the Dvaitavana[63] and was a constant wanderer, on the full moon day of the month of Kārttika[64] for the religious merit of his parents and of his own self. The grant was endowed with the same privileges and exemptions as enumerated in *ante,* III:VI-VII.[65] The villagers were asked to pay the *bhoga, bhāga* and other dues to the donee regularly and thus live happily in the village.

The grant portion is followed by the customary exhortation to the future

58. It has been identified with the modern village of Baidpali in the Bargarh tahsil of the Raigarh District, Madhya Pradesh.
59. Oṇi, the place after which the *bhoga* (sub-division) was christened, has not been identified.
60. In this inscription the officers *Samāhartṛ* and *Sannidhātṛ* are included among the same royal officials (*rāja-puruṣas*) dependent upon the king whereas in other records of the king they are mentioned separately from other royal officials.
61. Pandit Pandeya suggests that this temple was probably built by Śivagupta's ancestor Īśānadeva. The sole basis of this surmise is, however, the identity of the first component of the two names.
62. Pattana Khadirapadratala, which is probably the same as Khadirapadra referred to in the Sonepur plates of the Somavaṁśī king Mahā-Bhavagupta I Janamejaya (*EI*, xxiii, 251, text-line 18), is probably represented by the modern village of Khairapali, about ten miles from Baidpali.
63. Dvaitavana is familiar from the Great Epic as a forest where the Pāṇḍavas lived for some time during the period of their exile. According to the *Mahābhārata*, it was situated close to a desert and the river Sarasvatī flowed through it. Named after the Dvaita lake flowing through it, it was close to the Himalayas and lay between Taṅgaṇa on the northeast and Kurukṣetra and Hastināpura on the south-east. See *EI*, xxvii, 322; Sorensen, *Dictionary of Proper Names in the Mahābhārata*, s.v. Dvaitavana; *Mahābhārata ki Nāmānukramaṇikā*, s.v. Dvaitavana.
64. The full moon day of Kārttika was, as now, regarded as very sacred.
65. In place of *nidhi* and *upanidhi* we have in this inscription the words *nidhāna* and *upanidhāna.* There is also some difference in the order of the mention of these privileges and exemptions.

kings to maintain the grant and eight common benedictive and imprecatory verses, six of them in the name of the sage Vyāsa, are quoted.[66]

The charter is dated the **full moon day of the month of Kārttika**[67] **in the fifty-seventh year of the increasingly victorious reign**, the date being given both in words and figures.

The *Anuṣṭubh* verse on the seal is identical with that met with on the seals attached to the other grants of the same king and speaks of the charter as belonging to **Śivagupta**, son of the illustrious king Harṣagupta.

66. The last two verses are quoted only in this Pāṇḍavavaṁśin inscription.

67. Evidently the charter was issued on the same day on which the grant was made. In figures the full moon day of Kārttika is equated to the thirtieth day of the same month which shows that the months mentioned in the Pāṇḍavavaṁśin inscriptions have to be taken as *pūrṇimānta*.

III : IX

MALLAR PLATES[1] OF ŚIVAGUPTA BĀLĀRJUNA

Provenances: Mallar, Bilaspur District, Madhya Pradesh.
References: V.V. Mirashi and L.P. Pandeya, *EI*, xxiii, 113-22 and plates opposite pp. 120 and 121; S.N. Rajaguru, *IO*, iv, 60-64.
Language: Sanskrit. In prose with the exception of a few benedictory and imprecatory verses at the end and the legend on the seal.
Metres: Verse 1: *Vasantatilakā*; Verses: 2, 4-6 and 7: *Anuṣṭubh*; Verse 3: *Indravajrā*.
Script: Box-headed variety of the Central Indian alphabet.
Date: Regnal year not mentioned. About the middle of the eighth century A.D.

TEXT[2]

First Plate

1 सिद्धम्[3] [।*] स्वस्त्यशेषक्षिति(ती) शविद्याभ्यासविशेषासादितमहनि(नी)यविनयस–
2 म्पत्स(त्सं)पादितसकलविजिगि(गी)षुगुणो गुणवत्समा[4]श्रय[5]प्रकृष्टतरशौ–
3 य्य(र्य्यं)[6] प्रज्ञाप्रभावस(सं)भावितमहाभ्युदय [:*] कार्ति(त्त)केय इव कृति(त्ति) वाससो–
4 राज्ञ [:*]श्रि(श्री)[7]हर्षदेवस्य सु(सू)नु [:*] सोमवङ्कश[8]सम्भवः परममाहे–
5 श्वरो मातापितृपादानुध्यात [:*] श्रि(श्री)महाशिवगुप्तराज [:*] कुशलि(ली) ।।[9] त–
6 रडङ्श[10]कभोगि(गी)यकैलासपुरग्रामे ब्राह्मणा [न्*] सम्पूज्य सप्रधा–
7 नात्प्र(न्प्र)तिवासिनो यथाकालाध्यासिनस्समाहृत्त्ं सन्निधातृ[सु](प्र)–

Second Plate : First Side

8 मुखानधिकारिण [:*] सकरणानन्यान्श्चा[11]स्मत्पादोपजि(जी)विनः[12] सर्व्वं(रा)–

1. The plates, 8.4" long and 5" broad and about .1" thick (the middle plate is thicker than others), have a circular hole about the middle of the left margin for the passage of the ring (about .4" thick and 4.3" in diameter) the ends of which are secured under the seal.
2. From plates in *EI*, xxiii, opposite pp. 120 and 121.
3. Expressed by a symbol. Mirashi and Pandeya: *Om*.
4. Originally *mo* had been engraved, and then the medial sign for *e* was struck off.
5. In the Bonda and Lodhia plates (*ante*, III: VII and VIII) we have गुणवत्समाश्रयः.
6. Mirashi and Pandeya: °शौर्य्यं°
7. The subscript *r* here and at some other places closely resembles the medial *ṛ*.
8. Read °वंश°
9. These *daṇḍas*, the first of which has a hook on top, are superfluous.
10. Read तरडंशक°
11. Read °नन्यांश्चा°
12. The synthesis would require *svapāda* instead of *asmat-pāda*.

9 जपुरुषा[न्*][13]समाज्ञापयति[।*]विदितमस्तु भवतां यथास्माभिरयं ग्रा–
10 मः सनिधि [:*] सोपनिधिः सदशापराधः सर्व्वंकरसमेतः सर्व्वंपीडा–
11 वर्ज्जित [:*] प्रतिषिद्धचाटभटप्रवेशतया ।[14] तरडङ्शक[15]प्रतिष्ठि–
12 तकोरदेवभोय्यालकका[16]रितविहारिकानिवासिचातुर्दिशार्य्यंभि–
13 क्षुसङ्घाय श्रि(श्री)भास्करवर्म्मंमातुलविज्ञप्त्या ताम्व्र(म्र)शासनेनाच–
14 न्द्राक्कंसमकालम्मातापित्रोरात्मनश्च पुण्याभिवृद्धये ।[17] आषाढा–

Second Plate : Second Side

15 मावास्यासूर्य्यंग्रहोपरागे उदकपूर्व्वं[18] प्रतिपादित इत्यतश्च[19]
16 विधेयतया समुचितम्भोगभागादिकमुपनयद्भिभ(र्भं)वद्भिः सुखं–
17 म्प्रतिवस्तव्यमिति ।।[20] भाविनश्च भूमिपालानु[द्*] दिश्येदमभिधीयते [।*]
18 भूमिप्रदा दिवि ललन्ति पतन्ति हन्त हृत्वा महि(हीं)नृपतयो
19 नरके नृशङ्ससात्[21] ।[22] एत [द्*] द्वयं परिकलय्य्य चलाञ्च लक्ष्मीः(क्ष्मी)मायुस्त–
20 था कुरुत यद्भवतामभि (भी)ष्ठं(ष्टम्) [।।१।।*] अपि च [*] रक्षापालनयोस्तावत्प(त्फ-
लं सु–
21 गतिदुर्ग्गति(ती) [।*] को नाम स्वर्ग्गमुच्छि(त्सृ)ज्य नरकं प्रतिपद्यते ।[23] [।२।*] व्यास-
गीता(तां)–

Third Plate

22 श्चात्र श्लोकानुदाहा(ह)रन्ति [।*] अग्नेरपत्य(त्यं) प्रथम (मं) सुवर्ण्णं भूर्व्वैष्ण(वी)
23 सु(सू)र्य्यंसुताश्च गाव [:।*] दत्तास्त्रयस्तेन[24] भवन्ति लोका य [:*] काञ्चनं गाञ्चच म–
24 हि(ही)ञ्च दद्यात् ।[25] [।३।।*] षष्टि वर्षसहस्राणि स्वर्ग्गे मोदति भूमिदः [।*]आ–
25 क्षेप्ता चानुमन्ता च तान्येव नरके वसेत् । [।४।।*] बहुभिर्व्वसु–
26 धा दत्ता राजभि [:*] सगरादिभिः [।*]यस्य यस्य यदा भूमिस्तस्य तस्य त–

13. The portion referring to the addressees of the royal order in respect of the grant is exactly the same as that of the Bardula plates (*ante*, III:VI) of the same king.
14. The mark of punctuation is superfluous.
15. Read तरडंशक°
16. Mirashi and Pandeya read कोरदेवभोय्यीलक and think that the intended reading is कोरदेवभार्य्यलिका° (*i.e.*, Alakā, wife of Koradeva). The superscript *r* is, however, absent. In case what looks like the medial sign for *ā* is taken as superscript *r*, it will have to be read as °भोर्य्यलक°
17. The mark of punctuation is unnecessary. Better read पुण्याभिवृद्धय आषाढा°
18. Read° पराग उदकपूर्व्वं.
19. Read इति। अतश्च.
20. Both the *daṇḍas* are curved and the first one shows a hook on its top.
21. Read नृशंसाः.
22. The *daṇḍa* has a hook on its top.
23. The mark of punctuation consists of a slightly curved *daṇḍa* which, however, does not show a hook on its top. It has escaped the notice of the original editors.
24. Read दत्तास्त्रयस्तेन
25. The mark of punctuation shows a hook on its top.

27 दा फलं (लम्) [।।५।।*] स्वदत्ता (त्तां) परदत्ताम्वा[26] यत्नाद्रक्ष युधिष्ठिरः (र)[।*] महि
(हीं) महि(ही) मता (तां)
28 श्रेष्ठ दानात्श्रे (च्छे्)योनुपालनमिति[27] ।। [६।।*।

Seal[28]

राज्ञः श्रीहर्षगुप्तस्य
सूनोः सद्गुणशालिन [:।*]
शासनं **शिवगुप्तस्य**
स्थितमाभुवनस्थिते [:।।७।।*]

ABSTRACT

The *siddham* symbol, with which the inscription opens, is followed by the mention of the issuer of the charter, king **Śivagupta** (called **Mahā-Śivagupta-rāja**), who is described exactly in the same words as in the last three inscriptions.

After honouring the Brāhmaṇas at the village Kailāsapura[29] situated in the Taraḍaṁśaka *bhoga*[30] the king informed the inhabitants of the village together with their *Pradhāna, Samāhartṛ, Sannidhātṛ* and other officers together with their subordinates and all the other royal officials dependent upon him that at the request of his maternal uncle Bhāskaravarman he had given away the village, by means of a copper-plate charter, to the venerable Order of the monks of the four quarters (*cāturdiś-ārya-bhikṣu-saṅgha*)[31] residing at the small monastery (*vihārikā*) at Taraḍaṁśaka constructed by Alakā(?), wife of Koradeva,[32] on the occasion of a solar eclipse on the amāvāsyā of the

26. Read परदत्तां वा.
27. Better Read नुपालनम् ।। [६ ।।*] इति ।।
28. The circular seal, 3.5" in diameter, is exactly similar to those attached to the last three charters of the same king.
29. This village may be represented by one of the several villages named Keslā in the Bilaspur and Janjgir tahsils. Of them all, the closest to Mallar, the findspot of the record, is Keslā, some eight miles to its south-east, where remains of some old structures are noticeable.
    The employment of *pura* as the name-ending of a village is interesting.
30. Taraḍaṁśaka, the headquarters of the *bhoga* of that name, cannot be definitely identified. It has been suggested by Mirashi and Pandeya that it is probably identical with the Talahāri-*maṇḍala* mentioned in some later epigraphs (*vide* Bhandarkar's *List*, Nos. 1231, 1232 and 1240). According to one of these records (Ratanpur inscription of Pṛthvīdeva II and Brahmadeva, *ibid.*, No. 1240), Mallāla (modern Mallar, the provenance of these plates) was included in this *maṇḍala*. The Buddhist images at Mallar are reported to have been brought there from the village Jaitpur, nearly a mile to the north of Mallar. It is thus possible that the site of Taraḍaṁśaka, where the small Buddhist monastery mentioned in this inscription was situated, is presently represented by Jaitpur.
31. For the significance of the qualifying expression *cāturdiśa*, see the present author's *An Outline of Early Buddhism* (Varanasi, 1965), 145-50.
32. This interpretation is based on the correction *Koradeva-bhāryy-Ālakā* suggested by the original editors. Vide fn. 16 above. In case the proposed correction is not

month of Āṣāḍha, with the object of the increase of the religious merit of his parents as well as of his own self. To the grant were attached the same rights and exemptions as those enumerated in *ante*, III:VI.

Next comes the usual request to the kings to protect the grant followed by six customary benedictive and imprecatory stanzas the last four of which are ascribed to Vyāsa.

The *Anuṣṭubh* stanza on the seal, which is also met with on the seals attached to the last three charters, avers that this record belongs to king **Śivagupta** son of the illustrious Harṣagupta.

---

accepted, the expression in the original may refer to a monastery built by two persons named Koradeva and Bhayyālaka. Alternatively Koradevabhayyālaka may be a single name.

III : X

MALLAR PLATES[1] OF ŚIVAGUPTA

Provenance: Mallar, Bilaspur District, Madhya Pradesh.
Reference: Balchandra Jain, *Prāchya Pratibhā*, v(i), 48-53 and plates between pp. 50 and 51.
Language: Sanskrit. In prose except the benedictive and imprecatory verses at the end and the legend on the seal.
Metres: Verse 1: *Vasantatilakā*; Verses 2, 4-7: *Anuṣṭubh*; Verse 3: *Indravajrā*.
Script: Box-headed variety of the Central Indian alphabet.
Date: Latter half of the eighth century A.D.

TEXT[2]

First Plate

1 सिद्धम्[3] [।*] स्वस्त्यशेषक्षिति (ती) शविद्याभ्यासविशेषासादितः[4] महनि (नी) यविन–
2 यसम्पत्स (त्सं) पादितसकलविजिगि (गी) षुगुणोगुणवत्समाश्रय [ः*]प्र–
3 कृष्टतरशौर्य्यप्रज्ञाप्रभावसम्भावित महाभ्युदय [ः*] कार्त्तिकेय
4 इव कृति (त्ति) वाससो राज्ञः श्रि (श्री) हर्षदेवस्य सु (सू) नुः[5] सोमवङ्श (वंश)–
5 सम्भवः परममाहेश्वरो मातृपितृपादानुध्यातः श्रि (श्री) **महाशिवगु–**
6 **प्तराजः** कुशलि (ली) ॥ उ (ओ) णि भोगि (गी) य शुष्कसिरिल्लिकायां ब्र (ब्रा) ह्मणा [न्*] सम्पू–
7 ज्य [6]सप्रधानान्प्रतिवासिनोन्याङश्च (न्यांश्च) समाहत् (त्तं) सनि (न्नि) धातृप्रभि (भृ) तियथा–

Second Plate : First Side

8 कालाध्यासिनस्सर्वराजपुरुषाङस (न्स) माज्ञापयति [।*] विदितमस्तु
9 भवता (तां) यथास्माभिरयं ग्रामस्सनिधिस्सोपनिधिरचाटभटप्र–
10 वेशस्सर्व्वकरादानसमेतस्सर्वपि (पी) डावर्ज्जितः [ः*] सदशापराधः

1. The plates, rectangular in shape, are 12.5 cms. broad and 19 cms. long. The round hole for the passage of the ring has a diameter of 1.5 cms. and is bored about the middle of the left margin about 3 cms. from the edge. The ends of the ring are joined under a circular seal.
2. From photographs.
3. Expressed by a symbol.
4. The *visarga* is superfluous.
5. Jain: सूनुः
6. Jain: सप्रधानात्

11 कोसलानगरप्रतिष्ठितश्रि (श्री) शिवनन्दिने (ना) [6a] कारितकपा–

12 लेश्वरभट्टारकयो [:*] [7] खण्डस्फुटितसंस्कारकरणाय बलिचरु–

13 प्रवर्त्तनाय मु (उ) दकपूर्व्वमाचन्द्रार्क्कसमकालोपभोगाय माता–

14 पित्त्रोरात्मनश्च पुण्याभिबृ (वृ) द्धये श्रि (श्री) शिवनन्दिविज्ञप्त्या ताम्त्र (म्र) शासने–

Second Plate : Second Side

15 न प्रतिपादितः (त) इत्यवगम्य विधेयैर्भूत्वा यथोचितभोगभागमुप–

16 नयद्भि [:*] भवद्भि [:*] सुखं प्रतिवस्तब्य (व्य) मिति ।।भाविनश्च भूमिपालानु–

17 दि (द्दि) श्येदममिधि (धी) यते [*] भूमिप्रदा दिवि ललन्ति पतन्ति हन्त हृत्वा

18 महि (हीं) नृपतयो नरके नृश (शं) ङ्सात् (साः) । एत [द्*] द्वय (यं) परिकलै (ल) य्य

19 चलाञ्च [8] लक्ष्मि (क्ष्मी) मायुस्तथा कुरुत यद्भवतामभि (भी) ष्ट [म्*] [।।१।।*] श्रा (श्र) पि
च [।*]

20 रक्षापालनयोस्तावत्फल [9] (लं) सुगति दुर्गति (ती) [।*] को नाम स्वर्गमुच्छि (त्सृ)–

21 ज्य नरक (कं) प्रतिपद्यते ।।[२।।*] व्यासगि (गी) ता (तां) श्चात्र श्लोकानुदाहरन्ति [।*]
श्रा (श्र)–

Third Plate

22 ग्नेरपत्यं प्रथमं सुवर्ण्णं (र्णं) भूर्व्वैष्णवि (वी) सूर्य्यसुताश्च गाव [:।*] दत्ता–

23 त्र (स्त्र) यस्तेन भवन्ति लोका यः [10] काञ्चन (नं) गाञ्च [11] महि (ही) ञ्च [12] दद्यात् ।[।३।।*]

24 षष्टिवर्षसहस्राणि स्वर्गे मोदति भूमिदः [:*] अ (आ) च्छेता (त्ता) चानुमन्ता

25 चा (च) [13] तान्येव नरके वसेत् ।[।४।।*] बहुभिर्व्वसुधा दत्ता राजभि [:*]

26 सगरादिभि [:।*] यस्य यस्य यदा भूमिस्त स्यतस्य तदा फलं (लम्) [।।५।।*] स्व–

27 दत्ताम्परदत्ता (त्तां) म्वा (वा) यत्नाद्रक्षः (क्ष) युधिष्ठिरः (र) [।*] महि (हीं) महि (ही)
मता (तां) श्रेष्ठ

28 दानाश्रे (च्छे) योनुपालनमिति [13a] ।।[६।।*]

Seal[14]

1 राज्ञ (ज्ञः) श्रीहर्षगुप्तस्य सु (सू) नो [:*] सद्गुणशालिन [:।*]

2 शासनं **शिवगुप्तस्य** स्थितमाभुवनस्थिते [:।।७।।*]

6a. Really speaking, the case ending is not required.

7. Jain proposes to correct it to भट्टारकाय but adds in a note (*Prāchya Pratibhā*, v (i), 52, note 1) that the original may be correct in case two temples were built.

8. Jain: चलाञ्चु.

9. Jain:° त्पल.

10. Jain: काञ्चुन°.

11. Jain: गाञ्चु.

12. Jain: महिञ्चु.

13. A subscribed *t* appears to have been incised by oversight and cancelled.

13a. Better read पालनम् ।। ६ ।। इति ।।

14. The surface of the seal, 9.2 cms. in diameter, comprises three parts. The upper part has the figure of a couchant bull (Nandin) facing left with a trident in front and an auspicious pitcher (*maṅgalakalaśa*) behind. In the middle we have a two-line legend in the *Anuṣṭubh* metre and in the lowermost portion a full-blown lotus flanked by a leaf on either side.

ABSTRACT

Commencing with the auspicious words *siddham*, indicated by a symbol, and *svasti*, the charter was issued by the Somavaṁśa monarch **Śivagupta** who is described exactly in the same manner as in other grants. It aims at recording the grant, by the king, of the village Śuṣkasirillikā[15] forming part of the Oṇi *bhoga*[16] for the repairs to and the arrangement of *bali* and *caru* offerings for the temples of Kapāleśvara (Śiva) and Bhaṭṭāraka (probably Sūrya) built by Śivanandin, a resident of Kosalānagara,[17] at the latter's behest.[18] The addressees of the royal order concerning the grant and the privileges accompanying the grant are the same as those mentioned in the previous charter.

The customary exhortation to future kings to protect the grant, which follows, is sought to be strengthened by six imprecatory and benedictive stanzas four of which are ascribed to Vyāsa.

The verse on the seal is the same as that found on the other seals of Śivagupta.

15. Not identified.
16. It is also mentioned in no. III: VIII, text-line 6. But Oṇi, which gave its name to the *bhoga*, remains unidentified.
17. The town named Kosalānaara, which is mentioned here for the first time cannot be identified. Although Kosalānagara is explicitly referred to as the seat of Śivanandin, the builder of the temple, the temples were obviously built at this town.
18. The respectful manner in which Sivanandin is mentioned indicates that he held a high position and his word carried weight with the king. He may have been either Śivagupta's son of that name or a religious leader.

III : XI

SIRPUR LAKṢMAṆA TEMPLE STONE[1] INSCRIPTION OF THE TIME OF ŚIVAGUPTA BĀLĀRJUNA

Provenance: Sirpur, Raipur District, Madhya Pradesh.

References: Hira Lal, *EI*, xi, 184-201 and plate facing p. 190; *ICPB*, 99-105, No. 174,[2] Bhandarkar's *List, No.* 1654.

Language: Sanskrit. In verse with the exception of the *maṅgalā* at the beginning.

Metres: Verses 1-2: *Sragdharā*; Verse 3: *Hariṇī*; Verses 4, 6, 9, 12 and 15: *Vasantatilakā*: Verses 5 and 39: *Śikhariṇī*; Verses 7, 10-11, 13-14, 16, 18 and 21: *Śārdūlavikrīḍita*; Verse 8: *Praharṣiṇī*; Verses 17 and 40: *Upajāti*; Verses 19, 26 and 28-34: *Anuṣṭubh*; Verse 20: *Vaṁśasthāvila*; Verses 22 and 38: *Drutavilambita*; Verse 23: *Vaitālīya*; Verses 24-25, 27, 35-37 and 41-42: *Āryā*.

Script: Nāgarī of the northern class.

Date: About the middle of the eighth century A.D.

TEXT[3]

1 सिद्धम्[4] [।*] नमः पुरुषोत्तमाय ॥[4a] अन्योन्यप्रान्तरान्तर्विचलदुरुमरुत्पुञ्जगुञ्जारवोग्रैर-
गुडल्यग्रैरुदञ्चन्नखकिरणशिखास्पष्टदंष्ट्राकरालैः । क्रामन्वः पातु पञ्चानन इव चरणश्चक्रिण-
खेघनौघान्विध्वस्य ध्व(ा)-
2 न्तधाम्नः करिण इव किरन्मौक्तिकाभानिभानि ॥[१॥*] लब्धो निर्भेत्तुमेभिर्न रिपुरिति
रसाद्दत्तचक्षुर्नखेषु त्रासात्तत्क्रोड[5] रन्ध्रोदरकुहरदरीमेव लीनं विलोग्य । हासोल्लासावहेलं
तदितरकरजाग्रेण निर्भिद्य [सद्यः कोशा[6]] च्चिक्षेप तज्जं मलमिव
3 दनुजं यः स वोव्यान्न्ृसिङ्हः[7] ॥[२॥*] वहदिव[रु]चा शङ्ख्या [दंष्ट्रां] सचिह्नमिवासिना

1. The reddish stone on which the inscription is engraved was found while removing the debris of the *maṇḍapa* of the brick temple, locally known as the Lakṣmaṇa Temple, at Sirpur. The breadth of its upper corner is 3' 8½", while the height at the right side is 2' 3½" and at the left side 2' 1½".
2. The text of the inscription is also given in B.C. Jain, *Catalogue of the Antiquities in the M.G.M. Museum, Raipur:* vi, 36-44, pl. XX; and S.N. Rajaguru, *Inscriptions of Orissa, iv*, 70-73.
3. From plate in *EI*, xi.
4. Hira Lal: *Oṁ*. Expressed by a symbol.

4a Of the two *daṇḍas* forming the mark of punctuation, the first is corrected from an inadvertently engraved *visarga*.

5. Hira Lal reads °त्रोड° and suggests to correct it to त्रोढ° or °त्रोह°; but as pointed out by H. Krishna Sastri, the reading on the impression seems to be °त्क्रोड°
6. Read क्रोधा°
7. Hira Lal: नृसिह्नः. Read नृसिंहः.

ज्वलदिव दधच्चक्रेणास्यं गदां भ्रुकुटीमिव। ग्रसितुमसुरान्संभूयेव श्रितान्तकविभ्रमं दुरितमिति [वेषो][8] यं [विष्णो:]पि —⏑⏑—⏑—[9] ।।[३।।*] [ग्रासीच्छशी]व भुवनाद्भुतभूत[10]भूति–

4 रुद्भूतभूतपति [भक्तिसमप्र]भावः। चन्द्रान्वयैकति[ल]क [: खलु चन्द्रगुप्तरा]जाख्यया पृथुगुणः प्रथितः पृथिव्याम् ।।[४।।*] गरीयान् भारोयं दुरधिगमिदं वर्त्म पुरतो न मे प्रष्ठः कश्चिन्न च स मधुरः कश्चन सखा। इ————⏑⏑⏑⏑⏑———⏑गणशः स्वशक्त्या

5 निर्व्यूढि⏑⏑⏑⏑⏑———⏑⏑⏑— ।।[५।।*] दुर्धर्ष[वैरि]वरवारणदारुणेषु [11] सीरायुधः स इव कंसनिषूदनस्य राजाधिकारधवलः सबलो[12] बभूव यस्याग्रजोप्यनुचरश्चरतो रणेषु ।।[६।।*] कुम्भैरङ्कितमस्तकानतिमद[13] व्याहारमुग्धात्मनो वक्त्रन्यस्ततृणानधः कृतकरा–

6 न्मातङ्गकान्मारयन्। श्वेव श्वापदराट् न यस्य नृपतेः शौर्यं जगामोपमां हन्तुः कोशपराक्रमान्वयनयस्फीतत्विषां विद्विषाम्[14] ।।[७।।*] तस्याभूदवनिभृतामधीश्वरस्य प्रख्यातो जगति सुतो यथा हिमाद्रेः ।।[८।।*]

7 स्थानं चिरादुचितमेदतदभून्ममेति लक्ष्मीः प्रसूतिसमये यमुवाह हर्षम्। तेनावृतः सततमेव शुचामगम्यः श्रीहर्षगुप्त इति नाम ततो [य ऊहे] ।।[९।।*] संसक्ताः सकलोपभोगविषये धर्माध्वनि प्र(प्रा)ध्वराः सद्गोष्ठीषु निरन्तराः परबलध्व(ध्वं)न्से(से) प्यवन्ध्याः सदा। [ग्रक्षुणाः]सततं गुरूपचरणे

8 यान्ति स्म विस्मापिनो यस्यानेकसुखक्रियासु युगपत्संभाविनो वासराः ।।[१०।।*] क्षुण्णा भित्तिरनेकधा विघटिताः सर्वेप्यमी सन्धयो वीथ्यङ्गान्यपि विक्षतानि परितः शुष्कोस्थिव(ब)न्धक्रमः। चित्रं प्रच्युतमामुखादपि कथं किं वीक्षितेनामुना यस्येति द्विषतां कुनाटकमिव द्विष्टं पुरं

9 प्रेक्षकैः ।।[११।।*] तस्मादजायत महाशिवगुप्तराजो धर्मावतार[15] इति निर्वितथं प्रतीतः। भीमेन यः सुत इव प्रथमः पृथायाः पृथ्वीं जिगाय रणकेसरिणानुजेन ।।[१२।।*] भावी हन्त पितामहादपि महानाच (चा)र्यमप्योजसा जेष्यत्येष रणे बलेन भविता तत्कोस्य वैकर्त्तनः। ग्रस्त्राभ्यस्ति [ष यं समस्त]–

10 जयिनं मत्वेति **बालार्जुनं** स्वे देहेपि जहुः स्पृहामरिगणाः प्रागेव सम्पत्तिषु ।।[१३।।*] यः प्रद्वेषवतां वधाय विकृताकारास्थाय मा[या]मयीः कृष्णो [योव]तरन्नभूदिह स खल्वव्याजलूनद्विषः। नासीदेव समो हरिर्धवलतामात्यन्तिकीं बिभ्रतो यस्याकल्पमनेनं चापि भविता क[ल्की] भविष्यन्पुनः ।।[१४।।*]

8. Hira Lal: वेदो.
9. Hira Lal has left out the remainder of the stanza after विष्णोः undeciphered as the writing on this portion of the stone is worn out. The inscription, however, shows the letter *pi* after विष्णोः clearly. The rest cannot be read out.
10. Originally *ti* had been engraved, but later the medial sign for *i* was cancelled.
11. Hira Lal: °कौरवरदो रणदारुणषु; Jain: वैरिवरदारणदारुणेषु.
12. Jain: सकलो.
13. In the body of the text Hira Lal read it as °नति [ग?] दि° but in a footnote indicated the probability of the reading being नयच. But as pointed out by H. Krishna Sastri, on the impression the reading appears to be °नतिमद°.
14. Jain: विद्विषां.
15. Hiralal and Jain: धर्म्मावितार

11 तस्योरुजन्यजयिनो जननी जनानामीशस्य शैलत[न]येव मयू[रके]तोः। विस्मापनी विबुध-
लोकधियां बभूव श्रीवासटेति नरसिङ्ह[16][त]नोः सटेव ।।[१५।।*] निष्पङ्के मगधाधिपत्यमहतां
जातः कुले वर्मणां पुण्याभिः कृतिभिः कृती कृतमनःकम्पः [सुधा]भोजिनाम् ।।(।)
12 यामासाद्य सुतां हिमाचल इव श्रीसूर्यवर्मा नृपः प्राप प्राक्परमेश्वरश्वसुरतागर्वानिखर्वं पदम्
।।[१६।।*] गतेपि पत्यौदिव[मेक] रूपैः सदोपवासव्रतकर्शितैरपि। न मुक्तमेवावयवैर्यदीयैः[17]
स्वभावलीलामयमात्ममण्डनम् ।।[१७।।*] या वर्णाश्रमिणां त्रयीव शरणं राज्यस्य नीतिर्यथा
13 प्रज्ञेव प्रविवेचनी सदसतोस्तृष्णावतां श्रीः स्वयम्। उत्खाताखिलकल्मषप्रसरया किञ्चिश्च-
लन्ती स्थितेः सन्धानाय यया सखीव पृथिवी भूयः कृतं स्मारिता ।।[१८।।*] दमयन्त्या श्रपि[18]
पुरा यः स्थलं प्राप्य गर्वितः। स क[लि]ः स्वेपि समये हतमानः कृतो यया ।।[१९।।*] तया निजः
14 प्रेत्य पतिर्यथाविधे वसत्यसौ नित्यमुपासिताच्युतः। प्रकाशितुं तादृशमेव कारितं विभोरिदं
धाम हरेः सनातनम् ।।[२०।।*] दिव्यादेः सकलस्य जन्तुनिवहस्योच्चवचैः कर्मणां वैचित्र्यादय-
मद्भुतो बहुविधावस्थैर्वपुःपञ्जरैः ।।(।) [यः] प्रासादव्र(बृ)हच्छलेन[19] क–
15 थितः संसार एव स्फुटं पश्यत्त(न्त)स्तदिमं[20] मनः कुरुत भोः[21] पापेषु मा भूमिपाः ।।२१।।*]
क्षणमधः क्षणमुत्पतितैर्नभः पवनलोलतया[ध्व]जपल्लवैः ।।(।) हरणपालनयोरुचिते[22] गती
कथयति स्वयमेष महीभुजां (जाम्) ।।[२२।।*] तट एव भवाम्बुधेस्तरीतुं निहि–
16 तो धर्ममयः प्लवो महान्। परिपालयितव्य एष भूपै रवदीर्णोहिनिमज्जयत्यधः ।। [२३।।*]
इति वः प्रशस्तिकारः कविः स चिन्तातुराङ्क ईशानः ।।(।) यत्पालनार्थमर्थयति पार्थिवास्तां
स्थितिं शृणुत ।।[२४।।*] तोडङ्कणमधु–
17 वेढौ नालीपद्रश्च कुरपद्रश्च[23] [।*] स्थानेत्र वा(बा)णपद्रश्च पञ्च दत्ता इमे ग्रामाः ।।[२५।।*]
एषां भागास्त्रयः सत्रे खण्डस्फुटितसंस्कृतौ। पादमूलपरीवारपोषणे च त्रिधा कृताः ।।[२६।।*]
यस्तु [च]तुर्थो भाग : स पञ्चदशधाकृ–
18 तो विभागेन ।।(।) तत्र द्वादश विप्राः प्रतिवेदं प्रतिचतुष्केन ।।[२७।।*] ब्रह्मा त्रिविक्रमोर्कश्च
विष्णुदेवस्तथापरः ।।(।) तथा महिरदेवश्च चत्वारो बह्वचोत्तमाः ।।[२८।।*] एवं कपर्दो-
पाध्यायो भास्करो मधुसूदनः ।।(।) वेदगर्भश्च चत्वा–
19 रो यजुर्वेदस्य पारगाः ।।[२९।।*] तथा भास्करदेवश्च स्थिरोपाध्याय एव च ।।(।) त्रैलोक्य-
हन्सो[24] मोउट्ढश[25]चत्वारः सामपारगाः ।।[३०।।*] भाव्यं तत्पुत्रपौत्रैश्च [सा]ग्निहोत्रैः
षडङ्गिभिः ।।(।) द्युतवेश्याद्यनासक्तैरपिट्टाकैरसेवकैः ।।[३१।।*] य[स्तु]

16. Read नरसिहं.
17. Hiralal and Jain: °य्यंदीयैः.
18. Hiralal and Jain: ह्यपि.
19. Hiralal प्रासादवृहच्छलेन; Jain: प्रसाद°.
20. Hiralal and Jain: पश्यन्त°.
21. Hiralal and Jain: भो..
22. Jain: °रुचितं.
23. Read कुरपद्रः.
24. Read °हंसो.
25. Jain: मोउट्ठ°.

20 नैवंविधो[26] भावी[27] यश्चापुत्रो विपत्स्यते ॥(।)तयोर्ङशे[27a] प्रवेश्योन्यः पूर्व्वोक्त[28]गुणवान्द्विजः
॥[३२॥*] स चैषामेव सम्बन्धी सविद्यत्वे वयोधिकः ॥ (।) एभिरेव च साम्मत्यात्प्रवेश्यो
न नृपा[ज्ञ]या[29] ॥[३३॥*] ततो वासवनन्दीति [वि]प्रः

21 पु(स्तक)वाचकः[30] ॥(।)द्वौ च भागवतौ नाम्ना वामनः श्रीधरस्तथा ॥[३४॥*] एते पञ्च-
दशाङशा[31] विवर्जिता दानविक्रयाधानैः ॥(।) सर्व्वेपि च सद्भोज्याः ॥[32] लेखकश्चात्र[33]
गोण्ण इति इति[34] ॥[३५॥*] यस्तल एव ग्रामो वर्गुल्लक[35]संज्ञितः स दे–

22 व[स्य] । ब[लिचरुनिवेद्यसत्रो] पकरणहेतोः पृथग्दत्तः ॥[३६॥*] अत्र च साधिष्ठानैः सपाद-
मूलैश्च सर्व्वकार्याणि ॥(।) सं(स)म्भूय[36] विप्रमुख्यैः करणीयान्यैकमत्येन ॥[३७॥*] स्थिति-
रियं क्षितिपाः परिपाल्यतां चलतु

23 सैष क्र[तो]प[क्रतिक्रम] : ॥(।)[ननु भ] विष्यति का पुनरुत्तरा गतिरथो भवतामपि कीर्[त्ति]षु
॥[३८॥*] गज[स्ना]नं जातं [खलु] चरणकुद्दालनमिदं स्वयं पुण्योत्थानं[37] यदिह परकीर्त्ति-
क्षतिकृतां (ताम्) ॥(।)

24 मदक्लाम्यन्नारी[38]नयनतरलान्वीक्ष्य विभवानतः श्रेयः शुद्धं कुरुत ननु भोः क्षीरमदिरं(रम्)[39]
॥[३९॥*] भवाब्धिध[र्म][40]प्लवकर्ण्णधारो बभूव देव्याः कुलशीलशाली ॥(।)केदारनामा स
इदं समग्र–

25 मकारयत्पुण्यमहानिधानं(नम्) ॥[४०॥*] श्री**शिवगुप्तो** राजा हित्वा त्रैलोक्य–⏑–⏑
——⏑⏑———त्येन प्रादागगो (द्गो)लाय्य(र्य्यं) भट्टाय[41] ॥[४१॥*] भागमिहैकं
स्थाने[42] गुणव[द्*] द्विज भोज्यमुत्तमगुणा[य] ॥(।)

26 शास्त्रव्याख्याविदुषे विदुषे सा[ङ्गेषु[43] वेदे]षु ॥[४२॥*]

ABSTRACT

The inscription opens with the auspicious word *siddham*, expressed symbolically, followed by obeisance to lord Viṣṇu under the name Puruṣottama. The first three stanzas invoke the blessings of god Viṣṇu in his Trivikrama

26. Hiralal: नवंविधो.
27. Hiralal and Jain: सहे. 27*a* Read तयोरंशे.
28. Hiralal and Jain: पूर्वोक्त°.
29. There is a *tha*-like mark before the *daṇḍas* which is known to have been used at close of some records to indicate their end.
30. Hiralal and Jain: पुण्याह°.
31. Read °दशांशा.
32. The mark of punctuation is unnecessary.
33. Hiralal and Jain: लेखकश्चार्थं; V. Nenkayya: लेखकश्चात्र.
34. The second *iti* is redundant.
35. Hiralal: वग्गुंल्लक.
36. Hiralal and Jain: सम्भूय.
37. Hiralal and Jain: पुण्योस्थानं.
38. Hiralal and Jain: °म्यत्तन्वी°.
39. Hiralal and Jain: व्रतम [नुचर] न्कीर [नु?] दिरं.
40. Hiralal and Jain: धर्म्मं°.
41. Hiralal and Jain: °त्गोणार्य्यं°.
42. Hiralal and Jain: स्थानं.
43. Hiralal and Jain: शास्त्रेषु.

incarnation in which one of his feet tore asunder the clouds (v. 1)[44] and the man-lion (Nṛsiṁha) form in which he destroyed, with his claws, the demon Hiraṇyakaśipu (vv. 2-3).[45] Next is mentioned king Candragupta, the crest-jewel of the lunar race, whose dignity was commensurate with his devotion to the lord of goblins, *i.e.*, Śiva (v. 4). Even his elder brother, who also enjoyed regal power, followed him in the battle-fields even as the plough-weaponed (Balarāma) followed the destroyer of Kaṁsa, *i.e.* Kṛṣṇa (v. 6).[46] We have vague allusions to his victories over powerful enemies (v. 7).[47] From him sprang Harṣagupta even as did the Maināka mountain originated from Himādri (v. 8).[48] He is described in general terms in the next three stanzas which refer, *inter alia*, to his successful warfare (vv. 9-11).[49] From him was born king **Śivagupta** (here mentioned as **Mahā-Śivaguptarāja**), who was well-known as Dharmāvatāra (lit. an incarnation of virtue) and conquered the earth with the aid of his younger brother Raṇakesarin even as Pṛthā's first son (Yudhiṣṭhira) did with the help of his younger brother Bhīma (v. 12). The next verse mentions his *viruda* Bālārjuna and compares him to the epic hero Arjuna inasmuch as he was greater than his grandfather and would beat even his preceptor in battle by his prowess and there was none who could vanquish him even as Arjuna had excelled his grandfather Bhīṣma and surpassed his teacher Droṇa in prowess and states that Karṇa (Vaikarttana) was nothing before him in the practice of weapons.[50] The next verse tells us that Viṣṇu in his Kṛṣṇa and Kalki incarnations could not stand comparison with him.[51] His mother was Vāsaṭā even as the daughter of the moun-

44. Hiralal thought that this verse along with the following two stanzas praised the man-lion incarnation of Viṣṇu. But the reference to his feet destroying the multitude of clouds clearly shows that the verse actually points to the Trivikrama form.
45. This stanza purports to state that the terrific face of Nṛsiṁha resembled that of Yama. The various parts of the face are also compared to the attributes of Viṣṇu. Thus, the jaws, because of being white, are likened to the conchshell, the tongue to the sword, the face, being round, to the discus, and eye-brows to the mace. Thus, the verse is important iconographically.
46. H. Krishna Sastri suggests that Adhikāradhavala was the name or title of his elder brother. But the expression *rāj-ādhikāra-dhavala* may also be taken in the sense of 'one shining with regal power' as done by Hiralal.
47. This stanza seems to refer to an interesting practice connected with the code of warfare prevalent in ancient India, *viz.*, keeping straw in the mouth and the lowering of hands which symbolised the acceptance of one's own defeat.
48. This verse refers to the Maināka as an abode of jewels and as possessing large unchipped wings.
49. Verse 11, by employing words with a double entendre, alludes to a bad drama (*ku-nāṭaka*) detested by spectators (*prekṣaka*) even in the prologue (*āmukha*) because of torn curtains (*bhitti*), disjoined incidents (*sandhi*), broken dialogues (*aṅga*) and dry plot (*bandha*).
50. This verse compares the disappointed enemies of Śivagupta to Arjuna's enemies, *i.e.*, sons of Dhṛtarāṣṭra. The comparison was evidently suggested by the king's *biruda* Bālārjuna.
51. According to H. Krishna Sastri, this stanza also possibly refers to Atyantadhavala as a surname of Śivagupta.

tain (Pārvatī) was of the peacock-rider (god Kārttikeya) and she bewildered the minds of the wise men like the mane of the man-lion form of god Viṣṇu (v. 15). Her father was king Sūryavarman, born in the family of the Varmans great on account of their supremacy over Magadha,[52] who, by getting this daughter obtained the great honour of becoming the father-in-law of the lord of the East (*prāk-parameśvara*) even as in earlier times the snow-mountain (Himācala) had felt exalted by marrying his daughter Pārvatī to the great god (*Parameśvara*) Śiva (v. 16). She is praised vaguely in the following three stanzas (vv. 17-19)[53] and the only piece of historical information we get from these verses is that she survived her husband (v. 17). She built this eternal abode (temple) of lord Hari (Viṣṇu) to illustrate exactly the place (Vaikuṇṭha) where her deceased husband resided worshipping lord Acyuta (Viṣṇu) eternally (v. 20). The kings are then exhorted to protect the following gifts realising the ephemeral character of this world (vv. 21-24).[54] Five villages, namely Toḍaṅkaṇa, Madhuveḍha, Nālīpadra, Kurapadra and Nāgapadra, were given (v. 25). These were divided into four shares. Of these, three shares were meant for the maintenance of the almshouse, the repair of the breaks and cracks in the temple and to provide for the host of the attendants of the temple,[55] one share being allotted to each of these purposes (v. 26). The fourth share was sub-divided into fifteen parts. Twelve of them were for as many Brāhmaṇas, each four of them well-versed in one of the Vedas, as shown below.

Name of the Brāhmaṇa	*Veda*
Brahma-Trivikrama	*Bahvṛc* (*Ṛgveda*)
Arka	,,
Viṣṇudeva	,,
Mahiradeva	,,
Kapardopādhyāya	*Yajurveda*
Bhāskara	,,
Madhusūdana	,,
Vedagarbha	,,
Bhāskaradeva	*Sāmaveda*
Sthiropādhyāya	,,
Trailokyahaṁsa	,,
Mouḍḍha	,,

(vv. 27-30)

52. Roughly speaking, South Bihar or the area comprised in the Patna and Gaya districts of Bihar.
53. In verse 19 Kali is said to have had an access to Damayantī who, with the noble intention of getting back her husband, pretended to marry for a second time.
54. The outcome of the destruction and protection of the pious foundation is illustrated by the fluttering down and rising upward of the flag atop the temple tossed up by the unsteady wind (verse 22).
55. The word in the original is *pāda-mūla-parīvāra*. At the suggestion of Krishna Sastri, Hiralal takes the word *pāda-mūla* in the sense of 'the sanctuary' (*EI*, xi, 196, fn. 3), which is palpably incorrect. The word actually means 'a servant of the temple', 'a temple

These shares were to be inherited only by such of their sons and grandsons as perform *agnihotra*, are well-versed in the six limbs of the Vedas and are not addicted to gambling, prostitutes, etc., whose mouths are clean and who are not servants (v. 31). In case one does not satisfy these conditions or dies without leaving a male issue, his place was to be taken by a Brāhmaṇa possessing the aforesaid qualities (v. 32). He had to be their relative, learned and advanced in age and was to be appointed by their consent, and not by the order of the king (v. 33). Of the three remaining shares, Brāhmaṇa Vāsavanandin, the reciter of the books,[56] and the two Bhāgavatas, to wit, Vāmana and Śrīdhara, were to receive one part each (v. 34). These fifteen shares were not permitted to be alienated by gift, sale and mortgage. The writer of this portion was Goṇṇa[57] (v. 35).

The village known as Vargullaka was given separately for the *bali*, *caru*, *nivedya* and the almshouse attached to the god (v. 36). All the transactions were to be performed unanimously by the Brāhmaṇas in association with the local body (*adhiṣṭhāna*) and the temple-attendants[58] (v.37). The next two stanzas again exhort the rulers to maintain this pious foundation (vv. 38-39).

The temple was built by one Kedāra (v. 40).

The import of the last two stanzas (vv. 41-42) is not quite clear; but they seem to aver that king Śivagupta gave Golāryyabhaṭṭa, who was well-versed in the *śāstras* and their commentaries as well as the Vedas, one part of this gift which was to be enjoyed by a virtuous Brāhmaṇa.[59]

---

attendant' and is found employed in this sense in inscriptions and literature. The words *pādamūlika*, *Pādamūlattār*, etc. are also used in this sense. See F. Kielhorn, 'Pādamūla *IA*, xxvii, 252; D.C. Sircar, *IEG*, 224; Ajay Mitra Shastri, 'The Reading and Interpretation of a Verse in the Kuṭṭanī-mata in the Light of Archaeological and Puranic Evidence', *Purāṇa*, xiii, 60-66; *India as seen in the Kuṭṭanī-mata of Dāmodaragupta*, 66, fn. 3.

56. *Pustaka-vācaka* is also mentioned in some literary texts. Vide V.S. Agarwala, *Harṣa—Eka Sāṁskṛtika Adhyayana* (Hindi), 52. If Hira Lal's reading *Puṇyāha-vācaka* is accepted, Vāsavanandin will have to be regarded as a priest officiating at auspicious ceremonies and proclaiming by certain *mantras* a happy day for the ceremony and its performance.
57. Hira Lal reads the relevant portion of the stanza as *lekhakaśc-Ārya-Goṇṇa iti* and accordingly takes Ārya Goṇṇa to be the name of the writer.
    The mention of the writer, which normally comes at the end, at this point seems to indicate that the original record ended here and the remaining portion was appended later.
58. *Pāda-mūla* in the original has been wrongly rendered as 'worshipper' by Hira Lal.
59. Hira Lal takes the last verse to mean that one portion was to be reserved for one well-read in the *śāstras* and their commentaries as well as the Vedas and possessing an excellent character. We feel that verses 41-42 should be taken together as referring to Golāryabhaṭṭa.

III : XII

SIRPUR STONE SLAB[1] INSCRIPTION OF THE TIME OF ŚIVAGUPTA BĀLĀRJUNA

Provenance: Sirpur, Raipur District, Madhya Pradesh.
Reference: Moreshwar G. Dikshit, *EI*, xxxi, 197-98 and plate facing p. 198.
Language: Sanskrit. In verse except the concluding sentence giving the name of the engraver.
Metres: Verses 1, 6: *Sragdharā*; Verse 2: *Āryā*; Verse 3: *Śārdūlavikrīḍita*; 4, 7: *Anuṣṭubh*; Verse 5: *Vasantatilakā*.
Script: Early Nāgarī of the northern class.
Date: About the middle of the eighth century A.D.

TEXT[2]

1 [सिद्धम्[3]] ।[*] मुक्तश्रीको[न]जात:[4] सते(त)तमपि करैः स्पृश्यमानः सुधाङ्शोर्नो[5] वा म्लानः कदा–
2 चिन्न च हिमनिवहेनापि नीतोन्यथात्वं (त्वम्) । नोद्यत्प्रोद्दामकल्पक्षयसमयमरुत्प्रेरण–
3 स्यापि गम्यो रम्योन्यः[6] कोपि युष्मान्सुखयतु सुगतस्याङ्घ्रुतः पादपद्मः ।।[१।।*] ध [व]–
4 लकुलकमलभानौ भूभृति भूपालमण्डलीतिलके । प्रतिपक्षक्षतिदक्षे रक्षति
5 **वा(बा)लार्ज्जुने** क्षोणीं(णीम्) ।।[२।।*] दूरोत्सारितमत्सरः शमसुधास्वादप्रसक्तः सदा भिक्षुः स–
6 द्वसुधाधिपप्रतिकृतिर्दक्षः क्षमारक्षणे । आनन्दप्रभ इत्युदारकरुणाभारा–
7 द्रंभावो[7] भवद्भक्ति शास्तरि मारवैरिणि भृशं वि(बि)भ्रद्भवच्छेदिनि ।।[३।।*] स विहार-कुटीं
8 चक्रे क्रीत्वा मूल्येन सङ्घतः । व्यञ्जनाङ्शेन[8] सहितां सिततण्डुलसेतिकां(काम्) ।।[४।।*] सक्तं[9] (त्त्रं)त–
9 यानुदिनमत्र च कारयित्वा तद्व्यञ्जनाङ्श[10]सहितं यतिभिः स[म]स्तैः । प्रत्येकमा–

1. The inscribed slab, which is a yellowish variety of soft sandstone and measures about 14" long, $8\frac{1}{4}$" wide and 3" thick, was found on the floor of the northern verandah of the monastery at a depth of about 8 feet below the surface in the course of excavations at Sirpur.
2. From the plate in *EI*, xxxi, facing p. 198.
3. Dikshit: *Om*. Expressed by asymbol. The formula *Om* is entirely out of place in a Buddhistic record like the present one.
4. Dikshit: मुक्त श्रीकल्पजातः.
5. Read सुधांशोर्नो.
6. Dikshit: गन्धोरस्योन्यः.
7. Dikshit: करुणाभारात्प्रभावो.
8. Read व्यञ्जनांशेन.
9. Dikshit: सत्रं.
10. Read व्यञ्जनांश°.

10 त्मपरिपाटिवशेन भोज्यं यावन्नभस्तलमलंकुरूते विवस्वान् ।।[५।।*] वातोद्धूताव्ज (ब्ज) पत्रं (त्र)[11]–
11 स्थि[त] सलिलकणश्रेणिलीलाविलोलां लक्ष्मीमालोक्य लोकस्थितिमपि विपुलाप–
12 द्ग्रह[ग्र]स्यमानां (नाम्) । वु (बु) [द् *]ध्वा चोद्दामदुःखप्रभवभवगतौ वा (बा) न्धवं धर्ममेकं दानं दत्ता–
13 व[धानै रि[12]] दमिह यतिभिः सर्वदा पालनीयं (यम्) ।।[६।।*] सुमनोनुगतामेतां चक्रे स्रजमिवो–
14 [ज्ज्वलां] (लाम्) ।][13] सूनुः श्रीतारदत्तस्य प्रशस्ति श्रीसुमङ्गलः ।।[७।।*] उत्कीर्ण्णेयं प्रभाकरेण।।

ABSTRACT

The record opens with the auspicious word *siddham*, expressed by a symbol, which is followed by a stanza in praise of the lotus-feet of Sugata ((*i.e.*, Buddha). The next verse mentions the reigning Pāṇḍavavaṁśin King **Bālārjuna** (v. 2).[14] Then we are introduced to a monk named Ānandaprabha who cherished great devotion for the Buddha who is referred to as Śāstṛ and described as the enemy of Māra (*Māra-vairin*) and as the destroyer of the chain of life and death (v. 3). He established a free feeding house for the monks of the local monastery after purchasing, for this purpose from the Saṅgha, by paying a price, a hut in the monastery (*vihāra-kuṭī*) and a *setikā*[15] of white rice together with an appropriate quantity of condiment (*vyañjana*) for each of the monks per day for so long as the sun adorns the sky (vv. 4-5).[16] The monks are exhorted to maintain this gift keeping in mind the ephemeral character of the wealth and realising that *dharma* is the only succour in this worldly existence which is full of great sufferings (v. 6).

This eulogy (*praśasti*) was composed by Sumaṅgala, son of Tāradatta[17] (v.7), and engraved by Prabhākara.

11. Dikshit: °ताम्बुपत्र°.
12. Pointing out that two letters here are abraded in the original, Dikshit had left out the first four letters of this line undeciphered. Sircar in his editorial note restored this portion. The first *akṣara* is quite clear in the facsimile and traces of the second and fourth *akṣaras* are also visible.
13. The stone being damaged at this place, the *akṣaras* at the beginning of this line are lost. They have, however, been restored by Dikshit.
14. Bālārjuna is described, *inter alia*, as the very sun to the lotus that was his pure family (*dhavala-kula-kamala-bhānu*). D.C. Sircar (*EI*, xxxi, 198, fn. 8) points out that since the words *dhavala* and *pāṇḍu* are synonymous, the expression may have been intended to hint at Bālārjuna's descent from the epic hero Pāṇḍu.
15. *Setikā* is a measure equal to 4 *palas* or two handfuls. For some other references to it, see *ibid.*, xxv, 235, fn. 3; xxx, 177; *IEG*, s.v. *setikā*.
16. Dikshit had misunderstood the verses in question and taken them to mean that Ānandaprabha constructed a monastery and established a feeding house for the upkeep of which a white rice-field was given. According to him, the field was purchased from the Saṅgha and given together with the supplementary crops grown in it. The correct interpretation, followed in these pages, was suggested by D.C. Sircar (*ibid.*, xxxi, 197, fn. 2) who further pointed out that Ānandaprabha apparently paid a suitable amount of money to the monks who undertook the responsibility of securing the quantity of rice and condiments required for the purpose.
17. Sumaṅgala, son of Tāradatta, is also known from some other records found at Sirpur. *Vide* III: XV and appendix II below.

III : XIII

SIRPUR STONE INSCRIPTION OF ŚIVAGUPTA BĀLĀRJUNA

Provenance: Sirpur, Raipur District, Madhya Pradesh.
References: A. Cunningham, *ASR*, xvii, 25-26, pl. XVIII. A; F. Kielhorn, *IA*, xviii, 179-81; Hira Lal, *ICPB*, 98, No. 173; Bhandarkar's *List*, No. 1655, S N. Rajaguru, *IO*, iv, 91-94.
Language: Sanskrit. In verse with the exception of the invocatory formula at the beginning.
Metres: Verses 1-12: *Anuṣṭubh*.
Script: Early Nāgarī of the northern class.
Date: About the middle of the eighth century A.D.

TEXT[1]

1 ओं[2] नमः शिवाय ।। पायादालिङ्गिता युष्मान्क[ण्ठ]मेचकरोचिषा । शम्भोर्[र्भ]–
2 स्माङ्गरागस्य च्छाया कृ[ष्णा त]³नुच्छविः ।।[१।।*] आसीदुदयनो नाम नृपः [श]–
3 शधरान्वयः । अभूद्व (द्व) लभिदा तुल्यस्तस्मादिन्द्रव (ब) लो व (ब) ली ।।[२।।*] ततः श्री–
4 नन्नदेवोभूतभिमानमहोदयः । पूर्ण्णीनन्नेश्वराख्यो यश्चकारोर्व्वीं[शि]–
5 वालयैः ।।[३।।*] चन्द्रगुप्तो भुवो गोप्ता तस्य जज्ञे सुतोत्तमः । तत[:]
6 श्री हर्षगुप्तो भूज [गद्ध]⁴ र्षं निव (ब) न्धन[म्] ।।[४।।*] तस्याजनिष्टेष्टरणः
7 **शिवगुप्तो** महीपतिः । धनुर्व्विज्ञानमुख्यो यः ख्यातो **वा (बा) ला**–
8 **र्जुनाख्यया** ।।[५।।*] श्यामामसिलतां संख्ये कृत्वा यः करसङ्गिनीं (नीम्) ।
9 प्रियामिवालङ्कुरुते मत्तमातङ्गमौक्तिकैः ।।[६।।*] यस्य निर्ज्जित्य निर्ज्जित्य
10 सुभृत्य इव सायकैः । व्युत्थित राजकमिव स्त्रैणमर्प्पयति
11 स्मरः ।।[७।।*] तस्य भृत्य[वि]शेषोस्ति नागदेवो द्विजोत्तमः । केशवश्च
12 कलोदग्रो व्यग्रः सुकृतकर्म्मभिः ।।[८।।*] ताभ्यां संभूय साधुभ्यां गृही–
13 त्वा वित्तविस्तरैः । सर्व्वश्रीपुरवासिभ्यो मालिकेभ्यस्त्रिशूलिने ।।[९।।*]कृ–
14 [त्स्न]⁵ किल्विषविघ्नाय कष्टापत्प्रतिघातिने । पुरुषप्रमाणं दत्तं कुसु–
15 मस्रक्ष (च) तुष्टय [ं] (यम्) ।।[१०।।*] एतदामेदिनीनाशादामौदान्मदषट्पदम् । अस्तु
16 षट्पदकण्ठस्य श्रीकण्ठस्यार्च्चनाकृते ।।[११।।*] प्रशस्तिमतनोदेतां वैद्य
17 श्रीदेवनन्दिनः । श्रीकृष्णनन्दी तनयो नयप्रणयकेतनं (नम्) ।।[१२।।*]

1. The text is copied from *IA*, xviii, 180. Pl. XVIII.A in *ASR*, xvii, is not quite dependable.
2. Expressed by a symbol. But in *ASR*, xvii, pl. XVIII.A, it looks like *siddham*.
3. These *akṣaras* have become almost completely illegible.
4. These letters are almost entirely effaced.
5. This *akṣara* has become almost completely illegible.

ABSTRACT

The record opens with the famous Śaiva *mantra* paying obeisance to god Śiva. The opening stanza invokes the protection of the hue of the body of god Śambhu, who covers his body with the ashes, which is darkened by a shadow, encircled as it is by the dark blue lustre of his neck. Next follows the description of the ruling family to which **Śivagupta** belonged. It is said (v. 2) that in the family of the moon (*i.e.*, lunar race) there flourished a king named Udayana. From him was born the mighty Indrabala who was equal to the destroyer of the demon Bala (*i.e.*, Indra).[6] From him sprang Nannadeva, also known as Nanneśvara, who filled the earth with the temples of Śiva (v. 3). His son was Candragupta from whom sprang Harṣagupta (v. 4). To the latter was born **Śivagupta** who, because of his excellence in archery, was also famous by the appellation of **Bālārjuna** (v. 5). The following two stanzas make vague allusions to his victories over enemies in battles. Brāhmaṇa Nāgadeva and Keśava, the latter described as highly proficient in arts, were his servants (v. 8). They together acquired for abundant money four flower-garlands of the measure of man's height from all the gardeners residing at Śrīpura and gave them to the trident-bearer (*i.e.*, Śiva) for the worship of the (Lord) Śrīkaṇṭha (*i.e.*, Śiva) to last until the destruction of the earth (vv. 9-11).

This eulogy was composed by one Kṛṣṇanandin,[7] son of the physician Devanandin (v. 12).

6. The comparison with the Bala-destroying Indra is evidently suggested by the two components (Indra and Bala) of the king's name.
7. Kṛṣṇanandin is not known from any other record.

III: XIV

SIRPUR GANDHEŚVARA TEMPLE INSCRIPTION OF THE TIME OF ŚIVAGUPTA BĀLĀRJUNA[1]

Provenance: Gandheśvara Temple, Sirpur, Raipur District, Madhya Pradesh.

References: Beglar, *ASR*, vii, 169; A. Cunningham, *ibid.*, xvii, 26 and Pl. XVIII. B, lines 10-15; Henry Cousens, *ASI*, *AR*, Western Circle, 1904, 22; D.R. Bhandarkar, *ibid.*, 49-50, No. 2016; F. Kielhorn, *IA*, xviii; 179; Hira Lal, *ICPB*, 97-99, No. 173; S.L. Katare, *IHQ*, xxxiii, 129-34 and plate opposite p. 232; Ajay Mitra Shastri, *VIJ*, xvii, 200-202.

Language: Sanskrit. The preserved portion is in verse throughout.

Metres: Verses 1-5: *Anuṣṭubh.*

Script: Early Nāgarī of the northern class.

Date: About the middle of the eighth century A.D.

TEXT[2]

1 [सिद्धं][3] [।*] धारितं येन गंगाया:[4] श्रृंगोच्चं पतनाद्भुवि:(वि) [।*] जटाविटपसंस्थेन स हरः पातु वो

2 भवा[त्][5] ॥[१॥*] राज्ञः[6] श्री**शिवगुप्तस्य** विजिते[7] यस्य ईदृशाः [।*] सन्ति सन्ता(न्त)श्च धर्म्मंज्ञा:[8] पर—

3 लोकपरायणाः ॥[२॥*] भक्त्याहितेन मनसा जोर्ज्जराकेन तेन वै । [गन्ध]र्व्वेश्वरपूजा[र्थं] कु–

4 सुमं प्रतिपादितं(तम्) ॥[३॥उ][उ]च्चपौरुषप्रामाण्यं—⏑—प्रथितं शुचि । पु[ष्पं]—⏑⏑

5 —दिव्यं सुगन्धं सुमनोर[म](मम्) ॥[४॥*] मालाकाराश्च[9] यावन्तः(न्तो) नवहट्टनिवासिन:[10] ।

1. This inscription is inscribed on a stone-slab fixed to the wall of the Gandheśvara temple at Sirpur in continuation of another record which also appears to have belonged to the time of the Pāṇḍavavaṁśin king Śivagupta. The first nine lines on this stone represent the concluding portion of that record while the succeeding lines contain the beginning of the other inscription. S.L. Katare, who published them, has mixed them up. But we think it more reasonable to publish them as separate records.
2. From the plate in *IHQ*, xxxiii, facing p. 230.
3. Expressed by a symbol. Katare: *Om*.
4. Katare: गङ्गाया:°.
5. Katare: जना[न्].
6. Katare: राजा.
7. Katare: विजिता.
8. Katare: धर्मज्ञ:.
9. Katare: मालाकारश्च.
10. Katare: नवहट्टा निवासिना.

6 वोढव्या: कुसुमग्रामा:[11] [या]वच्च[न्द्रां]र्कतारका: ।।[५।।*]

ABSTRACT

What is preserved is only the initial portion of an inscription; but it is enough to give a clear idea of its purport. It commences with the auspicious word *siddham*, expressed symbolically, which is followed by a stanza invoking the favour of god Śiva, referred to as Hara, who is described as bearing the stream of the Gaṅgā on his matted locks of hair (v. 1). Next is mentioned the reigning King **Śivagupta** whose dominions are said to be full of people well-versed in *dharma* and devoted to acts leading to the other world, *i.e.*, heaven (v. 2). Last comes the purport of the epigraph which was to record that a certain Jorjjarāka[12] instituted the offering of a flower-garland, measuring a *puruṣa* in height, for the worship of the god Gandharveśvara[13] (vv. 3-4). Flowers for this purpose were to be supplied, as long as the moon, the sun and the stars last, by all the garland-makers residing at Navahaṭṭa[14] (v. 5).

It must be admitted that this portion is not quite clear in the facsimile accompanying Katare's paper, but the reading suggested above is the only one grammatically correct and should be preferred to that suggested by Katare.

11. There is a superfluous letter before *grā*.
12. Hira Lal gives the name as Jejuraka.
13. This shows that the original name of the temple was Gandharveśvara and that the modern name, Gandheśvara, is a contraction from it.
14. It was either a village situated very close to Sirpur on a newly established market place at Sirput itself. Another inscription on a stone slab built into the floor of the entrance of the Gandheśvara temple mentions Pranavahaṭṭaka, again in connection with the gardeners (*ICPB*, 98). This Pranavahaṭṭaka is apparently the same as Navahaṭṭa of the present record.

III : XV

SENKAPAT STONE SLAB[1] INSCRIPTION OF THE TIME OF ŚIVAGUPTA BĀLĀRJUNA

Provenance: Senkapat, Raipur District, Madhya Pradesh.

References: M.G. Dikshit and D.C. Sircar, *EI*, xxxi, 31-36 and plate opposite p. 34; V.V. Mirashi, *ibid.*, xxxiii, 251-54; D.C. Sircar, *ibid.*, xxxiii, 255-56; S.N. Rajaguru, *IO*, iv, 47-54.

Language: Sanskrit. In verse, with the exception of the introductory religious formula, i.e. *namaḥ Śivāya*.

Metres: Verses 1, 3-4, 6, 9-11, 13, 19, 24 and 29: *Vasantatilakā*; Verse 2: *Sragdharā*; Verses 5, 8 and 12: *Śārdūlavikrīḍita;* Verses 7, 18, 21, 27-28 and 30: *Āryā*; Verse 14: *Mālinī*; Verses 15-17, 20, 22-23 and 25-26: *Anuṣṭubh*.

Script: Early Nāgarī of the northern class.

Date: About the middle of the eighth century A.D.

TEXT[2]

1 सिद्धम् ।[×][3] नमः शिवाय ।। उद्वेल्लनातिभरनिर्भरहस्तषण्डचण्डाभिघातरभसोत्पल(त)द्
द्रिजालैः । यः कन्दुकैरिव कृतातुल[त]ालकेलिर्न्नृत्ते व(ब)भौ स भवभिद्भवताद्भवो वः
।।[१।।*। निर्द्दग्धोप्यत्र ने–

2 त्रज्वलनक[व]लनैस्तावकीनैर्म्मनोभूर्भूयो जन्मानुयाने गमित इति रुषा रुक्षितेन त्वयेयं (यम) ।
किं भोः शम्भो रणाम्भोनि[धि[मधिशयिता त्यज्ज्यते लज्ज्यते नो श्रृंङ्गीति प्रोक्तिकारी रि–

3 पुरशभि यया सावतात्पार्व्वती वः ।।[२।।*] शीताङशुवङश[4] विमलाम्व (म्ब)रपूर्णचन्द्रश-
चन्द्राङशु[5]निर्म्मलयशः प्रकट[ा]ट्टहासः । राजास्त्युपार्ज्जितसमूर्ज्जितभक्तिभार–
भावातिभावितशिवः **शिवगुप्तना**–

4 मा ।।[३।।*] यस्य प्रतापनमितोन्नतवीरचक्रचक्रप्रहारहतवैरिचमूचस्यस्य । श्रीसङ्गसङ्गल-
दुरुप्रमदस्य विष्णो**र्व्वा(र्बा)लार्ज्जुन**त्वमलमुन्नतियुक्तमुक्तं(क्तम्) ।।[४।।*] [न] व्या[सी]
विषयोपभोगगरिमा राजा द्विज–

5 न्माग्रणीर्न्नाम्ना श्रीशिवरक्षितः क्षितितलोद्भासी विवस्वानभूत(त्) । पद्मोद्भासन-

1. The slab, which is well-dressed, is of Vindhyan sandstone, reddish buff in colour. Rectangular in shape, it measures about 20" in length, 18" in width and 3" in thickness. It must have originally been fixed into one of the walls of the Śiva temple which the inscription engraved on it aims at recording.
2. From plate in *EI*, xxxi, facing p. 34.
3. Expressed by a symbol.
4. Read **शीतांशुवंश**°.
5. Read **चन्द्रांशु**°.

निर्भराद्भुतरुचिर्द्दोषोज्झितः सर्व्वदा सर्व्वाकारपरोपकारकरणव्यग्रीभवद्विग्रहः ॥[५॥*]
तस्माद् भूद् भुवनमण्डलमण्डनश्री (श्रीः)

6 श्रीदेवरक्षित इति प्रथितः पृथिव्यां(व्याम्)। श्रीनन्नराज इति गीततनोन्नृपस्य विश्वास-
भूमिरिह यो हृदयोपमानः ॥[६॥*] यो विन्ध्यधूद्र्धृ (द्ध्र्)रत्वं[5a] वरदातटपरिहृतां(तं)[5b]
च संप्राप्य। संप्राप्तवानिह यशोभाण्डागाराख्यया ख्या–

7 ति[6](तिम्)। [॥७॥*] अस्मादेव शशाङ्कशुद्धयशसः श्रीनन्नराजाख्याया विख्यातान्नरनाथ-
नाथतिलकाद्भूरिप्रसादोदयैः। संप्राप्तैर्व्विषयैश्चयस य विकृतिर्न्नाल्पाप्यभूदल्पकाः कम्पन्ते
[हि] समृद्धि [भिर्न्न] तु महौदार्यातिधै–

8 [र्या]त्मकाः॥[८॥*] तस्य प्रशस्यविकसद्गुणरत्नराजिसंराजिताविकललोकविलोकितस्य।
पुत्रोत्तमोस्त्यमलशीलधनाधिकश्रीः श्रीदुर्ग्गरक्षि[त] इति प्रथिताभिधानः[7] ॥ [९॥*] **बा**
[बा]लार्ज्जुनाख्यगुणमुख्यनराधिराजसंरा–

9 जदङ्घ्रि[8]कमलास्पदषट्पदोपि। क्षेपीय एव य इहोज्झितकृष्णपक्षः प[क्षैः] सितैश्चरति शोभि-
शुभाभिधानैः॥ [१०॥*] भक्त्या प्रणम्य न परं प[र]मेश्वरस्य रूपं निरूपयति वेश्मनि [लोच]
नाभ्यां (भ्याम्)। ध्यानात्मकैश्च

10 नयनैरतिनिश्चलैर्यो वर्यो विलोकयति शम्भुमयीं त्रिलोकीं (कीम्)॥ [११॥*] अर्थिभ्योपि
कृपान्वि(वि)लब्धि(ब्धि)विकसत्प्रीतिप्रदत्तैर्द्धनैर्द्धन्येनातिशयेन [येन] महती धर्म्मस्य
वृद्धिः कृता। आत्मीयैरतिनिश्चलैरविरलैर्ज्जे–

11 गीयमानैर्ग्गुणैरक्षिप्तैरपि सर्व्वतः प्रविसृतैरापूरिता मेदिनी। [१२॥*] [ते]नैतदायतनमायत-
भक्तिपूरसंपूरणा[ति]भरनिर्भरभावभाजा। अन्तर्गतातुलमहेश्वररूपर–

12 म्यमात्मोपमानमसमानमकारि शम्भोः ॥[१३॥*] प्रचलमवनिपालाः सर्व्वभस्मत्समानं
शुभमशुभभिदेकं निश्च[लं] तत्कुरुद्ध्वं (ध्वम्)। इति गदितुमिवोच्चैर्यस्य शम्योपशोभा

13 भवति पवनपातान्दोललोला ध्वजाली॥ [१४॥*] गुडशर्करकग्रामे [शा]सनेनोपपा[दि]ता।
द्विहली मदनारातेरत्रकृ[ष्ण]तल्लान्विता॥ [१५॥*] आसीत्सद्यःशिवाचार्यः श्रीमान्वर्य–

14 स्तपोवतां (ताम्)। श्रीमदामर्द्धकख्याततपोवनविनिर्ग्गतः॥ [१६॥*] श्रीमान्सदाशिवाचा-
[र्य]स्तस्यास्तिस्तुतिभाग् भुवि । भ्रातृप्र[शि]ष्यतिलकस्तिलकः शमधारिणां (णाम्)॥
[१७॥*] यो रविरन्यो मा–

15 न्यो राज्ञाति जगतीतलेस्तसंतापः। दोषोदयेप्यमन्दं भिन्दन्नज्ञानतिमिर मलं (लम्)॥ [१८॥*]
तस्यै (स्मै) तदायतनमर्प्पितमादरेण श्रीदुर्ग्गरक्षित इति प्रथितेन तेन। शिष्यप्रशिष्यप–

16 रिपाटिवशेन भोक्तुमाचन्द्रकालमनुपालयितुं च सम्यक् ॥[१९॥*] तस्य कृष्णतलोपेतं
शासनेन प्रकल्पितं (तम्)। कोडासीमाख्यया ख्याते ग्रामे द्विहलिकाद्वयं(यम्)॥ [२०॥*]
ग्रामे वियाण–

17 काख्ये द्वि(हली) द्विहली तथा सकृष्णतला। शासनविधिना विहिता लाटे श्रीपर्णिकाग्रामे
॥[२१॥*][9]

5a Mirashi: विन्ध्यधूद्घृ(द्धं)रत्वं, 5b Mirashi. वरदातट (or, rather कट) फलि(णि) हृतां.

6. Dikshit and Sircar: ख्याति°.
7. Dikshit and Sircar: प्रथाभिधानः.
8. Read संराजदङ्घ्रि°.
9. The first part of the inscription concluding with this stanza ends about the middle of this line the remainder of which is left blank.

18 [10]आषाढे कार्त्तिके मासे माघे च प्रतिवत्सरं(रम्) । पौर्ण्णमास्यां विधातव्यो विधिर्यागस्य यत्नत : ॥[२२॥*] निर्व्वाण [द] क्षरीक्षाया व्याख्यायाः समयस्य च । सत्रमत्र

19 विधानीयमन्नस्यच तपोधनैः ॥[२३॥*] वृद्ध्यर्थमर्थमसृजद्भिरपास्तरोवैरीशोपदेशकुशलैः कुशलैः शुभेषु । स्थेयं तपस्विभिरिह प्रशमाप्तिदीप्तिदीप्तात्मभिर्गुरुदयाद्द्र–

20 मनोमनोज्ञैः ॥[२४॥*] आ[च्च] सम्वमयीं[10a]गर्त्तामुत्तराशासमाश्रितां (ताम्) । यावच्छि-वसमुद्रं च दक्षिणस्यां दिशि स्थिरं(रम्) ॥[२५॥*] पूर्व्वपश्चिम[दि] ग्भागभागिमार्ग्ग-द्वयावधिः । तलपाटक इत्येषा

21 स्थितिरत्त्र नियोजिता ॥[२६॥*] आयुर्व्वायुविलोलं निवृतिधनं[11] चावबु (बु)द्ध्य वु(बु) द्धिधनैः । अशुभच्छिच्छुभमीहक्कामं पाल्यं च कृतमपरैः ॥[२७॥*] असमसमीरसमीरण[र] णदम्भोम्भोधिपूरपरि–

22 पूर्ण्णं (र्णम्) । न भवति यावद् भुवनं भवभवनं तावदिदमास्तां(स्ताम्) ॥ [२८॥*] श्री दुर्गरक्षितगुणेक्षणतत्क्षणोद्यदानन्दपूरपरिपूरितचित्तवृ[त्ति]: । श्रीतारदत्ततनयः श्रुतविश्रुतश्री श्रीमान् सुमङ्ग–

23 ल इमामकरोत् प्रशस्ति (स्तिम्) ॥ [२९॥*] ऋषिगणनाम्नः सूनुः सूत्रधृतः सकलकर्म्म-कृतिकृतिनः । उदकिरदिमां प्रशस्तिं वासुगणो गुणगणोन्नतिमान् ॥ [३०॥*] ॥[12]

ABSTRACT

The epigraph opens with the auspicious symbol for *siddham*, followed by the well-known formula (*namaḥ Śivāya*) paying obeisance to lord Śiva. Verse 1 invokes the blessings of god Bhava (Śiva)[13] and verse 2 of his spouse, the goddess Pārvatī.[14] Next is introduced the reigning king Śivagupta who is spoken of as belonging to the Śītāṁśu-vaṁśa (*i.e.*, the lunar dynasty) and as a devout worshipper of lord Śiva (v. 3). Verse 4 refers to him by his other name Bālārjuna and he is described as an incarnation of god Viṣṇu.[15] Next

10. The space for about six or seven letters at the beginning of this line has been left blank, probably to mark the beginning of the second part.

10*a*. The reading of the *akṣara* within parenthesis and the meaning of this word are uncertain.

11. Read निर्वृति° for the sake of meaning though it disturbs the metre.

12. There is a *tha*- like symbol between the double *daṇḍas*. It is found at the end of several records (e.g. *EI*, xviii, 298, text-line 30; xix, 81, text-line 41) and, like *cha* (*ibid.*, xxiii, 140-41, text-lines 4 and 15; xxv, 63, text-line 94; xxv, 221, text-line 141; xxx, 219, text-line 12) and a symbol midway between these two letters, denotes the conclusion of a record. *Cha* is recognised as a concluding mark in the *Śāsvatakośa* (Poona, 1930), 74; Śriharṣa's *Naiṣadhīya-carita*. xvi·98, and Hemacandra's *Ekākṣarakośa*, v. 13. See *JOI*, iii, 368; A.N. Jani, *Śrīharṣa's Naiṣhadhīya-charita: A Study*, *EI*, xxx, 218, note 2; *IE*, 94; *IEG*, 72.

13. There is an allusion in this stanza to the dance of Śiva in which the god plays with mountain-chains, as if with balls, which are uprooted by his swiftly moving arms.

14. This verse alludes to the legend of the burning of the god of love by Śiva with the fire emanating from his (third) eye.

15. Śivagupta is compared to Viṣṇu, for, like the latter, who had destroyed the host of enemy forces by hurling his *cakra* (discuss), Śivagupta had also subdued the circle (*cakra*) of arrogant brave men (*i.e.*, enemies) and had acquired *śrī* (royal fortune) even as goddess Śrī was Viṣṇu's consort. Kṛṣṇa's association with the epic hero Arjuna is also perhaps intended to be hinted at.

is mentioned a Brāhmaṇa called Śivarakṣita, who is styled king (*rājan*) and probably governed the district known as Navyāsī-viṣaya[16] (v.5). His son was Devarakṣita who earned the confidence and favour of king Nannarāja[17] (v. 6). He obtained, evidently from king Nannarāja, the governorship of the Vindhyan territory extending as far as the banks of the river Varadā[18] and became famous by the appellation Yaśobhāṇḍāgāra (v. 7). From this very 'king of kings' (*naranātha-nātha*) called Nannarāja he obtained many districts, evidently as a fief or for governing them (v. 8). His son was Durgarakṣita (v. 9), who was a devoted servant of king Bālārjuna and a devout devotee of god Śambhu, *i.e.*, Śiva (vv. 10-11). He built a unique temple of Śambhu (v. 13).[19] In the following verse mention is made of a row of flags on wooden posts, probably set up around the temple, fluttering with wind (v. 14). Two *halas*[20] of black-soil land in the village Guḍaśarkaraka[20a] were given away, evidently to this temple, by means of a charter (*śāsana*) (v. 15).[21] Next we are introduced to a Śaiva ascetic named Sadyaḥśivācārya who hailed from the penance-grove called Āmarddaka[22] (v. 16). Next is mentioned another

16. Navyāsī-viṣaya has not been located so far nor it is likely to be located as it appears to have denoted a district comprising eighty-nine villages. It was evidently a fiscal unit for revenue purposes situated in or near South Kosala and may be compared to several districtnames accompanied by figures.
17. We know of two kings named Nannarāja in the Pāṇḍuvaṁśa of South Kosala, *viz.*, (i) father of Mahāśiva Tivara and (ii) the latter's son known from his incomplete Aḍhabhāra plates (*ante*, III: V). As Durgarakṣita was a contemporary of Śivagupta Bālārjuna, Nannarāja of this inscription, who patronised Durgarakṣita's father Devarkaṣita, can only be identified with the second of the two Nannarājas.
18. It has been identified with the modern Wardha after which the well-known town of that name has been christened.
19. The slab bearing this inscription was evidently affixed to this temple.
20. *Hala* as a measure of land is frequently mentioned in literature and inscriptions. It on is variously defined in literature (*cf.* Hārīta quoted by *Sarvajñārāyaṇa* and Kullūka *Manu-smṛti*, vii· 119), indicating thereby that different kinds of *hala* measure were prevalent in different parts of the country and in different periods. Originally it appears to have signified a piece of land ploughable by a single plough. See my *India as Seen in the Kuṭṭanī-mata of Dāmodaragupta*, 194-95. Also vide *IE*, 134, 411, 417; *IEG*, 125. It is difficult to ascertain the area connoted by the word *hala* in the present context.
20*a*. Dikshit and Sircar hint at the possibility of one of the several villages called Sāṅkrā representing the ancient Guḍaśarkaraka. The village of this name nearest to the provenance of the inscription lies some 13 miles due west of Sirpur. But it is interesting to note that most of the villages mentioned in this record have their liguistically closer parallels in the Chanda district of the Vidarbha region of Maharashtra. For Guḍaśarkaraka, for instance, we have a village called Guḍasellā in the Rajura Tahsil of the Chanda District.
21. The charter, through which this plot of land was granted, has yet to be discovered. This piece of land is probably referred to as *tala-pāṭaka* in v. 26.
22. Āmardaka figures as an important place in connection with a line of Śaiva ascetics. In a stone inscription from Ranod, the spiritual predecessor of Purandara, the founder of the famous Mattamayūra line of Śaiva ascetics, is styled *Āmardaka-tīrtha-nātha*, *i e..*, lord of the *tīrtha* called Āmardaka (*EI*, i 355, verse 9). He had evidently established himself at Āmardaka. The Rajor inscription of Maṭhanadeva (*ibid.*, iii, 266, text-line 13) informs us that Āmardaka was the home of a line of the

Śaiva ascetic named Sadāśivācārya, who appears to have been Sadyaḥśivācārya's spiritual successor but is apparently described as the foremost of his brother's grand-disciples (v. 17). The temple was dedicated to him and his spiritual successors by Durgarakṣita for enjoyment and protection as long as the moon would endure (v. 19). Sadāśivācārya also received black-soil land measuring four *halas* in the village Koḍasīmā[23] which was made over to him by means of a charter (v. 20). Likewise two other plots of black-soil land, each of two *hala* measures, one in the village named Viyāṇaka[24] and the other at the place called Lāṭa[24a] within the village of Śrīparṇikā[25], were also given away to him (v. 21).

The next three stanzas mention certain obligations which the Śaiva ascetics had to fulfil. They were expected to arrange a sacrificial rite (*yāga*), the ceremony of initiation (*dīkṣā*) into the Śaiva faith, described as capable of securing final beatitude (*nirvāṇa-dakṣa*), the exposition of the Śaiva doctrine (*samaya*) and a free feeding house (*annasya sattram*) every year on the full moon day of the months of Āṣāḍha, Kārttika and Māgha (vv. 22-23). The ascetics were required to reside in the temple and were prohibited from taking to money-lending on interest (v. 24).

The boundaries of the *tala-pāṭaka*[25a] (gift-land) are defined in the next two

---

Śaiva *ācāryas* of the Sopurīya clan. Thus, Āmardaka was a prominent centre of the Śaiva Siddhānta school to which the Mattamayūra clan belonged. But it has not yet been identified satisfactorily. It has been held on the basis of a stanza from Brahmaśambhu's *Pañjikā* and some other considerations that it was situated in western Malwa. See *CII*, iv, clii. This view was once accepted by me also. See my *Tripurī*, 98. However, the Rāñjaṇā (Parbhani District) stone inscription of *Mahāmaṇḍaleśvara* Āmaṇadeva (Brahmanand Deshpande, *Śodhamudrā* (Marathi), 57) and the Ardhapur stone inscription of the Raṭṭa chief Ballāla (N.S. Pohnerkar, *Raṭṭavaṁśīya Ballāla yācā Ardhāpūra Śilālekha*) seem to favour its identification with Auṇḍhā Nāga- nātha (Parbhani District) which is known for its *jyotirliṅga.*

23. Dikshit and Sircar propose to identify it with a village called Korāsī, about two miles to the south-west of Sāṅkrā which lies about thirteen miles due west of Sirpur. But there is also a village called Koḍasī in the Rajura tahsil of the Chandrapur District.

24. It may be identified with modern village called Bināguḍā in the Sironcha tahsil of the Chandrapur District.

24*a*. It is probably represented by modern Lāṭa (Jhorā) in the Gadachiroli tahsil of the Chandrapur District.

25. It appears to be represented by modern Sivanapallī in the Sironcha tahsil of the Chandrapura District. Alternatively it may be identified with Sironcha itself.

25*a*. Here the term obviously refers to the gift-land mentioned in verse 15. Sometimes also spelt as *tala-vāṭaka* (Paharpur copper-plate grant of the Gupta year 159, *EI*, xx, 62 and 63, text-lines 14 and 18), it has been taken to denote 'the land granted for the maintenance of a temple or deity at the time of its consecration' (*IEG*, 333 and 335). It is evidently the same as *tala-bhoga* (*IA*, vii, 212, text-lines 44 and 48) and *tala-vṛtti* (Bankapur inscription of Someśvara I and Kadamba Arikesarin, *EI*, xiii, 171, text-line 35; Sudi plates of Someśvara I, *ibid.*, xv, 89, text-line 41; Sudi plates of Someśvara II, *ibid.*, 98, text-line 27; Gawarwad inscription of the time of Someśvara II, *ibid.*, 340, text-line 18, verse 8; Narendra inscription of the time of Vikramāditya VI and Jayakeśin II, *ibid.*, xiii, 308, text-line 111; Lakshmeshwar inscription, *IA*, vii, stanzas (vv. 25-26). On the north it was bordered by a pit, on the south by Śiva-samudra, probably a tank known by this name, and on the east and west by two roads. Verse 27 asks the intelligent people to realise the ephemeral character of life and protect the pious acts done by others, while the following stanza prays that the temple of god Bhava (Śiva) may endure till the end of this creation.

This eulogy (*praśasti*) was composed by Sumaṅgala, who was probably under the employment of Durgarakṣita, son of Tāradatta, and was engraved by Vāsugaṇa, son of the *sūtradhāra* Ṛṣigaṇa (vv. 29-30).[26]

105, text-lines 34-5, etc.) found mentioned in connection with land-grants in numerous inscriptions from different parts of the country, more particularly South India. As used in the Arjunawada inscription of Yādava Kannara, it has been taken as a tax (*EI*, xxi, 14, text-line 55). In the Deo-Baranark inscription of Jīvitagupta II (*CII*, iii, 216, text-line 7) *talavāṭaka* appears in the list of officials, and Bhagwanlal Indraji compared it to the modern *talāṭī* or *talāṭhī* and accordingly took it to mean 'the village accountant' (*ibid.*, 217, fn. 8). According to D.C. Sircar (*IEG*, 334), it denotes 'possibly the superintendent of temple property'. For Tala-pāṭaka as a place-name, see *EI*, xxi, 52, verse 4.

26. Vāsugaṇa, who engraved the record, and the poet Sumaṅgala, responsible for composing the *praśasti*, also figure in identical roles in some other inscriptions of the time of Śivagupa Bālārjuna. See *supra*, no. III: XII and *infra*, appendix II.

APPENDIX I

A FRAGMENTARY SIRPUR GANDHEŚVARA TEMPLE INSCRIPTION

This inscription, which is incised just above *ante,* III: XIV, appears to be the concluding portion of a record which is styled *praśasti.* Its initial portion has been lost irretrievably, and at present only the concluding nine lines comprising five stanzas are extant. Even of these, the whole of the first line and a few initial letters of the following line have become completely indistinct. The extant portion contains only some admonitory stanzas and supplies the names of the composer and the engraver. Of the opening verse in the extant portion only a few words are preserved and consequently their import cannot be made out. The import of the second stanza is also not quite clear, but it appears to threaten hell and other sufferings, evidently to those who might obstruct the enjoyment of the grant recorded in this epigraph. The next verse points to the ephemeral character of the world and exhorts people to perform pious acts as well as protect similar acts of others. The eulogy was composed by one Sumaṅgala, son of Tāradatta (v. 4), and incised by a certain Vāsugaṇa, son of the *sūtradhāra* Ṛṣigaṇa (v. 5).

Unfortunately, the purport of the record cannot be made out from the extant portion, but it was obviously to record some grant in favour of the Gandharveśvara temple. The name of the monarch during whose reign the inscription was incised is lost irretrievably in the lost portion. However, the composer and the engraver of the *praśasti* are known to have played the same role in some other records of the time of the Pāṇḍuvaṁśin king Śivagupta Bālārjuna. Moreover, as stated earlier, this epigraph is engraved immediately above another record of Śivagupta. These facts seem to indicate that this inscription also belongs to the same king. The details of references, language and script are the same as those concerning the record incised just below it.[1]

The text of the inscription is given below.

TEXT[2]

1 [3]— — ⏑ —⏑⏑⏑—⏑⏑—⏑—⏑——⏑—⏑⏑⏑—⏑⏑—⏑
—[।] ——⏑ —⏑⏑⏑

1. S.L. Katare, who edited this inscription originally, mixed it up with *ante*, III: XIII (see *IHQ*, xxxiii, 229-34 and plate facing p. 230). But as these are two distinct inscriptions they are published here separately. This inscription has been reedited by us in *VIJ.* xvii, 198-200.
2. From facsimile published in *IHQ*, xxxiii.
3. As stated by Katare himself in the impression published by him there is no trace of line 1, while Cunningham's photograph shows a few letters at the end. The next line contains only a few *akṣaras* of this stanza, a major portion of which was evidently contained

2 —⏑⏑—⏑—सम्पादिताभिमता [भोगभु]जो भवन्ति ।।[१।।*] यः कीर्त्तिभिर्भवति मोहि–

3 ⏑—[शरी][4]रमारोप्यते स नरके नरकेश्वरेण। ज्वालाकलापकपिलाकुलदेहिदेह–

4 माहार[वह्नि[5]] भरनिर्भरवह्निमेव ।। [२।।*] इत्याकलय्य सकलं सं(स)कलं च लोकमालोक्य

5 [वा]रि[6]हतवारिधिवारिलोलं(लम्) । सर्व्वादरेण सुकृतं कृतिभिर्विधेयमन्यैः[7] कृतं च

6 सततं परिपालनीयं (यम्) ।।[३।।*] एतद्गुणानणुमणिस्फुरणाभिवृद्धिवर्द्धिष्णुजिष्णु–[8]

7 परितोषवशाव(द्)शाङ्गं(गम्) । श्रीतारदत्ततनन्वयः प्रथितः श्रुतेन श्रीमान्सुमङ्गल

8 इमामकरोत् प्रशस्ति(स्तिम्)।। [४।।*] उत्कीर्ण्णवानृषिगण[स्य] गुणौद्यमुख्यसत्सूत्रधारसुत–

9 वासुगणः प्रशस्ति(स्तिम्) । अन्यस्तथा च सुर[9]रोधविधत्सयेव हा[10](ह्या)त्मस्तवं निज-
गुणैर्द्विगुणैस्तनोति ।।[५।।*]

---

in the first line. Katare thinks that in the beginning of the first line there was invocation of some deity (*ibid.*, 233, fn. 3). However, as the upper portion of the epigraph forms only the concluding portion of a record, the initial portion of which is not preserved, there is no room here for any invocation which is found normally at the beginning of a record.

4. Katare leaves out these two letters as illegible.
5. The reading of these letters, which have been left out as illegible by Katare, is very doubtful.
6. These two *akṣaras* are left out undeciphered by Katare.
7. Katare: विधेयं मंत्रैः
8. Katare relegates the last two letters to the next line whereas they actually form the concluding portion of this line.
9. In the text Katare leaves unread the four *akṣaras* following *sta* but suggests to read the relevant portion as अन्यस्तथा च भव° which undoubtedly gives better meaning than the reading given by us. However, the facsimile seems to support the reading given above.
10. **Katare: या.**

APPENDIX II

A STRAY PLATE OF ŚIVAGUPTA, YEAR 57

Sometime back Dr. I. Karthikeya Sarma of the Archaeological Survey of India invited my attention to a stray copper-plate found at the village of Burhikhar near Malhar in the Janjgir Tahsil of the Bilaspur District in Madhya Pradesh. The plate, which was found in possession of a school teacher at Malhar, is now deposited with the Temple Survey Project (Southern Circle), Madras. At my request, the then Chief Epigraphist, Dr G.S. Gai, supplied me with an excellent impression of the plate from which it is edited here.

The **plate** measures 21.5 cms. long and 14.2 cms. broad and is 0.3 cm. thick. Its weight is 730 grammes. There is a hole, measuring about 2 cms. in diameter, on the left margin of the plate through which a copper-ring meant to keep the plates of the charter in their proper position must have passed. The plate is engraved on one side only, the other side being blank. Its edges are not raised for the protection of the writing on it. However, the writing, which comprises only eight lines, is well-preserved. A perusal of the text on this plate as also the fact that it bears writing only on the inner face leaves no doubt that this is the last plate of a record which was probably engraved on three plates. The ring, which held the plates together, and the seal, if it was affixed to the ring, are now missing.

The **characters** bear a close resemblance to those of the other records in the box-headed alphabet, more particularly to those of the Pāṇḍuvaṁśins. Attention may, however, be invited to the use of *avagraha* in line 7 and of the decimal notation in the figure of 30 in line 8. As regards orthography, mention may be made of the use of *b* for *v*, occasional reduplication of the consonant following *r*, the use of *anusvāra* for final *m* and, sometimes, the use of *m* for *ṁ*.

The **language** of the record is Sanskrit.

The portion of the text engraved on this plate comprises the four admonitory and benedictory stanzas usually found at the end of copper-plate charters besides the concluding word of another such verse at the beginning of the plate and details about the date and the engraver of the record at the end. The **date** is given as the **30th day of the month of Māgha in the year 57 of 'increasingly victorious reign'.** The regnal year is given both in words and figures. Unfortunately, the name of the king in whose reign the record is dated is not given. The charter is said to have been incised by Nāgadeva, son of Golāryya, who is described as a *tāmra-paṭṭika*, 'engraver of copper-plate charters'.

As stated above, the plate in question is only the last plate of the charter and as such the names of the issuing chief and the dynasty to which he belonged are not known. Only the characters of the record, the date and the findspot can be of some help in this connection.

The inscription, as pointed out above, is incised in box-headed characters. The characters of this variety are known to have been employed in the records of the Gupta (at Eran), the Vākāṭakas, the Kadambas, the Śarabhapurīyas and the Pāṇḍuvaṁśins of South Kosala. The provenance of the record, Burhikhar, which lies in South Kosala, indicates that it has to be assigned either to the Śarabhapurīyas or to the Pāṇḍuvaṁśins. In the *Annual Report of Indian Epigraphy* for 1973-74 it has been sought to be attributed to the Śarabhapurīyas. But this attribution does not appear to be correct. The characters of the inscription are much more elongated and angular than those met with in the Śarabhapurīya records known so far. On the other hand, they bear very close resemblance to those of the undated Mallar plates[1] and the Lodhia plates dated in the 57th year[2] of the last known Pāṇḍuvaṁśin king of South Kosala, Śivagupta Bālārjuna. Moreover, no Śarabhapurīya king is known to have ruled for such a long time as the ruler responsible for issuing the present grant. On the other hand, the Pāṇḍuvaṁśin chief **Śivagupta Bālārjuna** ruled for at least fifty-seven years as we learn from his above-mentioned Lodhia plates. No other Pāṇḍuvaṁśin king had such a long reign. The present record may, therefore, be tentatively, nay, very probably, ascribed to the closing period of the reign of **Śivagupta Bālārjuna**. Another factor, which also precludes its attribution to an early date suitable to the Śarabhapurīyas, is the employment of the decimal notation involving the use of zero in the figure 30 (line 8) which appears comparatively late in Indian epigraphy. It may be pointed out, in this connection, that the figure 30 is given in the decimal notation in the Lodhia plates also.[3]

The Lodhia plates were given on the 30th day of the month of Kārttika whereas the present record is dated on the 30th day of Māgha. Thus the plate published here is dated exactly three months later than the Lodhia plates. This is thus the latest record of the reign of Śivagupta and, for that matter, the latest known inscription of the Pāṇḍuvaṁśin rulers of South Kosala.

The present as well as the Lodhia grant is one of the earliest inscriptions to employ the decimal notation. But the expression of the regnal year 57 in numerical symbols for 50 and 7 points to the transitional phase when both the numerical symbols and decimal notation were in vogue simultaneously. In fact, this state of affairs continued for a long time, and the complete replacement of the numerical symbols by decimal notation was effected long after.

1. See *supra*, Nos. III: IX-X.
2. See *supra*, No. III: VIII.
3. *Supra*, No. III: VIII, text-line 32.

This is the only copper-plate grant of Śivagupta Bālārjuna to name the engraver. Since this record is separated from the Lodhia plates only by a short period of three months, it is not unlikely that the latter were also incised by the same person. Nāgadeva, son of Golāryya, does not figure as an engraver in any other record of the dynasty. One Golāryyabhaṭṭa is, of course, mentioned as a recipient of a gift in the Sirpur Lakṣmaṇa Temple inscription of the time of Śivagupta.[4] But he is evidently different from the homonymous father of the engraver of our record.

TEXT[5]

1 वसेत्[6] । [।*] बहुभिर्ब्ब (र्व्वं) सुधा दत्ता राजभिः सगरादिभिः [।*] यस्य यस्य यदा
2 भूमिस्तस्य तस्य तदा फलं (लम्) । [।*] स्वदत्तां परदत्ताम्बा (त्तां वा) यत्नाद्रक्ष युधिष्ठिर ।
3 महीं महीभृतां श्रेष्ठ दानात् श्रेयो[7]नुपालनं (नम्) ॥ मा भूदफलश–
4 ङ्का वः परदत्वे (त्ते) ति पार्थिवाः [।*] स्वदानात्फलमानन्त्यं पर[8]दा (द) त्तानु–
5 पालने ॥ इति कमलदलाम्बुबिन्दुलोलां श्रियमनुचित्य (न्त्य) मनु–
6 ष्यजीवितं च । सकलमिदमुदाहृतं च बु[द्*]ध्वा न हि पुरुषैः परकीर्तयो विलो–
7 प्याः ॥ **प्रवर्द्धमानविजयराज्यसम्ब (संव) त्सरे सप्तपञ्चाशेऽङ्केनापि सं० ५० ७ मा–**
8 **घदिन ३०**[9] [।*] उत्कि (त्की) र्ण्णं ताम्त्र (म्र) पट्टि (ट्टि) कगोलाय्य (र्य्यं) सु (सू) नुना
नागदेवेनेति ॥[10]

4. *Supra*, No. III: X, verse 41.
5. From the facsimile supplied by the Chief Epigraphist.
6. This is the concluding word of a stanza which runs as follows:
षष्टिवर्षसहस्राणि स्वर्ग्गे मोदति भूमिदः ।
आच्छेत्ता चानुमन्ता च तान्येव नरके वसेत ॥
7. Better read दानाच्छ्रेयो°
8. Originally *rā* was engraved, but later the medial sign for *ā* was erased.
9. Note the simultaneous use of the old and new systems of numerical notations.
10. See for our edition of the record, *VIJ*, xv, 117-20 and plate facing p. 120.

IV

INSCRIPTIONS OF THE SOMAVAṀŚINS

IV : I

VAKRATENTALI[1] GRANT[2] OF MAHĀBHAVAGUPTA I JANAMEJAYA, YEAR 3

Provenance: Former Sonpur State, Sambalpur District, Orissa.

References: B.C. Mazumdar, *EI*, xi, 93-95 and plates opposite pp. 94 and 95; Bhandarkar's List, No. 1557; Ajay Mitra Shastri, *Studies in Indian Epigraphy,* iii, 153-54.

Language: Sanskrit. In prose with the exception of the usual benedictory and imprecatory verses at the end.

Metres: Verses 1-3 and 5-10: *Anuṣṭubh*; Verse 4: *Indravajrā*; Verse 11: *Śālinī*; Verse 12: *Puṣpitāgrā.*

Script: Northern class of alphabets.

Date: Regnal year 3, Śrāvaṇa śukla 5. Last quarter of the ninth century A.D.

TEXT[3]

First Plate

1 सिद्धम्[4] [।*] स्वस्ति [।*] **सुवर्ण्णपुर**समावासितश्रीमतो विजयस्कन्धावारात् पर–
2 मभट्टारकमहाराजाधिराजपरमेश्वरश्रीशिवगुप्तदेवपादानुध्या–
3 तपरममाहेश्वरपरमभट्टारकमहाराजाधिराजपरमेश्वरसो–
4 मकुलतिलकत्(त्रि)कलिङ्गाधिपति श्री **महाभवगुप्तराजदेवः** कुशली
5 लुपत्तराखण्डीयवक्रतेन्तलीग्रामे व्रा(ब्रा)ह्मणान् सम्पूज्य तत्प्र–
6 तिनिवासिकुटुम्वि(म्बि)नस्त [द्वि]षयीययथाकालाध्यासिनः समाहर्त्तृ स–
7 न्निधातृ (तृ) दाण्डपाशिकपिशु[नवे]त्रिकावरोधजनराजवल्लभादीनन्यांश्च चा–

1. Although the plates were found in the erstwhile Sonpur State attached to the Sambalpur District of Orissa, they are called Vakratentali plates after the village granted by the charter. This nomenclature, coined by B.C. Majumdar, is retained here for convenience of reference.
2. The plates of this grant are slightly broader in the middle than at the ends and their width is more at the ends than in the middle. It varies from 4¼" to 4¾" and the length from 8⅞" to 9". About the middle of the left margin there is a circular hole for the ring, the ends of which are secured into the lower portion of the lump of copper which bulges out on either side along the ring for a space measuring 1½". In the upper surface of the lump there is a deep depression, almost circular, nearly 2" in diameter, in which we have, in relief, the device of goddess Lakṣmī, probably squatting on lotus, being bathed by an elephant on either side, and alegend, which is not clear but conjectured to be *Śrī-Janamejayarājasya.*
3. From plates in *EI*, xi.
4. Majumdar: *Om.* Expressed by a symbol.

8 टभटजातीयान् समाज्ञापयति [।*] विदित[म*]स्तु भवतां यथा स्माभिरयं ग्रा–
9 मः सनिधिः सोपनिधिः सर्व्वंवा (बा)धाविवर्ज्जितः सगर्तोषरः साम्र–

Second Plate : First Side

10 मधुकः सजलस्थलः सर्व्वोपरिकरादानसहितः प्रतिनिषिद्धचाट–
11 भटप्रवेशश[च]तुः[5]सीमापर्यन्तः कौण्डीन्य[6]गोत्राय मैत्रावरुणवाशि–
12 ष्ठ[7]प्रवराय च्छन्दोगचरणाय राढायां वल्लिकन्दरविनिर्गताय[8] मेरण्डावा–
13 स्तव्याय भट्ट पुत्रजातरूपनम्ने भट्टपुत्रश्रीवच्छसु(सू)नवे सलिलधारा–
14 पुरःसरमाचन्द्रतारकार्क्कक्षितिसमकालाय भोगार्थं मातापित्रो–
15 रात्मनश्च पुण्ययशोभिवृद्धये विशुमति[9]संक्रान्त्यां ताम्रशासने–
16 नाकरीकृत्य प्रतिपादित इत्यवगत्य समुचितभोगभागकरहिरण्या–
17 दिकमुपनयद्भिर्भवद्भिः सुखेन प्रतिवस्तव्यमिति [।*] भाविभिश्च भूपतिभिर्द्द–
18 त्तिरियमस्मदीया धर्म्मगौरवादस्मदनुरोधाच्च स्वदत्तिरिवानुपालनीया [।*]
19 तथा चोक्तं धर्म्मशास्त्रे [।*] व(ब)हुभिर्व्वसुधा दत्ता राजभिः सगरादिभिः [।*] यस्य य–

Second Plate : Second Side

20 स्य यदा भूमिस्तस्य तस्य तदा फलं (लम्) [॥१॥*] मा भूदफलशङ्का वः परदत्तेति
21 पार्थिवाः [।*] स्वदानात्फलमानन्त्यं[10] परदत्तानुपालने [॥२॥*] शष्ठिं[11] वर्षसहस्राणि
22 स्वर्गे मोदति भूमिदः [।*] आक्षेप्ता चानुमन्ता च तान्येव नरके वसेत् [॥३॥*] अग्नेरप–
23 त्यं प्रथमं सुवर्ण्णं भूर्व्वैष्णवी सु (सू)र्यसुताश्च गावः [।*] यः काञ्चनं गाञ्च महीञ्च
24 दद्याद्दत्तास्त्रयस्तेन भवन्ति लोका [:॥४॥*] आस्फोटयन्ति पितरः प्रव–
25 लगयन्ति[12] पितामहाः [।*] भूमिदाता कुले जातः स नस्त्राता भविष्यति [॥५॥*]
26 भूमिं यः प्रतिगृह्णा(ण्हा)ति यश्च भूमिं प्रयच्छति [।*] उभौ तौ पुण्यकर्म्माणौ निय–
27 तं स्वर्गगामिनौ [॥६॥*] तडागानां सहस्राणि[12a] वाजपेयशतानि[12b] च [।*] गवां कोटिप्रदा–
28 नेन भूमिहर्त्ता न शुध्यति [॥७॥*] हरते हारयते यस्तु मन्दवु(बु)द्धिस्तमोवृतः [।*] सव(ब)द्धो
29 वारुणैः पाशैस्तिर्य्यग्योनिं च गच्छति [॥८॥*] स्वदत्तां परदत्तां वा यो हरेद्वसु–

5. The letter *tu* looks like *tta*.
6. Read कौण्डिन्य°.
7. Read वासिष्ठ.
8. Mazumdar: राढाफंवल्लिकन्दरविनिर्गताय
This reading is accepted by R.D. Banerji (*History of Orissa*, i, 206), H.C. Ray (*Dynastic History of Northern India*, i, 397), Hira Lal (*EI*, xi, 201) and others. The *akṣara* following *ḍhā* is, however, clearly *yāṁ*. The form of *yā* resembles that in *puṇyā°* in line 16 and in °*smadiyā* in line 18 below. For the use of this kind of medial *ā* with other letters see *śā* in *śāsanaṁ* in line 38 below. It is quite different from *pha* in *phalam* in line 20 below.
9. Read विषुवति.
10. The *akṣara ntyaṁ* looks like *ttyam*.
11. Read षष्टि°
12. Read प्रवलगन्ति
12*a*. Read °सहस्रेण
12*b*. Read °शतेन

Third Plate

30 न्धरां(राम्)[13] [।*] स विष्ठायां कृमिर्भूत्वा पच्यते पितृभिः सह [॥६॥*] आदित्यो वरुणो विष्णुर्व्वं(र्ब्र)–

31 ह्मा सोमो हुताशनः [।*] शूलपाणिस्तु भगवा:[14] आ(अ)भिनं(न)न्दन्ति भूमिद [म् ॥१०॥*] से(सा)मान्यो–

32 यं धर्म्मसेतुर्नृपाणां काल(ले) काले पालनीयो भवद्भिः [।*] सर्व्वानितान्भाविनो भूपती–

33 न्द्रा[न्] भूयो भूयो याचते रामचन्द्रः [॥११॥*] इति कमलदलाम्वु (म्बु) वि(बि)न्दुलोलं (लां)श्रियम–

34 नुचिन्त्य मनुष्यजीवितञ्च [।*] सकलमिदमु[दा*]हृतञ्च वुध्वा[15] न हि पु–

35 रुषैः परकीर्त्तयो विलोप्याः [॥१२॥*] परमभट्टारकमहाराजाधिरा–

36 जपरमेश्वरश्री**जनमेजयदेवस्य विजयराज्ये[16]सम्वत्सरे तृतीये श्रा**

37 **वणमाससितपक्षपञ्चम्यां यत्राङ्कतो सम्वत् ३ श्रावणशु दि ५ लिखि**–

38 तमिदं शासनं महासन्धिविग्रहप्रतिव(ब)द्धकायस्थकोद्घोषेण वल्ल[भ*] घोष[17]–

39 सुतेन संङ्ग्रामेन[18] उक्तं[19] शास[न*] मितिः[20] रयण[21]ओज्झासुतेन [।*] मङ्ग[लं] महाश्रीः ॥

Seal

श्री **जनमेजयदेव** [राजस्य ?]

ABSTRACT

Beginning with the auspicious symbol *siddham* and *svasti* and issued from the victorious camp (*vijaya-skandhāvāra*) situated at **Suvarṇapura,**[22] the charter first introduces king **Mahābhavagupta** (I)[23] who is described as a devout worshipper of Maheśvara, *Paramabhaṭṭāraka-Mahārājādhirāja-Parameśvara*, as belonging to the family of the Moon (*Soma-kula-tilaka*) and as the lord of Trikaliṅga[24] and is said to have meditated upon the feet of the illustrious

13. Read हरेत वसुन्धराम्.
14. Read भगवान्.
15. Read बुद्ध्वा.
16. Better read °राज्य°.
17. Restored on the basis of some other records of the same king.
18. Read सङ्ग्रामेण.
19. Read उत्कृतं.
20. This mark comprising a couple of small circles probably indicates the conclusion of the record. The words following it appear to be an afterthought.
21. In the Nagpur Museum plates (*infra*, no. IV : V) we have रयणा.°
22. The same as modern Sonpur in the Sambalpur District of Orissa where the plates have been found.
23. Later in this record he is mentioned as Janamejaya.
24. The location of Tri-Kalinga has been discussed in connection with the history of the Somavaṁśins in the introduction.

Śivagupta who is also given the imperial title *Paramabhaṭṭāraka-Mahārājādhirāja-Parameśvara.*

The king, being in good health and after worshipping the Brāhmaṇas in the village of Vakratentalī[25] situated in the division (*khaṇḍa*) called Lupattarā,[26] granted the village to the *Bhaṭṭaputra* Jātarūpa, son of the *Bhaṭṭaputra* Śrīvatsa, hailing from Vallikandara[27] in Rāḍhā,[28] an inhabitant of Meraṇḍā[29] and belonging to the Kauṇḍinya *gotra* and the Maitrāvaruṇa and Vāsiṣṭha *pravaras* and the Chandoga *caraṇa*, for the increase of the religious merit and fame of his parents as well as of his own self, on the occasion of the Viṣuva *saṅkrānti*. The granted village, which extended up to its borders on four sides, was turned into a rent-free holding by means of the copper-plate charter. The grant was intended to last as long as the moon, the sun and the earth endure and was endowed with the right to the *nidhis*, *upanidhis*, the pits and barren lands, the mango and *madhuka* trees, waters and land and the levy of all the *uparikaras*,[30] and was exempted from all the troubles and the entry of the *cāṭas* and the *bhaṭas*. The order in respect of the grant was addressed to the agriculturist householders inhabiting the village and the officers posted in the district from time to time such as *Samāhartṛ*, *Sannidhātṛ*, *Dāṇḍapāśika*[31], *Piśuna*[32], *Vetrika*[33] the inmates of the royal harem, favourites of the

25. It has been identified with modern Bantentuli or Bantentily in the former Sonpur State, 16 miles west of Sonpur town, See *EI*, xi, 201; Binayak Misra, *Dynasties of Medieval Orissa*, 66.
26. Lupattarā, the headquarters of the administrative division known after it, is probably the same as Lipatuṅgā mentioned in the Patna plates of the 6th year of Mahābhavagupta I (*infra*, no. IV:II text-line 15) and has been doubtfully identified with modern Leptā, 6 miles south-east of Bolangir. See *EI*, xi, 198 and 201; Binayak Misra, Op. cit. 66.
27. It has not been identified so far. Accepting B.C. Mazumdar's reading *Rāḍhāphaṁvallikandara* and taking it as referring to a single locality, Hira Lal proposed to identify it with the village of Rairākhol, 45 miles from Sonpur, the findspot of the plates. See *EI*, xi, 201. But as pointed out above, the correct reading is *Rāḍhāyāṁ Vallikandara*° and the reference is to the village Vallikandara situated in Rāḍhā.
28. It is a well-known geographical unit and roughly corresponded to south-west Bengal. See D.C. Sircar, *Studies in the Geography of Ancient and Mediaeval India*, 217.
29. Hira Lal identifies it with the village of Mendā, 17 miles west of Sonpur. Vide *EI*, xi, 201.
30. It has been variously explained as 'additional taxes', 'unfixed taxes', 'minor taxes' and 'tax paid by the temporary tenants'. In some records we find the word *parikara* (in the expression *saparikara*) employed in the same sense. Vide *IEG*, 352.
31. It has been taken to refer to the 'officer in charge of punishment, i.e. criminal justice' (*HDS*, iii, 986) or 'an officer entrusted with the punishment of criminals' (*IEG*, 81). For some other epigraphical references, see *HDS*, iii, 988.
32. It may denote an 'informant', 'a whisperer'. But most scholars take this word together with the following word as referring to a single official.
33. It seems to refer to the 'truncheon-bearing policemen' and is comparable to the term *yāṣṭika* which is found frequently used in literature (Vide my *India as Seen in the Kuṭṭanīmata of Dāmodaragupta*, 48-49 and P.V. Kane, *HDS*, iii, 1001). According to some scholars, it denotes 'the chamberlain'. But the words *piśuna* and *vetrika*

king,[34] etc. and officials of the rank of *cāṭa* and *bhaṭa*. The villagers were asked to make over to the donee the *bhoga, bhāga, kara, hiraṇya*, etc., as and when they fell due, and thereby live happily in the village.

The future rulers are exhorted to maintain the grant as if it were their own grant and twelve benedictory and imprecatory stanzas, said to have been extracted from Dharmaśāstra, are cited.

The charter is dated the **fifth day of the bright fortnight of the month of Śrāvaṇa in the third year**[35] **of the victorious reign (vijaya-rājya) of the Paramabhaṭṭāraka-Mahārājādhirāja-Parameśvara Janamejaya (Mahābhavagupta I).**

The inscription was written by the *Kāyastha* Koighoṣa, son of Vallabhaghoṣa,[36] who was attached to the office of the *Mahāsāndhivigraha* (minister of peace and war), and incised by Saṅgrāma, son of Rayaṇa Ojjhā.[37]

The inscription concludes with the auspicious formula *maṅgalaṁ mahāśrīḥ*.

---

are usually taken to form a single official designation in the sense of 'an officer who drives away undesirable persons with a cane' (*HDS*, iii, 991) or 'one engaged in a court for caning culprits' (*IEG*, 251).

34. *Rāja-vallabha* may denote 'a courtier' or 'a court-favourite'.
35. The date is expressed both in words and figures.
36. Kaighoṣa, son of Vallabhaghoṣa, figures as the writer in some other charters of the same king. See nos. IV: II-IV.
37. Saṅgrāma, son of Rayaṇa Ojjhā, is mentioned as the engraver in the Nagpur Museum plates of Mahābhavagupta I, dated in his eighth regnal year also. See infra, no. IV: V. The fact, however, that the expression describing the engraver as a son of Rayaṇa Ojjhā was added after the statement that the charter was engraved by Saṅgrāma and the mark indicating the conclusion of the record clearly reveal that this statement was an afterthought.

IV : II

PATNA PLATES[1] OF MAHĀBHAVAGUPTA I JANAMEJAYA, YEAR 6

Provenance: Somewhere in the erstwhile Patna State, Sambalpur District, Orissa.

References: Pratapachandra Ghosh, *JASB*, xlvi, 173-78; J. F. Fleet, *EI*, iii, 340-44 and plates between pp. 342 and 343; Bhandarkar's *List*, No. 1559; R. D. Banerji, *History of Orissa*, i, 206-08; H.C. Ray, *Dynastic History of Northern India*, i, 397-98; S. N. Rajaguru, *IO*, iv, 105-11.

Language: Sanskrit. In prose with the exception of some customary benedictive and imprecatory verses in lines 24-39 and a stanza at the end in praise of the issuing king under the name Janamejaya.

Metres: Verses 1-3 and 5-9: *Anuṣṭubh*; Verse 4: *Indravajrā*; Verse 10: *Śālinī*; Verse 11: *Puṣpitāgrā*; Verse 12: *Sragdharā*.

Script: Northern class of alphabets.

Date: Regnal year 6, Āṣāḍha śukla 8. Last quarter of the ninth century A.D.

TEXT[2]

1 सिद्धम्[3] [।*] स्वस्ति [।*] **मूरसीमस**मावासितश्रीमतो विजयकटकात् परमभट्टारकमहाराजाधि

2 राजपरमेश्वरश्रीशिवगू (गु) प्तदेवपादानुध्यातपरममाहेश्वरपरमभट्टारकमहारा–

3 जाधिराजपरमेश्वरसोमकुलतिलक तृ (त्रि) कलिङ्गाधिपति**श्रीमहाभवगुप्त**राजदे–

1. The plates measure about $9\frac{5}{8}$" by 5" at the ends and somewhat less in the middle. The ring, on which the plates are strung, is about 1/2" thick and $4\frac{1}{2}$" in diameter, and its ends are secured under a circular seal, nearly $1\frac{3}{4}$" in diameter. On countersunk surface within thick border it bears in relief in the centre a seated figure with what appears to be a chowri on either side. The figure in the centre is indistinct. Ghosha surmised it to be Rāmacandra seated on a lotus and surrounded by lotus leaves and flowers (*JASB*, xlvi, 174). But in all likelihood it must have been goddess Lakṣmī being bathed by an elephant on either side as on the seal of the previous charter. According to Ghosha, the lower portion probably contained the figure of Hanumān whereas Fleet thinks it more likely that there was a floral device.
2. From plates in *EI*, iii.
3. Fleet: *Om*. Expressed by a symbol.

4 वः ।।[4] कूषली[5] ।।[5a] श्रोङ्गा[6]तटविषयप्रतिव (ब) द्धवककवेड्डाग्रामे[7] तत्प्रतिनिवासिकुटुम्वि (म्बि) जनपदां[8]–

5 स्तद्विषयीययथाकालाध्यासिनः समाहर्तृ सन्निधातृचाटभटपिशुनधे (वे) त्रिका–

6 वरोधजनराजवल्लभादीन् सर्व्वान् राजपादोपजीविनः[9] सम (मा) ज्ञापयति[10] [।*] विदि–

7 तमस्तु भवतां ।[11] यथास्माभिरयं ग्रामः सनिधिः सोपनिधिः सर्व्वंवा (बा) धाविवाज्जि (र्ज्जि) तः ।

8 [12]सर्व्वोंपरिकरकरादानसहितः साम्रमधूकः सगर्त्तोषरः[13] ।[14]प्रसिद्धचतुःसि (सी) मा–

9 चच्छिन्वः[15] । [16]प्रतिनिषिद्धचाटभटप्रवेशः नानागोत्रप्रवरविनिर्गतवास्तव्ये–

Second Plate : First Side

10 भ्यो द्विजातिवरेभ्यः एक [:*] कौच्छ (त्स) गोत्रः अङ्गिरसवर्षयो[17] (यौ) वनाश्वप्रवरः यूवनाश्वदम्वरिष–

11 दङ्गिरश्रनुप्रवरः[18] सामवेदे कौथ (थु) मशारवाध्यायी पम्पासरसि (सी) विनिर्गत [:*] [18a]लेइश्शृङ्गावा–

12 स्तव्य [:*] भट्टपुत्रदामाकः[18b] ऐवुलिसू (सु) तः [।*] द्वितीयो गौतु (त) मगोत्रः अ (आ) ङ्गिरस-प्रवरः वा (बा) र्हस्पत्यानु–

4. These *daṇḍas* are superfluous.
5. Read कुशली
5*a*. The punctuation mark is redundant.
6. Ghosha: तुङ्गा°
7. Ghosha: वेद्द°
   In the Vakratentali plates (*supra*, IV: I) we have the expression ब्राह्मणान् सम्पूज्य after the word ग्रामे.
8. The *anusvāra* over *dā* is not visible in the plate accompanying Fleet's transcript, but is given here on the authority of Fleet.
   In the Vakratentali plates (above, IV:I) we have simply कुटुम्बिन° in place of कुटुम्बिजनपदान् of the present plates.
9. We have समाहर्तृ सन्निधातृदाण्डपाशिकपिशुनवेत्रिकात्ररोधजनराजवल्लभादीनन्यांश्च चाटभटजातीयान् in the Vakratentali grant (*supra*, IV: I).
10. Fleet: समाज्ञापयति
11. This mark of punctuation is unnecessary.
12. Read सर्व्वोपरिकरा°
13. The privileges and exemptions mentioned here are the same as those specified in the previous charter, but there is a difference in the order of their mention.
14. This *daṇḍa* is superfluous.
15. Read °वच्छिन्नः. In the previous record we have simply चतुःसीमापर्यन्तः which follows प्रतिनिषिद्धचाटभटप्रवेशः.
16. This mark of punctuation is unnecessary.
17. Read आङ्गिरसाम्बरीष°
18. Read युवनाश्ववदम्बरीष वदङ्गिरोवदनुप्रवरः.
18*a*. Ghosha: लेड़°
18*b*. Ghosha: ऐप्रालि°

13 प्रवर:[19] यजुव्वे (र्व्वे)दे काण्वशाखे(खी)[19a] ओडयशृङ्गा[19b]विनिर्गत [:*] खण्डक्षेत्रवास्तव्य [:*] भट्टपुत्रो[19c] नारपगण्डसू (सु)त [:।*] तृति(ती)य–

14 श्च कृषा(ष्णा)त्रेयगोत्र: अ(आ)र्च्चनानाश(स)प्रवर: श्यावाश्वन[19d] अनुप्रवर:[20]यजुर्व्वेद-(दे)काण्वशाखा–

15 ध्यायी कोङ्कलेड्डु[20a]विनिर्गत [:][20b] लिपतुङ्गावास्तव्य[:*]भट्टपुत्रवासू(सु)देव: रिशिकेश[21]सू(सु)–

16 त: [।*] चतुथ (र्थ)श्च ।[22] अगस्तिगोत्र: ।[22] ईध्मवाहवप्रवर:[23] च्यवा(व) [ना*] नुप्रवर: च[24] यजुव्वे (र्व्वे)दे

17 काण्वशाखाध्याई(यी) च[24] कलिङ्गविनिर्गत: ॥[25] पम्पासरसि (सी)वा–

18 स्तव्य: कोण्डदेवनाम(मा) रामशम्म(र्म्म)सू(सु)त: [।*]एतेभ्यो द्विजातिवरेभ्य: सलिल-धारा–

19 पू (पु)र:सरमाचन्द्रतार [का*] र्क्कक्षितिसमकालोपभे(भो)गार्थम् प्रतिवर्षदातव्यरु(रू)प्यकाष्ट पल

20 करदान(नं) विनिश्चित्य मातापित्रोरात्मनश्च पुण्ययशोभिवृद्धये ताम्रशासनेना–

Second Plate : Second Side

21 करि(री) कृत्य प्रतिपादि ई(इ) त्यवगत्य समू(मु)चितभोथं[26] मातापित्रोरात्मनश्च पुण्यय-शोभि–

22 वृद्धये ताम्रशासनेनाकरीकृत्य प्रतिपादित इत्यवगत्य समुचितभोगभाग[27]करहिर–

23 ण्यादिकमुपनयद्भिर्भवद्भि: सुखेन प्रतिवस्तव्यमिति [।*] भाविभिश्च भूपतिभिर्द्दत्तिरियमस्म–

24 दीया धर्म्मगौरवादस्मदतु (नु)रोधाच्च स्वदत्तिरिवातु (नु) पालनीथा [।*] तथा चोक्तं धर्म्मशास्त्रे [।*] व (ब) हुभि–

25 र्व्वसू(सु)धा दत्ता राजभि: सगरादिभि:[28] [।*] यस्य यस्य यदा भूमिस्तस्य तस्य तदा फलं (लम्) ॥ [१॥*] मा भु (भू) दफल–

19. Fleet: प्रवर [:*] clearly But the *visarga*, indicated by a couple of dots, is clearly visible in the facsimile.
19*a*. Ghosha: शाख्य
19*b*. Ghosha: उपशृङ्ग°
19*c*. Ghosha: नेरप°
19*d*. Ghosha: श्यवोश्वन°
20. Read श्यावाश्ववदनुप्रवर:
20*a*. Ghosha: कोष्कलड°
20*b*. Ghosha: लेप°
21. Read. हृषीकेश°
22. This *daṇḍa* is superfluous.
23. Read इध्मवाहप्रवर:
24. This word is superfluous.
25. This punctuation mark is uncalled for.
26. Read भोगार्थं
27. This portion from *mātāpitro*° in the preceding line is unnecessarily repeated. The repetition has been caused by a careless attempt to correct the immediately preceding word*samucita-bho[gār*]tha[ṁ*]* which was an error.
28. Fleet: सगरादिभि [:*]. But the *visarga* is clearly visible in the facsimile.

26 शङ्का वः परदत्तेति पार्थिवाः [।*] स्वदत्तात्फलमानन्त्यं[29] परदत्तानुपालने ॥[२॥*] षष्टि-
वर्षंस–

27 हस्राणि स्वर्ग्गे मोदति भूमिदः [।*] आक्षेप्ता चानू (नु)मन्ता च तान्येव नरके वसेत् ॥[३॥*]

28 अग्नेरपत्य(त्यं) प्रथमं सुवर्ण्णं (र्ण्णं) भूर्व्वो(र्व्वै)ष्णवि(वी) सूर्यसू (सु)ताश्च[30] गावः
[।*] यः काण्च(श्च) नं गाण्च (श्च) मही–

29 ण्च (श्च) दद्यात् दत्तास्त्रयस्तेन भवन्ति लोके(काः) [॥४॥*] आस्फोटयन्ति पितरः प्रवल्ग-
यन्ति[31] पि––

30 तामहा [।*] भूमिदाता कूल[32] जाता (तः) स नस्त्राता भविष्यति ॥ [४॥*] भूमि (मिं)
यः प्रतिगृह्णाति यश्च

31 भूमिं प्रयच्छति । उभौ तौ पुण्यकर्म्माणौ नियतं स्वर्ग्गगामिनौ ॥ [५॥*] तडागानां सह–

32 स्राणि[32a] वाजपेयशतानि[32b] च । गवां कोटिप्रदानेन भूमिहृत्ता(र्त्ता)न शू(शु) ध्यति।
[।६॥*] हरते हा–

Third Plate : First Side

33 रयते[33] यस्तु मन्द (बु)द्धिः तमोवृतः [।*] स व(ब)द्धो वारुणैः पाशैस्तीर्यग्योनीण्च[34] गच्छति
॥[७॥*]

34 स्वदत्तां परदत्ताम्वा[34a] यो हरेति(त) वसू(सु)न्धरां(राम्) [।*] स विष्ठायां कृमिभू(र्भू)
त्वा पितृभिः सह पच्यते ।[।८॥*]

35 आदित्यो वरुणो विष्णुर्व्र (ब्र)ह्मा सोमो हुताशनः [।*] शूलपाणिश्च [35]भगवारभिनन्द–

36 न्ति भूमिदं (दम्) । [।९॥*] सामान्योयं धर्म्मसेतुनृ (नृ)पाणां काले काले पालनि(नी)यो
भवद्भिः [।*] सर्व्वा–

37 नेतान् भाविनः पार्थिवेन्द्रां(न्द्रान्) ।[36]भूयो भूयो याचते रामचन्द्रः ॥ [१०॥*] इति कमल-
दलाम्बु(म्बु)विन्दू[37]–

38 लोला(लां)श्रियमनु(नु)चिन्त्य मनुष्यजिवितण्च[38] । सकलमिदमु(मु) दाहृतण्च(श्च)
वुध्वा[39]

39 न हि पू(पु)रुषैः परकि(की)र्त्तयो विलोप्या [:॥११॥*] इति परमभट्टारक महाराजाधि-
राजपरमे–

29. Fleet's suggestion to correct it to *ānandyaṁ* is uncalled for.
30. Fleet: °सुताश्च
31. Read प्रवलगन्ति
32. Read कुले
32*a*. Read सहस्त्रेण
32*b*. Read °शतेन
33. Its correction to *hārayet* suggested by Fleet is uncalled for.
34. Read तिर्यग्योनिञ्च
34*a*. Read °दत्तां वा
35. Read भगवान°
36. This mark of punctuation is not required.
37. Read °बिन्दु°
38. Read °जीवितञ्च
39. Read बुद्ध्वा

40 श्वरश्रीजनमेजयदेवस्य विजयराज्ये सम्वच्छ(त्स)रे षष्ठेः[40] आषाढ़-मासे सितपक्षे त(ति)–

41 थावष्टम्यां यत्राङ्कतोपि सम्वत् ६ अ(आ)षाढ़ शुदि ८ लिखितमिदं शासनं महासा(स)न्धि वि–

42 ग्रहिश्रीभल्लाधारदत्तसू (सु)तप्रतिव(ब)द्धकायस्थ कोइघोषेण वल्लभघोषसू(सु) तेनेति [।*]

43 आस्ति क्षोणीश्वराणाममलमणिरुचामन्वयत्[41] कौस्तुभाभः शौर्यत्यागाम्बु(म्बु)राशि–

Third Plate : Second Side

44 विरचितविधिवद्दानशुभ्रीकृताभ्रः [।*] श्रीमान् जन्मेजया[42]ख्यस्तृ(स्त्रि)दशपतिसमः

45 कृच्छ(त्स्न)गां भोक्तुकामः प्रख्यातद्वेशिवङ्शप्रविदलनपटू भूपतिः[43] सोमवङ्शि[44] ॥[१२॥*]

ABSTRACT

The record, which opens with the auspicious formulae *siddham*, expressed by a symbol, and *svasti*, was issued from the prosperous victorious camp (*vijaya-kaṭaka*) stationed at **Mūrasīma**[45] by king **Mahābhavagupta** (I) meditating upon the feet of king Śivagupta both of whom are described exactly in the same manner as in the preceding grant.

The object of the inscription is to record that the king (Mahābhavagupta I), being in good health, gave away the village Vakaveḍḍā[46] attached to the district (*viṣaya*) of Oṅgātaṭa[47] to the following four Brāhmaṇas :—

(i) *Bhaṭṭaputra* Dāmāka, son of Aivuli, belonging to the Kautsa *gotra* and the *pravaras* of Āṅgirasa, Āmbarīṣa, and Yauvanāśva and the *anupravaras* of Yuvanāśva, Ambarīṣa and Aṅgiras, a student of the Kauthuma *śākhā* of the *Sāmaveda*, an immigrant from Pampāsarasī[48] and a resident of Leiśṛṅgā;[49]

(ii) An unnamed son of Nārapagaṇḍa, also styled *Bhaṭṭaputra*, belonging to the Gautama *gotra*, with the Āṅgirasa *pravara* and the *anupravara* of Bār-

40. Read षष्ठे
41. Read °मन्वये
42. The spelling *Janmejaya* in preference to the correct *Janamejaya* is due to exigencies of metre.
43. Read °द्वेषिवंशप्रविदलनपटुर्भूपतिः
44. Read सोमवंशी
45. Sometimes spelt as Murasima, it has been identified with Mursingā or Moorsima on the bank of the river Ong about 13 miles south-west of Bolangir in the Sambalpur District. See *EI*, xi, 198; Binayak Misra, *Dynasties of Mediaeval Orissa*, 66.
46. Hira Lal identifies it with Bakti, about 15 miles north of Bolangir (*EI*, xi, 198) while Binayak Misra *Ibid.* proposes to equate it with Vankavira in the erstwhile Sonpur State in the Sambalpur District.
47. The district on the bank of the river Oṅgā, a tributary of the Mahanadi.
48. It has not yet been identified. But it must have been a locality situated near a lake called Pampā.
49. Probably identical with modern Loisinga or Loysingā, about eleven miles north of Bolangir in the Sambalpur District. See *EI*, xi, 198; Binayak Misra, Op. cit, 67; R.D. Banerji, *History of Orissa*, i, 207.

haspatya, a student of the Kāṇva *śākhā* of the *Yajurveda*, an immigrant from Oḍayaśṛṅga[50] and a resident of Khaṇḍakṣetra;[51]

(iii) *Bhaṭṭaputra* Vāsudeva, son of Hṛṣīkeśa, belonging to the Kṛṣṇātreya *gotra*, with the *pravara* of Ārccanānasa and the *anupravara* of Śyāvāśva, a student of the Kāṇva *śākhā* of the *Yajurveda*, an immigrant from Koṅkaleḍḍa[52] and a resident of Lipatuṅgā;[53]

(iv) Koṇḍadeva, son of Rāmaśarman, belonging to the Agasti *gotra*, with the *pravara* of Idhmavāha and the *anupravara* of Cyavana, a student of the Kāṇva *śākhā* of the *Yajurveda*, an immigrant from Kaliṅga[54] and a resident of Pampāsarasī.

The grant, which was meant for perpetual enjoyment, was subject to the payment of an annual tax fixed at eight *palas*[55] of silver.[56] It carried with it the same privileges and exemptions as specified in the previous grant. The order regarding the grant was addressed to all the royal officers such as *Samāhartṛ*, *Sannidhātṛ*, *cāṭas*, *bhaṭas*, *Piśuna*, *Vetrika*, inmates of the royal harem and the favourites of the king posted in the district from time to time as well as the agriculturist householders residing in the granted village. The village, it is stated, was turned into a rent-free holding by means of a copper-plate charter before being granted.[57] The villagers were asked to live happily in the village while paying *bhoga*, *bhāga*, *kara* and *hiraṇya* in time.

The rulers in future are requested to maintain the grant like their own grant and eleven imprecatory and benedictive stanzas, represented as taken from Dharmaśāstra, are quoted.

The grant was issued on the **eighth day of the bright fortnight of the month of Āṣāḍha in the sixth year of the victorious reign of the Paramabhaṭṭāraka-Mahārājādhirāja-Parameśvara Janamejaya.**[58]

50. Udayagiri, four miles from Bhubaneshwar in the Cuttack District according to Hira Lal (*EI*, xi, 198) and Oḍasing in the erstwhile Athamallika State in Orissa (*Dynasties of Mediaeval Orissa*, 67). The latter identification looks more probable.
51. Hira Lal proposes to identify it somewhat doubtfully with modern Khandapara in the erstwhile feudatory state of the same name touching the south-western boundary of the Cuttack District (*EI*, xi, 198). According to R.D. Banerji (*History of Orissa*, i, 207), however, Khandakṣetra ought not to be taken as a place-name as it simply means a field, and has been used in many inscriptions discovered in different parts of Orissa. But in the present context it appears to be a place-name.
52. Identified with Koknara or Konknara four miles from Narsinghnath in the Sambalpur District.
53. It has been doubtfully identified by Hira Lal with modern Lepta, six miles south-east of Bolangir in the Sambalpur District (*EI*, xi, 198).
54. Generally taken to denote the coastal area comprising Puri-Ganjam and adjoining area of Orissa and Andhra Pradesh with Mukhalingam as its capital.
55. A measure of weight equal to four *karṣas* or 320 *rattis*. See Kane, *HDS*, iii, 120-21 and note 161 on p. 120 (for references).
56. Thus, though not stated clearly, the record is actually a *kara-śāsana*, i.e. a charter recording a land-grant on the condition of payment of a fixed tax.
57. In view of the unambiguous stipulation of payment of a fixed annual tax, this is simply a meaningless pious statement.
58. The date is given both in words and figures.

The record was written by the Kāyastha Koighoṣa,[59] son of Vallabhaghoṣa, who was attached to the office of the *Mahāsandhivigrahin* Mallā,[60] son of Dhāradatta.[61]

The record closes with a stanza in praise of king **Janamejaya** who is described as an ocean of valour and liberality and skilled in routing the families of his famous foes and as desirous to enjoy the whole earth and is said to have belonged to the Somavaṁśa.

59. Koighoṣa was also the writer of some other charters of Janamejaya. See above, IV: I; below, IV : III.
60. We know from some other inscriptions (IV : III—X) that his full name was Malladatta. As such, the latter part of the name appears to have been dropped out by oversight. Following the wording of the relevant portion, Fleet took Mallādhāradatta to be the name of the occupant of the office of *Mahāsāndhivigrahin.*
61. Malladatta, son of Dhāradatta, figures as the *Mahāsāndhi-vigrahin* in some other records also. See *infra,* nos. IV : III—X. In no. IV : I his name appears to have been left out due to oversight.

IV : III

PATNA PLATES[1] OF MAHĀBHAVAGUPTA JANAMEJAYA, YEAR 6

Provenance: Erstwhile Patna State, Bolangir District, Orissa.

References: Ganga Mohan Laskar, *JASB*, New Series, i, 8-12 and 19-23; R.D. Banerji, *History of Orissa*, i, 207-08; H.C. Ray, *Dynastic History of Northern India*, i, 398-99; Bhandarkar's List, No. 1558; S.N. Rajaguru, *IO*, iv, 112-17 and plates facing p. 112 and between pp. 114 and 115.

Language: Sanskrit. In prose except the imprecatory and benedictory stanzas.

Metres: Verses 1–3 and 5–11; *Anuṣṭubh;* Verse 4: *Indravajrā*; Verse 11: *Śālinī*; Verse 12: *Puṣpitāgrā.*

Script: Northern class of alphabets.

Date: Regnal year 6, Kārttika śukla 13. Last quarter of the ninth century A.D.

TEXT[1a]

First Plate

1 सिद्धम् [।*।[2] स्वस्ति । **मुरसि (सो)** मसमावासितश्रीमतो विजयकटकात् परमभ–

2 ट्टारकमहाराजाधिराजपरमेश्वरश्रीशिवगुप्तदेवपादानुध्यातपरममा–

3 हेश्वरपरमभट्टारकमहाराजाधिराजसोमकुलतिलकतृ (त्रि) कलिङ्गाधिप–

4 तिपरमेश्वरश्री**महाभवगू (गु) प्त**[3]राजदेवः । [4]कुष (श) ली ।[4] पोताविषयप्रतिव (ब) द्धपा–

5 सितलाग्रामे व्रा (ब्रा) ह्मणां (णान्) सपू (म्पू) ज्य तत्प्रतिनिवासिकू (कु) टू (टु) म्वि (म्बि) जनपदा (दां) स्तद्विषयी–

6 ययथाकालाध्यु (ध्या) सिनः समाहर्तृ[5]सन्निधातृदाण्डपाशिकचाटभट–

7 [6]पिशू (शु) न वेत्रिकावरोधजनराजवल्लभादी [न्*][7] सर्व्वान् राजपादोपजी–

1. The plates measure about 7⅞″ in length and about 5″ in width, and ends of two of them are raised. There is a square hole bored about the middle of the left margin of the plates for the passage of the ring, the ends of which are secured under a circular seal, about 1⅞″ in diameter, which bears seated Abhiṣeka-Lakṣmī in the upper part; the legend, if any, in the lower part, has now become illegible.

1a. From plates in *IO*, iv.

2. Laskar: *Om.* Expressed by a symbol.

3. Laskar: गुप्त

4. This mark of punctuation is superfluous.

5. Laskar reads *samāhatṛ* and then supplies superscript *r* on his own.

6. Laskar: पिश्रून

7. Laskar's reading is *vallabh-ādīn*; but the final *n* is conspicuous by its absence in the original.

8 विनः समाज्ञापयति [।*] विदिमस्तु भवतां यथास्माभिरय (यं) ग्रामः

9 सनिधिः सोपनिधिः सर्व्ववा (बा) धाविवर्ज्जितः[8] सर्वोपरिकरकरादानस–

10 हितः साम्रमधुकः सगत्तो (र्त्तो) षरः प्रतिनिषिद्धचाटभटप्रवेशश्चतु [ः*]–

11 सि (सी) मापर्यन्तः[9] कौशिक[10]गोत्ताभ्यां ग्रौदल[11]देवराज (त) विश्वामित्रप्रव–

12 राभ्यां काण्वशाखाध्यायिभ्यां [12]कोम्मायिरविनिर्ग्गताभ्यां[13] लोइ–

13 [14]शृङ्गावास्तव्याभ्यां भट्टपुत्तश्री–

Second Plate: First Side

14 केशवश्रीग्रप्याभ्या (भ्यां) भट्टदाद्दीसू (सु) ताभ्या (भ्यां) सलिलधारापू (पु) रः–

15 सरमाचन्द्रतारकार्क्कक्षितिसमकालोपभोगार्थः (थं)[15] श्रीदेवमाता–

16 पित्रोरात्मनश्च पू (पु) ण्ययशोऽभिवृद्धये त्ता (ता) म्रशासनेनाकरीकृ–

17 त्य प्रतिपादित इत्यवगत्य समुचितभोगभागकरहिरण्यादि–

18 कम (मु) पनयद्भिर्भवद्भिः सुखेन प्रतिवस्तव्यमिति । भाविभिश्च भूप–

19 तिभिर्दत्तिरी (रि) यमस्मदीया धर्म्मगौरवादस्मदनुरोधाच्च स्व–

20 दत्तिरिवानुपालनीया [।*] तथा चोक्त (क्तं) धर्म्मशास्त्रे। [16]व (ब) हुभिर्व्वसू (सु) धा दता (त्ता)

21 राजभिः सगरादिभि [ः।*]र्यं (य) स्य यस्य यदा भूमिः (मि) त (स्त) स्य तस्य तदा फलं (लम्) । [।१।।*]

22 मा भूदफलशङ्का वः परदत्तेति पाथि (र्थि) वाः [।*] स्वदानात्फलमान–

23 न्त्यं परदत्तानुपालने ।।[२।।*] षष्टिं वर्षसहस्राणि स्वर्ग्गे मोदति भूमि–

24 द [ः।*] ग्राक्षेप्ता चानुमन्ता च तान्येव नरके वसेत् । [।३।।*] ग्रग्नेरपत्यं प्रथ–

Second Plate: Second Side

25 म (मं) सुवण (र्णं) भूर्व्वैष्णवी सूर्यसुताश्च गावः [।*] यः काञ्चनं गाञ्च म–

26 हि (ही) ञ्च दद्यात् (द) दत्तास्त्रयस्तेन भवन्ति लोके (काः) ।। [४।।*] ग्रास्फोटयन्ति पितर (रो)

27 प्रवल्गयन्ति[17] पितामहा [ः।*] भूमिदाता कुले जातः स नस्त्राता भविष्य–

28 ति ।।[५।।*] भूमिं यः प्रतिगृह्णाति यश्च भूमिं प्रयच्छति [।*] उभौ तो (तौ) पुण्यक–

8. Laskar: °विवर्जितः
9. Laskar: °पर्य्यन्तः
10. Laskar's reading is *Aukiśaka* while Rajaguru reads *Krauśika*.
11. Laskar omits *au* and reads the following letter as *di*. *Au* is also ignored by Rajaguru according to whom the letter next to it is *da*.
12. *Kommāpira* is Laskar's reading followed by Rajaguru though the letter in question is undoubtedly *yi*, not *pi*. The letters *p* and *y* are clearly distinguished in this inscription.
13. Laskar reads °विनिर्गताभ्यां
14. Space sufficient to accommodate ten or eleven letters on the left has been left blank.
15. The word *śrī-deva* is not found prefixed to the expression *mātā-pitroḥ* in other records.
16. Imprecatory and benedictive stanzas beginning in this and ending in line 40 have been omitted by Laskar.
17. Read प्रवल्गन्ति or वल्गयन्ति

29 र्म्माणौ नियतं स्वर्ग्गगामिनौ ।[६।।*] तडागाना(नां) सहस्राणि[18] वाजपेय–

30 शतानि[19]च [।*] गवां कोटिप्रदानेन भूमिहर्त्ता न शुद्धयति ।।[७।।*] ह–

31 रते हारयते भूमि (मिं) [20]मन्दवु(बु)द्धिस्तमोवृत्तः [।*] स व(ब)द्धो वारुणैः पाशै–

32 ति(स्ति)र्य्यग्योनिञ्च गच्छति ।[।८।।*] स्वदत्ता(त्तां) परदत्ताम्वा[21]पो(यो) हरेद्व(त व)सुन्धरां (राम्) [।*]स

33 विष्ठायां कृमिर्भूत्वा पितृभिस्सह पच्यते ।।[९।।*] सुवण्ण(र्ण्ण)मेक(कं) गामेकां

34 भूमेरप्यर्द्धमङ्गुलं (लम्) [।*] हरन्नरकमायाति यावदाहू(भू)तसंप्लवं (वम्) ।।[१०।।*] आ–

35 दित्यो वरुणो विष्णुर्व्र(र्ब्र)ह्मा सोमो हुताशनः [।*] शूलपाणिस्तु भग–

Third Plate

36 वानभिनन्दन्ति भूमिदं(दम्) ।।[११।।*] सामान्योयं धम्म (र्म्म) सेतुनृ(र्नृ) पाणां काले काले

37 पालनीयो भवद्भिः [।*] सर्व्वानेतान् भाविनः पार्थिवेन्द्रान् भूयो भूयो या–

38 चते रामचन्द्रः ।।[१२।।*] इति कमलदलाम्वु(म्बु)वि(बि)न्दुलोलां श्रियमनुचिन्त्य

39 मनुष्याजि(जी) वितञ्च [।*] सकलमिदमुदाहृतञ्च वु (बु)[द्*] ध्वा न हि पुरुषैः पर–

40 कीर्त्तंपो(यो) विलोप्या [:।।१३।।*] इति परमभट्टारकमहाराजाधिराजपरमेश्व–

41 **रश्रीजनमेजयदेवस्य विजयराज्ये सम्वच्छरे[22] षष्ठे ।।[23] कार्त्ति–**

42 **कमाससितपक्षत्रयोदश्यां यत्राङ्कतः सम्व (संव) त् ६ कार्त्तिक श्रु (शु) दि**

43 **१३** लिखितमिदं शासनं महासान्धिविग्रहिश्रीमल्लदत्तश्रीधारद—

44 त्तसुतप्रतिव(ब)द्धकायस्थकोइघोषेण वल्लभघोषसुतेन । प्रतिव–

45 र्षे[24] चात्र शासने करपञ्चरु(रू)प्यप्लानि[25] निष्टङ्क्य[26][।*]करशासनमिदं

46 दत्तं यत्र रूप्ल[27] ५ [।*]

ABSTRACT

Commencing with the auspicious words *siddham*, indicated by a symbol, and *svasti*, the grant was issued from the prosperous camp of victory stationed at **Murasīma**[28] by king **Mahābhavagupta I** who meditated on the feet of king

18. Read सहस्रेण
19. Read °शतेन
20. In the previous record we have यस्तु without which the verse will remain incomplete.
21. Read °दत्तां वा
22. Read संवत्सरे
23. These *daṇḍas* are uncalled for.
24. Read प्रतिवर्षं
25. Read °पलानि
26. Laskar's reading is निवृङ्क्य
27. The intended reading appears to have been रूपल which probably served as an abbreviation for रूप्यपलानि
28. The previous grant was also issued from the camp pitched at the same place though there the place-name is spelt as Mūrasīma.

Śivagupta, both of whom are described exactly in the same fashion as in the preceding charter.[29]

The king, after worshipping the Brāhmaṇas in the village Pāsitalā[30] attached to the Potā *viṣaya*,[31] granted the village in favour of the two Brāhmaṇa brothers *Bhaṭṭaputra* Keśava and Apya, sons of *Bhaṭṭa* Dāddī, who belonged to the Kauśika *gotra* having Audala, Devarāta and Viśvāmitra for its *pravaras*, were students of the Kāṇva *śākhā* (of the Śukla *Yajurveda*) and had immigrated from the village of Kommāyira[32] and resided at Loiśṛṅgā[33] at the time of the grant. The grant was accompanied by the same privileges and exemptions as specified in the preceding record. The order in respect of the grant was addressed to the agriculturist householders of the village and the very same officers posted in the district from time to time as mentioned in the previous epigraph with the exception of only the *Dāṇḍapāśika* who is not named in the present record. The granted village, which is said to have extended to its four borders, is said to have been rendered tax-free by means of a copper-plate charter, though at the end the charter is described as a *kara-śāsana*[34] involving the payment, evidently by the donees, of tax fixed at five *palas* of silver per annum.[35] The villagers were asked to live happily in the village by paying the *bhoga, bhāga, kara, hiraṇya* and other dues to the donee when due.

Next follows the exhortation to the future rulers to uphold the grant as if it were their own grant and in support of this request thirteen imprecatory and benedictive stanzas, said to have been extracted from Dharmaśāstra, are cited.

The date[36] of the charter is given as the **thirteenth day of the bright fortnight of the month of Kārttika in the sixth year of the victorious reign of the Paramabhaṭṭāraka-Mahārājādhirāja-Parameśvara Janamejaya.**[37]

29. The only difference is that in this inscription the title *Parameśvara* is employed just before Mahābhavagupta's name as against the previous record in which it is used, in keeping with the usual practice, immediately after *Mahārājādhirāja*.
30. Probably represented by the modern Pointalā or Pointil, some 2 miles east of Bolangir, Bolangir District.
31. Hira Lal (*EI*, xi, 200) and D.C. Sircar (*IHQ*, xx, 240 and fn. 9) favour the identification of Potā, the headquarters of the district christened after it, with Povā, the chief place of the district of that name, mentioned in one of the Chaudwar plates of Mahābhavagupta I (*infra*, IV: VIII-X). Potā *viṣaya* is also named in the Kālibhanā plates of the 6th regnal year of the same king (below, IV: IV). Binayak Misra identifies it with Porā in the erstwhile Sonpur State now included in the Bolangir District (*Dynasties of Mediaveal Orissa*, 66).
32. It has yet to be identified.
33. It is generally regarded as identical with Leiśṛṅgā mentioned in the preceding grant as the place of residence of one of the donees.
34. I.e. a charter granted on the condition of the payment of a fixed rent.
35. Cf. the previous grant which was made on the stipulation of the payment of eight *palas* of silver *per annum*.
36. Given both in words and figures.
37. The other Patna grant (above, IV: II) was made just about four months earlier in the same year.

The inscription was written by the *Kāyastha* Koighoṣa, son of Vallabhaghoṣa, attached to the *Mahāsāndhivigrahin* Malladatta, son of Dhāradatta.[38]

38. The same writer and the *Mahāsāndhivigrahin* also figure in the preceding charter. R.D. Banerji's description of the writer Koighoṣa as the *Mahāsāndhivigrahika* is evidently due to oversight.

IV : IV

KĀLIBHANĀ PLATES[1] OF MAHĀBHAVAGUPTA I JANAMEJAYA, YEAR 6

Provenance: Kālibhanā, Sambalpur District, Orissa.

References: D.C. Sircar and P.C. Rath, *IHQ*, xx, 238–44 and plates opposite pp. 242 and 243; S.N. Rajaguru, *IO*, iv, 100–04 and plates facing p. 100 and between pp. 102 and 103.

Language: Sanskrit. In prose except a stanza eulogising Janamejaya in lines 7–10 and the usual benedictive and imprecatory stanzas.

Metres: Verse 1: *Sragdharā*; *Verses* 2–4 and 6–12: *Anuṣṭubh*; Verse 5: *Indravajrā*; Verse 13: *Śālinī*; Verse 14: *Puṣpitāgrā*.

Script: Northern class of alphabets.

Date: Regnal year 6, Phālguna śudi 1. Last quarter of the ninth century A.D.

TEXT[2]

First Plate

1 सिद्धम्[3] [।*] ओम्[3] [।*] स्वस्त्यमलमणिकुट्टिमसदनचलदनेकवखारविलासिनीज–
2 नचरणनूपुर(पु)र रवत्रस्तपारावत्तस्वनवधिरितदशदिशो नानादिग्देशा–
3 न्तरादागतवन्दिवृन्दविस्तारितकीर्त्तेर्व्विविधविद्यालंकृतविद्वज्जनजनितविद–
4 ग्धकाव्यालापस्तुतधनपतिविभवस्पर्द्धितविपणिजनपरस्य संहर्षरचित–
5 विचित्रप्रासादाट्टालिकाविहारारामदेवकुलोद्यानवापीकूपतडागोप–
6 निर्ज्जितसुरसदनमहिम्न श्रीमतो **मूरसीम**पत्तनवरात् ।।[4]
7 अस्ति क्षोणीश्वराणामलमणिरुचामत्व(न्व)यात्[5] कौस्तुभाभः
8 शौर्यत्यागाम्बुराशिर्व्विरचितविंधिवद्दानशुभ्रीकृताभ्रः । श्रीम[ा*]न्जन्मेजया[6]––
9 रव्यस्तृ(स्त्र)दशपतिसमः कृच्छन(त्स्न)गां भोक्तुकामः प्रख्यातद्वेशि(षि) वङ्श (वंश) प्रविदलन–

1. The plates are slightly broader at the ends than in the middle and measure about 8″ in length and a little less than 5″ in width. About the middle of the left margin there is a circular hole for the passage of the ring. The seal is missing.
2. From plates in *IHQ*, xx.
3. Expressed by a symbol. Rajaguru reads both the signs together as *siddham*.
4. In the earlier records of Mahābhavagupta I the mention of the place of issue is a simple affair and this is the earliest known inscription of the dynasty in which this item is elaborated.
5. Read °मन्वये
6. In line 44 below the name is spelt as Janamejaya. It has been altered to Janmejaya here to suit the metre.

10 पटू(टु)भूंपतिः सोमवङशे(वंशे) ।।[१।।*][7] सो यं ।[8] परमभट्टारकमहाराज[9] परमेश्वर–
11 श्रीशिवगुप्तदेवपादानुध्यातपरममहेश्वरपरमभट्टारकमहा–
12 राजाधिराजसोमकुलतिलकतृ(त्रि)कलिङ्गाधिपतिपरमेश्वरश्री**महा**–

Second Plate: First Side

13 **भवगुप्तराज**देवः कुशली ।[10] पोताविषय[11]प्रतिव(ब)द्धजम्व(म्बू)ग्राम[12]ग्रामे व्रा(ब्रा)ह्म
14 णान् संपूज्य तत्प्रतिनिवासिकुटू(टु)म्वि(म्बि)जनपदा(दां)स्तद्विषयीययथाकालाध्यासि–
15 नः समाहर्तृसन्निधातृदाण्डपाशिकपिशुनवेत्री(त्रि)कावरोधजनराजवल्लभा–
16 दीन सर्व्वान्[13] समाज्ञापयति [।*] विदितमस्तु भवतां यथास्माभिरयं ग्रामः सनि–
17 धिः सोपनिधिः सदशापराधः[14] सर्व्ववा(बा)धाविवर्ज्जितः सर्व्वोपरिकरकरादा–
18 नसहितः साम(म्र)मधूकः ।[15] सगर्त्तोषरः प्रतिनिषिद्धचाटभटप्रवेशः[16]
19 पराशरगोत्रायः (य) वासिष्ठशक्ति[17]पाराशर्यप्रवरः (राय) वाजसनेयिमा-
20 ध्यदिनशाखाध्यायिने हस्तिपद[18]विनिर्गताय जम्बुग्रामा(म)वास्तव्याय
21 भट्टपू(पु)त्रश्रीगोविन्दनाम्ने भट(ट्ट)पू(पु)त्र कोण्डसुताय सलिलधारापुर[ः*]सरमा–
22 चन्द्रतारकार्क्कक्षितिसमकालोपभोगार्थं मातापित्रोरात्मनश्च पू(पु)ण्ययशो–
23 भिवृद्धये ताम्रशासनेनाकरीकृत्य प्रतिपादित इत्यवगत्य समु(मु)चित भा(भो)ग–
24 भागकरहिरण्य[।*]दिकमू(मु)पनयद्भिर्भवद्भिः सू(सु)खेन प्रतिवस्तव्यमिति [।*] भाविभि–

Second Plate: Second Side

25 श्च भूपितभिर्द्दत्तिरियमस्मदीया धर्म्मगौरवादस्म[द*]नुरोधाच्च स्वदत्तिरिवा–
26 नुपालनीया [।*] तथा चोक्तं [19]धर्म्मशास्त्रे [।*] व(ब) हू(हु)भिर्व्वसुधा दत्ता राजभिः सगरादि–

7. This stanza is also met with in one of the Patna grants of the 6th year (*supra*, IV: II), the Nagpur Museum plates of the 8th year (*infra*, IV: V) and the Gaintala plates of the 17th year (*infra*, IV: VII). But in the first and the third it occurs at the end and in the second grant after the mention of the place of issue as in the present grant.
8. This mark of punctuation is superfluous.
9. Instead of the usual *Mahārājādhirāja* noticed in other records *Mahārāja* has been used here inadvertently.
10. The *daṇḍa* is superfluous.
11. The Potā *viṣaya* is also referred to in one of the Patna plates issued by Mahābhavagupta I in his 6th regnal year (*supra*, IV: III).
12. In line 20 below the name of the village is spelt simply as Jambugrāma.
13. The expression राजपादोपजीविन: found after this word in the preceding two grants has been dropped out in the present charter.
14. This expression occurs for the first time in this record of the dynasty.
15. The mark of punctuation is unnecessary.
16. Note the omission of the expression चतु:सीमापर्यन्त: found hereafter in the preceding two records.
17. Sircar and Rath: °शाक्ति°.
18. This locality is found mentioned in several records of the dynasty.
19. Sircar and Rath: धर्म°.

27 भिः[20] [।*] यस्य यस्य यदा भूमिः (मि) त(स्त) स्य तस्य तदा फलं (लम्) ।।[२।।*] मा भूदफलशङ्का वः पर–

28 दत्तेति पार्थिवाः [।*] स्वदानात्फलमानन्त्यं परदत्तानुपालने ।।[३।।*] षष्टिं वर्षसहस्रा–

29 णि स्वर्ग्गे मोदति भूमिदः [।*] आक्षेप्ता चानु(नु)म[न्ता*] च तान्येव नरके वसेत् ।।[४।।*] अग्नेरप

30 त्य(त्यं) प्रथमं सुवर्ण्णं भूर्व्वैष्णवी सूर्य्यसुताश्च गावः [।*]यः काञ्चन(नं) गाञ्च

31 महीञ्च दद्याद्दत्तास्त्रयस्तेन भवन्ति लोके(काः) ।।[५।।*] आस्फोटयन्ति पित–

32 रः प्रवल्गयन्ति[21] पितामहाः [।*] भूमिदाता कुले जाताः (तः) स नस्त्राता भविष्यति ।।[६।।*].

33 भूमिं यः प्रतिगृह्णाति यश्च भूमिं प्र[य*]च्छति [।*] उभौ तौ पू(पु)ण्यकर्म्माणौ नियतं स्वर्ग–

34 गामिनौ ।।[७।।*] तडागानां सहस्राणि[22] वाजपेयशतानि[23] [च*][24] [।*] गवा(वां)[25] कोटिप्रदानेन भू–

35 मिहर्त्ता न सु(शु)ध्यति ।[।८।।*] हरते हारयते[26] यस्तु मन्दवु(बु)द्धितमोवृतः [।*] स व (ब)द्धो वा–

36 रुणैः पाशैः (शै)ती(स्ति)र्य्यग्योनिश्च गच्छति ।।[९।।*] सुवर्ण्णमेक(कं) गामेकां भूमेरप्यर्द्धम–

Third Plate: First Side

37 ङ्गुलं(लम्) ।।(।) हरन्नरकमायाति यावत(द)ाहू(भू)तसंप्लवं(वम्) ।।[१०।।*] स्वदत्ता (त्तां) परदत्ताम्वा[27] यो–

38 [28]हरेद्वसू(सु)न्धरां(राम्) [।*] स विष्ठायां कृमिर्भूतः पच्यते पितृभिः सह[29] ।।[११।।*] आदित्यो वरु–

39 शो(णो) विष्णुर्व्र(ब्र)ह्मा सोमो हू(हु)ताशनः [।*] शूलपाणिस्तु भगवानभिनन्दति भूमिदं (दम्)

40 ।।[१२।।*] सामात्यो(न्यो)यं धर्म्मसेतुर्नृपाणां काले काले पालनीयो भवद्भिः [।*] सर्व्वा- नेतान्

41 भाविनः पार्थिवेन्द्रान् भूयो भूयो याचते रामचन्द्रः ।।[१३।।*] इति कमल–

42 दलाम्वु(म्बु)वि(बि)न्दुलोलां श्रियमनुचिन्त्य मनुष्यजीवितञ्च [।*] सकलमिद–

43 मुदाहृतञ्च वु(बु)[द*]ध्वा न हि पुरुषैः परकीर्त्तयो विलोप्याः ।।[१४।।*] परमभट्टारक[30] महाराजा-

20. Sircar and Rath read this *akṣara* at the end of the preceding line.
21. Read प्रवल्गन्ति.
22. Read सहस्रेण.
23. Read °शतेन.
24. Rajaguru proposes to restore the missing *akṣara* as *vā*.
25. Sircar and Rath: गवां
26. In some records we have हारयेत् in place of हारयते
27. Read परदत्तां वा
28. Sircar, Rath and Rajaguru: हरेद्वसु°. Read हरेत वसु°.
29. In many other records we have स विष्ठायां कृमिर्भूत्वा पितृभिः सह पच्यते
30. The *akṣara ra*, which was at first left out due to inadvertence, is engraved below the line.

44 धिराजपरमेश्वरश्रीजनमेज[य*] देवस्य विजयराज्ये सम्वच्छरे[31] षष्ठे फाल्गुनमासाद्वि–
45 तीयपक्षतिथौ प्रतिपदि यत्राङ्कतोपि सम्वत्[32] ६ फाल्गु शुदि १ लिखितमिदं शा–
46 सनं महासात्धि (न्धि) विग्रही (हि) श्रीमल्लदत्तश्रीधारदत्तसुतप्रतिव (ब) द्धकायस्थकोइ–
47 घोषेण वल्लभघोषसुतेन ।।उत्कीर्ण्णं सुवर्ण्णकारवापूकेन शावदेवसुते–
48 नः ।।ढ[33]

ABSTRACT

The auspicious symbols for *siddham* and *om* and the word *svasti*, which inaugurate the record, are followed by an elaborate but purely conventional description of the town of **Mūrasīma,**[34] from where the charter was issued. Next comes a verse in praise of King **Janamejaya**, which is also found at the end of the previous inscription. Then follows the mention of king Śivagupta and his successor, king **Mahābhavagupta I,** both of whom are given exactly the same titles as in the last two records, except only that Śivagupta is, probably by oversight, styled simply *Mahārāja* instead of being given the more showy title *Mahārājādhirāja*.

The king, in good health, after worshipping the Brāhmaṇas in the village Jambūgrāma[35] comprised in the district (*viṣaya*) of Potā,[36] gave away the village to the *Bhaṭṭaputra* Govinda, son of the *Bhaṭṭaputra* Koṇḍa, who belonged to the Parāśara *gotra* with the *pravaras* of Vāsiṣṭha, Śakti and Pārāśarya and was a student of the Mādhyandina *śākhā* of the Vājasaneyi school of the *Yajurveda*, an immigrant from Hastipada[37] and a resident of Jambugrāma, for the increase of the religious merit and fame of his parents and of his own self. The grant was accompanied by all the privileges and exemptions specified in the earlier grants as well as the *daś-āparādhas* and was rendered

31. Read संवत्सरे
32. Better read संवत्
33. This mark is employed to indicate the completion of the record. In some other inscriptions also we come across certain marks employed for the same purpose.
34. While the last two records are said to have been issued from the victorious camp stationed at Mūrasiman, this and some of the subsequent charters are represented to have been given from the town itself.
35. Sircar and Rath propose to identify it with the modern Jāmgāon, a village contiguous to Kālibhanā, the provenance of the record. L.P. Pandeya, on the other hand, points out that there still exist two villages called Jāmgāon in the Chandrapur taluk of the Bilaspur District. Vide *IHQ*, xx, 240, fn. 9.
36. P.C. Rath identifies Potā, the headquarters of the district named after it, with the modern Porā or Purā in the erstwhile Sonepur State, Sambalpur District, Orissa. Vide *ibid.* Sircar appears to favour the identification of Potā *viṣaya* with the Povā *viṣaya* mentioned as situated in the Kosala country in the Chaudwar plates of Mahābhavagupta I (*infra*, IV: VIII-X) on linguistic grounds (*IHQ*, xx, 240 and fn. 9). Hira Lal (*EI* xi, 199) identified Povā with the modern Pow in the erstwhile Sonpur State, Sambalpur District. L.P. Pandeya (*IHQ*, xx, 240, fn. 9) invites attention to an old village called Potā in the Chandrapur taluk of the Bilaspur District.
37. It has yet to be identified; but Sircar points to the celebrated Hastigrāma, near Vaiśālī (mod. Basarh, Muzaffarpur District, Bihar).

tax-free by means of the copper-plate charter. The royal command in regard to the grant was addressed to the agriculturist householders living in the village and all the royal officers such as *Samāhartṛ*, *Sannidhātṛ*, *Dāṇḍapāśika*, *Piśuna*, *Vetrika*, inmates of the royal harem and the king's favourites posted in the district from time to time. The villagers were asked to pay the donee the dues like *bhoga*, *bhāga*, *kara* and *hiraṇya* at the proper time and thereby live happily in the village.

The future kings are requested to maintain the grant as if it were their own grant, and thirteen imprecatory and benedictive stanzas, said to have been borrowed from Dharmaśāstra, are quoted in support of the request.

The charter is dated the **first day of the second fortnight of the month of Phālguna in the sixth year of the victorious reign[38] of the Paramabhaṭṭāraka-Mahārājādhirāja-Parameśvare Janamejaya.**

The record was written by the *Kāyastha* Koighoṣa, son of Vallabhaghoṣa, who was attached to the *Mahāsāndhivigrahin* Malladatta, son of Dhāradatta,[39] and incised by the goldsmith Vāpūka, son of Śāvadeva.

38. The date is given both in words and figures.
39. Koighoṣa and Malladatta appear as writer and *Mahāsāndhivigrahin* respectively in some other records also.

IV : V

SATALMA[1] PLATES[1a] OF MAHĀBHAVAGUPTA I JANAMEJAYA, YEAR 8

Provenance: Not known.

References: E. Hultzsch; *EI,* viii, 138–43 and plates between pp. 140 and 141; Bhandarkar's *List,* No. 1560; R.D. Banerji, *History of Orissa,* i, 208–09; H.C. Ray, *Dynastic History of Northern India,* i, 399; Binayak Misra, *Dynasties Mediaeval of Orissa,* 66–7; S. N. Rajaguru, *IO,* iv, 118–23.

Language: Sanskrit. In a mixture of prose and verse.

Metres: Verse 1: *Sragdharā*; Verses 2–4 and 6–10; *Anuṣṭubh*; Verse 5: *Indravajrā*; Verse 11: *Śālinī*; Verse 12: *Puṣpitāgrā.*

Script: Northern class of alphabets.

Date: Regnal year 8, Kārttika śukla 12. Last quarter of the ninth century A.D.

TEXT[2]

First Plate

1 सिद्धम्[3] [।*] स्वस्त्यनेकवरविलासिनीचरणनो(नू)पूर(पु)रखोद्भ्रान्तमत्तपरावात–
2 कुलात(त) सकलदिगन्तरागतवन्दिजनविस्तारितकीर्त्तेः श्रीमतो **मुरसि(सी)म्नः** [।*]

1. Inscriptions are generally named after the findspot or the place of their deposit. And in case neither of these are known, they are referred to after places mentioned in them. Of the last category, the best example in the present volume is Vakratentali grant (no. IV: I). The inscription in question was so called by the original editor, E. Hultzsch, because at that time it was deposited in the Central Museum, Nagpur. But since the inscription is actually known to have been found at the modern village of Satalma, about thirty-two miles south-west of Sambalpur in the Sambalpur District of Orissa, the charter has been named here after the place of its discovery in keeping with the usual practice of naming the records after their provenance.

1*a*. The plates are broader in the middle than at the top or at the bottom. At the broadest part they measure about 9". Their width varies from 5⅜" to 5½". About the middle of the margin on the left there is a hole for the ring, which is not quite circular. The ends of the ring are secured in the base of a circular seal measuring about 1" in diameter. The seal bears in relief, on a countersunk surface, the figure of goddess Lakṣmi, apparently seated on a lotus and flanked by a couple of lamp-stands. The flower extends on both sides to the height of the shoulders of the goddess and is surmounted on each side by an elephant with an uplifted trunk. The base of the seal issomewhat damaged, and a nail seems to have been driven to fix the seal to the ring.

2. From plates in *EI*, viii.

3. Hultzsch: *Om.* Expressed by a symbol.

3 अस्ति क्षोणीश्वराणाममलमणिरुचामन्वयात[4] कौस्तुभाभः शौर्यत्यागा–

4 म्बु(म्बु)रा[शि]र्विरचितविधिवद्दाना(न)शुभ्रीकृताभ्रः [।*] श्रीमान्जन्मेजयाख्यस्तृ(स्त्रि) दश–

5 पतिसम [:*] कृत्छ्न (त्स्न)गां भोक्त(क्तु) कामः प्रख्यातद्वेषि वंशप्रतिदलनपटुर्भु(र्भू)- पति [:*] सो–

6 मवंशे [॥१॥*][5] सोयं परमभटा(ट्टा)रक[6]महाराजाधिराजपरमेश्वर[7]श्रीमहा–

7 शिवगुप्तराजदेव[8] पां(पा)दानुध्यात्प(तप)रमभटा(ट्टा)रकमहाराजाधिराजपरमे–

8 श्वरसोमकुलतिलकतृ(त्रि)कलिङ्गाधिपति**श्रीमहाभवगुप्तराज**देवः कु–

9 शली कशलोडाविषयप्रतिव(ब)द्धसतल्लमाग्रामे व्रा(ब्रा)ह्मणान् सम्पु(म्पू)ज्य त–

10 त्प्रतिनिवासिकुटुम्बि(म्बि) जनपदान(न) तद्विषयीययथाकालाध्यासिन [:*] समा–

11 हर्त्रि (तृं) सन्निधात्रि(तृ) चाट भटपिशुनवे(वै)त्रिकावरोध[9]जनराजवल्लभादीन(न) स–

Second Plate: First Side

12 र्वान(न) राजपादोपजि(जी)विन [:*] समाज्ञापयति [।*] विदितमस्तु भवतां यथा–

13 स्माभिरयं ग्राम [:*] सनिधिः सोपनिधिः सर्व्वा(बा)धाविर्वाजतः सर्वोपरिकर–

14 करादानसहितः साम्व्र(म्र) मधुक [:*] सगर्तोषरः प्रतिनिसि(षि)द्धचाटभटप्रवेश [:*]

15 चतुःसीमावाच्छिन्नः गौतमगोत्राय गौतमाङ्गिरसश्रौतथ्यत्रियारिष[10]प्र

16 वराय वाजसनेये(य) माध्यन्दिनशाख्या(खा) ध्यायिने[11] ओड्रदेशे पुरुषमण्डपग्राम–

17 विनी(नि)र्गताय मुरुजुंगग्रामवास्त्व्याय भट(ट्ट)पुत्रश्रीसान्थकरनाम्ने धृति–

18 करसुताय श(स)लिलधारापुरस्श(स्स)रमाचन्द्रतारकार्क्कक्षितिश(स)मकाला(लो)प–

19 भोगार्थं मातापित्रोत्मनश्च पुन्य (ण्य)यशोभिवृद्धयेताम्र(म्र)शासनेनाकरि(री)कृत्य

20 प्रतिपादित इत्यवगत्य समुचितभोगभाग[12]करहिरन्या(ण्या)दिकमुपनय–

21 द्भिभ(र्भ)वद्भिः सुखेन प्रतिवस्तव्यमिति [।*] भाविभिश्च भूपतिभिर्दत्तिरियमस्म–

22 दि(दी)या धर्म्मगौरवादस्मदनुरोधाच्च स्वदत्तिरिवानुपालनीया [।*] तथा चोक्तं ध–

23 र्म्मशास्त्रे [।*] व(ब)हुभिर्वसुधा दत्ता राजभिस्सगरादिभिर्य (भिः।य)स्य यस्य यदा भु (भू) मि–

Second Plate: Second Side

24 स्तस्य तस्य तदा फलं(लम्)[॥२॥*] मा भु(भू)दफलं(ल)शङ्का वः परदत्तेति पार्थिवाः[।*]

4. Read °मन्वये
5. This stanza is also met with in *supra* nos. IV: II and IV and *infra*, no. IV: VII, in IV: IV at the same place as in the present grant and IV: II and VII at the end or thereabout.
6. Originally *ka* had been engraved and later it was corrected to *ra*.
7. This *akṣara*, which was at first left out by oversight, was inserted subsequently.
8. The word *mahat* is not prefixed to the name of this ruler in any other record of his son and successor, Mahābhavagupta I.
9. *Dha* is engraved on an erasure.
10. Read °रसौतथ्यत्र्यार्षेय°
11. *Sandhi* rules would require °ध्यायिन
12. This letter, which was at first omitted by oversight, was inserted later.

25 स्वदानात्फलमत्यन्त[13] परदानानुपालने [।।३।।*] षष्टिं वर्षसहस्राणि स्वर्गे

26 मोदति भु(भू)मिदः [।*] आक्षेप्ता चानुमन्ता च तान्येव नरके वशेत (सेत्) [।।४।।*] अग्नेरप[त्यं] प्र–

27 थमं स्व(सु)वर्ण्णं भु(भू)र्व्वैष्णवी सु(सू)र्यसुताश्च गावः [।*] यः काञ्चनं गां च महीं च दद्यात् (द्)

28 दत्तास्त्रयस्तेन भवन्ति ला(लो)काः [।।५।।*] आस्फोट्ट(ट) यन्तिपितरः प्रवल्ग[य]न्ति[14] पिताम–

29 हाः [।*] भु(भू)मिदात्ता (ता) कुले जातः स नस्त्राता भविष्यति [।।६।।*] भु(भू)मि थः प्रतिगृह्ना(ह्णा)–

30 ति यश्च भु (भू)मि प्रयच्छति [।*] उभौ तौ पुन्य (ण्य) कर्म्माणौ नियतं स्वर्गगामि–

31 नौ [।।७।।*] तडागानां सहस्राणि[15] वाजपेयशतानि[16] च [।*] गवां कोटिप्रदानेन भूमिहर्ता

32 न शुध्यति [।।८।।*] स्वदत्तां परदत्ताम्वा [17]यो हरेद्व (त व)सुन्धरां(राम्)[।*] स विष्ठायां कृमिर्भूत्वा प-

33 च्यते पितृभिः सह [।।९।।*] आदित्यो वरुणो विष्णुव्र [ब्र]ह्मा सोमो हुताशनः[।*] शु(शू) लपा–

34 णिस्तु[18]भगवानभिनन्दन्ति भूमिदं (दम्) [।।१०।।*] सामान्योयं धर्म्मसेतुर्नृपाणां काल(ले)

Third Plate

35 काले पालनि(नी)यो भवद्भिः [।*] सर्व्वानेतान् भाविनः पार्थिवेन्द्रान्

36 भूयो भूयो याचते रामचन्द्र [:।।११।।*]इति कमलदलाम्वु (म्बु) वि(बि)न्दुलो–

37 [लं](लां) श्री (श्रि)यमनुचिन्त्य मनुष्यजीवितं(त)ञ्च [।*] सकलमिदमुदाहृ[तं](त)ञ्च

38 वे(बु)न्धा(द्ध्वा) न हि पुरुषैः परकीर्त्तयो विलोप्याः [।।१२।।*] परमभट(ट्टा) रकमहा–

39 राजाधिराजपरमेश्वरसोमकुलतिलकतृ(त्रि)कलिङ्गाधिपति–

40 **श्रीजनमेजयदेवस्य विजयराज्ये समवच्छरे [19]अष्टमे कार्त्तिकमा–**

41 **सद्वितीयपक्ष (क्षे) तिथौ द्वादश्यां यत्राङ्कतोपि सम्व (संव)त् ८ कार्त्तिक शुदि १२** [।*] द्यो (दू)–

42 तकश्च महामहत्तमभट(ट्ट) श्रीसाधारण [:*] शोभनसुतः [।*] लिखितमिदं शासनं

43 महासान्धिविग्रहिराणकश्रीमल्ला(ल्ल)दत्तधारदत्तसुतप्रतिव(ब)द्धेन कायस्थआ–

44 ल्लवेन कैविलाससुते[20]नः[21] उत्किरितं[22] संग्रामेन(ण) ।।[23] रयणाओज्झासुतेन[23a]

13. Elsewhere we generally have °मानन्त्यं
14. Read प्रवल्गन्ति
15. Read सहस्रेण
16. Read °शतेन
17. Read °दत्तां वा
18. Better read °पाणिश्च
19. Read संवत्सरे
20. Read कैलाससुतेन. *Vi* after *kai* has been written by oversight.
21. The sign for *visarga* appears to be intended to serve as a mark of punctuation.
22. Read उत्कीर्णं°
23. This punctuation mark, consisting of a couple of vertical lines the first of which is curved and the second straight, which differs from other punctuation marks used earlier and later in this very line, is superfluous.

23a. The *visarga* here is probably intended to serve as a punctuation mark.

ABSTRACT

The words *siddham,* represented symbolically, and *svasti* are followed by a brief description of the place of issue. **Murasīman,**[24] a stanza in praise of king **Janamejaya,** already familiar from some other records, and a prose passage referring to kings Śivagupta and **Mahābhavagupta** *I* both of whom are described in the same manner as in the earlier records except that Mahābhavagupta I's predecessor is called Mahāśivagupta and the sectarian title Paramamāheśvara, employed for Mahābhavagupta I in other records, has been dropped out, perhaps due to oversight.

It is next stated that Mahābhavagupta, after worshipping the Brāhmaṇas in the village called Satallamā,[25] attached to the district called Kaśalōḍā,[26] gave away the village to the *Bhaṭṭaputra* Sānthakara, son of Dhṛtikara, who belonged to the Gautama *gotra* with the *pravaras* of the three *ṛṣis,* to wit, Gautama, Āṅgirasa and Autathya, and the Mādhyandina *śākhā* of the Vājasaneyi school of the *Yajurveda* and was an immigrant from the village of Puruṣamaṇḍapa[27] situated in the Oḍra country[28] and a resident of the village called Murujuṅga.[29] The grant was endowed with the same privileges and exemptions as the earlier grants. The addressees of the royal command concerning the grant, which was turned into a rent-free holding by means of a copper-plate charter, included the agriculturist householders inhabiting the village and the *Samāhartṛ, Sannidhātṛ, cātas, bhaṭas, Piśuna, Vaitrika,* inmates of the royal harem, royal favourites and all the other royal officers posted in the district from time to time. The villagers were asked to make over to the donee the *bhoga, bhāga, kara* and *hiraṇya,* etc., as and when they fell due.

Then follow the usual request to the future kings for the protection of the grant and eleven customary imprecatory and benedictive stanzas said to have been extracted from the Dharmaśāstra.

The grant was issued on the **twelfth day of the bright half of the month of Kārttika in the eighth year**[30] **of the victorious reign of Janamejaya**.

24. It is described as prosperous, inhabited by many beautiful courtesans and as one the fame of which is spread by the minstrels coming from all the different quarters.
25. Identified with Satlamā, the findspot of the inscription, 32 miles south-west of Sambalpur, in the Sambalpur District. See *EI*, xi, 201; Binayak Misra, *Dynasties of Mediaeval Orissa*, 66.
26. It has been identified with the modern Kusardā, 10 miles north-west of Satlamā and 34 miles south-west of Sambalpur, in the Bargarh tahsil of the Sambalpur District.
27. Binayak Misra (Op. cit., 67) proposes to identify it with the modern Maṇḍapa in the erstwhile Baud State, Orissa.
28. Generally speaking, Oḍra *deśa* denotes lower Orissa.
29. It has yet to be identified.
30. The date is expressed both in words and figures. The *tithi* in question was evidently the *pāraṇā* (breaking the fast) day following the *devotthāna ekādaśī* which is regarded as very sacred. The grant, therefore, appears to have been made by the king to mark the breaking of his fast. Further, the equation of the second fortnight of the month with the bright half shows that *pūrṇimānta* months are referred to in our records.

The *dūtaka*[31] of the grant was *Mahāmahattama*[32] *Bhaṭṭa*[33] Sādhāraṇa,[33a] son of Śobhana.

The inscription was written by *Kāyastha* Āllava, son of Kailāsa, who was attached to the *Mahāsāndhivigrahin Rāṇaka*[34] Malladatta, son of Dhāradatta,[35] and incised by Saṅgrāma, son of Rayaṇā Ojjhā.[36]

31. I.e. conveyor of the royal order regarding the grant to the local officers who drew up and delivered the charter to the donee or donees. See *CII*, iii, 100, fn. 3; *HDS*, iii, 987-88; *IEG*, 104. But we have also instances of the request for grant being conveyed to the king by some people through the *dūtaka*. *Cf.* the Khalimpur plate of Dharmapāla, *EI*, iv, 250.
32. The meaning of this official designation is uncertain. Sircar takes *Mahattama* in the sense of the village headman or a member of the Panchayat board (*IEG*, 190) and regards *Mahāmahattama* as the same as *Mahāmahattaka* and *Mahāmahattara*, probably meaning 'the chairman of the council of the *Mahattaras* (*ibid.*, 179) mentioned in several inscriptions. Stein renders *Mahattara* as 'chamberlain' (*Rājataraṅgiṇī*, vii. 659). For references, see *HDS*, iii, 994, 998).
33. This title, applied to learned Brāhmaṇas, shows that Sādhāraṇa was a Brāhmaṇa.
33*a*. Sādhāraṇa figures in various important capacities in all the records of Mahābhavagupta I, issued from eighth to thirty-fourth years of his reign.
34. Derived from *Rājānaka* or *Rājānyaka*, this is a title enjoyed by nobles and feudatory chiefs in mediaeval period. *Vide HDS*, iii, 1003; *IEG*, 276.
35. While Malladatta, son of Dhāradatta, is referred to as the *Mahāsandhivigrahin* in several records, the *Kāyastha* is mentioned only in this inscription.
R.D. Banerji's statement that the charter was written by Malladatta (*History of Orissa*, i, 208) is incorrect.
36. Rayaṇā Ojjhā's son Saṅgrāma figures as an engraver in *supra*, IV: I also.
R.D. Banerji is wrong in averring that this record was incised by Āllava (*History of Orissa*, i, 208-09).

IV : VI

SONPUR PLATES[1] OF MAHĀBHAVAGUPTA I JANAMEJAYA, YEAR 17

Provenance: Sonpur, Sambalpur District, Orissa.
References: B. Ch. Chhabra, *EI*, xxiii, 248-55 and plate opposite p. 252; S. N. Rajaguru, *IO*, iv, 130-37.
Language: Sanskrit. In prose with the exception of twelve customary benedictive and imprecatory verses and another stanza eulogising the donor and his minister.
Metres: Verses 1–10: *Anuṣṭubh*; Verse 11: *Śālinī*; Verse 12: *Puṣpitāgra;* Verse 13 : *Sragdharā*.
Script: Northern class of alphabets.
Date: Regnal year 17, Āṣāḍha śukla 5. About the close of the ninth century A.D.

TEXT[2]

First Plate

1 सिद्धम्[3] [।*] स्वस्त्यमलमणिकुट्टिमसदनचलय (द) ने[4]कवरवारविलासिनीज–
2 नचरणनूपुरखत्रस्त्र (स्त) पाराप (व) त कुलपक्षस्वनव (ब) धिरितदशदिग्नाना[5]–
3 देसा (शा) न्तरादागतवन्दिजनविस्तारितकि (की) र्त्ते[6]र्व्विविधविद्यालंकृतविद्वज्जनज–

1. The plates were found preserved in a massive oblong stone coffer, measuring 16$\frac{3}{4}$″ long, with a slipping lid, which was obviously specially designed for the safe deposit of the charter.

 The plates are narrower in the middle and measure about 8$\frac{1}{4}$″ long and about 5$\frac{1}{4}$″ broad at either end. The ends of the copper ring (4" in diameter), which passes through the circular hole in the left margin on each plate, are secured under a circular seal, which is entirely defaced. But there are some very faint traces of Gaja-Lakṣmī.
2. From plate in *EI*, xxiii.
3. Chhabra: Oṁ. Expressed by a symbol.
4. Chhabra points out that the *e*-stroke (in *ne*) is parted into two at the end, whereby perhaps *ai* may be meant. Accordingly, in the text he reads the aksara as *nai.* But as admitted by him, it looks more like *ne.* Following some other records of Mahābhavagupta I, where we get similar description, we propose to restore the preceding three *akṣaras* as *calada.*°
5. Read दशदिशोनाना°
6. Cf. अनेकवरविलासिनीचरणनोपू (नूपु) र-
 रवोद्भ्रान्तमत्तपारावातकुलात (त्)
 सकलदिगन्तरागतवन्दिजनविस्तारितकीर्त्तेः
 in the Satalmā plates (above, IV: V) of the 8th year.

4 नित[7]काव्यालापस्तुतधनपतिविभवस्पर्द्धितरचित[8]विचित्रप्रासादाट्टा–
5 लिका[9]देवकुलोद्यानवापीकूपतडागोपसो (शो) भाजितसुरपुरम–
6 हिम्न:[10] । [11]प्रचण्डदोर्दण्डमण्डलाग्रतुण्डखण्डितारातिमत्त–
7 मातङ्गविमुक्ताफलप्रसाधितासे (शे) षमहीमण्डल[12]–
8 सकलभूपालमौलिमालाविला (ल) ग्नमाणिक्यमयु (यू) ख-व्राताभिरञ्जि–
9 तक्रमकमलयुगलात्[13] श्रीमदारामात् परमभट्टारकमहाराजा–
10 धिराजपरमेश्वरपरममाहेश्वरश्रीसि (शि) वगुप्तदेवपादानुध्या–
11 तपरममाहेश्वरपरमभट्टारकमहाराजाधिराजपरमेश्वर–

Second Plate: First Side

12 सोमकुलतिलकत्रिकलिङ्गाधिपतिश्री**महाभवगुप्तराजदेव**:कुस (श) –
13 ली कोसलायां[14] लुपुत्तरा[14a] खण्डप्रतिव (ब) द्धगोत्तइकेलाग्रामे ।[15] व्रा (ब्रा) ह्मणान् संपु (पू) ज्य तद्विष–
14 यीयथाकालाध्यासिन: समाहर्तृ सन्निधातृदाण्डपासि (शि) कपिसु (शु) नवेतृका[16]–
15 वरोधजनराजवल्लभादीन् सर्व्वान् समाज्ञापयति । विदितमस्तु भवतां ।[17] य–
16 थास्माभिरयं ग्राम: सनिधि: सोपनिधि: सर्व्ववा (बा) धाविवर्जित: सर्वोपरिक–
17 रकरादानसमेत: साम्ब्र (म्र) मधुक: सगर्त्तोषरश्चतु [:*]सीमाप
18 र्यन्त: सजलस्थलसहित:[18] ।[19] खदिरपद्रविनिर्गताय सुवर्ण्ण–

7. The word *vidagdha* found after *janita* in above, IV: V is missing here.
8. According to Chhabra, the intended reading probably is विभवस्पर्द्धिनो रचित°. But a comparison with the Kalibhana plates of the year 6 (*supra*, IV: IV), which appear to have been followed in this description, shows that between the words *sparddhita* and *racita* we have to add *vipaṇi-jana-parasya saṁharṣa*° which appear to have been left out due to oversight.
9. *Vihār-ārāma* found after this word in the Kalibhana plates (above, IV: IV) is dropped here.
10. In the Kalibhana plates (above, IV: IV) we have° *pa-nirjjita-sura-sadana-mahimnaḥ.*
11. This mark of punctuation is unnecessary.
12. Read °प्रसाधिताशेषरणमहीमण्डल:
13. Read °युगल:. This and the foregoing compound qualify the donor and not Ārāma. These attributes are found applied to Mahābhavagupta I in the Chaudwar plates of his 31st regnal year (below, IV: VIII-X, text-lines 34-37) and the Kalibhana plates of his 34th regnal year (below, IV: XI, text-lines 37-40), though the order of these compounds is changed.
14. The word *Kosalāyāṁ*, which was left out by inadvertence, is engraved in smaller characters on the space above the ring-hole opposite line 17 and that it is to be read after *kuśalī* is indicated by the *kākapāda* mark after each of the words. The *kākapāda* is in the form of a cross.

14*a*. Chhabra: लुपुतुरा°

15. The *daṇḍa* is superfluous.
16. Read °वैत्रिका.°
17. This puncuation mark is unnecessary.
18. Better read सजलस्थल:.
19. This *daṇḍa* is not required.

19 पुरवास्तव्याय श्रीकमलवनवणिक्स्थानाय सलिलधारापुरःसरमाच–

20 न्द्रतार[20]कार्कक्षितिसमकालोपभोगार्थं मातृ(ता)पित्रोरात्मनश्च पुण्ययसो (शो)–

21 ऽभिवृद्धये ताम्र(म्र)सा(शा)सनेनाकरीकृत्य प्रतिपादित इत्यवगत्य समुचित–

22 भोगभागकरहिरण्यादिभि[21]र्भवद्भिः सुखेन प्रतिवस्तव्यं (व्यम्)। अनेनापि प्रा–

23 प्रसा(शा)सनेन सुवर्ण्णपुरीयश्रीकमलवनवाणिक्स्थानेन व(ब)लिचरुनैवेद्य–

Second Plate : Second Side

24 खण्डस्फुटित प्रतिकरणार्य (य or र्थं) श्रीकेस(श)व श्रीआदित्यभट्टारकाभ्यां।[22] देवकुलो (ला)–

25 भ्यां सा(शा)सनीकृत्य प्रदत्त [:*]। भाविभिश्च भूपति[23]भिर्दत्तिरियं (य)मस्मदीया धर्मगौ

26 रवादस्मदनुरोहा (धा)च्च स्वदत्तिरिया(वा)नुपालनीया। तथा चोक्तं धर्मसा(शा)स्त्रे।

27 व(ब)हुभिर्वसुधा दत्ता राजभिः सगरादिभि।[24]र्य (भिः। य) स्य [यस्य*] यदा भूमितस्य तस्य तदा

28 फलं(लम्)। [।१।।*] मा भूदफलसं[25](शं)का वः परदत्तेति पार्थिवाः। स्वदानात्फल[मा*]नन्त्यं प–

29 रदत्तानुपालने। [।२।।*] षष्टिवर्षसहस्राणि स्वर्गे मोदति भूमिदः [।*][26]

30 आस्फोटयन्ति पितरो वल्गयन्ति[27] पितामहाः [।*] भूमिदाता कुले जा–

31 तः स नस्त्राता भविष्यति।[।४।।*]भूमिं यः प्रतिगृह्ना(ह्णा)ति यश्च भूमिं प्रयच्छति। उभौ

32 तौ पुण्यकर्माणौ नियतं स्वर्गगा(गा)मिनौ।[।५।।*] तडागानां सहस्राणि (स्रेण) वाजपेयस (श)–

33 तानि (तेन) च। गवां कोटिप्रदानेन भूमिहर्त्ता न शुध्यति। [।६।।*][28] स्वर्ण्णमेकं गामेकां भूमे—

34 रप्यर्द्धमङ्गलं[29] (लम्) हरन(न्न)रकमयाति यावदाहूतसंप्लवः (वम्)। [।७।।*] अन्यायेन हृता भूमि–

20. The letter *ra*, which was left out by oversight, is incised below the line.
21. This is evidently an error for °हिरण्यादिकमुपनयद्भिः° which is met with in several other records.
22. This mark of punctuation is uncalled for.
23. The impression shows a superfluous scratch attached to *ti* making it appear as *tri*. But, as pointed out by Chhabra, on the plate it is plain *ti*.
24. This mark of punctuation, quite clear in the impression, has not been noticed by Chhabra.
25. After *saṁ* a small vertical stroke is seen in the facsimile. But Chhabra points out that it does not appear on the plate.
26. The second half of the verse, to wit, आक्षेप्ता चानुमन्ता च तान्येव नरके वसेत् is left out by inadvertence.
27. Read प्रवल्गन्ति.
28. Read सुवर्ण्णम् as demanded by the metre and found in other records.
29. The *anusvāra* over *la* is not seen in the facsimile. But Chhabra informs us that it is clear on the plate.

35 रन्यायेन तु हारिता। हरतो हारयतश्चैव स हन्यात्सप्तमं कुलं (लम्) ।।[८।।*] स्वदत्तां परद–
36 त्तां म्वा (वा) ।[30]यो हरेच्च[31] वसुन्धरां (राम्) [*] स विष्ठायां कृमिभूमित्वा[32] पच्यते
पितृभिः सह। [।९।।*] आ–

Third Plate : First Side

37 दित्यो वरुणो विष्णुव्र (र्ब्र) ह्मा सोमो हुतास (श) नः। शु (शू) लपाणिश्च भगवान्।[33] अभिन–
38 न्दन्ति[34] भूमिदं (दम्)। [।१०।।*] सामान्योयं धर्मसेतुनृ (र्नृ) पाणां काले काले पालनीयो
भवद्भिः [।*]
39 रिति[35] सर्व्वानेतान् भाविनः पार्थिवेन्द्रान् भूयो भूयो याचते रामचन्द्र [:*] ।[।११।।*] इति
40 कमलदलाम्वु (म्बु) वि (बि) न्दुलोलां।[36] श्री (श्रि) यमनुचिन्त्य मनुष्यजि (जी) वितं च।
सकलमिदमु–
41 दाहृतं च वुद्धा[37] (बुद्ध्वा) न हि पुरुषैः परकि (की) र्त्तयो विलोप्याः।[।१२।।*] परमभट्टा-
रकमहाराजाधि–
42 राजपरमेश्वरसोमकुलतिलकत्रिकलिङ्गधिपतिश्री [म*]**ज्जन–**
43 **मेजयदेवस्य विजयराज्ये सम्व (संव) त्सरे सप्त–**
दस (श) मे[38] आषाढ–
44 **माससितपक्षपञ्चम्यां। यत्राङ्कतः।[39] सम्व (संव) त् १७ आषाढशुदि ५।** ज्ञेया–
45 ऽशेषार्थसा (शा) स्त्रस्मृतिविम [ल*] धिया वेदवेदाङ्गविद्या। सी (शि) क्षाल्पेतिहास[40] प्र–
46 कटसुरगुरुप्राप्तभूयिष्ठधाम्ना। नाम्ना साधारणेन द्विजवरतनुना म–
47 न्त्रिणा यस्य राज्यं निर्वू (र्व्यु) ढं सोयमुच्चैस्तृ (स्त्रि) जगति विदितो **देवजनमेजय–**
48 श्रीः[41]। [।१३।।*]. . . . . . . स . . सुत।
49 . . . वृ . . . सुत . . . त्कि . . . हरद . . .[42]

30. This mark of punctuation is not necessary.
31. We generally have हरेत.
32. Read कृमिर्भूत्वा.
33. This *danda* is unnecessary.
34. Read भगवानभिनन्दन्ति.
35. The letters *riti* are superfluous.
36. This mark of punctuation is redundant.
37. This word is written below the line.
38. Read सप्तदशे.
39. These punctuation marks are redundant.
40. The small stroke attached to *sa,* which is seen in the facsimile, is, as stated by Chhabra, conspicuously absent in the plate.
41. Read जन्मेजयश्रीः, if we are to conform to the requirements of the metre. The corresponding portion of the Chaudwar plates of the 31st year of Mahābhavagupta I's reign (below, IV: VIII-X) reads धर्म्मकन्दर्प्पदेवः.
42. The portion engraved in these two lines after the 13th verse was perhaps deliberately scooped out as some serious errors might have crept in. But from the few letters that are still legible, this portion appears to have contained the names of the writer, engraver, etc. These names are, however, found on the reverse of the plate where they were probably re-engraved.

Third Plate : Second Side

50 [43]ली (लि) खी (खि)तमी (मि) दं ताम्व्र (म्र) सा (शा) सनं महास (सा)न्धी (न्धि)वी (वि) ग्रही (हि) राणकश्रीमल्लदत्तः महाक्षपट–

51 ली (लि)ना[44] कैलाससुतेन श्रीग्रवलेन ॥ उत्कीर्ण्णश्च सीवृल्ला सुतेन हरदासेनेती (ति) ॥०॥[45]

ABSTRACT

Opening with the auspicious words *siddham*, represented by a symbol, and *svasti*, the charter was issued from **Ārāma**,[46] which is described much in the same way as Mūrasīman in *supra*, IV : IV,[47] by king **Mahābhavagupta**, meditating upon the feet of king 'Śivagupta, both of whom are described in the conventional manner.

After worshipping the Brāhmaṇas in the village Gottaikelā[48] attached to the Luputtarā *khaṇḍa*[49] in Kosalā[50], the king ordered all the royal officers including *Samāhartṛ*, *Sannidhātṛ*, *Dāṇḍapāśika*, *Piśuna*, *Vaitrika*, inmates of the royal harem and the king's favourites that he had given away the village to the illustrious *Kamalavana-vaṇik-sthāna*,[50a] which was resident at

43. As stated in the previous note, lines 50-51 seem to have contained the same matter in a revised form as that first written and then cancelled in lines 48-49. But the writing of lines 50-51 differs from that of the rest of the record and is apparently by a different hand. This, as observed by Chhabra, raises the suspicion as to whether it was the original engraver himself who was responsible for scoring out lines 48-49 and adding lines 50-51 or it was someone else who sometime later tampered with the portion of the grant in question. If the latter be the case, the intention of the tamperor cannot be made out.
44. Read °दत्तमहाक्षपटलिना.
45. This mark probably indicates the conclusion of the record.
46. Ārāma, from where these plates were issued, is also mentioned in the Gaintala plates of the 17th year (below, IV: VII), and the three Chaudwar plates of the 31st year (below, IV: VIII-X) of Mahābhavagupta I's reign as a place where the royal camp was pitched. Chhabra suggests that probably Ārāma was a place situated not far from Sonpur, the find-spot of the grant, where royal camp was often pitched. According to him, it is equally likely that Ārāma here denotes only 'a pleasure-garden' with a palace where the king occasionally resided.
47. The few changes that are noticed are insignificant. The fact that the same description, without any real change, is applied to two different localities leaves no doubt that these descriptions are of a conventional nature (*varṇaka*) and of absolutely no use for historical purposes. Such stereotyped descriptions of persons, places and things are frequently met with in medieval Sanskrit and Prakrit literature.
48. The village is now represented by Gotarkela, about three miles from Sonpur, Sambalpur District, Orissa.
49. Luputtarā *khaṇḍa* is also referred to in the Vakratentali grant (supra, IV: I). For its identification, see *supra*, fn. 26 in IV.I.
50. I.e. South Kosala comprising the Chhattisgarh region of Madhya Pradesh and the Sambalpur region of Orissa.

50*a*. Obviously the headquarters of traders' organisation which originally hailed from Kamalavana.

Suvarṇapura[51] and had migrated from Khadirapadra[52]. The grant, which was rendered tax-free by means of a copper-plate charter, carried with it the same privileges and exemptions as in the previous grant with the exception of the freedom from the entry of the *cāṭas* and the *bhaṭas*.[53] The villagers were instructed to bring to the donee proper *bhoga, bhāga, kara, hiraṇya* and other dues. Having received the charter, the *Kamalavana-vaṇik-sthāna* of Suvarṇapura also made the village over to the temples of the gods Keśava (Viṣṇu) and Āditya-bhaṭṭāraka (Sūrya), i.e. two temples, one of Viṣṇu and the other of Sūrya, for meeting the cost of *bali*, *caru* and *naivedya* and repairs to the temples, by means of a charter.

Next follow the usual entreaty to the future rulers for the maintenance of the grant and twelve customary imprecatory and benedictive stanzas quoted in the name of Dharmaśāstra.

This charter was issued on the **fifth day in the bright fortnight of the month of Āṣāḍha in the seventeenth year[54] of the victorious reign of Janamejaya.**

It is stated in a eulogistic stanza that the administration of Janamejaya well-known in the three worlds, was looked after by his Brāhmaṇa minister named Sādhāraṇa whose intellect was purified by the study of all the worth-knowing Arthaśāstra and Smṛti texts and who was verily the divine preceptor (i.e. Bṛhaspati) in the knowledge of the Vedas, Vedāṅgas, Śikṣā (phonetics), Kalpa and Itihāsa[55].

The record was written by *Mahākṣapaṭalin*[55a], the illustrious Avala, son of Kailāsa,[56] when *Rāṇaka* Malladatta held the office of *Mahāsāndhivigrahin*.[57] It was engraved by Haradāsa, son of Sivṛllā.

51. Modern Sonpur.
52. S.N. Rajaguru proposes to identify it with the modern village of Khairapadā in the Kalahandi District, Orissa. See *IO*, iv, 130.
53. Whether their omission is deliberate or by inadvertence cannot be ascertained.
54. The date is given in both words and figures.
55. This stanza is also met with in the Gaintala plates of the 17th year (below, IV: VII) and with slight modification in the Chaudwar plates of the 31st year (below, IV: VIII-X) and the Kalibhana plates of the 34th year (below, IV: XI) of Mahābhavagupta I.
55*a*. There is a difference of opinion about the connotation of this official designation. Fleet (*CII*, iii, 190, fn. 2 and 257, fn. 8) takes *Akṣapatalika* to mean 'keeper of records' while according to Stein (on *Rājataraṅgiṇī*, v. 301, 397-98) *akṣapaṭala* denotes 'accounts office'. *Mahākṣapaṭalika* may therefore be taken in the sense of 'chief record-keeper' or 'chief accountant'. But in the present context the former connotation appears more appropriate. For references, see *HDS*, iii, 975 and 995.
56. Kailāsa's son Avala appears to be the same as the *Kāyastha* Āllava who wrote the Satalma plates of Mahābhavagupta's 8th regnal year (above, IV: V). But in that record he is styled simply *Kāyastha* or 'a clerk'. He was evidently promoted to the post of the 'chief record-keeper' sometime prior to the date of the present record.
57. The intention was probably to state that Avala was attached to the *Mahāsāndhivigrahin* Malladatta, the word *pratibaddha* between the mention of Malladatta and Avala being dropped out by inadvertence. Malladatta is also mentioned in some other records of Mahābhavagupta I where he is said to have been son of Dhāradatta.

IV : VII

GAINTALA PLATES[1] OF MAHĀBHAVAGUPTA JANAMEJAYA, YEAR 17

Provenance: Gaintala, Bolangir District, Orissa.
References: S. N. Rajaguru and M.P. Dash, *OHRJ*, xi, 192–97 and plates between pp. 194–95 and 196–97; S. N. Rajaguru, *IO*, iv, 124–29.
Language: Sanskrit. In a mixture of prose and verse.
Metres: Verse 1–3 and 5–12; *Anuṣṭubh*; Verse 4: *Indravajrā*; Verse 13: *Śālinī*; Verse 14: *Puṣpitāgrā*; Verses 15–16; *Sragdharā*.
Script: Northern class of alphabets.
Date: Regnal year 17, Māgha śukla 13. About the close of the ninth century A.D.

TEXT[2]

First Plate

1 सिद्धम[3] [।*] स्वस्त्यमलमणिकुट्टिमसदनचलदनेकवार विलासिनीज–
2 नचरणनूपुर[4]खत्रस्तपारावतपुन्या (ञ्ज)स्वनवधिरित[4a] दशदिग्नानादिग्देशा–
3 न्न(न्त)रा गत[5]वन्दिजनविस्तारितकीर्त्तिर्व्विविधविद्यालंकृतविद्वजनजनतिकाव्यकलाप–
4 स्तुतधनपतिविभ[व]स्फूर्ज्जित[6]विपणिजनान्योन्यसंहर्षविचित्रप्रासादाट्टालिका[7]–
5 देवकुलोद्यानवापिकु(कू)पतडागारामोपशोभाजितसुरपुरमहिम्नः ।[8] **श्रारा–**
6 **मसमावसितश्रीमतो विजयकटकात्**प(प)रमभट्टारकमहा–

1. Each of the plates measures about 8.3'' in length and 5″ in width. The hole in the left margin, through which the ring passed, is ½″ in diameter.
2. From plates in *OHRJ*, xi. The plates are unfortunately very bad, and a considerable portion of the record has not come out at all. In all such cases we had to depend on the transcript of Rajaguru and Dash.
3. Rajaguru and Dash: Oṁ. Expressed by a symbol.
4. Rajaguru and Dash: नुपूर.
4*a*. Rajaguru and Dash are wrong when they suggest to correct it to वधीरित.
5. Rjaguru and Dash suggest to correct it to नबागत°. Elsewhere also they have not maintained distinction between *v* and *b*. Such cases being numerous, we shall ignore them.
6. Rajaguru and Dash: स्फुर्ज्जित. In other records we have *sparddhita*.
7. The last three letters of the line are not clear in the plate and Rajaguru and Dash read *prāsād-āṅka-śālina*. The reading given by us is based on other records where this passage occurs.
8. This mark of punctuation is unnecessary.

7 जाधिराजपरमेश्वरश्रीशिवगुप्तदेवपादानुध्यातपरमभट्टार–

8 कमहाराजाधिराजपरमेश्वरपरममाहेश्वरसोमकुलतिल–

9 कतृ(त्रि) कलिङ्गाधिपतिश्री**महाभवगुप्त**राजदेव [:*] कुशली। निमुनाविषयीय–

10 ऋ(ऋ) षिग्रामे (व्रा)(ब्र)ह्मणानी(न्)सम्पू(म्पू)ज्य[9] तद्विषयीययथाकालाध्यासिनः समाह

11 र्त सन्निधातृनियुक्तकाधिकारिकादाण्डपाशिकपिशुन वे (वै)तृ(त्रि)का[10]वरोधजन–

12 राणकराजपुत्रराजवल्लभादीन्[11] सर्वान्(न्)[12] समाज्ञापयति [।*] शिवमस्माक–

13 मन्यत्[13] [।*] विदितमस्तु भवतां यथास्माभिरयं ग्रामः सनिधिः सोपानिधः

Second Plate : First Side

14 सर्व्वबा(बा)धाविवर्ज्जितः सर्व्वोपरिकरादानसमेतश्चतुशी(तुस्सी)मापर्यन्तः सा

15 म्व्र(म्र) मधु(धू)कः सगर्त्तोषरः सजलस्थलसहितः[14] ।।[15] व(ब) ह्वृचशाखाध्यायिने।[15] वच्छ(त्स)गो–

16 त्राय भार्गवच्यवनआप्नुवान (न्) और्व्वय(ज) मदग्निप्रवराय।[15] य(ज्ञ)मदग्निऔर्व्व-आप्नुवान (न्)–

17 च्यवनभार्गवआ(अ)नुप्रवराय।[15]मध्यदेशीयशालुविग्रामविनिर्गल.य।[15] कोसलदे–

18 शीयलपुसोड्डाग्रामवास्तव्याय।[15]भट(ट्ट)पुत्रश्रीतिकुनाम्वेमधुसु(सू)दनसुताय।[15]सलिलधा–

19 रापुरस्सरमाचन्द्रतारकार्कक्षि तिसमकालोपभोगार्थं मातापित्रोरात्म–

20 नश्च पुण्ययशोभिवृं (वृ)द्धये ताम्व्र(म्र)शासनेनाकरि(री)कृत्य प्रतिपादित इत्य–

21 वगत्य समुचितभोग भागकर[16]हिरण्यादिकमुपनयद्भिर्भवद्भिः सुखे–

22 न प्रतिवस्तव्यमिति।। भाविभिश्च भूपतिभिर्दत्तिरियमस्मदीया धर्म्मगौरवादस्म–

23 दनुरोधाच्च स्वदत्तिरिवानुपालनीयाः (या)। तथा चोक्तं[17] धर्म्मशास्त्रे [।*] व(ब)हु-भिर्व्वसु–

24 धा दत्ता राजभिस्सगरादिभिर्यस्य(भिः[।*] यस्य) यस्य यदा भूमिस्तस्य तस्य तदा फलं(लम्) [।।१।।*] मा भूद–

25 दफलशङ्का वः परदत्तेति पार्थिवाः [।*] स्वदानात्फलमानन्त्यं परदत्तानुपा–

26 लने।[।२।।*] षष्टिवर्षसहस्राणि।[18] स(स्व)र्गे मोदति भूमिदः [।*] आक्षेप्ता चानुमन्ता च त(ता) न्ये–

27 व नरकं(के) वसेत्।[।३।।*] अ।(अ)ग्नेरपत्यं प्रथमं सुवर्णं भूर्व्वैष्णवी सूर्य्यसुताश्च गावः।

9. Rajaguru and Dash: संपुज्य.
10. Rajaguru and Dash propose to correct it to बेत्रका. In *IO*, iv, it is proposed to be corrected to *vetrakā*.° I feel that वेत्रिक need not be corrected to वैत्रिक. Some other scholars have left it uncorrected. In this Ms. itself, it has not been corrected in all cases.
11. Rajaguru and Dash: °भादान.
12. सर्व्वान is the reading of Rajaguru and Dash.
13. This expression is not met with in any other record and does not yield any satisfactory meaning.
14. Read सजलस्थलः or जलस्थलसहितः.
15. This mark of punctuation is superfluous.
16. This word has been left out by Rajaguru and Dash.
17. Rajaguru and Dash: चोत्कं.
18. This punctuation mark is not required.

Second Plate : Second Side

28 यः काञ्चनं गां च महीञ्च दद्यात् दत्ता[19]स्त्रयस्तेन भवन्ति लोकाः [॥४॥*] आस्फोटयन्ति पि–

29 तरः प्रवल्गयन्ति[20] पितामहाः । भूमिदाता कुले जातः स नस्त्राता[21] भविष्यति ॥[५॥*] भूमिं यः प्र–

30 तिगृह्णाति यश्च (श्च) भूमिं प्रयच्छति । उभौ तौ पुण्यकर्म्माणौ नियतं स्वर्ग्गगामिनौ [॥६॥*] तडागानां–

31 सहस्राणि[22] वाजपेयशतानि[23] च [।*] गवां कोटिप्रदानेन भूमिहर्त्ता न शुध्यति [॥७॥*] [24]सुवर्ण्णमेकं गामे–

32 कां[25] भूमेरप्यर्द्धमङ्गुलं (लम्) [।*] हरन्नरकमायाति यावदाहूतसंप्लवं (वम्) ।[॥८॥*] आ (अ) न्यायेन हृता भूमिर–

33 न्यायेन तु हारिता [।*] हरतो हारयतश्चैव स हन्यात्सप्तमं कुलं (लम्) [॥९॥*] हरते हार–

34 यते यस्तु मन्दव (ब) द्धिस्तमोवृतः । स व (ब) द्धो वारुणैः पाशैः (शै) स्तिर्यग्योनिं स ग–

35 च्छति ।[।१०॥*] स्वदत्तां परदत्तां वा यो हरेद्व (त व) सुन्धरां (राम्) [।*] स विष्ठायां कृमिर्भु (र्भू) त्वा पच्यते पि–

36 तृभिस्सह ।[।११॥*] आदित्यो वरुणो विष्णुर्व्र (ब्र) ह्मा सोमो हुताशनः [।*] शूलपाणिस्तु भगवानभिन–

37 न्दन्ति भूमिदं (दम्) ।[।१२॥*] सामान्योयं धर्म्मसेतुर्नृपाणां काले काले पालनीयो भवद्भिः [।*] सर्व्वानि–

38 तान् भाविनः पार्थिवेन्द्रान् भूयो भूयो याचते रामभद्रः ।[।१३॥*] इति कमलदलाम्वु (म्बु) वि (बि)–

39 न्दुलोलां श्रियमनुचिन्त्य मनुष्यजि (जी) वितं च । सकलमिदमुदाहृतं च वे (बु) [द्*]ध्वा न हि पु–

40 रु (रु) षैः परकीर्त्तयो विलोप्या [॥१४॥*] इति सकलभूपालमौलिमालाविलग्नमाणिक्य–

Third Plate

41 मयु (यू) ख व्राताभिरञ्जित क्रमकमल[26] युगलप्रचण्डदोर्दण्डमण्डलाग्रतुण्ड (?) खण्डिता–

42 राति[27] मत्तमातङ्गविमुक्तमुक्ताफलप्रसाधिताशेषरणमहीमण्डलः । (ल) परमभट्टा–

43 रकमहाराजाधिराजपरमेश्वरश्रीजनमेजदेवस्य पादप्रवर्द्धमानवि–

44 **जयराज्ये सम्व (संव) त्सरे सप्तशमे[28] माद्य[मा*] से शि (सि) तपक्षे त्रयोदश्या (श्यां) यात्राङ्कतः स–**

19. Better read दद्याद्दत्ता।°
20. Read प्रवल्गन्ति.
21. Rajaguru and Dash are wrong in suggesting to correct it to सन्नस्त्राता.
22. Read सहस्रेण.
23. Read °शतेन.
24. Rajaguru and Dash: स्वर्ण्ण°.
25. Rajaguru and Dash unnecessarily suggest the insertion of the *akṣara bā* after *kāṁ*.
26. Rajaguru and Dash read कर्ण. The relevant letters are not clear in the illustration. The restoration is based on other records which contain this passage.
27. Rajaguru and Dash: त्गति. But in *IO*, iv, these letters are correctly read.
28. Read सप्तदशे.

45 **म्व(संव)त् १७ माघ शुदि १३** [।*] आ(ग्र)स्ति क्षोणीश्वराणाममलमणिरुचामन्वया(यः) कौस्तुभाभः

46 शौर्यत्यागाम्बुराशे[29]र्व्विरचितविधिवद्दानशुभ्रीकृताभ्रः[30] [।*] श्रीमान्**जन्मेजया**–

47 ख्यस्तृ(स्त्रि)दशपतिसमः कृत्स्नगां[31] भोक्तुकामः प्रख्यातद्वेशि(षि) वङ्श[32]प्रविद[ल*]–

48 नपटुर्भू(र्भू)पतिः सोमवङ्शे[33] ।।[१५।।*।[34] ज्ञेयाशेषार्थशास्त्रस्मृतिविमलधिया[35] । [35a]वेद–

49 वेदाङ्गविद्याशिक्षाकल्पेतिहासप्रकटसुरगुरुप्राप्तभूयिष्ठधाम्नां[36] नाम्ना श्री–

50 साधारणेन[37] द्विजवरु(र)तनुना मन्त्रिणा यस्य राज्यं निर्व्यूढं सोयमुच्चैस्त्रिजगति विदितो

51 देव**जन्मेजय**श्रीः ।।[१६।।*][38] लिखितमिदं ताम्व्र(म्र) शासा(स)नं महासान्धिविग्रहो(हि)-राणकश्रीम–

52 ल्लदत्तप्रतिव(ब)द्धेन श्रीवच्छेन[39] शंकिल्लसुतेनेति ।। लिखितमिदं[40] ताम्व्र(म्र)शासन(नं) वणिक (क्) सि–

53 उल्लासुतहरदासेन लिखितमितिः (ति)[41] ।[।*]

ABSTRACT

The charter, opening with the auspicious formulae *siddham*, represented symbolically, and *svasti*, was granted from the prosperous and victorious camp pitched up at *Ārāma*[42] by king **Mahābhavagupta**,[43] who meditated upon the feet of king Śivagupta.[44]

29. Read राशि°. These letters have not come out in the illustration.
30. Rajaguru and Dash: कृताद्र: But in *IO*, iv, it has been correctly read.
31. Rajaguru and Dash: कृच्छगां. In *IO*, iv, Rajaguru reads कृच्छनगां. The relevant *akṣara* is not clear in the plate; but *kṛtsna-gāṁ*, suggested above, is found in some other charters containing this stanza.
32. Read वंश.
33. Read वंशे.
34. This verse is found in IV: II, IV and V also, though its position is not the same everywhere.
35. Rajaguru and Dash: ज्ञेया शेषार्थशास्त्रास्मृति विगणधिया. But in *IO*, iv, it has been read correctly.
35*a*. This mark of punctuation is unnecessary.
36. Rajaguru and Dash: धाम्ने.
37. Read साधारणेन without *śrī* as in other records where this verse occurs.
38. This stanza is met with in *supra*, IV: VI and *infra*, IV: VIII-X and XI also.
39. Read श्रीवत्सेन.
40. This is probably an error for उत्कीर्णमिदम्.
41. This is redundant.
42. The description of the camp at Ārāma is almost the same, and in the same words, as that of the town of Murasīman in IV:IV above and of Ārāma in IV:VI above which suffices to illustrate its unrealistic and conventional character.
43. Described as in the preceding charter, but the title *Parama-Māheśvara*, found in that record is conspicuous by its absence in the present inscription.
44. He is given the same titles as in the previous charter. The only difference is that here the sectarian style *Parama-Māheśvara* follows, and does not precede as in the previous inscription, the imperial title *Paramabhaṭṭāraka-Mahārājādhirāja-Parameśvara*.

Having honoured the Brāhmaṇas in the village Ṛṣigrāma situated in the district (*viṣaya*) of Nimunā gave away the village in favour of the *Bhaṭṭa-putra* Tiku, son of Madhusūdana, who was a student of the Bahvṛca *śākhā* and belonged to the Vatsa *gotra* with the five *pravaras* Bhārgava, Cyavana, Āpnuvan, Aurvva and Jamadagni and the same five *anupravaras*,[45] had migrated from the village of Śāluvi situated in Madhyadeśa and was a resident of the village Lapusoḍḍā[45a] situated in Kosala *deśa*, for the augmentation of the religious merit of his parents and of his own self. The gifted village was rendered tax-free by means of a copper-plate charter and was endowed with all the privileges and exemptions enumerated in the previous grant. The addressees of the royal command concerning the grant were all the officers posted in the district from time to time including, besides the *Samāhartṛ*, *Sannidhātṛ*, *Dāṇḍapāśika*, *Piśuna*, *Vaitrika*, the inmates of the royal harem and the royal favourites mentioned in the preceding charter, the *Niyuktaka*[46], *Adhikārika*,[47] *Rāṇakas* and *Rājaputras*.[48] The villagers were ordered to pay all the proper dues including the *bhoga*, *bhāga*, *kara* and *hiraṇya* to the donee.

Next follows the usual request to the future monarchs to uphold the grant and as many as fourteen imprecatory and benedictive stanzas, reported to have been taken from Dharmaśāstra, are cited in order to strengthen the entreaty.

The record is dated[49] the **thirteenth day of the white fortnight of the month of Māgha in the seventeenth year of the increasingly victorious reign of Janamejaya** whose pair of lotus-feet, it is stated, was variegated by the multitude of rays emanating from the jewels set in the garland adorning the crowns of all the kings and who had decorated the whole earth with the pearls drawn from the maddened elephants of the enemies vanquished by his terrible arms.[50]

We next find a couple of stanzas in praise of Janamejaya and his minister

45. But they are mentioned in a different order, viz. Jamadagni, Aurvva, Āpnuvān, Cyavana and Bhārgava.
45*a*. The localities have not been identified.
46. He is the same as *Niyukta*; but his function is not clear. See *HDS*, iii, 990, where some other epigraphical references are cited. According to Sircar (*IEG*, 221), he was probably a subordinate officer under *Āyuktaka*.
47. As in the case of *Niyuktaka*, the exact function of this officer also cannot be determined. It is generally taken as meaning a minister, magistrate, superintendent, governor or director. See *HDS*, iii, 977-78; *IEG*, 7. He is evidently the same as *Adhikārin*.
48. Literally meaning 'king's son', 'prince', this word as employed here and in some other records seems to denote 'nobleman' or 'knight'. *Vide CII*, iii, 218, fn. 1; *HDS*, iii, 1002; *IEG*, 272.
49. Both in words and figures.
50. This passage occurs in some other records also. See *supra*, IV: VI and *infra*, IV: VIII-X and XI. But here this description and the eulogy in the subsequent verses is intervened by the date.

Sādhāraṇa with which we are already familiar from some other records.[51]

The copper-plate charter was written by Śrīvaccha (Skt. Śrīvatsa), son of Śaṅkilla, who was attached to the *Mahāsandhivigrahin Rāṇaka* Malladatta.[52] It is again said to have been written by Haradāsa, son of the merchant (*vaṇik*) Siullā, which is evidently an error as elsewhere Haradāsa figures as an engraver.[53]

51. *Vide supra*, fns. 34 and 38.
52. While Malladatta is known from so many records of Mahābhavagupta I, the writer Śrīvatsa, son of Śaṅkilla, is not mentioned in any other inscription.
53. As Śrīvatsa has already been referred to as the writer, the mention of Haradāsa in the same capacity is obviously due to oversight. The intention appears to have been to refer to him as the engraver in which role he figures in the Sonpur plates of the 17th year of Mahābhavagupta I also (above, IV: VI). But in that inscription his father's name is spelt as Sīvṛllā.

IV : VIII, IX, X

CHAUDWĀR PLATES[1] OF MAHĀBHAVAGUPTA I JANAMEJAYA, YEAR 31

Provenance: Chaudwār, Cuttack District, Orissa.

1. Fleet, who re-edited one of these charters and noticed the remaining two grants, called them 'Kaṭak Copper-plate Grants' simply because they were found not very far from Cuttack. But while forwarding Rangalala Banerjea's article on one of these charters, John Beames stated that it was found at the village of Kapāleśvara on the north bank of the river Mahanadi opposite the city of Cuttack, about four miles distant from the Cuttack station (*IA*, v, 55). Banerjea, on the other hand, informs that the charter was actually found at Chaudwar, a place of considerable antiquarian interest, some 4½ miles north-east of the Cuttack post-office (*ibid.*, 58). This fact is also noticed by Fleet even though he preferred to christen the record after Cuttack. According to Rajendra Lal Mitra, one of the remaining two charters was also found at Chaudwar (*JPASB*, li, 9ff.). The findspot of the remaining grant is not quite certain, and Fleet, who noticed it, could only aver that the provenance 'appears to have been somewhere at, or closely in the neighbourhood of, Kaṭak' (*EI*, iii, 346). But it has to be remembered that this set of plates was received by Fleet from the same person (John Beames) who had forwarded Rangalal Banerjea's paper on the first-mentioned set of plates from Chaudwar. In view of this fact as well as the identity of contents it is very likely that this grant also was really found at the same place, i.e. Chaudwar. Therefore, we prefer to style these charters 'Chaudwār Plates'.

   Two of these charters have been published: one by Rangalala Banerjea (without plates, *IA*, v, 55ff) and later by J.F. Fleet (with plates, *EI*, iii, 347ff.) and the other by Rajendra Lal Mitra (*JPASB*, li, 9ff., without plates). Some information about the remaining charter has been furnished by Fleet (*EI*, iii, 346, c). The text engraved on the plates constituting this charter has not been published and their present whereabouts are also unknown. The transcripts of Banerjea and Mitra are full of errors; in the absence of the original plates or their impressions it is difficult to check Mitra's readings. S.N. Rajaguru has tried to restore the correct readings with the help of the plates attached to Fleet's edition of the record originally published by Banerjea. But as rightly pointed out by Fleet, the contents of all the three grants are literally identical except only the details about the villages granted. There is therefore no necessity of giving the text of each of these records separately, and it would suffice to give the text of only one record the readings of which can be checked with the help of the plates accompanying Fleet's transcript and to note the important differences noticed in other grants in the footnotes as has been done by Fleet. For the sake of convenience, following the chronological order of publication, the inscription published by Banerjea and Fleet may be numbered as VIII, that published by Mitra and Rajaguru (*IO*, iv, 145-50) and briefly noticed by Fleet (*EI*, iii, 346-47, D) as IX, and that only briefly noticed by him (*ibid.*, 346, C) as X.

   The plates of IV:VIII measure about 9. 3/8″ broad at the end and somewhat less in the middle, their edges being somewhat thicker than the inscribed portions so as to serve as rims for the protection of the writing. The ring, passing through the circular hole about the middle of the left margin of each plate, is circular, about ⅝″

References: Rangalala Banerjea, *IA*, v, 55-60;[2] R. L. Mitra, *JPASB*, li, 9-14;[3] J.F. Fleet, *EI*, iii, 345-51;[4] S. N. Rajaguru, *IO*, iv, 138-50;[5] R. D. Banerji, *History of Orissa*, i, 209-10; H. C. Ray, *Dynastic History of Northern India*, i, 400; Bhandarkar's *List*, Nos. 1562-1564.

Language: Sanskrit. In prose with the exception of the usual benedictive and imprecatory verses, a couple of eulogistic stanzas and a stanza probably referring to the *dūtaka* at the end.

Metres: Verses 1-3, 5-11 and 16: *Anuṣṭubh*; Verse 4; *Indravajrā*; Verse 12: *Puṣpitāgrā*; Verse 14: *Śārdūlavikrīḍita*; Verse 15: *Sragdharā*.

Script: Northern class of alphabets.

Date: Regnal year 31, Mārgaśīrṣa śukla 13. Beginning of the tenth century A.D.

TEXT[6]

First Plate

1 सिद्धम्[7] [*]स्वस्ति । श्रीम**दाराम**समावासिनः (त)[8]श्रीमतो विजयकटकात् । परमभट्टा–
2 रकमहाराजाधिराजपरमेश्वरश्रीशिवगुप्तदेवपादानुध्यातपरममाहेश्व–
3 रपरमभट्टारकमहाराजाधिराजपरमेश्वरसोमकुलतिलकत्रिकालिङ्गाधिपति–
4 [9]महाराजाधिराजश्री**महाभवगुप्तदेवः** कुशली । [10]कोश(स)लदेशे पोवाविश(ष)यीय–

---

thick and nearly $4\frac{1}{4}''$ in diameter, its ends being secured under a circular seal, nearly $1\frac{3}{4}''$ in diameter. It bears in relief on a somewhat countersunk surface the Abhiṣeka-Lakṣmī. The legend below it has become illegible.

The plates of IV: IX are $8\frac{5}{8}''$ broad and $5\frac{5}{8}''$ high and their edges are slightly thicker than the inscribed portions. The ring is about $\frac{5}{8}''$ thick with a diameter of 4″. The circular seal, which has a diameter of about $1\frac{3}{4}''$, is partly broken and its surface is completely effaced.

As regards IV: X, the plates measure about 9" in length and about $5\frac{3}{4}''$ in width and their edges are slightly raised with a view to protect the writing. The ends of the circular ring, about $\frac{5}{8}''$ thick and with a diameter of $4\frac{1}{8}''$, are soldered under the circular seal, nearly $1\frac{3}{4}''$ in diameter, bearing in relief on a somewhat countersunk surface the motif of Abhiṣeka Lakṣmī and, beneath it, a short legend referring to the issuer of the charter.

2. No. IV: VIII.
3. No. IV: IX.
4. No. IV: VIII edited and Nos. IV: IX-X briefly noticed.
5. Text of Nos. IV: VIII-IX.
6. From plates in *EI*, iii.
7. Expressed by a symbol. Fleet: oṁ.
8. IV: IX-X have समावासित:
9. The title *Mahārājādhirāja*, which has already been given in the preceding line, is repeated here by inadvertence.
10. This mark of punctuation is unnecessary.

5 रण्डाग्रामे[11] ।[12] तथा [13]ग्रलाण्डलाग्रामे[14] ।[15]ब्रा (ब्रा) ह्मणान् संपूज्य तद्विश (ष) यीयान्[16] यथाकाला–

6 ध्यासिनः समाहर्तृ सन्निधातृनियुक्तकाधिकारी (रि) क[17]दाण्डपाशिकचाट–

7 भट्ट (ट) पिशुनवेरि (त्रि) कावरोधजनराणक[राजपुत्र*][18] राजवल्लभादीन (न्) सर्व्वान् स–

8 माज्ञापयति । विदितमस्तु भवताम् यथास्माभिरयङ्ग्रामः ष (स) निधिस्सो–

9 पनिधिस्सदशापराधस्सर्व्ववा (बा) धाविवर्ज्जितस्सर्व्वोपरिककरादानसहितश्चतुः–

10 सीमापर्यन्तस्सा [म्र*][19] मधु (धू) कस्सगर्तोष [र*][20]स्सजलस्थलसहितः[20a] प्रतिनिषिद्धचाट भट्ट (ट) प्र–

11 वेशः ।[21]टृ (ट) कारी[22] विनिर्ग्गताय ।[23] कोश (स) ले तुर्व्वुनावास्तव्याय ।[23] भरद्वाजगोत्राय । वा (बा)–

12 र्हस्पत्याङ्गिरसप्रवराय ।[23] वाजसेन[24]शाखाध्यायिने भट्टश्रीमहत्तमसाधारणा–

13 य ।[25] भट्टश्रीशोभनसुताय ।[25] सलिलधारापुरस्सरमाचन्द्रतारकार्क्कक्षितिसम–

Second Plate : First Side

14 कालोपभोगाय ।[25] मातापित्रोरात्मनश्च पुण्ययशोभिवृद्धये ताम्र (म्र) शासनेनाकरी–

15 कृत्य प्रतिपादितमित्यवगत्य[26] समुचितभोगभागकरहिरण्यादिप्रत्यायमुपनय–

16 द्भिर्भवद्भिस्सुखेन प्रतिवस्तव्यमिति । भाविभिश्च भूपतिभिर्द्दत्तिरियमस्मदीया धर्म्म–

17 गौरवादस्मदनुरोधच्च स्वदत्तिरिवानुपालनीया ।। तथा चोक्तन्धर्म्मशास्त्रे । व (ब) हुभि–

18 र्व्वसुधा दत्ता राजाभिस्सगरादिभिः । यस्य यस्य यदा भूमिस्तस्य तस्य तदा फलम् ।[१।।*] मा भू–

11. Rangalala Banerjea: योधाविषयीदारण्डाग्रामे. In IV:IX, line 5 also we have the same incorrect spelling विशयीय for विषयीय.
12. This punctuation mark is superfluous.
13. Rangalala Banerjea: खलाण्डलग्रामे.
14. IV: IX, line 5, has कोश (स) लदेशे सन्दानाविश (ष) यीयत् (?तू) लेण्डाग्रामे and IV: X, lines 4-5, have कोश (स) लदेशे तुलुम्वखण्डीय अर्किआमाग्रामे.
15. This *daṇḍa* is not required.
16. In IV: IX, line 6, and IV:X, line 5, also we have विशयीयान् for विषयीयान्.
17. IV: IX, line 7, and IV: X, line 6, have the correct form °काधिकारिक.
18. This word has been supplied from IV:IX–X.
19. IV: IX, line 11, and IV: X, line 10 have साम्र.
20. This *akṣara* has not been dropped in IV: IX and IV: X.

20a. Read सजलस्थलः or जलस्थलसहितः.

21. This mark of punctuation is redundant.
22. In IV: X, line 11 also we have टृकारी for टकारी; but IV: IX, line 12 has टृकरा, obviously due to inadvertence.
23. This *daṇḍa* is superfluous.
24. IV: IX, line 13, and IV: X, line 12 also contain the same error. Read वाजसनेय.
25. This punctuation mark is uncalled for.
26. Read प्रतिपादित इत्यवगत्य.

19 दफलशङ्का व:[27]पपरदत्तेत्ति पार्थिवा: । स्वदानात्म(त्फ)लमानन्त्यं[28] परदाना[29]–

20 नुपालने [॥२॥*][30]षष्ठिम्वर्षसहस्राणि स्वर्ग्गे मोदति भूमिद: । आक्षेप्ता चानुम–

21 न्ता च द्वितीयन्नरकं[31] व्रजेत् ॥[3॥*] अग्नेरपत्यम् प्रथमम् सुवर्ण्णम् भूर्व्वैष्णवी

22 सूर्य्यसुताश्च गाव: । य: काञ्च (श्च)न(नं) गाञ्च(श्च) महीञ्च(श्च) दद्यात् दत्तास्त्रयस्तेन भवन्ति लोके (का:) [॥४॥*]

23 आस्फोटयन्ति पितर: प्रवल्गन्ति पितामहा: [।*] भूमिदाता कुले जात: स नस्त्राता भ–

24 विष्यति ॥[५॥*] भूमिं य: प्रतिगृह्णाति यश्च भूमिं प्रयच्छति । उभौ तौ पुण्यकर्म्माणौ नि–

25 यतं स्वर्ग्गगामिनौ ॥[६॥*] तडागानां[32] सहस्राणि[33] वाजपेयशता[नि*][34] च । गवां कोटिप्र–

26 दानेन भूमिहर्त्ता न शुध्यति ॥[७॥*] हरेत हारयेद्यस्तु मन्दवु(बु)द्धिस्तमोवृत:। सुव(ब)द्धो

Second Plate : Second Side

27 वा[रु*]णै:[35] पाशैस्तिर्य्यग्योनिं स गच्छति ॥[८॥*] सुवर्ण्णमेकं गामेकां भूमेरप्यर्द्धमङ्गुलम् ।

28 हरन्नरकमायाति यावदाभूतसंप्लवं (वम्) ॥[९॥*] स्वदत्ताम्परदत्ताम्वा यो हरेत वसुन्ध–

29 राम् । स विष्ठायाम् क्रिमिर्भूत्वा पितृभिस्सह पच्यते ॥ [१०॥*] आदित्यो वरुणो विष्णुर्व्व्र (र्ब्र)ह्मा

30 सोमो हुताशन: । शूलपाणिश्च भगवानभिनन्दति भूमिदम् ॥[११॥*] सामान्यो–

31 यं धर्म्मसेतुर्नृ (र्नृ) पाणां काले काले पालनीयो भवद्भि: । सर्व्वानेवं[36] भाविन: पार्थि–

32 वेन्द्रान् भूयो याचते रामभद्र: ॥[१२॥*] इति कमलदलाम्वु (म्ब) वि(बि)न्दुलो–

33 लां श्रियमनुचिन्त्य मनुष्यजीवितं च । सकलमिदमुदाहृत(तं) च वुद्वा[37]

34 न हि पुरुषै: परकीर्त्तयो विलोप्या: ॥[१३॥*] सकलभूपालमौलिमालावि–

35 लग्नमाणिक्यमयूख व्राताभिरञ्जि (ञ्जि) ताङ्घ्रि (ङ्घ्रि) कमलयुगल: प्रचण्डदोर्द्दण्डमण्ड–

36 लाग्रखण्डिताराति मत्तमातङ्गविमुक्तमुक्ताफलप्रसाधिताशेषरणमही–

37 मण्डल: ॥ यस्साध(धा)रण[38]नाम्नि मन्त्रितिलके विन्यस्य सर्व्वागमं धैर्य्योदन्वति ती–

38 व्रतेजसि धुरं राज्यस्य विप्रोत्तमे । नानाख्यानकविस्तरामृतरसास्वादाद–

27. Read पर°. This mistake is also found in IV: IX, line 21; but IV: X, line 19 has पर correctly.
28. Fleet reads मानन्द्य, but the last *akṣara* is undoubtedly *ntyaṁ*. Fleet informs that IV: X, line 20 also has *ānandyaṁ*; but IV: IX, lines 21-22, has *ānantyaṁ*, correctly.
29. Generally we get °*datt-ānu*°.
30. Better read षष्टिं वर्ष°.
31. The corresponding portion of this stanza in a majority of Somavaṁśin charters reads *tāny-eva narake*.
32. Fleet reads *taḍāgānā* and supplies *anusvāra*. But the *anusvāra* is quite clear in the lithograph accompanying his transcript.
33. Read सहस्रेण.
34. Read शतेन.. शतानि is also found in IV: IX, line 28 and IV: X, line 26, and Fleet wrongly regards it as correct.
35. In IV: IX, line 29 and IV: X, line 28, we have वारुणै: correctly.
36. We generally have *etān* instead of *evaṁ*.
37. Read बुद्ध्वा.
38. Fleet: साधारण.

39 मन्दस्फुरत्सन्तोषात्सुखमन्वभूदविरतं पृथ्थ्वीशचूडामिणः ।। [१४।।*] ज्ञा (ज्ञे) याश (शे) [षा*]र्थं[39]

Third Plate

40 शास्त्रस्मृतिविमलधिया वदवेदाङ्गविद्याशिक्षाकल्पेतिहासप्रकटसुरगु–
41 रुः प्राप्त[40] भूयिष्ठधाम्ना । नाम्ना साधारणेन द्विजवरविधिना मन्त्रिणा यस्य राज्यं नि–
42 व्यूढं सोयमुच्चैस्त्रिजगति विदितो **धर्म्मकन्दर्प्पदेवः** ।। [१५।।*][41]परममाहेश्वरपरम–
43 भट्टारकमहाराजाधिराजपरमेश्वरसोमकुलतिलकत्रिकलिङ्गाधिपतिश्री–
44 **महाभवगुप्तदेवपादपद्मप्रवर्द्धमानविजयराज्ये एकत्रिङशत्तिमे**[42] **सा (स) म्वत्स–**
45 **रे** [43] **। मार्ग शुदि तिथौ त्रयोदश्यां यात्राङ्के नापि सम्वत्**[44] **३१ मार्ग**
46 **शुदि १३** लिखितमिदं त्रिफलीताम्व्र (म्र) शासन (नं) महासान्धिविग्र[45]–
47 ही (हि) राणकश्रीमल्लदत्तप्रतिव (ब) द्धकायस्थश्रीमाहूकेन प्रियङ्करा–
48 दित्यसुतेनेति ।।[46] प्रणीतं कोश (स) लेन्द्रेण प्रतिवो (बो) ध्य मं (म) हत्तम [म्*] । श्रादत्त पुण्डरीका–
49 क्षः[47] शासनं ताम्रनिर्म्मितम् ।।[१६।।*] उत्किर्नित[48]माधवेन वासुषू (सु) तेनेति ।।[49]

ABSTRACT

The grants, inaugurated by the auspicious words *siddham* and *svasti*, the former represented by a symbol, were issued from the victorious camp stationed at **Ārāma**[50] by king **Mahābhavagupta** *I* who meditated upon the feet of king Śivagupta, both described exactly in the same manner as in the previous record.

39. In IV: IX, line 43 and IV: X, line 41 we have **ज्ञेयाशेषार्थं**, correctly.
40. Read °सुरगुरुप्राप्त°. IV: IX, line 44 and IV: X, line 42 have the correct reading.
41. The prose passage following verse 13 and verse 15, with **देवजन्मेजयश्रीः** instead of **धर्म्मकन्दर्प्पदेवः** found in these charters, are met with in IV: VI and IV: VII also, while stanza 14 is found in these records for the first time. In IV: VI the prose passage is wrongly used as an adjective of the place of issue.
42. Read **एकत्रिंशत्तमे**. IV: X, line 46 has **तिङशत्तिमे**.
43. Read **संवत्सरे**
44. IV: X, line 47 has **सम्वत**. Read **संवत्**.
45. Read °**सन्धिवि**°.
46. In IV: IX, line 51 we have **मूतेनेति** and in IV: X, lines 49-50 **सूषुनेति** for **सूनुनेति**.
47. Rangalala Banerjea: **श्रीदत्तपुण्डरीकाक्षः**.
48. Read **उत्कीर्णं**. Rangalala Banerjea: **तन्निर्म्मितं**,
49. Rangalala Banerjea: **वा सृष्टं लेनेति**. IV: IX, line 53 has **पूतेनेति** and IV: X, line 51 **षुतेनेति**, incorrectly.
50. The Gaintala plates (above, IV: VII) were also issued from the military camp located at Ārāma, while in the Sonepur charter (*supra*, IV: VI) Ārāma itself is mentioned as the place of issue.

After worshipping the Brāhmaṇas in the villages Raṇḍā[51] and Alaṇḍalā[52] situated in the Povā[53] *viṣaya*, the village called Tū (?Trū) leṇḍā[54] included in the Sandānā *Viṣaya*,[55] and the village named Arkigrāma[56] comprised in the Tulumva *khaṇḍa*,[57] all in the Kosala *deśa*, granted the same villages in favour of the *Bhaṭṭa*[58] *Mahattama*[59] Sādhāraṇa,[59a] son of the *Bhaṭṭa* Śobhana,[59b] who belonged to the Bharadvāja *gotra*, with the *pravaras* of Bārhaspatya and Āṅgirasa, and was a student of the Vājasaneyi *śākhā* of the *Yajurveda*, an immigrant from Ṭakārī[60] and a resident of the village Turvvunā.[61] The grant was accompanied by all the privileges specified in the previous record as well as the right to the *daś-aparādhas* and exemption from the entry of the *cāṭas* and

51. It has been identified with the modern Reṇḍā, six miles east of Bolangir, the headquarters of the district of the same name in Orissa (*EI*, xi, 199). According to Rangalala Banerjea, the name of the village is Dāraṇḍā, whereas S.N. Rajaguru (*IO*, iv, 144, fn. 5) states that it may be Nuṇḍā.
52. Modern Alandā, three miles east of Bolangir (*EI*, xi, 199). Rangalala Banerjea reads the name of the village as Khalāṇḍala while Rajaguru says that it may be Alaṇḍilā (*IO*, iv, 144, fn. 6).
53. Possibly the same as Potā, the headquarters of the Potā *viṣaya*, mentioned in the Patna plates of the 6th year and the Kālibhanā plates of the same year of Mahābhavagupta I (*supra*, IV: III and IV: IV), Povā, the headquarters of the *viṣaya* named after it, has been identified with the modern Pow in the former Sonpur State, 19 miles south of Binkā, 12 miles north-east of Bolangir and 8 miles north-east of Reṇḍā (*EI*, xi, 199) or Pua in the erstwhile Sonpur State (Binayak Misra, *Dynasties of Mediaeval Orissa*, 66). Rangalala Banerjea, however, reads the name of the district as Yodhā (*IA*, v, 55) which John Beames identifies with the Pargaṇā of Jodh, a few miles north of Cuttack.
54. Hira Lal doubtfully identifies it with the modern Tulendi, 6 miles north of Bolangir (*EI*, xi, 199) whereas others identify it with the modern Tiluṇḍa or Tulunda in the former Sonpur State (B. Misra, *Dynasties of Mediaeval Orissa*, 68). R.L. Mitra, however, gives, the name of the village as Ntralenu.
55. Sandānā, the headquarters of the *viṣaya* of the same name, is proposed to be identified with Sonda, 11 miles east of Sonpur (*EI*, xi, 199) or Saranda in the Bargarh Tahsil (B. Misra, , *Ibid*, 68). R.L. Mitra gives Sammānī as the name of the district.
56. Probably modern Harigan in the former Sonpur State (*ibid*.).
57. Identified with the modern Turum on the Mahanadi, 27 miles south of Sambalpur.
58. A title of the learned Brāhmaṇas.
59. In the Satalma grant of Mahābhavagupta I's 8th regnal year (above, IV:V), however, Sādhāraṇa, who figures as the *dūtaka* of that charter, is given the higher title *Mahāmahattama*. Why the lower title is employed in this record is not clear.

59*a*. He figures as the minister of Mahābhavagupta I in these and some other records, but as a donee he is mentioned only in these charters.

59*b*. Mitra wrongly reads the name in IV:IX as Khagadeva.

60. It is evidently the same as the famous Brāhmaṇa village in Madhyadeśa variously called Ṭakkārikā or Tarkārikā which is known to have supplied Brāhmaṇas to distant regions. For references see, *EI*, iii 350, fn. 13. Hira Lal proposes to identify it with the place of this name, 16 miles north-west of Gya (*EI*, xi, 199).
61. Not yet located.

bhaṭas, and the king's order concerning the grant was addressed to the same district officials posted from time to time as named in the preceding charter together with the *cāṭas* and *bhaṭas*. The villagers were asked to make over to the donee the *bhoga*, *bhāga*, *kara*, *hiraṇya* and other incomes as and when they fell due.

The ruler to follow in future are beseached to maintain the grant, and in support of this request thirteen benedictive and imprecatory stanzas, reportedly belonging to the Dharmaśāstra, are cited.

We next find a short prose passage and a couple of stanzas extolling the king, here named **Dharmmakandarpadeva**, and the minister Sādhāraṇa. Of these the prose passage and the second verse (v. 15) are already familiar to us from the previous record with the only difference that in the verse met with here the king's name Janamejaya, found in the preceding grant, is replaced by the new name **Dharmmakandarpadeva**. The other verse (v. 14), which is found for the first time, states that the king left the burden of the kingdom to the care of his Brāhmaṇa minister Sādhāraṇa and himself whiled away his time enjoying an uninterrupted pleasure derived from a variety of tales.

The charter is dated[62] the **thirteenth day of the bright half of the month of Mārgaśīrṣa in the thirty-first year of the increasingly victorious reign of Mahābhavagupta.**[63]

This charter, said to have comprised three plates of copper (*tri-phalī-tāmraśāsana*),[64] was written by *Kāyastha* Māhūka, son of Priyaṅkarāditya, who was attached to the *Mahāsāndhivigrahin Rāṇaka* Malladatta.[65] It is said that this charter on copper-plates, which was made (i.e. given) by the lord of Kosala[66] (i.e. Mahābhavagupta), was received by Puṇḍarīkākṣa after informing the *Mahattama* (v. 16).[67] It was written by Mādhava, son of Vāsu.

62. Both in words and figures.
63. In all other charters the name of the king in connection with the date is given as Janamejaya, the name Mahābhavagupta in this context being peculiar to these three charters.
64. Fleet, however, takes the expression *tri-phalī-tāmra-śāsana* to mean a 'set of three connected charters' (*EI*, iii, 345).
65. In the preceding six records also Malladatta is mentioned in connection with the writing of the charters. R.D. Banerji (*History of Orissa*, i, 209) is wrong in crediting him with the writing of these grants. *Kāyastha* Māhūka is not named in any other record.
66. It is only in this record that Mahābhavagupta I is styled *Kosalendra*.
67. Puṇḍarīkākṣa appears to have acted as the *dūtaka*. The *Mahattama*, who is said to have been informed of the grant, was probably Sādhāraṇa himself who is given this title earlier in these records. Fleet's rendering of *pratibodhya mahattamam* as 'intended to give information to the *Mahattama*' (*EI*, iii, 350-51) is not correct.

IV : XI

KĀLIBHANĀ PLATES[1] OF MAHĀBHAVAGUPTA I JANAMEJAYA, YEAR 34

Provenance: Kālibhanā, Sambalpur District, Orissa.

References: D. C. Sircar and P. C. Rath, *IHQ*, xx, 245–50 and plates between pp. 248 and 249; D.C. Sircar, *ibid.* 364; S.N. Rajaguru, *IO*, iv, 151–56 and plates facing pp. 152 and 156 and between pp. 154 and 155.

Language: Sanskrit. In prose except the usual benedictive and imprecatory stanzas and those eulogising the minister Sādhāraṇa and the king, about the end.

Metres: Verses 1–3 and 5–11: *Anuṣṭubh*; Verse 4: *Indravajrā*; Verse 12: *Śālinī*; Verse 13: *Puṣpitāgrā*; Verse 14: *Śārdūlavikrīḍita*; Verse 15: *Sragdharā*.

Script: Northern class of alphabets with an admixture of Devanāgarī and proto-Bengali alphabets.

Date: Regnal year 34, Āśvina vadi 8. Early tenth century A.D.

TEXT[2]

First Plate

1 सिद्धम्[3] [।*]ओम् [।*] स्वस्ति [।*] श्री**सुवर्णपुरसमावासितश्रीमद्विजयकटकात्** ।[4] परममा–
2 हेश्वरपरमभट्टारकमहाराजाधिराजश्रीशिवगुप्तदेवपादानुध्यात–
3 परममाहेश्वरपरमभट्टारकमहाराजाधिराज परमेश्वरसो–
4 मकुलतिलकत्रिकलिङ्गाधिपतिश्री**महाभवगुप्त**राजदेवः[3a] कोष(स्)लदे–
5 से(शे) ।[4] टोक्काराविषयीयकोन्नयिल्लाग्रामे ।[4] व्रा(ब्रा)ह्मणान् (न) संपूज्य तद्विषयीयय–
6 थाकालाध्यासिनः समाहर्तृ: (र्तृ) सनि(न्नि)धातृनियुक्तकाधिकारिक[दा*]ण्डपाशि–
7 कचाटभा(भ)टपिशुनवेत्रिकावरोधजनराणकराजपुत्रराजव–

1. The plates measure about 6¼" in breadth and about 8½" in length and are held together by a copper ring the ends of which are secured under a circular brass seal, a little over 1½" in diameter. The seal bears the goddess Lakṣmī, seated in *padmāsana* on a fully blossomed lotus, being bathed by an elephant standing on a full-blown lotus on either side. There is no legend.
2. From plates in *IHQ*, xx and *IO*, iv.
3. Expressed by a symbol. Rajaguru takes both the symbols together to stand for *om*.
3a. The expression *kuśali*, generally met with after the king's name, is missing here.
4. This *daṇḍa* is superfluous.

8 ल्लभादीन् सर्वान्[5] । [6]समाज्ञापयति । विदितमस्तु भवतां यथास्माभिरयं ग्रा–

9 मः सनिधिः ।[6] सोपनिधिः।[6] सदसा (शा) पराधः सर्व्वबा (बा) धाविवर्जितः[7] सर्वोपरिक[8]–

10 रकरादानसहितः चतुः [:*] सीमापर्यन्तः साम्रमधुकः सगर्त्तोषरः सज–

11 लस्थलसहितः[9] प्रतिनिसि (षि) ध (द्ध) चाटभा (भ) टप्रवेस (श) : श्रावस्त्यां मुक्तावथिग्रा–

12 मविनिर्गताय सदाकटकवास्तव्याय ।[10] कास्य (श्य) पगोत्राय ।[10] कास्य (श्य) पावच्छा[11]र–

13 नै ध्रुवप्रवराय ।[12] रि (ऋ) ग्वेदचरणाय ।[12]कालदेशी (शि) भट (ट्ट) पुत्रश्रीदेवुनाम्ने

Second Plate: First Side

14 **अञ्जिणिग्रामे** वास्तव्याय गाङ्गेयसुताय ।[12] अर्जुननप्त्रे सलिलधा–

15 रापुरस्सर (रं) ।[12] चन्द्रतारकाशिक्षितिसमकालोपभोगाय[13] मातापित्रोरात्मन–

16 स्च (श्च) पुण्ययसो (शो) भिवृद्धय (ये) ताम्त्र (म्र) सा (शास) नेनाकरीन्द्र (कृ) त्य प्रति-
पादितमित्यवगत्य[14] स–

17 मुचितभोगभागकरहिरण्यादिकमुपनयद्भिः (द्भि) भ (र्भ) वतिभ (द्भि) : सुखेन प्रतिवस्त––

18 व्यामिति । भाविभिस्च (श्च) भूपतिभिर्दत्ति[15] रियमस्मदीया धर्म्मगौरवादस्मदनु–

19 रोधाच्च स्वदत्तिरिवानुपालनीया । ता (त) था चोक्तं धर्म्मशास्त्रे । व (ब) हुभिर्वसुधा द- ।[16]

20 त्ता राजभिस्सगरादिभिः । यस्य यस्य यदा भूमिस्तस्य तदा फलं (लम्) [।।१।।*]

21 मा भू [द*] फल[श*] ङ्का वः परदत्तेति पार्थिवा [:*] स्वदानात्फलमनन्तं[17]परद–

22 त्तानुपालने । [।२।।*] षष्ठि (ष्टि) म्व (व) र्षसहस्राणि स्वर्गे मोदति भूमिदः । आक्षे–

23 प्ता चानुमन्ता च ।[18] द्वावेव नरकं व्रजेत[19] । [।३।।*] अग्नेरपत्यम् (त्यं) प्रथमम् (मं)
सुवर्ण्ण–

24 मू (र्ण्णं) भूर्व्वैष्णवी सु (सू) र्यसुत (ता) श्च गावः । यः काञ्चनम् (नं) गां चा (च) महीश्च
दद्यात् (द्) ।[20]

5. Sircar and Rath: सर्व्वान्.
6. This mark of punctuation is unnecessary.
7. Sircar and Rath: विवर्ज्जितः.
8. Sircar and Rath: सर्व्वो.
9. Better read सजलस्थलः.
10. This *daṇḍa* is uncalled for.
11. Read काश्यपवात्स्य°
12. This punctuation mark is not required.
13. In the Kālibhanā plates of the 6th year of Mahābhavagupta I (above, IV: IV) and in most other Somavaṁśin charters we have° रमाचन्द्रतारकार्क्कक्षितिसमकालोपभोगार्थं.
14. Read प्रतिपादित इत्यवगत्य.
15. Sircar, Rath and Rajaguru: °र्द्दत्ति°
16. This *daṇḍa* is redundant.
17. In the corresponding verse in the Kālibhanā grant of the 6th year of Mahābhavagupta I (*supra*, IV: IV) and in most of the Somavaṁśin grants we have °लमानन्त्यं.
18. This mark of punctuation is redundant.
19. As suggested by Sircar and Rath, द्वितयं नरकं व्रजेत् as in the Katak plates of Mahābhavagupta I's 31st regnal year (*supra*, IV: VIII) will be a better reading. In many other records we have तान्येव नरके वसेत् in place of द्वावेव नरकं व्रजेत्.
20. This *daṇḍa* is not required.

25 दत्तास्त्रयस्तेन भवन्ति लोके:(का:)। [।४।।*] आस्फोटयन्ति पितरं(रो) वल्गयन्ति[21] पिता-महा[:।*]

26 भूमिदाता कुले जात: स नत्रा(स्त्रा) ता भविष्यति ।[।५।।*। भूमी (मिं) य [:*] प्रतिगृह्णा(ह्णा)ति ।[22] यश्च

27 भूमिमीम्प्रयच्छति[23] । उभौ तौं पुण्यकर्म्मार्णौ नियतम् (तं) स्वर्ग्गगामिनौ ।।[६।।*]

Second Plate : Second Side

28 ता(त) डागानां सहस्राणि (स्रेण) वाजपेय(यैं)स्तथौ (थैं) व[24] च [।*]गवां कोटिदप्रदानेन भूमिहर्ता–

29 न शुध्यति ।[।७।।*] हरते हारयते[25] [य*] स्तु मन्दबुद्धिस्तमोवृत: [।*]सुव(ब)द्धो[26] वारुणौ (णैं): पासौ (शैं)ति(स्ति)–

30 यंक्(ग्) योनि: (निं)स गच्छति ।[।८।।*] सुवर्ण्णमेकं गामेकं (कां) [27] भूमेरध्यर्द्धमङ्गुलम् । हरन्न–

31 रकमायाति यावदाहू(भू)तसंप्लवम् [।।९।।*] स्वादा(द) त्तां परदत्त(त्तां)म्वा(वा) यो हरेद्वसुन्धराम्[28] ।

32 स विष्ठायां कृमिर्भूत्वा पितृभि: सह प्य (प) च्यते[29] । [।१०।।*] आदित्यम् (त्यो) वरुणो विष्णु:[30] (ष्णु)–।[31]

33 व्र(ब्र)ह्मा सोमो हुताशन: [।*] शूलपाणिस्तु भगवान् अभिनन्दन्ति[32] भूमिदम् ।।।११।।*।

34 सामान्योयं धर्म्मसेतुर्नृपाणां काले काले पालनीयो भवत्भि(द्भि) : [।*]

35 सर्व्वान्ने(ने)ता न्पा(न्भा) [विन:*] पार्थिवेन्द्रान(न्) भूयो भूयो याचते रामभद्र: ।[।१२।।*] इति कम–

36 लदलाम्वु (म्बु)[बिन्दु*] लोलाम् (लां) श्री(श्रि)यमनुचित्यं (न्त्य) मनुष्यजीवितम् (तं) [च*] । सकलमिदमुदा–

37 हृतम् (तं) व(च) वु (बु)द्धा न हि पुरुषौ(षैं): परकीर्त्तयो विलोप्या: । [१३।।*] सकल-भूपालमौलि–

21. In the Kālibhanā plates of the 6th year of the reign of Mahābhavagupta I (above, IV: IV) we have पितर: प्रवल्गयन्ति.
22. This mark of punctuation is superfluous.
23. Read भूमिं प्रयच्छति.
24. In most other Somavaṁśī records we have वाजपेयशतेन or वाजपेयशतानि, which latter is incorrect.
25. Read हारयेद् for the sake of metre.
26. In most other Somavaṁśin grants we have स बद्धो which is correct and gives better sense.
27. This mark of punctuation is uncalled for.
28. Read हरेत वसुन्धराम् for the sake of metre.
29. In the other Kālibhanā plates of the same ruler (*supra*, IV: IV) the second half of the stanza reads स विष्ठायां कृमिर्भूत: पच्यते पितृभि: सह.
30. Sircar and Rath: विष्ण:.
31. This *daṇḍa*, which is superfluous, has been left unnoticed by Sircar, Rath and Rajaguru.
32. Read भगवानभिनन्दन्ति.

38 मालविलग्नमाणिक्यमयूखव्राताभि[र*]ञ्जितक्रमकमलयू(यु)गलः प्रच–

39 दोण्डर्द्दण्ड (ण्डदोर्द्दण्ड) मण्डलाग्रतुण्डखण्डितारातिमत्तमातङ्गविमुक्तमुक्ताफ–

40 लप्रशा(सा)धितासे(शे)षरणमहीमण्डलः ।[33] यस्साधारणनाम्निमन्त्रिति–

Third Plate : First Side

41 लके विन्यस्य सर्व्वागमे ग्रामोदन्वति[34] तीव्रतेजसि धुरं राज्यस्य विप्रोत्त–

42 मे [।*] नानाख्यानकविस्तरामृतरसस्वादानु(द) मन्दस्फुरत्संतोषात्सुखम–

43 न्वभूदविरतम् (तं) पृथ्वीशचूडामणिः । [।१४।।*] ज्ञेयाशेषार्थशास्त्रस्मृतिविमलधि–

44 यो (या) वेदवेदाङ्गविद्याशिक्षाकल्पेतिहासप्रकटसुरगुरुप्राप्तभू–

45 मि(थि)ष्ठधाम्ना [।*] नाम्ना साधारणेन द्विज वरविधिना[35] मन्त्रिणां (णा) यस्य राज्य (ज्यं) नि–

46 व्यूढं सौ (शौ)र्यमुच्चैं (च्चै) [36]स्त्रि [ज*] गति विदितो[37] धर्म्मका(क)न्दर्पदेवः[38] ।। [१५।।*] परममा–

47 हेश्वरपरमभट(ट्ट)ारकमहाराजाधिराजपरमेश्वरसोमकु–

48 लतिलकतृ(त्रि)कलिङ्गाधिपतिश्री**जनमेजयदेवस्य प्रवर्द्धमाने**

49 **वि[ज*] ये (य) राज्ये स(सं)म्ब(व)त्सरे चतुस्त्रि (स्त्रिं) ङश(श)त्तमे अ[ा*]श्विन वदि अष्टम्याम् (म्यां) तिथौ**

50 **स(स)म्व(व)त् ३४ अ[ा*]श्विन वदि ८ ल्लि(लि) खितमिदं** ताम्रसा(शा)सनं महासा–

51 न्धिविग्रही(हि) कराणकश्रीधारदत्तस्याभिमतेन । श्रीइयोकेन

52 श्रीयपसुतेन उत(त्) कि (की)र्ण्णम्: ।।

ABSTRACT

The charter, opening with *siddham*, *om*, both represented by symbols, and *svasti*, was given away from the victorious camp located at **Suvarṇapura**[39]

33. With a slight change of words this passage and the following two stanzas describing the king and his minister Sādhāraṇa are also found in the Chaudwār plates of the thirty-first year of the reign of Mahābhavagupta I (*supra*, IV: VIII-X). The prose passage and verse 15, with *deva-Janmejaya-śrīḥ* in place of *Dharmma-kandarpa-devaḥ*, are also met within the Sonpur (above, IV:VI) and Gaintala (above, IV: VII) charters of the 17th year, but in the former it is erroneously employed as an epithet of the place of issue.
34. Read सर्व्वागमग्रामोदन्वति. The Chaudwār charters of the 31st year have सर्वागमं धैर्योदन्वति. (*supra*, IV: VIII-X text-line 37).
35. In the Sonpur (*above*, IV: VI) and Gaintala (above, IV: VII) plates of the 17th regnal year we have तनुना in place of विधिना.
36. The Sonpur (*supra*, IV: VI), Gaintala (above, IV: VII) and Chaudwār (above, IV: VIII-X) charters have सोयमुच्चै° which is correct and should be substituted here.
37. Sircar, Rath and Rajaguru: धम्म° but the superscript *r* is quite clear in the facsimile.
38. In the Sonpur (above, IV: VI) and Gaintala (above, IV: VII) grants we have देवजनमेजयश्रीः instead.
39. Modern Sonpur, Sambalpur District, Orissa.

by the king **Mahābhavagupta** I, who meditated on the feet of the king Śivagupta, both of whom are given the same titles as in the preceding grant, with the only difference that the sectarian epithet *Paramamāheśvara* is applied here to Śivagupta also whereas the title *Parameśvara*, used with reference to the same ruler in the previous grant, is dropped.

The king, after worshipping the Brāhmaṇas, granted the village of Konnayillā[40] situated in the Ṭokkārā *viṣaya*[41] in the Kosala-*deśa*[42] in favour of the Brāhmaṇa *kāladeśin*[43] *Bhaṭṭaputra* Devu, son of Gāṅgeya and grandson of Arjuna, who was an immigrant from the village named Muktāvathi[44] situated in Śrāvastī[45] and a resident of the village called Añjiṇi[46] but always lived at the royal camp[47] and belonged to the Kāśyapa *gotra*, with the *pravaras* of Kāśyapa, Vātsya and Naidhruva, and was a student of the *Ṛgveda* together with the same privileges and exemptions as specified in the previous records. The addressees of the king's order in respect of the grant were also the same as those mentioned in the preceding grant. The villagers were ordered to pay the donee all the dues including the *bhoga*, *bhāga*, *kara* and *hiraṇya* when due.

Future kings are entreated to keep up the grant and this entreaty is sought to be supported by thirteen customary benedictory and imprecatory stanzas attributed to the Dharmaśāstra.

Next follows a brief eulogy of the king and his minister Sādhāraṇa in a mixture of prose and verse, which is also met with in the previous inscription.

40. It has not been identified. But Sircar and Rath are reminded of Kanarllā on the river Tel; but as pointed out by them, this locality lies more than a hundred miles from Ṭukrā which is supposed to represent Ṭokkārā.
41. According to Sircar and Rath, the site of Ṭokkārā, the headquarters of the district named after it, is probably represented by the modern village of Ṭukrā, well-known for its brass and bell-metal industry, some fourteen miles to the east of the town of Bargarh in the Sambalpur District, Orissa. Rajaguru regards it as identical with the place called Ṭakkārikā mentioned in some other inscriptions; but this suggestion is simply untenable.
42. I.e. South Kosala.
43. I.e. an astrologer predicting auspicious and inauspicious moment for military march and other purposes.
44. Evidently the same as Muktāvastu (or its variants) referred to in the three grants of Paramāra Arjunavarman (*JASB*, v, 379; *JAOS*, vii, 27 and 32) and the Mandhata plates of his successor Devapāla (*EI*, ix, 111] as well as in early Bengal inscriptions [R.C. Majumdar (ed.), *History of Bengal*, i, 579] as a prominent Brahmanical centre which supplied Brāhmaṇa migrants to a larger number of places situated at long distances. Unfortunately, it has not been identified so far.
45. Modern Set-Mahet on the border between the Gonda and Bahraich districts of Uttar Pradesh.
46. It has not been identified so far.
47. The expression in the original is *sadā-kaṭaka-vāstavyāya*. As the donee is clearly described as a resident of the village Añjiṇi, the word *sadā-kaṭaka* cannot be taken as the name of a locality and the expression has to be explained as referring to one who had to reside permanently at the royal camp for discharging his duty.

The grant was issued on the **eighth day of the dark fortnight of the month of Āśvina in thirty-fourth year[48] of the increasingly victorious reign of Janamejaya.**

The epigraph was written with the permission of the *Mahāsāndhivigrahika Rāṇaka* Dharadatta,[49] and incised by the illustrious Iyoka, son of the illustrious Yapa.

48. The date is specified both in words and figures.
49. As indicated by the Chaudwār plates (above, IV: VIII-X), up to the 31st year of Mahābhavagupta I's reign, Malladatta, son of Dhāradatta, occupied the office of the *Mahāsāndhivigrahin*. Dhāradatta must have evidently taken over as the *Mahāsāndhivigrahin* sometime between the 31st and 34th years. The relationship of this Dhāradatta with his predecessor Malladatta is not specified. But it seems likely that he was the son of Malladatta.

IV : XII

ORISSA STATE MUSEUM PLATES[1] OF MAHĀŚIVAGUPTA I YAYĀTI, YEAR 4

Provenance: Not known.

References: S.N. Rajaguru, *IO*, iv, 159-66 and plates between pp. 160 and 161 and 162 and 163; *ARIE*, 1964-65, No. A-48; P.R. Srinivasa, *EI*, xxxviii, 186-91 and plates facing pp. 188 and 189.

Language: Sanskrit. In a mixture of prose and verse[1a].

Metres: Verses 1-4: *Śārdūlavikrīḍita*; Verses 5-8 and 10-15: *Anuṣṭubh*; Verse 9: *Indravajrā*; Verse 16: *Śālinī*; Verse 17: *Puṣpitāgrā*.

Script: Northern class of alphabets.

Date: Regnal year 4, Kārttika śukla 5. First half of the tenth century A.D.

TEXT[2]

First Plate

1 सिद्धम्[3] [।*] स्वस्ति [।*] श्री**विनि(नी)तपुरात** (त्) समावाशि(सि)तश्रीमतो विजय-
कटकात (त्)[4] [स्व]-

2 स्त्यस्तु [॥*] [5]समस्तस(श)त्रु[6]नृपतिप्रारव्ध[7](ब्ध)सेवाविधि[8]व्यग्राकारविनीतदूर[9]निचित-
स्यामाश्रम-

3 द्रा(?)रत:[10] । धम्मर्थोचितशास्त्रनिश्चितनयण्यापारपौरप्रजाख्यातामात्यम-

1. The plates, the sides of which are not straight, measure approximately 20.5 cm in length and 14.8 cm in breadth and their edges are slightly raised. The ring, which passed through the circular hole in the left margin, and the seal, if any are missing.

1a. The text of the initial metrical portion is very corrupt and does not yield satisfactory meaning.

2. From plates in *IO*, iv, and *EI*, xxxviii.

3. Rajaguru: Om. Expressed by a symbol.

4. It ought to be corrected to श्रीविनीतपुरसमासितश्रीमद्विजयकटकात्.

5. A few more *akṣaras* are required at the beginning of the verse in order to complete the metre as well as to bring out its meaning. According to P.R. Srinivasan, the missing *akṣaras* may have been उत्खातात्म.

6. Srinivasan: शत्रु Rajaguru wrongly proposes to correct it to शतृ.

7. Srinivasan: प्रारब्द.

8. Rajaguru: °वधि.

9. Rajaguru: दूत.

10. The reading and interpretation of this portion are very doubtful. Rajaguru reads स्यामाश्रमज्ञा(?)रत: Srinivasan reads °स्यामाग्रमा [द्वा?] रत:. and proposes to correct it to °स्तदा मार्गम्. It does not, however, help in getting the sense.

4 तद्विनीतपुरतोन्वर्थ[11]प्रसिद्धाह्वयात(त्) ।[१।।*] सोमादिस्वकुलोद्गतक्षितिरु(भु)जां देवत्व–

5 भाजामपि [12]क्ष्मायाश्चात्ममनोभवाञ्छित[13]प्रतिप्रेप्सा[14]नुरूपश्रियः । नागाना–

6 मत्र[15]भूतसौहृदजुषामाकस्मिकानुग्रहा(हो)[16] यज्ञात्मा [17]प्रहणक्षणस्तिभुवने(न)क्षे–

7 माय[वै][18] लक्षितः[19] ।।[२।।*] प्रख्याताख्ययुधिष्ठिरान्वयमहासिङ्घा(सिंहा)सना[20]–

8 रोहणव्याप्त्या(प्ता)रावसराहितोत्सवमनोलोकामिनन्द्योदयः [।*] निः–

9 शेषागमतत्व(त्त्व)वेतृ(त्तृ)विमलप्रज्ञाव(ब)लाल(लं)कृतः स्फूर्ज्जत्सौ(च्छौ)र्य्यविनिर्ज्जितोर्ज्जि–

10 तरिपुक्ष्मापालवेलोद्गमः[21] ।।[३।।*] सप्तद्वीपविभूषणं क्षितितलं य[ः*] प्रोद्द–[22]

11 यालंकृतं त(त्*) प्रोतस्थितसोमराजविभुताम्धत्ते[23] त्तमन्यैद्यतः[24] । देवः श्रीजन–

12 मेजयस्तदधुना तत्रावतीर्य स्वयं त[त्*] कुर्यामिति यः कृतावतरणः स श्रीययाति–

13 तिप्रभुः ।।[४।।*] परममाहेस्व(श्व)रपरमभट्टारकमहाराजाधिराजपरमे–

14 श्वरसोमकुलतिलकत्रिकलिङ्गाधिपतिश्रीमहाभवगुप्तरा–

Second Plate : First Side

15 जदेवपादानुध्यायी ।।[25] परममाहे[श्व*]रपरमभट्टारकमहाराजाधिराज–

16 परमेश्वरसोमकुलतिलकत्रिकलिङ्गाधिपतिश्री**महाशिवगुप्त**रा–

17 जदेवः[26]कुस(श)ली । [27]उड्देसे(शे)[28] ।[29] गण्डितमविषय(ये) कुड्कुलोखण्डक्षेत्रे

11. Rajaguru: °न्यर्थः.
12. As pointed out by Srinivasan, the *akṣara kṣmā* is not properly formed. Rajaguru reads म्मार्या° and proposes to correct it to क्ष्मापा°.
13. Rajaguru: वान्छित.
14. Srinivasan first reads wrongly °प्राप्सा° and then suggests to correct it and the preceding two letters as परिप्रेप्सा°
15. Rajaguru suggests to correct it to °*mantra*° and Srinivasan to °*mati*°. The latter meets the metrical requirements.
16. Srinivasan reads °नुम्र[हा] and proposes to correct it to °नुग्रहः.
17. Rajaguru: यज्जत्नाग्र'
18. Traces of this letter are clear in the facsimile given by Rajaguru while it is completely blurred in the plate accompanying the transcript of Srinivasan who ignores it altogether even though this or some such letter is required by the metre.
19. Srinivasan feels that probably संलक्षितः is intended.
20. Srinivasan: सिङ्घांहसना°.
21. Srinivasan: °लोद्यमः.
22. Srinivasan: यद्..; but in the facsimile प्रोद्द appears to be quite clear.
23. Rajaguru: °तामुन्ने°.
24. Srinivasan: °द्यैतः. He thinks that the intended reading may be दब्दोर्द्दयालंकृतं तत्पौत्रस्थितसोमराजत्रिभुतां धत्तेत्र मन्येद्य तत्.
25. This mark of punctuation is unnecessary.
26. Srinivasan: कुशली.
27. This *daṇḍa* is superfluous.
28. Srinivasan: देशे.
29. This punctuation mark is uncalled for.

18 तद्विषयीयव्रा(ब्रा)ह्मणानापुक्त[30] यथाकालाध्यासिनः[31] समाहर्तृ:(र्तृ)सन्निधातृ(तृ)नि–

19 युक्तकाधिकारिकदाण्डपासि(शि)का(क)चाटभा(भ)टपिसु(शु)न[32] वे(वै)त्रिका[33] वरोधजनराणकरा–

20 जपुत्रराजवल्लभादीन (न्) [34]समाज्ञापयति[35] [।*] विदितमस्तु भवतां ।[36] यथास्माभि–

21 रय(यं) ग्रामः सनिधिः सोपनिधिः सदसा(शा)पराधः [37]सर्व्ववा(बा)–

22 धाविवर्ज्जितः [स*]र्व्वोपरिकरादानसहितः (त) श्चतुःसीमापर्य–

23 न्तः [38]स(सा)म्रमधुकः सगर्त्तोषरः[39] सज[ल*]स्थलसहितः [40]द्व(अ)चाटभटप्रप्रवेस(श)क–

24 :।[41] कौसि(शि)कगोत्वा(त्र) त्रिरिषय[42]प्रवराय [43]श्रावस्थालेखडियांग्रामविनिर्ग्गता–

25 य।[44] सदा[45]कटकवास्तव्याय [46]भट्टपुत्रदामोदरनप्त्रेमधुसुताय।[47] श्रीका—

26 कोनाम्ने सलिलधारापुरस्सरं ग्राचन्द्रतारक[48] (का)र्कशिक्षितिसमकालोपभो–

27 गार्थम्[49] मातापित्रोरात्मनश्च पुण्ययशोभिवृद्धये ताम्रशासनेनाकरीकृ–

28 त्य प्रतिपादित इत्यवगत्य यथादीयमानकरभरहिरण्यभोगभागा–

29 [दिकं] च ददद्भिः भवद्भिः सुखेन प्रतिवस्तव्यमिति । भा[50]–

Second Plate : Second Side

30 विभिश्च भूपतिभिर्द्दत्ति[51]रियमस्मदीया[52] धर्म्मगौरवादस्मदनुरोधाच्च स्वदत्ति–

31 रिवानुपालनीया [।*] तथा चोक्तं धर्म्मशास्त्रे [।*] व(ब)हुभिर्व्वसुधा दत्ता राजभिः सगरा–

32 दिभिः [।*] यस्य यस्य यदा भूमिस्तस्य[53] तस्य तदा फलं(लम्) ।[।५।।*] माभूदफलस(श)ङ्का

30. Rajaguru पुक्ष; Srinivasan: °युक्त. Read °नापूज्य.
31. Srinivasan: °ध्यायिनि. Following the usual draft, the relevant portion ought to have been worded as follows: कुडुकुलोखण्डक्षेत्रे ब्राह्मणानापूज्य तद्विषयीययथाकालाध्यसिनः.
32. Rajaguru: पिसुल.
33. Srinivasan: वेतृकाः°.
34. Rajaguru reads वलभादीन्.
35. समाज्ञापयती is Srinivasan's reading.
36. This *daṇḍa* is not required.
37. Rajaguru: पराधं° ; Srinivasan: °शापराधः.
38. Rajaguru: साम°
39. The suggestion of Rajaguru to correct it to सगर्त्तोसरः is wrong.
40. Better read सजलस्थलः.
41. This mark of punctuation is redundant.
42. Read °र्ष्यार्षेय°
43. Rajaguru reads °स्थीलिख°.
44. This punctuation mark is superfluous.
45. Srinivasam: यस(श)°.
46. Srinivasan: भट°.
47. This *daṇḍa* is unnecessary.
48. Rajaguru: तारका°.
49. Rajaguru: °भोगार्थः.
50. After this letter space sufficient to accommodate seven or eight letters has been left unutilised.
51. Srinivasan reads °र्दति°
52. Rajaguru's suggestion to correct it to *ddha* is uncalled for.
53. Srinivasan: भूमिः तस्य.

33 वः पर [दत्तेति पार्थिवाः । स्व] दत्तात्फलमानु(न)न्त्यं परदत्तानुपालने ।।[६।।*] आ-

34 स्फोटयन्ति [पितरः प्रवल्गन्ति] पितामहाः [।*] भूमिदाता कुले जातः स

35 नस्त्राता भविष्यति [।।७।।*] [षष्टिवर्षसह] स्राणि स्वर्ग्गे मोदति [54]भूमिदाः (दः) [।*] आक्षेप्ता

36 चानुमन्ता च द्वौ तौ नरकगामिनौ[55] । [।८।।*] अग्नेरपत्यं प्रथमं सु-

37 [वर्ण्णं भू]र्व्वैष्णवी सूर्यसुताश्च गावः [।*] यः काञ्चनञ्गां च [म*] हीञ्च

38 [दद्यादत्ता] स्त्रयस्तेन भवन्ति लोकाः ।। [९।।*] भूमिं यः प्रतिगृह्णाति यश्च भूमिं

39 प्रयच्छति [।*] उभौ तौ पुण्यकर्म्माणौ नियत(तं) स(स्व)र्गगामिनौ [।।१०।।*] तडागा-

40 [नां सहस्रेण वाज] पेयस(श) तेन[56] च [।*] गवा(वां) कोटिप्रदानेन भूमिहर्त्तान सु(शु)ध्य-

41 ति ।।[११।।*] हरेत हारयेद्यस्तु मन्दवु(बु)द्धस्तिमोवृतः [।*] [57]सुव(ब)द्धो वारुणौ(णैः)[58] पासै (शैः)

42 [तिर्य्यग्योनिं स] गच्छति ।।[१२।।*] [59]सुवर्ण्णमेका(कं) गामेकां[60] [61]भूमि(मे)रप्यर्द्धमङ्गलं (लम्) हरन्नरकमाया-

43 ति यावदाभूतसंप्लवं(वम्) ।।[62] [१३।।*] स्वदत्तां[63] परदत्ताम्वा(त्तां वा)यो हरेत वसुन्धरां (राम्) ।

Third Plate

44 [म]विष्ठायां कृमि[र्भूत्वा] पितृभिस्सह पच्यते ।।[१४।।*] आदित्यो वरुणो विष्णुर्व्र(र्ब्र)ह्मा [सो]-

45 मो[64] हुतास(श)नः । शूलपाणिस्तु[65] भगवानमिनन्दन्ति[66] भूमिदं (दम्) ।।[१५।।*] सामान्योयं ध[र्म्म]-

46 सेतुर्नृपानां(णां) काले काले पालनीयो भवद्भिः [।*] सर्व्वानेतान् भाविनः पा[र्थि]-

47 वेन्द्रान् भूयो भूयो याचते रामभन्द्रः ।। [१६।।*] इति कमलदलाम्वु(म्बु)वि(बि)न्दुलोलां श्रि-

54. Srinivasan: भूमिदः.
55. Rajaguru reads °वासिनौ.
56. Rajaguru: सतानि; Srinivasan: शतेन.
57. Rajaguru reads स्व°.
58. Rajaguru: वारुण्यै. Srinivasan: वारुणैः.
59. Rajaguru: स्वर्ण्णमेकां वा.
60. These words, which had been left out by oversight, were later engraved in small letters below the line between the *akṣaras sva* and *da* in the next line. At the end of these words we find the mark + showing that this is a letter insertion of what was originally omitted.
61. Rajaguru: भूमे°.
62. Rajaguru's reading is यावच्चन्द्रदिवाकरम्.
63. Rajaguru reads गामेकां between *sva* and *dattāṁ*; but as pointed out above, it actually forms part of the previous line and has absolutely nothing to do with this line.
64. Rajaguru is wrong in taking the full word as forming part of this line.
65. Srinivasan: °पाणिश्च.
66. Srinivasan's reading is °नन्दति.

48 यमनुचिन्त्य मनुष्यजीवितञ्च [।*] सकलमिदमुदाहृतं च वु(बु)द्ध्वा न हि पु[रु*]षैः[67] पर–
49 कीर्त्तयो विलोप्याः ॥[१७॥*] परममाहेस्व (श्व)रपरमभट्टारकमहाराजा–
50 धिराजपरमेस्व(श्व)रसोमकुलतिलकत्रिकलिङ्गाधिपति–
51 श्रीम**द्ययातिराजदेवविजयराज्ये [68]चतुर्थसम्वत्सरी**[69]–
52 **यआर्तिकमाससितपक्षपञ्चम्यां अङ्कतः सं॰वत्**[70] ४[71] **कार्त्तिक**–
53 **शुदि**[72] ५। लिखितमिदं ताम्रसा(शा)सन(नं) मा(म) हासान्धिविग्रहिराण–
54 कश्रीच्छिछटेस्व(श्व)रस्यावगतेन।[73] महाश्राक्षपटल[74] श्रीशान्ति–
55 नागाभिमत्तेन[75] ॥[76] श्रीपन्नाकेन[77] उत्कीर्ण्णमिदमिति ॥[78]

ABSTRACT

The auspicious words *siddham*, represented symbolically, and *svasti*, which mark the commencement of the record, are followed by the mention of the prosperous and victorious camp pitched at **Vinītapura**[79] from where the charter was issued and which is described in a conventional manner in the opening verse. The stanza, of which a few initial letters are missing and which suffers from considerable textual corruption, seems to state that the city of Vinītapura had a meaningful name inasmuch as it looked verily as an entry to the hermitages pitched up by the humble messengers of all the enemy kings anxious to render various kinds of service, evidently to the victor (Mahāśivagupta I), and was well-known for its ministers who had earned great renown among the townsfolk on account of their following proper policies based on the Dharmaśāstra and Arthaśāstra works.[80] The following three stanzas contain in a eulogy of king Janamejaya and his son and successor, **Yayāti**, the issuer of the grant. These verses do not admit of

67. Srinivasan: पुरुषैः. But the letter *ru* is conspicuously absent in the facsimile.
68. Rajaguru's reading is चतु ४. But the last letter is clearly *rtha*. The untenability of Rajaguru's reading is also indicated by the fact that the regnal year in figure is given in the following line.
69. Read संवत्सरी°.
70. Read संवत्.
71. The two curved strokes following *t* appear to be intended for 4.
72. Rajaguru and Srinivasan: सुदि.
73. This mark of punctuation is uncalled for.
74. Read महाक्षपटल°
75. °*Nāg-ābhidhānena* seems to be the intended reading so that the record was drafted by Śāntināga himself.
76. A single *daṇḍa* would have done.
77. Rajaguru's reading is यल्लाकेन.
78. After this there are traces of a couple of indistinct lines of writing which have led Rajaguru to conclude that the record is a palimpsest.
79. Probably represented by the modern Binkā on the Mahānadī in the erstwhile Sonpur State, some 16 miles up, now included in the Bolangir District, Orissa.
80. This interpretation is based on the reading adopted by us.

a satisfactory interpretation owing to textual corruption. Verse 2 seems to allude to the claim of the Somavaṁśin rulers to divinity because of the origin of their family from the moon and their descent on the earth in spite of their divinity for the welfare and prosperity of the earth (i.e. world). It also refers to the favour done by Janamejaya to the Nāgas[81] who were friendly with him, his devotion to sacrifices and efforts for the wellbeing of the three worlds. Verse 3 states that his rise to power (i.e. coronation) was welcome by the people who were reminded of the festivities marking the occasion of the accession to the great throne belonging to the lineage of the well-known epic hero Yudhiṣṭhira; he was adorned by the pure intellect which had mastered the essence of all the *āgamas* as well as by his power and he had vanquished his powerful enemies by his rising valour. In the following stanza he is described as an ornament of the seven *dvīpas* (i.e. the entire world) and as possessing the greatness of the moon[82] and as verily an incarnation of the homonymous epic hero; then came king **Yayāti** who was eager to emulate the meritorious deeds of his illustrious father.

The *Paramabhaṭṭāraka-Mahārājādhirāja-Parameśvara*, the illustrious **Mahāśivagupta**, a devout devotee of Maheśvara, an ornament of the Soma-kula and lord of Trikaliṅga, who meditated on the feet of the *Paramabhaṭṭāraka-Mahārājādhirāja-Parameśvara*, the illustrious Mahābhavagupta, a devout devotee of Maheśvara, an ornament of the Soma-kula and lord of Trikaliṅga, being in good health, after worshipping the Brāhmaṇas in the village called Kuḍukul okhaṇḍakṣetra[83] included in the Gaṇḍitama *viṣaya*[84] in the Uḍra *deśa*, ordered the *Samāhartṛ*, *Sannidhātṛ*, *Niyuktaka*, *Ādhikārika*, *Dāṇḍapāśika*, *Cāṭas*, *Bhaṭas*, *Piśuna*, *Vaitrika*, inmates of the royal harem, *Rāṇaka*, *Rājaputra*, the king's favourites and others stationed in the district from time to time that he had given away the village in favour of the Brāhmaṇa named Kāko, son of Madhu and grandson of the *Bhaṭṭaputra* Dāmodara, who belonged to the Kauśika *gotra* with the three *pravaras*, and immigrated from the village Śrāvasthālekhaṇḍiya-grāma[85] and was a permanent resi-

81. Possibly here we have an allusion to the help which Janamejaya might have given to a contemporary Nāga chief of some adjoining area. But it is difficult to say any thing definite in the absence of details.
82. Alternatively the reference may be to a ruling chief named Somarāja who was defeated and deprived of his position by Janamejaya. It is also possible that there is an allusion here to Janamejaya trying to emulate the eminence and prosperity of the grandson of Yudhiṣṭhira, Parīkṣit, who, like the Somavaṁśī kings, also claimed descent from the moon. The comparison may have been suggested by the sameness of the names of Parīkṣit's son Janamejaya and the homonymous Somavaṁśin ruler.
83. It is not impossible that the name of the village was only Kuḍukulo, the second part of the name, viz. *khaṇḍa-kṣerta*, being used in the sense of a field as in some other records from Orissa. Cf. R.D. Banerji, *History of Orissa*, i, 207.
84. Neither Kuḍukulo nor Gaṇḍitama has been identified.
85. It has yet to be identified. It is also not unlikely that this is not the correct form of the name and reference may be to a village situated in the Śrāvastī area from which several Brāhmaṇa donees are known to have migrated to and settled at different places in eastern India, notably Orissa and Bengal.

dent of the royal camp,[86] for the increase of the religious merit of his parents and of his own self and for enjoyment as long as the moon, the stars, the sun and the earth endure. The granted village, which extended to its four boundaries and was rendered tax-free by means of a copper-plate charter, carried with it all the usual privileges and exemptions named in the preceding record. The villagers were ordered to make over to the donee all the dues such as *kara*, *bhara*,[87] *hiraṇya*, *bhoga* and *bhāga* as they were paid (to the state) hithertofore and live happily in the village.

Future kings are exhorted to uphold the grant as if it were their own grant, and this request is sought to be supported by thirteen customary benedictive and imprecatory stanzas said to have been extracted from the Dharmaśāstra.

The grant is dated the **fifth day of the bright half of the month of Kārttika in the fourth year of the victorious reign of the Paramabhaṭṭāraka-Mahārājādhirāja-Parameśvara, the illustrious Yayāti,** a devout worshipper of an ornament of the Soma-kula and lord of Trikaliṅga.[88]

This copper-plate charter was written by a person, whose name has not been given, with the knowledge of the *Mahāsāndhivigrahin*, *Rāṇaka* Cchichaṭeśvara and at the behest of the *Mahākṣapaṭala* Śāntināga[89] and was engraved by one Pannāka.

86. According to Srinivasan's reading, the donee was a resident of the village called Yaśakaṭaka which is proposed to be identified with the modern Cuttack. However, this identification cannot be taken seriously as the antiquity of Cuttack does not go to the period of the Somakulī rule in Orissa. The expression *sadā-kaṭaka-vāstvya* occurs in *supra*, IV: XI, line 12, also.
87. This revenue-term, of which the connotation is not clear, is not known to occur in any other record.
88. The date is expressed both in words and figures.
89. In case the intended reading was *Śāntināg-ābhidhānena*, as stated above, Śāntināga himself was the writer. He appears to have belonged to the same Nāga family a few members of which are mentioned in some other records of Mahāśivagupta I Yayāti.

IV: XIII

PĀTṆĀ PLATES[1] OF MAHĀŚIVAGUPTA I YAYĀTI, YEAR 8

Provenance: Somewhere in the erstwhile Pāṭṇā State, Bolangir District, Orissa.

References: Ganga Mohan Laskar, *JASB*, New Series, i, 6–7 and 14–16; R.D. Banerji, *History of Orissa,* i, 213; H.C. Ray, *Dynastic History of Northern India,* i, 402–03; Bhandarkar's List, No. 1565; D.C. Sircar, *JAS*, Letters, xix, 117–24 and plates between pp. 124 and 125;[2] S.N. Rajaguru, IO, iv, 167–75; K.C. Panigrahi, *Chronology of the Bhauma-Karas and the Somavaṁśīs of Orissa,* 49–52.

Language: Sanskrit. In prose except the benedictory and imprecatory and eulogistic stanzas at the end.[2a]

Metres: Verses 1–4 and 6–11; *Anuṣṭubh*; Verse 5: *Indravajrā*; Verse 12; *Śālinī*; Verse 13: *Puṣpitāgrā*; Verse 14: *Rathoddhatā;* Verses 15–17: *Upajāti.*

Script: Northern class of alphabet.

Date: Regnal year 8, Mārgaśīrṣa śukla 13. First half of the tenth century A.D.

TEXT[3]

First Plate

1 सिद्धम्[4][।*] ओ[म्*] स्वस्ति । श्रीवि(नि)नी)तपू(पु)रात(त्)[5] कटकात् पर[म*] माहेस्व (श्व)रपरमभ–

1. Each of the plates is 8·2″ long and 5·6″ broad and between ·1 to ·15″ in thickness. The ring-hole is about ·8" in diameter. The edges of the plates are raised for the protection of the writing. The seal, which is soldered to the joint of the ring, is about ·6″ thick and and 3·6″ in diameter. The circular surface within a raised rim bears the familiar device of Abhiṣeka-Lakṣmī.
2. Sircar calls this charter 'Bolangir Museum Plates' as the plates are now deposited in the Bolangir Museum.

2a. The text of the inscription is very carelessly drafted and full of errors. Such important items as the list of government officers normally mentioned in connection with the order about the grant and privileges and exemptions have been altogether omitted or seriously curtailed.

3. From plates in *JAS*, *Letters*, xix.
4. Expressed by a symbol. Laskar takes both the symbol and the letter following it as standing for *om*.
5. Laskar reads °पूरात्; while Sircar's reading is °पुरात.

2 ट्टारकमहाराजाधिराजश्रीमहाभवगू(गु)प्त[6]राजदेवपा[दा*]नू(नु)ध्यायी ।[7]

3 परममाहेस्व(श्व)रपरमभट्टारकमहाराजाधिराजपरमेस्व(श्व)रसो–

4 मकू(कु)लतिलकत्रिकलिङ्गाधिपतिश्रीमहाशिव[8]गू(गु)प्तराजदेवः कू(कु)स(श)–

5 लीः (ली) कोसलदेसे(शे)[9] ।[10] सनूलाविषयीय तलकज्जग्रामसम्व(म्ब)न्धो(द्धो)–

6 त्तरदी(दि)शा(श्य)वरीय[11]नदीसमेतभूमिश्चतुःशी(सी)मयाक्षिप्रे–

7 वतः[12] . . . . . .[13] व्रा(ब्रा)ह्मणान्सम्पूज्य चद्विषयीयः[14]

8 निषिद्धचाटभटप्रवेश(शा) कस्य ।[15] गोत्रय[16] क(का)श्यपावत्सा[र*] नैध्रु[व*] प्रव–

9 राय ।[17] वादशेन[18] म(मा) ध्यन्दिनश(शा)खाध्यायी(यि)ने।[19] [20]माध्वालविनि[र्ग]-ताय

10 कोसलजलजडुवास्तव्याय ।[21] [22]श्रीकामदेवनाम्ने ।[23] हर्षनप्त्रे ।[23a] न–

11 रसिंह(सिंहि) सू(सु)ताय[24] ।[25] [सलिलधारा*] पू (पु) रःसरमाचन्द्रतारकार्क्कक्षितिसम-कालाय भो–

12 गार्थं[26] मातापित्रोरात्मनश्च पुण्ययसो(शो)[27]ऽभिवृद्धये ताम्रशासनेना–

6. Laskar: गुप्त.
7. This mark of punctuation is superfluous.
8. Laskar's reading is सिव°.
9. Laskar: देशे.
10. This punctuation mark is superfluous.
11. Laskar: °तुरदाशानरीय°.
12. Laskar proposes to correct it to *kṣiptavataḥ*. Sircar reads *kṣiptivataḥ* and suggests to correct it to *kṣiptivatī*, the entire expression beginning with *catuḥ* being an adjective of the preceding *bhūmiḥ* and referring to the practice of demarcating the boundary of the granted land by burying charcoal, husks of grain, etc. It may be pointed out, however, that the last letter of line 6 cannot be read anything but *pre*. Cf. *pta* in earlier lines.
13. Here a few letters had been incised and were erased later.
14. Sircar: वद्विषयीः. Read तद्विषयीय°. Normally the words ब्राह्मणान् सम्पूज्य come immediately after the mention of the village to be donated and the expression तद्विषयीय precedes the list of officers to whom the royal order in respect of the grant is addressed. The present charter, however, contains no such list. Sircar suggests to read तद्विषयीय before ब्राह्मान्.
15. This *daṇḍa* is uncalled for.
16. Read काश्यपगोत्राय.
17. This *daṇḍa* is unnecessary.
18. Sircar: वादसेन. Read वाजसनेय.
19. This punctuation mark is redundant.
20. Laskar: माध्वील.
21. This *daṇḍa* is superfluous.
22. The letter *śrī* has escaped the notice of Sircar.
23. This mark of punctuation is uncalled for.

23*a*. Laskar has left this mark of punctuation, which is, of course, superfluous, unnoticed.

24. Laskar: सुताय.
25. This *daṇḍa*, which has not been noticed by Laskar, is unnecessary.
26. Laskar's reading is °कालोपभोगार्थं which is usually found in other copper-plate charters.
27. Laskar: यशो°.

13 करीकृत्य प्रतिपादी(दि)त(ता)इत्यवगत्य यथादीयमानकरहिरण्य–

Second Plate: First Side

14 भोगभागादिकं[28] ।[29] ददद्भी(द्भिः) भवद्भिः सू(सु)खेन[30] प्रतिवस्तव्यमिति ।[31] भाविभिस्च (श्च)[32] भू–

15 पतिभिर्द्दन्ति(त्ति)[33] रियमस्मदीया [34]धर्म्मगौरवादस्मदनू(नु)रोधाञ्च[35] ।[36] [37]स्वदत्तिरि–

16 वान(नु) पालनीया[33] । तथा चोक्तं धर्म्मसा(शा)स्त्रे[39] [।*][40] व(ब)हुभिर्व्वसू(सु)धा दत्ता राजभिः सग–

17 रादिभिः । यस्य यस्य यदा भूमिस्तस्य तस्य तदा फलः (लम्) [।।१।।*] मा भूदफलस(श)–

18 ङ्का वः ।[41] परदत्तेति पार्थिवाः । स्वदत्तात्फलमानन्त्यं परदत्तानू(नु)पा–

19 लने ।[।२।।*] आस्फोटयत्ति(न्ति) पितरो वल्गयत्ति(न्ति) पितामहाः [।*] भूमिजा(दा) ता कू (कु) ले

20 जातः स नस्त्राता भविष्यति ।[।३।।*] षष्टिवर्षसहस्राणि स्वर्गे मो–

21 दति भूमिदः [।*] आक्षेप्ता चानू(नु)मत्ता(न्ता)च ।[41]द्वौ तौ नरकगामिनौ

22 ।[।४।।*] अग्नेरपत्य(त्यं) प्रथम(मं) सू(सु)वर्ण्ण (र्ण्णं) भूवौ(र्वै)ष्णवि(वी) सूर्यसू(सु) तास्च (श्च) गावः [।*] यः क(का)ञ्च–

23 नङ्गा(ङ्गां) च महीञ्च दद्य (द्या) द्दत्तास्त्रयस्तेन भवत्ति(न्ति) लोकाः ।[।५।।*] भूमि(मिं) यः प्रतिगृ–

24 ह्ला(ह्णा)ति यस्च (श्च) भूमि (मिं) प्रयच्छति । उभौ तौ पू(पु)ण्यकर्म्माणौ नियतं स्वर्ग्गगा–

25 मिनौ ।[।६।।*] तडागाना(नां) सहस्रेण वाजपेयस(श)तेन च । गवां कोटिप्रदा–

26 नेन भूमिहर्त्ता न सुध्यति[42] ।[।७।।*] हरति(ते) हारयेद्यस्तु मन्दवु(बु)द्धिस्तमोवृतः ।

27 सुव(ब)द्धो वारुण्यै (णै):[43] पाशैः (शै)ति(स्ति)र्य्यग्योनिषु[44] गच्छति ।।[८।।*]

28. Sircar: °भागादीकं.
29. This superfluous *daṇḍa* has escaped Laskar's notice.
30. Laskar: सुखेन.
31. This punctuation mark, which is redundant, has escaped the notice of the previous editors.
32. Laskar: भाविभिश्च.
33. Laskar: °द्दंत्ति°.
34. Laskar: धर्म्मा°.
35. Laskar: °दनुरोधा°.
36. This *daṇḍa*, which is superfluous, has not been noticed by Laskar.
37. Laskar: दत्ति; ; Sircar: सदत्ति°.
38. Laskar: °नुपालनीया.
39. Laskar: धर्म्मशास्त्रे.
40. The imprecatory and benedictory stanzas found hereafter have been omitted by Laskar.
41. This *daṇḍa* is not required.
42. Read शुध्यति.
43. Sircar: पासैः
44. We generally have °योनिं स.

Second Plate: Second Side

28 सुवर्ण्णमेका(कं) गामेका(कां) भूमेरप्यर्द्धमङ्गुलं (लम्)। हरन्नरकमायाति यावदा–

29 हूतिसंप्लवं (वम्) ।।[९।।*] स्वदत्ताम्परदत्ताम्वा[45] यो हरेत वसुन्धरां (राम्)। स विष्ठायां कृमिभू(र्भू)ते[46]

30 पितृभिः सह पच्यते ।[।१०।।*] ग्रादित्यो वरुणो [47] विष्णू(ष्णु)व्र(र्ब्र)ह्मा सोमो हू(हु)तास(श)नः [।*]

31 सू(शू)लपाणिस्च(श्च) भगवानभिनन्दन्ति भूमिदं(दम्)[48]। [।११।।*] सामान्योयन्धर्म्मसे–

32 तुर्नृपाणा(णां) काल(ले)[49] कल(काले) पालनीयो भवद्भिः [।*] सर्व्व(र्व्वा) नेतान(न्) भ (भा)विनः पा–

33 र्थिवेन्द्रान(न्) भु(भू)यो भु (भू)यो याचते रामभद्रः ।[।१२।।*] इति कमलदलाम्वु (म्बु)–

34 वि(बि)न्द(न्दु)लोलां श्रियमनुचिन्त्य मनुष्यजीवितञ्च ।[50] सकलमिदमु–

35 दाहृतञ्च वु(बु)द्धा(द्ध्वा)न हि पुरुषैः परकीर्त्तयो कि(वि)लोप्याः ।[।१३।।*] परममाहे–

36 श्वर[51]परमभट्टारकमहाराजाधिराजपरमेस्व(श्व)रसोमाकुलति–

37 लकत्रिकलिङ्गाधिपतिश्रीम**द्ययातिदेवस्य**[52] **विजयराज्ये साम्व(संव)**–

38 **त्राषमे**[53] **म(मा)र्गशिर(रो)मासे शुक्लपक्षे त्रयोदश्यामङ्के सम्व(संव)त् ८**

39 **मार्ग्गशुदि**[54] **१३** लिखितमिदं ताम्रशासनं महासन्धिविग्रहिराण–

40 कश्रीधारदत्तस्यावगतेन[55] ।[56] [57]उत्थितासनी(नि)श्रीउच्छवणागस[58]–

Third Plate

41 [59]मक्षेणाल्लवसुतेन[59a]। उत्कि(त्की)र्ण्ण(र्ण्णं) विज्ञानी(नि)माधवेन वासुसुतेनेति। सम्वा (म्प)–

42 दो जलजपर्ण्णजलाभा जीवितं मरणसन्ततिसंस्थं(स्थम्) [।*] भोगभुक्ती(क्ति) रचिरा–

43 य[60]विलोक्याः (क्या) कीर्त्तयो नृपतिभिर्न विलोप्या [।।१४।।*] इतिः[61] सोभु(भू) नृ(न्नृ)पः सो––

45. Read दत्तां वा.
46. Read °र्भूत्वा which is Sircar's reading.
47. Sircar: विष्णु°
48. Sircar: भूमिदः.
49. Sircar: काले.
50. This *daṇḍa* has been left unnoticed by Sircar.
51. Sircar: माहेश्वर.
52. Laskar reads °द्ययातिदेवराजस्य.
53. Read °राष्टमे which is the reading of Laskar.
54. Laskar: श्रुदि.
55. Laskar: °स्मावगतेन.
56. This mark of punctuation is superfluous.
57. Laskar doubtfully read उत्तृिता° and thought that the second letter probably ought to be read as *tvi*.
58. Read श्रयुतसवनाग°.
59. Laskar: मम्फे° Rajaguru: °म्पे°
59*a*. ठच्छवणागेणाल्लपसुतेन seems to be the intended reading.
60. Laskar: °रतिनां° प्र°.
61. Read *iti* which is Sircar's reading.

44 मकुलाञ्ज(ब्ज) भानु: स्वभावतुङ्गो निजपौरुषेण। य: कोसला–
45 पालनकौमू(मु) दे (दी)न्दु[62]र्विजित्य चौ(चै)द्यान्वितताना[63]लक्ष्मी: (क्ष्मीम्)। [।१५।।*]
रामाह–
46 रा(रां)श्चेदिपवद्धटान्[64] स भट(ट्ट) पेड्डिप्रभृति(ती)न् (नु)[पेत्य*][65] मुण्डं [66] निका–
47 त्प्राहितशर्व्वराम:।[67] सलक्ष्मणो राम इवाप्तसे
48 तु:।[।१६।।*] तस्मात(त्) सू(सु)तो विष्णुरिवाजनिष्ट[68]।[69] स्व[70] दूर्गराजम्वी घटप्रता–
49 पं[71] [।*] तृणाय चइद्यं[72] वत मन्यमनो[73] दग्धा डहाला[74] विजना[75]–
50 श्चकार।–।[१७।।*]

ABSTRACT

Commencing with the auspicious formulae *siddham,* indicated symbolically, *om* and *svasti* and issued from the camp pitched up at **Vinītapura**[76] by the *Paramabhaṭṭāraka-Mahārājādhirāja-Parameśvara*, the illustrious **Mahāśiva-gupta,** a devout worshipper of Maheśvara, an ornament of the Soma-kula and lord of Trikaliṅga, who meditated on the feet of the *Paramabhaṭṭāraka-Mahārājādhirāja*, the illustrious Mahābhavagupta, a devout worshipper of Maheśvara, the charter records that the king, being in good health and after worshipping the Brāhmaṇas, granted a piece of land situated in the northern part of the village of Talakajja[77] included in the Sanūlā *viṣaya*[78] in the Kosala

62. Laskar: कौमुदिन्दु,°; Sircar: कौमुदेन्दु°
63. Laskar: लक्ष्या:.
64. Laskar: ; °शिदेपवद्धभटान्; Rajaguru: श्चेदिपवद्ध(जा*)त्थान्. Read बद्धपट्टान्. A few syllables have been omitted in this as well as in the next foot of the verse by oversight.
65. This restoration of missing letters is suggested by Sircar.
66. Laskar: मृकुमिकल्पान्तितशखं राम:; Rajaguru reads विकल्प्याहित°. S.K. Mookerjee, quoted by Sircar, thinks that the intended reading probably is निकृत्या हृतसर्व्वराम:. Sircar: निकण्या°.
67. This *daṇḍa* is superfluous.
68. Laskar reads तस्मादसुते विषुरिवाजक्षिष्ट.
69. This mark of punctuation is not required.
70. Read *sa* which is Sircar's reading.
71. Laskar: सदृगराजम्वीघटप्रणीप; Sircar दुर्गराजम्विघटं. Read दुर्गराजं विकटप्रतापम्.
72. Read चैद्यं. Laskar reads these and the preceding three letters as तृणायजईषु.
73. Read मन्यमानो which is Sircar's reading.
74. Read दग्ध्वा डहालां. Laskar' reads दश्चाडहाणा.
75. Laskar reads विजंना°.
76. The relevant expression is *Vinītapurāt kaṭakāt*, and Sircar is in favour of taking the word in the sense of 'city'.
77. Probably represented by the modern village of Talagaja, ten miles south-east of Bolangir, in the former Patna State, now incorporated in the Bolangir District, Orissa.
78. The headquarters of the district, Sanūla, has been identified with Soinnūla, 20 miles south of Bolangir and 22 miles south-west of Talagaja (*EI*, xi, 200) or Somara (Binayak Misra, *Dynasties of Mediaeval Orissa*, 68), Bolangir District.

country together with the bed of the lower (flow of the) river[79] and extending to its borders on all the four sides in favour of a Brāhmaṇa named Kāmadeva, son of Narasiṁha and grandson of Harṣa, who belonged to the Kāśyapa *gotra* with the Kāśyapa, Āvatsāra and Naidhruva *pravaras,* was a student of the Mādhyandina *śākhā* of the Vājasaneya *caraṇa* (of the *Yajurveda*), an immigrant from Mādhvāla[80] and a resident of Jalajaḍḍa[81] situated in Kosala. The granted land, which was meant for enjoyment as long as the moon, the stars, the sun and the earth endure and was given away for the augmentation of the religious merit and fame of the donor's parents and of his own self, was turned into a rent-free holding by means of a copper-plate charter. The villagers were exhorted to pay the *kara, hiraṇya, bhoga, bhāga* and other dues to the donee as paid hitherto.

Thirteen familiar imprecatory and benedictory stanzas, said to have been taken from Dharmaśāstra, are quoted in order to strengthen the customary entreaty to the future kings to maintain the grant as if it were their own grant.

The record is dated the **thirteenth day of the bright fortnight of the month of Mārgaśīrṣa in the eighth year of the victorious reign of king Yayāti,**[82] who is described exactly in the same words as in the previous inscription.

This copper-plate charter was written, with the permission of the *Mahāsandhivigrahin Rāṇaka* Dhāradatta,[83] by Utsavanāga,[84] son of Āllava,[85] and incised by the *vijñānin* (artisan) Mādhava, son of Vāsu.[86]

79. The relevant expression, *avariya-nadī,* is according to Sircar, the name of a river which he proposes to identify with the modern Aurag, a feeder of the Mahānadī. Laskar, who reads the relevant portion as *tura-Dāśānarīya-nadī,* thinks that the donated lands were situated on the northern part of the Dāśānarīya river or the river of the Daśārṇa country.
80. Not yet identified.
81. Probably modern Jalajoḍo near Talagaja, 10 miles south-east of Bolangir, Bolangir District.
82. The date is given both in words and figures.
83. Dhāradatta figures in the same role in the Kālibhanā plates of the 34th year of Mahābhavagupta I Janamejaya (above, IV: XI) and in a later record of the fifteenth regnal year of Mahāśivagupta I Yayāti (below, IV: XV).
84. Utsavanāga is described as *utthit-āsanin,* lit. 'one occupying a raised (or high) seat', which evidently denotes a high status though its exact technical connotation cannot be ascertained. Sircar think that it may have indicated a noble of the king's court. He is referred to as *Mahākṣapaṭalaka* in IV: XV below and appears to have enjoyed the same position at the time of the present record also.
85. This Āllava is evidently the same as *Kāyastha* Āllava son of Kaivilāsa, figuring in the same role in the Satalma plates (above, IV: V) of Mahābhavagupta I and *Mahākṣapaṭala* Avala, son of Kailāsa, the writer of the Sonepur plates of the same ruler (*supra,* IV: VI). Āllava was evidently succeeded by his son sometime after the 17th year of Mahābhavagupta I when the Sonepur plates were issued.
86. Mādhava, son of Vāsu, is mentioned as the engraver in the three Chaudwār plates of Mahābhavagupta I (*supra,* IV: VIII-X) as well as in the Cuttack plates of Mahāśivagupta I (below, IV: XIV), though in the latter record his father's name has been omitted.

Next follow four verses which form something like a supplement.[87] The first of these stanzas partakes of the nature of the imprecatory and benedictory stanzas and states that the wealth is as unsteady as water on the lotus-leaves, the life is terminated by death and mundane pleasures are ephemeral and therefore kings ought not to destroy pious acts (of others).[88] The next three stanzas refer to an important historical episode. Verse 2 avers that there was a king named Svabhāvatuṅga,[89] verily the sun (causing the blossoming) of the lotus that was the Soma-kula and the moon for the moonlit night that was the protection of the Kosalā country, who defeated the Caidyas, i.e. Kalacuris, by his own prowess, thereby augmenting his prosperity. The following stanza, of which the text is highly corrupt and the reading not beyond doubt, seems to state that the soldiers of the Cedi king under the leadership of *Bhaṭṭa* Peḍi raided the Somavaṁśin kingdom and carried away some women and thereby earned their master's favour symbolised by the tying of the head-band (*paṭṭa*);[90] however, Svabhāvatuṅga, assisted by his general named Lakṣmaṇa, chased and beheaded the enemies and recovered all the women and thereby resembled Rāma, accompanied by Lakṣmaṇa, who had rescued his spouse after crossing the *setu*.[91] We are told in the concluding verse that to Svabhāvatuṅga was born a son,[92] who resembled Viṣṇu and caring a hoot for the powerful Caidya king Durgarāja[93] burnt Ḍahālā[94] which consequently became depopulated.[95]

87. Such additional material is found in the Mahada plates of Someśvaradeva varman II of South Kosala also. See *EI*, xxviii, 292.
88. This verse is found at the end of some other later records of the Somavaṁśins also. See *infra*, IV: XV.
89. This was obviously another name or *viruda* of Mahābhavagupta I.
90. This *paṭṭa* must have been of the nature of the *senāpati-paṭṭa* or *prasāda-paṭṭa* described by Varāhamihira. For details see, my *India as seen in the Bṛhatsaṁhitā of Varāhamihira*, 229-30.
91. This comparison was evidently suggested by the general's name, Lakṣmaṇa, and the rescue of women.
92. Evidently Mahāśivagupta I Yayāti.
93. Caidya, i.e. Kalacuri king Durgarāja is not known from any other source, and it has therefore to be regarded as a *viruda* or secondary name of a later member of the Kalacuri dynasty of Ḍāhala.
94. I.e. Baghelkhand or region round Jabalpur, Madhya Pradesh.
95. K.C. Panigrahi's reading and interpretation of the last two verses, which differs from the one adopted in these pages, is given below:

४५. रामाह-
४६. रा(रां).श्चेदिप(द्विप)वद्धा(द्धान्) [घ*] टान् सभटचेढि(डी)प्रभृति (ती)न्[।*] मण्डनिका-
४७. न्प्रा (न्प्रा) हितश (स) व्वंरामा: सलक्ष्मणो राम इवाप्तसे-
४८. तुः (तुम)[।*] तस्मात(त्) सू (सु) तो विष्णुरिवाजन्येष्टा (ष्टम्) य्व(य)द्ज्यु (यु) [ब*] राजम्विघटप्रता-
४९. पं (पम्।) तृणाय चैद्यं वत (नच) मन्यमाना दग्धा (दग्ध्वा) डहाला (डाहलां) विजना-
५०. ञ्चकार ।०।

Translation: His son, like Viṣṇu, without caring a fig for the immensely powerful Caidya (Kalachuri) Yuvarāja, the best among those unfit to be born, depopulated Ḍāhala by burning it; and like Rāma in the company of Lakṣmaṇa, took to the boundary (of his own kingdom) the troops of elephants belonging to the king of Cedi (the Cedi or Kalacuri country) and engaged in carrying away women, along with the soldiers, maidservants, etc., the decorators and the captured women.

IV: XIV

CUTTACK PLATES[1] OF MAHĀŚIVAGUPTA YAYĀTI, YEAR 9

Provenance: Not known.

References: Rangalala Banerjee, *JASB*, xlvi, 149–57 and pl. x; J.F. Fleet, *EI*, iii, 351–55; R.D. Banerji, *History of Orissa*, i, 213–15; H.C. Ray, *Dynastic History of Northern India*, i, 403; Bhandarkar's List, No. 1566; S.N. Rajaguru, IO, iv, 177–83.

Language: Sanskrit. In a mixture of prose and verse.

Metres: Verses 1–3, 6 and 19–20: *Śārdūlavikrīḍita*; Verse 4: *Upajāti* of *Indravajrā* and *Upendravajrā*; Verses 5 and 7: *Vasantatilakā*; Verses 8–16: *Anuṣṭubh*; Verse 17: *Śālinī*; Verse 18: *Puṣpitāgrā*.

Script: Northern class of alphabets.

Date: Regnal year 9, Jyeṣṭha śukla 13. First half of the tenth century A.D.

TEXT[2]

First Plate

1 सिद्धम्[3] [।*] स्वस्ति ।[4] प्रेमनिरुद्धमुग्धमनसोः स्फारीभवच्चक्षुषोर्य्यूनोर्य्य–
2 त्र विचित्रनिर्भररतक्रीडाक्रमं तन्वतोः । विच्छिन्नोपि कृतातिमात्रपुलकै–
3 राविर्भू(र्भ)वत्सीत्कृतैराश्लेषैर्ग्गलपितक्लमैः स्मररसः काममुहुस्ताय्य–
4 ते[5] ॥१॥[6] यता(त्रा) शेषविशेषरूपमहिमापास्ताप्सरः[7]कान्तिभिज्जतिर्ष्य[8]कल–
5 हेष्वपि प्रणनिः कर्ण्णोत्पलैस्ताडिताः । जायन्ते प्रविशङ्क[9]तस्मरशर–
6 प्रोत्थापितान्तर्व्यथा [:*] सान्द्रि(न्द्र) स्वेदजलाविसेचनवशान्निर्य्यातरोमाङ्ग(ङ्कु)रा–
7 :॥२॥[10]अत्युत्तुङ्गकरीन्द्रदन्तमुसलै [:*] प्रोद्भासिरोचिश्चयैर्ध्व–

1. Each of the plates measures about 8″ in length and 6¼″ in width. They have a circular hole in the left margin for the passage of the ring which held the plates together. The ring and the seal are lost.
2. From pl. x in *JASB*, xlvi.
3. Banerjea and Fleet: Om. Expressed by a symbol.
4. This mark of punctuation is unnecessary.
5. Banerjea: स्थापते; Fleet: मुहु[:*] स्ताय्यन्. The reading adopted here, which is also found in *infra*, IV: XVI and XVII, gives a satisfactory meaning.
6. The serial number of the verse is wrongly placed after the end of verse 2.
7. Banerjea: °यास्त्वप्सरः.
8. Banerjea: जातेर्षा.
9. Better read प्रविशच्छित which gives a satisfactory sense and is met with in *infra*, IV: XVI.
10. This number is erroneously placed at the end of the second quarter of the next verse.

8 स्तध्वङ्कसन[11]निष्फलीकृतशरच्चन्द्रोदयौ (यैं): सर्वदा[12]। यत्रासीदसत(ती)[13]–

9 जनस्य विशदं मुक्तामयं मण्डनं सङ्केतास्पदमप्यतीव धवल(लं)

10 प्रासादश्रृंङ्गाग्रतः ।[।*]३।। महानदीतुङ्गतरङ्गभङ्गस्फारोत्स (च्छ)–

11 लच्छीकरबद्भिराराात्। यस्मिन् रतारान्तिगवङ्गनाना(नां) श्रमापनो

12 दः क्रियते मरुद्भिः ।[।*]४।। तस्मात् **श्रीविनीतपुरात्**। लोकत्रयप्र–

13 थितशुभ्रयशोवितानव्याप्ताष्टदिक्प्रसभनिर्ज्जितवैरिवर्गः।

14 राजा व (ब) भूव भुवि भावितभव्यमूर्त्तिः श्रीमान् सरोजवदनो ज–

Second Plate: First Side

15 नमेजयाख्यः ।।५।। यः खड्गाग्रविदारितद्विप[14]घटाकुम्भस्थ–

16 लादुल्लसन्मुक्त(क्ता)जालविभूषितम् (तं) प(प्र)तिरणं पृथ्वीवधूरः स्थल (लम्)। च–

17 क्रे [15]चारुतरन्नराधिपशिरोरत्ना(त्नां) शु[15a]जालामला [16]यत्पादाम्वु (म्बु)जरे–

18 णवः समतया तद्रश्मिलक्ष्मीं दधुः[17] ।।६।। निर्द्दारिता[18]रिकरिकुम्भस–

19 मूहमुक्तमुक्ताफलप्रकरद[न्तुरखङ्ग]धारः[19] तस्मादजायत जगत्त–

20 त्रय[20]गीतकीर्त्तिहेलाविनिर्ज्जितरिपुर्न्न(न्नृं)पतिर्य्ययातिः[21] ।।७।। पर–

21 ममाहेश्वरपरमभट्टारकमहाराजाधिराजपरमेश्वर–

22 सोमकुलतिलकत्रिकलिङ्गाधिपतिश्रीमहाभवगुप्तराज–

23 देवपादानुध्यातपरममाहेश्वरपरमभट्टारकमहारा–

24 जाधिराजपरमेश्वरसोमकुलतिलकत्रिकलिङ्गाधिपति**श्रीम**–

25 **हासि(शि)वगुप्तराजदेवः** कुशली ।।[22] दक्षितोसलायां[23] मरडविषयी–

11. Read ध्वान्तध्वंसन which is Banerjea's reading.
12. This word was originally left out by inadvertence and was then inserted below the line.
13. Banerjea: °दसतो.
14. श्रृङ्गाग्रविदारितद्विपघरis Banerjea's reading.
15. Banerjea: चारुतरामराधिप°. The reading adopted by us not only yields a good sense but is also supported by *infra*, IV: XVI and XVII.

15*a*. Fleet. °रत्नाग्र.°

16. Banerjea's reading is यूथाद्यम्बुज°.
17. Banerjea: लक्ष्मीवधूः.
18. Banerjea: निर्द्धारिता°.
19. The letters within square parenthesis are not clear in the original but can be restored with the help of *infra*, IV: XVI. Banerjea reads मुद्रमुक्तमुक्ताफलप्रकरयुक्तनखांग्रधारः while Fleet doubtfully reads the letters within square parenthesis as °त्तरयाङ्ग.°
20. Read जगत्त्रय.
21. Banerjea's reading is यजातिः.
22. This mark of punctuation is uncalled for.
23. Fleet thinks that this is probably a mistake for दक्षिणकोसलायां. Banerjea gives this very reading in his transcript even though the reading adopted in these pages is quite clear in the lithograph given by him. In our opinion it is more likely that the intended reading was दक्षिणतोसलायां or दक्षिणतोसल्यां; for, Tosalā or Tosali is a well-known geographical name.

26 यचान्दग्रामे[24] ।[25] तद्विषयीयव्रा (ब्रा) ह्मणानापूज्य[26]यथाकालाध्यासिन [:*]

27 समाहर्तृ सन्निधातृतलहि (?) तसामता (न्ता) सिक[27] नियुक्तकाधिकारिकदा–

28 ण्डपासि (शि) कपिशुनवेत्रे (त्रि) काव[28]रोधजनराणकराजपुत्रा[ज*]वल्ल–

29 भादी [न्*] सव्वा (ब्र्वा) न् समाज्ञापयति [।*] विदिमस्तु भव[ता] म् यथास्मभिर–

Second Plate: Second Side

30 य (यं) ग्रामः सनिधिस्सोपनिधिः सर्व्ववा (बा) धाविवर्ज्जितः सर्व्वोपरि–

31 करादानसहिस्तालादितरुसंयुक्तः सगत्तो (र्त्तो) षर [:*] सजलस्थ

32 लश्चतुःसि (सी) मावच्छिन्नः मध्यदेशीयश्रीवल्लग्रामवे (वि) निर्ग्गताय

33 ओड्रदेशे श्रीशिलाभ ञ्जपाटीवास्तव्याय ।[29] टक्कार[30] पूर्व्वभार–

34 द्वाजगोत्राय ।[31] आङ्गिरस ।[31] वा (बा) र्हस्पत्यभारद्वाजप्रवराय ।[31] [32]च्छन्दो–

35 गकौथुमशाखाध्यायिने भट्टपुत्रानन्तनप्त्रे[33] श्रीशङ्खपाणी (णि) ना[34]–

36 म्ने दिनकर[35]पुत्राय ।[36] आज्यपाल . . . .[37] सलिलधारा–

37 पुरस्सरमाचन्द्रतारकार्क्क [क्षि*]तिसमकालोपभोगार्थ–

38 म् मातापित्रोरात्मनश्च पुण्ययशोऽभिवृद्धये ताम्व्र (म्र) शासने–

39 नाकरीकृत्य प्रतिपादित इत्यवगत्य [38]यथादीयम (मा) नकरभरहिर–

40 ण्यभोगभागादिकं ।[39] ददद्भिः सुखेन प्रतिवस्तव्यमिति [।]

41 भाविभिश्च भूपतिभिर्दत्तिरियमस्मदीया धर्म्मगौरवादस्मद–

42 नुरोधाच्च[40] । [41] स्वदा (द) त्तिरिवानुपालनीया । तथा चोक्तं धर्म्मसा (शा) स्त्रे [।*] व (ब)–

43 हुभिर्वसुधा दत्ता राजभिः सगरादिभिः । यस्य यस्य यदा भूमि–

24. Banerjea: चान्द्र°.
25. This mark of punctuation is superfluous.
26. Banerjea: ब्राह्मणानां पूज्य; Fleet: ब्राह्मणान्स (सं)पूज्य.
27. Banerjea reads समाहृतसन्निवीतवर्ण्णाहितसामवायिक. The meaning of the portion after *sannidhātṛ* is not clear. But looking to the context, it obviously refers to some officials.
28. Banerjea's reading is विधिकार.
29. This *daṇḍa* is not required.
30. Banerjea: टङ्कार.
31. This mark of punctuation is redundant.
32. Fleet reads च्छान्दोग.
33. Banerjea reads भट्टपूर्व्वानन्त.
34. गङ्गापाणी° is Banerjea's reading.
35. Banerjea's reading is दिवाकर.
36. This mark of punctuation is unnecessary.
37. Banerjea restores this portion as आजाख्यानेति यजुः पुरस्तात्.
38. Banerjea reads: यथास्मदीयमृण.
39. This *daṇḍa* is superfluous.
40. Banerjea and Fleet: °दनुरोधात्. *Contra* the last letter here with *t* in line 12 above.
41. This mark of punctuation, which is superfluous, has been left unnoticed by the previous editors.

Third Plate: First Side

44 स्तस्य तस्य तदा फल [म्*] ।[८।।*] मा भूदफलस(श)ङ्का वः ।[42] परदत्तेति पाथि(र्थि)व (वाः) [।*]

45 स्वदत्तात्फलमानन्त्य (न्त्यं) परदत्तानुपालने ।।[९।।*] आस्फोटयन्ति पित–

46 रो वल्गयन्ति पितामहाः [।*] भूमिदाता कुलेः[43] जातः स नस्त्राता भविष्यति ।।[१०।।*]

47 भूमि (मिं) यः प्रतिगृह्णाति ।[44]यश्च भूमिम्प्रयच्छति ।। (।) उभौ तौ पुण्यकर्म्माणो

48 नियत (तं) स्वग्ग(र्ग) गामिनौ ।।[११।।*] तडागानां सहस्रेण वाजपेयस(श) तेन च [।*]

49 गवां कोटिप्रदानेन भूमिहर्त्ता न सु(शु)ध्यति[45] ।। [१२।।*] हरते हारयेद्यस्तु मन्दवु(बु)–

50 द्धिस्तमोवृतः [।*] सुव(ब)द्धो[46] वारुणौ (णै): पासै (शै)स्तिर्यग्योनि(निं) स गच्छति ।।[१३।।*] सु–

51 वण्ण(र्ण)मेकं गामेका(कां) भूमेरप्यर्द्धङ्गुलम्[47] । हरन्नरकमायाति

52 य (या) वदाभूति (त) स (सं) प्लवं (वम्)।। [१४।।*] स्वदत्ताम्परदत्ताम्वा[47a] यो हरेत व[सु*]न्धरा [म्*]

53 । स विष्ठाया(यां) कृमिभू (र्भू)त्वा पितृभिः सह पच्यते ।। [१५।।*] आदित्यो वरु–

54 णो विष्णुव्र(र्ब्र)ह्मा सोमो हुतास (श)नः । सू(शू)लपाणिश्च भगवानभिनन्द–

55 न्ति भूमिदं (दम्) ।। [१६।।*] सामान्योधन्धर्म्मसेतुर्नृपाणा(णां) काले काले पाल–

56 नीयो भवद्भिः [।*] सर्व्वानेतान (न्) भाविनः पार्त्थिवेन्द्रान (न्) ।[48] भूयो भूयो या–

57 चते रामभद्रः ।।[१७।।*] इति कमलदलाम्वु(म्बु)वि(बि)न्दोलोलां ।[48] श्री(श्र)यम–

58 [49]नुचिन्त्य मनुष्यजीवितञ्च । सकलमिदम(मु) दाहृतञ्च वुद्धा[50] न हि पु–

59 [रुषैः] परकीर्त्तयो विलोप्याः ।[।१८।।*] प्रज्ञा यस्तु गुणात्मकस्तदधि[51] (?) [।।१९।।*]

Third Plate: Second Side

60 येनात्यन्तसुरासुराधिपगुरुः (रु)प्रज्ञाभिमानोजितो[52] राज्ञारोपितराज्यभा–

61 रमतुलं यश्चावहली (ल्ली)लया । यस्यासीन्नयविक्रमद्वयमपि प्रेयान्

42. This *daṇḍa* is uncalled for.
43. Read कुले.
44. This superfluous *daṇḍa* has not been noticed by the previous editors.
45. Fleet: सुध्यते.
46. Fleet first reads सवधो and then corrects it to सुबद्धो.
47. Fleet: भूमेरप्य (प्ये) कमङ्गुलम्.
47*a*. Read दत्तां वा.
48. This *daṇḍa* is not required.
49. Rajaguru is wrong in taking *nu* as forming part of the last line.
50. Read बुद्ध्वा.
51. This is the initial portion of a verse in the *Śārdūlavikrīḍita* metre which has, for some unknown reason, been left incomplete. The reading of this portion is also highly doubtful. Banerjea read it as सृष्टा यस्तु गुणात्मनस्तूदधेः and Fleet as स्र(?)ष्टा(?) यस्तु गुणात्मकस्त दधि(?).
52. Banerjea's reading is प्रज्ञाभिमानोजितो° Fleet correctly reads प्रज्ञाभिमानोजितो but suggests to correct it to प्रज्ञाभिमानैर्जितो which, however, is unwarranted.

62 सखा सर्व्वदा य:[53] ख्यातो धृतसा(स)न्धिविग्रहपद: श्रीच्छिच्छटेश्व(श):[54] कृती ॥[२०॥*]
63 परममाहेश्वरपरमभट्टारकमहाराज[55]परमेश्व[र*]सोमकुलति-
64 लकत्रिकलिङ्गाधिपतिश्रीज(य)**याति**[56] **राजदेवप्रवर्द्धमानवे (वि)जयराज्ये**
65 **नवमे सम्वत्सरे**[56a] **६ ज्येश्ठशि(सि)तत्रयोदश्या(श्यां)** ।[57] १० ३ :[58] उत्कीर्ण्णा
66 विज्ञानी (नि)माधवेनेती(ति) [।*] ओम्[59] ओम्[59] । [।*]

ABSTRACT

The auspicious formula *siddham,* expressed symbolically, is followed by four stanzas describing the city of **Vinītapura,**, whence the grant was issued, as follows:—

"where the enjoyment of love is being continually intensified and still more intensified by the close embraces (of lovers), by which fatigue is removed, in which hissing sound often appears and in which hairs often stand on their ends, although such enjoyment often suffers interruption as the ardent young couple show their skill in the various processes of conjugal enjoyment with their eyes dilated (with excitement) and with their minds subdued and fascinated by amorous thoughts; where, even in the midst of quarrels arising from jealousy, lovers, beaten by the lotuses from the ears of women who have cast the beauty of the celestial damsels into shade by the greatness of their endless and peculiar charms, have all their mental anguishes roused to action by the entrance of the sharp arrows of Cupid, with their hairs standing in the ends (lit. sprouting up) on account of the sprinkling of the drops of sweat (from the persons of the objects, of their love); where, at the tops of houses beautifully white-washed, the places of assignation of unchaste women and their pearl-ornaments were whitened by the clusters of rays issuing from the club-like tusks of very lofty elephants—the rays which rendered the autumn moon useless in the matter of dispelling darkness; (and) where the fatigue of women enjoying conjugal caresses with ardent attachment is removed by the breezes surcharged with the particles of water sent up by the breaking and swelling of the high waves of the Mahānadī" (verses 1–4).

In the next two verses king Janamejaya is described as one endowed with a pure and mild appearance, and lotus-like face, the expanse of whose spotless fame had covered the eight quarters like a canopy and who had vanquished

53. Read स:.
54. Banerjea reads श्रीच्छिञ्चटेश्चम्पती. Rajaguru thinks that Banerjea's reading is more probable.
55. This is evidently an error for महाराजाधिराज.
56. Banerjea reads यजाति.
56*a*. Read संवत्सरे.
57. This mark of punctuation is superfluous.
58. As suggested by Fleet, the word *divasaḥ* has to be supplied in apposition.
59. Expressed by an ornate symbol.

the enemies forcibly; the point of whose sword rent asunder the foreheads of an array of elephants from which heaps of pearls came out and adorned the bosom of the lady that was the earth in every battle; and the dust of whose lotus-feet, as pure as the multitude of the rays of jewels on the heads of the kings (bowing at his feet), bore, through similarity, the lustre of their rays. The next verse says that from him was born king **Yayāti**, whose fame was sung in the three worlds, who had defeated his enemies with ease and the edge of whose sword had been rendered rugged by the heaps of pearls emanating from the casket-like frontal globes on the foreheads of the elephants cut asunder by it.

Next follows a prose passage describing Mahābhavagupta and **Mahāśiva-gupta,** the issuer of the grant, who meditated on the feet of the former, both of whom are styled *Parama-Māheśvara, Paramabhaṭṭāraka-Mahārājādhirāja-Parameśvara, Somakula-tilaka* and *Trikaliṅgādhipati.*

Mahāśivagupta, after worshipping the Brāhmaṇas in the Cāndagrāma[60] situated in the Marada *viṣaya*[61] in Dakṣiṇa Tosalā[62] ordered all the district officers posted from time to time including the *Samāhartṛ*, *Sannidhātṛ*, *Talahi* (?) *ta*,[63] *Sāmanta,*[64] *Āsika,*[65] *Niyuktaka, Ādhikārika, Dāṇḍapāśika, Piśuna, Vaitrika,* inmates of the royal harem and the king's favourites that he had given away the village in favour of the Brāhmaṇa Śaṅkhapāṇi, son of Dinakara and grandson of the *Bhaṭṭaputra* Ananta, who had immigrated from the village Śrīvalla[66] situated in Madhyadeśa and was a resident of Śrī-Śilābhañjapatī[67] situated in the Oḍradeśa, belonged to the Takkāra-Bhāradvāja[68] *gotra*, with the Āṅgirasa, Bārhaspatya and Bhāradvāja *pravaras* and was a student of the Kauthuma *śākhā* of the *Chandogya* (i.e. *Sāmaveda*). The grant was meant to be enjoyed by the donee in perpetuity (lit. as long as the moon, stars, sun and the earth endure), and the granted village, extending to its four boundaries, was rendered rent-free by means of a copper-plate charter. The grant was

60. Probably modern Chandgaon, 32 miles south-east of Cuttack. See Binayak Misra, *Dynasties of Mediaeval Orissa*, 68.
61. Binayak Misra (*ibid.*) identifies Maraḍa, the chief place of the district of that name, with either Barada or Marada Hariharapura in the Cuttack District.
62. Generally speaking, it comprised the modern Puru-Cuttack-Ganjam region of Orissa. Tosali, the headquarters of this territorial-administrative division, is now represented by the famous Dhauli in the Ganjam District of Orissa where a set of Aśokan inscriptions has been found. Aśoka had posted a *Mahāmātra* here.
63. Both the reading and interpretatian are uncertain.
64. = feudatory chief, here probably referring to land-owners or jagirdars.
65. Literally 'swordsmen'. It may refer to the policemen carrying swords.
66. It has not been identified.
67. This village, which has yet to be identified, was evidently named after one of the two Śilābhañjas belonging to the Bhañja dynasty.
68. As pointed out by Fleet, the expression *Ṭakkāra-pūrva-Bhāradvāja gotra* may also refer to a branch of the Bhāradvāja *gotra*, which was formerly settled at Ṭakkāra, which is probably the same as the famous Ṭakkārikā whence Brāhmaṇas are known to have migrated to several distant localities.

accompanied by the right to the *nidhis, upanidhis,* the collection of all the *uparikaras,* palm and other trees, low-lying areas, barren lands, and waters and lands and was exempted from all the oppressions. The villagers were asked to pay the donee all the dues as specified in the preceding grant.

Next follows the usual exhortation to the future monarchs to maintain the grant, and eleven imprecatory and benedictive verses, reported to have been taken from the Dharmaśāstra, are cited in support of this entreaty.

The import of verse 19, which has been left incomplete, is not clear. The following stanza mentions Cchicchaṭeśvara, who occupied the office of the minister of peace and war. It is said that he surpassed the preceptors of lords of the gods (i.e. Bṛhaspati) and the demons (i.e. Śukra), who were proud of their intellect, bore, with ease, the immense burden of the statecraft entrusted to him by the king and always had both policy and valour at his command.

The grant was issued on the **thirteenth day of the bright fortnight of Jyeṣṭha in the ninth year of**[69] **the increasingly victorious reign of king Yayāti,** who is described exactly as in the preceding grant.

The charter was incised by the artisan Mādhava.[70]

69. The date is indicated both in words and figures.
70. He is evidently identical with the homonymous engraver of the Chaudwār plates of Mahābhavagupta I (above, IV: VIII-X) and the Pāṭṇā plates of the 8th year of the reign of Mahāśivagupta I (above, IV: XIII). Strangely enough, the name of the writer, which is generally found in the Soma- vaṁśin records, has been omitted in this record.

IV: XV

NIBINNA[1] PLATES[2] OF MAHĀŚIVAGUPTA YAYĀTI, YEAR 15

Provenance: Former Sonpur State, Bolangir District, Orissa.

References: B.C. Mazumdar, *EI,* xi, 95–98 and plates facing pp. 96 and 97; R.D. Banerji, *History of Orissa,* i, 215; H.C. Ray, *Dynastic History of Northern India,* i, 403–04; Bhandarkar's List No. 1567; S.N. Rajaguru, *IO*, iv, 184–89.

Language: Sanskrit. In prose except the benedictive and imprecatory stanzas.

Metres: Verses 1–3 and 5–11: *Anuṣṭubh*; Verse 4: *Indravajrā*; Verse 12: *Śālinī*; Verse 13: *Puṣpitāgrā*; Verse 14: *Rathoddhatā*.

Script: Northern class of alphabets.

Date: Regnal year 15, Mārgaśīrṣa śukla 13. First half of the tenth century A.D.

TEXT[3]

First Plate

1 सिद्धम्[4] [।*] स्वस्ति [।*] श्री [म]तो **विनि(नी)तपुरात्पप**[5]रमभट्टारकमहाराजाधिराजप–

2 रमेश्वरमा(म)हाभवगुप्तराजदेवपादानुध्यात्प(तप)रममाहेश्वरपर–

3 मभट्टारकमहाराजाधिराजपरमेश्वरसोमकुलतिलकत्रिक–

4 लिङ्गाधिपतिश्री**महाशिवगुप्तराज**देवः कुशली कोसलदे–

1. Although the grant was found in the erstwhile Sonpur State, now included in the Bolangir District of Orissa, it is styled Nibinna plates after the name of the village granted through it. It may, however, be pointed out that in the inscription the name of the village is spelt as Niviṇḍā and Nivinnā. The name given by B.C. Mazumdar is retained in these pages for the convenience of reference.
2. The plates are about 8¼″ to 8½″ in length and about 5¾″ in breadth. and are strung together on a circular ring passing through a hole cut on the left margin of each plate at a distance of about 1″ from the edge. The ends of the ring, which is 4½″ in diameter and about ¾″ thick, are secured under a lump of copper which spreads out into a circular seal, 1⅓″ in diameter. The seal is said to bear a squatting figure cut in relief. Nothing else is clear. The device on the seal must have been the well-known Abhiṣeka Lakṣmī motif as on most other seals attached to the Somavaṁśin copper-plate charters.
3. From plates in *EI*, xi.
4. Mazumdar: Om. Expressed by a symbol.
5. Read पुरात्परम°.

5 स[6]प्रतिव (ब) द्धगन्धटपाटिलमण्डले[7] चोत्तरपल्लीयनिवण्डाग्रामे[8]

6 व्रा (ब्रा) ह्मणान् सम्पूज्य तद्विषयीयान् यथाकालाध्यासिनः समा–

7 हर्तृसनि (न्नि) धातृयुक्ताधिकारिकद (दा) ण्डपासि (शि) कचाटभटपिसु (शु)–

8 नवे (वै) [त्रि]कावरोधजनराणकराजपुत्रराज्ञीराजव[ल्ल]–

9 भ (भा) दीन् सर्वान् राजपादोपजि (जी) विनः समाज्ञापयति [।*] विदितमस्तु

10 भ[व*]तां यथासा (स्मा) भिरय (यं) ग्रामः सनिधिः सोपनिधिः सदसा (शा) पराधः

11 सर्ववा (बा) धाविवर्जितः सवो (र्वो) परिकरादानसहितश्चतुःसि (सी) माप–

12 र्यन्तः साम्रमधुकः सगर्तोस (ष) रः सजलस्थलः प्रतिनिषिद्धचाट–

13 भटप्रवेशः भारद्वा (द्वा) जसगोत्राय ।[9] श्राङ्गिरसवा (बा) र्हस्पत्यभार–

14 द्वाज[10]प्रवराय ।[11]उल्लास[12]शर्म्मणः पौत्राय ।[13]न (ना) रायणश[र्म्मा]–

Second Plate: First Side

15 ण[:*] पुत्राय ।[13] भटपरोलीविनी (नि) र्गताय ।[13] कोसलीय[14]मरमेण्डा[ग्रा]–

16 मे (म) वास्तव्याय श्रीपुण्डरिकसर्म्मणे[15] दीक्षिताय ।[15a] गन्धडपाटी[15b]–

17 मण्डले उत्तरपल्लिकाया[16] निविन्नाग्रामः[16a] [सलिलधारा*] पुरःसर[17]माचन्द्रतार–

18 काक्क (र्क्क) क्षितिसमके (का) लोपभोगार्थ (र्थं) मातापित्रोरात्मनश्च पुन (ण्य)–

19 यसो (शो) वृद्धये ताम्त्र[18] ताम्रसा (शा) सनेनाकरीकृत्य प्रतिपादित इत्यव–

20 गम्य[19] समुचित भोगभागकरहिरण्य (ण्या) दिप्रत्यय[20] मुपनयद्भिर्भव–

21 द्भिः सुखेन प्रतिवा (व) स्तव्यमिति [।*] भाविभिश्च भूपतिभिर्द्दन्ति (त्ति) रि–

22 यमस्मदीया धर्मगौरवादस्मदनुरोधाञ्च स्वदत्ती (त्ति) रिवानुप (पा)–

6. Read कोसलदेश. Cf. line 15 below where the name of the country has been correctly spelt with dental *s*.
7. Mazumdar doubtfully read the name as Ganuṭapāṭa. Cf. line 16 below where the name of the *maṇḍala* has been spelt as Gandhaḍapāṭī.
8. In line 17 below the name of the village is given at Nivinnā.
9. This mark of punctuation is superfluous.
10. Mazumdar: भारद्वज.
11. This *daṇḍa* is not required.
12. Read उल्लास°.
13. This punctuation mark is redundant.
14. In line 4 above the name has been wrongly spelt with palatal *ś*.
15. Read पुण्डरीकशर्म्मणे
15*a*. This mark of punctuation is not required.
15*b*. Mazumdar's reading is *Ganuḍapāṭī*. In line 5 above the name is given as Gandhaṭapāṭi.
16. In line 5 above the name is given as ending in *pallī*.
16*a*. Mazumdar reads *Nibinnā*. Cf. line 5 above where the name of the village has been spelt as Nivinḍā.
17. Mazumdar: पुर [स]सर°. Read पुरस्सर°.
18. These letters are superfluous.
19. Read इत्यवगत्य°.
20. Read प्रत्याय°.

23 लि(ल)नीय(या) । तथा [चो*]क्त(क्तं) धर्म्मसा(शा)स्त्रे[।*] व(ब) हुभिर्वसुधा दत्ता ।[21] राजभिः सग–

24 रादिभिः । यस्य यस्य यदा भूमिस्तस्य तस्य तदा फलं (लम्) ।।[१।।*] मा भू–

25 तफलसङ्का[22] वः परदत्तेति पार्थिवाः। स्वदानात्फलमानन्त्यं

26 परदत्तानुपालने ।[।२।।*] सष्ठि[23] वर्षसहस्राणि स्वर्गे मोदति भूमि– ।[24]

27 दः । आक्षि (क्षे) प्ता चानुमन्ता च द्वावेत्तौ नरकग्रा(गा)मिनौ[25] ।[।३।।*] अग्नेरपत्य(त्यं)

28 प्र[थ]म(मं)सुवर्ण्णं(र्ण्णं)। भु(भू)र्व(र्वै)ष्णवी सु(सू)र्यसुताश्च गावः। यः काञ्चन(नं) गाश्च

Second Plate: Second Side

29 महीञ्च दद्यात्(द्) द[त्तास्त्र]यस्तेन भवन्ति लोके (काः) ।[।४।।*] अ(आ) स्पोटयन्ति पितरः

30 प्रवल्गयन्ति[26] पितामहा : । भूमिदाता कुले जातः स नस्त्रे(स्त्रा)ता

31 भविष्यति ।[।५।।*] भूमि (मिं) य। प्रतिगृह्णाति यश्च भुमि[27] प्रयच्छति । उभो (भौ)[28]

32 तौ पुण्यकर्म्माणौ नियतौ(तं) स्वर्गगामिनौ ।[।६।।*]तडागाना(नां) सहस्रे–

33 ण वाजपेयसतानि[29]च[।*] गवा (वां) कोटिप्रदानेन भूमिहर्त्ता न सु(शु)ध्य–

34 ति ।[।७।।*। हरते हारयते यस्तु मन्दवु(बु)द्धिस्तमोवृतः [।*] सुव(ब)द्धो वारुणै[ः *]

35 पासै(शै)स्तिर्यगोनृ[30] स गच्छति ।[।।८।।*] सुवर्ण्णमेक(कं) गामेका(कां) भूमि (मे)–

36 रप्यर्द्धमङ्गुल[म्।*] हरं[31] न [र*] कमायाति ।[32] यावदाहुतसंप्लवः[33] ।[।९।।*]

37 [स्वद]त्ता (त्तां) पसारदत्ताम्वा[34] । [34a]यो हरद्वसुन्धराः[35] । स विष्ठायां कृमि–

38 [र्भूत्वा] पितृभिस्सह पच्यते ।[।१०।।*] आदित्यो वरुणो विष्णु(ब्रह्मा*] सोमो हु–

39 तास(श)नः [।*] सु(शू)लपाणिश्च भगवा[न*]भिन[न्द*]न्ति भूमिदः (दम्) ।[।११।।*]. सामान्यो–

40 य(यं) धर्म्मसेतुर्नृपाणा (णां) काले काले पालनीयो भवद्भिः [।*] स [र्वा]–

21. This mark of punctuation is unnecessary.
22. Read °भूदफलशङ्का.
23. Read षष्टि°.
24. This *daṇḍa* is uncalled for.
25. Read तान्येव नरके वसेत् which would be in consonance with the metre.
26. Read प्रवल्गन्ति.
27. Read भूमिं.
28. Mazumdar: उभ[ौ].
29. Read° शतेन.
30. Read °स्तिर्यग्योनि°.
31. Read हरन्.
32. This mark of punctuation is redundant.
33. Read यावदाभूतसंप्लवम्.
34. Read परदत्तां वा.
34*a*. This *daṇḍa* is superfluous.
35. Read हरेत वसुन्धराम्

41 नेतान(न्) भाविनः पार्थिवेन्द्रान(न्) भु(भू)यो [भूयो*] याचते रामभद्रः [36]। [।१२।।*]

Third Plate

42 इति कमलदलाम्वु(म्बु) वि(बि)न्दुलोला(लां) श्री(श्रि)यमनुचि[न्त्य]मनुष्यजीवि–
43 तञ्च ।[*] सकलमिदमुदाहरिञ्च[37] वुद्धा[38] न हि पुरुषै [:*] परकीर्त्तयो
44 विलोपा(प्या)[39] इति ।[।१३।।*][40] परममाहेश्वरपर[म*]भटा(ट्टा)रकमहाराजाधिरा—
45 जपरमेश्वरसोमकुलतिलकत्रिकलिङ्गाधिपतिश्री**मद्यया–**
46 **तिराजदेवस्य पादानुप्रवर्द्धमानविजयराज्ये पञ्चदस(श)मे[41]**
47 **सम्वत्सरे[42] ।[42a] [43]मर्ग्गसिमासे ।[43a] सु(शु)क्लपक्षे त्रयोदस्या (श्या)न्तिथौ सम्व–**
48 **त्[44] १५ मार्ग्ग सुदि १३** ।[*] लिखि[त*]मिदं सा(शा)सन(नं) महासान्धि–
49 विग्रहिकराणकश्रीधारदत्त[45]स्यावगतेन महाक्षप–
50 ट[ल]क[46] श्रीउच्छवणागेनाल्लवनागसुतेने(नो)त्कीर्ण(र्ण्ण)[47] ढुक्कुरपना–
51 केनेति। सम्पदो जलजपर्ण्णजलाभा[48] ।[49] जीवित्त[50]मरणसन्त–
52 तिसस्थ[51] भोगभू (भु)क्तिरचिराय विलोक्यः[52] कीर्त्तयो नृपतिभिर्न्नृ (र्न)
53 [वि*]लोप्या [:।।१४।।*] इति।

ABSTRACT

The charter, inaugurated by the auspicious formulae *siddham,* represented by a symbol, and *svasti*, was issued from **Vinītapura** by **Mahāśivagupta** who meditated upon the feet of Mahābhavagupta. The former is described in a conventional manner with full titles met with in the preceding record while the latter is given only the imperial title *Paramabhaṭṭāraka-Mahārājādhirāja-Parameśvara*.

36. Following the *daṇḍa* there are faint traces of the initial *i* which has been imperfectly erased as the same letter is engraved at the beginning of the following line.
37. Mazumdar: °मुदाहृरिञ्च. Read °मुदाहृतञ्च.
38. Read बुद्ध्वा.
39. Mazumdar: विलोप्या.
40. Better read विलोप्याः ।।१३।। इति.
41. Read पञ्चदशे.
42. Read. संवत्सरे.
42*a*. This mark of punctuation is not required.
43. Read मार्गशिर°.
43*a*. This *daṇḍa* is uncalled for.
44. Read संवत्.
45. चारुदत्त is Mazumdar's reading.
46. Read महाक्षपटलिक.
47. Read ठक्कुर.
48. Read °जलाभा°.
49. This mark of punctuation is redundant.
50. Read जीवितं.
51. Read °संस्थम्।.
52. Read विलोक्या.

The king, after worshipping the Brāhmaṇas in the village called Niviṇḍā[53] in Uttara-pallī[54] situated in the Gandhaṭapāṭi-*maṇḍala*[55] attached to the Kosala-deśa, gave away the village[56] to the Brāhmaṇa *Dīkṣita* Puṇḍarikaśarman, son of Ullāsaśarman and grandson of Nārāyaṇaśarman, who belonged to the Bhāradvāja *gotra*, had the Āṅgirasa, Bārhaspatya and Bhāradvāja *pravaras* and was an immigrant from the village of Bhaṭaparolī[57] and a resident of the village named Maramenḍā[58] situated in Kosala. The grant was endowed with all the usual privileges and exemptions enumerated in the Orissa State Museum plates of the same king[59] and the royal order concerning the grant was also addressed to all the royal officers stationed in the district from time to time mentioned in the same record with the only difference that in the present record the *Niyuktaka* is replaced by the *Yukta*[60] and in addition to the favourites of the king (*rāja-vallabha*) the favourites of the queen (or queens) are also referred to. The villagers were exhorted to make over all the incomes including *bhoga, bhāga, kara* and *hiraṇya* as due to the donee and continue to live happily in the village.

Next follows the usual entreaty to the future monarchs to uphold the grant, and thirteen benedictory and imprecatory stanzas, reportedly borrowed from the Dharmaśāstra, are quoted in support of this exhortation.

The date is specified as the **thirteenth tithi of the bright half of the month of Mārgaśīrṣa in the fifteenth year of the increasingly victorious reign of king Yayāti,** who is described with full usual titles.

This copper-plate charter was written by the *Mahākṣapaṭalaka* Ucchavaṇāga[61] (Skt. Utsavanāga), son of Āllavanāga, with the approval of the *Mahā-*

53. Identified with the modern Libina in the Bargarh Tahsil of the Bolangir District. See Binayak Misra, *Dynasties of Mediaeval Orissa*, 68.
54. This appears to have been the name of the *viṣaya* which must have comprised the northern part of the Gandhaṭapāṭi-*maṇḍala*.
55. Mazumdar points out that no such name is retained for any village or pargana in the erstwhile Sonpur State but at the same time invites our attention to Ghaṇṭāpāra in the nighbourhood. (*EI*, xi, 96, fn. 5). Evidently founded by or named after the Bhañja king Śatrubhañja I Gandhaṭa, Gaṇḍhaṭapāṭī has been identified with Gandharāḍhi in the Phulbani District. The reference to Uttarapallī suggests that the *maṇḍala* must have been divided, for administrative purposes, at least into two parts, the other being known as Dakṣiṇa-pallī.
56. The *deśa, maṇḍala, pallī* and the village are mentioned twice which was not the common practice. But this peculiarity enables us to know that their names were not spelt uniformly and were pronounced differently. Thus, they are also spelt as Kosala, Gandhaḍapāṭī, Uttara-pallikā and Nivinnā.
57. It has yet to be identified.
58. Not yet identified. Mazumdar suggests that the word *mara* was probably prefixed with the object of distinguishing the village from other places bearing the name Meṇḍā.
59. See *supra*, IV: XII.
60. The difference is perhaps not deliberate.
61. Utsavanāga figures in the same capacity in the Pāṭṇā plates of the 8th year of the reign of Mahāśivagupta I; but there he is styled *utthitāsanin* and his father's name is given without the name-ending or surname *nāga*.

sāndhivigrahin, *Rāṇaka* Dhāradatta[62] and engraved by *Thakkura*[63] Panāka.[64]

The records concludes with a stanza dilating upon the ephemeral character of wealth and life as well as wordly enjoyments and exhorting monarchs not to hinder the pious acts of others.[65]

62. Dhāradatta is mentioned as *Mahāsāndhivigrahin* in the Pāṭṇā plates of the 8th year of Mahāśivagupta I's reign (IV: XIII) also; but in the Orissa State Museum plates of the 4th year (IV: XII) and the Cuttack plates of the 9th year (above, IV: XIV) of the same king Chicchaṭeśvara figures in the same capacity.
63. S.N. Rajaguru reads *ṭakura* in the text and *ṭukura* in a footnote and suggests to correct it to *taṭhakāra* which he takes in the sense of 'smith'. But both the reading and proposed correction are totally unwarranted as *ṭhakkura* is known to have been popularly employed as an honorific in the medieval period.
64. He is evidently the same as Pannāka mentioned as the engraver in the Orissa State Museum plates of the 4th year of the reign of the same king (above, IV: XII). But in that inscription he is not styled *Thakkura*.
65. This stanza is earlier met with in the Pāṭṇā plates of the 8th year of Mahāśivagupta I's reign (*supra*, IV: XIII).

IV: XVI

PĀṬṆĀ PLATES[1] OF MAHĀŚIVAGUPTA I YAYĀTI, YEAR 24

Provenance: Somewhere in the former Pāṭṇā State, Balangir District, Orissa.
References: Ganga Mohan Laskar, *JASB*, New Series, i, 7–8 and 16–18; R.D. Banerji, *HO*, i, 215–16; H.C. Ray, *DHNI*, i, 404; Bhandarkar's List, No. 1568; S.N. Rajaguru, *IO*, iv, 190–95 and plates facing pp. 190 and 194 and between pp. 192 and 193.
Language: Sanskrit. In a mixture of prose and verse.
Metres: Verses 1–3; *Śārdūlavikrīḍita*; Verse 4: *Upajāti* of *Indravajrā* and *Upendravajrā*; Verses 5–6; *Vasantatilakā*; Verse 7: *Sragdharā*; Verses 8–10 and 12–18: *Anuṣṭubh;* Verse 11: *Indravajrā;* Verse 19: *Śālinī;* Verse 20: *Puṣpitāgrā.*
Script: Northern class of alphabets.
Date: Regnal year 24, Āṣāḍha śukla 5. About the middle of the tenth century A.D.

TEXT[2]

First Plate

1 सिद्धम्[3] [।*] स्वस्ति प्रेमनिरुद्धमुग्धमनसोः स्फारीभवच्चक्षु–
2 षो[4]र्यूनोर्यत्र विचित्रनिर्भररत क्रीडाक्रमं तन्वतोः । विच्छिन्नो–
3 पि कृतातिमात्रपुलकैराविर्भवत्सीत्कृतैराश्लेषैर्ग्लं[5]पिलक्ल–
4 मैः स्मररसः कामं मुहुस्ताय्यते ॥ [१॥*] यत्राशेषविशेषरूप–
5 महिमापास्ताप्सरः कान्तिभिर्जातेर्ष्याकलेह्ष्वपि प्रणयिन
6 :[6] कण्णोंत्पलैस्ताडिताः [7]। जायन्ते प्रविशच्छितस्मरशरप्रोस्थापि–
7 तान्तर्व्यथा [:*]स्यन्दिस्वेदजलावसेचनवशान्निर्यातरोमा–
8 ङ्कुराः ॥[२॥*] अत्युत्तुङ्गकरीन्द्रदत्त[8](न्त) मुसलप्रोद्भासिरोचिश्चये–

1. The plates measure by 8½" by 6½" and have a circular hole bored about the middle of the left margin for the passage of the ring which keeps them together. The surface of the seal, which has a diameter of 2¼", bears the usual Gaja-Lakṣmī motif.
2. From impressions.
3. Expressed by a symbol. Laskar reads it as *om.*
4. Laskar is wrong in taking it as the concluding letter of the last line.
5. Laskar first reads '°राश्लेषग्ल° and then proposes to correct it to °राश्लेषैर्ग्लं°.
6. A shallow *visarga* was engraved at the end of line 5 also. But evidently finding it not sufficiently clear, the engraver incised another bold *visarga* at the beginning of this line.
7. Laskar: कर्णो°.
8. Laskar and Rajaguru: दन्त°.

9 द्धवात्त[9]ध्वन्सन[10] निष्फलीकृतशरच्चन्द्रोदयैः सर्व्वदा ।[11] यत्रासी–

10 दसतीजनस्य विशदं मुक्तामयं मण्डनं सङ्केतास्पदमप्यतीवध–

11 वलप्रासादशृङ्गाग्रतः ॥[३॥*] महानदीतुङ्गतरङ्गभङ्गा[12]स्फारोच्छ–

12 लच्छीकरवाद्भिरारात् । यस्मिन्नतासक्तिमदङ्गनानां श्रमापनोद–

13 :[13]क्रियते मरुद्भिः ॥[४॥*] तस्मात् **श्रीययातिनगरात्** ॥ लोकत्रयप्रथि–

14 त शुभ्रयशोवितानव्याप्तप्राष्टदिक्प्रसभनिर्जितवैरिवर्गः । राजा

15 व(ब) भूव भुवि भावितभव्यमूर्तिः श्रीमान्सरोजवदनो जनमेजया–

Second Plate: First Side

16 [14]रव्यः ॥ [५॥*] निर्द्दारितारिकरिकुम्भसमुद्गमुक्तमुक्ताफलप्रकरदन्तुरखड्ग–

17 धारः । तस्मादजायत जगत्त्रयगीतकीर्त्तिर्हेलाविनिर्जितरिपुर्नृपतिर्य–

18 **याति**:[15] ॥[६॥*][16] माद्यल्लोलालिमालाकुलकरटपुटस्यन्दिदानप्रवाहान् सिन्दूरार[17]–

19 क्तकुम्भान् शितपृथुलरदान् कामदेवादिसंज्ञान्[18] । जित्वाऽजापालमाजौ ज–

20 नितसुखधूविस्मयः स्मेरवक्त्रः स द्वात्रिंशत्करीन्द्रान्[19] शरनिकरहतारो–

21 हक(का)नग्रहीद्यः ॥[७॥*] परममाहेश्वरपरमभट्टारकमहाराजाधिराजपर–

22 मेश्वरसोमकुलतिलकत्रिकलिङ्गाधिपतिश्रीमहाभवगुप्तराजदेव

23 पादानुध्यातपरममाहेश्वरपरमभट्टारकमहाराजाधिराजप–

24 रमेश्वरसोमकुलतिलकत्रिकलिङ्गाधिपतिश्री**महाशिवगु**–

25 प्तराजदेवः कुशली ।[20] कोसलदेशे तेलातटविषये

26 [21]डेलडेलीग्रामे व्रा(ब्रा)ह्मणान्वसम्पूज्य तद्विषयीययथाकाला–

27 ध्यासिनः समाहर्तृ[22] सन्निधातृनियुक्ताधिकारिकद(दा)ण्डप(पा)शिक[23] च—

28 ट्ट[24]भट्टपिशुनवे (वै)तृ(त्रि) कावरोधजनराज्ञीराजपुत्र[25]राणकराज–

29 वल्लभादीन् सर्व्वा[26]न्राजपादोपजीविनः समाज्ञापयति [।*] वि–

9. Read °द्धवन्ति° which is the reading of Laskar and Rajaguru.
10. Read °ध्वंसन°.
11. Laskar supplies this *daṇḍa* on his own though it is quite clear in the impression.
12. Read °भङ्ग°.
13. Laskar reads this *visarga* at the end of the previous line.
14. Both Laskar and Rajaguru take this line as forming the concluding line of the first plate.
15. Laskar: °यर्यातिः.
16. Laskar: मद्योल्लोला°.
17. Laskar: सिन्दुरार°.
18. Laskar and Rajaguru: °सज्ञान्.
19. We have सद्द्वात्रिंश in the Pāṭṇā plates of Yayāti's twenty-eighth year. See IV: XVII below.
20. This mark of punctuation is superfluous.
21. Laskar: डलाडेली; Rajaguru ड़ेलाड़ेली.. The distinction between *ḍ* and *h* being not quite clear in our record, the name of the village may as well be read as हेलहेली.
22. Laskar reads समाहतृ and proposes to correct it to समाहर्तृ°
23. Laskar: दाण्डपाशिक; Rajaguru: दण्डपाशिक.
24. Laskar reads this letter at the end of the last line.
25. Laskar: राजपुत्र.
26. Laskar: सर्वा°.

30 दितमस्तु भवतां यथास्माभिरयं ग्रामः सनिधिः सोपनिधिः
31 सदशपराधः सर्व्ववा(बा)धा विर्वाजितः सर्व्वोपरिकरादानसहि–

Second Plate: Second Side

32 तः ।[27] चतुः सीमापर्य्यन्तः साम्रमधुकः सगर्तोषरः[28] सजलस्थ–
33 लः प्रतिनिषिद्धचट्टभट्टप्रवेशः कौशिकगोत्राय देवरात–
34 औदल[29] विश्वामित्रप्रवराय गौतमशाखाध्यायिने श्रावस्ति[30] (स्ती)म–
35 ण्डले कासिलीविनिर्गतायलावडाविषयेन्तरडिवास्तव्याय
36 परमेश्वरनप्त्रे सिद्धेश्वरसुताय भट्टश्रीमहोदधये उ–
37 दकधारापुरःसरं आचन्द्रतारकार्क्कक्षितिसमकालोपभोगा–
38 र्थो[31] मातापित्रोरात्मनश्च पुण्ययशोऽभिवृद्धये ताम्रशास–
39 नेनाकरीकृत्य प्रतिपादित इत्यवगम्य[32]समुचितभाग–
40 भोगकरहिरण्यादिप्रत्यायमुपनयद्भिर्भवद्भिः सुखे–
41 न वस्तव्यमिति [।*] ता(भा)विभिश्च भूपतिभिर्दतिरियमस्मदीया धर्म्मगौ[33]–
42 रवादस्मदनुरोधाच्च [34]स्वदत्तिरिवानुपालनीया [।*] तथा चोक्तं धर्म्म–
43 शास्त्रे [।*] [35]व(ब)हुभिर्व्वसुधा दता(त्ता) राजभिः सगरादिभिः [।*] यस्य यस्य यदा
44 भूमिस्तस्य तस्य तदा फलं (लम्) ।।[८।।*] मा भूदफलशङ्का वः परदत्तेति पा–
45 र्थिवाः [।*] स्वदानात्फलमानन्त्यं परदत्ता [नु*]पालने ।।[७।।*] षष्टिवर्षसहस्रा–
46 णि स्वर्गे मोदति भूमिदः [।*] आक्षेप्ता चानुमन्ता च द्वौ तौ नरकगामि–

Third Plate

47 नौ ।।[१०।।*] अग्नेरपत्यं प्रथमं सुवर्णं भूर्व्वैष्णवी सूर्यसुताश्च गावः [।*] यः काञ्चनं गाञ्च म–
48 हीञ्च दद्यादृत्त(त्ता)त्र(स्त्र)यस्तेन भवन्ति लोके(काः) ।[।११।।*] आस्फोटयन्ति पितरो वल्गयन्ति पितामहाः [।*]
49 भूमिदाता कुले जातः स नस्त्राता भविष्यति ।[।१२।।*] भूमिं यः प्रतिगृह्णा (ह्णा)ति यश्च भूमिं प्रयच्छ–
50 त्ति [।*] उभौ तौ पुण्यकर्म्माणौ नियतं स्वर्ग्गगामिनौ ।[।१३।।*] तडागानां सहस्रेण वाजपेयश
51 तेन च [।*] गवां कोटिप्रदानेन भूमिहर्त्ता न शुध्यति ।[।१४।।*] हरते हारयते यस्तु मन्दवु(बु)द्धिस्त–

27. This mark of punctuation is unnecessary.
28. Laskar: सगर्त्तोषिरः.
29. Better read देवरातौदल°.
30. Rajaguru: श्रावस्थि°.
31. Read °य उदकधारापुरः सरमाचन्द्रतारकार्क्कक्षितिमकालोपभोगार्थं.
32. Read इत्यवगत्य which is Laskar's reading.
33. The letter *gau* is omitted in Laskar's transcript, obviously due to oversight.
34. Laskar: स्वदर्त्ति°.
35. This and the subsequent benedictive and imprecatory stanzas have been deliberately left undeciphered by Laskar.

52 मोवृत्तः [।*] सुव(ब)द्धौ वारुणैः पाशैस्तिर्यग्योनिं स गच्छति ।[।१५।।*] सुवर्ण्णमेकं ग्रामेकां
भूमेरप्य–
53 र्द्धमङ्गुलं (लम्) [।*] हरन्नरकमायाति यावदाहू (भू) तसंप्लवं (वम्) ।[।१६।।*] स्वदत्तां
परदत्ताम्वा[36] यो हरेत
54 वसुन्धरां(राम्) [।*] स विष्टायां कृमिर्भूत्वा पितृभिः सह पच्यते ।[।१७।।*] आदित्यो
वरुणो विष्णुर्व्र(ब्रं)ह्मा
55 सोमो हुताशनः [।*] शूलपाणिश्च भगवानभिनन्दन्ति भूमिदं (दम्) ।[।१८।।*] सामान्योयं
ध–
56 र्म्मसेतुर्नृपाणां काले काले पालनीयो भवद्भिः [।*] सर्वानितान् भाविनः पार्थि–
57 वेन्द्रान(न्) भूयो भूयो याचते रामभद्रः [।।१७।।*] इति कमलदलाम्वु(म्बु)वि(बि)न्दु-
लोलां श्री(श्रि)य–
58 मनुचिन्त्य मनुष्यजीवितञ्च [।*] सकलमिदमुदाहृतञ्च वु[37](बु) [द्*]ध्वा नहि पुरुषैः परकी–
59 र्त्तयो विलोप्याः [।।२०।।*] परममाहेश्वरपरमभट्टारकमहाराजाधिराजपरमेश्व–
60 रसोमकुलतिलकत्रिकलिङ्गाधिपति**श्रीमद्ययातिदेवपादप्र–**
61 **वर्द्धमानविजयराज्ये[38] चतुर्व्विङशति[39] सम्व (संव)त्सरे आषाढ शुक्लपक्षे ति–**
62 **थौ पञ्चम्यां यत्राङ्केनापि सम्वत[40] २४ आषाढ शुदि ५** लिखितमिदं शा–
63 सनं महासान्धिविग्रहि[41]राणकश्रीधारदत्तावगतेन महासान्धिविग्रह–
64 कायस्थतथातेनेति [।*] विनाणिवासुकेनोत्करितम्[42] ।।

ABSTRACT

The auspicious formula *siddham*, expressed symbolically, is followed by the description of **Yayātinagara,** whence the charter was issued, king Janamejaya and his son and successor **Yayāti** in seven stanzas. Of these, the first six stanzas are already met with in IV: XIV.[43] The seventh verse, which is introduced for the first time and found repeated in some later grants of the family,[44] tells us that Yayāti defeated in battle a certain Ajapāla and captured thirty-two rutting elephants known as Kāmadeva, etc., with their riders already killed by an array of arrows.[45]

36. Read परदत्तां वा.
37. There is a superfluous punctuation mark-like stroke after *vu*.
38. Laskar: °राज्य.
39. Read °बिशति°.
40. Read संवत्.
41. Laskar: °विग्रह°.
42. Read विज्ञानिवासुकेनोत्कीर्णम्.
43. Verses 1-6 of the present record are identical with verses 1-5 and 7 of IV: XIV. Verse 6 of the latter record describing Janamejaya has been omitted in the former, whether deliberately or by oversight we cannot ascertain. In the next inscription this verse is retained, but it is wrongly applied to Janamejaya's son Yayāti.
44. It is met with as verse 8 in IV: XVII and XVIII and as verse 7 in IV: XX.
45. Some scholars take the word *ajapāla* as a common nown in the sense of 'protector of the drove'. See K. C. Panigrahi, *op. cit.*, 48. But it is untenable.

This *praśasti* is followed by the formal prose portion which refers to kings Mahābhavagupta and Mahāśivagupta, the latter meditating upon the feet of the former, with the usual imperial titles.

It is next stated that after honouring the Brāhmaṇas in the village named Ḍelāḍelī[46] included in the Telātaṭa-*viṣaya*[47] situated in the Kosala country, **Mahāśivagupta** donated the village extending up to its four boundaries to *Bhaṭṭa* Mahodadhi, who belonged to the Kauśika *gotra* and had Devarāta, Audala and Viśvāmitra for his *pravaras* and was a student of Gautama *śākhā*, originally hailed from Kāsilī[47a] situated in the Śrāvastī-*maṇḍala*[48] and was at the time of the grant living at Antaraḍi[48a] in the Lāvaḍā-*viṣaya*[49], and was the son and grandson respectively of Siddheśvara and Parameśvara. The privileges conferred on the dones and the royal officers to whom the king's order concerning the grant was addressed are the same as those enumerated in the preceding charter except that while the queen (*rājñī*) is separately mentioned, there is no reference to her favourites (*rājñī-vallabha*) and that the *Yukta* is replaced by the *Niyukta*. The villagers were asked to live happily by regularly offering to the grantee regular income including the *bhāga, bhoga, kara and hiraṇya* as due.

Future kings are requested to protect the grant like their own grant, and this entreaty is sought to be strengthened by citing thirteen imprecatory stanzas reportedly extracted from the Dharmaśāstra.

The charter was issued on the **fifth day of bright fortnight of the month of Āṣāḍha in the twenty-fourth year of the increasingly victorious reign of Yayāti,** who is mentioned with full imperial titles.[49a]

The charter was written by *Kāyastha* Tathāgata attached to the office of the minister of peace of war with the knowledge of the *Mahāsandhivigrahin Rāṇaka* Dhāradatta.[50]

46. Identified with the modern village of Dedil (20-22" N. 83-21" E.), a few miles from the Tel river in the erstwhile Patna State. See Binayak Misra, *DMO*, 68. R. D. Banerji (*HO*, i, 216) spells the name as Delāḍelī.
47. The district was evidently so called because it comprised territory along the river Tel, a tributary of the Mahānadī rising in the former Kalahandi State and joining it at Sonpur in the Balangir District. See *EI*, xi, 201; *HO*, i, 216; *DMO*, 68, *DHNI*, i, 404, fn. 3. This district is mentioned in the next inscription also.

47*a*. Not identified. But it must have been situated somewhere in the region round Set-Mahet (ancient Śrāvastī) in the Gonda-Bahraich area of Uttar Pradesh.

48. Region round Śrāvastī, modern Set-Mahet.

48*a*. Indentified with Antarida in the former Sonpur State. See Binayak Misra, *DMO*, 69.

49. Hira Lal (*EI*, xi, 201) doubtfully identifies it with modern Lebda, 48 miles south-west of Balangir.

49*a*. The date is specified both in words and figures.

50. R. D. Banerji (*HO*, i, 216). is wrong in taking the text under consideration to mean that 'the order was written by the *Mahāsāndhivigrahī Kāyastha* Tathāgata with the consent of the *Mahāsāndhi-vigrahika* and *Rāṇaka* Dhāradatta.'

IV: XVII

PĀṬṆĀ PLATES[1] OF MAHĀŚIVAGUPTA I YAYĀTI, YEAR 28

Provenance: Somewhere in the former Pāṭṇā State, Bolangir District, Orissa.

References: Ganga Mohan Laskar, *JASB*, New Series, i, 8–12 and 19–23; R.D. Banerji, *History of Orissa,* i, 216–17; H.C. Ray, *Dynastic History of Northern India,* i, 404, No. 6; Bhandarkar's List, No. 1569; S.N. Rajaguru, *IO*, iv, 196–204 and plates facing p. 196 and between pp. 198 and 199 and 200 and 201.

Language: Sanskrit. In a mixture of prose and verse.

Metres: Verses 1–3, 7 and 23: *Śārdūlavikrīḍita;* Verse 4: *Upajāti* of *Indravajrā* and *Upendravajrā;* Verses 5–6: *Vasantatilakā;* Verse 8: *Sragdharā;* Verses 9–11, 13–20 and 24: *Anuṣṭubh;* Verse 12: *Indravajrā;* Verse 21: *Śālinī;* Verse 22: *Puṣpitāgrā.*

Script: Northern class of alphabets.

Date: Regnal year 28, Bhādrapada śukla 5. About the middle of the tenth century A.D.

TEXT[1a]

First Plate

1 सिद्धम्[2] [।*] स्वस्ति प्रेमनिरुद्धमुग्धमनसोः स्फारीभवच्चक्षुषो–
2 र्यूनोर्यत्र विचित्रनिर्भररतक्रीडाक्रम(मं) तत्वतोः ।[3] विच्छिन्नोपि कृता–
3 तिमात्रपुलकैराविर्भवत्सीत्कृतैराश्लेषैर्ग्लपितक्लमैः स्मरर–
4 सः कामं[4] मुहुस्ताय्यते [।।१।।*] यत्राशेषविसे(शे)षरूपमहिमापास्ता–
5 प्सरःकान्तिभिर्जातेर्ष्याकलहेष्वपि प्रणयिनः कर्णोत्पलै–
6 स्ताडिताः [।*] जायन्ते[5]प्रविशत्सतस्मरशरप्रोत्थापितान्तर्व्यथा [:*] स्यन्दी(न्दि)[5a]–
7 स्वेदजलावसेचनवशान्निय्यातिरोमाङ्कुराः ।।[२।।*] श्रा(श्र)त्युत्तुङ्गक–
8 रीन्द्रदन्तमुसलप्रोद्भासिरोचिश्चयैध्वन्ति ध्वन्सन[6]निष्फ–

1. The plates measure about 9⅓" in length and 7" in width. The ends of the ring, which was passed through the circular hole bored on the left margin of each plate, are secured under a lump of copper which bulges out into a circular seal bearing the representation, in relief, of the Gaja-Lakṣmī motif.

1a. From plates in *IO*, iv.

2. Laskar: Om. Expressed by a symbol.

3. This mark of punctuation has escaped the notice of Laskar who supplies it on his own.

4. The *anusvāra*, which is slightly on left, has escaped the notice of Laskar.

5. Read प्रविशच्छित°.

5a. In above, IV: XIV, we have *sāndra.*

6. Read ध्वंसन°.

9 लीकृतशरच्चन्द्रोदयै: सर्व्वदा ।[7] यत्रासीदसतीजन–
10 स्य[8] विशदं मुक्तामयं मण्डनं सङ्केतास्पदमप्यतीवध–
11 वल(लं) प्रासादशृङ्गाग्रतः ।।[३।।*] महानदीतुङ्गतरङ्गभङ्गस्फा–
12 रोच्छलत्सी(च्छी) [क*][9]रवद्भिरारात् [।*] यस्मिन्नताश(स)क्ति[10]मदङ्गनानां श्रमापनो–
13 दः क्रियते मरुद्भिः ।।[४।।*] तस्मात् **श्रीययातिनगरात**(त्) । लोकत्रयप्र–
14 थितशुभ्रयशोवितानव्याप्ताष्टदिक्प्रसभनिर्ज्जितवैरिवर्गः ।
15 राजा व(ब)भूव भुवि भावितभव्यमु(मू)र्त्तिः श्रीमान् सरोजवदनो जनमे–
16 जयाख्यः ।।[11][५।।*] निर्द्दारिकरिकुम्भसमुद्गमुक्तमुक्ताफलप्रकरद–
17 न्त(न्तु)रखड्गधारः [।*] तस्मादज(जा)यतजगत्र(त्त्र)यगीतकीर्त्तिहे(र्हे)लाविनिर्ज्जित–

Second Plate: First Side

18 रिपुन्न(र्न्न)पतिर्**ययातिः** ।।[६।।*] यत्खड्गाग्रविपाटितद्विपघटाकुम्भस्थ–
19 लादुल्लसन्मुक्ताजालविभूषितं प्रतिरणं पृथ्वीवधूर [:*] स्थलं (लम्) । शश्व–
20 द्द्व(द्वा)रन्मन्न[12]राधिपशिरोरत्ना(त्नां) शुजालामला यत्पादाम्वु(म्बु)जरेणवः सम–
21 तया तद्रश्मिलक्ष्मीं दधुः ।।[७।।*] माद्यलो[ल्लो]लालिमालाकुलकरटपुटस्य–
22 न्दिदानप्रवाहान् सिन्दूरारक्तकुम्भान् शित[13]पृथुलरदान् कामदेवादि–
23 संज्ञान् [।*] जित्या(त्वा)ऽजापालमाजौ जनितसुखधूविस्मय [:*] स्मेरवक्त्रः स
24 द्द्वात्रिंशत्करीन्द्रान् शरनिकरहत(ता)रोहकानग्रहीद्यः ।।[८।।*] परममा–
25 हेश्वरपरमभट्टारकमहाराजाधिराजपरमेश्वरसोमकुल–
26 तिलकत्रिकलिङ्गाधिपतिश्रीमहाभवगुप्तराजदेवपादानु–
27 ध्यातपरममाहेश्वरपरमभट्टारकमहाराजाधिराजप–
28 रमेश्वरसोमकुलतिलकत्रिकलिङ्गाधिपति **श्रीमहाशिवगुप्त**–
29 राजदेवः कुशली ।[14] षण्णवत्यां तेलातट[15] विषयीयलुत्तरुमा[16]–
30 ग्रामे तद्विषयीयव्रा(ब्रा)ह्मणानापूज्य[17] समाहृतूं[18] सन्निधातृ नियू(यु)
31 क्ताधिकारिकद(दा)ण्डपासि(शि)कपशिुनवे(वै)त्रिकावरोधजनराण–

7. This *daṇḍa* has been left unnoticed by Laskar who proposes to supply it on his own.
8. This letter has been wrongly taken by Laskar as forming part of the last line.
9. The letter *ka*, which is omitted by inadvertence in the original, is given by Laskar as if it were present on the plate.
10. The medial sign for *i* looks like that of *e*.
11. These *daṇḍas* are supplied by Laskar on his own as if they were absent in the original.
12. Note the difference in the wording of this quarter in this inscription and in the Cuttack plates (above, IV: XIV).
13. Laskar suggests to correct it to सित.
14. This mark of punctuation is superfluous.
15. Laskar reads °तट्ट.
16. Laskar suggests that this letter should be read as *yā* so that the name of the village would be Luttaruyā. Rajaguru reads लु(लु)तरुमा.
17. Laskar reads सम्पूज्य. The adjective *tad=viṣayiya*, which should correctly come before the list of officers named subsequently, is wrongly used here.
18. Laskar reads समाहृत्.

32 कराजवल्लभादीन् सर्व्वान्राजपादोपजीविनः समाज्ञापय–

33 ति[।*] विदिमस्तु भवतां यथास्माभिरयं ग्रामः सनिधिः सोप–

34 निधिः सदशापराधः सर्व्ववा(बा)धाविर्वाजतः[19] सर्वोपरिकरादा–

35 नसहितः।[20] चतुः[21] सीमापर्यन्तः साम्रमधुकः सगर्तोष–

Second Plate: Second Side

36 र[:*] सजलस्थलः प्रतिनिषिद्धच (चा)टभट[22] प्रवेशः कौशि–

37 कगोत्राय[23] देवरातऔदलविश्वामित्रप्रवराय गौतमशा–

38 खाध्यायिने श्रावस्ति(स्ती) मण्डले कासिलीविनिर्गताय लावडावि–

39 षयेन्तरडी[24] वास्तव्याय परमेश्वरनप्त्रे सिद्धेश्वरसुता–

40 य भट्टश्रीमहोदधये उदकधारापुरःसरश्रा(मा)चन्द्र–

41 तारकार्कक्षितिसमकालोपभोगार्त्थं मातापित्रोरात्मन–

42 श्च पुण्ययशो[24a]भिवृद्धये ताम्व्र(म्र)शाश(स)नेनाकरीकृत्य प्रतिपाद–

43 त इत्यवगत्य समुचितकरनिकरभोगभागादिकमु–

44 पनयद्भिर्भवद्भिः सुखं प्रतिवस्तव्यमिति ॥ भाविभि–

45 श्च भूपतिभिर्द्दत्तिरियमस्मदीया धर्म्मगौरवादस्मदनु–

46 रोधाच्च स्वदत्तिरिवानुपालनीया ॥ तथा चोक्तं धर्म्मशास्त्रे [।*][25]व(ब)हुभि–

47 र्वसुधा दत्ता राजभिः सगर(रा)दिभिः। यस्य यस्य यदा भूमिस्तस्य त–

48 स्य तदा फलं (लम्) ॥[९॥*] मा भूदफलशङ्का वः परदत्तेति पार्थिवाः।[*] स्वदा–

49 नात्फलमानन्त्यं परदत्तानुपालने ॥[१०॥*] [26]षष्टिम्वर्षसहस्राणि स्व–

50 र्गे मोदति भूमिदः। आक्षेप्ता चानुमन्ता च [27]द्वयमेव नरकं व्र–

51 त् ॥[११॥*] अग्नेरपत्यं प्रथमं सुवर्ण्णं भूर्वैष्णवी सूर्यसुत(ता)श्च गावः। यः

Third Plate: First Side

52 काञ्चनं गाञ्च महीञ्च दद्याद्दत्तास्त्रयस्तेन भवन्ति लोके (काः) ॥[१२॥*] आस्फो–

53 टयन्ति पितरो वल्गयन्ति पितामहाः। भूमिदाता कुले जातः

54 स नस्त्राता भविष्यति ।[।१३॥*] भूमिं यः प्रतिगृह्णाति यश्च भूमिं प्रयच्छ–

55 ति। उभौ तौ पुण्यकर्म्माणौ नियतं स्वर्गगामिनौ ॥[१४॥*] तडागानां सहस्रेण

19. Laskar's reading is विवर्ज्जितः.
20. This *daṇḍa* is redundant.
21. Laskar reads चतु[:*] while the *visarga* is clearly legible in the plate.
22. Laskar reads चट्टभट्ट.
23. Better read वरातौदल°.
24. In the previous grant we have °*ntaraḍi*, so that the name might have been spelt with long as well as short *i*.

24*a*. After *śo* Laskar reads an *avagraha* which is not to be seen in the plate.

25. The imprecatory and benedictory verses in lines 46—66 have been omitted by Laskar.
26. Read षष्टिं वर्ष°.
27. In other inscriptions we generally have तान्येव नरके वसेत् or द्वौ तौ नरकगामिनौ which are more suitable metrically.

56 वाजपेयशतेन च। गवां कोटिप्र [दा*]नेन भूमिहर्त्ता न शुध्यति ॥[१५॥*] स्वर्ण्णं (सुवर्ण्णं)-
मेकं गामेकां

57 भूमेरप्यर्ध्धं (र्द्धं) मङ्गुलं (लम्)। हरन्नरकमायाति यावदाहू (भू) तस (सं) प्लवं (वम्)
॥[१६॥*][28]अन्यायेन

58 हृता भूमिरन्यायेन तु हारिता ॥[१७॥*] हर्त्ता हारयति (यिता) यस्तु मन्दवु (बु) द्धिस्त-
मोवृतः। सु–

59 व (ब) द्धो वारुणैः पाशैस्तिर्यग्योनिं स गच्छति ।[।१८॥*] स्वदत्ता (त्तां) परदत्ताम्वा (त्तां
वा)

60 जो (यो) हरेत वसुन्धरां (राम्) [।*] स विष्ठाया (यां) कृमिर्भूत्या (त्वा) पितृभिः सह
पच्यते ॥[१९॥*] आ–

61 दित्तो (त्यो) वरुणो विष्णुर्व्र (ब्रं) ह्मा सोमो हुताशनः [।*] शूलपा–

62 णिश्च भगवानभिनन्दन्ति भूमिदं (दम्) ।[।२०॥*] सामान्योयं धर्म्मसे–

63 तुर्न्नृपाणां काले काले पालनीयो भवद्भिः। सर्व्वानेतान् भावि–

64 नः पार्थिवेन्द्रान् भूयो भूयो याचते रामभद्रः[28a] ।[।२१॥*] इति कमल–

65 दलाम्वु (म्बु) वि (बि) न्दुलोलां श्रियमनुचिन्त्य मनुष्यजीवितञ्च [।*] सकलमिद–

66 मुदाहृतञ्च वु (बु) द्धा न हि पुरुषैः परकीर्त्तयो विलोप्याः ॥[२२॥*] येनात्यन्त–

67 सुरासुराधिपगुरुप्रज्ञाभिमानो जितो राज्ञारोपितराज्यभारम–

68 तुलं यश्चावहल्लीलया [।*]यस्यासीन्नयविक्रमद्वयमपि प्रेयां (यान्) सखा स–

69 र्व्वदा स श्रीमान्धृतसा (स) न्धिविग्रहपदः श्री सिङ्घ[29]दत्ताहयः ।[।२३॥*] कोसलीयसन्धिविग्रही
(हि) स (से) वक[30]–

Third Plate: Second Side

70 कायस्थसूर्यसेणेन[31] लिखितं शाशन[32] स्थास्नु यावच्चन्द्रार्कता–

71 रकं (कम्) ॥[२४॥*][33] परममाहेश्वरपरमभट्टारकमह (हा) राजाधिराजपरमे–

72 श्वरसोमकुलतिलकत्रिकलिङ्गाधिपति**श्रीमद्ययातिदेवस्य प्र–**

28. This is only the first part of the verse, the remaining portion, which is left out due to inadvertence, being अतीतागामिपापानां दहत्यासप्तमं कुलम्. The second *caraṇa*, is sometimes worded as हारिता वानुमोदिता. See *IE*, 178.

28*a*. Rajaguru: रामचन्द्रः.

29. Read सिंह°.

30. The last three letters in line 69 are not quite clear in the original. Laskar gives the reading *satāka* in the body of the text and thinks that *sattāka* or *sattvaka*, derived from the root √ *as* and equivalent in meaning to *pratibaddha* met with in other grants, is the correct intended word. But at the same time he points that the three letters under consideration may also be read as *savaka*, an error for *sevaka*, 'servant'. We prefer the latter reading.

31. Read सूर्यषेणेन. Laskar omits the letter *se* before *ṇe*.

32. Read शासनं which is Laskar's reading.

33. This is a portion of a verse in the *Anuṣṭubh* metre. The remainder of the stanza has been apparently omitted.

73 **वर्द्धमानविजयराज्येऽष्टाविशतिमे[34] सम्व(संव)त्सरे भाद्रपदमासे**
74 **सितपक्षे तिथौ पञ्चम्यां यत्राङ्के [ना*]पि सम्व(संव)त् २८ भाद्रपद–**
75 **सु (शु)दि ५** शिवं (वम्) ।। विनाणीमधुमथनेनोत्कीरितम् ।।[35]

ABSTRACT

After the auspicious word *siddham*, indicated by a symbol, the town of **Yayātinagara**, the place of issue of the charter, king Janamejaya and his son and successor, **Yayāti**, are described in eight verses which are already known from epigraphs IV: XIV and XVI.[36]

In the prose passage that follows kings Mahābhavagupta and **Mahāśivagupta**, who meditated upon the feet of the former, are described with full titles exactly as in the previous grant.

The inscription next records that after worshipping the Brāhmaṇas in the village of Lluttarumā[37] included in the Telātaṭa-*viṣaya* situated in Ṣaṇṇavati,[38] **Mahāśivagupta** granted the village, extending up to its four boundaries, in favour of *Bhaṭṭa* Mahodadhi who is described exactly in the same manner as in the previous record. The addressees of the royal command regarding the grant are the same royal officers posted in the district as those referred to in the preceding epigraph with the exception of only the *cāṭas* and *bhaṭas*, and the privileges and exemptions bestowed on the donee are also exactly the same. The inhabitants of the village were ordered to pay the donee all the *karas, bhoga*, *bhāga*, etc., as due and live happily in the village.

The usual request to the future monarchs to protect the grant is sought to be strengthened by fourteen imprecatory and benedictive verses said to have been extracted from the Dharmaśāstra.

Verse 23, which describes Siṁhadatta, the occupant of the office of the minister of peace and war, is worded almost identically as verse 20 of the Cuttack plates of the 9th regnal year of the same king mentioning Chicchaṭeśvara who held the same office.

34. Read °विशतितमे which is the reading of Laskar.
35. Read विज्ञानिमधुमथनेनोत्कीर्णम्. Laskar reads विनानिमधुमथनेनोत्करितम्.
36. Of these verse 7, which is conspicuously absent in the preceding record and is employed in the Cuttack plates of the 9th year of the reign of Mahāśivagupta Yayāti (above, IV : XIV, verse 6) to describe his father Janamejaya, is erroneously applied here to Yayāti himself.
37. Binayak Misra proposes to identify it with the modern Leter in the former Kalahandi State, about 12 miles north of the river Tel (*Dynasties of Mediaeval Orissa*, 70).
38. Literally meaning 96, this territorial division cannot be identified. But as according to the preceding charter the Telātaṭa-*viṣaya* was situated in the Kosala-*deśa*, Ṣaṇṇavati appears to have been employed as another name of Kosala or might have denoted a part of Kosala. it was probably so called in consequence of its containing ninety-six towns.

The record was written by the *Kāyastha* Sūryasena, a servant of the *Sandhivigrahin* of Kosala.[39]

The inscription is dated[40] the **fifth tithi of the bright fortnight of the month of Bhādrapada in the twenty-eighth year of the increasingly victorious reign of Yayāti.**

The charter was incised by the artisan Madhumathana.[41]

39. The *Sandhivigrahin* of Kosala is evidently the same as Siṁhadatta named in the preceding stanza.
40. Both in words and figures.
41. As normally the writer and the engraver are mentioned together at the end, the separation of these two items by the insertion of the date portion between them is a little interesting.

 This as well as the previous record reminds one of the three Chaudwār plates which also record grants to one and the same person. But the similarity does not go beyond it. All the three Chaudwār plates are literally identically worded except only the names of the granted villages and the districts wherein they were situated. The two Pāṭṇā plates, on the other hand, were issued in different years, their writers, engravers as well as the *Sandhivigrahins* connected with their execution are different, and two verses not found in the grant dated in the 24th year are incorporated in that of the year 28. There are some other differences also.

IV: XVIII

CUTTACK PLATES[1] OF MAHĀBHAVAGUPTA II BHĪMARATHA, YEAR 3

Provenance: Cuttack or its neighbourhood, Cuttack District, Orissa.[2]

References: J.F. Fleet, *EI*, iii, 355-59 and plates facing pp. 356 and 357; Hira Lal, *ibid.*, xi, 200; R.D. Banerji, *History of Orissa*, i, 220; H.C. Ray, *Dynastic History of Northern India*, i, 406-07; Bhandarkar's List, No. 1570; K.C. Panigrahi, *Chronology of the Bhauma-Karas and the Somavaṁśīs of Orissa*, 48-49; S. N. Rajaguru, *IO*, iv, 205-11.

Language: Sanskrit. In a mixture of prose and verse.

Metres: Verses 1-3, 7, 9 and 22: *Śārdūlavikrīḍita;* Verse 4: *Upajāti* of *Indravajrā* and *Upendravajrā*; Verses 5-6: *Vasantatilakā*; Verse 8: *Sragdharā*; Verses 10-12, 14-19 and 23: *Anuṣṭubh*; Verse 13: *Indravajrā*; Verse 20: *Śālinī*; Verse 21: *Puṣpitāgrā.*

Script: Northern class of alphabets.

Date: Regnal year 3, Mārgaśīrṣa śukla 3. Latter half of the tenth century A.D.

TEXT[3]

First Plate

1 सिद्धम्[4] [।*] स्वस्ति प्रेमनिरुद्धमुग्धमनसोः स्फारीभवच् [च*]क्षुषोर्यूनोर्यत्र

2 विचित्रनिर्भररतक्रीडाक्रम(मं) तन्वतोः । विच्छिनो (न्नो)पि कृतातिमात्रपु–

3 लकैराविर्भवत्सीत्कृतैराश्लेषैर्ग्लपितक्लमैः स्मरसरसः कामं मु–

4 हुस्ताय्यते[5] ।[।१।।*] यत्राशेषविशेषरूपमहिमापास्ताप्सरः कान्तिभिर्जा–

1. Each plate measures about 9¾″ long and 7″ broad at the ends and somewhat less in the middle. The ring, which is passed through the round hole in the left margin of each plate and holds the plates together, is about ½″ thick and 5″ in diameter, and its ends are secured under a circular seal, nearly 1½″ in diameter, of which the surface is very much damaged resulting in the complete breaking away of whatever legend and devices may have been on it.
2. Fleet states that there is no precise information as to where these plates were found; but they appear to have been found somewhere at Cuttack or closely in its neighbourhood.
3. From plates in *EI*, iii.
4. Fleet: Om. Expressed by a symbol.
5. मुहु[:*] खाद्यते is Fleet's reading. The reading adopted here is also found in the Cuttack plates of the 9th year and the Pāṭṇā plates of the 24th and 28th years of the reign of Mahāśivagupta-I (above, IV: XIV, XVI and XVII).

5 तेष्यकिलहेष्वधि प्रणयिनः कर्ण्णोत्पलैस्ताडिताः। जायन्ते प्रविश–

6 च्छित[6]स्मरशरप्रोत्थापित्ता (ता) न्तर्व्यं थ [:*]स्यन्दि[7]स्वेदजलावशे (से) चनवशान्निर्व्वा (र्य्या)

7 तरोमाङकुराः ॥[२॥*] अ्रत्युतु (त्तु) ङ्गकरीन्द्रदन्तमुसलप्रोद्भासिरो[चि*]श्चयैर्द्धा (द्ध्वा) न्तध्वं–

8 सननिष्फलीकृतशरच्चन्द्रोदयैः सर्व्वदा ॥(।) यत्रासीदसतीजनस्य

9 विशदं मुक्तामयं मण्डनं सङ्केतास्पदमप्यतीव धवलं प्रा–

10 सादशृङ्गाग्रतः ।[।३॥*]महानदीतुङ्गतरङ्गभङ्गस्फारोच्छलच्छी–

11 करवद्भिरारात् ।[*] यस्मिन् रतासक्तिमदङ्गनाना (नां) श्रा (श्र) मा[प*]नोदः क्र (क्रि) य–

12 ते मरुद्भिः ।[।४॥*] तस्मात् श्री**ययातिनगरात्** । लोकत्नयप्रथितशुभ्रय–

13 शोवित्तानव्याप्ताष्टदिक्प्रसभनिर्जितवैरिवर्गः । राजा व (ब) भूव भुवि

14 भावितभव्यमूर्त्तिः श्रीमान् सरोजवदनो जनमेजयाख्यः ॥[५॥*] नि[8]–

15 र्दारितारिकरिकुम्भसमुद्‌ग[9]मुक्तमुक्ताफलप्रकरदन्तुरखङ्ग[10]धा–

16 रः[।*] तस्मादजायत जगत्त्रय[11]गीतकीर्त्तिर्हेलाविनिर्जितरिपुर्नृप–

17 **तिर्ययातिः** ॥[६॥*] यत्खड्गाग्रविपाटितद्विपघटाकुम्भस्थलादुल्लस–

18 न्मुक्ताजालविभूषितं प्रतिरण (णं) पृथ्वीवधूरः[*]स्थलं (लम्) [।*] शश्वद्द्वारनम–

Second Plate : First Side

19 न्नराधिपशिरोरत्नाङशु[12]जालामला यत्पादाम्वु (म्बु) जरेणवः समतया तद्र–

20 शिमलक्ष्मीं दधुः ॥[७॥*] माद्यल्लोलालिमालाकुलकरटपुटस्यन्दि[13]दानप्रवाहा–

21 न् सिन्दूरारक्तकुम्भान् सि (शि) तपृथुलरदान् कामदेवादिसंज्ञान् । जि–

22 त्वाजापाल[14]माजौ प (ज) नित[15]सुखवधूविस्मयस्मेरवक्त्रः स द्वात्रिंशत्क[16]–

23 रीन्द्रान् शरनिकरहतारोहकानग्रहीद्यः ॥[८॥*] पुत्रस्तस्य व (ब) भूव ध–

24 र्म्मनिरतः **श्रीभीमपूर्व्वो** रथः ख्यातः क्ष्मापनिषेव्यमानचर[ण]–

25 श्चूडामणिर्भूभुजा (जाम्) । योसौ शौचमहाधनोपि समरे लक्ष्मीः (क्ष्मीं) परे–

6. Fleet reads प्रविशङ्कित, but the last but one letter is clearly *cchi*. Our reading also finds support from the Cuttack and one of the Pāṭṇā plates of Mahāśivagupta (supra, IV: XIV and XVI).
7. Fleet: सान्द्रि(न्द्र). The reading adopted in these pages is vouched for by the Cuttack plates and two of the Pāṭṇā plates of Mahāśivagupta (above, IV: XIV, XVI and XVII) which also contain this verse.
8. Fleet reads the last letter of this line as *nir*, evidently by oversight.
9. Fleet reads समूह. But the last letter cannot be read as *ha*. *Cf. ha* in line 10 above.
10. दत्तरथाङ्ग° is Fleet's reading. The reading given by us finds support not only from other records containing this verse (above, IV: XIV, XVI and XVII) but also from the facsimile accompanying Fleet's transcript.
11. Fleet: जगत्रय.
12. Read रत्नांशु.
13. Fleet's reading is पुटास्वान्दि which he proposes to correct to पुटास्यन्दि.
14. Fleet reads जित्वा जावाल°.
15. Fleet: पतित.. Panigrahi proposes to correct, it to जित्वाजपालमजोपनीत° which, however, violates against the metre.
16. Fleet's reading is खङ्गी त्रिंशत्के.

26 षां व(ब) लाज्जग्राह क्षतवैरिवर्गविभवः सौन्दर्यशोभास्पदं(दम्) ।।[६।।*][17]

27 परममाहेश्वरपरमभट्टारकमहाराजाधिराजपरमे–

28 श्वरसोमकुलतिलकत्रिकलिङ्गाधिपतिश्रीमहाशिवगु–

29 प्तराजदेवपादानुध्यातपरममाहेश्वरपरमभट्टार–

30 कमहाराजाधिराजपरमेश्वरसोमकुलतिलकत्रिकलिङ्गा–

31 धिपतिश्रीमहाभवगुप्तराजदेवः कुशला(लीं) ।[16] कोसलसारवङ्ग–

32 द्यन्हाविषयीय ।[18] गौडसिमिणिल्लिग्रामे ।[18]तद्विषयीय[18a] व्रा(ब्रा)ह्मणाना–

33 पूज्य समाहर्तृ सन्नियुक्ताधिकारिकदाण्डपासि(शि)कपिसु(शु)नवे(वै)त्रिका–

34 वरोधजनराज्ञीराणकराजपुत्रराजवल्लभादीन् सर्व्वान्

35 समाज्ञापयति । विदितमस्तु भवताम् यथाऽ[19]स्माभिरयङ्ग्राम–

36 :सनिधिः सोपनिधिः सर्व्ववा(बा)धाविवर्जितः सर्व्वोपरिकरादा–

Second Plate : Second Side

37 नसही(हि)तः ।[20] चतुः[21] साम्रमधुकः सगर्त्तोषरः सजलस्थलः ।[22]

38 श्रावस्तीमण्डने(ले) कासील्ली[23] भट्टग्रामविनी(नि)र्गताय[24] कोसले दे–

39 वीभोगवी(वि)षयीयसीङ्गोश्राग्रामवास्तव्याय कौशिकगोत्रा–

40 य ।[25] विश्वामित्रदेवरातऔदल्य(ल)प्रवराय कौथुमचरणाय च्छन्दो–

41 गशाखाध्य(ध्या)यिने भट्टपरमेश्वरपौत्राय भट्टवसिष्ठसुताय ।[25]

42 राणकश्रीराच्छोनाम्ने सूर्यग्रहणे सलिलधारापुरः सरमाच–

43 न्द्रतारकार्कक्षितिष(स)मकालोपभोगार्थ(थं)मात्रापित्रोरात्मनश्च

44 पुण्ययशोभिवृद्धये ताम्रशास[ने*]नाकरीकृत्य प्रतिपादी(दि)त इत्य[व*]ग–

45 त्य[26] समुचितकरनिकरभोगभागादी(दि)कमुपनयद्भिः[26a]सु—

17. While the first eight verses have been taken verbatim from the records of Mahāśivagupta I Yayāti (*supra*, IV : XIV, XVI—XVII), this stanza describing his son and successor Mahābhavagupta II Bhīmaratha is met with only in this inscription.
18. This mark of punctuation is unnecessary.
18a. This word should come immediately prior to *Samāhartṛ*, etc., which it normally qualifies.
19. The use of *avagraha* is interesting.
20. This *daṇḍa* is superfluous.
21. This word by itself conveys no intelligible sense in the present context. The intended reading was, of course, चतुः सीमापर्यन्तः.
22. The mark of punctuation is not required.
23. Kāsilī, which is met with in two of the Patna plates of Mahāśivagupta I (*supra*, IV : XVI and XVII), appears to be the intended reading.
24. Fleet: विनिर्गताय.
25. This *daṇḍa* is uncalled for.
26. Fleet reads इयेगत्य and suggests its correction to इत्यवगत्य. The second *akṣara* of this word may, however, be read as *tya*, *t* being similar in form to the same letter in *ātmanaś-ca* in line 43. It must, however, be admitted that the form of the second *tya* in this word would then be different from the first one.
26a. Hereafter we expect the word भवद्भिः which is dropped by oversight.

46 खेन प्रतिवस्तव्यमिकि (ति) [।*]भाविभिश्च भूपतिभिः दत्तिरियम–
47 स्मदीया धर्म्मगौरवादस्मदनुरोधाञ्च स्वदत्ती (त्ति) री (रि) वानुपालनी–
48 य (या)॥ तथा चोक्तं धर्म्मशास्त्रे ॥ व (ब) हुभिर्वसुधा दत्ता राजभिः सग–
49 रादिभिः । यस्य यस्य यदा भूमिस्तस्य तस्य तदा फलम् ॥[१०॥*] माभूद–
50 फलशङ्खा (ङ्का) वः परदत्तेते (ति) पार्थिवाः [।*] स्वदत्तात्फलम (मा) नन्त (नत्यं) परद–
51 त्तानुपालने ॥[११॥*] षष्टं (ष्टि) वर्षसहस्राणि स्वर्गे मोदति भूमिद : ॥ (।) आ–
52 क्षेप्ता चानुमन्ता च द्वौ तौ नरकगामिनौ ॥[१२॥*] अग्नेरपत्यं प्रथमं
53 सुवर्ण्णं भूर्वैष्णवी सूर्यसुताश्च गावः । यः काञ्चन (नं) गान (ञ्च) महीञ्च
54 दद्याद्दत्तास्त्रयस्तेन भवन्ति लोके (काः) ॥[१३॥*] आस्फोटयन्ति पितरो व

Third Plate

55 ल्गयन्ति पितामहाः [।*] भूमिदाता कुले जातः स नस्त्र (स्त्रा) त (ता) [भ]वि[ष्य]–
56 ति ॥[१४॥*] [भूमिं]यः प्रतिगृह्णाति यश्च [भूमिं] प्र[यच्छति [।*] उभौतौ पुण्यकर्माणौ]
57 निय[तं] स्वर्गगामिनौ ॥[१५॥*] तडागानां सहस्रेण वा[जपेयशतेन च] [।*]
58 गवां कोटिप्रदानेन भूमिहर्त्ता न शुध्यते ।[।१६॥*]हर[ते हा]रयेद्यस्तु
59 मन्दवु (बु) द्धिस्तमोवृतः [।*] ष (सु) व (ब) द्धो वारुणैः पाशैस्तिर्यग्योनिं स ग–
60 च्छति ।[।१७॥*] स्वदत्ताम्परदत्ता (त्तां) म्वा (वा) यो हरेद्वसुन्धरां[27] [।*] स विष्ठायां कृ–
61 मिर्भूत्वा पितृभिः सह पच्यते ।[।१८॥*] आदित्यो वरुणो विष्णुर्व (ब्र) ह्मा सोमो
62 हुतास (श) नः [।*] शूलपाणिश्च भगवानभिनन्दन्ति भूमिदं (दम्) ।[।१९॥*] स (सा) मान्योयं धर्म्मसेतु–
63 र्नृपाणा (णां) काले काले पालनीयो भवद्भिः । रा (स) र्व्वानेतान् भाविनः पार्थिवेन्द्रान्
64 भूयो भूयो याचते रामभद्रः ।[।२०॥*] इति कमलदलामु (म्बु) वि (बि) न्दुलोलां श्री (श्रि) य–
65 मनुचिन्त्य मनुष्यजीवित (तं) च [।*] सकलमिदमुदाहृतं च वुद्वा[28] न हि पु–
66 रुषैः परकीर्त्तयो विलोप्याः ।[।२१॥*] येनात्यन्तसुरासुराधिपगुरुप्रज्ञाभिमानैं (नो)
67 जितो[29] राज्ञारोपितराज्यभारमतुल (लं) यश्चावहल्लीलया । यस्यासीन (न्न) यविक्र–
68 मं (म) द्वयमपि[30] प्रेया[न्*] सखा सर्व्वदा स श्रेयान्[30a] धृतसनि (न्ति) विग्रहपदः श्रीसि–
69 ङ्गदत्तः[31] कृती ।[।२२॥][32] नाम्ना मङ्गलदत्तेन कायस्थेन स (सु) वु (बु) द्धिना[33] [।*] अलेखि शासनं स्था–

27. Read हरेत वसुन्धराम्.
28. Read बुद्ध्वा.
29. Fleet restores the entire portion as °गुरु [:*] प्रज्ञाभिमानैजि(र्जि)तो. Our reading is not only supported by *supra*, IV : XIV and XVII, which also contain this stanza with only a slight modification but also yields a better sense.
30. Fleet: विक्रम°. But *anusvāra* is quite clear in the facsimile illustrating his transcript.
30a. In other records we have श्रीमान् which is preferable.
31. Read सिंहदत्त.
32. This verse is taken verbatim from the Pāṭnā plates of the 28th year of the reign of Mahāśivagupta I (above, IV : XVII) with only श्रीमान् and सिङ्गदत्ताह्वयः substituted by श्रेयान् and सिङ्गदत्त कृती respectively.
33. Fleet could read only the first letter of this word as *sa*.

70 सं (स्नु)[34] ।[34a] यावच्चन्द्रार्कतारकाः ।[।२३।।*][35] परममाहेश्वरपरमभटा(ट्टा)रकमहा-राजाधिराज-
71 परमेश्वरसोमकुलतिलकत्रिकलिङ्गाधिपतिश्रीमद्भीमरथदेवस्य[36] प्र-
72 वर्द्धमानवविजयराज्ये तृति[37] संवत्सरे मार्गशीर्षमासीयशुक्लपक्ष (क्षे) तिथौ तृत(ती)-
73 यायां यत्राङ्केनापि सम्वत् ३ मार्ग शु दि ३ :[38] ।। विज्ञानिमधुमल्लेन[39] उत्करितं[40] [।।*]

ABSTRACT

The initial portion including the first eight stanzas, describing, in a conventional manner, the city of **Yayātinagara**, whence the plates were issued (1-4), the king Janamejaya (5) and his son and successor, Yayāti (6-8), is already familiar from the two preceding charters.[41] Verse 9, which is new, mentions Yayāti's son and successor, *Bhīmaratha*, who is described, equally conventionally, as devoted to the observance of his duties, a crest-jewel among kings, destroyer of the prosperity of the multitude of his enemies, an abode of beauty and as one whose feet were served by kings and who, though endowed with purity of character, seized forcibly the fortunes of his enemies in the battle. The prose passage following it refers to the reigning king **Mahābhavagupta II**, who meditated on the feet of Mahāśivagupta (I), both of whom are described with all the conventional titles, viz. *Parama-Māheśvara, Parama-bhaṭṭāraka-Mahārājādhirāja-Parameśvara, Soma-kula-tilaka* and *Trikaliṅgādhipati.*

Having worshipped the Brāhmaṇas in the village called Gauḍasimiṇilli[42] situated in the Kosalasākhaṅgadyanha-*viṣaya*[43], the king ordered all the district officers including *Samāhartṛ, Sanniyukta,*[44] *Ādhikārika, Dāṇḍapāśika, Piśuna, Vaitrika,* innates of the royal harem, the queen (or queens), *Rāṇaka,*

34. The first letter of this word was left unread by Fleet. This letter is, however, quite clear in the facsimile. The second letter has been corrected on the basis of the Pāṭṇā plates of the 28th year of Mahāśivagupta I's reign (*supra*, IV : XVII).
34a. This *daṇḍa* is superfluous.
35. The concluding portion of this stanza is found in the Pāṭṇā plates issued by Mahāśivagupta I in his 28th regnal year.
36. Fleet reads श्रीभीमरथदेवस्य.
37. Read तृतीय.
38. I.e. तृतीयः.
39. Is it an error for मधुमथनेन found in the previous record?
40. Read उत्कीर्णम्,.
41. The erroneous employment of the 7th verse, which originally described Janamejaya, (*supra*, IV: XIV), with reference to his son Yayāti, first and met with in above, IV: XVII, is retained here.
42. Binayak Misra (*Dynasties of Mediaeval Orissa*, 70) suggests its identification the village of Gaisama in the Bargarh tahsil.
43. Probably 'Sākhaṅgadyanhā in Kosala, ' it has not been identified yet. Hira Lal (*EI*, xi, 200) doubtfully proposes to read the name as Sākhaḍgīyanhā.
44. Probably the same as *Niyuktaka* of other inscriptions.

Rājaputras, the favourites of the king and others that on the occasion of an eclipse of the sun[45] he had given away the village in question to the *Rāṇaka*[46] Rāccho, son of the *Bhaṭṭa* Vasiṣṭha and grandson of the *Bhaṭṭa* Parameśvara, who belonged to the Kauśika *gotra* and had the *pravaras* of Viśvāmitra, Devarāta and Audala, was a member of the Kauthuma *caraṇa* and a student of the Chandogya *śākhā*[47], an immigrant from the *bhaṭṭa-grāma*[48] of Kāsīllī[49] situated in the Śrāvastī-*maṇḍala*[50] and an inhabitant of the village named Sīṅgoā[51] included in the Devībhoga-*viṣaya*[52] in Kosala. The grant bestowed on the donee all the privileges and exemptions mentioned in the preceding grant except *daś-āparādha* and the ban on the entry of the *cāṭas* and the *bhaṭas*, and the gifted land was, as usual, rendered rent-free by means of a copper-plate charter.

Next follows the usual request to future kings to maintain the grant and thirteen imprecatory and benedictive stanzas, reportedly borrowed from Dharmaśāstra, are cited in support of this entreaty.

Verse 23, which is also found in the previous grant, describes the *Sandhi-vigrahin* Siṁhadatta[53] while the following stanza states that the charter was written by the *Kāyastha* named Maṅgaladatta.

The record is dated[54] **the third day of the bright half of the month of Mārgaśīrṣa in the third year of the increasingly victorious reign of Bhīmaratha,** again described with the same usual titles.

The inscription was engraved by the artisan Madhumalla.[55]

45. This allusion is interesting as references to occasions of gift in the Somavaṁśin records are rare.
46. The use of the title *Rāṇaka* for a Brāhmaṇa donee is not quite common in our records.
47. The intention probably was to state that the grantee was a student of the Kauthuma *śākhā* of the Chandoga, i.e. *Sāmaveda*. Chandoga as the name of a Vedic *śākhā* is unknown.
48. *I.e.*, a Brāhmaṇa village.
49. The correct form of the name was probably Kāsilī. This village is referred to in the Pāṭṇā plates of the 24th and 28th years of the reign of Mahāśivagupta I (above, IV : XVI and XVII) also; but it is called a *bhaṭṭa-grāma* only in the present inscription.
50. The donees of the two latest Pāṭṇā plates of Mahāśivagupta I also originally belonged to the same place.
51. According to Hira Lal (*EI*, xi, 200), it is probably represented by the village Singhar in the erstwhile Khariar zamindari in the Raigarh District, Madhya Pradesh.
52. Hira Lal (*ibid.*) identifies Devībhoga, the chief town after which the district was named, with the modern Deobhog in the Bindra Nawagarh zamindari in the extreme south of the Raipur District.
53. Siṁhadatta is mentioned in the same capacity in the Pāṭṇā plates of the 28th year of Mahāśivagupta I's reign (above, IV: XVII) also; but there he is said to have been *Sandhivigrahin* of Kosala.
54. Both in words and figures.
55. Is he identical with Madhumathana of the preceding record and the difference in spelling the name due to the scribe?

IV : XIX

KUDOPALI PLATES[1] OF THE TIME OF MAHĀBHAVAGUPTA II BHĪMARATHA, YEAR 13

Provenance: Kudopali, Sambalpur District, Orissa.

References: F. Kielhorn, *EI*, iv, 254-59 and plates facing pp. 258 and 259; Hira Lal, *ibid.*, xi, 201; R.D. Banerji, *History of Orissa*, i, 220-21; H.C. Ray, *Dynastic History of Northern India*, i, 407-08; Bhandarkar's List, No. 1561; S.N. Rajaguru, *IO*, iv, 237-41.

Language: Sanskrit. In prose except the customary imprecatory and benedictory verses at the end.

Metres: Verses 1-10: *Anuṣṭubh*; Verse 11: *Puṣpitāgrā*.

Script: Northern class of alphabets.

Date: Regnal year 13. Latter half of the tenth century A.D.

TEXT[2]

First Plate : Second Side[3]

1 सिद्धम्[4] [।*] स्वस्ति [*] श्रीययातिनगरे परम[5]माहेश्वरपरमभट्टा–
2 रकमहाराजाधिराजपरमेश्वरसोमकुलतिलकतृ(त्रि)क–
3 लिङ्गाधिपतिश्रीमहाशिवगुप्तराजदेवपादानुध्यातपरम[6]मा–
4 हेश[व]रपरमभट्टारकमा(म)हाराजधिराजपरमेश्वरसांमकु–
5 लतिलकतृ(त्रि)कलिङ्गाधिपतिश्रीमहाभवगुप्तराजदेवमही–
6 प्रवर्द्धमानकल्यान(ण)विजयराज्ये त्रयोदशसम्वत्सरे आत्राङ्के स–
7 म्वत[7] १३[8] व्वामण्ड[9]पाट्टी(टी) समावासकात(त्) परममाहेश्वरमठर–

1. Each plate measures about 7-5/8″ long by 4″ broad. The ends of the circular ring, which is passed through the round hole bored in the left margin, are soldered under a circular seal.
2. From plates in *EI*, iv.
3. At the top of the first side of the first plate is engraved the following line in characters closely resembling those of the inscription itself :—पेंटापम्हालातलिकतम्वोलभोलिछ्त्रसतो ॥ Kielhorn reads the first two letters doubtfully as *peṁṭṭā*, but the second syllable appears to be *ṭā*, not *ṭṭā*. The line yields no sense.
4. Kielhorn: Oṁ. Expressed by a symbol.
5. Originally पमम was engraved.
6. Originally °ध्याता/परम was engraved.
7. Read संवत्सरेत्राङ्केन संवत्.
8. As pointed out by Kielhorn, from here to the end of this plate the writing appears to have been engraved over a cancelled passage.
9. Read वामण्डा°. As will be pointed out in the sequel, at three places below *vv* is engraved in place of *v*. Rajaguru reads वापण्डा°.

8 वंषो(शो)द्भवकुलतिलक[10] कालेश्वरि(री)[11] वरलव्ध(ब्ध)प्रसादपञ्चदशपल्लिका–

9 धिपतिसमधिगतपञ्चमहाशव्द(ब्द)माण्डलिकराणकश्रीपुण्ज (?)[12]

Second Plate : First Side

10 [13]व्वो(?)डासुत [:*] कुशलि(ली) शिडाण्डा[14]मण्डलप्रतिव (ब)द्धलोइसराग्राम्य[15]

11 सगर्त्तोश(ष)र सजलस्थल साम्व्र(म्र) मधु स(वा ?)ट्टविट्टपारन्य(ण्य)चा (च)–

12 तु:सि(सी)म(मा)पर्या(र्य)न्त श्रा(श्र)चाट्ट (ट)भा(भ)टप्रवेस(श) सर्व्वंवा(बा) धा-
विर्वाजि–

13 त सर्व्वोपरिकरकरवां(दान)सहित त्रा(ब्रा)ह्मणां(णाने)संपु(पू)ज्य तत्र प्रतिनिवा–

14 सिनो राजपुत्रतलर्वागि[16]सामवाजि च सर्व्वे (र्व्वान्) जनपदां(दान्)

15 समाज्ञापयति [।*] विदितमस्तु भवतां हस्तिपदविनिर्गत[17] कौण्डिन्य–

16 गोत्र[18] मित्राव्व(व)रुणप्रवर[19] कन्व(ण्व)शाखाध्यैं[20] भट्टपुत्रश्रीनारायण[21] द(ज)नार्दनसुत[22]

17 [23]ससलिलधारापुरश्चरेणमचन्द्रतार्कार्कखितिसमकालोप–

18 भोगार्त्थम् मातापित्रोरात्म [न*]श्च पुन्य(ण्य)यशोपिवर्द्धए[24] ताम्व्र(म्र)शा–

Second Plate : Second Side

19 सनेनाकरि(री)कृत्य प्रतिपादितोस्माभि[:*]शासनगौरगौर–

20 धर्म्मगौवणा च भवद्भी प्रतिपालनिपा[25] [।*] तथा चोक्तं धर्म–

21 शास्त्रे [।*] व (ब)हुभिर्व्वसुधा दत्ता राजन(भिः) सगरा[दि*]भि[:।*] यस्य यस्य यदा

10. Read either मठरवंशोद्भव or मठरकुलतिलक.
11. Kielhorn suggests that the actual reading may have been कुलेश्वरी.
12. Read पुञ्जो. Rajaguru reads पुर्ण्णं.
13. Read वोडा.
14. Kielhorn's reading is गिडाण्डा and that of Rajaguru शिद्राण्डा. But the first letter is quite unlike elsewhere in the record whereas it bears greater resemblance to *ś*.
15. From here to line 15 the arrangement and the details of the text are very much confused. On the analogy of other records the intended arrangement appears to be as follows:—
लोइसराग्रामे व्राह्मणान् संपूज्य तत्र प्रतिनिवासिनो राजपुत्रलर्वागि (?) सामवाजि [कादीन्*] सर्वाञ्जनपदान् समाज्ञापयति । विदितमस्तु भवतां [यथायं ग्रामः*] सगर्त्तोषरः सजलस्थलः साम्रमधूकः सवाटविटपारण्यश्चतुः सीमा पर्यन्तोचाटभर प्रवेशः स्र्वबाधाविवर्जितः सर्वोपरिकरादानसहितो हस्तिपद°.
16. Originally तलर्व्वागि was engraved, but the upper *v* of the letter *vva* was later cancelled.
17. Read विनिर्गताय.
18. Read गोत्राय.
19. Read प्रवराय.
20. Read शाखाध्यायिने
21. Read °यणाय.
22. The word सुत is incised below the line. Read सुताय.
23. Read सलिलधारापुरःसरमा चन्द्रतारकार्कक्षिति°.
24. परिव्वर्द्धय् was originally incised, but the lower *v* of *vva* was later cancelled. Read °भिवृद्धये.
25. Read शासन गौरवाद्धर्म्मगौरवाच्च भवद्भिः परिपालनीयः.

22 भु(भू)मि तस्य[26] तस्य तदा फल[म् ॥१॥*] मा भु(भू)दः(द)फलशंका व[:*][27] परदते(त्ते) ति

23 पार्थिव(वाः) [।*] स्वदानात्फलमन्यन्तं[28] परदता(त्ता)नुपालने [॥२॥*] [29]षष्ठिं वर्श(र्ष)–

24 सहस्राणि स्वर्गे मोदति भु(भू)मिद[:*] ।[।३।][30] भुमी[31] यः प्रतिगृह्नन्ति[32] यस्य[33] भुमि[34]

25 प्रयछ(च्छ)ति ।[*] उभौ तौ पुन्य(ण्य)कर्म्माणौ नियतौतं[35] स्वर्गगामिनौ ।[४॥*] आदित्य-(त्यो) वरु–

26 णो विष्णु ब्रह्म[36] सोमो हुताशन[:।*] शु (शू)लपाणिस्तु भगवां(वा)म(न)भिनन्दन्ति भु(भू)–

27 मिद[म् ॥५॥*] भु(भू)मिदाता कुलेजाता (तः) स न्य(न)स्त्राता भविश्य(ष्य)ति [॥६॥*][37] उभौ[तौ*] पुन्य(ण्य)–

Third Plate

28 कर्म्माणौ नियतौतं[38] स(स्व)र्ग्गगामिनौ ।[।७॥*] [39]तडागानां सहस्राणि[40] वा–

29 जपेयशतानि[41] च[।*] गवां कोट्टि(टि) प्रदानेन भु(भू)मिहर्त्ता न शु–

30 ध्यति ।[।८॥*] हरते हारयते यस्तु मन्दवु(बु)द्धिस्तमा(मो)वृत[:।*] सवद्ध[42] वारु–

31 णौ[:*] पासै(शै)ति(स्ति)र्य्यग्योनि(नि) स गछ(च्छ)ति ।[।९॥*] स्वदत्त(त्तां) परदत्ता-म्वा (त्तां वा) यो

32 हरेद्वसुन्धरा[43] [।*] स विष्ठा(ष्टा)यां कृमिर्भु[र्भू]त्वा पिति(तृ)भि(भिः) सह प–

33 च्यते ।[।१०॥*] इतिः[44] कमलदलाम्वु(म्बु)वि(बि)न्दुलोला(लां) श्रीमनुचिन्त्य[45] मनुष्य-जि(जी)–

26. Read भूमिस्तस्य.
27. Kielhorn takes it to be meant for मा भूद् वः which is met with in the Ganjam plates of Pṛthivīvarmadeva (*EI*, iv, 201, line 27). But on the analogy of other Somavaṁśin charters we feel that it is actually intended for मा भूदफलशंका वः which we come across in several records of the dynasty.
28. Read °लमानन्त्यं.
29. Read षष्टि°.
30. The second half of this stanza (आक्षेप्ता चानुमन्ता च द्वौ तौ नरकगामिनौ has been omitted.
31. Read भूमिं.
32. Read प्रतिग्रह्णाति.
33. Read यश्च.
34. Read भूमिं.
35. Read नियतं.
36. Read विष्णुर्ब्रह्मा.
37. The first half of the verse (आस्फोटयन्ति पितरः प्रवल्गन्ति पितामहाः) has been omitted.
38. Read नियतं.
39. This is an unnecessary repetition of the second half of the verse no. 4 above.
40. Read सहस्रेण.
41. Read °शतेन.
42. Read सुबद्धोः.
43. Read हरेत वसुन्धराम्.
44. Read इति.
45. Read श्रियमनुचिन्त्य.

34 वितां(तं) च [१*] सकलमिदमुदाहृतं[46] वुद्धा:[47] न हि पुरुषां(षैः) परकिर्तिम[48] विलो-
35 प्यते(प्याः) ।।[११।।*] लेनपुरश्रेष्ठिश्रीकिरणसुतपु(पू)र्ण्णंदते(त्ते)न इदं[49] ताम्म्र[50] यलिखि-
36 तां[51] तत्प्रमाणमिति[51a]- [।।*]

Seal[52]

राणकश्री [पुंज]

ABSTRACT

After the conventional auspicious words *siddham*, represented symbolically, and *svasti,* the record mentions the Somavaṁśīn capital Yayātinagara[53] and states that in the **thirteenth year[54] of the increasingly auspicious and victorious reign of the king Mahābhavagupta**, who meditated on the feet of the king Mahāśivagupta, both of whom are given full conventional titles, his feudatory, the *Rāṇaka* Puñja,[55] son of Voḍā, who was a devout worshipper of Maheśvara and belonged to the Māṭhara family, who had obtained fifteen *pallikās*[56] by the grace of the goddess Kāleśvarī[57] and acquired the five *mahāśabdas*, gave away, from his residence at **Vāmaṇḍāpāṭi,**[58] the village of Loi-

46. Insert *ca* after it.
47. Read बुद्ध्वा.
48. Read परकीर्तयो.
49. Originally इमं was engraved.
50. Read ताम्रं.
51. Read लिखितं.
51a. This line is engraved on the extreme right corner at the bottom.
52. The seal bears in high relief the figure of a sitting swan, facing proper left and surmounted by a crescent, and below the swan, the legend.
53. The mention of the capital Yayātinagara is only with reference to the Somavaṁśī overlord of the donor and as the place of issue of the charter which, as stated in line 7, was issued from the residence at Vāmaṇḍāpāṭī.
54. Given both in words and figures.
55. According to Rajaguru, Pūrṇṇa.
56. Probably villages, though sometimes the word seems to have referred to an administrative division like pargana comprising several villages. *Cf.* the Nibinna plates of Mahāśivagupta I (above, IV: XV) where the village Niviṇḍā or Nivinnā is said to have been included in Uttara-*pallī* or Uttara-*pallikā*.
57. If Kielhorn's suggestion about the intended reading being *kuleśvarī* is conceded, the reference would be not to any particular goddess, but to the family deity whosoever she was.
58. Now represented by Bāmrā, or Bāmrāgarh, locally called Bāmaṇḍā, about sixty miles north-east of Binka in the Bolangir District, Orissa.

sarā[59] attached to the Śiḍāṇḍā-*maṇḍala*[60] in favour of the *Bhaṭṭaputra* Nārāyaṇa, son of Janārdana, who was an immigrant from Hastipada[61] and a student of the Kāṇva *śākhā* (of the *Yajurveda*), belonged to the Kauṇḍinya *gotra* and had the *pravara* of Mitrāvaruṇa[62]. The grant land, which extended up to its four boundaries, was freed from taxes by means of a copper-plate charter, and the order conveying the grant, which was issued after worshipping the Brāhmaṇas, was addressed to the *Rājaputras*, *Talavargins,*[63] *Sāmavajins*[64] and to all the residents of the village. The grant carried with it the right to the pits and barren lands, waters and lands, mango and *madhūka* trees, paths, trees and forests as well as the privilege of collecting all the *upari-karas* and the exemption from the entry of the *cāṭas* and the *bhaṭas* and freedom from all the troubles.

The addressees are entreated to protect the grant, and the request is sought to be strengthened by quoting eleven imprecatory and benedictive stanzas reportedly extracted from the Dharmaśāstra.

This copper-plate charter was written by one Pūrṇadatta, son of the *śreṣṭhin* Kiraṇa, an inhabitant of Lenapura.[65]

The legend on the seal mentions the *Rāṇaka* Puñja.

59. Identified with a village of the same name in the Bargarh Tahsil of the Sambalpur District, 13 miles south-east of Bargarh, 16 miles south-west of Sambalpur and 3 miles south of Kudopali, the findspot of the plates.
60. Gidāṇḍā according to Kielhorn. Taking Siḍāṇḍā to be the correct reading, Hira Lal (*EI*, xi, 201) proposes to identify the headquarters of the *maṇḍala* with the modern Saraṇḍā, Bargarh Tahsil, 11 miles south-west of Sambalpur.
61. Not yet identified.
62. As stated by Kielhorn, a Brāhmaṇa of the Kauṇḍinya *gotra* ordinarily has the three *pravaras* Vāsiṣṭha, Maitrāvaruṇa and Kauṇḍinya.
63. An official designation of which the meaning is not clear. It is not met with anywhere else.
64. The same as *Sāmavājika*, found mentioned in the Ganjam plates of Pṛthivīvarmadeva (*EI*, iv, 200) and *Sāmavāyika* mentioned, according to Rangalala Banerjea and Keilhorn, in *supra* IV: XIV, line 27. According to Kielhorn, *Sāmavāyika* is the original of *Sāmavājika.* It is probably an official designation, but its connotation is not clear.
65. It has yet to be identified.

IV : XX

MAHULPARA[1] PLATES[1a] OF MAHĀŚIVAGUPTA II DHARMARATHA, YEAR II

Provenance: Mahulpara, Puri District, Orissa.

References: S.C. De, *OHRJ*, xii, 60-71 and plates xv-xvii; S.N. Rajaguru *IO*, iv, 280A-80F; Ajay Mitra Shastri, *Studies in Indian Epigraphy*, i, 85-96; *ARIE*, 1964-65, No. A 53; P.R. Srinivasan, *EI*, xxxvii, 225-32 and plates between pp. 228 and 229.

Language: Sanskrit. In a mixture of prose and verse.

Metres: Verses 1-3, 6, 8-10 and 24-25: *Śārdūlavikrīḍita;* Verse 4: *Upajāti* of *Indravajrā* and *Upendravajrā*; Verse 5: *Vasantatilakā*; Verse 7: *Sragdharā*; Verses 11-13 and 15-21: *Anuṣṭubh*; Verse 14: *Indravajrā*; Verse 22: *Śālinī*; Verse 23: *Puṣpitāgrā*.

Script: Northern class of alphabets.

Date: Regnal year 11, Phālguna kṛṣṇa 3. Second half of the tenth century A.D.

TEXT[2]

First Plate

1 सिद्धम्[3] [।*] ओम्[4][।*] स्वस्ति प्रेमनिरुद्धमुग्धमनसोः स्फारीभवच्चक्षुषोर्यूनोर्यत्र [वि]-[च्चि*][5]–

2 प्रनिर्भररतक्रीडाक्रमन्तन्वतोः[6] । विच्छिन्नोपि कृतातिमात्रपुलकैराविर्भवत्सीत्कृ–

3 तैराश्लेषैर्ग्लपितक्लमैः स्मररसः कामम्मुहुस्ताय्यते[7] ।।[१।।*] यत्राशेषविशेषरु(रू)–

1. De, Rajaguru and myself published the charter under the name 'Khandpara plates'. But as the plates were actually found at the village of Mahulpara, it is more appropriate to call them 'Mahulpara plates'.

1a. The plates are approximately 26.1 cm long and 18.4 cm broad at the maximum and are held together by a circular ring, 1.3 cm thick, of which the ends are secured under a circular seal with a diameter of 5.5. cm. Broken at the top, the seal bears, in low relief on its countersunk surface the figure of Gajalakṣmī, two-armed and seated on a lotus-flower in the *padmāsana* posture, with her left hand placed on the lap. On either side of the goddess a beautiful stalked lotus-flower rises upward, and on the fully blossomed flower is carved a standing elephant facing the goddess.

2. From plates in *OHRJ*, xii, and *EI*, xxxvii.

3. Expressed by a symbol, this is ignored by De.

4. Expressed by a symbol.

5. The portion of the plate where the letters *vi* and *ci* were engraved is broken. *Vi* is partially preserved whereas *ci* is altogether lost.

6. De reads °क्रमन्तन्धतोः.

7. Srinivasan reads °ताप्यते. The reading adopted here is supported by some earlier records of the dynasty containing this verse (*supra*, IV: XIV, XVI-XVIII).

4 पमहिमापास्ताप्सर[8] कान्तिभिर्ज्जतिर्प्या(ष्या)कलहेष्वपि प्रणयिनः कर्णोत्पलैस्ताडि–

5 ताः[9] । जायन्ते प्रविशत्सित[10]स्मरशरप्रोत्थापितान्तर्व्यथा[11][ः*]स्यन्दिस्वेदजलावसेच–

6 नवशान्वि(न्नि)ज्जति[12]रोमाङकुराः ॥[२॥*] अत्युत्तुङ्गकरीन्द्रदन्तमुसलप्रोद्भासिरोचिश्चयै-
र्द् ध्वान्त[13]–

7 ध्वन्सन[14]निष्फली[15]कृतशरच्चन्द्रोदयैस्सर्वदा[16] । यत्रासीदसतीजनस्य विस(श)दम्मुक्ता–

8 मयम्मण्डनं[17] सङ्केतास्पदमप्यतीव धवल(लं) प्रासादसृ(शृ)ङ्गाग्रतः ॥[18][३॥*] महानदी-
तुङ्गत–

9 [19]रङ्गभङ्गस्फारोच्छलच्छीकरवद्भिराराता(त्) ।[20] यस्मिन्रतासक्तिमदङ्गनानां श्रमापनो–

10 दः क्रियते[21] मरुद्भिः ॥[४॥*] तस्मात् **श्रीययातिनगरात्** [22] ।[23]लोकत्रयप्रथितशुभ्रयशो–

11 वितानव्याप्ताष्टदिक्प्रसभनिर्जितवैरिवर्गः । सोमान्वये किल व(ब)भूव सुगीतकीर्त्ति–

12 : श्रीमान्सरोजवदनो नृपतिर्ययाति[24] ॥[५॥*] यत्खड्गाग्रविपाटित[25]द्विपघटाकुम्भ–

13 [26]स्थलादुल्लसन्मुक्ताजालविभूषितं प्रतिरणं पृथ्वीवधूरः स्थलं[27](लम्) ।[28]स(श)स्व(श्व)-
दृ(दृ)रनमन्नराधिप–

14 शिरोरत्नाङशु[29]जालामला यत्पादाम्मुज[30]रेणवस्समतया तद्रस्मि(श्मि)लक्ष्मीन्दधुः[31]॥[६॥*]
माथल्लो–

15 लालिमालाकुलकरटपुटस्यान्दिदानप्रवाहान्[32]सिन्दूरारक्त[33] कुम्भान् सि(शि)तपृथुल–

8. De: °मायास्ताप्सरः°.
9. De: स्ताड़िताः.
10. Better read प्रविशच्छित which is met with in some records of Mahāśivagupta I and Mahābhavagupta II also. See above, IV: XVI, XVIII.
11. De is wrong in suggesting to correct it to °व्यथा.
12. De: °निज्जति. In some records of Mahāśivagupta I we have °न्नियति°. *Vide supra*, IV: XIV, XVI-XVIII.
13. De reads °द्ध्वन्ति° while Srinivasan's reading is °ध्वांन्त°.
14. Read ध्वंसन which is De's reading.
15. De wrongly suggests to correct it to निस्फली.
16. De is wrong in reading °सर्वदा and proposing to correct it together with the preceding portion as शरच्चन्द्रोदयेः सर्वदा.
17. Better read मुक्तामयं मण्डनं, which is De's reading.
18. These *daṇḍas* are inscribed below the line.
19. Before *raṅga*, De reads *ta* which is neither seen in the plate nor necessary.
20. De: यस्मिन्व्रतासक्ति°.
21. De: क्रियतिः.
22. De: नगरात.
23. Note that this verse is applied to Janamejaya in the earlier charters of the family.
24. De: °र्ययति°.
25. De: °विपातित°.
26. De: °स्थलोदु.
27. Srinivasan: °स्थलम्.
28. De: सस्वदूर°.
29. Read रत्नांशु which is the reading of De.
30. Read °दाम्बुज which is Srinivasan's reading.
31. Better read लक्ष्मीं दधुः.
32. De: सिन्दुरा°.
33. The letter *ku* is engraved below the line.

Second Plate : First Side

16 रदान् ।[34] कामदेवादिसंज्ञान् । जित्वाजावालमाजौ जनितसुखवधूविस्मयस्मेरवक्त्र:[35] स द्वा–

17 त्रिङ्श (त्रिंश) त्करीन्द्रा[36]न्शरनिकरहतारोहकानग्रहीद्य: ॥[७॥*] तस्माद्विस्मयहेतुहेतिल-
डित[37]प्रस्तावनाक–

18 ण्ण (र्ण्ण)[38]नैर्द्धूताकम्पितपूर्व्वं[39]रुद्रमुकुटप्रीते[40]न्दुनिर्व्वर्ण्णित: । भ्राम्यत्कीत्ति (र्त्ति) रजायता-
हवतस्व–

19 व्यारिगीतोदय: श्रीमान्भीमरथो यत: स्वमुदरन्ताराचिरादच्चर्चति:[41] (ति) ॥[८॥*] य:
काव्यामृतनिर्झर–

20 स्य महत: सोता[42] महीभृत्पतिस्त्याग: सत्यमिति द्वयं[43] कलिं[44]भयादभ्येत्य यम्मोदते[45] । यत्के–

21 लिज्वलितान्ध्रगौडनगरीधूमावलीढौ[46] किताम्वि (म्ब्र) भ्रद्धाति मसीम्विधु[47]न्नि (र्न्नि)
जकुलप्रीत्या कल–

22 ङ्कीकु (कृ) त:[48] ॥[९॥*] यो धर्मेण च विक्रमेण च धिया चाश्चर्यकार्येण च प्रागल्भ्येन च
देवराजपद–

23 वीं प्राप्तो महीमण्डले । स[49] श्री**धर्म्मरथ**स्ततोरिनिवहध्व (ध्वं) न्सै (सै) कहेतु: कृती दानान–

24 न्दितवन्दिवृन्दमुखरक्ष्मामण्डलो जातवान् ॥[१०॥*] परममाहेश्वरपरमभ–

25 ट्टारकमहाराजाधिराज[50] परमेश्वरसोमकुलतिलकत्रिकलिङ्गाधिपतिश्रीमहा–

26 भवगुप्तराजदेवपादानुध्यातपरममाहेश्वरपरमभट्टारकमहाराजाधि–

27 राजपरमेश्वरसोमकुलतिलकत्रिकलिङ्गाधिपति**श्रीमहाशिवगुप्तराजदे**–

28 व: कुशली अन्तरुदविषयस (स्य) अभपराखण्डीयभिल्विग्रामे[51] । [51a]अतस्तद्विशषयीयव्रा
(व्रा)–

34. This mark of punctuation is superfluous.
35. De: वक्त्र.
36. De: करिन्द्रा°.
37. De: लडित.
38. De: °कर्ण्णं°.
39. De's reading is °द्धूंताकम्पितपूवं.
40. De: °प्रीति°.
41. De proposes to correct it to समुदरन्ताराश्चिरादच्चर्चति. Srinivasan does not take cognisance of the *visarga* following *ti* which is clear in the facsimile.
42. De: स्नाता.
43. The *anusvāra* here takes the form of a semi-circle open at the bottom, the left lower end of which is joined to the top of *ya*.
44. There is a superfluous small dot on *li*. Srinivasan is wrong in taking it as an *anusvāra* and stating that it ought to have been placed on *ya* of the preceding word *dvayam*. As we have seen, there is *anusvāra* on *ya*.
45. Better read यं मोदते. De is wrong when he suggests to correct it to य: मोदते.
46. Srinivasan: °ठौकिता°.
47. Read मसीं विघु:.
48. Srinivasan: कृत:.
49. De: श्रीधर्मं.
50. Subscript *v* is wrongly engraved at the bottom of this letter.
51. De: अभप्पराखण्डय भिल्लोग्रामे; Srinivasan: अभयनाखण्डीय°.
51a. This *daṇḍa* is redundant.

29 ह्मणान्स(सं)पूज्य[52] समाहर्तृ सन्निधातृनियुक्ताधिकारिकदाण्डपासि(शि)कपिशुनवे(वै)-
त्रिकावरोध–

30 जनराज्ञीराणकराजपुत्रराजवल्लभभोगि[53]जनप्रमुखसमस्तजनपदान(न्) समाज्ञा–

31 पयति। विदितमस्तु भवतां यथाऽ[54]स्माभिरय(यं)ग्रामः सप्रतीहारः[55] अन्धारुवा[56]पदाति–

Second Plate : Second Side

32 जीव्यहस्तिदण्डवरव(ब)लीवर्द्दचिङ्गोल[57] अदत्तादिसहितः सनिधिः सोपनि–

33 धिः [58]सव्व(र्व्व)वा(बा)धावर्जितः सर्व्वोपरिकरादानसमेतश्चतुःसीमापर्यन्तः[59] साम्रमधू–

34 कः सगर्त्तोषरस्सजलस्थलः काश्यपसगोत्राय।[60]त्र्यार्षप्रवराय।[60] दामो–

35 दरपौत्राय।[60] वासुपुत्राय।[60] [61]राण[क*]श्रीअभिमन्युनाम्ने सलिलधारापुरस्सर।[62] आ[63]–

36 चन्द्रतारार्क्कक्षितिसमकालोपभोगार्थं मातापित्रोरात्मनश्च पुण्ययशोऽ–

37 भिवृद्धये।[64] सप्रतीहारेण[65] ताम्रशासनेनाकरीकृत्य[66] प्रतिपादित इत्यवगत्य स्व(स)–

38 मुचितकरभोग भागादिकमुपनयद्भिर्भवद्भिः सुखेन प्रतिवस्तव्यमिति। भा–

39 विभिश्च भूपतिभिर्द्दत्तिरियमस्मदीया।[67] धर्म्मगौरवादस्मदनुरोधा-

40 च्च स्वदत्तिरिवानुपालनीया। तथा चोक्तं धर्म्मशास्त्रे। व(ब)हुभिर्व्वसुधा द–

41 त्ता राजभिः सगरादिभिः। यस्य यस्य यदा भूमिस्तस्य तस्य तदा फलं(लम्) ॥[११॥*]

42 मा भूदफलशङ्का वः परदत्तेति पार्थिवाः [।*] स्वदत्तात्फलमानन्त्यम्परदत्तानुपाल–

43 ने ॥[१२॥*][68] षष्ठि(ष्ठि)म्वर्षसहस्राणि स्वर्गे मोदाति भूमिदः। आक्षेप्ता चानुमन्ता च
द्वौ तौ नर–

44 कगामिनौ ॥[१३॥*] अग्नेरपत्यं प्रथमं सुवण(र्णं)[69] भूर्व्वैष्णवी सूर्यसुताश्च गावः। यः
काञ्च–

45 नं गाञ्च महीञ्च दद्याद्दत्तास्त्रयस्तेन भवत्ति(न्ति) लोके(काः) ॥[१४॥*] आस्फोटयत्ति
(न्ति) पितरो व–

52. De: ब्राह्मणानां पूज्य.
53. De: °भोगी°.
54. The *avagraha* has escaped the notice of Srinivasan.
55. De: सप्रतिहारः.
56. Srinivasan: अन्धारुवी°
57. De: चिहोल. But *contra ha* earlier in the same line.
58. De: सर्वं°.
59. De ignores *visarga*.
60. This mark of punctuation is superfluous.
61. De: राणो.
62. This punctuation mark is not required.
63. Read °पुरस्सरमा°.
64. This *daṇḍa* is unnecessary.
65. De: सप्रतीडारेण; Rajaguru: सप्रत्याहारेण.
66. De: °नाकरिकृत्य.
67. This mark of punctuation is uncalled for.
68. Srinivasan: षष्टि°. Read षष्टिं वर्ष° or षष्टिवर्ष°.
69. Srinivasan: सुवर्णं.

46 ल्गयत्ति(न्ति) पितामहाः। भूमिदाता कुले जातः स नस्त्राता भविष्यति ॥[१५॥*] भूमिं यः प्र–

47 तिगृह्ना(णा)ति[70] यश्च भूमिं प्रयच्छति। उभौ तौ पुण्यकर्म्माणो नियतं स्वर्ग्गगामि–

Third Plate

48 नौ ॥[१६॥*] तडागानां सहस्रेण वाजपेयशतेन च। गवाङ्कोटिप्रदानेन भूमिहर्त्ता

49 न शुद्धयति ॥[१७॥*] सुवण्ण(र्ण्णं)मेकं गामेकां भूमेरप्यर्द्धमङ्गुलं(लम्) हरन्नरकमायाति यावदाहू(भू)त–

50 सम्प्लवं (वम्) ॥[१८॥*] हरते हारयेद्यस्तु मन्दवु(बु)द्धिस्तमोवृतः। सुव(ब)द्धो[71]वारुणैः पाशैस्तिर्य–

51 ग्योनिं स गच्छति ॥[१९॥*] स्वदत्ताम्परदत्ताम्वा[72] यो हरेत वसुन्धरां (राम्)। स विष्ठायां कृमिर्भूत्वा

52 पितृभिः सह पच्यते ॥[२०॥*] आदित्यो वरुणो विष्णुव्व्र(र्ब्ब्र)ह्मा सोमो हुताशनः। शूलपाणि–

53 श्च भगवानभिनन्दन्ति भूमिदं (दम्) ॥[२१॥*] सामान्योऽयं धर्म्मसेतुर्नृपाणां काले काले पा–

54 लनीयो भवद्भिः।[73] सर्व्वानेतात्भाविनः पार्थिवेन्द्रान्भूयो भूयो याचते रामभ–

55 द्रः ॥[२२॥*] इति कमलदलाम्वु(म्बु)वि(बि)न्दुलोलां श्रियमनुचिन्त्य मनुष्यजीवित–

56 ञ्च। सकलमिदिमुदाहृतञ्च वु(बु)द्ध्वा न हि पुरुषैः परकीर्त्तयो विलोप्याः ।[।२३॥*]

57 निण्णा(ष्णा)तौ(त)स्सहदेवराजगुरुणा [74]मैत्रीम्मनीषागुणैर्व्वि(र्ब्बि)भ्राणः परमा(मां) गुणैकव–

58 सतिः[75] कुम्भण्डिपालः[76] कृती। कुर्व्वाणः[77] किल सन्धिविग्रहपदं यश्चन्द्रसूर्यात्मिकी(कीं)[78] मू–

59 त्ति(र्त्ति)न्तत्व(त्त्व)निविप्त(ष्ट)धीः प्रकटयत्याश्चर्यवर्षी[78a] सतां(ताम्) ॥[२४॥*] यत्कीर्त्तिप्रसरप्रभूतमा(म)हिम(मा)–

60 प्रोद्वीक्षणामीलित[79] व्रीडावेगवशादयम्मलिनतामत्त(न्त)र्व्विधत्ते[80] शसी(शी)। स श्री–

70. De and Srinivasan: °गृह्णाति.
71. De: सुबन्धो.
72. Read °दत्तां वा.
73. De: सवनिताभा°.
74. De: मैत्री मनीषागुण°.
75. De is wrong in suggesting to correct it to वसत्ति.
76. Srinivasan reads कुमुण्डिपालः and proposes to correct it to कूमुण्डिपालः for the sake of metre. But the stroke taken as medial *u* in what is read as *mu* is quite different from the medial sign of *u* in the preceding letter.
77. De and Srinivasan: कुर्वाणः.
78. Srinivasan: °त्मिकां.
78a. De: °वर्षो.
79. De: °मिलित.
80. De reads °दयमलिनतामतुर्विधत्ते.

61 मत्रि(न्त्रि)वरी[81] महाक्षपटलाध्यक्ष: सतामग्रणीरेकश्शासनम[82]भ्यलीलिख–
62 दिदं श्रीनेत्नदेव: स्वयं(यम्)॥[२५॥*]। **सम्वत्[83] ११ फाल्गुनवदि ३**॥ विज्ञानिसोर्ण्णङ्गाकेन[84] लि–
63 खितमिति॥[85]

ABSTRACT

The charter opens with the auspicious symbols for *siddham* and *om* which are followed by four stanzas describing **Yayātinagara,** the place of issue of the grant. Next three verses, which are well-known from earlier records,[86] eulogise king Yayāti. His son and successor, Bhīmaratha, claims the following verse which, besides containing vague allusions to his roving fame and success against his enemies, refers to a certain Rudra, probably described as a ruler of the east (*pūrva-Rudra*), who is stated to have been pleased to hear the account of the movements of Bhīmaratha's sword and looked at the latter with his crown somewhat tremulous as a gesture of appreciation. Verses 9-10 are eulogistic of **Dharmaratha,** the son and successor of Bhīmaratha. Verse 9 speaks of him as a great source of the poetic nectar and as an abode of liberality and truth which had taken refuge with him out of fear of the Kali age and refers to the chain of smoke rising from the cities (capitals) of Andhra and Gauḍa which were put aflame by him with ease as if in a sport. It is stated that the moon, out of love for his lineage,[87] bears the black spot caused by this smoke. The next stanza avers that he had secured for himself the status of the lord of gods, i.e. Indra, on this earth by means of the observance of duties, valour, intellect, wonderful deeds and eloquence and was the cause of the destruction of the multitude of his enemies and that the circuit of the earth became resonant with (the songs of) the host of minstrels

81. De wrongly suggests the correction मन्त्री.
82. De: °रेक शासन°. That Srinivasan is wrong in proposing to correct it to रेतच्छासन° is clearly indicated by the word *idaṁ* found later in the verse.
83. Read संवत् which is Srinivasan's reading.
84. De: विज्ञारिसोर्ण्णङ्ग°; Srinivasan: °सोल्लङ्गाकेन. The intended reading seems to be स्वर्ण्णाङ्गकेन.
85. These letters are written at the bottom right corner.
86. These as well as the four preceding verses are met with in some records of Mahāśivagupta I and Mahābhavaguta II also. However, verse 5, which is employed for describing Janamejaya (Mahābhavagupta I) in the earlier inscriptions, is applied here with slight changes in the second half, to his son and successor, Yayāti; This is evidently due to oversight. Verse 7 of *supra*, IV: XIV, and verse 6 of *supra*, IV: XVI-XVIII, describing Yayāti, has been dropped, which is probably responsible for the erroneous application of verse 5 to Yayāti and the dropping of all reference to his father Mahābhavagupta I. The wrong application of verse 6 of supra, IV: XIV, to Yayāti, first met with in *supra*, IV: XVII, is, of course, continued in this inscription also.
87. The Somavaṁśins, as indicated by the dynastic name, claimed descent from the moon,

delighted by gifts. This description is followed by a prose passage mentioning king Mahābhavagupta and the reigning king **Mahāśivagupta,** who meditated upon the former's feet. Both are given full conventional titles, i.e., *Parama-Māheśvara, Paramabhaṭṭāraka-Mahārājādhirāja-Parameśvara, Soma-kula-tilaka* and *Trikaliṅgādhipati.*

Next is mentioned the village named Bhilvi[88] included in the Abhaparā-*khaṇḍa*[88a] attached to the Antaruda-*viṣaya*[89] and it is stated that after worshipping the Brāhmaṇas of the district the king ordered all the people such as the *Samāhartṛ, Sannidhātṛ, Niyukta, Ādhikārika, Dāṇḍapāśika, Piśuna, Vaitrika,* inmates of the royal harem, the queen (or queens), *Rāṇakas, Rāja-putras,* king's favourites and *Bhogins*[90] to the effect that he had donated the village to the Brāhmaṇa *Rāṇaka* Abhimanyu, son of Vāsu and grandson of Dāmodara, who belonged to the Kāśyapa *gotra* with the three *pravaras,* and that they should live happily paying the *kara, bhoga, bhāga,* etc., as due to the donee. The grant was accompanied by the privileges *pratīhāra,*[91] *andhā-ruvā,*[92] *padāti-jīvya,*[93] *hasti-daṇḍa,*[94] *vara-balīvardda,*[95] *ciṅgola*[96] and *adatta,*[97] etc., besides the usual *nidhis, upanidhis,* exemption from all the troubles, right to collect all the *uparikaras,* the mango and *madhūka* trees, the pits and barren spots and waters and lands. The granted village is stated to have been made rent-free by means of a copper-plate charter accompanied by the *Pratī-hāra.*[98]

88. It has yet to be identified. As suggested by the name, it may have been a hamlet inhabited by the Bhils.
88a. Not yet identified.
89. Evidently the same as the Antarudra-*viṣaya* referred to in the Chaurashi plates of the Bhauma-Kara king Śivakaradeva, dated in the year 73 of the Bhauma-Kara era (*JBORS*, xiv, 292ff.). it chief town is probably represented by the Antarodh Pargana of the Puri District. See Binayak Misra, *DMO*, 16.
90. The word *bhogin* has been taken in the sense of a 'village headman' or '*ināmdār*', preferably the latter. See *EI*, xxviii, 323.
91. Sircar (*IE*, 402; *IEG*, 259) takes it to mean a tax for entry into the royal palace or 'a levy for the maintenance of the door-keepers of the city gates'. Rajaguru reads प्रतीहार and points out that in Orissa it is used as the household designation of the caste of agricultural class.
92. An Odiya term denoting a levy of an uncertain nature, it has been taken to be a variant reading of *arthāruva* (*IEG*, 19), perhaps derived from Sanskrit *artha-rūpya*, 'a levy from the money-lenders on the amounts loaned out' (*ibid.*, 29).
93. Debala Mitra takes it in the sense of 'subsistence for the infantry' (*EI*, xxxiii, 264). But it is better to take it to refer to a tax levied for the maintenance of foot-soldiers; perhaps the same as Oḍiyā *pāikāli* (*IEG*, 224).
94. Evidently a levy for maintaining elephants.
95. It has been taken to denote a tax on the maintenance of superior bulls (*EI*, xxxiii, 264) or a tax on choice bullocks for bull-fights (*IEG*, 363).
96. A levy of an indefinite import. Rajaguru reads *riddola* in the body of the text and *ciddola* in a footnote and states that the latter may be the same as *dolī* or *hāndolā*.
97. A levy of an indefinite import; perhaps interest or fine on arrears of taxes (*IEG*, 5).
98. Literally, 'a gate-keeper' or 'chamberlain', the *Pratihāra* had something to do with the grant. Probably he acted as the conveyor of the royal order about the grant.

The future rulers are entreated to uphold the grant as if it were their own grant, and thirteen benedictive and imprecatory stanzas, stated to have been taken from the Dharmaśāstra, are quoted.

Verse 24 refers to the royal preceptor (*rājaguru*) Sahadeva and to Kumbhaṇḍipāla who held the office of the minister of peace and war (*Sandhivigrahin*) who is described in a general manner as shining with qualities like friendship and intelligence, the only abode of virtues, possessed of wisdom capable of grasping the essence and as performing wondrous deeds. The following verse mentions the *Mahākṣapaṭalādhyakṣa* Netradeva who wrote the charter. He is said to have been a minister (*mantri-vara*) and described in a conventional manner.

The date is the **third day of the dark half of the month of Phālguna in the thirteenth year.**[99]

The inscription was incised by the artisan Sorṇṇāṅgaka.[100]

99. As against the common practice of indicating the date both in words and figures, here it is given only in figures and there is no explicit reference to the regnal reckoning though the year under reference is undoubtedly regnal.

100. Instead of *utkīrṇṇam* the word *likhitam* is erroneously employed with reference to incising.

IV: XXI

JATESINGA-DUNGRI[1] PLATES[1a] OF MAHĀŚIVAGUPTA III YAYĀTI, YEAR 3

Provenance: Boundary of Jatesinga and Dungri villages, Bolangir District, Orissa.

References: B.C. Mazumdar, *JBORS*, ii, 45-59 and plates between pp. 52 and 53 and 54 and 55; D.R. Bhandarkar, *IA*, lxi, 241; Bhandarkar's List, No. 1556; R.D. Banerji, *HO*, i, 212-13; H.C. Ray, *DHNI*, i, 401-02; P. Acharya, *PIHC*, 7th Session, 180-95; K.C. Panigrahi, *Chronology of the Bhauma-Karas and the Somavaṁśīs of Orissa*, 61-64; S.N. Rajaguru, *IO*, iv, 218-24.

Language: Sanskrit. In prose except only the benedictive and imprecatory stanzas.

Metres: Verses 1-8 and 10: *Anuṣṭubh*; Verse 9: *Śālinī*; Verse 11: *Puṣpitāgrā.*

Script: Northern class of alphabets.

Date: Regnal year 3, Vaiśākha śukla 5. First half of the eleventh century A.D.

TEXT[2]

First Plate

1 सिद्धम्[3][।*] स्वस्त्यपगत[4]व(ब)हलकलिकलष[5]घम्मर्मामृत[6][व]मलशिशिरकिरणावलिपरि-
घटितचन्द्रवि(बि)[7]-

1. B.C. Mazumdar calls the record Mārañja-Mura charter after one of the villages granted through it while H.C. Ray christens it as Sonpur grant, evidently after the place of issue described at length in the beginning of the record. But as the plates were actually found at the boundary of the villages Jatesinga and Dūṅgrī, it is preferable to style it Jatesiṅga-Dungri plates following the usual practice of naming the plates after their findspots. The designation 'Jatenginga and Dungri Plates' proposed by Rajaguru is simply inappropriate.

1a. The plates measure approximately 8″ in length and about 4″ in width. The 2nd plate is thicker than the remaining plates, the 3rd plate being very thin. The ends of the ring, about 3-1/2″ in diameter and 1/2″ in thickness, which is passed through the circular holes bored on the left margin of the plates, are soldered under a lump of copper, the upper surface of which spreads out into an oval seal bearing, in relief on a countersunk surface, the device of Gaja-Lakṣmī.

2. From plates in *JBORS*, ii.
3. Mazumdar and Rajaguru: Om. Expressed by a symbol.
4. Rajaguru unnecessarily inserts the letter *da* between *svasty-a*° and °*pagata.*
5. Read कलुष which is the reading of Mazumdar and Rajaguru.
6. Rajaguru: °धम्मर्वृत°.
7. Rajaguru is wrong in taking the last two letters of this line as forming part of the following line.

2 म्वो (म्बो) दय[8]स्यदित[9]फेनकुसु[म]संर्दभित[10]तरलतरतरङ्गमालविरचिततेलामहा–

3 नदीसङ्गमविमलजलपवी (वि) त्रीकृतधर्मधर्मा[11]भिनिवेशित्तसकलजनकारिताने–

4 कविविधदेवकुलायतनविहारारामण्डपोद्यानविचित्रकुसुम[12]विटपतला (ल)[13]–

5 मञ्जरीविकम्पितस्तव (ब) कसुरभिकुसुमरजोधूसरितवपुमनोहरविदग्धभुजङ्ग–

6 जनानुसङ्गमाविक्र (ष्क्र) त (?)[14]मदमुदितजन्मविभ्रमस्फुरितकमलवदन–

7 समुल्लसितभ्रूभङ्गविक्षेपस्फुटित कुवलयोद्योतित[15]वरकामिनी–

8 सुरतकरणव्यापारानेकपतत्रि[16]गणसमुत्कण्ठितमुरे (रो) विनिर्गत[17]मयूररुत[18]–

9 [19]तूर्यनिर्घोषविरचितावसरभवनादवतीर्य[20] सकललोकाभिलषित[21]वरप्रदाना–

10 नुग्रहकाम्यया भगवत्या श्रीपञ्चाम्व (म्ब) रिभद्रांवि (बि) का (क) या[22]धिष्ठितात्पत्तन-[23]
सुवर्ण्ण[24]पु–

11 रावासित श्रीमद्विजयकटकादतिशयोर्जितप्रतापभरावनत[25]समस्तनृपतिकुरु (कद)–

12 म्व (म्ब)[26] चूडामणिपरिचुम्वि (म्बि) तपादपीठः प्रथितानेकनलनहुषमान्धातृद्वि (दि) लीप[27]
भरतभगी[28]–

8. Mazumdar and Rajaguru : °बिम्बोदय°.
9. Read °स्यन्दित° which is the reading of Mazumdar followed by Rajaguru. The letter *y* resembles *p*.
10. Mazumdar and Rajaguru : °सन्दर्भित°.
11. Mazumdar and Rajaguru : °पवित्रीकृतधर्म्मधर्म्मा°. Read कृतधर्माभिनिवेशित°.
12. Between *ku* and *su* a letter was first engraved and then cancelled.
13. Mazumdar, followed by Rajaguru, doubtfully reads विटायतणो and suggests it to correct as विटपीतल which is, however, grammatically incorrect.
14. Mazumdar reads जनानोसङ्गमाधिकृत (?) which is followed by Rajaguru.
15. Mazumdar : °योद्दोतित°. Read °योद्घोतित°.
16. Mazumdar and, following him, Rajaguru : °पतत्री°.
17. Mazumdar : °मुरे (?) घिनिर्गत°; Rajaguru : मुरे (री) घिनिर्गत°.
18. Mazumdar : °रूत°; Rajaguru : °ऋत°.
19. Mazumdar and Rajaguru : °तूर्य्यं°.
20. Mazumdar and Rajaguru : °दवतीर्य्यं°.
21. Mazumdar followed by Rajaguru : °भिलसित°.
22. Mazumdar : °भद्राम्विकया°; Rajaguru: °भद्राम्बिकाया°. A glance at the illustration will show that what has been read *mvi* or *mbi* is undoubtedly only *vi*. Between it and the preceding letter *drā* there is a small slanting stroke which may perhaps stand for *anusvāra*. It must be pointed out, however, that it is different in form from other *anusvāra* signs met with elsewhere in this record.
23. Mazumdar and Rajaguru : °धिष्ठिता पत्तन°.
24. Mazumdar : सुवर्ण°.
25. Mazumdar : °भारावनत°; Acharya : °भारवनत°; Rajaguru reads °भावावतन°, and then suggests to correct it to °भारावनत°.
26. Mazumdar reads °कुरुम्ब° and wrongly takes *mva* as the concluding *akṣara* of the previous line. Acharya : °कदम्ब°; Rajaguru : °कुऋम्ब°.
27. Mazumdar, Acharya and Rajaguru read दिलीप. But the subscript *v* is quite clear in the facsimile.
28. Mazumdar : भगि°; Rajaguru : भागि°.

Second Plate : First Side

13 रथादिराजचरितः।[29] कर्ण्णाटलाटगुर्ज्ज[रे*]श्वर[30]दाहज्वरो[31] भूविटकलत्रकाञ्चीकलापा[32]–

14 भरणलम्पटः। [32a]कलिङ्गकोङ्गोदोत्कलक[33] कोसला[34]स्वयम्वरः[35] प्रसिद्ध[36] गौडराढाम्व (म्ब)र (रा)–

15 [37]पकर्षणोद्धातमारुतः[38] शीताङशुवङश[39] विमलाम्व(म्ब)रपूर्ण्णचन्द्रः[40]। [41]स्वभुजोपार्जित त्रि–

16 कलिङ्गाधिपतिः परममाहेश्वरः[42] परभट्टारकः[42] श्रीमहाभवगुप्तपादानुध्या–

17 तमहाराजाधिराजपरमेश्वर[:*][43]प्रणमतराजन्योपसेवितपादारविन्दयुगलः श्रीमहा–

18 शिवगुप्तश्रीयय(या)तिदेवः[44] कुशली ।।[45] [46]कोष(स)लप्रतिव(ब)द्धोङ्गाडविषयीयव(बृ)-द्भु–

19 साईग्राम ।[47] गन्धरवाडिमण्डलसंतोनर्ताखण्डीयमारञ्जमुरा[48]–

20 ग्रामयोर्व्रा(ब्रा)ह्मणान्संपूज्य तत्प्रतिनिवासिकुटुम्वि(म्बि)नस्तद्विषयीय[49] जानपदान्[50] यथा–

29. This mark of punctuation, which is unnecessary, has been left out unnoticed by Mazumdar and Rajaguru.
30. Mazumdar : गुर्ज्जेश्वर°; Acharya and Rajaguru : °गुर्ज्जरेश्वर°.
31. Acharya : °दाहज्वर°; Panigrahi reads दाहज्वरो and proposes to correct it to दाहज्वरे.
32. Rajaguru : °कलाप°.
32a. This *daṇḍa* is superfluous.
33. Rajaguru ignores this letter.
34. Mazumdar: कोशला; Acharya and Rajaguru: कोशल.
35. Rajaguru and Acharya have left out this *visarga* unnoticed.
36. Read °स्वयंवरप्रसिद्धः.
37. Mazumdar, Acharya and Rajaguru: °प्रकर्ष°.
38. Mazumdar: °णोत्घातमारुत.
39. Mazumdar and Panigrahi : शीताङ्ग वङ्ग. Read शीतांशुवंश°.
40. Mazumdar : पूर्णचन्द्रः. Rajaguru has failed to notice *visarga*.
41. This mark of punctuation, which is superfluous, has escaped the notice of Mazumdar and Rajaguru.
42. This *visarga* has escaped the notice of Rajaguru and Acharya.
43. Mazumdar, Acharya and Rajaguru : प्रणमित. Read प्रणमद्रा°.
44. Mazumdar : °यजाति°; Acharya and Rajaguru : ययाति.
45. This mark of punctuation is left out by Mazumdar. It is, however, superfluous.
46. Mazumdar reads कोशलप्रतिवद्धोभ्रांडविषयीबृहद्भुसायीग्राम and Rajaguru follows him except substituting भ्रांड़ and वृहद्भूसायी for भ्रांड and बृहद्भुसायी respectively. What has been taken as subscript *r* in what has been wrongly read as भ्रांड is in all likelihood just a scratch.

    Note the use of the word *bṛhat* as a part of the name of the village which was obviously intended to distinguish this village from another village of the same name in the neighbourhood. This practice of prefixing *bṛhat* and *laghu* to the names of localities was in vogue in other regions also. Words of similar import are even now found attached to the names of villages.
47. This mark of punctuation has eluded earlier editors. It is, however, not required.
48. Mazumdar and, following him, Rajaguru read this passage as शम्वरवाडिमण्डलसन्तोवडीखण्डीयमारंजमुरा°.
49. Mazumdar reads कुटुम्विन तद्विषयीय° and Rajaguru follows him.
50. Mazumdar reads °अ(?)वप्रदान°, which is followed by Rajaguru.

21 कालाध्यासिनः समाहर्तृ[51]सन्निधातृप्रभृतीनन्यांश्च[52] राजपादोपजीविनो द(दा)ण्डपासिक[53]–
22 चट्टभट्ट[54]पिशुनवे(वै)तृ(त्रि)काव[55][रोध*]जनराजवल्लभादीन्सर्वान्समाज्ञापयति[56] विदित-
मस्तु भव–
23 तां[57] । [58]यथाऽस्मा[भि*][59] ग्रा(ग्रा)मावेतौ सनिधि(धी)[60] सोपनिधि (धी)[61] सगर्त्तोषर
(रौ)[62] साम्रमधुकौ[63] सखटविटप(पौ)[64] सपद्रा—
24 रण्य(ण्यौ)[65]सजलस्थलौ[66] [67]सदशापराध(धौ) सर्वोपरिकरादानसमेत(तौ)[68]सर्व्वंवा(बा)-
धापरिर्वाज–

Second Plate : Second Side

25 तो(तौ)[69] प्रतिनिःषिद्धचाटभटप्रवेशौ[70] ।[71] मध्यदेशीयहस्तिग्रामविनिर्गताय पराशरसगो[72]–
26 त्राय त्र्यार्षेयष्र(प्र)वराय[73] नारायणनप्त्रे शान्तिकरसुताय ।[73a] यजुर्वेदकान्व[74] शाखा-
ध्यायि–

51. Mazumdar : समाहर्त्तृ.
52. Rajaguru : °नन्यां च.
53. Read °पाशिक° which is the reading of Mazumdar and Rajaguru.
54. Read चाट भट which is adopted by Mazumdar and Rajaguru.
55. Mazumdar's reading वेत्रिक is followed by Rajaguru.
56. Mazumdar, who reads °वल्लभां संभाण्य समा° is followed by Rajaguru.
57. Mazumdar : भवता.
58. This punctuation mark, which is redundant, has escaped the attention of the earlier editors.
59. Rajaguru follows Mazumdar's reading यथास्मिन.
60. Both Mazumdar and Rajaguru read सनिधिः.
61. Mazumdar and Rajaguru: सोपनिधिः.
62. Mazumdar and Rajaguru: सगर्त्तोषरः.
63. Mazumdar reads साम्ब्रमधुकौ and Rajaguru साम्ब्रमधुको.
64. Mazumdar's reading is सगूठविषय, Rajaguru reads सगूडविषय in the body of the text but regards सगुल्म as the probable reading of the first part.
65. Mazumdar and Rajaguru read सपङ्काल.
66. Mazumdar, followed by Rajaguru, reads °स्थल.
67. There are indistinct traces of one or two letters before *sa*. These letters are doubtfully read as भर (?) ण by Mazumdar and Rajaguru.
68. Mazumdar and Rajaguru : सर्वापरिकरादानसमेत°.
69. Mazumdar and Rajaguru : सर्व्वंवाधाविवर्जितः.
70. Mazumdar and Rajaguru : °प्रवेश.
71. This mark of punctuation, which is, however, redundant, has escaped the notice of the earlier editors.
72. Mazumdar : परासर°. The letter *sa* preceding *go* has been overlooked by Rajaguru.
73. Mazumdar: आत्रेय प्रवराय. The transformation of *pra* into *ṣra* is due to carelessness on the part of the scribe who, by oversight, joined the notch in the left limb of *p* to the right vertical. This fact has not been noticed by the previous editors.

73a. This *daṇḍa* is superfluous.

74. Read काण्व which is Mazumdar's reading followed by Rajaguru.

27 ने भट्टपुत्रस(स्व)रोदयी(यि) श्रीयशकराय पुण्यतिथावस्यां[74a] ।[75] उदकपूर्वक(कं)[76] । [77]आचन्द्रतारकार्क्क[78]–

28 स्थि(क्षि)तिसमकालोपभोगार्थं मातापित्रोरात्मनश्च पुण्ययशोभिवृद्धये ।[79] ताम्रशास[80]–

29 नेनाकरीकृत्य प्रतिपादिता[वि]त्यवगत्य[81] समुचितभोग(?)भार(ग)करहिरण्यादिकमुप[82]–

30 नयद्भिः[83] सुखेन प्रतिवस्तव्यं[84](व्यम्) ।[85] भाविभिश्च भूपतिभिर्दत्तिरियमस्मदी–

31 या[86] स्वदानमिव परिपालनीया[87] ।।[88](।) तथा चोक्तं धर्म्मशास्त्रे ।।[89](।)व(ब)हुभिर्वसुधा दत्ता राजभि[90]–

32 [91]स्सगरादिभिः । यस्य यस्य यदा भूमिस्तस्य तस्य तदा फलं (लम्)।।[92] [१।।*] मा भूद-फलशङ्कावः

33 परदत्तेति पार्थिवाः । [93]स्वदानान्फ(त्फ)लमानन्त्यं परदत्तानुपालने ।।[२।।*][94]षष्ठिम्वर्षसह–

34 स्राणि स्वर्ग्गे[95] मोदति भूमिदः । आक्षेप्ता चानुमन्ता च तान्येव [96]नरकम्वसेत् ।। [३।।*] भूमिं यः[97] प्रति–

35 गृह्णा(ह्णा)ति यश्च भूमिं प्रयच्छति । तावुभौ[98] पुण्यकर्म्माणौ नियतौ[99] स्वर्ग[100]गामिनौ ।।[101] ।।[४।।*] आस्फोटय–

74a. Rajaguru erroneously reads °तिथ्यावस्यां which he proposes to correct to °तिथ्यामावाश्यां.
75. This superfluous *daṇḍa* has eluded the earlier editors.
76. Mazumdar : ओदकपूर्व्वकं; Rajaguru : औदकपूर्व्वकं.
77. This mark of punctuation, which is not required, has escaped the attention of Mazumdar and Rajaguru.
78. Mazumdar : °तारकार्क°.
79. Earlier editors have left this mark of punctuation, which is redundant, unnoticed.
80. Mazumdar : ताम्त्र°. Rajaguru : ताम्ब्र°.
81. Mazumdar and Rajaguru : °पादित इ°.
82. Mazumdar and Rajaguru : हिरण्यदिकमुपा°.
83. In other charters we normally have भवद्भिः between उपनयद्भिः and सुखेन. It is evidently left out by oversight.
84. Mazumdar : °वास्तव्यं°.
85. Earlier editors have ignored this mark of punctuation which is quite relevant.
86. Mazumdar and Rajaguru : °स्मदीय.
87. In most other charters of the family we have *sva-dattir-iv-ānupālanīyā*.
88. Only a single *daṇḍa* has been noticed by the earlier editors.
89. Mazumdar has noticed only one *daṇḍa* while Rajaguru has altogether left out the punctuation mark.
90. Mazumdar and, following him, Rajaguru unnecessarily read a *visarga* at the end of the line which is neither present in the plate nor necessary.
91. Mazumdar and Rajaguru : सगरा°.
92. Here as well as in the following lines one of the strokes of the punctuation mark, indicating the completion of the stanza, has escaped the notice of the earlier editors.
93. Mazumdar and Rajaguru : सदाना°.
94. Mazumdar and Rajaguru : षष्ठीम्वर्षं. Read षष्टिं वर्ष°.
95. Mazumdar : स्वर्गे.
96. Mazumdar : नरकं वसेत्; Rajaguru : नरके वसेत्. In other records we generally have the latter expression which is preferable.
97. The *visarga* has eluded Mazumdar and Rajaguru.
98. We normally have *ubhau tau*.
99. Read नियतं which is the reading of Mazumdar and Rajaguru.
100. Mazumdar : स्वर्ग°.
101. This mark of punctuation has been left out unnoticed by Mazumdar.

Third Plate

36 [न्ति पि]तरो वल्गयन्ति[102] पिताम[हा:][103]। भूमिदाता कुले जा[त:][104] स नस्त्राता भविष्यति ।।[५।।*] सुवर्ण्ण[मेकं]

37 गामेकां भूमेरप्यर्द्धमङ्गलं (लम्)। हरन्नरकमायाति यावदाभूतसंप्लवं[105] (वम्) ।।[६।।*] स्वदत्तां परद[त्तां वा]

38 यो हरेत वसुन्धरां (राम्)। स विष्ठायां कृमिर्भूत्वा पितृभिः सह पच्यते ।।[७।।*] हरते हारयते यस्तु म[न्द वु (बु)]–

39 द्धिस्तमोवतः। सवद्धो[106] वारुणैः पासै (शै) स्तिर्यग्योनिषु[107] गच्छति[108] ।।[८।।*] साम (मा) न्योयं [109]धर्मसे[तुर्नृ]–

40 पाणां काले काले पालनीयो भवद्भिः। सर्व (र्वा) नेतान् भाविनः[110] पार्थिवेन्द्रान (न्) भूयो भूयो[111] याच[ते]

41 रामभद्रः[111a] ।[।९।।*] अस्मद्वङशान्वये[112] काले यः कश्चिन्नृपतिर्भवेत्। तस्याहं पादलग्नोस्मि मया[दत्तं]

42 न लोपयेत्[113] ।।[१०।।*] इति कमलदलाम्वु (म्बु) वि (बि) न्दुलोलां श्रियमनुचिन्त्य[114] मनुष्यजीवित[ञ्च।]

43 सकलमिदमुदाहृतं च वु (बु)[द्*]ध्वा न हि पुरुषैः परकीर्तयो[115] [वि*]लोप्याः[116] ।।[११।।*] श्री**महाशिव**–

44 **गुप्तश्रीययातिराजदेव पादप्रवर्द्धमान[117] विजयराज्ये सम्वत्[118] तृतीये[119] वैसा (शा) खसित-पंचम्यां[120]**

102. Mazumdar: प्रवल्गयन्ति; Rajaguru: प्रवलगन्ति.
103. Mazumdar and Rajaguru : पितामहः.
104. This *visarga* has escaped the notice of Mazumdar and Rajaguru. The latter erroneously suggests the correction जाता.
105. Mazumdar and Rajaguru : °संप्लभं.
106. Read सुबद्धो.
107. Mazumdar : पाशैस्तिर्य्यंक योनिषु; Rajaguru : पाशैस्तिर्य्यक्.
108. Rajaguru follows Mazumdar in reading जायते.
109. Mazumdar and Rajaguru: धर्म्म°.
110. Mazumdar: भाविनो पार्थिवेन्द्रान्; Rajaguru: सर्व्वानेतान् भाविनो पार्थिवेन्द्रान्.
111. Mazumdar : भुयो भुयो.
111a. The reading of the last two letters in doubtful. Mazumdar and Rajaguru read them as *candra*.
112. Mazumdar : अस्मद्वङ्गान्वये. Read अस्मद्वंशान्वये which is Rajaguru's reading.
113. The second half of this stanza was not deciphered satisfactorily by the earlier editors. Mazumdar read it as पादरजोस्मिययाति and Rajaguru as तस्मादायादयोमस्मिन्.
114. Mazumdar : °मनुचिन्ह्य.
115. Mazumdar and Rajaguru : °कीर्त्तयो.
116. The form of the *akṣara* is quite unusual.
117. Mazumdar : °पादवर्द्धमान°. Rajaguru also ignores *pra* which is quite legible in the original and supplies it on his own.
118. Mazumdar and Rajaguru : संवत्सरे. Read संवत्.
119. Rajaguru : तृतीय.
120. Mazumdar, followed by Rajaguru, reads वैशाकसितपञ्चम्यां.

45 अङ्केनापि[121] सम्वत्[122] ३ वैसा(शा)ख[123] सुदि ५ लिखितमिदं ताम्र(म्र) शासनं सन्धि-विग्रहिश्री–

46 हर्षदत्तनप्तृणा[124] सिंहदत्तभा(भ्रा)तृसुतेन राणक[125] श्रीरुद्रदत्तेन इति[126] ॥०॥

ABSTRACT

As usual, the record opens with the auspicious expressions *siddham* and *svasti*, the former indicated symbolically, followed by the mention of the victorious camp stationed at the town (*pattana*) of **Suvarṇapura** whence the charter was issued. It is described in a long prose passage in a purely conventional manner and the only factual information we get is that it was situated on the confluence of the rivers Telā[127] and Mahānadī[128] and that the goddess Pañcāmbari-Bhadrāmbikā, who had descended over there with the desire of favouring all the people by granting their desired boons, was its presiding deity.[129] Next is introduced the king **Mahāśivagupta Yayāti,** who meditated upon the feet of Mahābhavagupta[130] and is styled *Paramamāheśvara, Paramabhaṭṭāraka-Mahārājādhirāja-Parameśvara*[131] and said to have acquired the title of *Trikaliṅgādhipati* by (the prowess of) his own arms. It is further stated that his foot-stool was kissed by the crest-jewels of the multitude of all the ruling chiefs humbled by his great valour, he had emulated the deeds of the renowned kings like Nala, Nahuṣa, Māndhātṛ, Dilīpa, Bharata

121. Mazumdar : साङ्केनापि.
122. Read संवत्.
123. Mazumdar : वैशाक°.
124. Mazumdar : नप्तृना. Rajaguru, who accepts Mazumdar's reading, proposes to correct it to नप्ताना which is unwarranted.
125. Mazumdar : राण्क.
126. This word, which is quite clear in the facsimile, has escaped the notice of both Mazumdar and Rajaguru. The same is the case about the following strokes marking the conclusion of the record. Mazumdar concludes his transcript without any punctuation mark while Rajaguru supplies a full stop on his own.
127. The same as the modern Tel, a tributary of the Mahanadi.
128. The modern town of Sonpur, which represents Suvarṇapura, literally agrees with this description.
129. Mazumdar points out that at Sonpur there is still a temple of the goddess Bhagavatī, but it is not known as Pañcāmbari-Bhadrāmbikā and it is not possible to ascertain if it actually represents the shrine of that goddess.
130. Strange as it might apear, not a single title is applied to the donor's father. In all other official records of the dynasty the donor's father is given almost the same titles as are applied to the donor himself.
131. The manner in which the titles are mentioned is peculiar to this record. The titles *Trikaliṅgādhipati* and *Paramamāheśvara* and a part of the imperial title, *viz.*, *Paramabhaṭṭāraka*, each separately in nominative singular, are mentioned before the name of the donor's father whereas the remaining part of the imperial title, *viz.*, *Mahārājādhirāja-Parameśvara,* precedes the donor's name. In other official records all these titles are found compounded with the monarch's name in a single passage.

and Bhāgīratha; he was the burning fever to the Karṇāṭa, Lāṭa and Gurjara kings, like a lustful person he carried away the girdles (*kāñci-kalāpa*) of the ladies of Bhūviṭa,[132] he had attained fame by being the self-chosen husband (*svayaṁvara*) of Kaliṅga, Koṅgoda,[133] Utkala and Kosalā,[134] he was verily the wind in carrying away the cloths of Gauḍa and Rāḍhā and a full moon in the clean sky that is the lineage of the moon and that his lotus-feet were served by the saluting kings.

It is recorded that after honouring the Brāhmaṇas of the villages Bṛhad-Bhusāī[135] and Mārañjamurā,[136] the former included in the Uṅgāḍa-*viṣaya*[137] and the latter in the Santonartā-*khaṇḍa*[138] included in the Gandharavāḍi-*maṇḍala*,[139] both attached to Kosala, the king ordered the agriculturist householders residing there and the people of the district as well as all the royal officers posted from time to time including the *Samāhartṛ*, *Sannidhātṛ*, others serving the king like the *Dāṇḍapāśika*, *Piśuna*, *Vaitrika*, inmates of the royal sareglio and the king's favourites that he had given away the two villages on an auspicious *tithi* in favour of the *Bhaṭṭaputra* Yaśakara,[140] son of Śāntikara and grandson of Nārāyaṇa, who had immigrated from Hastigrāma[141] in Madhyadeśa,[142] belonged to the Parāśara *gotra*, had the Ātreya *pravara* of three *ṛṣis* and was a student of the Kāṇva *śākhā* of the *Yajurveda*. The grant was accompanied by the privileges including the right to the *nidhis*, *upanidhis*, pits and barren spots, mango and *madhuka* trees, bushes and shrubs, habita-

132. It is mentioned in such a manner as to leave the impression that it is the name of a country. If so, it cannot be identified. D.C. Sircar (*The Struggle for Empire*, 211) regards it as a mistake for Draviḍa referring to the Colas. A vague claim to some military success against Kāñcī, which was at this time under the Colas, might also have been intended.
133. Generally speaking, region round Ganjam.
134. It appears to be intended only as an allusion to his authority over these countries.
135. Not yet identified. Mazumdar is wrong in taking it as the chief place of the *khaṇḍa* in which it was situated.
136. Mazumdar erroneously takes Mārañja and Murā as the names of the two villages granted through this charter. Mārañjamurā was just one of the donated villages, the other being Bṛhad-Bhusāī-grāma. Mazumdar points out that there are many villages in the Sambalpur tract bearing the names Mārañja and Murā with slightly altered pronunciation. One of these villages may represent ancient Mārañjamurā.
137. It has not been identified. D.C. Sircar (*The Struggle for Empire*, 224, fn. 20) erroneously takes the name of the district to be Uṅgoḍa.
138. It has yet to be identified.
139. Gandharavāḍi, the chief town of the *maṇḍala* christened after it, is probably the same as Gandhaḍapāṭī, the headquarters of the *maṇḍala* of that name, mentioned in the Nibinna plates dated in the fifteenth year of Mahāśivagupta I (*supra*, IV : XV) and Gandharāḍhi of the Bhauma-kara records.
140. Sanskrit, Yaśaskara. He is styled *svaroday in* which probably refers to his skill in reciting.
141. Probably the same as Hastipada mentioned as the original home of some of the Brāhmaṇa donees in a few other records of the dynasty. See above, IV: XIX.
142. Mazumdar's contention that Madhya deśadenotes the tract covered by the northern portion of the district of Balasore and the subdivision of Contai in Orissa is quite untenable.

tions and forests, waters and lands, *daś-āparādhas,* all the *upari-karas* and exemption from all the troubles and the entry of the *cāṭas* and *bhaṭas.* The grant was turned into a rent-free holding and the villagers were asked to pay the donee all the dues like the *bhoga, bhāga, kara* and *hiraṇya* as due and thereby live happily.

Next follows the customary entreaty, supported by eleven stanzas from the Dharmaśāstra, to the future ruling chiefs for the upkeep of the grant as if it were their own grant.

The grant is dated[143] the **fifth day of the bright fortnight of the month of Vaiśākha in the third year of the increasingly victorious reign of the illustrious Mahāśivagupta Yayāti.**[144]

This copper-plate charter was written by the *Sandhivigrahin*[145] *Rāṇaka* Rudradatta, grandson of Harṣadatta and son of the brother of Siṁhadatta.[146]

143. The date is indicated both in words and figures.
144. It may be noted that absolutely no regal title is attached to the name of the donor in connection with the specification of the date as in other official records.
145. The title *Sandhivigrahin*, which was evidently meant for Rudradatta, the writer of the record, appears to have been prefixed to his grandfather's name by oversight. Otherwise one will have to believe that while the writer of the record, who obviously occupied a high position at the time, is given no official title, his grandfather, who was probably no more, is mentioned with a high official designation, which is quite unusual.
146. He is evidently identical with the homonymous person who is mentioned as the *Sandhivigrahin* in the Pāṭṇā plates of the 28th regnal year of Mahāśivagupta I Yayāti and the Cuttack plates of Mahābhavagupta II Bhīmaratha (above, IV : XVII and XVIII).

IV : XXII

BĀLIJHARI PLATES[1] OF MAHĀBHAVAGUPTA IV UDDYOTAKESARIN, YEAR 4

Provenance: Bālijhari, Cuttack District, Orissa.

References: Binayak Misra, *JBORS*, xvii, 1-24 and plates between pp. 24 and 25; Debala Mitra, *IHQ*, xxxv, 93-108; S.N. Rajaguru, *IO*, iv, 225-34.

Language: Sanskrit. In a mixture of prose and verse.

Metres: Verses 1, 3-7, 24: *Śārdūlavikrīḍita*; Verses 2, 8: *Vasantatilakā*; Verse 9: *Upajāti*; Verse 10: *Āryā*; Verse 11: *Rathoddhatā*; Verses 12-13, 15-21, 25-26: *Anuṣṭubh*: Verse 13: *Indravajrā*; Verse 22: *Śālinī*; Verse 23: *Puṣpitāgrā*.

Script: Northern class of alphabets.

Date: Regnal year 4, Mārgaśirṣa kṛṣṇa 10. The latter half of the eleventh century A.D.

TEXT[2]

First Plate

1 सिद्धम्[3] [।*] जो(ज्यो)स्ना(त्स्ना)सा(शा)लिसमृद्धिभूः[4] कुमुदिनीहासौ(सैं)कसम्पा-

2 दनाधूर्त्तो धूर्जटि[5]मौलिसौधव[स*]तिः पीयूस(ष)धारागृहं(हम्) । तारान्त[ः*]पु-

3 रनायको रतिपतेःशस्त्रैकशानो (णो)पलः[6] क्षीरोदार्ण्णव-

4 नन्दनो विजयते देवः सुधादीधितिः ।।[१।।*] अस्यान्वये महति सान्द्रतमः-

1. Binayak Misra, who first published the inscription, called it Narasinghpur charter since it was found in the erstwhile Narasinghpur State and he is followed by Rajaguru. But as the plates were actually found at the village of Bālijhari it is more appropriate to designate them as Bālijhari plates, as has been done by Mitra.

   The plates, measuring 8¾″ × 6″, are strung on a ring, 1½″ thick and 2″ in diameter, which is passed through the holes bored in the middle of the margin on the left. The ends of the ring are secured under a seal, 1½″ in diameter, which bears in relief on a countersunk surface, the figrure of Gaja-Lakṣmī seated on lotus and being bathed by elephants. No legend is discernible.
2. From facsimiles in *JBORS*, xvii. Since the published facsimiles are faint at places and since the original plates are not traceable, one cannot be quite certain about the correctness of some of the readings.
3. Misra : Om. Expressed by a symbol.
4. Misra : जोत्स्नासालि समुद्विभः.
5. Misra : धृजटि°.
6. Misra reads शस्त्रे कृशानो पलः and suggests to correct the last word to फलः.

5 कलङ्कविच्छायदिग्वलयमार्ज्जनकूर्च्चकस्य[7]। उत्पेदिरे सकलसद्गुण–

6 जन्मकन्दाः कुन्दावदातयशसो जगती[8]भुजस्ते। ।[२।।*] राजाभूज्जनमेजयो–

7 ऽथ नृपतिर्जा(र्जा)तो ययातिः(ति)त(स्त)तः श्रीमान् भीमरथोऽभवत्तदनु च

8 क्ष्माचक्ररक्षामणिः [।*] भ्रष्टा(ष्ट)षे(स्वे)व दिगन्तरेषु(षु) विजयस्तम्भावालिच्छ–

9 द्मना हृच्छल्यानि दिशाभु[जा*]मपि समारोप्त(प्य)[न्त*]यैंव्वि(व्वि)स्फुटं(टम्) [।।३।।*] तस्माद्धर्म्म–

10 रथो मनोरथफल(लं) शीता(तां)न्सु(शु)व(वं)ङश(श)श्रियो निस्त्रि(स्त्रि)ङशै(शैं)-कश(स)खा शिखा–

11 [9]मणिरभूसनिःशेषभूमि(मी)[10]भुजाः(जाम्) [।*] यस्मिन् दिग्विजयावतारिण(णि) पु[रा*]–

12 विद्वेषिभूमि(मी)[10]भुजा(जः) प्राती(ति)थ(ष्ठ)न्त्य(न्त) दिगन्तर(रं) तदनु च स्फीता-श्चमूरेणवः।।[४।।*]से–

13 तूपान्त[11]वनान्तरे हिमवतः पर्य्यन्तभूसीमनि।[12] प्रागम्भोधितटीवनेषु[13] कट–

14 के पूर्व्वेतरक्ष्माभृतः [।*] यस्योत्ताम्यदराती(ति)[14]राजयुवतीनि[ः*]श्वासझञ्झानिल–

15 व्यासङ्गस(स्व)नदन्तरालमुखरैंर्ग्गि(र्ग्गी)तं यशः कि(की)चकैः।।[५।।*] भ्राता तस्य व(ब)भूव

16 भूतलपते[15][र्भूते*[16]]शतुल्यप्रभः प्रख्यातः(तं)क्षितिभूषणं नघुष इत्युव्वी(र्व्वी)[17]प–

17 ती[नां पति*]ः[18] [।*] यद्दोर्द्दण्ड[19]भुजङ्गमेन विलसन्निस्त्रि(स्त्रि)न्स(श)[20]जिह्वाभृता पीता[स्ते][21]

Second Plate : First Side

18 परिपन्थिपार्थिवचमूकण्ठान्तरे[22] मारुताः।।[६।।*] अत्रास्ते करिवृन्दमुन्मद–

19 मिह प्रौढोस्ति पञ्चाननः सन्त्येतासु जग[द्*]द्रुहो[23] गिरिदरीकुम्भीषु कु–

7. Misra reads it as कृच्चक्रस्य which he proposes to correct to कृत्करस्य.
8. Misra reads जगतां.
9. Read °मणिरभून्निःशेष°.
10. This rather unusual correction is necessary to suit the metre.
11. The correction to सेतु-प्रान्त suggested by Misra is uncalled for.
12. This mark of punctuation is superfluous.
13. Misra : °तटावनिषु.
14. Misra reads यस्योत्कम्पदराति°.
15. Misra : °पतिः; Rajaguru : °पति.
16. The restoration of these two missing letters is based on the corresponding verse in the Ratnagiri plates of Karṇa.
17. Misra :इत्युर्व्वि°; Mitra : इत्युवी°.
18. These three missing letters have been restored from the corresponding stanza of the Ratnagiri plates of Karṇa.
19. Mitra : °दंण्ड°.
20. Misra: °निस्त्रिंश°; Mitra: °निस्तृंस°.
21. Misra: पीतासौ.
22. Misra's reading is °कण्ठान्तरि° which he proposes to correct to कण्ठान्तरी.
23. Misra: °जगद्गुहो.

20 म्भीनशा(सा): । स्नेहादित्यभिधाय वृद्धशवरीवर्गेण व(ब)द्धाश्रुणा[24] यद्वै[रि]–

21 प्रमदाजनो वनभुवः सञ्चारमध्यापितः ॥ [७॥*] तस्यानुजो नतसमस्तस–

22 पत्नमौलिरत्ना(त्नां)न्सु(शु)मीलित[25]पादसरोजरोचिः[।*] विद्यानिधिः प्रतिनिधिर्म–

23 धुसूदनस्य जातोथ विश्वविजयी नृपतिर्ययातिः ॥ [८॥*] भटै रवष्टव्ध(ब्ध)मि–

24 दं नरेन्द्रैः राष्ट्र(ष्ट्र) द्वयं कोष(स)लमुके(त्क)लञ्च । अकण्टकं साधयतः स[26]

25 समन्ताद्भुजद्वय(यं) यस्य कृतार्थमासीत(त्) ॥[९॥*] तस्य ततः सुकृत–

26 [फलं] सफलीकृतलोकलोचनस्तनयः [।*] समजनि गुणैकसीमा

27 श्रीमानु[द्*]**द्योतकेसरी** नृपतिः ॥[१०॥*] भक्तिदूरनतकुन्तलस्खलन्म[27]ल्लिका—

28 कुसुम[दाम[28]*]राजयः । ढौक[य*]न्त इव कीर्त्तिसन्ततीर्यं प्रणेमुरहि(भि)तो[29] महि(ही)
भुज [:॥११॥*]

29 स्वस्ति[30] श्री**ययातिनगरात**(त्) । परममाहेश्वरप[र*]मभट्टारकमहाराजाधि–

30 राजपरमेश्वरसोमकुलतिलकत्रिकलिङ्गाधिपतिश्रीमहाशिवगु–

31 प्तराजदेवपादानुध्यात[31] ।[32] परममाहेश्वरपरमभट्टारकमहा–

32 राजाधिराजपरमेश्वरसोमकुलतिलकत्रिकलिङ्गाधिपतिश्री**महा**–

33 **भवगुप्त**राजदेवः कुशली । ओड्रे[33](ड्र)देशीयऐरावट्टमण्डलसं[34][बद्ध*]स–

34 [रा]वखण्डीयकोन्तलण्डाग्राम[:*] एतस्मिन(न्न) तस्त[त्*]खे(ख)ण्डीय[35]व्रा(ब्रा)ह्म–

Second Plate : Second Side

35 णाना[36]पूज्य समाहर्तृ सन्निधातृनियुक्ताधिकारिदाण्डपाशिकपिशु–

36 नवेत्रिकावरोधजनराज्ञीराणकराजपुत्र ।[37]राजवल्लभ ।[37] भोगिजनप्र–

37 मुखजनपदान(न्) ।[37] समाज्ञापयति [।*] विदितमस्तु भवत्तां(तां) ।[37] यथास्माभिरयं

38 ग्रामः सगर्त्तोषरो महानदीअर्द्धं[38]श्रो(स्रो)तःसमेतच(श्च) तुःसीमावच्छि–

39 न्नः साम्र[39]मधूकतालप्रभृतिनानावृक्षः[39a] सनिधिः सोपानिधिः हस्तिदण्डव–

24. Rajaguru: **वद्धशृणा**.
25. Read °सम्मिलित° to meet the metrical requirements. Mitra proposes to correct it to मांसलित and Rajaguru adds सु before **पाद**.
26. This *akṣara* is superfluous.
27. Misra: °**स्खलन**°.
28. The restoration of these two missing letters is based on the Ratnagiri plates of Karṇa.
29. Misra reads **य (:) प्रणि(णी)त्यरहितो.**
30. Mitra: **स्वस्ती.**
31. Mitra's suggestion to add *visarga* after *ta* is unwarranted. In other carefully drafted records also we do not come across *visarga* at this place.
32. The *daṇḍa* is superfluous.
33. Misra reads it as *Oḍri* and Rajaguru *Oḍi.*
34. In the Ratnagiri plates of Karṇa also only *saṁ* is employed for *saṁbaddha.*
35. Misra reads **तस्मिन् तस्य (स्थित) खेण्डीय.**
36. Rajaguru unnecessarily adds *anusvāra* after *nā.*
37. This mark of punctuation is unnecessary.
38. Read महानद्यर्द्धं°.
39. Perhaps *śiṁśapā* is intended.

39a. Read °**वृक्षसहितः.**

40 र व(ब)लीवर्न्द(र्द्दं)-।[40]चिटोल[41]।[42] अन्धारुवा-।।[42] प्रत्यन्धारुवा-।[42] अदत्ता।[42] पदाति-
जीव्य-।।[42]

41 अहिदण्ड-।[42] अन्तरावड्डि-।[42] व(ब)न्धदण्ड-।[42] विजयवन्दापना-।[42] मार्ग्गणिकप्रभृति–

42 भविष्यत्करसहितः सप्रतीहारः सर्व्वा(र्व्वं)[बा*]धा[विव*]जी(र्जि)तः सर्व्वोपरिकरा-
दानस–

43 हितः ति(ती)र भुक्तिमण्डे(ण्ड)लि(ली)यपलास(श)ग्रामविनिर्ग्गताय।[42] मार्ग्ग(र्ग्य)
गो–

44 त्राय।[42] त्रार्ष (त्र्यार्षे)यप्रवराय।[42] ऋग्वेदाध्यायिने।[42] भट्टपुत्रवटेश्वर[43] पौ–

45 त्राय भट्टपुत्रवामनपुत्राय।[44] भट्टपुत्रश्रीशङ्करस(श)र्म्म–

46 णे।[44] सलिलधारापुरःसरं (र) आ(मा) चन्द्रार्क्क[45]क्षितिसमकालोपभोगार्त्थ[46]

47 मातापित्रोरात्मनश्च पुन्य(ण्य)यसो(शो)भिवृद्धये[47] ताम्व्र(म्र) शासनेनाकरीकृत्य

48 सम्प्रदत्तः [।*] ऐरावट्टमण्डलसं (बद्ध*]सरावखण्डीयलोवाकरडाग्रामश्च ए[48]–

49 तस्य[49] सोदरभ्रातृश्रीव(ब)लभद्र।[50] स(श)र्म्मणे एवं सम्प्रदत्त।[50] इत्यवग–

50 त्य समुचितकरभोग भागादिकमुपनयद्भिर्भवद्भिः सुखेन प्रतिवस्त–

51 व्य[म्।*] स[51] दे(द)त्तिरियमस्मदीया धर्म्मगौरवादस्मदनुरोधाच्च स्वदत्तिरिवा–

52 नुपालनीया। तथा चोक्तं धर्म्मशास्त्रे [।*] व(ब)हुभिर्व्वसुधा दत्ता राजभिः

Third Plate : First Side

53 सगरादिभिः [।*] यस्य यस्य यदा भूमिस्तस्य तस्य तदा फलं(लम्)। [।१२।।*]मा भूदफ–

54 लशङ्का वः [परदत्तानुपालने*][52]। स्वदत्तात्फलमा[न*]न्त्यं परदत्तानुपालने ।।[१३।।*]
षष्ठि (ष्टि)वर्षसहस्रा–

55 णि स्वर्ग्गे मोदति भूमिदः। आक्षेप्ता चानुमन्ता च द्वौ तौ नरकगामिनौ।।[१४।।*]

56 अग्नेरपत्यं प्रथमं सुवर्णं भूर्व्वैष्ण(ण्ण)वि(वी) सूर्यसुताश्च गावः। य[:*] काञ्चनं

57 गाञ्च महि(ही)ञ्च दद्यादृत्तास्त्रयस्तेन भवन्ति लोकाः ।।[१५।।*] आस्फोटयन्ति पि–

58 तरो वल्गयन्ति पितामहाः ।।(।) भूमिदाता कुले जातः स नस्त्राता भविस्य(ष्य)ति।
[।१६।।*]

59 भूमिं यः प्रतिगृह्णाति यश्च भूमिं प्रयच्छति। उभौ तौ पुन्य(ण्य) कर्म्माणौ निय–

40. This *daṇḍa* is uncalled for.
41. Misra reads °चोटाल°.
42. This *daṇḍa* is not required.
43. Misra reads चतेश्वर.
44. This mark of punctuation is redundant.
45. Misra: आचन्द्रार्क°.
46. Misra and Mitra: °भोगार्थं.
47. Misra: पुन्याय सिद्धिवृद्धये.
48. This letter is left out unread by Misra and, following him, Rajaguru.
49. Better read ग्रामश्चैतस्य.
50. This punctuation mark is not required.
51. This letter is superfluous.
52. The omission of this portion of the stanza is due to oversight.

60 तं स्वर्गगामिनौ ।।[१७।।*] तडागानां सहस्रेण वाजपेयशतेन[53] च। गवां

61 [को]टी-[54] प्रदानेन भूमिहर्त्ता न्न[55](न) शुध्यति ।।[१८।।*] स्वदत्तां परदत्ताम्वा[56] यो

62 हरेद्व(त व)सुन्धरां (राम्) [।*] स विष्ठायां कृमिर्भूत्वा पितृभिः सह पच्यते ।।[१९।।*]

63 गामेकां [57]सुवर्ण्णमेकं [वा*] भूमेरप्यर्द्धमङ्गुलं (लम्) [।*] हरन्नरकमायाति यावदाहू (भू)त–

64 सम्प्लवं[58](वम्) ।।[२०।।*] हरते हारयेद्व(द्य)स्तु[59] मन्दवु(बु)द्धिस्तमोवृतः। स(सु) व(ब)द्धो वारुणैः

65 पाशैस्तिर्यग्योनिं[60] स गच्छति ।।[२१।।*] सामान्योयं धर्म्मंशे(से)तुर्न पाणां काले का–

66 ले पालनीयो[61] भवद्भिः। सर्व्वानितान्भावी (वि)नः[62] पार्थिवेन्द्रान्भूयो भूयो या–

67 चते रामभद्रः[63] ।।[२२।।*] इति कमलदलाम्वु (म्बु)वी(बि)न्दु[64]– लोलां श्रियमनुचिन्त्य मनुष्यजी–

68 वितञ्च। सकलमिदमुदाहृतं[65] [च*] वु(बु)द्वा(द्ध्वा)न ही(हि) पुरुषैः परकीर्त्तयो वी-(वि)लोप्या[ः*]।। [२३।।*]

69 यत्कीर्त्तिर्भुवनत्रयस्य[66] कुहरे स(श)श्वत्तनी पु(पू)र्णयन्मन्त्रेण[67] चिरप्रणाम[68]–

70 रहितक्षोणीभुजो भोगी(गि)न [:।*] यद्दोर्दण्ड[69]भवप्रतापशिक्षी(खि)नो नी(नि)स्त्रिस (श)[70]–

Third Plate : Second Side

71 —⏑———⏑⏑–⏑–⏑⏑⏑——⏑––⏑– ।।[२४।।*][71] उ–

53. Misra reads °शतानि.
54. Read कोटि° which is Misra's reading.
55. Misra: न.
56. Read °दत्तां वा.
57. Read स्वर्ण्णं° for the sake of metre.
58. Misra: सम्भावः; Rajaguru: सम्प्लवः. What is read as *visarga* by them is actually just another form of *anusvāra. Contra visarga* later in the same line.
59. Misra: हरति हारयेद्वसु. Rajaguru wrongly suggests to correct it to हारयते भूमि.
60. Misra: तीर्य्यग्योनिं.
61. Misra: पालनीय; Rajaguru: पालनीयः.
62. Rajaguru: भाविनः.
63. Rajaguru: रामचन्द्रः.
64. Rajaguru: °बिन्दु°.
65. Misra: मुदाहृतञ्च.
66. Misra: यत्कीर्त्तिभु°.
67. Misra reads पर्ण्णयन्मन्त्रिणः. Rajaguru proposes the correction मन्त्रीणः which is unwarranted.
68. Better read मन्त्रेणातिचिर° to meet the metrical requirements.
69. Misra: यद्दोर्द्दण्ड°.
70. Misra: निस्त्रिंश.
71. This portion has been read by Misra as धूम-च्छटा दूरस्थोपि ⏑—— ⏑—— ⏑⏑⏑——— मनष्यामहं. But in the published facsimile accompanying Misra's transcript the concluding portion of line 69 and the whole of the following two lines are so faint that they cannot be fully restored and one cannot be sure even regarding the correctness of what has been read. Consequently it is impossible to make out any intelligible sense,

72 तकले कोष(स)ले[72] देशे स महासन्धिविग्रही । अश्वा(?)ङ्गणगणाधारो **रुद्रद**[73]–
73 **त्त** इति श्रुतः ॥ [२५॥*] महाक्षपटलाध्यक्ष [:*] श्रीमहद्दक्षः सता (तां) मतः[74] । अली–
74 ली(लि) खदिद(दं)[75] ताम्र(म्र)शासन(नं) शत्रुसा(शा)सनः(नम्) ॥॥२६॥.। महा-
राजाधिराजपर–
75 मेश्वरश्रीमदुद्द्योतकेसरिराजदेवस्य **प्रवर्द्धमानविजय**–
76 **राजे(ज्ये)**[76] चतुर्थे[77] **स(सं)म्व(व)[त्स*]रे मार्ग्गवदि दशम्यां(म्याम्) । यत्राङ्के स(सं)**
म्व(व) त(त्)[78] ४
77 **मार्ग्गवादि** १० [।*] सुवर्ण्णवि(वी)थिविज्ञानिवाहेरुमङ्गाकाभ्यां(भ्या)उ(मु)क्ती(त्की)
[र्ण्ण*]–
78 मिदं (दम्) ॥

ABSTRACT

The epigraph opens with the symbol for *siddham*. Thereafter is given a versified eulogy of the ruling family on conventional lines. In the great lineage of the nectar-bright moon god, an abode of the wealth that is moon-light, clever in the unique production of the smile (i.e. blooming) in the cluster of the lilies, residing in the palace that is the head of Dhūrjaṭi (god Śiva), the home of the streams of nectar, the hero of the inner apartment of the stars, the unique touchstone of the weapons of the lord of Rati, the offspring of the ocean of milk and the brush for wiping out the ring of the quarters dimmed by the stain of dense darkness, were born the enjoyers (*i.e.*, rulers) of the earth, who were the roots of the birth of all the virtues and had jasmine-white fame (vv. 1-2). In that family there was king Janamejaya and from him was born king Yayāti. After him came the illustrious Bhīmaratha, the protecting gem of the orb of the earth. All these kings (Janamejaya, Yayāti and Bhīmaratha) had manifestly planted thorns in the form of a row of columns of victory raised in the regions of all the eight directions even in the hearts of the enjoyers (i.e. lords) of the directions (v. 3). From Bhīmaratha was born Dharmaratha, the fruit of the heart's craving of the goddess of fortune of the lunar lineage, who had sword for his only companion and was the crest-jewel of all the kings. When, in yore, he launched upon the conquest of the quarters, the enemy kings left (ran away) for the different quarters followed by the dusts raised by his armies. His fame was sung by the bamboos which were resonant with their sounding interstices brought close by the storm-

72. Misra: कोशले.
73. Misra, followed by Rajaguru, takes *da* to be the first letter of the next line whereas in the facsimile it is clearly seen at the end of this line.
74. Misra: शतामतः.
75. Misra reads अणलिखविद.
76. Misra: राज्ये.
77. Mitra: चतुर्थं.
78. Misra: सम्वतत्.

winds in the form of the sighs of the distressed young ladies of the hostile chiefs-in the forest region in the vicinity of the Setu, on the bounds of the earth adjoining the Himavat, in the forests on the shores of the eastern ocean[79] and in the capital of the king of the west[79a] (vv. 4-5). Thereafter came the brother of that king, Naghuṣa by name, whose lustre was akin to that of the lord of the creatures (Śiva), who was a famous adornment of the earth and the chief of the lords of the earth. The serpent in the form of his staff like arm, which had the shining sword for its tongue, drank the vital winds inside the throats of the soldiers of the armies of the hostile kings.[80] The womenfolk of his enemies were instructed in the manner of wandering about in the forest-regions by a group of old Śavara women, holding back their tears, saying with affection, 'here resides a flock of maddened elephants', 'here is a mature lion', 'there are venomous snakes hostile to all inside these hill-caves' (vv. 6-7). Next followed his younger brother, king Yayāti, the lustre of whose lotus-feet was rendered variegated by the rays emanating from the head-jewels of all the hostile kings as they bent down to salute him, who was an abode of learning, the representative of the destroyer of the demon Madhu (god Viṣṇu) and conqueror of the universe. His two arms achieved their objective by freeing from enemies on all sides the two kingdoms of Kosala and Utkala when besieged by combatant kings (vv. 8-9). Then was born his son, the illustrious king **Uddyotakesarin,** who was the reward of good deeds, who had rendered the eyes of the people fruitful and was the unique climax of virtues. On his (Uddyotakesarin's) both sides bowed down kings who, with the rows of the garlands of *mallikā* flowers slipping down from the locks of hair, when they bent down at a distance through reverence, gave the appearance of offering him chains of fame (vv. 10-11).

Next is mentioned **Yayātinagara,** whence the charter was issued, followed by a prose passage referring to the kings **Mahābhavagupta** and Mahāśivagupta, on whose feet the former meditated. Both the kings are given the usual titles, *viz., Paramamāheśvara, Paramabhaṭṭāraka-Mahārājādhirāja-Parameśvara, Soma-kula-tilaka and Trikaliṅgādhipati.*

The inscription next records that the king (**Mahābhavagupta IV Uddyotakesarin**) gave away the village Kontalaṇḍā[81] situated in the Sarāva-*khaṇḍa*[82]

79. The expression *prāg-ambhodhi-taṭi-vaneṣu* may also be taken to mean 'in the forests on the shores of the ocean in the east'.

79a. The word *kaṭaka* also means an 'army camp'. *Kṣmā-bhṛt* can be taken in the sense of a mountain also. Yet another meaning of *kaṭaka* being 'mountain-ridge', the passage *kaṭake pūrv-etara-kṣmā-bhṛtaḥ* may also yield the meaning 'on the ridge of the western mountain', the reference being to the mythical mountain of sunset.

80. Such metaphors are often met with in classical Sanskrit literature.

81. Probably represented by the modern Kaṇṭilo (20°22' N, 85°14'E) in the erstwhile Khandpara State.

82. As pointed out by Mitra, the name of the hill Sorap (lat. 20° 18'; long. 85°26'), 16 miles south-east of Kaṇṭilo, reminds one of Sarāva, the headquarters of the *khaṇḍa* named after it.

which was attached to the Airāvaṭṭa-*maṇḍala*[83] in the Oḍra-*deśa* together with half the stream of the Mahānadī in favour of the *Bhaṭṭaputra* Śaṅkaraśarman, son of the *Bhaṭṭaputra* Vāmana and grandson of the *Bhaṭṭaputra* Vaṭeśvara, who had immigrated from the village of Palāśa[84] situated in the Tīrabhukti-*maṇḍala*,[85] belonged to the Gārgya *gotra* with the three *pravaras* and was a student of the *Ṛgveda*. It further registers the grant of the village of Lovākaraḍā[86] situated in the Sarāva-*khaṇḍa* attached to the Airāvaṭṭa-*maṇḍala* to the Brāhmaṇa Balabhadraśarman who was a uterine brother of the aforesaid grantee. As usual, these grants were rendered tax-free by means of a copper-plate charter. The royal order concerning the grant was addressed to the same royal officers and other personages as specified above in, IV: XX. The grant carried with it the right to all the varied trees including, *śiṁśapā*, *madhūka* and palm, the *nidhis, upanidhis, hasti-daṇḍa, vara-balīvardda, ciṭola,*[87] *andhāruvā, pratyandhāruvā,*[88] *adattā, padāti-jīvya, ahi-daṇḍa,*[89] *antarāvaḍḍi,*[90] *bandha-daṇḍa,*[91] *vijaya-vandāpanā,*[92] *mārgganika*[93] and other future taxes, *pratīhāra*, the collection of all the *uparikaras* and exemption from all the oppressions. The villagers were exhorted to pay the donee *kara*, *bhoga* and *bhāga* as due.

Eleven stanzas said to have been extracted from the Dharmaśāstra are cited in support of the request to the future ruling chiefs to protect the grant.

As a considerable portion of verse 23 cannot be made out, its import is

83. Probably identical with the modern Raṭāgarh in the erstwhile Banki States, about 16 miles from Māraḍā, proposed to be identified with Lovākaraḍā.
84. Not yet identified.
85. Tirhut in Bihar.
86. Misra identifies it with the modern Māraḍā, about four miles from Kaṇṭilo, in his article on the inscription (*JBORS*, xvii, 4) and with Karaḍā (20°28' N, 85°24'E) in the erstwhile Baramba State in his *Dynasties of Mediaeval Orissa*, 72.
87. Evidently the same is *ciṅgola* mentioned in the Mahulpara plates of Mahāśivagupta II Dharmaratha. See *supra*, IV:XX.
88. An Odiya revenue-term, probably derived from Sanskrit *pratyartha-rūpyaka*, denoting a levy of an uncertain nature. It may refer to a tax levied on loans realised with interest by money-lenders. See *IE*, 402–03; *IEG*, 261.
89. Probably a levy imposed on snake-charmers. According to Sircar, it may alternatively refer to a tax payable for the maintenance of snake-charmers. *Vide IE*, 402; *IEG*, 12.
90. It is a variant of *āturāvaḍḍi*, probably a tax levied for the treatment of the king or members of the royal family when sick. *Ibid.*, 23, 37; *IE*, 403.
91. Perhaps a fine in lieu of imprisonment. See *ibid.*, 402; *IEG*, 45.
92. An Odiya revenue term, perhaps meaning something like the *nazrānā* offered to the king on his triumphant return after a military expedition. Alternatively, it may refer to a tax levied for meeting the expenses on such expeditions. *Vide ibid*, 372; *IE*, 402. Also see *EI*, xxxiii, 264.
93. Not found in lexicographical texts, it probably denoted a levy imposed on the hunters or for the maintenance of the hunters. *Mārgaṇa* = an arrow; therefore *mārgaṇika* = one who uses arrow, a hunter. Sircar (*IEG*, 199) equates it with *mārgaṇaka*, mentioned in some Cālukya inscriptions and taken to mean 'benevolences of a general character as distinguished from special types called *prasthaka* and *skandhaka*'.

not quite clear; but this together with the following stanza refers to Rudradatta,[94] the *Mahāsandhivigrahin* of Utkala and Kosala.[95] Verse 25 states that this charter was written by the *Mahākṣapaṭalādhyakṣa* Dakṣa.

The record is dated[96] on the **tenth day of the month of Mārgaśīrṣa in the increasingly victorious reign of Mahārājādhirāja-Parameśvara, the illustrious Uddyotakesarin.**

The record was incised by Vāheru and Maṅgāka, artisans of the goldsmiths' lane.[97]

94. Evidently the same as the *Rāṇaka* Rudradatta, grandson of Harṣadatta, brother's son of Siṁhadatta, who figures as the writer in the Jatesinga Dungri plates of Mahāśivagupta III Yayāti. *Supra,* IV: XXI.
95. In the previous record Rudradatta is styled just *Sandhivigrahin* and there is no reference there to Utkala and Kosala in this connection. Probably he was elevated to a higher rank sometime in the intervening period. The Somavaṁśin kingdom was, during this period, apparently divided into two main parts, Utkala and Kosala, each of which had probably a separate *Sandhivigrahin*. *Cf.* IV: XVII which refers to the *Sandhivigrahin* of Kosala.
96. Both in words and figures.
97. The goldsmiths' quarters appear to have been located together in a particular part of the town.

IV : XXIII

LALĀṬENDUKESARI'S CAVE INSCRIPTION OF MAHĀBHAVA-GUPTA IV UDDYOTAKESARIN, YEAR 5

Provenance: Back wall of the Lalāṭendukesari's Cave or the Lion Gate on the Khaṇḍagiri Hill, Puri District, Orissa.

References: R.D. Banerji, *EI*, xiii, 166, No. XVI, and Pl. III.XVI; Bhandarkar's List, No. 1571.

Language: Sanskrit, very corrupt.

Script: Northern class of alphabets.

Date: Regnal year 5. Latter half of the eleventh century A.D.

TEXT[1]

1 सिद्धम्[2] [।*] श्रीउ[द्*]द्योतकेसरिविजयराज्यसम्व(संव)त् ५

2 श्रीकुमारपर्व्वतस्थाने जिर्न्नं वापि जिर्न्नं इसण

3 उद्योतित तस्मीन थाने चतुर्विन्सति तीर्थं(र्थं) कर–

4 स्थापित प्रतीष्ठाकाले हरिश्रोपा जसनन्दिक

5 क्न(?) द(?) ति(?)द्रथा(?) श्रीपारस्यनाथस्य कर्म्मखय: [।*][2a]

ABSTRACT

After the auspicious symbol for *siddham*, the inscription proceeds to record that in the **fifth year of the victorious reign of the illustrious Uddyotakesarin,** at the sacred place (*sthāna*) on the illustrious Kumāraparvata,[3] the decayed

1 From Pl. III.XVI, facing p. 166 in *EI*, iii.

2 Banerji: Oṁ. Expressed by a symbol.

2a. K. C. Panigrahi has given his own reading and translation of this inscription in his *Chronology of the Bhauma-Karas and the Somavamsis of Orissa*, 53. In line 1 he finds a reference to *samvat* 549 which he proposes to refer to the Ganga era. In other respects also his reading differs very considerably from that given above. But it is not borne out by the facsimile given by Banerji and his English rendering is simply fantastic.

3. Kumāraparvata is the ancient name of the Khaṇḍagiri hills. In the famous Hathigumpha inscription of Khāravela it is referred to under the slightly differently spelt name Kumārīparvata. See *EI*, xx, 80, text-line 14.

stepped well (*vāpī*)[4] and decayed temples[5] were caused to shine (*i.e.*, to be repaired) and the twenty-four Tīrthaṅkaras (*i.e.*, their images) were installed. At the time of the installation one Hariopā Jasanandika was probably present.[6] Next we find mention of the *karmakhaya,* Skt. *karma-kṣaya*[7] of the illustrious Pārasyanātha.[8]

4. According to Banerji, the word *vāpī* most probably refers to the numerous rock-cut reservoirs on the Khaṇḍagiri hills.
5. The word employed in the original is *isaṇa*, Skt. *Iśāna*, which, according to Banerji, most probably denotes a temple. It is also found used in the Sarnath inscription of the Pāla king Mahīpāla, dated V. E. 1083, where J. Ph. Vogel takes it in the sense of Śiva.
6. The reading of the first few letters of the concluding line is extremely doubtful and the doubtfully conjectured reading does not yield any meaning.
7. Banerji seems to doubtfully take the word *karma-kṣaya* in the sense of a temple. But we think that the word is employed here in the normal sense of 'the destruction of *karma*' which was evidently intended to accrue from the installation of the images of the twenty-four Tīrthaṅkaras recorded in this epigraph.
8. Banerji takes Pārasyanātha to stand for the name of the twenty-third Jaina Tīrthaṅkara, Pārśvanātha, and the passage पारस्यनाथस्य कर्म्मखय: to refer to a temple of Pārśvanātha. As pointed out in the previous note, it is more reasonable to take the expression *karma-kṣaya* to mean destruction of *karma.* As such there does not seem to be any reference to a temple of Pārśvanātha. It seems that the pious acts recorded in the inscription were performed by a Jaina devotee named Pārasyanātha with the wish that it should lead to the destruction of his accumulated action which, according to Jain view, is most vital to the attainment of liberation.

IV : XXIV

MAHAKOSALA HISTORICAL SOCIETY'S PLATES[1] OF MAHĀBHAVA GUPTA IV, UDDYOTAKESARIN, YEAR 11

Provenance: Not known.
References: L.P. Pandeya, *EI*, xxii, 135-38 and plate facing p. 137; S.N. Rajaguru, *IO*, iv, 212-17.
Language: Sanskrit. In prose with the exception of benedictive and imprecatory verses and a stanza craving for the indulgence of the learned readers at the end.
Metres: Verses 1-5 and 9: *Anuṣṭubh*; Verse 6: *Indravajrā*; Verse 7: *Śālinī*; Verse 8: *Puṣpitāgrā.*
Script: Northern class of alphabets.
Date: Regnal year 11, Bhādrapada kṛṣṇa 6. Latter half of the eleventh century A.D.

TEXT[2]

First Plate

1 सिद्धम् [।*][3] ओं[4] नम[:*] शिवाय[5] ।। स्वस्ति [।*] **किसरकेल्लासभावसितमहाविजय–**
2 **कटका**त्परममाहेश्वरमातापितृपादानुध्यात[6]महाराजाधिरा–
3 जपरमेश्वरपरमभट्टारकसोमकुलतिलकस्त्रिकलिङ्गाधिप–
4 तिश्री**महाभवगुप्तराज**देवः कुशली ।।[7] पृथुराभुक्त्यन्त [:*]पा–
5 तिलिञ्जिरग्रामे व्रा(ब्रा)ह्मणान्सम्पूज्य[8] तत्प्रतिनिवासिकुटुम्वि(म्बि)नः समा–

1. D.C. Sircar calls this charter Kesarakalla plates after the place of issue. But as information about its findspot is wanting, we prefer to retain the original nomenclature under which it was published for the first time.

   Each of the plates measures about 8·1″ in length and 4·2″ in breadth. The circular ring, on which the plates are strung, is 4·2″ in diameter and its ends are secured under a circular seal.
2. From plate in *EI*, xxii.
3. Pandeya: Om. Expressed by a symbol.
4. Expressed by a symbol which looks exactly like the numeral 3 and probably represents the primitive form of the *praṇava.* It evidently forms part of the famous Śaiva *mantra.* Pandeya actually reads it as 3.
5. This is the only record of the dynasty to contain this *mantra.*
6. This expression is not met with in any other record of the dynasty.
7. This mark of punctuation is unnecessary.
8. Read सम्पूज्य which is the reading of Pandeya.

6 हतृ॑सनि (न्नि) धातृ॑ (तृ) [9]द (दा) ण्डपाशिकचाटभटराजवल (ल्ल) भादीत्स (न्स) र्व्वा[न्*] समा–

7 ज्ञापयति [।*] विदितमस्तु भवतां यथास्माभिस्सनिधिः सोपनिधि–

8 स्सदशापराधो निषिद्धचाटभटप्रवेशः सर्व्वोपरिक–

9 रिकरकरादान[10]समेत[ः*] सर्व्वपीडा[11]परिवर्ज्जितः कपि–

Second Plate : First Side

10 ष्ठल्ल (ल) गोत्राय एकार्षे (र्षि) वसिष्ठप्रवराय मैत्रायि (य) णीशा–

11 खाध्यायिने मध्यदेशमधुरविनिर्ग्गत[12] उल्लखेटवास्त–

12 व्य[13] भट्टव्रा (ब्रा) ह्मणाय चक्रधरसुताय [14]सिङ्घसङ्कान्तौ माता–

13 पित्रोरात्मानश्च[15] पुन्या (ण्या) भी (भि) वृद्धये सलिलद्धा (धा) रापुरःस–

14 रेण चन्द्रतारकार्कक्षितितलसमकालो (लमु) पभोक्तु[16]न्ताव्र (म्र)–

15 शासनेनाकरीकृत्य प्रतिपादितोयमित्यवगत्य स–

16 मुचितभोगभागकरहिरण्या[दि*]क[17]मुपनयद्भिर्भवद्भिः

Second Plate : Second Side

17 सुखेन प्रतिवस्तव्यमिति ।। भाविभिश्च भूपत्ती (ति) भि (भि) र्द्धर्म्मगौ–

18 रवादस्मा (स्म) दनुरोधा[च्च*] [18]स्वस्वदत्तिरिवानुपालनीया [।*] तथा चैव–

19 म्पठ्यते धर्म्मशास्त्रे[19] ।। व (ब) हुभिर्व्वसुधा दत्ता राजभिः सग–

20 रादी (दि) भिर्यस्य[20] यस्य यदा भूमिस्तस्य तस्य तदा फ–

21 लं (लम्) [।।१।।*] मा भूः (भू) दफलशङ्का वः परदते (त्ते) ति पाथि (र्थि) व[21] ।। (।) स्वदा–

22 नात्प (त्फ) ल[22]मानन्त्यम्परदत्तानुपालने [।।२।।*] भूमिं यः

23 प्रतिगृह्णा (ह्णा) ति यश्च भूमी (मि) म्प्रयच्छती (ति) [।*] उभौ तौ

Third Plate : First Side

24 पुन्य (ण्य) कर्म्माणौ नी (नि) यतौ[23] स्वर्ग्गगामी (मि) नौ [।।३।।*] षष्टिम्वर्ष[24]–

9. Pandeya: सन्निधातृ॑.
10. Read सर्व्वोपरिकरकरादान°.
11. Pandeya: पीड़ा°
12. Read विनिर्ग्गताय.
13. Read वास्तव्याय.
14. Read सिंह°.
15. Read °रात्मनश्च which is Pandeya's reading.
16. In other Somavaṁśi records we generally have °पुरःसरमाचन्द्रतारकार्कक्षितिसमकालोपभोगार्थं°.
17. Pandeya proposes to correct it to हिरण्यक.
18. Read स्वदत्ति°.
19. In other records of the family we generally come across the pasasage तथा चोक्तं धर्म्मशास्त्रे.
20. Read भिः [।*] यस्य.
21. Better read पार्थिवाः.
22. Pandeya: त्फलं.
23. Read नियतं.
24. Read षष्टिं वर्षं°.

25 सहस्राणी (णि) स्वर्ग्गे मोदति भूमी (मि) दः [।*] आच्छेत्वा (त्ता) चानुम–

26 न्ता च तावे (न्ये) व नरके वसेत् [।।४।।*] सुवर्ण्णमेकङ्गामेकाम्भूमेरप्य–

27 र्द्धमङ्गुलन्हरतनरकमायाति[25] यावदाहूतसंम्प्ल (प्ल) वम् ।।[५।।*]

28 अग्नेरपत्यम्प्रथम (मं) सुवर्ण्णं म्भूर्व्वैष्णवी[26] सु (सू) र्यसुताश्च[27] गावो (वः) [।*]

29 दत्तास्त्रयस्तेन भवन्ति लोका यष्काञ्चनङ्गा[28]ञ्च महीञ्च दद्या–

30 त्सा (त् [।।६।।]*सा) मान्योयन्धर्म्मसेतुनृ (नं) पाणा (णां) काले काले पालनीयो भवद्भी (द्भिः) [।*]

31 सर्व्वान्नि (ने) ताम्भा (न्भा) वी (वि) नः पार्थिवेन्द्रा [न्*।।][29] भूयो भूयो याचते रामभद्रः [।।७।।*]

32 इति कमलदलाम्वु (म्बु) वि (बि) न्दुलोला (लां) श्री (श्रि) यमनुचिन्त्य मनुष्यजीव (वि) तञ्च[30] [।*] सक–

33 लमिदमुदाहृतञ्च वु (बु) [द्*]ध्वा न हि पुरुषैः परकीर्तयो विलोप्य (प्याः) ।।[८।।*][31] **प्रवर्द्धमा–**

34 **नविजयराज्यसम्वत्सरे[32] एकादशमे[33] भाद्रपदवदिदी (दि) न[34]**[६][35] [36]महासान्धिविग्रहीकश्री–

Third Plate : Second Side

35 रुद्रदते (त्ते) न[37] देवदत्तस्य सुतेन अयोध्यापुरविनिर्गतेन

36 ल्लि (लि) खी (खि) तमिदं शासा (स) न[म्*] ।।⊙।।[38] यदि आक्षरपरी भ्रष्टं[39] मात्राहीनस्तु[40] यद्भे (द्भवेत्) [।*] क्षान्तमरहशीविद्वाङस कस्य न

37 स्खलते मन[ः*]।। [41][९।।*]

Seal[41a]

1 श्रीमहाभवगुप्त

2 राजदेवस्य

25. Read °मङ्गुलम् । हरन्नरकमायाति.
26. Pandeya: भूर्व्वैष्णवी. Reade either सुवर्ण्णं भूर्व्वैष्णवी or सुवर्ण्णम्भूर्व्वैष्णवी.
27. Pandeya: सूर्यसुताश्च.
28. Read यः काञ्चन°. It is possible that य ⋌ काञ्चन was intended to be written.
29. These *daṇḍas* are superfluous.
30. Pandeya: जीवितञ्च.
31. The floral device seems to indicate the end of the main part of the record.
32. Read संवत्सरे.
33. Read एकादशे.
34. Better read भाद्रपदवदि.
35. The numerical symbol is not visible in the facsimile.
36. Pandeya :महासन्धी [वि] ग्रहीक. Read महासान्धिविग्रहिक.
37. Pandeya: रुद्रदत्तेन.
38. This mark seems to indicate the conclusion of the record.
39. Read यद्यक्षरपरिभ्रष्टं or better यदक्षरपरिभ्रष्टं.
40. Read मात्राहीनञ्च.
41. After the *daṇḍa* we have a rather peculiar mark which appears to be just another concluding mark.

41a. The round seal is 1·6″ in diameter and bears, in the middle, a crudely represented figure of a standing humped, horned bull to right surmounted by a crescent and below it a two-line legend.

ABSTRACT

The charter, which opens with the *siddham* symbol, the well-known Śaiva formula paying obeisance to god Śiva[42] and the word *svasti*, was issued from the great victorious camp[43] pitched up at **Kisarakella**[44] by the king **Mahābhavagupta,** who is given the usual titles *Paramamāheśvara, Mahārājādhirāja—Parameśvara-Paramabhaṭṭāraka*,[45] *Soma-kula-tilaka* and *Trikaliṅgādhipati* and is said to have meditated upon the feet of his mother and father.[46]

The inscription records that on the occasion of the *Siṁha-saṅkrānti* the king, after honouring the Brāhmaṇas at Liñjiragrāma[47] included in the Pṛthurā-*bhukti*[48] gave away the village (Liñjira) in favour of a Brāhmaṇa,[49] who was a son of Cakradhara, belonged to the Kapiṣṭhala *gotra* and the Vasiṣṭha *pravara*, and was a student of the Maitrāyaṇī *śākhā* (of the Black *Yajurveda*), an immigrant from a place called Madhura[50] in Madhyadeśa and a resident of Ullakheṭa.[51] The king's order concerning the grant was addressed to the agriculturist householders residing in the village as well as all the royal officers including the *Samāhartṛ, Sannidhātṛ, Dāṇḍapāśika, cāṭas, bhaṭas* and the royal favourites, and the grant carried with it the usual privileges including the right to the *nidhis, upanidhis, daśāparādhas*, exemption from the entry of the *cāṭas* and *bhaṭas* and levying all the *uparikaras* and taxes. The villagers were ordered to pay the donee the *bhoga, bhāga, kara, hiraṇya*, etc., as due.

42. Even though the Somavaṁśin kings were devout worshippers of Śiva and are styled *Paramamāheśvara*, this formula is not met with in any other epigraph of the dynasty.
43. Original *mahā-vijaya-kaṭaka*. In no other record of the dynasty the camp is called great.
44. The same is the modern village of Kesarkelā, about six miles to the east of Bolangir, Bolangir District.
45. In all other official charters of the dynasty the word *paramabhaṭṭāraka* is the first component of the regal title.
46. In other official records of the Somavaṁśins the ruling chief is described as meditating upon the feet of his rather who is mentioned by name with practically the same titles as are employed for the ruler himself. In no other record of the dynasty the king is said to have meditated upon the feet of his mother. The non-specification of the king's royal predecessor is typical of this record.
47. It has been identified with the village of the same name close to Baramakelā in the erstwhile Sarangarh feudatory state.
48. Pṛthurā, after which the *bhukti* was named, has been identified with the present-day Pithoṛā in the Padampur tract, some forty-five miles to north-west of the Sambalpur town.
49. The Brāhmaṇa is called simply Bhaṭṭa. Whether it was his personal name or a title indicating his scholarship, cannot be ascertained. If the latter was the case, it will have to be assumed that the personal name has been dropped, evidently due to oversight.
50. Not identified. But perhaps the celebrated city of Mathura in Uttar Pradesh is intended.
51. It may be the present Ulakhara village in the erstwhile Sarangarh feudatory state, about 20 miles to the west of Liñjira.

Next follows the usual request to the future ruling chiefs to maintain the grant, and eight imprecatory and benedictive stanzas, reportedly taken from the Dharmaśāstra, are quoted.

The record is dated on the **sixth day of the dark fortnight of the month of Bhādrapada in the eleventh year of the increasingly victorious reign (of Mahābhavagupta).**[52]

The epigraph was written by the *Mahāsāndhivigrahika* Rudradatta,[53] son of Devadatta and an immigrant from Ayodhyāpura.[54]

The record concludes with a verse which seems to crave the indulgence of the learned for errors of omission and commission that may have crept in the text.

52. The date is here indicated partly in words and partly in figures.
53. He is mentioned in *supra*, IV:XXI and XXII also. From this inscription we know that Devadatta was Siṁhadatta's brother whose son Rudradatta is said to have been in above, IV: XXI.
54. Probably modern Ayodhyā in the Faizabad District of Uttar Pradesh.

IV : XXV

NAVAMUNI CAVE INSCRIPTION OF MAHĀBHAVAGUPTA IV UDDYOTAKESARIN, YEAR 18

Provenance: Inner side of the architrave of the Navamuni Cave on the Khaṇḍagiri hill, Puri District, Orissa.

References: J.D.M. Beglar, *ASR*, xiii, 85, note (Cunningham's rendering); R. D. Banerji, *EI*, xiii, 165—66 and Pl. III. 14; Bhandarkar's List, No. 1573.

Language: Sanskrit.

Script: Northern class of alphabets.

Date: Regnal year 18. Latter half of the eleventh century A.D.

TEXT[1]

1 सिद्धम्[2] [।*] श्रीमदु[द्*]द्योतकेसरिदेवस्य प्रवर्द्धमाने विजयराज्ये सम्व (संव) त् १८

2 श्री आर्यसंघप्रतिव (ब) द्धग्रहकुलविनिर्गतदेशीगणआचार्य [3]श्रीकुलचन्द्र–

3 भट्टारकस्य तस्य शिष्यसु (शु) भचन्द्रस्य ।।[4]

ABSTRACT

The inscription purports to register some pious act, evidently in connection with the Navamuni cave, performed by Śubhacandra, the disciple of Kulacandra, an *ācārya* of the Deśī *gaṇa*, derived from the Graha *kula* attached

1. From Pl. III. 14, facing p. 166, in *EI*, xiii.
2. Banerji: Oṁ. Expressed by a symbol.
3. Read देशिगणाचार्य.
4. After this the impression shows some traces of scribbling which is evidently due to visitors to the cave and has nothing to do with the original record. But the device comprising two circles (or dots) placed one over the other and followed by a hollow vertical stroke with a short hollow triangle attached in the middle on left: <[]

   Must be taken as belonging to the original record and as marking its conclusion. The same mark is found in Pl. iii.xv*b* also.

   In his *Chronology of the Bhauma-Karas and Somavaṁśis of Orissa*, 55, K.C. Panigrahi has proposed an amended reading and translation of the inscription. In line 2 he reads *grahdvāla* and *ṛśi(ṣi)gaṇa* in place of *grahakula* and *deśigaṇa* respectively. In place of *ācārya* he proposes to read *āvā[sā*]ya*. According to him the epigraph registers the causing of the excavation of the cave temple by Śubhacandra for the abode of the sages belonging to the Āryasaṅgha and coming from Garhwal. At the end he finds reference to one cave temple.

   However, the amendations in the reading and corresponding alterations in the meaning suggested by Panigrahi are quite untenable.

to the illustrious Ārya *saṅgha*, in the **eighteenth year of the prosperous and victorious reign of the illustrious Uddyotakesarideva.**[5]

5. In his translation of the record, Banerji takes the description of Kulacandra in the second line to mean, '(who) belonged to the Graha Kula, of the illustrious Ārya congregation (and belonged. to) the Deśigaṇa'. The editor, F.W. Thomas, suggested certain corrections to Banerji's rendering which have been adopted in these pages.

Another inscription of Śubhacandra has been found incised on the partition between the two inner chambers in the Navamuni Cave. (*EI*, xiii, 166, No. XV). Although there is no mention of Uddyotakesarin, the record must belong to his reign or thereabouts. It consists of two parts. The first part is imcomplete as it contains only an incomplete sentence, *viz.*, *Śrīdhara-chātra* = the student of Śrīdhara, about whom we have no other information. The second part comprises three lines of writing and seems to record a pious act performed by a certain Vīja, a pupil of Khalla Śubhacandra, who was himself the disciple of the illustrious *ācārya* Kulacandra. The record runs as follows:—

१ सिद्धम् [।*] श्री आचार्यकुलचन्द्रस्य तस्य
२ शिष्यरचेल्लसु (शु) भचन्द्रस्य
३ छात्र वि विजो [।*].

IV : XXVI

BRAHMEŚVARA TEMPLE[1] INSCRIPTION OF MAHĀBHAVAGUPTA IV UDDYOTAKESARIN

Provenance: Brahmeśvara Temple, Bhubaneswar, Orissa.

References: James Prinsep (and Kamalakanta Vidyalankara who prepared the text), *JASB*, vii, 557-62 and plate xxiv;[2] R.L. Mitra, *Antiquities of Orissa*, ii, 87-89; Bhandarkar's List, No. 1572; Binayak Misra, *JBORS*, xvii, 1-24; P. Acharya and D.C. Sircar (ed.), *JRASB, Letters*, xiii, 63-74 and eye-copy on p. 74;[3] S.N. Rajaguru, *IO*, iv, 244-52 and plate facing p. 246.

Language: Sanskrit. In verse except the last line giving details of date.

Metres: Verses 1-4, 7-9, 11, 13, 15 and 16: *Śārdūlavikrīḍita*; Verses 5 and 6: *Vasantatilakā*; Verses 10 and 12: *Sragdharā*; Verse 14: *Mandākrāntā*; Verse 17: *Mālinī*.

Script: Northern class of alphabets.

Date: Regnal year 18, Phālguna śukla 3. Latter half of the eleventh century A.D.

TEXT[4]

1 सिद्धम्[5] [।*] ओम्[5a] [।*] ब्रह्मोपेन्द्रमहेश्वरेन्द्रबलि [भी रज्जू कृता]हीश्वरै र्भ्रा*]
म्यन्मन्दरपर्व्वतेन [मथितात् क्षीरोदधेर्मध्यतः ।
विस्फीतामतकौ]मुदीभि[र]खिलं[त्रै][लो*]क्यमुद्द्योतय[न्राजेन्दुः सकला सम*]
2 ग्रवसतिः सार्द्धं श्रिया जातवान् ।। [१।।*]
तद्व[ङ्शेजनि[6] शुभ्रकीर्त्तिरतुलो वि*]श्वम्भ[रावल्लभो]
रा[जा श्री*] [जनमे]जयः [स रिपुहा भू]त[स्त्रिलि]ङ्गाधिपः[7] ।

1. The stone bearing this inscription originally belonged to the Brahmeśvara temple at Bhubaneswar. It was removed from Bhubaneswar and deposited in the the Museum of the Asiatic Society of Bengal, Calcutta, and later, in 1837, returned to Bhubaneswar. Its whereabouts are now unknown.
2. The text was deciphered by Kamalakanta Vidyalankara and the translation was provided by Sarada Prasad.
3. The paper was edited and revised by D.C. Sircar.
4. From eye-copy in *JRASB, Letters*, xiii.
5. Expressed by a symbol. The fact that this symbol is followed by the symbol for *om* seems to indicate that the symbol normally found at the beginning of a vast number of inscriptions stands for *siddham*.

5a. Expressed symbolically.

6. Read तद्वंशे°.
7. Sircar states that the eye-copy published by Prinsep probably suggests the reading स्त्रिलिङ्गाधिपः; but it appears that the tracing was influenced by Vidyalankara's

दन्ता[8][दन्तिक][राकरिश्रममिषाद् भग्ने रिपूषां*]
3 द्विपे
य: कुन्ताग्रहतौड्रदेशनृपतेर्ल्म[क्ष्मीं][समाकृष्टवान् ।।] [२।।]
[तत्सूनु:[9] सु*] भटारिराजरमणी[10]सीमन्त[विभ्रान्तिहृ–
द्विरव्यातो नयविक्रमादभु]त[मति:] [सप्ताङ्गराज्येश्वर: ।
बाल्यादक्षतवैधकर्म्म*]–
4 चरितस्त्यागी महाधार्म्मिको
राजा शौर्यमयो यया[तिरभवंद यो*][11] मेदिनीमण्डन: ।। [३।।*]
तस्यान्ते क[लि]कालकल्प[विट]पी भूपाल[चू]डाम[ण*]–
र्म्म[र्य*][दा][मृतसत्व(त्त्व)[धैर्यक*]मला[गा*][म्भी][र्यरत्नकर: ।*]
5 माङ्गल्योदयशक्तिसिद्धिविदुर: प्रख्यातकीर्त्ति:[सदा*]
[र]ाजा भी[म*]रथो[12] महारथगुण: शूरो बभूवारिहा ।। [४।।*]
तस्मादजय्य भुजव [ज्र]विनि[र्जि]ता[रि]–
रु(रू)[र्ज]स्वल: परशुराम इव द्वि[तीय]: ।
6 मध्यन्दिनार्क इव तीव्रतरप्रतापो
राजा बभू[व भु*]वि धर्मरथोग्रवीर]:[13] ।। [५।।*]
तस्मिन गते दिवमपुत्रिणि राजमल्ले
नाना भटैरु [पहते] सकलेपि राष्ट्रे ।
देशान्तरस्थितव[ति प्रब]ल–
7 प्रवीरे
काल: कियानगमदत्र यथाकथञ्चित् ।। [६ ।।*]
त[त्र श्री[14]*] जनमेजयस्य तनयो भूत: प्र[सि]द्ध: क्षितौ
सर्व्वत्रापि विचित्रवीर इति यस्तस्मादजन्यात्मज: ।
धन्योसा[व]भिमन्युरित्यतिबली
8 तस्यो[प]तेजा: सुत:

---

reading. This reading goes against certain known facts of history. Even if it is accepted, one may suggest an expression like पराभूतस्त्रिलिङ्गाधिप: to indicate 'one who has defeated the king of Striliṅga (Triliṅga)'.

8. As pointed out by Sircar, the reading दत्ता° is not supported by the eye-copy.
9. This restoration (i.e. तत्सूनु:) is suggested by Sircar in preference to तस्यान्ते proposed by Acharya as the latter expression actually occurs at the beginning of the next verse.
10. Vidyalankara's reading was सम्राड्भर्त्तरिराजकम्रमणी which does not yield any satisfactory meaning.
11. This reading, suggested by Acharya in place of Vidyalankara's ययातिनृपवद्यो is preferable as it gives better meaning.
12. Vidyalankara read दीर्घरवो which, as pointed out by Acharya, is not borne out by the facsimile print.
13. Vidyalankara's reading was राज बभूव कविधर्मपरोपवार:. The last three letters of the verse were read as प्रतीत: by Acharya. But as pointed out by Sircar, this reading is rendered improbable by the change of *visarga* into *o* in the preceding letter *tho*. The reading adopted here has been suggested by Sircar.
14. This restoration, which has been suggested by Sircar in place of ततोपि of Acharya, is adopted here as it gives better meaning. Moreover, ततोपि would offend the metre.

8 श्रीचण्डीहर इत्यभून्नरप[तिः*]स्सर्व्वैरमात्यैः कृतः ।। [७।।*]
भत्यामात्यसुहृत्प्रजाश्रितजनज्ञातीष्टबन्धून्यथा–
योगं सम्परिपाल्य राष्ट्रमुभयं निष्कण्टकीकृत्य यः ।
9 भूतोनेकनरेन्द्रशेखरमणिप्रोद्ग[च्छ*] दङ्शु[15] [च्छटा लोको*]द्भासितपादप[द्मयुग] लः
स[र्व्वावनी*] [वन्दि]तः [16]।। [८।।*]
श्रीमानाचतुरब्धिसीमव[सु[धा च[क्रै]करक्षामणिम्मर्मान्धातेव पृथूपमो
10 भरतवद्राजा जगज्जित्वरः ।
सूर्याचन्द्रम [सोः] [समैर्न्नि*] जकरैरुद्दीपयन्रोद [सी] पूर्व्वाद्रिः सवितेव सू [नु] रुदगादु-
द्द्योतकः केसरी ।।[९।।*]
बालक्रीडाभिरेव प्रतिभटमखिलं डाहलं चोड्र-गौडौ[17]
11 युद्धे सन्नद्धयोधद्वि [रदबल*] घटास [ङ्ग] [र यो वि*] जित्य ।
उद्दृप्ताक्षौहिणीपद्गु [रु] गतिविनमद्भूभराका [क्रा] न्तपृ [थ्वी][18]
[राज्ञः] कुर्व्वन्नशेषानवनतशिरसो जिष्णुरुर्व्वीमजै (षीत्) ।।[१०।।*]
12 तन्माता दिनकृत्कुलस्य दुहिता **कोलावती** नामतो
[यासौ*] शीतकरान्वयस्य महिषी दू [दु] र्गेवल[क्ष्मी] रिव ।
यस्याः कीर्त्तनमूर्द्धसु[19] ध्वजत्रयो वात्याभिरूद्र्ध्वङ्गतो
हस्ताभः शशिलक्ष्म लोप्तुमिव
13 रवे सोत्साहमुद्गच्छति ।। [११।।*]
श्रीमद्ब्रह्मेश्वरस्य प्रण [तमल*] [हृ] तः स्पर्शतो मुक्तिदस्य
प्रासादोम्रङ्क शाग्रस्तरणिरथरयव्या [हृ] ति स्थाणुकल्पः ।
एकाम्रे सिद्धतीर्थे चतुरमरकुली [चारू] शाला-
14 समेतः
कोलावत्या तयैष [:*] क्षितिमुकुटनिभः [कारितः*] कीर्तिराजः ।।[१२।।*]
लोकालोकमहीध्रसप्तजलधिद्वीपस्थलीपिण्डिका
मध्यस्था (यु)कमेरुलिङ्गमुपरि ब्रह्माण्डहेमालयम् ।
15 गङ्गाद्भिः स्नपयन्नहर्निशमसौ देर्वा [स्त्रलोकी] [पति
ब्रं*] ला स्वचर्चति यं शिवं स भगवान् ब्रह्मेश्वरोय[20] म्विभुः[21] ।।[१३।।*]
अर्द्धंवभ्राजत्ककनककलशोत्तिष्ठदङ्शू[22]त्करार्चिच-
दी (दो) प्रा (पा) लोकप्रस[रक्त्त*]-

15. Read °दंशु°.
16. नन्दनः is Vidyalankara's reading. Sircar points out that such of the traces as are legible, support neither the reading of Vidyalankara nor that of Acharya (i.e. वन्दितः).
17. Acharya's reading सिंहलं चोड्रगौडौ is not borne out by the eye-copy which clearly supports Vidyalankāra's reading adopted in these pages.
18. Sircar observes that the use of the three synonyms *bhū, pṛthvī* and *urvī* in the same stanza would make the suggested reading rather doubtful.
19. Acharya: मूद्ध्र्वसु.
20. This letter has been left out by Acharya.
21. Read °यं विभुः.
22. Read °दंशू°.

16 दिक्चक्रवालप्रसादः ।
प्रासा [दो] स्य त्रिदशयु [व] [तीव्रा]* तस [न्ध्य] ाप्र [दीपो]
मूर्छ्वाद्रेः[23] सकलगगनं मण्डयन्नुच्चकास्ति ॥[१४॥*]
रत्नालङ्कृतिभूषिताङ्गसुषमा देदीप्यमाना दि[वः] [क्रीडन्त्य*]
17 स्तडितः स्थिरा इव कुचश्रोणीभरव्याकुला : ।
[सु] [न्दर्योक्षि*] कनीनिकां । इव[24] द्दशामन्तः प्रविष्टा नणा-
मस्मै चञ्चलकर्ण्णजाहनयना[25] दत्तास्तया दारिकाः ॥[१५॥*]
वेद[व्या]करण[ार्थशास्त्रकविता*] –
18 तर्क्कादिविद्याधरो
ब्रह्मेवावितथप्रसन्नवि [नयो*] [द्बु] द्धिर्व्विशुद्धान्वयः ।
ताराधीश्वरवङश[26] जावनिभुजां शुभ्रं यशस्तन्वती–
म्भट्टः श्रीपुरुषोत्तमः कविवरोका [र्षीदिमां वर्णणाम्॥] [१६॥*]
19 सनगवनसमुद्रा मेदिनी याव [दास्ते]
[त्रिभु*] वननिजनेत्रे [पु] ष्पवन्तौ च याव [त्] ।
अतिजगदुपरिस्थो यावदौत्तान [प] ादि-
र्जनवदनसुधेयन्तावद [स्तु] [प्रशस्तिः ॥*] [१७॥*]
20 परममाहेश्वरमहाराजाधिराजसो[27]म [कुलतिल*] [क] त्रिकलिङ्गाधिपति[28] **श्रीमदुद्-
द्योतकेसरिराजदेवस्य विजयराज्ये सम्वत**[29] **१८ फाल्गुन शुदि ३** सूत्रधाररा [ये] [णि
उत्कीर्णम्[30] ॥*]

ABSTRACT

The record opens with the auspicious words *siddham* and *om*, both expressed symbolically, and next is given account of the family to which king **Uddyota-kesarin** belonged. We are told that the moon was born together with the goddess Śrī from the midst of the ocean of milk when it was churned with the Mandara mountain, tied with the lord of serpents[31] serving as the churning rope, by gods Brahmā, Upendra (Viṣṇu), Maheśvara (Śiva), Indra and the demon Bali (v. 1). In his (moon's) lineage was born king Janamejaya, the lord of Triliṅga,[32] who seized the fortune of the king of the Oḍra country who was killed in a battle by spear after his elephants had been destroyed (v.2). He was succeeded by his son Yayāti, who is described in vague terms

23. Acharya reads मूद्र्ध्वेवाद्रेः.
24. Read °कामिव.
25. Vidyalankara read चञ्चलखञ्जनाभनयना.
26. Read वंश°.
27. In the eye-copy this letter looks like *sye*.
28. Vidyalankara read सोमवंशोद्भवभूपति which is not borne out by the portion preserved in the eye-copy.
29. Read संवत्.
30. This restoration is due to Acharya. Vidyalankara had read स्या/स्ये at the end of the record.
31. *I.e.* Vāsuki.
32. Obviously an error for Trikaliṅga.

(v. 3).[33] After the end of his reign came king Bhīmaratha, about whom absolutely no information of historical interest is given (v. 4). From him sprang king Dharmaratha, who was, as it were, a second Paraśurāma (v. 5). After that Rājamalla[34] had expired sonless, the entire kingdom was laid waste by the various warriors and a little time somehow elapsed (v. 6). Thereafter all the ministers installed Caṇḍīhara, son of Abhimanyu, grandson of Vicitravīra and great-grandson of Janamejaya,[35] as king (v. 7). He ruled properly and freed both the kingdoms[35a] from disturbances. His lotus-feet shone with the rays emanating from the crest-jewels of numerous chiefs (v. 8). Next came his son **Uddyotaka Kesarin (i.e. Uddyotakesarin)**, who was the sole protecting gem (*rakṣā-maṇi*) of the circle of the earth bounded by the four oceans and a conqueror of the earth comparable to Māndhātṛ, Pṛthu and Bharata (v. 9).[36] He defeated, as if in a childish sport, the entire armies of Ḍāhala, Uḍra and Gauḍa, subdued all the kings and conquered the earth (v. 10).

His (Uddyotakesarin's) mother, Kolāvatī by name, was a descendant[37] of the lineage of the Sun and the chief queen of the family of the Moon (*i.e. Soma-kula*) and was verily like the goddesses Durgā and Lakṣmī (v. 11). That Kolāvatī caused to be erected a lofty shrine of god Brahmeśvara, the remover of the dirt (*i.e.* sin) of one paying obeisance and grantor of salvation at touch, accompanied by four miniature shrines (*catur=amara-kulī*), on the spot called Siddhatīrtha at Ekāmra[38] (v. 12). It is said that the God is the same as Śiva (i.e. *liṅga*) whose pedestal is formed by the Lokāloka mountain, the seven oceans and islands,[39] at whose centre stands the Meru mountain, whose peak is formed by the Hemālaya (*i.e.* Himālaya) mountain,[40] and whom god Brahmā, the lord of the three regions, worships with the waters of the river Gaṅgā day and night (v. 13). The temple was adorned with golden pinnacles (v. 14). Kolāvatī also made over to the temple some beautiful maids decked with gem-set ornaments (v. 15).

33. According to the restored reading, he was the lord of the *saptāṅga rājya*, *i.e.*, kingdom endowed with seven limbs. For the seven limbs of a state, see *Kauṭilīya Arthaśāstra*, vi.1.1; *Manu-smṛti*, ix. 294; *Yājñavalkya-smṛti*, i. 353, etc. Some of the writers give the number of the *aṅgas* as eight. For details, see P.V. Kane, *HDS*, iii, 17; A.S. Altekar, *State and Government in Ancient India*, 39ff.
34. Literally meaning 'a wrestler among the kings', it may have been a *viruda* of Dharmaratha.
35. The word *tanaya* in the original has been rendered as 'a lineal descendant' by Acharya.
35a. *Viz.* Kosala and Utkala.
36. The birth of Uddyotaka Kesarin from Caṇḍīhara is compared to the rising of the sun from the mythical eastern mountain (Pūrvādri).
37. *Duhitṛ* in the original.
38. Ekāmra is the ancient name of Bhubaneswar. It is equally likely that *siddha-tīrtha* is employed here as an adjective of Ekāmra.
39. It is not unlikely that the intention of the poet was to refer to the islands marked out by the seven oceans.
40. In the translation, Acharya unnecessarily inserts the word *liṅga* after Hemālaya which is again erroneously spelt as Himālaya.

This eulogy (*varṇanā*), spreading the fame of the kings born in the family of the lord of stars (*tār-ādhīśvara-vaṁśa, i.e.* moon, was composed by *Bhaṭṭa* Puruṣottama, the best of the poets and well-versed in the Vedas, grammar, *arthaśāstra*, poetry, logic and other disciplines (v. 16). Verse 17 expresses the wish that this *praśasti* may endure as along as the earth with its mountains, forests and oceans, the sun and the moon and the *auttānapādi* (pole-star) last.

The inscription gives the following date:[41] **the third day of the bright half of the month of Phālguna in the eighteenth year of the victorious reign of Uddyotakesarin,**[42] who is styled *Paramamāheśvara, Mahārājādjhirāja. Trikaliṅgādhipati* (1. 20).

41. The date is indicated in figures.
42. This is based on the restoration suggested by Acharya which has been adopted here.

IV : XXVII

RATNAGIRI PLATES[1] OF MAHĀŚIVAGUPTA V KARṆA, YEAR 6

Provenance: Ratnagiri, Cuttack District, Orissa.

References: Narayana Tripathi, *JBORS*, xvi, 206-10 and plate facing p. 206; Debala Mitra, *EI*, xxxiii, 263-68 and plates opposite pp. 266-68; D.C. Sircar, *ibid.*, 269-74 and plate facing p. 269;[2] S.N. Rajaguru, *IO*, iv, 253-64.

Language: Sanskrit. In a mixture of prose and verse.

Metres: Verses 1, 3-7: *Śārdūlavikrīḍita*; Verses 2, 8, 16: *Vasantatilakā*; Verses 9, 13: *Upajāti*; Verses 10, 12, 17: *Āryā*; Verses 11, 15: *Rathoddhatā*; Verse 14: *Vaṁśastha*; Verses 18-20, 22-27, 30-32: *Anuṣṭubh*; Verse 21: *Indravajrā*; Verse 28: *Śālinī*; Verse 29: *Puṣpitāgrā*.

Script: Northern class of alphabets.

Date: Regnal year 6, Āśvina śukla 12. End of the eleventh or early twelfth century A.D.

TEXT

First Plate[3]

1 सिद्धम्[4] [१*] ज्योत्स्नाशालिसमृद्धिभूः कुमुदिनीहासैकसम्पादनाधूर्तो धूर्ज्जटिमौलिसौ-

2 धवसतिः पीयूषधारागृहं (हम्) । तारान्तःपुरनायको रतिपतेः शस्त्रैकसानोपलः[5] क्षी–

3 रोदार्ण्णवनन्दनो विर्ज (ज)यते देवः सुधादीधितिः ॥[१॥*] अस्यान्वये महति सान्द्रतमः-कलङ्कवि-

4 च्छाय[6]दिग्वलयमार्ज्जनकूर्च्चकस्य[7] । उत्पेदिरे सकलसद्गुणजन्मकन्दाः कुन्दावदातय–

1. The three plates, on which the present charter is engraved, are not of a uniform size. The first plate measures 15.1½″ x 8.9″; the second, 14″ x 8.9″; and the third, 14″ x 8.7;. There is a circular ring-hole, .7″ or .8″ in diameter, bored at the centre of the left margin. The third plate has a raised rim.
2. The part of the record incised on the first plate was edited by Naryana Tripathi and re-edited by D.C. Sircar. The remainder of the inscription engraved on the second and third plates was published by Debala Mitra and interpretations of certain passages were suggested by Sircar.
3. From facsimile in *JBORS*, xvi, and *EI*, xxxiii.
4. Expressed by a symbol which Tripathi takes as standing for ओं सिद्धिः.
5. Tripathi: शाणोपल; Sircar: साणोपलः. Read शाणोपलः.
6. Tripathi: विच्छाप.
7. Tripathi कुच्छकस्य.

5 शसो जर्ग (ग) ती भुजस्ते ।।[२ ।।*] राजा **भूज्जनमेजयोऽथ** नपतिर्ज्ज (र्ज्जा)तो[8] ययाति-स्ततः श्रीमा–

6 न् भीमरथोऽभवत्तदनु च क्ष्माचक्ररक्षामणिः । अष्टास्वेव दिगन्तरेषु विजयस्तम्भाव–

7 लिहु (च्छ) द्भूना हृच्छल्यानि दिशाभुजामपि समारोप्यन्त यैः[9] विस्फुटं (टम्)[10] ।।[३।।*] तस्माद्धर्म्मरथो मनो–

8 रथफलं शीतांशुवंशश्री (श्रि) यो निंस्त्रिशैकसखा शिखामणिरभून्निः शेषभूमीभुजां (म्) । य–

9 स्मिन्दिग्विजयावतार (रि)णि पू (पु)रा विद्वेषिभु (भू)मीभुजः प्रातिष्ठन्त दिगन्तरं तदनु च

10 स्फीताश्चमु (मू) रेणवः ।। [४।।*] सेतूपान्तवनान्तरे हिमवतः पर्यन्त[11] भूशी (सी)मनि प्रागम्भोधित–

11 टीवनेष (षु) कटके पु(पू)र्व्वेतरक्ष्माभृतः । यस्योत्ताम्यदरातिराजयुवतीनिश्वासझञ्झा-

12 निलव्या सङ्गस्वनदन्तरालमुखरैर्ग्गीतं यशः कीचकैः।।[५।।*] भ्राता तस्य व(ब) भूव भूतलपते–

13 र्भू तेशतुल्यप्रभः प्रख्यातं क्षितिभूषणं नघुष[12]इत्युर्व्वीपतीनां पतिः । यद्दोर्दण्डभु–

14 जङ्गमेन विलसन्निस्त्रिस(श)जिह्वाभृता[13]पीतास्ते परिपन्ति(न्थि)पार्थिवचमूकण्ठान्तरे मारुता–

15 ः।।[६।।*] अत्रास्ते करिव(वृ)न्दमुन्मदमिह प्रौढोस्ति पञ्चाननः सन्त्येतासु[14] जगद्द्रुहो गिरिदरीकु–

16 म्भीषु कुम्भीनशा(सा)ः । स्नेहादित्यभिधाय वृद्धशवरीवर्ग्गेण व(ब) द्धाश्रुणा यद्वैरिप्रम-दाजनो वन–

17 भुवः सञ्चारमध्यापितः ।।[७।।*] तस्यानुजो नतस[म]*स्तसपत्नमौलिरत्नात्सुमा त्सलित[15] पादसरो–

18 [जरो][16] चिः । विद्यानिधिः प्रतिनिधिर्म्मधुशू (सू) दनस्य जातोऽथ विश्वविजयी नृपतिर्य-यातिः ।।[८।।*]

Second Plate : First Side[17]

19 भटैरवष्टब्ध(ब्ध)मिदं नरेन्दै राष्ट्रद्वयं कोष(स)लमुत्कलञ्च । अकण्टकं साधयतः समन्ताद्भू (द्रू)जद्व–

8. Tripathi and Sircar: °ज्जातो.
9. Tripathi: जैः.
10. Read **यैर्विस्फुटम्**.
11. Tripathi and Sircar: **पर्य्यन्त**.
12. Read **नहुष** which is the correct form of the name.
13. Tripathi reads °भुता.
14. There is a superfluous stroke after this letter.
15. Read °रत्नांशुसंमिलित° रत्नांशुमांसलित°.
16. These two letters are cut off and have been restored on the basis of the Bālijhari plates of Uddyotakesarin (above, IV: XXII) which also contain this stanza.
17. Text on the second and third plates is edited from the facsimile accompanying Mitra's transcript in *EI*, xxxiii.

20 यं यस्य कृतार्थमासीत् ।।[९।।*] तस्य ततः सुकृतफलं सफलीकृतलोकलोचनस्तनयः । सम–

21 जनि गुणैकसीमा श्रीमानु[द्*] द्योतकेसरी[18] नृपतिः ।।[१०।।*] भक्तिदु(दू)र नतकुन्तलस्खलन्मल्लिकाकुसु–

22 मदामराजयः । ढौकयन्त इव कीर्त्ती(र्त्ति)सन्ततीर्यम्प्रणेमुरभितो महीभुजः ।।[११।।*] तनयस्तस्य न–

23 मस्यन्नरेन्द्रमौलीन्द्रनीलमणिमधुपैः [।*] शृङ्गारितपदपद्मः समजनि जनमेजयो नृपतिः ।।[१२।।*]

24 कृपाणधाराधरधौतवौ(वै)रिभूपालकान्ताम(मृ)गनाभिपङ्कः । वसुन्धरा भारमहाधुरि(री)णदोः काण्ड–

25 निर्भत्सि(र्त्सि)तनागराजः ।।[१३।।*] ततस्तन्(नू)जो मनुजोत्तमोभवत्पुरञ्जयो वैरिपुरञ्जयो नृपः [।*] नमत्क्षि–

26 तीशार्च्चितपादपङ्कजः स्फुरत्सुनासी(शी)रसमानविक्रमः ।। [१४।।*] गौडडाहलकलिङ्गवङ्गजा भूभु–

27 जो भुजनिवारितारयः । तेपि यस्य भुजभारशङ्कया कम्पमानमनिशम्मनो दधु–

28 : ।।[१५ ।।*] तस्यानुजो निजभुजार्ज्जितशौर्यसूर्य प्रौढ प्रभाशमितशत्रुयशः शशाङ्क–

29 : । श्री**कर्ण्णदेवनृ**पति : क्षितिपालमौलिसंलीनरत्नचयचुम्वि(म्बि)तपादपीठः ।।[१६।।*] त्रिभुव–

30 नकुटीरपटले सर्पति निजकीयकीर्त्तिवल्लि(ल्ली)यं(यम्) । यस्यसमुन्नतिभाजं भुजयुगनिःश्रि(श्रे)णि–

31 कां श्रित्वा ।।(१७।।*) स्वस्ति । श्री**ययातिनगरात** (त्) । परममाहेश्वरपरमभट्टारकमहाराजाधि–

32 राजपरमेश्वरसोमकुलतिलकत्रिकलिङ्गाधिपतिश्री**महाशिवगुप्त**राजदेव :

33 कुशली ।[19] उत्तर[19a] तोष(स)लीयव्र(ब्र) ह्मे[20] (?) श्रट्ठावीस[21]खण्ड सं[22] कोणाग्रामः । श्रतस्ततिखण्डीय[23] व्रा (ब्रा) ह्म–

34 णानापूज्य । समाहर्तृ सन्निधातृ-। नियुक्ताधिकारिक-। दाण्डपाशिक-। पिशुनवे(वै)-त्रिकावरोध–

35 [24][ज] न-। राज्ञीराणक-। राजपुत्र-। राजवल्लभ-। भोगिजन-प्रमुखनिवासिसमस्तजनपदान–

36 [नु] नयति वो (बो) धयति समाज्ञापयति [।*] विदितमस्तु भवतां(ताम्) । यथास्माभिरयङ्ग्रामः

18. Rajaguru is wrong in reading at first °केसरि and then proposing to correct it to °केसरी which latter is quite clear in the facsimile.
19. The mark of punctuation here and in most of the cases up to line 45 is superfluous.
19a. Rajaguru: उत्तर°.
20. The reading of this word is very doubtful. Mitra reads *vrahmo* which she doubtfully proposes to correct to *brahme*. Sircar reads it as *vrajme* and doubtfully regards it as an error for *rājye* (*EI*, xxxiii, 273).
21. This is a vernacular form of the Sanskrit word *aṣṭāviṁśa*.
22. *Saṁ* is a contraction of the word *saṁbaddha*.
23. Sircar appears to be right in proposing to correct it to अतस्ततखण्डीय°.
24. The opening letter in this as well as the following line is cut off.

Second Plate : Second Side

37 सजलस्थलः । सगर्त्तोषरः । साम्रमधूकप्रभृतिनानावृक्षः । सनिधिः । सोपनिधि–

38 : । हस्तिदण्ड-। वरव (ब) लीवर्द्द-। चिट्टोल-। अन्धारुआ-। प्रत्यन्धारुआ-। अदत्ता-। पदाति-जीव्य-। अ–

39 न्तरावड्डि-। रिन्तकावड्डि-। वसावकी-। विषयाली-। आ (अ) हिदण्ड-। हलदण्ड-। व(ब) न्धदण्ड । वन्दापना–

40 । विजय-वन्दापनाप्रभृतिनानामार्ग्गणीसमेत भविष्यत्करसहितः । सखण्डपालीयः ।

41 सर्व्वंवा(बा)धावार्ज्जितः । सर्व्वोपरिकर(रा)दानसहितः । चतुःसीमावच्छिन्नः । उत्कलदेशीयश्री–

42 सलोणपुरमहाविहारविनिर्ग्गतायै । कास्य(श्य)पसगोत्रायै । त्र्यार्षप्रवरायै । उदयम–

43 तीनाम्न्याः पौत्र्ये । महारी[25] माहूणदेवि(वी) नाम्न्याः पुत्र्यै । राणीश्रीकर्प्पूरश्रीनाम्नौ (म्न्यै) । सलि–

44 लधारापुरस्सरं(रम्) । आचन्दा (न्द्रा) र्क क्षितिसमकालोपभोगार्थं (र्थम्) । मातापित्रोरा-त्मनश्च पु–

45 ण्ययशोभिवृद्धये । ताम्रशासनेनाकरीकृत्य । सम्प्रदत्त इत्यवगत्य । समुचि–

46 तकर भागभोगमुपनयद्भिभ(र्भ)वद्भिः सुखेन प्रतिवस्तव्यमिति । भाविभिश्च भूपति–

47 भिर्द्दत्तिरियमस्मदीया। धर्म्मगौरवादस्मदनुरोवा(धा) च्च स्वदत्तिरिवानुपालनीया।[25a] तथा

48 चोक्तन्धर्म्मशास्त्रे ॥ व (ब) हुभिव (र्व)सुधा दत्ता राजभिः सगरादिभिः । यस्य यस्य यदा भू–

49 मिः(मि)त (स्त)स्य तस्य तदा फलं (लम्) ॥ [१८॥*] मा भूदफलशङ्का वः परदत्तेति पार्थिवाः । स्वदत्तात्फल–

50 मानन्त्यं परदत्ता(त्ता) नुपालने ॥[१६ ॥*] षष्टि वर्षसहस्राणि स्वर्ग्गे मोदति भूमिडः । आक्षेप्ता

51 चानुमन्ता च द्वौ तौ नरकगामिनौ ॥ [२० ॥*] अग्नेरपत्यं प्रथमं सू (सु)वर्ण्णं भूर्व्वैष्णवी सूर्यसू (सु) ता–

52 श्च गावः । यः काञ्चनं गाञ्च महीञ्च दद्यात् ।[26] दत्तास्त्रयस्तेन भवन्ति लोकाः ॥[२१॥*] आस्फोट [य][27]–

53 न्ति पितरो वल्गयन्ति पितामहाः । भूमिदाता कुले जातः स नस्त्राता भविष्यति ॥[२२॥*] भू[मिं]–

54 यः प्रतिगह्णाति यश्च भूमिं प्रयच्छति । उभौ तौ पुण्यकर्म्माणौ नियतं स्वर्ग्गगामि [नौ ॥] [२३ ॥*]

25. Sircar states that this letter may also be read as *cī* and the name in question may thus have been Mahācīmā (*ibid.*, 267, fn. 3). In view of the close similarity between the forms of *r* and *c* there is no difficulty in accepting this suggestion. However, elsewhere (*ibid.*, 272) he accepts the reading given above and regards *mahārī* as an adjective of Māhūṇadevī.

25a. This *daṇḍa* is superfluous.

26. Read दद्याद्. The mark of punctuation is redundant.

27. An *akṣara* each at the end of lines 52-54 is cut off.

Third Plate

55 तडागानां सहस्रेण वाजपेयशतेन च । गवां कोटिप्रदानेन भूमिहर्त्ता न शु–

56 ध्यति ।।[२४ ।।*] हरति(ते) हारयेद्यस्तु[28] मन्दवु(बु)द्धिस्तमोवृतः । सुव(ब)द्धो वारूणैः पाशैस्त्रि(स्ति)य(र्य) ग्योनिं

57 स गच्छति ।।[२५ ।।*] स्वदत्ताम्परदत्ताम्वा[29] यो हरेत(त)वसुन्धरा[म्*] । स विष्ठायां कृमिभू (र्भू)त्या(त्वा) पितृभिः सह

58 पच्यते ।। [२६।।*] गामेका (कां) स्वर्ण्णमेकञ्च भूमेरप्यद्ध (र्द्ध)मङगुलं (लम्) । हरन (न्न)रकमायाति यावदाहू(भू)–

59 तस(सं) प्लवः (वम्) ।। [२७।।*] सामान्योयं धर्म्मसेतुन्न (र्न्नृ) पा(पा)णां काले काले पालनीयो भवद्भिः । सव्वा (र्व्वा) नेतान् (न्)

60 भाविनिः पार्थिवेन्दा (न्द्रा) न् भूयो भूयो याचते रामभद्रः।। [२८ ।।*] इति कमलदलाम्वु (म्बु)वि(बि)न्दुलोला(लां)

61 श्रियमनुचिन्त्य मनू (नु)ष्य[30] जीवितञ्च [।*] सकलमिदमुदाहृतञ्च वु (बु)द्ध्वा न हि पुरुषैः परकीत्त(र्त्त) यो

62 विलोप्याः ।। [२९।।*] यज्द(द्)ण्ड[31] मण्डलाग्रेण खैण्डितैरहितैरयं(यम्) । सू(सु) नासी[32] रोऽर्थवान् पुथ्यी[33] पात्रे य—

63 त्र वसुन्धरा।। [३०।।*] यस्यवु(बु)द्धिव(ब) लाल्लक्ष्मीरेकपत्नीव(व्र)तर्स्थि(स्थि) ता[34] [।*] स श्रीमान् कृष्णदेवोभू [द*] भूप–

64 तेः सन्धिविग्रही ।। [३१।।*] महाक्षपटली श्रीमान (न्) वीरश्छित्तल्लदेवकः । सोलीलिखत्

65 खलानन्दनाशन[35]स्ताम्रशासनं (नम्) ।। [३२।।*] परममाहेश्वरपरमभट्टारकमहाराजाधि–

66 राजपरमेश्वर श्रीमत्**कर्ण्णराजदेवस्य प्रवर्द्धमानविजयराज्ये । सट (षष्ठ) सम्व (संव) त्सरे। आ–**

67 **शि(श्वि)न शुविद्वादश्यां(याम्) । अङ्के स (सं)म्व(व) त्**[36] **आश्विन शुदि १२** स्वर्ण्ण-वीथिप्रतिव(ब)द्धसुन्नहि[37]विज्ञानि–

28. Read हरेत हारयेद्यस्तु or हरते हारयते यस्तु.
29. Better read स्वदत्तां परदत्तां वा.
30. Mitra: मनुष्य°.
31. Mitra reads *pahṛṇḍa* and states that the first *akṣara* may also be read as *ya* and the second as *jṛ* or *ju*. According to her, this is an error for *pracaṇḍa*.
32. Mitra and Rajaguru: °सिरो°.
33. There being little distiction between *p* and *y* and between the medial signs for *ā* and ī, the word may also be read as *yuthyā*. Sircar reads *puthvī* and proposes to correct it to *pṛthyāḥ*.
34. The corrections adopted here are those suggested by Sircar. According to Mitra, the intended reading is °पत्नीव तत्स्थिता which is equally probable.
35. Rajaguru thinks that खलानन्ददासेन should probably be the correct reading. This suggestion is simply absurd.
36. As pointed out by Sircar, the figure looks more like 5. But in view of the definite reading *saṭa* (= 6) in the previous line, there is no alternative but to take it as 6.
37. As stated by Sircar (*ibid.*, xxxiii, 268, fn. 7; 273), the first letter may alternatively be read as *sva*.

68 शङखुकेन[38] ताम्रशासनमिदमुत्कीर्णमिति [।।*]

ABSTRACT

The first eleven stanzas following the *siddham* symbol giving an account of the reigns of the kings Janamejaya (Mahābhavagupta I), Yayāti (Mahāśivagupta I), Bhīmaratha (Mahābhavagupta II), Dharmaratha (Mahāśivagupta II), Naghuṣa, Yayāti (Mahāśivagupta III) and Uddyotakesarin (Mahābhavagupta IV) have been copied from the Bālijhari plates of Uddyotakesarin (*supra*, IV: XXII). The next six verses, which are not found in any other record, describe the history of the dynasty after Uddyotakesarin up to the time of **Karṇṇa**, the donor of the grant. It is said that Uddyotakesarin's son was king Janamejaya whose lotus-feet were adorned by the bees that were the blue jewels decorating the heads of the chiefs bowing down in the act of paying obeisance (v. 12). His sword resembled clouds in as much as it washed away the decorations of the women of the enemy kings made with musk-paint and he threatened[39] the Nāga king by his staff-like arms eminently capable of bearing the burden of the earth (v. 13).[40]

Thereafter came his (Janamejaya's) son king Purañjaya, the best of men and the conqueror of the cities of the enemies, whose lotus-feet were worshipped by the chiefs saluting him and who rivalled Indra in prowess (v. 14). Even the minds of the kings of Gauḍa, Ḍāhala, Kaliṅga and Vaṅga, who had kept at bay their enemies by the valour of their arms, constantly trembled because of the fear of the prowess of his arms (v. 15).

Purañjaya was succeeded by his younger brother king **Karṇṇa** who, by the mature lustre of the sun of the valour acquired by his own arms, extinguished the moon that was the fame of his enemies and whose foot-stool was kissed by the multitude of jewels set on the heads of kings (v. 16). The creeper of his fame, having betaken itself to his ladder-like exalted pair of arms, creeps upon the roof of the cottage of the three worlds[41] (v. 17).

Next is mentioned **Yayātinagara** whence the grant was issued by the king **Mahāśivagupta** who is styled *Paramamāheśvara, Paramabhaṭṭāraka, Mahārājādhirāja-Parameśvara, Somakulatilaka* and *Trikaliṅgādhipati*. The epigraph records the grant of the village of Koṇā[42] situated in the Brahme-

38. शङ्कुकेन appears to be the intended reading.
39. *Nirbhartsita* in the original may also mean 'surpassed'.
40. It is difficult to ascertain if the reference to the Nāga king has any historical significance.
41. The idea is that his fame spread in all the three worlds.
42. It is not possible to identify it definitely. But at a distance of about three miles from Ratnagiri, the findspot of the record, there is a village Anikoṇā which may represent ancient Koṇā.

Aṭṭhāvīsa *khaṇḍa*[43] of Uttara Tosali[44] in favour of *Rāṇī* Karpūraśrī[44a], grand-daughter of a lady called Udayamatī[45] and daughter of the lady named Mahārī Māhūṇadevi,[46] who hailed from the *mahā-vihāra* of Saloṇapura[47] situated in Utkala *deśa* and belonged to the Kāśyapa *gotra* having three *pravaras.*[48] The grant was made after worshipping the Brāhmaṇas of the *khaṇḍa* in question[49] and bestowed upon the grantee right to waters and lands, pits and barren lands, various trees like mango and *madhūka*, *niddhis*,

43. It is difficult to be sure if the modern village of Brahmapur, 1½ miles north-east of Ratnagiri, has anything to do with the Brahme-Aṭṭhāvīsa *khaṇḍa*. It is not improbable that it was the chief place of the sub-division comprising twenty-eight villages.
44. Roughly corresponding to the modern Ballasore District and parts of the Cuttack and Mlidnapur Districts.
44a. As indicated by the title *Raṇī*, Karpūraśrī was perhaps the wife of some feudal chief or more probably a queen or concubine of king Karṇa. The non-mention of the name of her husband appears to favour of the second alternative.
45. Mitra takes the word *pautrī* in the original to mean 'the daughter of the son of' and naturally regards Karpūraśrī as the daughter of the son of Udayamatī. But, as pointed out by Sircar, the description of Karpūraśī as the grand-daughter of a woman and daughter of another woman and the non-mention of the names of her father and grandfather appear to indicate that she was born of a harlot. Harlots are known to have been mentioned similarly in some other records also (*IA*, x, 103; xi, 125; *SII*, x, no. 249).
46. Mitra splits the name as Mahārīmā-Hūṇdevī and accordingly takes Karpūraśrī's mother as of Hūṇa origin. According to her, the name is not a pure Sanskrit one which may be due to her Hūṇa origin. But Sircar rightly points out that her name was Māhūṇadevī, the word mahārī being her title. *Mahārī* is evidently the same as Oriya *māhārī* or Prakrit *mehārī* meaning a songstress or dancing girl or a *devadāsī* or harlot. It is thus clear that Māhūṇadevī, who was a harlot or *devadāsī* had, nothing to do with the Hūṇas.
47. As *devadāsīs* are associated with Brahmanical temples and not with Buddhist monasteries, Sircar finds it impossible to believe that the ladies in question originally resided at the great monastery at Saloṇapura. He therefore thinks that *Saloṇapura-mahāvihāra* is here employed as the name of a locality which probably comprised the entire area under the possession of the monastery at Saloṇapura or the village or township around the monastery. The harlots may have been residents of this locality. In our opinion, however, this explanation is uncalled for and the expression in question seems to indicate the association of the *devadāsīs* with the Buddhist establishments in Orissa during the period in question.

    Saloṇapura, evidently the same as Saloṇapur-ādhivāsa in Uttara Tosali referred to in the Neulpur grant of the the Bhauma-Kara chief Śubhakara (*EI*, xv, 2f.), is probably identical with the modern Solaṇapura (20°-53′ N., 86°-11′; E) on the north bank of the Vaitaraṇī, some 2 miles from Jajpur, a town in the Bhadrak Sub-division of the Balasore District.
48. Sircar is of the opinion that Kāśyapa must have been the *gotra* of one of Karpūraśrī's direct female ancestors, who first adopted the profession of a harlot and refers, in this connection, to a Bengali saying that one having no *gotra* can claim the Kāśyapa *gotra*.
49. This follows the acceptance of the emendation (*atas-tat-khaṇḍīya*) suggested by Sircar. Otherwise it will be difficult to explain as to why the king honoured the Brāhmaṇa residents of a *khaṇḍa* different from the one in which the donated village was situated.

upanidhis, the various *mārgaṇīs*[49a] including *hasti-daṇda, varabalīvarda, ciṭṭola,*[50] *andhāruā,*[51] *praty-andhāruā,*[52] *adattā, padāti-jīvya, antarāvaḍḍi, rintakāvaḍḍi,*[53] *vasāvakī,*[54] *viṣayālī,*[55] *ahi-daṇḍa, hala-daṇḍa,*[56] *bandha-daṇḍa, vandāpanā,*[57] and *vijaya-vandāpanā* and future taxes[58] and *khaṇḍapālīya,*[59] exemption from all the oppressions as well as the right to levy all the *uparikaras.* The addresses of the royal order regarding the grant were the same as those specified in the Bālijhari[60] plates of Uddyotakesarin. As usual, the grant-land was made tax-free and made over by means of a copper-plate charter. The villagers were asked to pay the donee *kara, bhāga* and *bhoga* as due and thereby live happily.

Twelve stanzas, represented to have been extracted from the Dharmaśāstra, are quoted in support of the entreaty to the future kings for the maintenance of the grant.

Verses 30-31 describe the king's *sandhivigrahin* Kṛṣṇadeva. The first of these stanzas, which is somewhat obscure, seems to state that it was Kṛṣṇadeva who, by killing the enemies, made Karṇṇa the lord of the earth in the real sense and the earth take refuge with a deserving lord. The second verse states that by means of his wisdom he made Lakṣmī behave like a faithful

49a. *Mārgaṇi* as used here is a general revenue term denoting a number of levies some of which are listed in this inscription and has to be distinguished from *mārgaṇika* which is mentioned as a specific cess in the Bālijhari and Sankhameri plates of Uddyotakesarin.
50. The same as *ciṅgola* referred to in the Mahulpara plates of Mahāśivagupta II Dharmaratha (above, IV: XX) and *ciṭṭola* mentioned in the Balijhari and Sankhameri plates of Uddyotakesarin (*supra,* IV: XXII).
51. In the Mahulpara plates of Mahāśivagupta II Dharmaratha and the Balijhari plates of Uddyotakesarin (*supra,* IV: XX and XXII) it is spelt as *andhāruvā.* The same is true of the Sankhameri plates of Uddyotakesarin.
52. The word is spelt as *praty-andhāruvā* in Uddyotakesarin's Balijhari and Sankhameri plates.
53. A levy of an uncertain nature.
54. A revenue term of uncertain connotation. It may perhaps denote a kind of tax collected by the officer (or for his maintenance) called *Vāsāpaka* or *Vāsāvaka* who was probably entrusted with the duty of assigning places of residence to strangers. See *IA*, xii, 189; xiii, 69, fn. 11; *EI*, vi, 292, line 58; *CII*, iv, 141, line 36; 171, line 33; 173, note 1; cxliv.
55. Probably the same as *viṣaya-dāna* of the Gāhaḍavāla records (*EI*, xi, 21; xiv, 196) and *viṣayadānika* or *viṣayādānika* of the Kalacuri inscriptions (*CII*, iv, 390, line 35). The former expression has been taken in the sense of 'a regional tax or taxes realisable from a particular district' (*IEG*, 377) or 'district dues' (L. Gopal, *Economic Life in Northern India*, 63). The official called *Viṣaya-dānika* was probably responsible for collecting this levy.
56. Literallʎ, 'plough-tax'.
57. Probably offerings made while paying visits to the king or landlord; the same as *nazrānā*. See *IEG*, 362.
58. The expression *bhaviṣyat-kara-sahitaḥ* in the original is not met with in any other record of the dynasty.
59. Tax realised for the maintenance of swordsmen. See *ibid.*, 155.
60. As well as Sankhameri.

wife.[60a] The charter was written by the brave Chittalladeva who occupied the office of *Mahākṣapaṭalin* (v. 32).

The record is dated[61] on the **twelfth day of the bright fortnight of the month of Āśvina in the sixth year of the increasingly victorious reign of Paramamāheśvara, Paramabhaṭṭāraka-Mahārājādhirāja-Parameśvara Karṇṇa.**

The inscription was engraved by the artisan Śaṅkhuka, an inhabitant of an area named Sunnahi situated in the goldsmiths' quarters (*svarṇa-vīthi*).[62]

60a. The idea intended to be conveyed is that he made the goddess of royal fortune stay with the king permanently.

61. The date is indicated both in words and figures.

62. *Cf.* Balijhari and Sankhameri plates of Uddyotakesarin which are also said to have been written by the artisans of *suvarṇa-vīthi*. The expression *sunnahi* or *svannahi* is, however, not met with there.

IV : XXVIII

KELGA PLATES[1] OF SOMEŚVARADEVA, YEAR 1

Provenance: Kelga, Bolangir District, Orissa.

References: B.C. Mazumdar, *EI*, xii, 237-42 and plates facing pp. 240 and 241; D.C. Sircar, *ibid.*, xxviii, 322-26; S.N. Rajaguru, *IO*, iv, 268-75.

Language: Sanskrit greatly influenced by the local dialect. In prose except the customary benedictive and imprecatory stanzas.

Metres: Verses 1-6: *Anuṣṭubh*; Verse 7: *Puṣpitāgrā*.

Script: Northern class of alphabets.

Date: Regnal year 1, Māgha (*tithi* is left unspecified). First half of the twelfth century A.D.

TEXT[2]

1. Mazumdar and, following him, Rajaguru call the record Sonpur plates since the plates on which it is incised were found in the erstwhileSonpur State. But it is more reasonable to call them Kelga plates after the findspot.

When originally discovered, there were four plates strung on a circular copper-ring to which was soldered a brass seal shaped like a double-petalled lotus. The ring was found cut open at the lower end in such a manner that all the plates could be taken out of it. Unable to arrange the plates in their proper order, Mazumdar believed that the grant originally consisted of four plates engraved on one side only and that at a later date in place of the second and fourth plates two forged plates incised on both sides were substituted and one concluding line was unnecessarily attempted to be engraved on the reverse of what was originally the third plate. Sten Konow thought it more probable that the original record comprised of three plates one of which, engraved on both sides, was missing (*EI*, xii, 238, fn. 1). D.C. Sircar, who examined the plates, now deposited in the Asutosh Museum of the University of Calcutta, for the first time arranged them in a proper order and found that the three plates of equal size, marked A, B and C by Mazumdar, actually constitute a complete charter of the Somavaṁśin king Someśvara and that plate C is actually its middle or the second plate. Likewise, as pointed out by him, the fourth plate, termed D by Mazumdar, is the second or middle plate of another three-plate charter (*tri-phalī-tāmraśāsana*), and not forged as suggested by Mazumdar.

The plates called A and B generally measure 8″ long and 4″ broad; plate C is about 8[illegible]″ in length and 4[illegible]″ in breadth; and plate D is 7″ long and 4.1/8″ broad.

The seal to which the circular ring is attached is fashioned in the imitation of a lotus. The inner side of the seal is hollow. Its lower external ring consists of fifteen petals, while there are fourteen petals in the middle ring. The seal bears the representation of the seated figure of a goddess, evidently Lakṣmī, with her right arm outstretched to the knee, within the enclosure of a blossoming creeper.

2. From plates in *EI*, xii.

First Plate

1 सिद्धम्[3] [।*] स्वस्ति [।*] **श्रीसुवर्ण्णपुरात**(त्)[4] । ।।[5] परममाहेस्व(श्व)रपरमभ[6]–
2 ट्टारकमहाराजाधिराजपरमेश्वर ।।[7] सोमकुलतिलकत्रि–
3 कलिङ्गाधिपतिश्रीमहाभवत(गु)प्त[8]राजदेवपादानुध्यात ।। श्री–
4 मदुद्ये(द्द्यो)त[9] केसरिराजदेवप्रसादि(दी)कृतकोसलराज्याभिसि(षि)–
5 क्तश्री**अभिमत्यु** (न्यु)[10] दि(दे)वस्यातीतराज्ये ।। परममाहेश्वरप–
6 रमभडा (ट्टा) रक[11] कुम (मा) राधिराजपरमेस्व (श्व) रपश्चिमलङ्काधि–
7 पतिसोमकुलकमलकलिकाविकासभाज्य (स्क) रकुम्व (मा)र[12] श्री–
8 **सोमेश्वर**देवपादाः कुस(श)लिनः ।। उत्तरवाल्लिविषयसं[13]–
9 **केसलोगा**[14]खण्डीय ।। [15]**अत्तेण्डा**ग्रामे ।। प्रतिवासिनो व्रा(ब्रा)ह्म–
10 णपु(पु)रःसरान (न्)[16] ।। भोगिभोगिरूपप्रमुखसमस्त–

Second Plate : First Side

11 जनपदान (न्)[17] यथाकालाध्यायि(सि)नश्च मण्डलपति ।। विषय–
12 पति ।। खण्डपति ।। दाण्डपासि(शि)कादीन (न्) समस्तराजपादोपजीविनो
13 यथार्हं ।। मानय(न्ति) ।। वो(बो)धयन्ति ।। समाष्ण (ज्ञा)पयन्ति[18] [च ।*] विदिमस्तु
14 भवता (तां) ।। उपरिलिखितग्रामोयं ।। प्रसिद्धचतुः सीमावच्छिन (न्नः)
15 सजलस्थलः ।। समत्स्यकच्छपः ।। सविटपारण्यः ।। स–
16 निधिः ।। सोपनिधिश्च ।। साम्व्र(म्र)मधुवनाकीर्ण्णः[19] ।। सुवर्ण्णदण्ड–
17 [20]अहिदण्ड ।। [21]वर्त्मदण्ड ।। वन्दापना ।। विजयवन्दापना ।। तृणोदक–

3. Mazumdar: *Oṁ*. Expressed by a symbol.
4. Mazumdar: °पुरात्.
5. There is one *daṇḍa* to the left of the ring-hole and two to the right. They are, however, superfluous.
6. At the end of this line we have a small *daṇḍa* which is not required.
7. These *daṇḍas* are superfluous. In fact, all the *daṇḍas* up to line 29 are redundant.
8. In view of the description of Mahābhavagupta IV Uddyotakesarin as the son of Mahāśivagupta in the Balijhari and Sankhameri plates, it seems to be an error for Mahāśivagupta.
9. Mazumdar: °द्द्योत°.
10. Mazumdar: °मन्यु°. Sandhi rule would require श्र्यभिमन्यु°.
11. Mazumdar: °भट्टारक°.
12. Sircar: कुमार°.
13. The *akṣara saṁ* is an abbreviated form of *saṁbaddha* and is also met with in the Balijhari plates of Uddyotakesarin (above, IV: XXII) and Ratnagiri plates of Karṇa (above, IV: XXVII).
14. Mazumdar: केसलोरा[ज्य*] °.
15. The observance of *sandhi* rule would have required °खण्डीयात्तेण्डा°.
16. Mazumdar: °सरान्.
17. Mazumdar: °दान्.
18. Sircar: समा [ज्ञा]पयन्ति.
19. Better read आम्रमधुवनाकीर्ण्णः.
20. *Sandhi* rule, if observed, would require °दण्डाहि°.
21. Mazumdar: वन्धदण्ड.

18 सा (शा)सनार्द्धिक ।। चरव(ब)लीवद(र्द) ।। अर्थारुवा[22] ।। प्रत्यार्थारुवा[23] पदातिजी–

19 व्य आदत्ता ।। आतुरावड्डि[24] ।। भविष्यत(त्)करादिसहितः ।। गोगौड–

20 समेतः ।। सखण्डपालनीयः ।। सर्व्वंवा(बा)धाविवर्जित [:*] ताम्व्र(म्र)सा(शा)–

Second Plate : Second Side

21 सनेनाकरीकृत्य ।। सलिलधारापुरः सरं ।। [25]आचन्द्रार्क[क्षि]ति [का]ल–

22 समभोगार्थं ।। [26]मातापित्रोरात्मनश्च पुण्ययसो(शो)भिवृद्धये ।। भगव–

23 न्तं महेस्व (श्व) रभट्टारकमुद्दिस्य(श्य) ।। महासन्धिविग्रडि (हि)[27] र (रा) णकनायकश्री–

24 महीपतिभट्टश्रीअनिरुद्ध ।। अनयोः[28] परिष्णत्न[29] ।। **प्रवर्द्धमानविजयरा–**

25 **ज्ये ।। प्रथमसम्व (संव) त्सरे ।। माद्यमासीय ।। पु (:)(पु) ण्य[30] तिथौ ।।** कुम्मा (मा) रह (हा)रित्र(त)[31] गो–

26 त्राय ।। पञ्चार्षप्रवराय ।। माध्यन्दिनक(का)र्ण्ण[32] (ण्व)सा(शा)खाध्यायिने ।। [33]सावत्थमण्ड–

27 लीय ।। महुवालिवी (वि) निर्गताय ।। कमलपुरवास्तव्याय ।। भट[34](ट्ट)पुत्रल–

28 क्ष्मीधरप्रपौत्राय ।। भट्टजयकरपौत्राय । भट्टविद्याकरपुत्राय

29 भट्टपुत्रउदयकर[35]स(श)म्म(र्म्म)णे[36] सम्प्रदत्तो[37]ऽस्माभिः ।। [38]आत्रेयगोत्रैः ।।

30 आ(त्या)र्ष(र्षे)यप्रवरैः ।। अतोस्य विधेयीभूय यथादीयमानभोगभाग–

31 करनिकरादिकं समुपनयद्भिः भवद्भिः सुखेन प्रतिवस्तव्यं (भा)–

Third Plate : First Side

32 विभिश्च भूपतिभिः [39]दानमिदमस(स्म)दीयं ।।[40] धर्म्मगौरवादस्मदनुरो–

33 धाच्च ।।[40] स्वदानमिवानुपालनीयं (यम्) ।।[40] तथा चोक्तं धर्म्मसा(शा) स्ते (स्त्रे)[41] (।*) भूमिं यः

22. Mazumdar: अन्धारुवा.
23. Mazumdar: प्रत्यन्धारुवा.
24. Observance of *sandhi* rules would require पदातिजीव्यादत्तातुरावड्डि.
25. *Sandhi* rule would require °सरमा°.
26. Mazumdar: °भोगान्तं. Better read °क्षितिसमकाल°.
27. Mazumdar: °विग्रहि.
28. Read °कद्धयोः.
29. Sircar: परिज्ञत्व्य. Read परिज्ञप्त्या.
30. Mazumdar: पूर्ण°.
31. Mazumdar: कुमारहारित्र.
32. Mazumdar: कण्ण.
33. Mazumdar: सावत्थि. *Śrāvastī* seems to be the intended reading.
34. Mazumdar: भट्ट°.
35. Observance of *sandhi* rule would have required °पुत्रोदय°.
36. Mazumdar: °सर्म्मणे.
37. Mazumdar: सम्य[ग्*]दत्तो°.
38. Adherence to the sandhi rule would have changed it to °भिरात्रेय°.
39. *Sandhi* has not been observed. Otherwise it would have become °भिर्दान°.
40. These *daṇḍas* are uncalled for.
41. Mazumdar: °सास्त्रे°

34 प्रतिगह्णाति ॥[42] यस्व[43](श्च) भूमिं प्रयच्छति [।*] उभौ तौ पुण्यकमा(र्मा)णौ[44] नियतं स्वर्ग-

35 गामिनौ ॥ [१ ॥*] आस्फोटयन्ति पितरो वल्क(ल्ग)यन्ति च[45] पितामहाः ॥ (।) भूमि-दाता कु-

36 ले जातः स नस्ता (स्त्रा)ता[46] भविष्यति ॥[२॥*] व(ब) हुति(भि)र्व्वसुधा दत्ता राजभिः सगरादिति(भि): ॥ (।) य-

37 स्य यस्य यदा भूमिस्तस्य तस्य तदा फलं (लम्) ॥[३॥*] मा भूदफलस(श)ङ्का वः परद-

38 त्तेति [47]कीर्त्तनात(त्) ॥ (।) स्वदत्तात्फलमानन्त्यं पददत्तानुपालनात(त्)[48] ॥ (४॥*) स्वदत्तां प-

39 रदत्ताम्वा[49] यो हरे (त*) द्व(व)सुन्धरां (राम्) ॥ (।) स विष्टा(ष्ठा)यां[50] कृमिर्भूत्वा[51] पितृभिः सह

40 पच्यते ॥ (५॥*) गमिकां स्वर्ण्णमेकञ्च भूमेरप्यर्द्धमङ्गुलं(लम्)[।*] हरन्नरकमाया-

41 ति[52] यावदाहू(भू) ति (त)र्स (सं) प्लवं(वम्)[52a] ॥ [६॥*]इति कमलदलाम्बु (म्बु) व (बि)न्द (न्दु) लोलां श्री(श्रि)यमनु-

42 चिन्त्य मनुष्यजीवितञ्च [।*]सकलमिदमुदाहृतं [च*]वु (बु) [द्*]ध्वा न हि सत (त्) पुरु-

Third Plate : Second Side

43 षैः[52b] परकीर्त्तयो वि [लोप्याः ॥] [७॥*] [52c]

ABSTRACT

Inaugurated by *siddham*, indicated by a symbol, and *svasti*, the charter was issued from **Suvarṇapura** by *Kumārā*[52d] **Śomeśvaradeva,** who is styled

42. These *daṇḍas* are unnecessary.
43. Mazumdar: यस्च.
44. Mazumdar: °कर्माणौ.
45. Delete it for the sake of metre. Sircar has altogether left it out.
46. Mazumdar: नस्त्राता.
47. Mazumdar: कीर्त्तनात्. We generally have पार्थिवाः in place of कीर्त्तनात्.
48. Mazumdar: °पालनात्. We generally find °पालने.
49. Read °दत्तां वा.
50. Mazumdar: विष्ठायां.
51. Sircar: °भूंत्वा.
52. Mazumdar: °माप्नोति.

52a. Mazumdar: संप्लवं.

52b. Read पुरुषैः instead of सत(त्)पुरुषैः for the sake of metre.

52c. Sircar points out that this line has suffered from corrosion and that there are traces of a few letters after this but they cannot be deciphered. Probably they contain details of the date and the name of the engraver. It may, however, be pointed out that the details of date, though incomplete, have been given earlier in the record.

52d. The title *kumāra* is not applied to any other Somavaṁśin ruler.

Paramamāheśvara, Paramabhaṭṭāraka-Kumārādhirāja[53], *Parameśvara* and is described as the lord of Paścima Laṅkā[54] (*Paścima-Laṅk-ādhipati*) and as the sun for the blossoming of the lotus-petals that is the Soma-kula.[55] Someśvaradeva is represented to have come to power after the cessation of the rule of the illustrious Abhimanyu who had been installed in the kingdom of Kosala which Uddyotakesarin, who meditated upon the feet of *Paramamāheśvara, Paramabhaṭṭāraka-Mahārājādhirāja-Parameśvara, Soma-kula-tilaka, Trikaliṅgādhipati* Mahābhavagupta,[56] was pleased to present to him.

The inscription records that king Someśvaradeva granted the village of Atteṇḍā[57] situated in the Kesalogā *khaṇḍa*[58] attached to the Uttaravallī *viṣaya*[59] to the Brāhmaṇa, *Bhaṭṭaputra* Udayakaraśarman, great-grandson of *Bhaṭṭaputra* Lakṣmīdhara, grandson of *Bhaṭṭa* Jayakara and son of *Bhaṭṭa* Vidyākara, who belonged to the Kumārahārīta *gotra*[60] with five *pravaras* and was a student of the Mādhyandina-Kāṇva *śākhā* of the *Yajurveda*, an inhabitant of Kamalapura[61] and an immigrant from Mahuvāli[62] situated in the Sāvattha *maṇḍala*,[62a] **on an auspicious tithi in the month of Māgha[62b] in**

53. The epithet *Kumārādhirāja*, which is not employed for any other Somavaṁśin chief, is reminiscent of the title *Mahākumāra* assumed by some of the Paramāra kings, and may perhaps indicate similar political uncertainty. See H.C. Ray, *DHNI*, ii, 889; Pratipal Bhatia, *The Paramāras*, 127-35.
54. According to Sircar, literally meaning 'the western island', Paścima Laṅkā was situated somewhere in South Kosala. As Someśvaradeva is styled *Paścima-Laṅk-ādhipati* and as his only known charter was issued from Suvarṇapura, the region round Sonpur in the Bolangir District was undoubtedly included in it. Mazumdar informs us that according to a popular tradition the erstwhile Sonpur State was once known by such a name and that a small rock in the bed of the Mahānadī at a distance of a stone's throw from the Maharaja's palace is still called Laṅkeśvarī which is referred to as Laṅkāvarttaka in the Mahada plates of Yogeśvaradevavarman (*EI*, xii, 219). The limits of Paścima Laṅkā, however, cannot be determined.
55. This description stylistically differs from that found in other records where the Somavaṁśin rulers are styled *Soma-kula-tilaka.*
56. This is obviously a mistake for Mahāśivagupta.
57. Mazumdar has identified it with the modern Acaṇḍa, about 7 miles from Kelga, the findspot of the charter.
58. Kesalogā, the headquarters of the sub-division which was named after it, is evidently represented by the modern Kelgā.
59. Now represented roughly by the Uttara-tīra division of the erstwhile Sonpur State, now in Bolangir District.
60. This *gotra* has not been traced elsewhere.
61. Even now known by the same name and situated within a short distance from the village of Kelga in the Uttara-tīra division of the former Sonpur State. Sten Konow's observation (*EI*, xii, 238, fn. 2) that 'Kamalapur is perhaps a Sanskritisation of Kelga' is unwarranted.
62. Not traceable.
62a. Evidently a corrupt or colloquial form of Śrāvastī which is now represented by the village of Set-Mahet on the borders of the Gonda and Bahraich Districts of Uttar Pradesh. The *maṇḍala* christened after it must have denoted the region round it.
62b. The full moon day of Māgha, still regarded as sacred, may have been intended, though it is difficult to be sure on this point.

the first year of the increasingly victorious reign (of Someśvaradeva). The grant was made at the request of the *Mahāsandhivigrahin, Rāṇaka, Nāyaka*[63] Mahīpatibhaṭṭa and Aniruddha[63a] and in favour of god Maheśvara-bhaṭṭāraka.[64] The king's command in respect of the grant was addressed to all the inhabitants of the village including the Brāhmaṇas,[65] *Bhogins* and *Bhogi-rūpas*[66] as also all the royal officials posted from time to time including the *maṇḍala-pati,*[67] *viṣaya-pati,*[68] *khaṇḍa-pati*[69] and *dāṇḍapāśika.* The privileges transferred to the donee included mastery over the waters and lands, fish and tortoises, trees and forests, *nidhis* and *upanidhis,* mango and *madhūka* groves, the right to collect *suvarṇa-daṇḍa,*[70] *ahi-daṇḍa, vartma-daṇḍa,*[71] *vandāpanā, vijaya-vandāpanā, tṛṇodaka,*[72] *śāsanārdhika,*[73] *cara-balīvarda,*[74] *arthāruva, praty-arthāruva,*[74a] *padāti-jīvya, ādattā,*[75] *āturāvaḍḍi,*[76] all the future taxes, *go-gauḍa,*[77] and *khaṇḍapālīya* and freedom from all the

63. Found in Kauṭilya's *Arthaśāstra* (i.12) and the *Śukranītisāra* (i.192), it has been taken by Kane (*HDS*, iii, 990) to mean 'head of (ten) villages'. Here, however, it seems to denote a subordinate ruler or a royal officer. See *IEG*, 214.
63a. According to Sircar, the titles or designations *Mahāsandhivigrahin* and *Rāṇaka* appear to have been used for both, Mahīpatibhaṭṭa and Aniruddha. The same may be the case with the title *Nāyaka*.
64. The donee was probably the priest of a Śiva temple and the grant may have been made for the maintenance of himself as well as the temple.
65. In most other copper-plate charters the grant is said to have been made after honouring the Brāhmaṇas of the village or the district.
66. It has been explained as 'one who is a mere title-holder, but is not in actual possession of the land in question' (*EI*, xxviii, 323) or as 'one who enjoys a free-holding as a representative of the real free-holder', (*IEG*, 56).
67. The same as *maṇḍalika, maṇḍalīka, māṇḍalika, maṇḍaleśa* and *maṇḍaleśvara*, it denoted a ruler or governor or officer-in-charge of a *maṇḍala* or district. Also employed as a title of a feudatory chief.
68. Governor of a *viṣaya* or district. *Cf. viṣaya-pāla, viṣayeśa* or *viṣayeśvara* found mentioned in several other records.
69. Governor or ruler of a sub-division of a district.
70. A tax on goldsmiths.
71. Road cess or 'tolls collected on the roads for the passage of articles of merchandise through a village' (*IEG*, 366).
72. Literally, 'a tax for grass and water', it may be taken to refer to some kind of grazing tax. See *IE*, 401; *IEG*, 344. For the use of this term in the sense of some fixed charges imposed on donated villages in some medieval Orissan copper-plate inscriptions, see *IE*, 111-12.
73. It has been explained as 'an additional share of the produce payable by the tenants engaged in cultivating rent-free lands' (*IE*, 402) or 'as 'the half of the cultivator's share of the produce of the land in the gift village' (*IEG*, 304).
74. Probably an error for *vara-balivarda* found in some other records.
74a. Probably the same as *andhāruvā* and *pratyandhāruvā* mentioned in some other records of the dynasty.
75. In some other records it is spelt with short initial *a*.
76. Perhaps the same as *antarāvaḍḍi* mentioned in a few other epigraphs.
77. Probably a levy imposed on cowherds or milkmen.

troubles. As usual, the village was turned into a tax-free holding and was given by means of a copper-plate charter.

The villagers were exhorted to live happily by offering the *bhoga, bhāga, kara*, etc., to the donee as were being paid hithertobefore.

Future kings are requested to maintain the grant as if it were their own grant and, in support of this entreaty, seven conventional stanzas, reportedly borrowed from the Dharmaśāstra, are quoted.

APPENDIX I

BANPUR PLATES OF INDRARATHA, YEAR 6

This charter consists, like other official records of the dynasty, of a set of three plates of copper and is reported to have been found at Banpur, about five miles from the Chilka Lake, in the Puri District of Orissa. It was first published by Dr. Kunja Behari Tripathy in the Oriya magazine *Jhaṅkāra*, x, 661-68 and later in the *JAS*, viii, 271-76 without facsimiles[1] and line numbers. It has been edited in a paper presented by Professor K.S. Behera at the fourteenth annual conference of the Epigraphical Society of India held at Guwahati on December 8-10, 1987, from the original plates now deposited in the Utkal University Museum, Bhubaneswar. He was kind enough to supply me a set of photographs of the plates and a copy of his text which form the basis of the present edition.[2]

The **plates** measure 27.5 x 19.3 cms. The first and the third plates bear writing only on the inner side, while the middle plate is inscribed on both the sides. There are in all 71 lines of writing, and the distribution of lines is as follows: first plate and second plate, first side, 18 lines; second plate, second side, 19 lines; and third plate, 16 lines. These plates are held together by a copper ring with a diameter of about 11.5 cms. The ends of the ring are joined under a **seal** which bears the usual device of seated Gajalakṣmī.

The **characters** belong to the Nāgarī of the northern class and bear a close resemblance to those of other records of the dynasty assignable to about the eleventh century A.D. They show certain features of the Oriya script in their rudimentary form and as such may be designated proto-Oriya. The **language** is Sanskrit, and the record is composed partly in verse and partly in prose, the *praśasti* (eulogy) portion being versified and the grant and the date portion in prose. In the latter portion some influence of the local dialect is evident as in some other contemporary records of the dynasty.

Issued from **Yayātipura,** the record aims at registering the grant of the village Laghukumbhi included in the subdivision (*khaṇḍa*) of Saghṛtakhallā in the *viṣaya* (district) of Thoraṇa in the province (*maṇḍala*) of Koṅgoda for defraying the expenses on the *bali, caru, naivedya* and *dolā* (swing) of the goddess Khadiravanī-bhaṭṭārikā, perhaps identical with the Buddhist goddess Tārā in the form of Khadiravanī, by king **Indraratha** who is described with the usual titles, *viz., Paramabhaṭṭāraka, Mahārājādhirāja Parameśvara* and *Tri-Kaliṅg-ādhipati.*

1. Only one plate was illustrated by way of sample.
2. This has necessitated some change in the text of Tripathy which we had followed earlier. However, the photographs of the first plate and the first side of the second plate are not of the desired quality, and our text in places differs from that of Behera.

The charter was written by Amṛtacandra, who held the office of the chief of the records office (*Mahākṣapaṭalin*) and was attached to the office of the minister of peace and war (*Sāndhivigrahin*). It was inscribed by the smith Vāheruka and issued on the **second day of the bright half of Kārttika in the sixth year of the issuing monarch's reign.**

Next as to the **contents.** The opening stanza pays obeisance to god Śiva and refers to the moon on the matted locks of his hair, the third eye on the forehead resembling flames of fire and poison in the neck which symbolised the trinity of qualities, to wit, *sattva, rajas* and *tamas.* The following four verses describe Yayātinagara, the place of issue of the grant and obviously the capital, in a conventional manner. Next follows an account of the family to which Indraratha, the issuer of the charter, belonged. We are told that having learnt from the people about the pitiable state of *dharma* on the earth, god Pinākin (Śiva) ordered Vivasvat (*i.e.*, the sun) to go to the earth immediately in order to restore *dharma* in its proper place (v. 6).[3] He, too, took the vow in Śiva's presence that having taken birth in a non-Kṣatriya family[4](?) together with his kinsmen he would do something very wonderful (v. 7). The first-born of his sons, who was devoted to Maheśvara, meditated upon the consort of Ambikā (*viz.,* Śiva), the rescuer from the worldly existence (v. 8). By the favour of the lord when his family was sanctified by the Moon, he received the boon of obtaining the kingdom of Indra (v. 9). In accordance with the command of Śiva the Vivasvat was born in this world as Bhīma (*i.e.,* Bhīmaratha) who had a queen named Durgā (v. 10).[5] He had from her three sons, the first of whom was Indraratha, followed by Vaṅkaratha and Śaṅkararatha one after the other (v. 11). Indraratha, who hailed from the lunar family (*Somānvaya*), is said to have obtained in battle by the prowess of his arms, from a certain Vajrahasta the kingdom of Kaliṅga (*Kaliṅga-Śrī*) through the favour of illustrious Dharmaratha (v. 12). After the passing away of king Dharma (*viz.,* Dharmaratha), on hearing from the people that king Vatsarāja was torturing the (royal), servants and the subjects, he came from Kaliṅga and killed him (*viz.,* Vatsarāja). Reference is also made to Abhimanyu (v. 13) who is said to have acquired the sovereignty of the earth (*i.e.,* kingdom) in a wrong manner and was, therefore, killed in the battlefield by Indraratha, who enjoyed his vanquished enemy's kingdom with the approval of the Brāhmaṇas and thereby became master of the three kingdoms (*trai-rājya,* v. 14). Indrarathārājadeva is next described in a prose passage with the full complement of usual imperial titles and is said to have made the grant as stated

3. It looks somewhat strange that the Sun was asked to take birth in a ruling family that claimed descent from the Moon.
4. *A-Kṣatriya-kule* is the reading in the original and it goes well with the metre. It would mean that the Somavaṁśins regarded themselves as non-Kṣatriyas, which would look somewhat strange. It is not impossible that there is some error in the wording of the text.
5. The import of the second half of the stanza is not quite clear.

above. The villagers were ordered to make over to the donee (*viz.*, trustees in charge of the shrine of the goddess) the *kara, bhoga, bhāga*, etc., as due. First respect was paid to the Brāhmaṇas of the *viṣaya* (district) and then the royal order concerning the grant was addressed to all the residents of the village (*samasta-janapadas*) including the *Samāhartṛ, Sannidhātṛ, Niyukta, Ādhikārika, Dāṇḍapāśika, Piśuna, Vaitrika,* the inmates of the royal harem, the queen, *Rāṇaka, Rāja-putra,* the king's favourites, *Bhogins*, etc. The grant was accompanied by the usual privileges and exemptions including the *pratihāra*, exemption from all the troubles, *padātijīvya, andharuvā, pratyandhāruvā, adattādāna, hasti-daṇḍa, ciṭṭola, di(de)śāvara-dānakaraṇa, chāyā, antarāvaḍḍi, vara-balīvarda,* the right to collect all the *upari-karas*, waters and lands, pits and barren spots, various trees including mango, and *madhūka*, and the *nidhis* and the *upaniddhis*.

The future rulers are entreated to maintain the grant as their own, and this request is sought to be strengthened by thirteen imprecatory and benedictive stanzas extracted from the Dharmaśāstra.

Two verses describe in a conventional but hyperbolic manner the occupant of the office of the minister of peace and war who has, however, been left unnamed (vv. 28-29). Then follows the description of the *Mahākṣapaṭalin*, Amṛtacandra by name, who wrote the charter (vv. 30-31).

Next are given the details of the date and the name of the engraver as stated above.

The record is of great historical value as it forms the only source of our information about the place in the dynasty of the king Indraratha and certain events of his life. From it we learn that Bhīmaratha, his father, had at least two queens, one (probably second) was Durgā from whom were born three sons, *viz.*, Indraratha, the issuer of the present charter, Vaṅkaratha and Śaṅkararatha. Indraratha was, thus, a step-brother of Mahāśivagupta II Dharmaratha whom he appears to have aided in his campaigns. It was obviously at his order that he invaded Kaliṅga and wrested it (or a part thereof) from king Vajrahasta who may be identified with the Eastern Gaṅga monarch Vajrahasta II-Aniyaṅkabhīma who is known to have ruled from 980-1015 A.D.[6] Dharmaratha obviously appointed Indraratha as governor or viceroy of the conquered province of Kaliṅga which was added for the first time to the growing Somavaṁśin empire. Dharmaratha died issueless, and his death was followed by a chaos which was exploited by some contemporary powers including his own kinsmen. King Vatsarāja, who is said to have oppressed the subjects, might have been a feudatory of the Paramāra king Sindhurāja as suggested by Behera.[7] Merutuṅga connects him with the early life of Bhoja who claims to have won a victory over Indraratha. And, as has been shown above, the kingdom itself was occupied by his cousin Abhimanyu who is

6. D.C. Sircar in the *History and Culture of the Indian People*, iv: *The Age of Imperial Kanauj* (ed. R.C. Majumdar), 143. Also see 516.
7. In his above-mentioned paper. Also see *OHRJ*, xxxiii, 164.

actually identical with the homonymous chief killed by Indraratha. But Indraratha's rule was short-lived; he was captured by the Coḷa emperor Rājendra Coḷa, and it was Abhimanyu's line that finally got entrenched in the rule over the Somakula kingdom.

As for the **localities** mentioned in this charter, Yayātinagara is already known from earlier charters. Koṅgoda-*maṇḍala,* which now formed part of the Somakula kingdom, was earlier under the Śailodbhavas and included the Puri-Ganjam region. Thoraṇa, which is mentioned in a Śailodbhava record also,[8] may be identical with Sorana in the Puri District.[9] Ghṛtakhallā is now probably represented by the village Ghiakhalla[10] under the Banpur police station in the Puri District.

TEXT[11]

First Plate

1 सिद्धम्[12][।*]इन्दु[:]जटासु विशदो[ऽ]ग्निशिखापिशङ्गी लालाटचक्षु[षि] गले विषभञ्ज-
नाभम् । सत्त्वंरजस्तम इ–
2 ति त्रिगुणस्य तस्य स्थानक्रमङ्गतवते[ऽ] नमः शिवाय ।।[१।।*] स्वस्ति श्रीमति यत्र सौध-
शिखरन्यस्तै–
3 रतीव स्फुरद्भाभिः काञ्चनकुम्भकैरतिशयप्रोद्दीपित व्योमनि । लोकैरुत्कटविस्मयव्यति–
4 करस्फारीभवल्लोचनैः स्थानरथानगतिक्रमेण कथमप्यालक्ष्यतें(ऽह्ः)पतिः ।।[२।।*]प्रासाद-
मौलिषु–
5 कराब्जपरम्पराभिराकृष्यमाणपरिलम्बिनभःप्रचारं(रम्)।[13] यस्मिन्निशासु निशितद्युति च–
6 न्द्रबिम्बमायोज्यते मकुरकृत्यविधौ वधूभिः।।[३।।*] यस्मिन्नस्पृशतः क्षितिं खुरपुटैर्वाहा–
7 नसंख्यानपि प्रत्येति सुदृशी जनो न तु रजोभारैः समुत्सर्पिभिः । श्रन्यद्यस्य ज–
8 लाशयेषु युगपद्दन्तावलानाङ्गणैरन्योन्यप्रतिपन्नडिण्डिमरवैरम(म्भः) समु[त्*]पीयते ।।[४।।*]
9 यद्भूमीवलयस्य भूषणविधिर्यस्यापि सौधश्रियो यत्सौधस्य मृगीदृशो
10 मृगदृशां यद्वर्त्तिनीनान्नवः । यद्या(स्याः) तोरणचित्रकर्मकनकग्रैवेयकादि स्फु–
11 टम्वीथीभूतमथेदमप्यन् मुहुः क्रीडेति सम्पाद्यते।।[५।।*] तस्मात् श्री**ययातिनगरात्** [।*]

8. The Khurda charter of Mādhava.
9. The identification has been proposed by Kedarnath Mahapatra who thinks that Sorana might be a corruption of Thoraṇa.
10. As pointed out by Tripathy, the word *khallā*, modern Oriya *khāla*, denotes an area which is rather shallow or marshy, and the Chilka lake and the surrounding region is undoubtedly a shallow or marshy area.
11. From photographs supplied by Professor K.S. Behera.
Metres: Verses 1 and 3: *Vasantatilakā;* Verses 2, 4-5, 11-14 and 29-30: *Śārdūlavikrīḍita;* Verses 6 and 10: *Śikhariṇī;* Verses 7, 15-17 and 19-25: *Anuṣṭubh;* Verses 8-9: *Mātrā;* Verse 18: *Indravajrā;* Verse 26: *Śālinī;* Verse 27: *Puṣpitāgrā;* Verse 28: *Sragdharā; Verse* 31: *Pṛthvī.*
12. Expressed by a symbol.
13. Tripathy: प्रचारः

12 पिनाकी लोकेभ्यः क्षितिपरिसरे धर्मविगतिम् विदित्वैवाहूय स्वयमनयदादेशपदवीम् ।

13 विकवस्वन्नी(न्तं) मान(न्यं) खचरमचिरादेव भवता धरित्री गन्तव्या शमयेत(यितु) मधर्मोजितमिति ।।[६।।*] अक्ष–

14 त्रियकुले भूत्वा सकुटुम्बो महाद्भ (द्भु)तम् । करिष्यामीति तेनापि प्रतिजज्ञे शिवाग्रतः ।।[७।।*] तस्य

15 तनयेषु मध्ये महानुभावो महेश्वरे भक्तः । भगवन्तमम्बिकापतिमवतारि[णं][13a] पूर्वजो द–

16 ध्यौ ।।[८।।*] भगवति च सानुकम्पे निजकुलभूषाञ्च पावितरि चन्द्रे । पितुराशयस्य च बलाद–

17 लम्भि तेनेन्द्रराज्यवरलाभः ।।[६।।*] शिरसि कृतशिवाज्ञा(ज्ञो) मर्त्यलोके विवस्वानजनि च कुलपुत्रो भीम–

18 नामोत्तमश्रीः । अयमलभत दुर्गा(र्गां) पूर्वपत्नीञ्च पत्नीमजनयदथ तस्यां पूर्वपुत्री(त्रं) च पुत्रान् ।।[१०।।*]

Second Plate: First Side

19 श्रीमा**निन्द्ररथो**[ऽ]जनि प्रथमतः सौन्दर्यसौ(शौ)र्य क्षमाधर्मत्यागदयाविवेकविनयप्राग–

20 ल्भ्यसत्याश्रयः । प्राभूतामथ विक्रमादिकगुणग्रामै कलीलास्पदे पूर्वम्व(र्वं व)ङ्करथो[ऽ]थ

21 शङ्कररथस्तस्यानुरूपानुजौ ।।[११।।*] यो[ऽ]साविन्द्र रथो रथाङ्कमहिमा सोमान्वय-क्ष्मापतिः श्री–

22 मद्धर्मरथस्य वल्लभतया लेभे कलिङ्गश्रियम् । सञ्जग्राह च विग्रहे भुजबलात्ताम्वज्र[14]–

23 हस्तादहो [।*] विक्रान्तिर्महती पदातिबहुताल्पत्वे तु न्यस्तादरः ।।[१२।।*] स्वर्गन्ध(र्गं ध)र्म–धरापतौ

24 गतवति श्रीवत्सराजो नृपा(पो)भृत्यान्सादयति प्रजामिति मुहुः श्रुत्वा जनेभ्यो गिरः । य

25 आगत्य कलिङ्गतो निजभुजाद(द्द?)र्पेण दृप्तात्मक[ः*] व्याहत्यैनमुदात(त्त)वृत्तिहृदयो धत्ते[ऽ]–

26 भिमन्यौ मतः ।।[१३।।*] यो विद्वानभिमन्युमप्यनुचित प्राप्ताधिपत्यन्भु(त्यं भु)वो वङ्श(वंश)स्यानधिकारिण(णं)

27 रणभुवि व्यापादयद्दे(द्द्वे)षिणं (णम्) [।*]तल्लक्ष्मी(मीं) द्विजसत्तमैरनुमतामासाद्य स्तम्या(सेना–)

28 द्यप(धिपैः) वैराज्यंञ्च तुरङ्गकेण जगृहे येनाथ राज्यान्तरं(रम्) ।।[१४।।*] परम-माहेश्वरमा–

29 तापितृपादानुध्यातपरमभट्टारकमहाराजाधिराजपरमेश्वरसोमकुल–

30 तिलकत्रिकलिङ्गाधिपति**श्रीमन्द्रिरथ**राजदेवः कुशली ।। कोङ्गोद[15]मण्डलीयथोर–

31 णविषयसघ(घृ)तखल्लाखण्डीयलघुकुम्भि[16]ग्रामो(मे)अतस्तद्विषयीयब्राह्मणानापूज्य समा–

13a. Probably the intended reading is °भवितारं.
14. Tripathy: 'तामुड्°.
15. Tripathy: कोङ्गद°.
16. Tripathy: लपुखम्व°.

32 हतृ(र्तृ)सन्निधातृनियुक्ताधिकारिकदाण्डपाशिकपिशुनवेत्रिकावरोधजनराज्ञीराणकराज–
33 पुत्रराजवल्लभभोगिजनप्रमुखसमस्तजनपदान् समाज्ञापयति। विदितमस्तु भव–
34 तां यथास्माभिरयं ग्रामः सप्रतीहारः सर्व्ववा(बा)धावर्ज्जितः।[17]पदातिजीव्य-अन्धरुवा-प्रत्यन्धा–
35 रुवा-अदत्तादान-हस्तिदण्ड-चिट्टोल-दिशावरदान[18] करणछाया-अन्तरावड्डि-वरव(ब)लीवर्द-स–
36 र्वोपरिकरादानसहितः सजलस्थल[:*]सगर्त्तोस(ष)रच(श्च)तुः सीमापर्यन्त[:*]साम्र(म्र)मधु(धू)क-प्रभृति–

Second Plate: Second Side

37 नानावृक्षः सनिधिः सोपनिधिः श्रीखदिरवणीभट्टारिकाया बलिचरूनैवेद्यप्रदीपदो–
38 लोपचे(च)यो आचन्द्रार्कक्षिति समकालोपभोगाय मातापित्रोरात्मनश्च पुण्ययसो(शो)भिवृद्ध–
39 ये सलिलधारापुरः सरस्ता(रं ता)म्रशासनेनाकरीकृत्य प्रतिपादित इत्यवगत्य समुचित
40 करभोगभागादिकमुपनयद्भि[:*]भवद्भिः सुखेन प्रतिवस्तव्यमिति॥ भाविभिश्च भूपतिभिः
41 दत्तिरियमस्मदीया धर्मगौरवादस्म दनुरोधच्चि स्वदत्तिरिवानुपालनीया॥ तथा चोक्त(क्तं)धर्मशा–
42 स्त्रे॥ व(ब)हुभिर्वसुधा दत्ता राजभिः सगरादिभिः। यस्य यस्य यदा भूमिस्तस्य तस्य पदा फ–
43 लम्॥[१५॥*] मा भूदफलशङ्का वः परदत्तेति पार्थिवाः। स्वदत्तात् फलमानन्त्यं परदत्तानुपा–
44 लने॥[१६॥*]षष्टि(ष्टिं)म्व(व)र्षसहस्राणि स्वर्गे मोदति भूमिदः। आक्षेप्ता चानुमन्ता च द्वौ तौ नर–
45 कगामिनौ॥[१७॥*] अग्नेरपत्यम्प्र(त्यं प्र)ध(थ)मं सुवर्णं भूर्वैष्णवी सूर्यसुताश्च गावः। यः
46 काञ्चनङ्गा(नं गा)ञ्च महीञ्च दद्याद्दत्तास्त्रय-स्तेन भवन्ति लोके(काः)॥[१८॥*] आस्फोटयन्ति
47 पितरो वल्गयन्ति पितामहाः। भूमिदाता कुले जातः स नस्त्राता भविष्यति॥[१९॥*]
48 भूमिं यः प्रतिगृह्ला(ह्णा)ति यश्च भूमिम्प्र(मिं प्र)यच्छति उभौ तौ पुण्यकर्माणौ नियतं स्वर्गगा–
49 मिनौ॥[२०॥*] तडागनां सहस्रेण वाजपेयशतेन च। गवाङ्को(वां को)टिप्रदानेन भूमिहर्ता
50 न शुध्यति॥[२१॥*]सुवर्णमेकङ्गा(कं गा)मेकां भूमेरप्यर्द्धमङ्गुलम्। हरन्नरकमायाति
51 यावदाहतसम्प्लवम्॥[२२॥*] हरते हारयेद्यस्तु मन्दवु(बु)द्धिस्तमोवृतः। स व(ब)द्धो
52 वारुणैः पाशैस्तिर्यग्योनिं स गच्छति॥[२३॥*] स्वदत्ताम्परदत्ता(त्तां)म्वा (वा) यो हरेत वसु–
53 न्धराम्। स विष्ठायाङ्कृमिर्भूत्वा पितृभिः सह पच्यते॥[२४॥*] आदित्यो वरुणो वि–
54 ष्णुर्व्र(र्ब्र)ह्मा सोमो हुताशनः। शूलपाणिश्च भगवानभिनन्दति(न्ति) भूमिदम्॥[२५॥*] सामा–

17. This mark of punctuation is superfluous.
18. Tripathy: शावरदान

55 न्योयन्ध (यं ध)र्मसेतुनृ(र्नृ)पाणां काले काले पालनीयो भवद्भिः। सर्वानेतान् भावि–

Third Plate

56 नः पार्थिवेन्द्रान् भूयो भूयो याचते रामभद्रः[19]।।[२६।।*] इति कमलदलाम्वु(म्बु)वि(बि)न्दु–
57 लोलां श्रियमनुचिन्त्य मनुष्यजीवित्तञ्च । सकलमिदमुदाहृतञ्चवु(बु)द्ध्वा
58 न हि पुरुषैः परकीर्त्तयो विलोप्याः।।[२७।।*] यद्वा(बा)णाः पक्षपालीपवनर–
59 यपरिष्वङ्गसन्दीप्तविद्युद्वह्निज्वालासमूहैरनुमितजलदव्यूहसंचा–
60 रलीलाः । उद्गच्छन्तो घनेभ्यस्तदनु च सि(शि)खया गुम्फितानेकतारासन्तान–
61 ग्रन्थिलास्ते कथमपि धरणीपृष्ठपर्यन्तमीयुः।।[२८।।*]तस्यान्त[ः*]स्थितचन्द्रसे(शे)खर–
62 पदद्वन्द्वस्य मन्दाकिनीतोयादस्यधिकादरद्विजपदाम्भोभिः समभ्युक्षितः । विद्या–
63 [यां*]निजवेश्मनो जलनिधि[ः*] लोकानुकम्पामति[ः*]विश्वाराधिनि सन्धिविग्रहप–
64 दे स्वामिश्रिये जाग्रति ।।[२९।।*]उद्घाट्य प्रतिकुम्भिकुम्भफरु(ल)कन्त(कं त)न्मौक्तिक-श्रेणि–
65 भि[ः*]कृत्वाथो निजदेहमण्डनविधिं यत्खड्गलेखानर्टी । सङ्ग्रामाङ्गणरङ्गभूमि–
66 मुमुहुः(षु मुदा?) स्वच्छन्दतो लीलया नृत्यन्ती हृदयङ्गमा समभवद्विद्वेषि भूमी भुजां (जाम्) ।।[३०।।*] असौ
67 निजभुजास(श)निक्षपितवैरिभूभृतकुलो महाक्षपटली यशः पटलकौमुदीचन्द्रमा[ः*]। क–
68 लानिवहजन्मभूरमृतचन्द्रनामा निधिः समस्तगुणसम्पदामिदमलीलिखच्छास–
69 नं(नम्)।।[३१।।*]परमम(मा)हेश्वरमहाराजाधिराज **श्रीमदिन्द्ररथराजदेवस्य प्रवर्द्धमान–**
70 **विजयराज्ये षष्ठे सम्वत्सरे कार्तिकमासि शुक्लपक्षद्वितीयायां** तिथौ लिखितमि–
71 दम् यत्राङ्केनापि[20] सम्वत् ६ कार्तिकशुदि २ विज्ञानिवाहेरुकेण उत्कीर्ण्णं(र्णम्) ।।

19. Tripathy: रामचन्द्रः
20. Tripathy: पत्राङ्कितमपि

APPENDIX II

A STRAY PLATE OF UDDYOTAKESARIN FROM MAHADA

The plate under consideration was brought to the notice of scholars by Shri B.K. Rath, Curator, Orissa State Archaeology, Bhubaneswar, on the occasion of the fourth annual congress of the Epigraphical Society of India at Madras in January 1978 and I am thankful to him for allowing me to incorporate the same in the present volume.

The plate was discovered at the village of Mahada in the Birmaharajpur Tahsil of the Bolangir District, Orissa.[1] It measures 16.5 cm. in length and 7.8 cm. in breadth[2] whereas the thickness, which is uniform all through, is 0.1 cm. The circular hole for the passage of the ring is on the right, which is rather unusual. Although the edges of the plate are neither raised nor fashioned thicker, the writing on it is in a fairly good state of preservation.

This is the second or middle plate of a three-plate charter (*triphalītāmra-śāsana*) of the Somavaṁśin dynasty and the ring and seal, if there were any, are missing together with the remaining two plates.

The plate bears in all fourteen lines of writing, there being seven lines on each side. The characters belong to the Nāgarī of the northern class as prevailing in Ọrissa during the eleventh century A.D. and bear very close resemblance to those of the Balijhari plates of Uddyotakesarin.[2a] The language is Sanskrit, and the portion of the record accommodated on the plate is in prose throughout and is highly corrupt.

The plate belongs to the illustrious **Uddyotakesarideva,** son of the illustrious Caṇḍīhara, as stated in the first two lines on the first side of the plate. There is no doubt that this Uddyotakesarin is identical with the homonymous Somavaṁśin ruler who is already known to us from several other official and private records.[3] That he was son of Caṇḍīhara is known from the Brahmeśvara Temple inscription (Bhubaneswar) of his mother.[4] But the name Caṇḍīhara does not figure in any official record of the dynasty and in the formal portion of the copper-plate inscriptions he is referred to by his official name Mahāśivagupta in keeping with the prevailing practice.[5] It is only in

1. The village has already yielded a copper-plate charter of the 23rd year of the Telugu-Coḷa chief Someśvaradevavarman II. See *EI*, xii, 218-21; xxviii, 283-92.
2. The size of the plate is unusually small as compared to most other records of the dynasty.

2a. See *supra*, IV: XXII.
3. *Vide supra*, IV: XXII-XXVI and suppl. III.
4. See *supra*, IV: XXVI.
5. See *supra*, IV: XXII, text-lines 30-31; suppl. III, text-line 30.

this charter that he is mentioned by the name Caṇḍīhara and herein lies the uniqueness of this record.

The object of the inscription is to register the grant by Uddyotakesarin of the village Gomuṇḍallā attached to the administrative division (*khaṇḍa*) known as Yamalā in favour of the *paṇḍita Bhaṭṭaputra* Dharmapāla, son of the illustrious Savyasācin, who belonged to the Jātukarṇya *gotra* and the Vasiṣṭha *pravara* and was a student of the *śākhā* of the *Yajurveda*[6] and an immigrant from Madhyadeśa. The grant was made by issuing a copper-plate charter on the occasion of an eclipse of the moon for the religious merit and fame of the donor's parents and of himself. It carried the usual privileges including right to the mango and *tāla* trees, alkaline spots, waters and lands, bushes and trees, inhabited lands and forests, fishes and tortoises, the usual *bhoga*, *bhāga*, all the taxes, gold (tax paid in cash), *nidhis* and *upanidhis*, *daś-āparādhas*, the collection of all the *uparikaras* and *karas* as well as exemption from all the troubles. If some more privileges and exemptions were granted, they may have been listed on the third plate which is missing.

The date, the name of the *Sandhivigrahin* and/or *Mahākṣapaṭala* responsible for the drafting of the charter and the name of the scribe cannot be made out as the same must have been given on the missing third plate.

As regards the **localities** named in our charter, the donated village Gomuṇḍallā may be identified with the present Gunurdula[7] which is situated beside the village of Mahada, the findspot of the record. Yamalā, the headquarters of the *khaṇḍa* known after it, cannot be identified.[8]

TEXT[9]

First Side

1 श्रीचण्डि (ण्डी) हरदेवस्य सुत[:*] श्रीउद्दयोतकसरि–
2 देवः कुशली यमलाडखण्डप्रतिव (ब) द्धगोमुण्ड–
3 ल्लाग्रामे (मः) साम्व्र (म्र) मधुतालसगर्तोषर[:*] सजलस्थ–
4 ल[:*]सख (खे) टविटप[:*]सपद्रारण्य[:*]–समच्छाकच्छप[10] चतु[:*]–
5 सि (सी) मा[11] भूमिच्छिद्रान्यपि ना (आ) चन्द्रतारकार्कक्षितिसम–
6 कालोपभोगार्थं (थँ) मात्रापित्रोरात्मनश्च पुन्य (ण्य) यशोभिवृ–

6. Strangely enough, the *śākhā* has not been named.
7. approximately, 84.0° East and 20.62° North.
8. I owe the facsimile and the information about the provenance as well the identification of the granted village to Shri B.K. Rath.
9. From facsimile.
10. Read समत्स्यकच्छपः
11. In other records we generally have चतुःसीमापर्यन्तः.

7 द्वये सोमग्रहेन (ण)[12] (म*) ध्यदे[13]–

Second Side

8 शवि[निर्ग]ताय जातो (तु) कण (ण्वं) [स*]गोत्राय वसिष्ठप्रव–

9 राय परेप्रवराय (?) यज (जु) र्वेदशाखाध्यायिने प–

10 ण्डितभट्टपुत्रधर्म्मंपाला[य*] श्रीसर्वं (व्य) शा (सा) ची (चि) सुताय

11 [14]गोमुण्डल्लाग्रामो (म) ता (स्ता) म्त्र (म्र) शासनीकृत्य प्रतिपा–

12 दित मि (इ) त्यवगत्य च समुचितभोग-भागकर–

13 निकरहिरण्याद्दि[15] स्व (स) निधि[:*] सोपनिधि-[:*] त्यास्मि (?) [स*]द–

14 शापराध[:*] सर्ववा (बा) धावहि[16]सर्वोपरिकर-करा[17]–

12. Read सोमग्रहणे.
13. This portion is engraved in only half the line; the remaining space of the line has been left uninscribed because enough space to accommodate the height of the *akṣaras* was not available.
14. As the name of the village has already been mentioned in lines 2-3 above, its repetition in this line is unnecessary.
15. An expression like *sahitaḥ* is required here.
16. Read °धावर्जितः.
17. The record was completed on the third plate which has not been traced.

APPENDIX III

GANDHIBEDHA SURYA IMAGE INSCRIPTION OF MAHĀŚIVA-GUPTĀ V KARṆA

This inscription is found engraved on the back of an image of Sūrya, now deposited in the Orissa State Museum, Bhubaneswar. The image is reported to have been secured from the village of Gandhibedha in the Balasore District of Orissa. The epigraph has been published by D.C. Sircar in *EI*, xxxiii, 273-74. Later, S.N. Rajaguru also gave his reading of the record in his *Inscriptions of Orissa*, iv, 265-67.

The **characters** of the inscription bear a close resemblance to those of the Ratnagiri plates of Karṇa (*ante*, IV: XXVII) and it is composed in Sanskrit.

The record is fragmentary. The halo of the image bearing this record is broken into two, or rather three, parts. The left half of the epigraph is broken away and lost whereas the extant portion of the writing is reported to have been deliberately rubbed off by means of chiselling. According to Rajaguru, the inscription contains in all ten lines of writing, of which only the first two lines of the extant portion can be read definitely as follows:—

1 धिराजपरमेश्वरसोमकुलतिलकतृ (त्रि)–
2 श्री**कर्ण्णराजदेवस्य** प्रवर्द्धमानवि–

In view of the general structure of the Somavaṁśin records, it may be easily conjectured that the lost portion of line 1 before °*dhirāja* must have contained *Siddham* (expressed by a symbol) *paramabhaṭṭāraka-mahārājā*° while *kaliṅgādhipati* must have been the letters lost at the beginning of line 2 probably followed by the sectarian title *paramamāheśvara*, both *Trikaliṅgādhipati* and *Paramamāheśvara* being well-known titles of the Somavaṁśin chiefs. The letters at the beginning of line 3 following *vi* at the end of line 2 must have been *jayarājye* or more probably *jayarājya-samva*(*saṁva*)*tsare,* followed by the mention of the regnal year. Thus, the portion of the inscription that admits of a definite reconstruction is as under:—

1 सिद्धम्।[*] परमभट्टारकमहाराजाधिराजपरमेश्वर-सोमकुलतिलकतृ (त्रि)–
2 कलिङ्गाधिपतिपरममाहेश्वरश्री**कर्ण्णराजदेवस्य** प्रवर्द्धमानवि–
3 जयराज्य (or ज्ये) सम्व (संव) त्सरे . . .

The inscription was thus intended to record the installation of the image on which it is incised during the reign of the Somavaṁśin king **Karṇṇa**. Rajaguru conjecturally reads at the beginning of line 3 the figure 3 and guesses that it may have been preceded by the figure 1 so that a reference to the 3rd or 13th regnal year was intended. But these readings are extremely doubtful and much cannot be built upon them. The same is true about the reading of the following letters in line 3 proposed by Rajaguru. He also proposes to read *śrī* at the beginning of line 7, [*ga*]*dabhaḥ* at the beginning of line 7 and a *visarga* at the beginning of the following line and takes *śrī*-Garttabha to be the name of the person responsible for the dedication of the Sūrya image on which the inscription is incised.[1] But all this is untenable and leads us nowhere.

1. Forgetting all other things for the moment, it is strange that while Rajaguru reads *Gadabha* in the inscription he credits one Garttabha with the installation of the image.

APPENDIX IV

A STRAY PLATE OF A SOMAVAṀŚĪN OR TELUGU-COḌA GRANT FROM KELGA

The plate was found buried in a field in the village of Kelga in the Uttaratīra division of the erstwhile Sonpur State, now in the Bolangir District, of Orissa. Alongwith three other plates forming a charter of the Somavaṁśin king Someśvara it was strung on a circular copper ring to which a brass seal of the shape of a double-petalled lotus bearing the usual Gaja-Lakṣmī device was affixed. B.C. Mazumdar, who first published it [*EI*, xii, 241-42 and plate (nos. *Da-Db*) facing p. 241], regarded it as a forgery (*ibid.*, 238). However, after a careful examination of the plate D.C. Sircar rightly concluded that Mazumdar's view was incorrect and that in reality it constitutes the second or middle plate of a three-plate charter (*tri-phalī-tāmra-śāsana*).

Measuring 7″ x 4⅛″ and weighing 33½ *tolās*, the plate bears writing on both sides, there being fourteen lines on each side. The **characters** are exactly the same as met with in the Somavaṁśin records of the twelfth century A.D. and the language is Sanskrit. The draft is full of errors. It contains the concluding portion of the king's address regarding the grant followed by the description of the privileges and exemptions attached to the grant and the grantee, the request for the maintenance of the grant and some of the imprecatory and benedictory stanzas.

The name of the king responsible for issuing the charter of which the present plate forms part cannot be ascertained as it must have been engraved on the first plate which is missing. But as will be seen in the sequel, in all probability he was either the Somavaṁśin chief Someśvara himself known from the above-mentioned Kelga plates or the homonymous Telugu-Coḍa king who replaced him at Suvarṇapura.

The object of the inscription is to register the grant of the village Pārśvagrāma together with a couple of plots of land (*khaṇḍa-kṣetras*) named Gudhvamāla and Kahapura belonging to Vuravuḍa-grāma situated in the Roṅgaḍā *maṇḍala* in favour of the Brāhmaṇa, *Bhaṭṭaputra* Ābhābhakaraśarman, son of *Bhaṭṭaputra* Udayakara, grandson of *Bhaṭṭa* Vidyākara and great-grandson of *Bhaṭṭa* Jayakara, who belonged to the Kumārahārīta *gotra* having five *pravaras* and was a student of the Mādhyandina-Kāṇva *śākhā* of the *Yajurveda*. His family originally hailed from Mahuvālī situated in the Sāvatha (Śrāvastī) *maṇḍala* though he was himself a resident of Kamalapura. The grant carried with it a number of privileges including the *nidhis*, *upanidhis*, elephant's tusk (ivory), tiger-skin and various wild animals, waters and lands, fish and tortoises, outposts and bushes, low and high lands, habitations and jungles, shrubs and creepers, mango, *madhūka,* tamarind, palm and other trees. The king's order regarding the grant appears to have been conveyed through a certain Ṣaṣṭhī-gābhura.

Next follows the conventional request to future rulers, including those belonging other ruling families, to maintain the grant and some imprecatory and benedictory verses are quoted.

It is noteworthy in this connection that the father of the donee of the present charter, *Bhaṭṭaputra* Udayakara, was the recipient of a land-grant made by *Kumāra* Someśvara through his Kelga plates. The grant under consideration, therefore, may have been made either by the Somavaṁśin Someśvara himself or his Telugu-Coḍa namesake who ousted him from Suvarṇapura.

As for the **localities** mentioned in the record, Sāvatha *maṇḍala* and Kamalapura have been already identified in connection with Someśvara's Kelga plates. Other localities cannot be identified.

TEXT[1]

First Side

1 प्रमुख: चत्वारि सीमन्तजानपदा: [2]।[3] षष्ठीगाभुरप्रमुख[4]–

2 तः । यथार्ह(र्हं)मानयति । समाद(दि)शति [च*] ।। विदितमस्तु भव–

3 ता(तां) रोङ्गडामण्डलवुरवुडा[5]ग्रामगुध्वमालखण्डक्षेत्रकह्न[6]–

4 पुरखण्डक्षेत्रप्रविशग्र[7](ग्रा)मे(मः) चतु[:*]सीमायावः[8](वत्) । निध्यो(ध्यु)पनिधिहस्ति[9]–

5 दन्तवा(ण्धा)घ्रचर्मनानावनचर[10][समेत:*]: सजलस्थल[:*] समच्छ(त्स्य)कच्छप[:*]

6 सख(खे)टविटप[:*][11]सखल्लउन(न्न)त[:*] सपद्रारण्यक[:*]।।[12] सगुल्मल्ल(ल)–

7 ता(त)[:*] ।। सभ्र(म्रा)म्व्र(म्र)मध(धु)क[:*] ।। सतन्तलिक[:*][13] सतालकै:(क:) नानावृक्ष[समेत:] शा–

8 सनीकृत्य प्रतिपादित[:*] ।। कुमारहारीत्र(त)गोत्रायपञ्चरिष (ञ्च ार्षे)–

9 यप्रवराय ।। माध्यन्दिनक(का)र्ण्ण[14](ण्व)शाखाध्याय(यि)ने सावथ[15]मण्डल–

1. From facsimile in *EI*, xii.
2. As suggested by Sircar, the intended reading may have been प्रमुखचतु:सीमान्तजनपदान्.
3. This mark of punctuation is superfluous. The same is the case with many other marks of punctuation in subsequent lines.
4. Mazumdar: °प्रमाण.°
5. Originally *Vuravyaḍā* was engraved. Trace of subscript *y* is clear.
6. Sircar: कह°.
7. Mazumdar: भविश (?). Perhaps प्रविष्ट is intended.
8. Mazumdar: सीमायनः.
9. Mazumdar: हस्त°.
10. Mazumdar: वनेचरः.
11. Read सखल्लोन्नतः.
12. These *daṇḍas* are unnecessary. Many other double punctuation marks in the following lines are likewise superfluous.
13. Sanskrit सतिन्तिरीकः.
14. Mazumdar: कण्ण°.
15. Probably the intended reading is श्रावस्ती

10 । महुवालीविनी(नि)गंताय ॥ **कमलपुरवास्तव्याय** ॥ भट[16](ट्ट)पु–

11 त्रजयकरप्रपौत्राय ॥ भट[16](ट्ट)विद्याकरपौत्राय ॥ भट[16](ट्ट)पुत्र–

12 उदयकरपुत्राय[17] ॥ भट[17a](ट्ट)पुत्रा**भाभकर**[18]श्र(श)श(र्म)णें[19] ॥ विधिव(वि)धाने–

13 न स(सं)विधाय । ताम्ब्र(म्र)शासनेन [20]प(प्र)तिपादितो पारंपर्यंक(क्र)भाग–

14 तसर्ववचनेन ॥ य[21]–

Second Side

15 था काण्डात्काण्ड(ण्डा)त्प्ररोहन्ती । [22]या स(श)तेन प्रतनोषि[23] ॥ [24]एवं राच(ज)शास–

16 नेन प्रतिपादितं(तः) । एवं वधाः परावह्म परतो वंशकारेणः[24a]

17 ठ यायस्मादनुराधर्म्मं ॥ [गौ]रवा[25] न तेन वि ॥ अन्येपवाधः[26]

18 रणाय[27] ॥ [28]तस्यागे(ग्रे) कोसि(स्ति) धम्म(र्म्म)वित(त्)[29] ॥ शासेदृषा[30] धमहि नद[31] ॥

19 तासविजं सस्थमेदिनि ॥ यावत्सुय[32]कथाल्लोके तावत्सगे[33] माद–

20 यत ॥ वेदवाकमया जाह्वा वदन्ति ॥ षा[34] देवताः ॥ भूमिहृत्ता[35] तथा–

21 न्ये च । अहो[36] मोहन मा हर्[॥*] यथायं पतितः शक्र । तेन वेन्द[37] ति–

16. Mazumdar: भट्ट°.
17. Read °पुत्रोदय°.
17a. Mazumdar: भट्ट°.
18. Mazumdar suggests to add *ya* between *trā* and *bhā*. In that case the donee's name would be Bhābhakara.
19. Mazumdar: °शर्मणे.
20. Sircar: प्रति°.
21. These *akṣaras* have been engraved in a little space available on the right side below the concluding portion of the previous line.
22. Here onward the text containing imprecatory and benedictive stanzas is extremely corrupt.
23. After this we have सहस्रेण विरोहति in some other records, e.g. Baudh charters of Raṇabhañjadeva, *EI*, xii, 324, 327. Also *cf. Vājasaneyī Saṁhitā*, xvi. 20f.
24. As pointed out by Sircar, the intended reading is एवं बुद्ध्वा परार्धञ्च परतो वंशावतारेणापि भवद्भिरस्मदनुरोधाद् धर्मगौरवाच्च न केनापि स्वल्पोऽप्यपराधः करणीयः.
24a. Sircar: °कारिणः.
25. Sircar: गौरव°.
26. Sircar: °पराधः.
27. Mazumdar: करणीया.
28. Here we generally have तथा चोक्तं धर्मशास्त्रे तस्याग्रे etc. is part of an incomplete stanza.
29. Mazumdar: धर्म्मवेत.
30. Mazumdar: शासेदूपा°; Sircar: शास°.
31. Mazumdar: नदा.
32. Mazumdar: °सूर्य°.
33. Mazumdar: सर्गे.
34. Mazumdar: या.
35. Mazumdar: °दत्ता.
36. Mazumdar: आह.
37. Mazumdar: वेवृ; Sircar: °विन्द.

22 सपति । एवं भूमिकृत दान । सशे सशे प्ररोहिति ॥[38] आदित्या (त्यो)

23 वरुणो विष्णु । व्र (ब्रुर्ब्र) ह्मा सोम (मो) हुताशनः [।*] श (शू) लपाणिस्तु भगवान अ । (वान)–

24 भिनन्दन्ति भूमिदं (दम्) ॥ अ (आ) सो (स्फो) टयंति (यन्ति) पितरः ॥ प (प्र) वल्स (ल्ग) न्ति[39] पितामहाः ॥ (।)

25 भूमिदाता कुले जाता (तः) ॥ स ते दाता[40]भविष्यति ॥ व (ब) हुभिव (र्व) सुधा दत्त (त्ता)

26 । राजान (जभिः) सगरादिभिः [41]॥ मा रोधः पलतत्कय परदत्तषु पाणित[42]

27 । यस्य यस्य [य*]दा भ (भू) मि । त (मिस्त) स्य (तस्य*) तदा प (फ) लं (लम्) । (॥)[42a] तस्म (स्मात्) त्वया[43] न हत (तं) व्य (व्यं) । सा (शा)– ।

28 श्वतीङ्गतिमाप्नुयात (त्) ॥ स्वदत्ता (त्तां) परदत्ताम्वा (त्तां वा) यो हर (रे) ति (त) वसुन्धर (राम् ।)[44]

38. The three verses beginning with शास्त्रे° in line 18 and ending with प्ररोहति in this line should be correctly read as follows:

फालकृष्टां महीं दद्यात् सबीजसस्यमेदिनीम् ।
यावत् सूर्यकृतालोकस्तावत् स्वर्गे महीयते ॥
वेदवाक् स्मृतयो जिह्वा वदन्ति ऋषिदेवताः ।
भूमिहर्त्ता तथान्ये च अहो मोहेन मा हर ॥
यथाप्सु पतितः शक्र तैलबिन्दुर्विसर्पति ।
एवं भूमिकृतं दानं सस्ये सस्ये प्ररोहति ॥

39. Mazumdar: पवल्गन्ति.
40. Read स नस्त्राता.
41. The second half of this stanza (यस्य यस्य यदा भूमिस्तस्य तस्य तदा फलम्) is given in line 27 below, and not omitted as stated by Sircar.
42. Mazumdar: तङ्क य परदत्त प्रपालिता.
Read मा भूदफलशङ्का व परदत्तेति पार्थिवाः । The second half of this verse (स्व दानात्फलमानन्त्यं पददत्तानुपालने) is dropped.
42a. The first half of this stanza has come earlier in lines 25-26.
43. Mazumdar: न्वया.
44. The remainder of this stanza as well as possibly some other stanzas were evidently engraved on another plate which is now missing.

SUPPLEMENTARY INSCRIPTIONS

I

SAMBALPUR UNIVERSITY MUSEUM PLATES[1] OF THE TIME OF MAHĀBHAVAGUPTA I JANAMEJAYA, YEAR 23

Provenance: Sambalpur, Sambalpur District, Orissa.
Reference: J.K. Sahu, *The Journal of Orissa History*, ii (i), 1-5 and plates facing pp. 4 and 5.
Language: Sanskrit. In prose with the exception of customary benedictive and imprecatory stanzas.
Metres: Verses 1-3 and 5-11; *Anuṣṭubh;* Verse 4: *Indravajrā*; Verse 12: *Śālinī*; Verse 13: *Puṣpitāgrā*.
Script: Northern class of alphabets.
Date: Regnal year 23, Bhādrapada śukla 13. About the close of the ninth century A.D.

TEXT[2]

First Plate

1 सिद्धम्[3][।*]स्वस्ति । परमभट्टारकमहाराजाधिराजपरमेश्वरश्रीशि[4]--
2 वगुप्तदेवपादानुध्यातपरममाहेश्वरपरमभट्टारकमहाराजाधि[4]–
3 राजसोमकुलतिलकत्रिकलिङ्गाधि[5]पतिश्रीमहाभवगुप्तदेवपाद प्रवर्द्धमा–
4 नविजयराज्ये ।[6] कोल्लेडासमावासकात् ।[6] महाराजाधिराजमहामण्डलेश्वर–
5 राष्ट्रकुलतिलकाण्डजोद्भवराणकश्रीशंकिल्लसुतपरमवैष्णव–
6 खंभेश्वरीवरल्ल(ल)व्ध[6a](ब्ध) प्रसादसमधिगता-शेषपंचमहाशब्द(ब्द) महाम–
7 ण्डलाधिपतिराणकश्रीदेवप्य: कुशली इहैव[7] कोल्लेडामण्डले डे–

1. The record was procured from a bell-metal worker of Sambalpur and was in all probability found originally somewhere in the vicinity of this town. It is now deposited in the History Museum of the University of Sambalpur.

   The plates, which measure about 7″ x 4.5″, are tied to a ring of copper passing through the hole bored about the middle of the margin on the left. The ring was not removed while photographing the plates.

   The seal, under which are joined the ends of the ring, bears only a short prose legend giving the name of the issuing chief preceded by the honorific *śrī* in genitive singular.
2. From original plates.
3. Expressed by a symbol.
4. Last few letters of the first two lines and the concluding letter of the next few lines have been damaged and almost effaced in the course of chemical treatment.
5. Sahu: सोमवंशकुलतिलकत्रिकलिंगाधि°.
6. The punctuation mark is superfluous.
6a. Sahu: °लब्धं.
7. Sahu: इहथेव

8 रिन्धग्रामे व्रा (ब्रा) ह्मणान् संपु (पू) ज्य यथाकालाध्यासिनः समाहर्तृ सन्निधातृ–

9 [8]दाण्डपाशिकवेत्रिकावरोधजनराजपुत्रराजवल्लभादीनन्यांश्च चा–

10 टभटजातीयान् ।[6] मानयति वो (बो) धयति समादिशति [।*] विदितमस्तु भव–

Second Plate: First Side

11 तां[8a]यथास्माभिरयं ग्रामः सनिधिः सोपनिधिः सर्व्वावा (बा) धाविवर्जि–

12 तः सर्वोपरिकरकरादानसमेत[:*] सगर्त्तोषरः सवल्लिलताविट–

13 पसाम्र (म्र) मधु (धू) क[:*] सजलस्थलश्चतुः सीमापय (र्य) न्तः [8]प्रतिनिषिद्धचाट–

14 भटप्रवेशश्छ (श्छा) [8b]न्दोगचरणाय अगस्तिगोत्राय आशीतिप्रवरा–

15 य तालीविनिर्गताय धर्मनगरवास्तव्याय भट (ट्ट) पुत्रश्रीवा–

16 मननाम्ने वापिल्ल[8c]सुताय सु (सू) र्यग्रहोपरागे महानदीती–

17 रोपकण्ठे सलिलधारापुरः सरमाचन्द्रतारकार्क्कक्षितिसमका–

18 लोपभोगार्त्थं मातापित्रोरात्मनश्च पुन्य (ण्य) यशोभिवृद्धये ताम्र (म्र) शा–

19 सनेनाकरीकृत्य प्रतिपादित इत्यवगत्य समुचित भोगभागक–

Second Plate: Second Side

20 रहिरण्यादिकमुपनयद्भिर्भवद्भिः सुखेन प्रतिवस्तव्यमिति[।*] भा–

21 विभिश्च भूपतिभिद (र्द) त्तिरियमस्मदीया धर्म्मगौरवादस्मदनुरोधा–

22 च्च स्वदत्तिरिवानुपालनीया । तथा चोक्तं धर्म्मशास्त्रे[।*]व (ब) हुभिर्वसु[8d]

23 धा दत्ता राजभिः सगरादिभिः[।*]यस्य यस्य यदा भूमिःतस्य तस्य त–

24 दा फलं (लम्) ।[।१।।*] मा भूदः (द) फलशंका वः परदत्तेति पार्थिवाः [।*] स्व–

25 दानात्फलमानन्त्यं[9] परदत्तानुपालने ।[।२।।*] षष्टिं (ष्टि) वर्षसह–

26 स्राणि स्वर्गे मोदति भु (भू) मिदः [।*]अ (आ) क्षि (क्षे) प्ता च्चा (चा) नुमन्ता च्च (च) तान्येवनरकेव–

27 सेत (त्) ।[।३।।*] अग्नेरपत्यं प्रथमं सुवर्ण्णं भु (भू) वे (र्वै) ष्णवी सु (सू) र्यसुताश्च गावः [।*]य[:*]

28 काञ्चन (नं) गां च महीं च दद्या[द्*]दत्तास्त्रयस्तेन भवन्ति ल्लो (लो) के (काः) ।[।४।।*] आस्फोट–

Third Plate: First Side

29 यन्ति पितरः प्रवल्गयन्ति[10]पितामहाः[।*] भूमिदाता कुले जातः स नस्त्रा–

8. Sahu: दण्ड°.
8a. Sahu: °ता (तां).
8b. Sahu: श्चा°.
8c. Sahu: वायिल्ल°.
8d. Sahu. वह (हु) भिवसु°.
9. Read °लमत्यन्तं.
10. Read प्रवल्गन्ति.

30 ता भविष्यति ।[।५।।*] भूमीं (मिं) यः प्रतिग्रि (गृ) ह्ना (णा) ति यश्च भूमीं (मिं) प्रयच्छति [।*] उभौ तौ

31 पुन्य (ण्य) कर्माणौ नियतौ स्वर्गगामिनौ ।[।६।।*] सुवण्ण (र्ण्ण) मेकं गामेकां भूमेरप्य–

32 र्द्धमंगुलं (लम्) [।*]। हरं (र) न (न्न) रकमायाति यावदाहूतसंप्लवं (वम्) ।[।७।।*] हरते हारयते

33 भूमीं (मिं) मन्दवु (बु) धि (द्धि) स्तमोवृतः [।*] सव (ब) द्धो वारुणैः पाशैस्तिर्यग्यो–

34 नीश्च[10a]गच्छति ।[।८।।*]तडागानां सहस्राणि[11]वाजपेयशतानि[12] च । गवां

35 कोटिप्रदानेन भूमिहर्त्ता न शुध्यति ।।[९।।*] अन्यायेन हृता भूमिरन्यायेन तु हा[13]

36 हारिता [।*] हरते हारयते श्चै (चै) व स हन्यात्सप्तमं कुलं (लम्) ।।[१०।।*] आदित्यो वरुणो

37 विष्णुव्र (ब्र) ह्मा सोमो हुतास (श) न[:*]। शूलपाणिस्तु भगवां (वा) ग्र (न) [13a]भिनन्दंतु (ति) भूमिदं (दम्)।।[११।।*]

Third Plate : Second Side

38 सामान्योयं धर्मसेतुर्नृपाणां काले काले पालनीयो[13b] भवद्भिः[।*] सर्वानेता[13c]–

39 नभाविनो भूपति (ती) न्द्रान् भूयो भूयो याचते रामचन्द्रः।[।१२।।*]इति कमलद–

40 लांवु (बु) वि (बि) न्दुल्लो (लो) लांश्रियमनुचिन्त्य मनुष्यजीवितं च [।*] सकलमिदि (द) मुदाहृतं

41 च वु (बु) द्ध्वा न हि पुरुषैः परकीर्त्तयो[13d]विलोप्या ः।[।१३।।*] परमभट्टारक–

42 महाराजाधिराजश्री**जनमेजयदेवस्य राज्ये स (सं) म्व (व) त्सरे त्र–**

43 **योविंशति [त*]मे भाद्रपदमासशुक्लपक्षतिथौ त्रयोदस्यां (श्यां)** यत्रां–

44 कतः **स (सं) म्व (व) त २३ भाद्रपदशुदि १३** लिखितमिदं ताम्व्र (म्र) शासनं काय–

45 स्थश्रि (श्री) गुर (रु) सुतेन[13e] श्रीकण्ठेनेति[।*] मंगलमाभा श्रीः[14] ।।

SEAL

श्रीदे[व*]प्यस्य

ABSTRACT

Beginning with the auspicious words *siddham* (indicated symbolically) and *svasti,* the charter first refers to the reign of Mahābhavagupta I, who meditated on the feet of Śivagupta, both of whom are described exactly in the

10a. Sahu: नी (नि) घ्रि°.
11. Read सहस्रेण.
12. Read शतेन.
13. This *akṣara* is superfluous.
13a. Sahu: भगवाण (न).
13b. Sahu: पालनीया.
13c. Sahu: सर्वोनिवं.
13d. Sahu: °कीर्त्तये.
13e. Sahu: श्री गुर सुतेन श्रीकण्ठनेति.
14. Read मंगलं महाश्रीः.

same manner as in the numerous records of the former. Next is mentioned the residence at Kolleḍā[15] whence the grant was issued by Devapya, son of Śaṅkilla, who is said to have belonged to the Rāṣṭra-kula and is further described as born of an egg.[16] Śaṅkilla is given the titles *Mahārājādhirāja*, *Mahāmaṇḍaleśvara* and *Rāṇaka*, while his son and successor Devapya is styled *Paramavaiṣṇava, Mahāmaṇḍalādhipati* and *Rāṇaka*[17] and is said to have acquired all the five *mahāśabdas* by the grace of the goddess Khambeśvarī (Skt. Stambheśvarī).[17a]

The inscription aims at recording Devapya's grant of the village Derindha[18] included in the Kolleda *maṇḍala*[19] to *Bhaṭṭaputra* Vāmana, son of Vāpilla, who was an immigrant from Tālī and resident of Dharmanagara[20] and belonged to the Chandoga (*caraṇa,* Agasti *gotra* and Āśīti *pravara,* on the bank of the Mahānadī on the occasion of a solar eclipse. The order about the grant was addressed to the *Samāhartṛ*, *Sannidhātṛ*, *Dāṇḍapāśika*, *Vaitrika,* inmates of the royal harem, *Rājaputras*, royal favourites and other officers of the class of *Cāṭas* and *Bhaṭas* posted from time to time and was issued after worshipping the Brāhmaṇas. The grant carried with it the same privileges and exemptions as specified in other records of Janamejaya with the exception of the income accruing from the ten offences (*daś-āparādhas*) and

15. According to Sahu, the modern villages named Baḍa-Karalā and Sāna-Karalā on the borders of the Sambalpur and Balangir Districts probably represent Kolleḍā. It has been suggested further that Kolleḍā is perhaps identical with Korāḷa mentioned in the Allahabad pillar inscription of Samudragupta as one of the kingdoms of Dakṣiṇāpatha whose king, Maṇṭarāja, was defeated and reinstated by him.
16. Although the expression *aṇḍaj-odbhava* is used in connection with Śaṅkilla, in all probability it refers to the belief that the family to which he belonged claimed to have originated from an egg.

    It is difficult to ascertain if the Rāṣṭra-kula to which the grantor and his father belonged was the same as the Rāṣṭrakūta family. It is noteworthy in this connection that some Rāṣṭrakūṭa chiefs are known to have ruled in a part of western Orissa as vassals of some powerful rulers including the Somavaṁśins. See no. II below. For a later record of this family issued from Koleḍā, see *infra*, no. V.
17. It will be noticed that the title *Mahārājādhirāja*, which is applied to Śaṅkilla, is conspicuous by its absence in connection with his son Devapya. It is difficult to ascertain if this omission indicates any change in the fortunes of the family or is due to oversight on the part of the writer.

17a. She was apparently the family deity.

18. Not yet identified.
19. This administrative division obviously covered the region round Kolleḍā which served as its headquarters.
20. Tālī has been identified with Tala on the confluence of the Maniari and Seonath in the Bilaspur District. This village is also called Sangama and is mentioned under the name Saṅgama-nagara in the Mallar plates of Śūrabala *alias* Udīrṇavaira (see II: II above). Dharmanagara is proposed to be identified with the modern village of Dhamā on the bank of the Mahanadi. See Sahu, *op.cit.*, 3.

the addition of creepers and trees.[21] The villagers were asked to pay the donee the *bhoga, bhāga, kara, hiraṇya* and other dues and live happily in the village.

Future kings are entreated to protect the grant as if it were their own grant, and twelve stanzas, said to have been extracted from the Dharmaśāstra are quoted in support of this exhortation.

The grant was issued on the **thirteenth tithi of the bright fortnight of the month of Bhādrapada in the twenty-third year of the reign of Janamejaya.**

The charter was written by Śrīkaṇṭha, son of the *Kāyastha* Śrīgura.[22] The grant ends with the auspicious formula *maṅgalaṁ mahāśrīḥ.*

21. *Daś-āparādhas*, which are mentioned in nos. IV:IV, VIII-X and XI, are omitted in other records of Janamejaya's reign. Trees and creepers are found listed along with the privileges conferred on the grantee only in the present grant.
22. The name may as well have been only Gura (correctly, Guru), *śrī* being only an honorific.

The fact that the record was written by Śrīkaṇṭha may be taken to indicate that he was also a *Kāyastha*, the omission of this word in connection with him being due to the scribe's carelessness. Alternatively it may be suggested that the designation was actually intended to be used for Śrīkaṇṭha, but it has been erroneously placed before his father's name. Such instances are not wanting in inscriptions.

II

DEGAON PLATES[1] OF THE TIME OF MAHĀBHAVAGUPTA I JANAMEJAYA

Provenance: Degaon, Balangir District, Orissa.
Language: Sanskrit. In a mixture of prose and verse.[2]
Metres: Verses 1, 3-6 and 8: *Vasantatilakā;* Verses 7 and 16: *Indravajrā*; Verse 9: *Mandākrāntā*; Verses 10-11, 13-15 and 17-18: *Anuṣṭubh* Verse 12: *Śālinī.*[3]
Script: Northern class of alphabets.
Date: About the end of the ninth century A.D.[4]

TEXT[5]

First Plate

1 सिद्धम्[6][।*]स्वस्ति स्फुरद्गजतुरङ्गसम(मु)द्गरै(तै)[7]घाद्ध(र्द्ध)निकधन्यजनै: सुसे–
2 व्य(व्या)त(त्) [।*] स्वर्गदेवेन्द्रिय[8]सुभोगसुखाभिरम्यात(त्)स्थानादित: प्रकटचित्तयो (वा)–

1. The plates are 22 cms. long and 11.9 cms. broad. The edges of the plates are raised a little. There is a circular hole bored about the centre of the left hand margin for the passage of the copper ring which held the plates together. The ends of the ring are soldered under a circular seal, 4 cms. in diameter, which bears, on its countersunk surface, the representation of Garuḍa with outstretched wings and beak-nose in low relief in running posture with its left hand extended to front as if to catch a serpent which is shown below.
2. Grammatically speaking, the text is highly incorrect and badly drafted.
3. The verses have been badly composed, and no care has been taken to comply with metrical rules as a result of which it often becomes difficult to recognise the metres. Verse 6 has been left incomplete. A few amendations of original readings have been suggested below which suit the metres better and give better sense. In this I have received some help from my esteemed friend Professor P.S. Sastry.
4. As will be seen from the abstract, the inscription gives the occasion of the gift, but the regnal year has been left unspecified. But as the engraver, Rayaṇa Ojhā's son Saṅgrāma, is also mentioned in the records of the third and eighth years of the reign of Mahābhavagupta I Janamejaya (see IV: I and V above), this inscription also appears to belong to the early years of his reign. This date is also supported by the mention of the tax stipulated to be paid annually by the donees in terms of a certain number of *palas* of silver in a couple of records of the sixth year of his reign (IV: II and III above) and the occurrence of the expression *rūpyapla* in one of them (*vide* IV: III above).
5. From impressions supplied by Dr. Snigdha Tripathy.
6. Expressed by a symbol.
7. *Ghā* is superfluous.
8. The metre would require something like स्वर्ग्गं तथेन्द्रिय°.

3 टिकाभिधानात(त्)[9] ।।[१।।*] नानामनोज्ञो मतिमान(न्) सुदक्षो यो व(ब)न्धुवर्गम्प्रति कल्प–

4 वृक्षः [।*] दुर्व्वारवीरवरवैरिशि(शि)रोविदाराः(रः) सु(शू)खा(रा)र यारुणतर[:*][10] सु(स)रणाङ्गण–

5 स्थः [।।२।।*]श्रीमङ्गलास्पदपदा(दं)म्वि(वि)[11]पदामभु(भू)मिः श्रीमत्**खड्गशिव**माण्ड–

6 लिक(कौ)[12] व(ब)भु(भू)वः(व)[।*] तस्यैव सु(सू)नू(नु)म(र्म)ली(लि)नि(नी) कृतारि[:*][13]स्फु(स्फू)र्जत्करालकरवालललत्क–

7 राग्रः[।।३।।*] आरुढतुङ्गसुतुरुङ्गवलसेदङ्गे[14] लक्ष्मीम्वहन(न्) ।।[15] स(स्व)कुलजां कुलना–

8 थभूतः दानाभिमानना(न)यविक्रमसत्प्रतापः सत्यातिसत्व(त्त्वो)धृतिसंयतिभु(भू)तिवास [:।।४।।*]

9 ख्यातस्सता(तां) गुणगणंग्ग(र्ग)णिकौ(तो)म(व)दान्यो श्री**मद्बालतुङ्ग**[16]इति माण्डलिक [:]की(लि)ला–

10 सीत(त्) । अस्य सुतः[17] प्रवरभद्रगजेन्द्रकल्पवृक्षः[17a] प्रोद(द्द)र्प्यशत्रुदलनोतिविनी–

11 तमूर्ति [:।।५।।*] आलम्व(म्ब)[18]पीवरकरोतिसुचारुशूरसद्दानसन्ततिसदाविलसज्जय–

12 श्रीः[19]।[।६।।*][20]

Second Plate: First Side

13 चक्रेण चक्री गदयाच भीमः सल्लाङ्गलेः(लै)ला(र्ला)ङ्गलिको म(व)दान्यो(न्यः) [।*] चापेन पार्थ[:*] प्र–

14 थित[:*] पृथिव्याः(व्यां) शस्त्रेण शस्त्रा(स्तः) तुरगैरतुल्यः [।।७।।*] श्रीमज्**जन्मेजयदेव** नृपेसततं

9. A reading like प्रकटचित्तवटाभिधानात् would suit the metre better.
10. The intended reading probably is शूरारिदारुणतरः. But शरारिमृत्यै would suit the metre better.
11. There is a superfluous stroke attached to the left lower portion of the letter.
12. For the sake of the metre we need something like श्रीखड्गतुङ्गशिवमाण्डलिको. It is noteworthy in this connection that the next ruler also had a name with the word *tuṅga* forming one of its components, and names terminating with this word were common among the Rāṣṭrakūṭas.
13. This *caraṇa* of *Indravajrā* does not go well with the verse which is in the *Vasantatilakā* metre.
14. आरूढतुङ्गचतुरङ्गबलैः समेतः appears to be the intended reading.
15. These marks of punctuation are superfluous.
16. For the sake of the metre, read श्रीबालतुङ्ग.
17. Better read अस्यात्मजः which would suit the metre without affecting the meaning adversely.
17a. Omit *vrkṣaḥ* for the sake of metre.
18. The use of *ālamba* instead of *lamba* is apparently inspired by metrical considerations.
19. This *akṣara* is incised at the right bottom of the plate. (below the last two but one letters).
20. This gives only half of the verse.

15 प्रसन्ने सामन्तचक्रशिरसा परिचुम्बिताङ्घ्रेः (ङ्घ्रौ) [।*] यस्य प्रतापशिखिनः (ना) प्रसभं

16 प्रतप्ताः प्र (प्रा) ज्ञा भवन्ति सकलाः खलु मण्डलेशाः [।।८।।*] त्यक्त्वा शीघ्रं सुकरकटकं ।।[21] काम–

17 रु (रु) पञ्च गत्वा [।*] क्षिप्त्वा कांञ्चि (ञ्चीं) समतटमनुः (नु) प्राप्य सन्मध्यदेशं यस्या-मार्ज्यप्र[22]–

18 थितविभः (भ) वा कुन्तलं शोधयित्वा कीर्ति[ः*] स्नाता सपदि जलधौ भाति लव्धा (ब्धा) म्व (म्ब) रेति [।।९।।*]

19 स[ः*] परममाहेश्वर[ः*] समधिगतपञ्च महाशब्द (ब्द) [ः*] महाराजाधिराज[ः*] माता–

20 पितृपादानुध्यातः लत्तलोरपुरविनी (नि) र्गतः वद्धांकुलभट्टारकस्य लव्ध (ब्ध) वर–

21 प्रसादः[23] राष्ट्रकु (कू) टामलकुलतिलक[ः*] परकुलमण्डलाधिपति [ः*] राणकश्री**मुग्ध**–

22 **गोन्दल** [ः*]कुशली तेलातट्टविषयीयकिरङ्केलाग्रामे महासामन्तराजनकराज–

23 पुत्रान (न्) विषयपतीन (न्) ग्रामभुजोधिकारिणः भोगिगण्डाप्रभृतयः[24] ज (जा) नपदानः (न्) ।।[25]

Second Plate: Second Side

24 अन्यानपि राजप्रसादिनश्चाट्ट (ट) भट्टवल्लभजातीयान (न्) घटपालद (दा) ण्डपासि (शि) का–

25 दीन (न्) मानयति वो (बो) धयति समादिशति च[।*] सर्व्वतः शिवमिहान्यत्[26][।*]विदित-मस्तु भव–

26 ताः (तां) ग्रामोयं चा (च) तु[ः*]सीमापर्यन्त[ः*] सजलस्थलारण्य[ः*] सगर्त्तोस (ष) रपाषाणः साम्र (म्र)–

27 मधुकपद्रसहितेन[27]।।[28] अचाटभट्टप्रवेशः निधिश्चोपनिधिवर्जितः[29] वखौडविनी (नि)–

28 र्गतः अन्तरलावास्तव्यः भट्टपुत्रश्रीभवणा (ना) गस्य सुतः[30] नारायणदासः अस्यै–

29 व[31] नप्त्या (प्त्रे) श्रीभुवणांग[32] कौण्डिन्यगोत्रवसिष्ठप्रवरमित्रावरुणानुप्रव–

30 राय काण्वशाखाय मातापित्रोरात्मनश्च पुण्याभिवृद्धये ताम्र (म्र) शासनीकृ–

31 त्य प्रदत्तोस्याभिः यतस्ताम्र (म्र) शासनात् अवलोक्य अस्याज्ञाविधि (धे) यीभूय उचितानुचितं

32 तादव्यं (व्यम्) [।*] पुष्य शुदि १४ अस्य शासनस्य प्रतिवार्षिकदाने सो (शो) भनरूप्य प्ल ३ दातव्य[म्।*]

21. These *daṇḍas* are redundant.
22. °मार्यप्र° appears to be the intended reading.
23. Better read °भट्टारकलब्धवरप्रसादः.
24. Read प्रभृतीन्.
25. These punctuation marks are uncalled for.
26. Read शिवामिहान्यच्च.
27. Read साम्रमधूकः.
28. These *daṇḍas* are not required.
29. Read निध्युपनिधिवर्जितः Normally we have the expression सनिधिः सोपनिधिः. Here it is just the opposite.
30. Read सुताय.
31. Read नारायणदासस्य.
32. Read श्रीभवनागाय.

33 धर्म्मश्लोकोनुलिख्यते [।*] स्वदत्ताम्परदत्ताम्वा[33] यो हरेद्वसुन्धराः[।*][34] स विष्ठायां कृमिभु(र्भू)त्वा

34 पितृभिः सह पच्यते [।।१०।।*]स्वदानात्फलमात्यन्त[35] परदत्तानुपालने [।*] मा भूत्फलशङ्का वा[36]

Third Plate

35 परदत्तेति पार्थिवाः [।।११।।*] सर्व्वं(र्व्वा)नेतान(न्) [भाविनः*]पार्थिवेन्द्रान(न्) भूयो भूयो याचते राम–

36 भद्रः[।*] स(सा)मान्योयं धर्म्मसेतुर्नृपाणां काले काले पालनीयो भवद्भिः[।।१२।।*][37]

37 हिरण्यमेकं गामेकं भु(भू)मि(मे)म(र)प्यर्द्ध[म*]ङ्गुलं(लम्) [।*]हरन(न्न)रकमायाति यावदाहु(भू)य(त)–

38 संप्लव[म्।।१३।।*] हरते हारयते भु(भू)मि(मिं) मन्दवु(बु)धि(द्धि)स्तमा(मो)वृतः [ः।*]स व(ब)द्धोवारुणैः[ः*] पासै(शै)ति(स्ति)र्ज्ज(र्य्य)–

39 यो(ग्यो) निशु(षु)गछ(च्छ)ति [।।१४।।*] ग्राखे(क्षे)प्ता च(चा)न(नु)मन्ता च ताने (न्ये)व नरके वसेत्[।।१५।।*][38] ग्रग्नेरप्रत्यय[39]

40 प्रथमः(मं) [सुवर्णं*] भु(भू)र्व्वं(र्व्वै)ष्णि(ष्ण)वि(वी) [सूर्यसुताश्च गावः ।*] यः काञ्चनं गाञ्च न[40]महि(ही)ञ्च दद्या[त्*] दता(त्ता)स्त्रयं(य)न्ति(स्ते)न भवं(व)–

41 न्ति लोका[ः।।१६।।*] [ग्रा*]स्फोष्ट(ट)यन्ति पितरः प्रवर्ग(ल्ग)न्ति पितामहा[ः।*] भु(भू)मिदाता कुलेजात[ः*] स नस्त्राता भ–

42 विष्यति[।।१७।।*] भु(भू)मि(मिं) यः प्रतिगृह्णा(ह्णा)ति यश्च भु (भू)मि(मिं) प्रयच्छति[।*] उभौ तौ पुण्यकर्म्माणौ नियते(तं) स्व–

43 र्गगामिनौ [।।१८।।*] न्यूनाक्षरमधिकाक्षरम्वा(रं वा) यदि (त्) परिलिखितं तत्सर्व्वम्प्र-माणमिति [।*] लिखित–

44 ञ्च (इ*)द(दं) ताम्र(म्र)शासन(नं) सान्धिविग्रहिघालाकेनेति ।।:: रयणाग्रोझासुतेन सं(स)ङग्रामेन(ण) उत्कि(त्की)र्ण्णे–

45 तं[41] ताम्र(म्र)शास[न*]मितिः[42] ।।

33. Read दत्तां वा.
34. Read हरेत वसुन्धराम्.
35. Read फलमत्यन्त.
36. Read मा भूदफलशङ्का वः.
37. The two halves of the stanza have changed place.
38. This is only the second half of the stanza, the first half being षष्टिं वर्षसहस्राणि स्वर्गे मोदति भूमिदः.
39. Read °रपत्यं.
40. This letter is superfluous.
41. Read उत्कीर्ण्णमिदं
42. This *visarga* is superfluous.

ABSTRACT

The versified *praśasti* following the *siddham* symbol describes **Prakaṭacittayoṭika**,[43] the place of issue of the charter, and gives an account of a Rāṣṭrakūṭa feudatory family which is said to have originally hailed from Lattalorapura.[44] Prakaṭacittayoṭika is said to have been endowed with numerous elephants, horses and the pleasures enjoyable by heavenly deities and inhabited by the affluent people.

The first member of the Rāṣṭrakūṭa feudatory line mentioned in the present record is Khaḍgaśiva who is described in a conventional manner and said to have vanquished powerful enemies in battle (vv. 2-3). He was followed by his son Bālatuṅga who is also described in equally conventional terms (vv. 3-5). Bālatuṅga was succeeded by his son **Mugdhagondala**[45] whose description[46] claims the remainder of the eulogy (vv. 5-9). He is compared to the epic heroes Kṛṣṇa, Bhīma, Balarāma[47] and Pārtha (v. 7) and described as a feudatory under Janamejaya whose feet are said to have been kissed by the heads of the circle of feudal chiefs (v. 8). His fame is said to have reached Kāmarūpa,[48] Kāñcī,[49] Samataṭa,[50] Madhyadeśa, Kuntala,[51] the ocean and the heaven[52] (v. 9).[53] He is stated to have acquired the five *mahāśabdas*, meditated upon the feet of his parents, obtained the favour of god Baddhāṅkulabhaṭṭāraka,[54] hailed from the city of Lattalora, belonged to the Rāṣṭrakūṭa

43. This is a rather strange name and the expression in question does not suit the metre. It has not been identified but must have been situated somewhere in the Balangir region.
44. Sometimes spelt as Lattalūra, it has been identified with modern Latur in the Oosmanabad District of Maharashtra. The Rāṣṭrakūṭas are often styled *Lattalūra-pura-varādhīśvara*. The Rāṣṭrakūṭa feudatory line in question obviously traced its origin from the Imperial Rāṣṭrakūṭas.
45. Though Mugdhagondala is described in detail, his name does not figure in the versified *praśasti* and is mentioned only in the formal portion in connection with the grant.
46. Referred to as *Cakrin* after *cakra* which is a well-known emblem of Vāsudeva-Kṛṣṇa and Viṣṇu.
47. Mentioned under the name Lāṅgalin as *lāṅgala* (plough) is one of his famous cognisances.
48. Region round Guwahati in Assam.
49. Modern Kanjivaram in the Chingleput District, Tamil Nadu.
50. A part of south-eastern Bengal, now in Bangladesh. Probably it had its capital at Karmānta which has been identified with modern Baḍ-Kāntā near Comilla. See D.C. Sircar, *Select Inscriptions bearing on Indian History and Civilization*, i, 265, fn. 4.
51. Northern Karnataka and the adjoining area of southern Maharashtra.
52. This reminds one of the Allahabad pillar inscription which speaks of Samudragupta's fame covering the whole earth and then reaching the heaven. See *ibid.*, 267, text-lines 29-30.
53. It is not quite clear whether the verse in question describes Mugdhagondala or his overlord Janamejaya. But it appears more reasonable to take it to refer to the former.
54. Obviously family deity of the Rāṣṭrakūṭa feudatory line brought to light by the present inscription.

family and to have been the lord of the circles of other (hostile) ruling families. He is given the titles of *Paramamāheśvara, Mahārājādhirāja* and *Rāṇaka.*

The object of the inscription is to record that Mugdhagondala gave away the village of Kiraṅkelā[55] situated in the Telātaṭṭa-*viṣaya*[55a] to Bhuvaṇāga (Bhavanāga), son of Nārāyaṇadāsa and grandson of *Bhaṭṭaputra* Bhavaṇā-(nā)ga, who belonged to the Kauṇḍinya *gotra*, the Vasiṣṭha *pravara,* the Mitrāvaruṇa *anupravara* and the Kāṇva *śākhā* (of the *Yajurveda*), hailed from Varavauḍā[56] and was a resident of Antaralā.[57] The chief's order concerning the grant was addressed to the *Mahāsāmantas,*[58] *Rājanaka,*[59] *Rājaputras,*[60] *Viṣaya-patis,*[61] village headmen (*Grāmabhuj*), *Bhogins,* Gaṇḍā[62] and other people.[63] The grant carried with it the usual privileges barring only the right to the major and minor deposits (*nidhis* and *upanidhis*)[64] and was subject to an annual payment of three *palas* of pure silver (*śobhana-rūpya*).[65] It was made on the fourteenth day of the bright fortnight of the month of Puṣya, *viz.,* Pauṣa.

Nine imprecatory verses (*dharma-ślokas*) have been cited. The charter was written by the *Sāndhivigrahin* Ghālāka[66] and engraved by Saṅgrāma, son of Rayaṇa Ojhā.[67]

55. Not identified.
55a. Telātaṭṭa (or Telātaṭa) *viṣaya* is mentioned as situated in Kosala in a couple of charters of Mahāśivagupta I Yayāti (see IV: XVI and XVII above) and comprised the territory on the bank of the river Tel, a tributory of the Mahānadī.
56. Not identified.
57. It has been identified with the modern village of Antaraḍā under the Tarava Police Station in the Balangir District, approximately 20°42′E and just by the side of Degaon, the provenance of the plates.
58. It looks a little strange that Mugdhagondala, who was himself a feudatory, addresses his order about the grant, *inter alia,* to the *mahāsāmantas.*
59. It is a title of feudatory chiefs or of the nobility and is also spelt as *Rājānaka, Rājanyaka* and *Rājanika.* Cf. *Rāṇaka* which is its derivative. See D.C. Sircar, *IEG,* 271-72.
60. A title of nobility. See *ibid.,* 272.
61. Literally meaning 'lord of the district', the *Viṣaya-pati* was an officer in charge of the administration of a *viṣaya* or district. Sometimes he is referred to as *Viṣayādhipati, Viṣayeśa, Viṣayeśvara,* etc. See *ibid.,* 378.
62. As the term *gaṇḍā* is connected with the monetary system, it is not impossible if it referred to an officer connected with minting or examination of coins. He is obviously the same as the *Gaṇḍaka* or *Gaṇḍakā* mentioned in the Bamhani plates of Śūrabala *alias* Udīrṇavaira (II: I) and the Malga plates of *Sāmanta* Indrarāja (II: Appendix).
63. The word in the original is *ja(jā)napada, i.e.,* inhabitant of the *janapada.* It is not met with in other Somavaṁśin records.
64. Most other copper-plate charters specifically state that the grant was accompanied by the right to the *nidhis* and *upanidhis.* In this case the donor reserved these rights for himself.
65. It two other grants of Janamejaya (IV: II and III above) also we find similar allusion to payment of tax by the donee; but the word *śobhana* is not met with in those records.
66. As no other record of Janamejaya refers to Ghālāka as *Mahāsandhivigrahin,* he was apparently a minister of war and peace under Mugdhagondala.
67. As stated above (note 4), the engraver of this record, Saṅgrāma, was responsible for engraving some other records of the earlier part of Janamejaya's reign also.

III

SANKHAMERI PLATES[1] OF MAHĀBHAVAGUPTA IV UDDYOTAKESARIN, YEAR 4

Provenence: Sankhameri, Cuttack District, Orissa.
Language: Sanskrit. In a mixture of prose and verse.
Metres: Verses 1, 3-7, 24: *Śārdūlavikrīḍita;* Verses 2, 8: *Vasantatilakā*; Verse 9: *Upajāti;* Verse 10: *Āryā*; Verse 11: *Rathoddhatā*; Verses 12-14, 16-21, 25, 26: *Anuṣṭubh;* Verse 15: *Indravajrā*; Verse 22: *Śālinī;* Verse 23: *Puṣpitāgrā*.
Script: Northern class of alphabets.
Date: Regnal year 4, Mārgaśīrṣa kṛṣṇa 10. About the middle of the eleventh century A.D.

TEXT[2]

First Plate

1 सिद्धम्[3][।*]ज्योत्स्नाशालिसमृद्धिभूः कुमुदिनीहासैकसम्पादनाधूत्तो धूर्ज्ज-
2 टी(टि)मौलिसौधवसतिः पीयूषधारो(रा)गृह[म्।*] तारान्तःपुरनायको रतिप-
3 [तेः*]शत्रे(स्त्रै)कशानो(णो)पलः क्षीरोदाण्ण(र्ण्ण)वनन्दनो विजयते देवः सुधादीधितिः [॥१॥*]
4 अस्यान्वये महति सान्द्रतमःकलङ्कविच्छायदिग्व[4]लयमार्ज्जनकूचकस[5][।*]
5 उत्पेदिरे सकलसद्गुणज्ज(ज)न्मकन्दाः कुन्दावदातयशसो जगति(ती)भुजस्ते [॥२॥*]
6 राजाभूज्जनमेजयोऽथ नृपतिर्ज्जातो ययातिः(ति)त(स्त)तः[6] श्रीमान् भीमर-
7 थोऽभवत्तदनु च क्ष्माचक्ररक्षामणिः [।*] अष्टाष्वे(स्वे)व दिगन्तरेषु विजय-
8 स्तम्भावलिच्छद्मना हृच्छल्यानि दिशाभुजामपि समारोप्यन्त यैर्व्वि-

1. The plates measure 25.5 x 17.7. cms. The set was originally attached to a copper ring which is found to be broken and half of the ring is now lost. At the end of the other half of the ring is soldered the royal seal in bronze which is very much corroded. The diameter of the surface of the seal measures 5 cms. Traces of the motifs are slightly visible on its countersunk surface, bearing in relief, the seated Gaja-Lakṣmī in the *padmāsana* posture, flanked by an elephant on either side, with raised trunk, standing on the lotus stalks with rising stems. When discovered, the plates were found covered with a coating of greenish verdigris.
2. From estampages.
3. Indicated by a symbol.
4. *Va* is not legible.
5. Read कूर्च्चकस्य as in nos. IV: XXII and XXVII.
6. This mark of punctuation is superfluous.

9 स्फुटम् ।[।३।।*] तस्माद्धर्म्मरथो मनोरथफल(लं) शीता(सां)न्सु(शु)व(वं)ङश(श) श्रियो

10 निस्त्रि(स्त्रिं)ङशै(शै)कश(स)खा शिखामणिरभू ।[6] नि(न्नि):शेषभूमीभुजा:(जाम्) [।*] य–

11 स्मिन् दिग्विजयावतारिणि पुरा विद्वेषिभूमीभुजा(ज): प्रातान्त्य[7] दिगन्तर(रं) तद–

12 नु च स्फीताश्चमूरेणव: [।।४।।*] स्वे(से)तूपान्तवनान्तरे हिमवत: पर्यन्तभूसीमनि

13 प्रागम्भोधितटीवनेषु कटके पूर्व्वरक्ष्माभृत: [।*]यस्योत्ताम्यदरातिरा–

14 जयुवतीनि[:*] श्वासभुञ्ज(ञ्झा)निलव्यासङ्गस्वनदन्तरालमुखरैर्ग्गीतं[यश:*]

15 कीचकै:[।।५।।*] भ्राता तस्य व(ब)भूव भूतलपतेर्भूतेशत्तु(तु)ल्यप्रभ: प्रख्यात–

16 :(तं) क्षितिभूषणं नघुष[8]इत्युर्व्वीपतीनां पति:यद्दोर्द्दण्डभुजङ्ग–

17 मेन विलसन्निस्त्रि(स्त्रिं)न्स्य(श) जिह्वाभृता पीतास्ते परिपन्थिपार्थिवचमू–

Second Plate: First Side

18 कण्ठान्तरे मारुता: [।।६।।*] अत्रास्ते करिवृन्दमुन्मदमहि प्रौढोस्ति पश्चान [न:*][9]

19 सन्ते(न्त्ये)तासु जगद्द्रुहो गिरिदरीकुम्भीषु कुम्भीनशा(सा): [।*]स्नेहादित्यभिधा [य][10]

20 वृद्धशवरीवर्ग्गेण व(ब)द्ध(द्धा) शृ(श्रु)णा यद्वैरिप्रमदाजनो वनभुव: सञ्चारम–

21 ध्यापित: [।।७।।*] तस्यानुजो नतसमस्तसपत्नमौलिरत्ना(त्नां)न्सु(शु)मीलित[11] पादसरो–

22 जरोचि: । विद्यानिधि: प्रतिनिधिर्म्मधुसूदनस्य जातोथ विश्वविजयी नृप–

23 तिय(यं)ययाति: ।[।८।।*] भटैरवष्टव्ध(ब्ध)मिदं नरेन्द्रै: राष्ट्रद्व(यं) कोष(स)– लमुत्कलञ्च अ–

24 कण्टक(कं) साधयत: समन्ताद् भुजद्वय(यं) यस्य कृतार्थमासीत् [।।९।।*] तस्य तत:

25 सुकृतफल(लं.) सफलीकृतलोकलोचनस्तनय: । समजनि गुणैक–

26 सीमा श्रीमानु **[द्]योतकेसरी** नृपति: [।।१०।।*] भक्तिदूरनतकुन्तलस्खलन्म–

27 ल्लिकाकुसुम[दाम*] राजय: । ढौकमन्त इव कीर्त्तिसन्ततीर्य(यं) प्रणेमू(मु)–

28 रभिरभितो[12] महीभुज: [।।११।।*] स्वस्ति [।*] श्री**ययातिनगरात्**[।*] परममाहेश्वर–

29 ष(प)रमभट्टारकमहाराजाधिराजष(प)रमेश्वरसोमकुलतिलकत्रिक–

30 लिङ्गाधिपतिश्रीमहाशि[वगु*]प्तराजदेवषा(पा)दानुध्यातष(प)रममाहेश्वरप–

31 रमभट्टारक ।।[13] महाराजाधिराजपरमेश्वरसोमकुलतिलकत्रिकलिङ्गाधिप–

32 ति**श्रीमहाभवगुप्त**राजदेव: कुशली ।[14] सङ्गाणमण्डलीयकोन्तङ्गाखण्डी–

33 य आगरवाडमुलाग्राम: अतस्तदिष [यी*]यवा(ब्रा)ह्मणानापूज्य समाहतृ(तृं)सन्निधातृ–

7. Read प्रातिष्ठन्त as in the corresponding stanza of nos. IV: XXII and XXVII.
8. Read नहुष.
9. This portion was actually engraved in the right upper corner of the plate which is cut and missing.
10. The letter is engraved very shallow and is practically illegible.
11. Read संमिलित.
12. Read प्रणेमुरभितो.
13. These *daṇḍas* are superfluous.
14. This punctuation mark is superfluous.

34 नियुक्ताधिकारिकदाण्डपाशिकपिशुनवे (वै) त्रिकावरोधजनराज्ञीराण–

Second Plate: Second Side

35 कराजपुत्रराजवल्लभभोगिजनप्रमुख[स*] मस्तजनपदान् समाज्ञा–

36 पयति। विदितमस्तु भवता (तां) यथाऽस्माभिरय (यं) ग्रामः सजलस्थलः सग–

37 र्त्तोस (ष) रः साम्रमधुकप्रभृ[ति*]नानावृक्षः सनिधिः सोपनिधिः हस्तिदण्ड ।[14] व–

38 रव (ब) लीर्व (व) र्द्द ।[14] चिट्टोलग्रन्धारुवाप्रत्यन्धारुवा ।[14] पदातिजीव्य ।[14] ग्रदत्ता ।[14] ग्र–

39 न्तरावड्डि ।[14] ग्रहिदण्ड ।[14] व (ब) न्धदण्ड ।[14] विजयवन्दापनादि ।[14] भविष्यत्करस–

40 मेतः सखण्डपालि (ली) यः सर्व्ववा (बा) धावर्ज्जितः सर्व्वोपरिकरादानसहि–

41 तः चतुःशी (सी) मावच्छिन्नः मध्यदेशविनिर्ग्ग (र्ग) ताय[14] कृष्णात्रेयगोत्र (त्रा) य

42 ।[14] [15]त्रियार्षप्रवराय ।[16]ऋग्वेदीयषडङ्गाध्यायिने ।[16]सु (शु) भाकर–

43 प्रपौत्राय ।[16]ग्रङ्गपौत्राय ।[16] रि (ऋ) षिकरपुत्राय ।[16] श्रीगोविन्दक–

44 राय ।[16] श (स) लिलधारापुरःसरं (र) ।[16] ग्रा (मा) चन्द्रार्क्कक्षितिसमकालोप–

45 भोगाथं (र्थं) मातापित्रोरात्म[न*]श्च पुण्ययशोभिवृध (द्ध) ये ताम्रशासरे (ना) करी–

46 कृत्य सम्प्रदत्त इत्यवगत्य समुचितकरभागभोगमुपनयन्दि (द्भि) र्भव–

47 द्भिः सुखेन प्रतिवस्तव्यमिति ।। भाविभिश्च भूपतिभिः [17]स्वद्द (द)–

48 ति (त्ति) रियमस्मदीया धर्म्मगौरवादस्मदनुरोधाच्च स्वदत्तिरि–

49 वानुपालनीय (या)।। तथा चोक्तं धर्मशास्त्रे [।*]व (ब) हुभिर्व्वसुधा दत्ता राजभिः स–

50 गरादिभिः[।*] यस्य यस्य यदा भूमिस्तस्य तस्य तदा फलम्[।।१२।।*] मा भू[18]–

Third Plate: First Side

51 दफलशङ्का वः परदति (त्ते) तिपार्थिवाः स्वदत्तात् फलमानन्त्यं परद–

52 त्तानुपालने ।।[१३।।*] षष्ठिं (ष्टिं) वर्षसहस्राणि स्वर्गे मोदति भूमदिः ग्राक्षे–

53 प्ता चानुमन्ता च दौ तौ नरकगामिनौ ।।[१४।।*] ग्रग्नेरपत्यं प्रथमं सुवर्ण्णं (र्णं) च[19]

54 भूर्वी (वैं) ष्णवी सूय (र्य) सुताश्च गावः। यः काञ्चनं गाश्च महीञ्च दद्यत् दत्तास्त्र–

55 यस्तेन भवन्ति ला (लो) काः ।।[१५।।*] ग्रास्फोटयन्ति पितरो वल्गयन्ति पितामहाः [।*] भू–

56 मिदाता कुले जातः स नस्त्राता भविष्यति ।।[१६।।*] भूमि (मिं) यः प्रतिगृह्णाति य–

57 श्च भूमिः (मिं) प्रयच्छति। उभै (भौ) तै (तौ) पुण्यकर्म्मो (र्म्मा) णै (णौ) नियतं स्वर्गगा–

58 मिनौ ।।[१७।।*] तडागानां सहस्रेण वाजपेयशतेन च [।*] गवां कोटि–

59 प्रदानेन भूमिहर्त्ता न शुध्यति ।।[१८।।*] हरते हारयते भूमिं मन्द–

60 वु (बु) द्धिः।[20] तमे (मो) वृतः [।*]सु (स) व (ब) द्धो वारुणैः पाशैः तिर्यग्योनिं स गच्छ–

61 ति ।।[१९।।*] स्वदता (त्तां) परदत्ताम्वा (त्तां वा) यो हरेत् (त) वसुन्धरां (राम्) [।*]
स विष्ठायाम् (यां) कृमिर्भूत्वा

15. Read त्र्यार्षेय°.
16. This mark of punctuation is unnecessary.
17. *Sva* is superfluous.
18. The portion of the plate bearing this letter is cut off.
19. This letter is redundant.
20. This mark of punctuation is uncalled for.

62 पितृभिः सह पच्यते।।[२०।।*] सामान्योऽयं धर्म्मंशे(से)तुर्नृपाणाम्(णां) काले काले
63 पालनीयो भवद्भिः। सर्वानितान् भाविनः पार्थिवेन्द्रान् भूयो भूयो य(या)–
64 चते रामभद्रः ।।[२१।।*] इति कमलदलाम्वु(म्बु)वि(बि)न्दुलोलां श्रियमनुचिन्त्य
65 मनुष्यजीवितञ्च । सकलमिदमुदाहृतञ्च वु(बु)द्धा(द्ध्वा) न हि पुरुषैः प–
66 रकीर्त्तयो विलोप्याः ।।[२२।।*] यत्कीर्त्तिभु(भुं)वनत्रयस्य कुहरे श(श) श्वत्तनी
67 [पूर्ण्णय]न्मन्त्रेण [सु*]चिरप्रणामरहिताः क्षौ(क्षो)णीभुजो भोगी(गि)न [:।*] यदो(द्दो)
दंण्डभवप्रताप–

Third Plate : Second Side

68 शिक्षी(खि)नो निस्त्रि(स्त्रिं)ङ्कश(श)। [20]धूमच्छटा दूरस्थापि चकार वैरियुवती रित्नेषुका–
69 श्याहमं ।।[21][२३।।*] उत्कलेकोष(स)ले देशे स महासन्धिविग्रही ।[22]श्राशी(सी)द्गुणग–
70 णाधारौ रुद्रदत्त इति श्रुतः ।।[२४।।*] महाक्षपटलाध्यक्ष [:*] सता(तां) म–
71 तः। श्रलीलिखददिदं ताम्रशासनं शत्रुसा(शा)सनः(नम्) ।।[२५।।*]महाराजाधिराज–
72 परमेश्वरश्रीमद्द्योतकेश(स)रिराजदेवस्य **प्रवर्द्धमानविज–**
73 **यराजे (ज्ये) चतुर्थे स(सं)म्व(व)[त्स*] रे** ।[23] मार्ग्ग व दि दशम्यां ।[23]यत्राङ्के
स(सं)म्व(व)त् ४
74 मार्ग्ग व दि १० [।*] सुवर्ण्णवि(वी)थिविज्ञानिवाहेरुमङ्गाकाभ्याउ(मू)क्ती(त्की)–
75 [र्ण्ण*]मिदं(दम्)[।।*]

ABSTRACT

The inscription aims at recording the grant, by **Mahābhavagupta IV Uddyotakesarin,**[24] of the village Āgaravāḍamulā situated in the Kontaḍḍā-*khaṇḍa* included in the Saṅgāṇa-*maṇḍala*[25] in favour of Govindakara, son, grandson and great-grandson respectively of Ṛṣikara, Aṅga and Śubhākara, who was a student of the six branches of the *Ṛgveda*[26] and hailed from Madhyadeśa and belonged to the Kṛṣṇātreya *gotra* with the three *ṛṣipravaras* on the **tenth day of the dark half of the month of Mārgaśīrṣa in the fourth regnal year.**

All other details are exactly the same as found in no. IV: XXVII.[27]

21. The reading of this word as well as of most of the previous line is extremely doubtful due to careless engraving as in the corresponding verse in no. IV: XXII.
22. In the corresponding stanza in no. IV: XXII this word has been doubtfully read as अश्वाङ्गण° which gives no sense.
23. This mark of punctuation is redundant.
2. The historical portion describing Uddyotakesarin and his predecessors is identical with the corresponding portion of no. IV: XXII.
25. Saṅgāna-*maṇḍala* may be the same as the present Sankhameri, the findspot of the record, on the bank of the Mahānadī in the Baramba Police Station and Tahsil, Cuttack District. Kontaḍḍā-*khaṇḍa* may be identical with Kontapādā on the bank of the same river in the same P.S. and Tahsil and adjoining the village Sankhameri. Āgaravādamūla cannot be satisfactorily identified. But there is a village called Barimula under the same Tahsil. However, it is quite afar from Sankhameri.
26. The expression in question (*Ṛgvedīya-ṣaḍ-aṅg-ādhyāyin*) may also be taken to mean a student of the *Ṛgveda* and the six *aṅgas* (*i.e.*, Vedāṅgas).
27. This is as one may naturally expect in view of the fact that both the grants were issued on the same day and incised by the same scribes.

IV

NUAPATNA PLATES[1] OF THE TIME OF MAHĀŚIVAGUPTA IV JANAMEJAYA, YEAR 5

Provenance: Nuapatna, Cuttack District, Orissa.
Reference: *Journal of the Orissa Research Society,* i, 29-33 and pls. 3-8.
Language: Sanskrit. In prose except only imprecatory and benedictive stanzas.
Metres: Verses 1-5: *Anuṣṭubh.*
Script: Northern class of alphabets.
Date: Regnal year 5, Phālguna kṛṣṇa 14. Close of the eleventh century A.D.

TEXT[2]

First Plate

1 सिद्धम्[3][।*] स्वस्ति [।*] श(स)ज्जनसमावासित श्रीमद्विजयपाटकात(त्) ।[4] परममा–
2 हेश्वर परमभट्टारकमहाराजाधिराजपरमेश्वर सोमुकु–
3 लतिलकत्रिकलिङ्गाधिपति श्रीमज्जनमेजयदेवदेवस्य प्रवर्द्ध–
4 मानविजयराज्ये पञ्च मे सम्व(संव)त्सरे फाल्गुने(न)माससित[पक्षे]
5 तिथौ चतुर्द्दश्यामङ्के सम्वत(संवत्) ५ फाल्गुन व दि १४ [।*] परममाहे–
6 श्वरपरमभट्टारकसोमकुलकमलकलिकाविकासभास्क–
7 र[:*]दुर्द्दण्डचण्डिमोद्रेकदुर्द्दमारिक्रमरमारमाचाङ्कशङ्क–
8 र[:*]सकलभुवनतलव(ब)लव(वा)न्कुम(मा)रशिर:[5]शेख–

Second Plate: First Side

9 र:[*]खरतरकरवालदावा[न[ल]जालकवलितारिकानन[:*]प–
10 श्चिमकलिङ्गाधिपतिमहाकुम(मा)राधिराजपरमेश्वर युवराजश्री–
11 धर्म्मरथदेववर्म्मा कुस(श)ली ।[6]सन्तममण्डलीय वावन्नखण्डे ।[6] ड–
12 लहारवेत्रजोङ्गसहिततुण्डिमखण्डक्षेत्रे ।[6] अतस्तद्वि[7]षयी–

1. The plates measure 15.8 cms. in length and 8.6 cms. in breadth. The seal attached to the ring, which holds the plates together, bears the figure of seated Gaja-Lakṣmī.
2. From plates 3-6 in the *Journal of the Orissa Research Society*, i.
3. Expressed by a symbol.
4. The mark of punctuation, which is unnecessary, is indicated by a vertical line with a small curved horizontal stroke attached to it on the left in the middle.
5. *Visarga* here and elsewhere, unless stated otherwise, is indicated by a couple of (pellets (hollow inside) joined to one another.
6. The mark of punctuation is superfluous.
7. The medial *i* is formed here in the usual manner. It differs from the same sign elsewhere in the record where it consists of just an inverted semi-circle on the top-line.

13 यव्ना(ब्रा)ह्‌मणानापु(पू)ज्य समाहत्तं सन्निधातृ।[8] नियुक्ताधिकारि–

14 दाण्डपासि(शि)क।[8] पिशुन।[8] वेत्रिकावरोधजन।[8] राज्ञी।[8] राणक–

15 राजपुत्र।[8] राजवल्लभ।[8] भोगिजनप्रमुखसमस्त जनपदा–

16 न् समाज्ञापयति। विदितमस्तु भवताम्। कोष्ठा[9]दाक्–

Second Plate: Second Side

17 ष्य खण्डक्षेत्रमिदमस्माभिः सजलस्थल(लं) सगर्त्तोषर(रं) सविटपा–

18 रण्य(ण्यं)समत्स्यकच्छप(पं) सनिधि सोपनिधि चतुःशी(सी)मावच्छिन्न(न्नं) स(सा)म्र मधु–

19 कप्रभृति[10]नानावृक्षादिसमेतं।[11] हस्तिदण्ड।[11] वरव(ब)लीवर्द्द।[11] चिट्टोल[12]।[13]

20 अन्धारुवा।[13] प्रत्यन्धारुवा।[13] पदातिजीव्य[13]। अदत्ता।[13] वसावका।[13] वि–

21 षय[14]वाली।[15] रिन्तकावडि।[15] अन्तरावड्डि। अहिदण्ड।[15] हलदण्ड।[15]व(ब)न्धद–

22 ण्ड।[15] वन्दापना।[15] विजयवन्दापनादिभविष्य[16]त्करसमेतं सखण्डपा–

23 लीयं सप्रतिहारं सर्व्वंवा(बा)धावर्ज्जितं[17] सर्व्वोपरिकरादानसमेतं।[18] म–

24 ध्यदेशीयशोणभद्रविनिर्ग्गताय।[18] वत्ससगोत्राय।[18] पञ्चार्षप्रव–

25 राय।[18] वैनतेयशर्म्मपौत्राय माधवशर्म्मपुत्राय।[18] साम–

Third Plate: First Side

26 वेदाध्यायिपण्डितश्रीजनपतिशर्म्मणे व्रा(ब्रा)ह्मणाय।[18] सलि–

27 लधारापुरःसरमाचन्द्रार्क्कक्षितिसमकालोपभोगात्थं(र्थं)माता–

28 पित्रोरात्मनश्च पुण्ययशोभिवृद्धये।[18] विषुवत्स(त्सं) क्रान्तिसम–

29 ये।[18] ताम्रशासनेनाकरीकृत्य सम्प्रदत्तमित्यवगय(त्य) समुचि–

30 तकरभोगभागमुपनयद्भिर्भवद्भिः सुखेन प्रतिवस्तव्यमिति।[19] भा–

31 विभिश्च भूपतिभिर्द्दत्तिरियमस्मदीया धर्म्मगौरवादस्मदनुरोधाच्च

32 स्वदि(द)त्तिरिवानुपालनीया।[19] तथा चोक्तं धर्म्मशास्त्रे।[19] व(ब)हुभिर्व्वसुधा दत्ता

8. This punctuation is uncalled for.
9. Behera: कोष्टा°.
10. Behera: प्रभृती°.
11. The punctuation mark is superfluous.
12. Behera: चिट्टाल.
13. The punctuation mark is uncalled for.
14. Behera: विसय°.
15. The mark of punctuation is superfluous.
16. Behera reads *bhaviṣa* and proposes to correct it to *bhaviṣya*. But *ṣya* is very clear in the facsimile.
17. *Anusvāra* in this as well as in the preceding cases has escaped Behera's notice. His suggestion to supply *visarga* after this as well as two earlier expressions is unwarranted. We expect *anusvāra* as the word *khaṇḍa-kṣetra* which these words qualify is in neuter singular.
18. This punctuation mark is superfluous.
19. This punctuation, which is required by the context, is ignored by Behera.

33 राजभिः सगरादिभिः [।*] यस्य यस्य यदा भूमिस्तस्य तस्य [20]तदा फलं (लम्) ।[।१।।*]

Third Plate: Second Side

34 स्वदत्तां परदत्ताम्वा (त्तां वा) यो हरेद्ध (रेत व) सुन्धराम् । स विपा (ष्ठा) यां कृमिर्भूत्वा

35 पितृभिः सह पच्येते: (पच्यते) [।।२।।*] मा भूदफलस (श) ङ्का वः परदत्तेति पार्त्थिवाः।। (।) स्व–

36 दानात्फलमानन्त्यं परदत्तानुपालने ।।[३।।*] गामेका (कां) स्वण्ण (र्ण्ण) मे–

37 कञ्च भूमेरप्यर्द्धमङ्गुलं (लम्) ।। (।) हरन्नरकमायाति यावदाभूतस–

38 म्प्लवं (वम्) [।।४।।*] निर्व्वंशो निर्द्धनो रोगी क्षीणायुः[21] शत्तुभिर्ज्जितः।। (।) भवेद्य–

39 :कुरुते वा (बा) धां विप्राणान्ताम्व्र (णां ताम्र) शासने ।।[५।।*] भूमिं यः[22] । ग्रास्फोटय–

40 यन्ति पितरः प्रवल्गन्ति पितामहाः । भूमिदाता कुले जातः को (स) न

41 स्त्राता भविष्यति ।[।६।।*] सन्धिविग्रहिराणक श्रीमल (ल्ल) दत्तः शासन–

42 मिदमलीलिखदिति ।। विज्ञानि (नी) हेरुकदास[23][:।।*]

ABSTRACT

Beginning with *siddham,* expressed symbolically, and *svasti,* the charter was issued from **Vijayapāṭaka**[24] on the **fourteenth day of the dark fortnight of the month of Phālguna in the fifth year of the increasingly victorious reign of the illustrious Janamejaya (II)** who is given the usual imperial titles met with in the Somavaṁśin records, *viz., Paramamāheśvara, Paramabhaṭṭāraka-Mahārājādhirāja-Parameśvara, Soma-kula-tilaka* and *Trikaliṅgādhipati,*[25] by the *Yuvarāja* (crown prince) Dharmmaratha[26] who is described as the very sun for the blossoming of the lotus-buds that is the Somakula and given the titles

20. *Ta,* which was left out by oversight, is incised below the line.
21. The *visarga* here and in the following line consists of two circles placed one above the other.
22. The remaining part of this well-known and oft-quoted imprecatory verse is omitted by oversight. The punctuation mark following *yaḥ,* which here consists of a single vertical line, is uncalled for.
23. These two words are engraved at the right end of the line after leaving a long gap following the punctuation mark.
24. It is difficult to ascertain whether *pāṭaka* forming part of this word is an error for *kaṭaka* met with in so many records of the dynasty or Vijayapāṭaka is to be taken here as the name of a locality which is yet to be identified. The first alternative appears more likely. *Pāṭaka* is, of course, a dictionary word and one of its meanings is 'part of half of a village' (see V.S. Apte, *The Student's Sanskrit-English Dictionary,* s.v. *pāṭaka*); but it does not suit the context.
25. Janamejaya mentioned here is to be distinguished from the first king of this name represented by nos. IV: I-XI and Suppl. I-II and may be identified with the homonymous son of Mahābhavagupta IV Uddyotakesarin known from the Ratnagiri plates.
26. If *yuvarāja* is here to be taken in its literal sense of heir-apparent cannot be ascertained.

Paramamāheśvara, Paramabhaṭṭāraka, Paścima-Kaliṅgādhipati[27] and *Mahākumārādhirāja-Parameśvara.*[28] Next we find mention of the plot of land (*khaṇḍa-kṣetra*) of Tuṇḍima together with Ḍalahāra and Vetrajoṅga situated in the Vāvanna-*khaṇḍa* included in the Santama-*maṇḍala*[29] and the statement that Dharmaratha worshipped the Brāhmaṇas of the district (*viṣaya*) and informed all the people[30] that he had donated plot of land belonging to his own fief (*koṣṭhād=ākṛṣya*) to the Brāhmaṇa *Paṇḍita* Janapatiśarman, son of Mādhavaśarman and grandson of Vainateyaśarman, who hailed from Śoṇabhadra[31] in Madhyadeśa, belonged to the Vatsa *gotra*, had five *pravaras* and was a student of the *Sāmaveda*. The grant was accompanied by the customary privileges and exemptions[32] and made on the occasion of a *viṣuvat saṅkrānti.*

Six imprecatory and benedictory stanzas, said to have been extracted from Dharmaśāstra, are quoted in support of the request to the future kings to protect the grant.

The charter was written by *Sandhivigrahin Rāṇaka* Malladatta and executed by the artisan Herukadāsa.[33]

27. Paścima-Kaliṅga cannot be identified satisfactorily. According to some [K.S. Behera, 'Administrative System of the Later Somavaṁśis', *Early Indian Political and Administrative Systems* (ed. D.C. Sircar), 89-90], it may be the same as Paścima-Laṅkā and may have denoted the Kosala part of the Somavaṁśin kingdom.
28. *Mahākumārādhirāja* is comparable to *Kumārādhirāja* used for Someśvara in no. IV: XXVIII and *Mahākumāra* employed for some later members of the Paramāra dynasty. Note the use of titles indicating that Dharmaratha ruled as an independent sovereign monarch for all practical purposes.
29. These localities have not been identified so far.
30. The addressees of the royal order are exactly the same as those in no. IV: XX.
31. It is yet to be identified.
32. Enumerated in lines 17-23, these exemptions and privileges are the same as those met with in later Somavaṁśin grants beginning with no. IV: XX.
33. Cf. Heruka who figures as the engraver in no. IV: Appendix 1. Whether the two were identical cannot be determined.

V

KAMALPUR PLATES[1] OF THE TIME OF MAHĀŚIVAGUPTA V KARNA, YEAR 4

Provenance: Kamalpur, Balangir District, Orissa.
Reference: K.C. Panigrahi, *The Journal of Orissa History,* i, 1ff. and plates.
Language: Sanskrit. In prose with the exception of usual benedictive and imprecative stanzas at the end.
Metres: Verses 1-4: *Anuṣṭubh.*
Script: Northern class of alphabets.
Date: Regnal year 4. About the beginning of the twelfth century A.D.

TEXT[2]

First Plate

1 सिद्धम्[3][।*]ओम्[3][।*]स्वस्ति [।*] स्त्री (श्री) **ययातिनगरात्** परममा-
2 हेस्व (श्व) रम[हा*]भटा (ट्टा) रक सो[म*]वंस (श) कू (कु) ल[4]कमले (ल)-
3 तिलकभास्करमा (म) हाराजाधी (धि) राजपरमेस्व (श्व)-
4 रश्री**कण्ण (र्ण) देवपादा: (द) प्रवर्द्धमाने (न) वी (वि) जय-**
5 **राजे (ज्य) स (सं) म (व) त (त्)** ४[।*]स्वस्ति[।*]**कोलेडापाटात्** परम-
6 वैष्णव (वा) [:*]समधी (धि) गु (ग) प्र (त) पञ्चमा (म) हास (श) व्द (ब्दा) [:*]स (श)
व्द (ब्द)[5]स (श)) द्व-
7 द्वयस (श) व्दा (ब्दा) भिनन्दित (ता) [:*]अनेकनिजनिखिलप्रज्ञा-
8 लङ्कृत (ता) [:*] डक[5a]डमर (रू) तृ (त्रि) वल (ली) कुय[6]खोत्रासित्-

Second Plate: First Side

9 तत[7] शतेचतुस्ठयस्तुवेलाण्डजवंसा (शो) द्भव (वा) [:*]शी (श्री)-

1. The plates measuring 17.5 x 11.2 cms. are held together by a circular ring passing through a roughly circular hole bored about the middle of the margin on the left. The surface of the seal fastened to the ring is covered with a lump of lead, making illegible whatever devices and/or legend may have been there.
2. From impressions.
3. Expressed symbolically.
4. In view of the employment of the word *vaṁśa* immediately before, *kula* is redundant.
5. This word is rendered superfluous by the same word following *śaṅkhadvaya* which is its more appropriate place.
5a. Read कनक.
6. Read तूर्यं.
7. Read खोत्रासितारातिचक्रा:. Almost the same expression is met with in the Banda plates of the Rāṣṭrakūṭa chief Paracakraśalya. See *EI,* xxx, 139, text-lines 4-6.

10 खम्भेस्व (श्व) रीवरलन्ध (ब्ध) प्रसाद (दा) [:*]स्वे (श्वे) लच्छत्ववि–

11 भूषित (ता) [:*]मा (म) हाराष्ट्रामलकुलतिलक (का) [:*]महामा–

12 ण्डलिक (का) [:*] महामण्डलेस्व (श्व) र (रा) [:*]राणकश्रीजयार्ण्णमपा–

13 दा:[।*] तस्य[8] सुत[।:*][9] गङ्गार्ण्णमस्य सुता[:*] **जयार्ण्णम**पादा [:*]

14 कोलेडामण्डले वाडकेलाग्रामे चतु (तुः) पत्रालप्र–

15 तिग्रहसति उभे पातुव[10]। मध्यदेशविनिर्ग–

16 त[11] महाप्रप्वाण[12] यजुर्वेदाध्यायिके (ने) मा (हा) रि–

Second Plate: Second Side

17 तगोत्र (त्राय) पञ्चारीषयान्वितविपा (प्रा) करो (र)–

18 भू (सु) त।[13] भा भ (व) करसुतरहशकर [14]सुत–

19 व (ध) रम[15]कर (राय) सासैत्वा[15a] तत सुत:[16] मार्गणे–

20 क (कं) दत्वा (त्वा) धान्यव (ब) न्धाच्छमुरिकृते[17] २ कापडव–

21 न्दापने १[।।*] भूमि (मिं) ज: (य:) प्रतिगृह्ला (ह्णा) ति ये च[18] भूमि (मिं)

22 प्रयच्छते (ति) [।*] उभो (भौ) द्वौ (तौ) पुन्य (ण्य) कर्म्माणौ नियतौ (तं)

23 स्वर्गगामे (मि) नो (नौ) ।[।१।।*] स्वदतं (त्तां) परदत्तं (त्तां) वा यो ह–

24 रेते (त) वंसोधरा[19] [।*] स विष्टा (ष्ठा) यां कृमिर्भूत्वा पि–

Third Plate

25 तृभि: सह पची (च्य) ते ।।[२।।*]सजलस्थलसविट–

26 पारण्यसगुरु (ल्म) ला (ल) तासमछ (त्स्य) कछपम (स) गु–

27 ल्मलता[20] च तक दता (त्ता) सि (सी) मा ।। मम वंस (श) परी–

28 क्षणे ये (य:) केचित्[20a] नृपभि (र्भ) वेत (त्) [।*]तस्याहं पा–

29 दलग्नानां मम किति[21]न लोपयेत (त्) ।।[३।।*] यस्य य–

8. Here we should expect *teṣāṁ* in view of the employment of plural in the immediately preceding word, *viz., pādāḥ*.
9. We should expect hereafter गङ्गार्ण्णम: or गङ्गार्ण्णमपादा: which is missing. In case गङ्गार्ण्णमपादा: were intended, the preceding word should also have been सुता:.
10. The meaning is not clear.
11. Read विनिर्गताय.
12. The intended reading perhaps is महापवणि.
13. This mark of punctuation is superfluous.
14. Panigrahi: रहणकर. The intended reading appears to have been रहस्यकर
15. Panigrahi: परम°.

15a. Read शासित्वा.

16. These words seem to be redundant.
17. Panigrahi reads चान्यवन्दाछमुरिकृतात् which gives no sense.
18. Read यश्च.
19. Read वसुन्धराम्.
20. This is unnecessarily repeated.

20a. Read कश्चिन्.

21. Read पादलग्नोस्मि मम कीर्ति.

30 स्य यदा भूमिः तस्य तस्य तदा फव्ल(ल)म् [।।४।।*][22] तस्य(स्या)हं
31 पादलग्नानां मम कृति न ला(लो)पय(ये)त(त्)[22a] [।।*]

ABSTRACT

After the triple auspicious formula consisting of *siddham* and *om* symbols and the word *svasti,* the inscription refers itself to the **fourth year** of the reign of the Somakula king **Karṇa** who is given the titles *Paramamāheśvara, Mahābhaṭṭāraka,*[23] *Mahārājādhirāja* and *Parameśvara*[24] and said to have been ruling from **Yayātinagara.** We are next introduced to the feudal chief **Jayārṇṇama,** son of Gaṅgāraṇṇama and grandson of Jayārṇṇama, who were evidently ruling from **Koleḍāpāṭa,**[25] whence the grant was issued. Jayārṇṇama is described as an ornament of the spotless Mahārāṣtra[26] family, sprung from egg-born family,[26a] having acquired the five *mahā-śabdas,* and as heralded by the music of a couple of conch-shells and is styled *Paramavaiṣṇava, Mahāmāṇḍalika, Mahāmaṇḍaleśvara* and *Rāṇaka.* He is further said to have been adorned by the white umbrella and to have secured a boon from the goddess Khambeśvarī.[27]

The object of the charter is to record the grant of a piece of land in the village Vāḍakelā[28] situated in the Koleḍā-*maṇḍala*[29] to the Brāhmaṇa Dharmakara, son of Rahasyakara, grandson of Bhābhakara and great-grandson of Viprakara who hailed from Madhyadeśa, was a student of the *Yajurveda* and belonged to the Hārita *gotra* and the Pañcārṣeya-*pravara.* The grant was

22. This is only the half of the well-known imprecatory stanza, the remaining half having been dropped.
22a. This is unnecessarily repeated from the second half of the third stanza.
23. We usually have *Pramabhaṭṭāraka*, not *Mahābhaṭṭāraka.*
24. The title *Trikaliṅgādhipati* and the official name Mahāśivagupta are missing here.
25. Evidently the same as Kolleḍā-samāvāsaka of Suppl. Inscr. I.
26. The intention may be to refer to the Mahārāṣṭra extraction of the family. Alternatively, it may be an error for Mahārāṣṭrakūṭa or Rāṣṭrakūṭa. For Mahārāṣṭrakūṭa (the same as Rāṣṭrakūṭa) as the name of ruling family, see *Bombay Gazetteer*, i (ii), 384, fn. 4; *EI*, xxx, 138.
26a. The claim to have sprung from the egg-born family is, as in the Sambalpur University Museum plates of Devapya (Suppl. Inscr.) I, due to local influence. The Bhañjas of Khiñjili-*maṇḍala,* too, regarded themselves as belonging to the egg-born family.
27. Devapya of the Sambalpur University Museum plates also professed his devotion to goddess Khambheśvarī, but the reference to white umbrella is conspicuous by its absence in that record. The mention of white umbrella together with the description that the circle of enemies was frightened by the sound of the golden *ḍamaru, trivalī* and *tūrya* occurs in the present record as well as in the Banda plates of Rāṣṭrakūṭa Paracakraśalya (*EI*, xxx, 139, text-lines 4-6 and 7), showing thereby that Jayārṇṇama also was a Rāṣṭrakūṭa chief.
28. Not identified.
29. The same as Kolleḍā-*maṇḍala* of the Sambalpur University Museum plates of Devapya.

subject to the payment by the donee of the *mārgaṇeka*[30] *dhānyabandhā*,[31] *cchamurikṛta*[32] 2 and *kāpaḍa-vandāpanā*[33] 1. The grant carried with it right to marshy and dry lands, trees, shrubs and creepers, and fish and tortoises, evidently within the donated land.

Four imprecatory stanzas are cited in support of the request for the protection of the grant.

30. Same as *mārgaṇika* mentioned in nos. IV: XXII and XXVIII and Suppl. Inscr. IV above.
31. Probably 'a fixed quantity of paddy' to be paid to the donor at regular intervals.
32. A tax to be paid in cash; its meaning is not clear.
33. Literally, 'a nazraṇa or present in the form of cloth'. This may have been a customary tax levied from the subjects, probably on the occasion of a religious ceremony like Durgā-pūjā when it was a custom to present a piece of cloth together with other presents in cash or kind to the king.

SELECT BIBLIOGRAPHY

A. Original Sources

I. *Sanskrit, Prakrit and other Indian Texts*

: *Divyāvadāna,* ed. by E.B. Cowell and R.A. Neil, Cambridge, 1886; ed. by P.L. Vaidya, Buddhist Sanskrit Text Series, No. 20, Darbhanga, 1959.

: *Mahābhārata,* with Nīlakaṇṭha's commentary, Chitrashala Press, Poona, 1929-33; Critical Edition, Bhandarkar Oriental Research Institute, Poona, 1927-66; Gita Press Edition, V.S. 2015.

: *Mahābhārata kī Nāmānukramaṇikā,* Gita Press, Gorakhpur, V.S. 2016.

: *Mahāvastu,* ed. by E. Senart, Paris, 1882-97.

: *Manusmṛti,* ed. by J. Jolly, London, 1887; with Kullūka's commentary, N.S.P., Bombay, 1929; with Medhātithi's commentary, Bombay, 1920; Engl. Tr. by G. Bühler, SBE, Vol. 25, Oxford, 1886.

: *Śukranītisāra,* Calcutta, 1890; Engl. Tr. by B.K. Sarkar, SBH, 2nd ed., Allahabad, 1923.

: *Yājñavalkya-smṛti,* with Aparārka's commentary, Anandashram Sanskrit Series, Poona, 1903-04; with Vijñāneśvara's Mitākṣarā commentary, Bombay, 1909.

Bāṇa : *Harṣa-carita* with Śaṅkara's gloss, BSS, Bombay, 1909.

: Kādambarī with the commentary of Bhānucandra and Siddhacandra, 9th ed., NSP, Bombay, 1948.

Candabaradāi : *Pṛthvīrāja-rāso,* Nagari Pracharini Sabha, Varanasi, 1907.

Dhoyin : *Pavana-dūta,* ed. by Manomohan Chakravarti (*JASB,* 1905, pp. 53-68); ed. by Chintaharan Chakravarti, Calcutta, 1926.

Hemacandra : *Abhidhāna-cintāmaṇi,* Bhavanagar, Vira Era, 2441.

Joshi, Tarkatirtha Laksmanasastri (Ed.) : *Dharmakośa,* Vol. I, Parts I-II, Wai, 1937-38.

Kalhaṇa : *Rāja-taraṅgiṇī*, ed. by M.A. Stein, Delhi, 1960.

Kauṭilya : *Arthaśāstra,* text edited by R.P. Kangle, Bombay, 1960; Engl. Tr. by R.P. Kangle, Bombay, 1963.

Kṣemendra : *Bṛhatkathā-mañjarī,* ed. by Sivadatta and K.P. Parab, 2nd edn., Bombay, 1931.

Rājaśekhara : *Kāvya-mīmāṁsā*, ed. by C.D. Dalal, Gaekwad Oriental Series, No. I, Baroda, 1934.

: *Viddhaśāla-bhañjikā,* ed. by J.B. Chaudhuri with the Camatkāra–taraṅgiṇī and Prāṇa-pratiṣṭhā commentaries, Calcutta Oriental Series, No. 10, Calcutta, 1943.

Sandhyākaranandin : *Rāma-carita,* ed. by H.P. Sastri, Memoirs of the Asiatic Society of Bengal, No. 5, Calcutta, 1910; Re-edited by R.C. Majumdar, R.G. Basak, and N.G. Banerji, Rajashahi, 1939.

Śāśvata : *Śāśvata-kośa,* Poona, 1930.

Somadevasūri : *Kathā-sarit-sāgara,* ed. by Durga Prasad and K.P. Parab, 4th edition, Bombay. 1930; Engl. Tr. by H.C. Tawney and Introductory Notes, etc. by N.M. Penzer, 10 vols., London 1924-28.

Śrīharṣa : *Naiṣadhīya-carita,* ed. with Nārāyaṇa's commentary by Sivadatta, 7th edition revised by W.L. Pansikar, Bombay, 1933.

Tulasidāsa : *Rāma-carita-mānasa,* Gita Press, Gorakhpur.

Vākpati : *Gauḍa-vaho,* ed. by S.P. Pandit and re-edited by N.B. Utgikar, BSS, No. XXXIV, Poona, 1927.

II. *Inscriptions*

Bhandarkar, D.R. : *List of Inscriptions of Northern India in Brāhmī and its Derivative Scripts, from about 200 A.C.,* Appendix to *EI,* xix-xxiii.

: *Inscriptions of the Early Gupta Kings, CII,* iii, ed. by B. Ch. Chhabra and G.S. Gai, Delhi, 1981.

Fleet, J.F. : *Inscriptions of the Early Gupta Kings and their Successors, CII,* iii, Calcutta, 1888. Indian Reprint with Notes and a Bibliography by A.K. Narain, Varanasi, 1970.

Hira Lal : *Inscriptions in the Central Provinces and Berar,* 2nd revised ed., Nagpur, 1932.

Jain, B.C. : *Mahanta Ghāsīdāsa Saṁgrahālaya: Purātattva Upavibhāga meṁ Saṁgṛhīta Vastuoṁ kā Sūcīpatra,* Part IV; *Utkīrṇa Lekha,* Raipur, 1961.

Lüders, H. : *A List of Brāhmī Inscriptions from the Earliest Times to about A.D. 400 with the exception of those of Aśoka, EI,* x, Appendix.

Majumdar, N.G. : *Inscriptions of Bengal*, iii, Rājashahi, 1929.

Mirashi, V.V. : *Inscriptions of the Kalachuri-Chedi Era, CII*, iv, Ootacamund, 1955.

: *Inscriptions of the Vākāṭakas, CII*, v, Ootacamund, 1963.

: *Inscriptions of the Śilāhāras, CII*, vi, New Delhi, 1977.

Rajaguru, S.N. : *Inscriptions of Orissa*, iv, Bhubaneswar, 1966.

Sircar, D.C. : *Select Inscriptions bearing on Indian History and Civilization*, i, 2nd revised ed., Calcutta, 1965; ii, Delhi, 1983.

III. *Numismatics*

Allan, John : *Catalogue of Indian Coins in the British Museum: Catalogue of the Coins of Ancient India*, London, 1936. British Museum Reprint, London, 1967.

: *Catalogue of Indian Coins in the British Museum: Catalogue of the Coins of the Gupta Dynasties and of Śaśāṅka, King of Gauḍa*, London, 1914. British Museum Reprint, London, 1967.

Altekar, A.S. : *Catalogue of the Gupta Coins in the Bayana Hoard*, Bombay, 1954.

: *The Coinage of the Gupta Empire*, Corpus of Indian Coins Series, iv, Varanasi, 1957.

IV. *Non-Indian Sources*

Beal, S. : *The Life of Hiuen Tsiang*, by Shaman Hwui Li, London, 1911.

McCrindle, J.W. : *Ancient India as described by Megasthenes and Arrian*, ed. by S.N. Majumdar Sastri, Calcutta, 1926.

: *Ancient India as described in Classical Literature*, Westminster, 1907.

Sachau, E. : *Alberuni's India*, 2 vols., London, 1910.

Watters, T. : *On Yuan Chwang's Travels in India*, 2 vols., London, 1904-05.

B. Modern Works

Agrawala, V.S. : *Harṣa-carita: Eka Sāṁskṛtika Adhyayana*, Patna, 1953.

: *Kādambarī: Eka Sāṁskṛtika Adhyayana*, Varanasi, 1958.

Altekar, A.S. : *State and Government in Ancient India*, 3rd ed., Delhi, 1958.

: *Rāshṭrakūṭas and their Times*, Poona, 1934.

Bajpai, K.D. & Pandey, S.K. : *Malhar 1975-77*, Sagar, 1978.

Banerji, R.D. : *History of Orissa*, i, Calcutta, 1930.

Basak, R.G. : *History of North-Eastern India*, Calcutta, 1967.

Bhatia, Pratipal : *The Paramāras*, New Delhi, 1970.

Bühler, G. : *Indian Palaeography*, Indian Reprint, Calcutta, 1959.

Burnell, A.C. : *Elements of South Indian Palaeography, from the Fourth to the Seventeenth Century A.D.*, 2nd ed., London, 1878.

Chattopadhyaya, S. : *Early History of Northern India*, 2nd ed., Calcutta, 1968.

Cunningham, A. : *The Ancient Geography of India, the Buddhist Period*, Indian Reprint, Varanasi, 1963.

Deshpande, Brahmanand : *Śodhamudrā* (Marathi), Aurangabad, 1977.

Dikshit, M.G. : *Madhya Pradesh ke Purātattva kī Rūparekhā*, Sagar, 1954.

Dubreuil, J.G. : *Ancient History of the Deccan* (Eng. Tr. from the French by V.S. Swaminadha Dikshitar), Pondicherry, 1920.

Ghoshal, U.N. : *Contributions to the History of the Hindu Revenue System*, 2nd ed., Calcutta, 1972.

Gopal, Lallanji : *Economic Life of Northern India* (*c. 700-1200 A.D.*), Varanasi, 1965.

Goyal, S.R. : *A History of the Imperial Guptas*, Allahabad, 1967.

Gupta, P.L. : *The Imperial Guptas*, i, Varanasi, 1974.

Jani, A.N. : *A Critical Study of Śrī-Harṣa's Naiṣadhīyacarita*, Baroda, 1957.

Jayaswal, K.P. : *History of India 150 A.D. to 350 A.D.*, Lahore, 1933.

Kane, P.V. : *History of Dharmaśāstra*, vols. i-v, Poona, 1930-62.

Khare, G.H. : *Dakṣiṇacyā Madhyayugīna Itihāsācī Sādhane* (*Sources of the Mediaeval History of the Deccan*), ii, Poona, 1934.

Law, B.C. : *Ancient Mid-Indian Kshatriya Tribes*, i, Calcutta, 1924.

: *Some Kshatriya Tribes of Ancient India*, Calcutta, 1924.

: *Tribes in Ancient India*, Poona, 1943.

: *Historical Geography of Ancient India*, Paris, 1954.

Majumdar, R.C. (Ed.) : *History of Bengal*, i, Dacca, 1943.

Majumdar, R.C. (ed.) : *History and Culture of the Indian People*, ii: *The Age of Imperial Unity*, 2nd ed., Bombay, 1953.

: *History and Culture of the Indian People*, iii: *The Classical Age*, Bombay, 1954.

: *History and Culture of the Indian People*, iv: *The Age of Imperial Kanauj*, Bombay, 1955.

: *History and Culture of the Indian People*, v: *The Struggle for Empire*, 2nd ed., Bombay, 1966.

: *The Classical Accounts of India*, Calcutta, 1960.

Majumdar, R.C. and Altekar, A.S. (Eds.) : *A New History of the Indian People*, vi: *The Vākāṭaka-Gupta Age*, Delhi, 1960.

Mazumdar, B.C. : *Orissa in the Making*, Calcutta, 1925.

Mirashi, V.V. : *Studies in Indology*, i, Nagpur, 1960 (1st ed.) and 1968 (2nd ed.); ii, Nagpur, 1961; iii, Nagpur, 1962; iv, Varanasi, 1963.

: *Literary and Historical Researches in Indology*, Delhi, 1975.

: *Indological Research Papers*, Nagpur, 1982.

: *Studies in Ancient Indian History*, Nagpur, 1984.

: *The History and Inscriptions of the Sātavāhanas and the Western Kshatrapas*, Bombay, 1981.

Mahtab, H.K. : *History of Orissa*, 2 vols., Cuttack, 1959-60.

Misra, B. : *Dynasties of Mediaeval Orissa*, Calcutta, 1933.

: *Orissa under the Bhauma-Kara Kings*, Calcutta, 1934.

Mitra, R.L. : *Antiquities of Orissa*, 2 vols., Reprint, Calcutta, 1961.

Nair, S. Bhaskaran (Ed.) : *Bhāratī-Bhānam* (Dr. K.V. Sarma Felicitation Volume), Hoshiarpur, 1980.

Nema, S.R. : *Political History of the Somavaṁśī Kings of South Kosala and Orissa*, New Delhi, 1978.

Ojha, G.H. : *Bhāratīya Prācīna Lipimālā*, Ajmer, 1918.

Panigrahi, K.C. : *Chronology of the Bhauma-Karas and the Somavaṁśīs of Orissa*, Bhopal, 1961.

Pargiter, F.E. : *The Purāṇa Text of the Dynasties of the Kali Age*, Indian Reprint, Varanasi, 1961.

Pillai, L.D.S. : *Indian Ephemeris, 700 A.D. to 2000 A.D.*, Madras, 1922.

Pohonekar, N.S. : *Raṭṭavaṁśīya Ballāla yācā Ardhāpura Śilālekha* (Marathi), Bombay, 1965.

Premi, Nathulal : *Jaina Sāhitya aur Itihāsa*, 2nd ed., Bombay, 1956.

Rajurkar, A.J. : *Candrapūracā Itihāsa* (Marathi), Chandrapur, 1956.

Ramesh, K.V. : *Indian Epigraphy,* i, Delhi, 1984.

Rath, B.K. : *Cultural History of Orissa,* Delhi, 1983.

Ray, H.C. : *Dynastic History of Northern India,* 2 vols., Calcutta, 1931, 1936.

Raychaudhuri, H.C. : *Political History of Ancient India,* 6th ed., Calcutta, 1953.

: *Studies in Indian Antiquities,* 2nd ed., Calcutta, 1958.

Roy, S.N. : *Historical and Cultural Studies in the Purāṇas,* Allahabad, 1978.

Sankaranarayanan, S. : *The Vishṇukuṇḍis and their Times,* Delhi, 1977.

Sastri, K.A. Nilakanta : *The Colas,* 2nd ed., Madras, 1955.

Shastri, Ajay Mitra : *An Outline of Early Buddhism,* Varanasi, 1965.

: *India as seen in the Bṛhatsaṁhitā of Varāhamihira,* Delhi, 1969.

: *Tripurī* (Hindi), Bhopal, 1971.

: *Yādava Inscriptions from Ambe Jogai,* Hoshiarpur, 1972.

: *India as seen in the Kuṭṭanīmata of Dāmodaragupta*, Delhi, 1975.

: *Kauśāmbī Hoard of Magha Coins,* Nagpur, 1979.

: *Ajantā* (Hindi), Delhi, 1980.

: *Early History of the Deccan: Problems and Perspectives,* Delhi, 1987.

Shastri, Ajay Mitra (Ed.) : *Coinage of the Sātavāhanas and Coins from Excavations*, Nagpur, 1972.

: *Coins and Early Indian Economy,* Varanasi, 1976.

: *Foreign Elements in Indian Indigenous Coins,* Varanasi, 1982.

Sinha, B.P. : *The Decline of the Kingdom of Magadha,* Patna, 1954.

: *Dynastic History of Magadha,* Delhi, 1977.

: *Readings in History and Culture,* Delhi, 1978.

Sircar, D.C. : *Successors of the Sātavāhanas in the Lower Deccan,* Calcutta, 1939.

: *Indian Epigraphy,* Delhi, 1965.

: *Studies in Indian Coins,* Delhi, 1968.

: *Studies in the Geography of Ancient and Mediaeval India,* 2nd ed., Delhi, 1971.

: *Studies in the Yuga Purāṇa and Other Texts,* Delhi, 1974.

Sircar, D.C. (Ed.) : *Early Indigenous Indian Coins,* Calcutta, 1971.

: *Early Indian Political and Administrative Systems,* Calcutta, 1972.

Subrahmanyam, R. (Ed.) : *Sri Mallampalli Somasekhara Sarma Commemoration Volume, JAHRS*, xxxv, Hyderabad, 1976.

Subudhi, Umakanta : *The Bhauma-Karas of Orissa*, Calcutta, 1978.

Thakur, U., and Misra, Y.K. (Eds.) : *The Heritage of India* (L.N. Mishra Commemoration Volume), Bodh Gaya, 1978.

Yazdani, G. (Ed.) : *Early History of the Deccan*, 2 vols., Oxford, 1960.

C. Glossaries

Apte, V.S. : *The Student's Sanskrit-English Dictionary*, Delhi, 1965.

Sircar, D.C. : *Indian Epigraphical Glossary*, Delhi, 1966.

Williams, Monier-Monier : *A Sanskrit-English Dictionary*, Oxford, 1899; Indian Reprint, Delhi, 1981.

D. Journals and Periodicals

Ancient India.
Annals of the Bhandarkar Oriental Research Institute.
Annual Bibliography of Indian Archaeology.
Annual Report on Indian Epigraphy.
Annual Report on South Indian Epigraphy.
Archaeological Survey of India, Annual Reports.
Archaeological Survey of India, Western Circle, Progress Reports.
Archaeological Survey Reports.
Asiatic Researches.
Corpus Inscriptionum Indicarum.
Indian Antiquary.
Indian Archaeology—A Review.
Indian Culture.
Indian Historical Quarterly.
Indian Museum Bulletin.
Indian Numismatic Chronicle.
Indica.
Epigraphia Andhrica.
Epigraphia Indica.
Itihas.
Journal and Proceedings of the Asiatic Society of Bengal.
Journal of the American Oriental Society.
Journal of Ancient Indian History.
Journal of the Andhra Historical Research Society.
Journal of the Asiatic Society.

Journal of the Asiatic Society, Letters.
Journal of the Asiatic Society of Bengal.
Journal of the Bihar and Orissa Research Society.
Journal of the Bihar Research Society.
Journal of the Bombay Branch of the Royal Asiatic Society.
Journal of the Department of Letters, Calcutta University.
Journal of the Epigraphical Society of India.
Journal of Indian History.
Journal of the Kalinga Historical Research Society.
Journal of the Madhya Pradesh Itihas Parishad.
Journal of the Numismatic Society of India.
Journal of the Oriental Institute, Baroda.
Journal of Orissa History.
Journal of the Orissa Research Society.
Journal of the Royal Asiatic Society.
Journal of the Royal Asiatic Society of Bengal, Letters.
Mahakosala Historical Society's Papers.
Mysore Archaeological Department, Annual Reports.
Nāgarī Pracāriṇī Patrikā.
New Aspects of the History of Orissa.
Numismatic Digest.
Orissa Historical Research Journal.
Prācya Pratibhā.
Proceedings of All-India Oriental Conference.
Proceedings of Indian History Congress.
Purāṇa.
Quarterly Journal of the Mythic Society.
South Indian Inscriptions.
Sri Venkateswara University Oriental Journal.
Studies in Indian Epigraphy (*Journal of the Epigraphical Society of India*).
The Journal of Orissa History.
Vidarbha Saṁśodhana Maṇḍala Vārṣika (Vidarbha Research Society's Annual).
Vishveshvaranand Indological Journal.

ADDENDA

SOME MORE PĀṆḌUVAṀŚIN AND SOMAVAṀŚIN INSCRIPTIONS

On 2 June 1990, Shri Rahul Kumar Singh, Curator, Government Museum, Bilaspur, and Shri Ved Prakash Nagayach, Archaeologist, Directorate of Archaeology and Museums, Raipur, visited me and my colleague Dr. Chandrashekhar Gupta and drew our attention to some important epigraphic finds, bearing on the Pāṇḍuvaṁśins, made recently and yet to be published in detail. Since publications like the present one seldom go through quick editions, I am appending here some important details regarding these inscriptions, as supplied by Shri Singh and Shri Nagayach, without prejudice to their detailed publication later. I take this opportunity to mention here a few other records of the Pāṇḍuvaṁśins casually noticed by some earlier scholars but yet lying unpublished till date. The sources of information about these inscriptions have been duly acknowledged.

I

KHAROD LAKṢMAṆEŚVARA TEMPLE INSCRIPTION OF ĪŚĀNADEVA

This long inscription, running into thirty-six lines, is incised on a stone-slab, measuring 24½" × 23", fixed on one of the walls of Lakṣmaṇeśvara (locally called Lakhneswar) Temple at Kharod in Bilaspur district, Madhya Pradesh. Composed in ornate Sanskrit stanzas and containing important historical information, it is unfortunately fragmentary and has not been published in full as yet.

It describes the Pāṇḍuvaṁśin king Indrabala as one whose lotus-like feet looked resplendent with the rows of crest-jewels of all the kings (*Sarvv-āvan-īśvara-śiromaṇi-rāji-rājat-pād-āmbujaḥ śaśi-kul-āmbara-pūrṇa-candraḥ| Āsīd=bhuvaḥ patir=avārita-vīra.....pāsta-ripur=Indrabal-ābhidhānaḥ||*). His son Īśānadeva (*Śrīmān=Īśānadevaḥ kṣitipati-tilakas=tasya putr-ottamo=bhūd*) erected the temple at Kharod and gifted to it some villages including Sāṭṭhapadrakagrāma.[1] It also refers to a place called Indrapura, evidently named after Indrabala, and mentions a district (*viṣaya*) called Kośīra-Nandapura-*viṣaya*, obviously named after the twin localities of Kośīra and Nandapura,[2]

1. The name of this village was tentatively read as Ghoṭhapadraka-*grāma* by Hira Lal (*ICPB*, 125). But it is clearly readable as Sāṭṭhapadraka-*grāma* in the estampage given by Shri Singh. It is not yet identified.
2. This *viṣaya* is also mentioned in the Bardula plates of Śivagupta (see *supra*, 119, text-lines 6-7). Kosir and Nandapur are two adjoining villages in Sarangarh tehsil of Raigarh district of Madhya Pradesh and the district was evidently named after the villagers. As per the information supplied by Shri Singh, some antiquarian remains in the form of some brickwork, probably datable to the Pāṇḍuvaṁśin period, and a fortification with a moat as well as the rumours of the discovery of copper-plates and old coins indicate the antiquity of Kosir.

and a number of villages including Mekalapadraka, which was apparently named after the Mekalā country.[3]

II

A HOARD OF NINE COPPER-PLATE GRANTS OF ŚIVAGUPTA BĀLĀRJUNA FROM SIRPUR

A hoard of nine sets of copper-plates of the Pāṇḍuvaṁśin king Śivagupta Bālārjuna was found accidentally while digging a small mound at Sirpur (ancient Śrīpura) in Raipur district of Madhya Pradesh in April 1987. It is now deposited with the Archaeologist at Raipur. All the sets, which have been found together with their seals and rings (either attached or separately), are incised on three plates. This is indeed a very important discovery in the history of Pāṇḍuvaṁśin epigraphy and sheds welcome light on the politico-religious history of South Kosalā. While the records are yet to be published in detail, brief information about this epoch-making find was given at a seminar on the Art of Chhattisgarh organised by the Directorate of Archaeology and Museums, Madhya Pradesh, at Raipur on 22 March 1990. A few important details from these plates are given below in a chronological sequence, on the basis of information supplied by Shri Nagayach, Shri Singh and Shri G.L. Raikwar, Registering Officer, Bilaspur.

Set 1

Engraved on three plates with 7/8/8/8/2 lines on inscribed faces barring the obverse of the first plate which is left blank, it records the grant of the village Ravituṅga included in the Kikkiḍa-*bhukti* to the Śaiva teachers (*gurus*) of the penance-grove (*tapovana-sthāna*) attached to the shrine of Muktataleśvara installed in the low-lying land (*tala*) at Śrīpura. The teachers are described as hailing from Phuṭṭapāṁṭi and belonging to Nandapura. Kikkiḍa-*bhukti* is apparently the same as Kikkiḍā-*ābhoga* mentioned in a Durg stone inscription, Kikkiḍa (or Kikkiḍā) being probably identifiable with the village of Kukḍa, about 18 miles from Durg,[4] while Nandapura may be the same as the locality of that name known from the Pipardula plates of the Śarabhapurīya king Narendra.[5] The charter was issued on the fourteenth day of the first fortnight of Māgha in the twenty-fifth year of Śivagupta's reign and is thus about three years later than his Bonda plates.

3. For earlier notices, see H. Cousens, *Progress Report*, 1904, 54; Hira Lal, *ICPB*, 125; V.V. Mirashi, *Studies in Indology*, I, 2nd ed., 257-58. The fuller reading of the verse referring to Indrabala and Īśānadeva has been possible with the help of an impression supplied by Shri Singh.
4. Hira Lal, *ICPB*, 36.
5. *Supra*, 5, text-line 6.

Set 2

Consisting of three plates bearing 7/7/6/6 lines on the inscribed faces, the first and the third plate being incised only on the inner side, and issued on the fifth day of the first fortnight of Vaiśākha in the thirty-seventh year of Śivagupta, it registers the grant of the village Hastipadraka located in the division called Svalpaśarkarāmārga to thei llustrious (*bhagavat-pāda*) Īrhācārya belonging to Nandapura at the time of the installation of the temple of Bāleśvara. While Nandapura is already known, Śarkarā-mārga may have something to do with the village Śarkarāpadraka mentioned in the Pipardula plates of Narendra as situated in the Nandapura-*bhoga*[6] or Śarkarāpāṭaka mentioned in the Bonda plates of Śivagupta.[7] But in view of the fact that the donee hailed from Nandapura, the former alternative looks more likely. The addition of the prefix *svalpa* indicates that there were two villages of this name, larger and smallar, the latter being intended in the present context. The shrine of Bāleśvara is mentioned in numerous plates.

Set 3

It is incised on a set of three plates which bear 7/7/7/7/4 lines of writing on the inscribed faces, the outer side of the first plate being left blank. It records the grant of the village Bhāṇḍāgāracuttāka (?) situated in the Aryyaṅka-*bhoga* to Śaivācārya Aho(gho)raśiva of Nandapura at the time of the establishment of the monastic residence (*maṭhikā*) attached to the shrine of Bāleśvara-bhaṭṭāraka erected by the king himself (*sva-kārita*) on the low-lying land at Śrīpura on the full-moon day of Śrāvaṇa in the thirty-eighth year of his reign. While the donated village cannot be identified, Aryyaṅka is evidently Arang in Raipur district and was apparently the divisional headquarters.

Set 4

It is engraved on a set of three plates which bear on incised faces (barring the first side of the first plate) 7/7/7/7/4 lines and is dated on the full-moon day of Śrāvaṇa in the forty-sixth regnal year. Its object is to register the grant of the village Bhāṇḍāgāra-takkaḍaṅśaka included in the Devī-*bhoga* on the occasion of the establishment of the shrine of Dayeśvara-bhaṭṭāra within the *maṭhikā* of the Bāleśvara-bhaṭṭāraka temple in the low-lying land of Śrīpura for the purpose of its repairs (when needed) and for the maintenance of its employees. The shrine of Dayeśvara-bhaṭṭāraka is said to have been built by the king himself. Devī-*bhoga* cannot be located.

Set 5

Issued on the twenty-fifth day of the month of Phālguna in the forty-eighth year of the reign and inscribed on the engraved sides of the three plates,

6. *Ibid.*
7. *Supra*, 124, 126.

bearing 7/7/7/7/4 lines, it records the donation of the village Devapadrullaka attached to Bhāṇḍāgār-Āśvatthaka forming part of the Cullāṭasīmā-*bhoga* to the illustrious teacher Aho(gho)raśiva also known as Īrhācārya, belonging to Nandapura on the occasion of the installation of the shrine of the god (*āyatana-deva-bhaṭṭāraka-pratiṣṭhā*) Amareśvara built by the illustrious Amaradevī[8] in the *maṭhikā* attached to the shrine of Bāleśvara-bhaṭṭāraka built on the low-lying land at Śrīpura.

Of the localities mentioned in the record, Cullāṭasīmā-*bhoga* is already known from the Kurud plates of Narendra,[9] while the villages Bhaṇḍāgār-Āśvatthaka and Devapadrullaka cannot be identified at present. Śrīpura and Nandapura are well-known from several records.

Set 6

Engraved on a set of three plates bearing on their inscribed sides 7/7/7/8/3 lines and issued on the fourth day of the first fortnight of the month of Śrāvaṇa in the fifty-fifth regnal year, it records the grant of the village Virttoḍaka situated in the Uṇi-*bhoga* at the time of the installation of a shrine within the premises of the temple of Bāleśvara-bhaṭṭāraka.[10] The Uṇi-*bhoga* is obviously identical with the Oṇi-*bhoga* known from the Lodhia plates of the fifty-seventh year[11] and the undated Mallar plates[12] of Śivagupta himself, while it is difficult to say anything definitely regarding the location of the village Virttoḍaka located in this *bhoga*.

Set 7

This record is incised on a set of three plates of which the first and third bear writing only on the inner sides and the middle one on both sides, each inscribed face bearing seven lines of writing. It records the gift of the village Katambapadūllaka situated in the Cullāḍaśimā-*bhoga* in favour of a shrine in the *maṭhikā* attached to the temple of Bāleśvara. The village Katambapadūllaka evidently reminds one of the locality called Kadambapadrullaka mentioned in the Mallar plates of the Śarabhapurīya king Jayarāja, dated in his fifth regnal year,[13] on account of the closeness of the two names phonetically; but there it is stated to have formed part of the administrative division called Antaranālaka, whereas the village in question was situated in the Cullāḍaśimā-

8. The shrine was apparently named after herself.
9. *Supra*, 8, text-lines 2-3, with the only difference that the first part of the name is spelt as Cullāḍa instead of Cullāṭa.
10. The name of the shrine appears to be doubtful: the reading as supplied to us is *śrī-Bāleśvara-bhaṭṭāraka-pratidvābbaśvara-bhaṭṭāraka-praviṣṭa-kāle* which shows clearly that the shrine in question was definitely attached to the temple of Bāleśvara-bhaṭṭāraka. The word *prati* probably stands for *pratibaddha*.
11. *Supra*, 128, 132.
12. *Supra*, 138, 140.
13. *Supra*, 17, 19.

bhoga as is known from several records. Thus, they cannot be identified without assuming some change in the boundaries of the two administrative divisions, of which no evidence is forthcoming.

This as well as the next two records are undated but, as will be seen in the sequel, are closely connected with the records noticed so far.

Set 8

The set of three plates employed for this record bears writing on the inner side of the first plate while both sides of the middle and last plates are incised. The first four inscribed faces bear seven lines each and the last inscribed face has only two lines. The inscription records the grant of the village Kośambraka included in the Svalpa-Śarkarāmārga to the shrine of Ammeśvara-bhaṭṭāraka built by Ammādevī[14] near the Bāleśvara temple in the low-lying land at Śrīpura.

Set 9

This record is also engraved on a set of three plates with the obverse and reverse of the first and last plates respectively left blank. The first three inscribed sides bear seven lines each, while the last incised side has six lines. It registers the grant of the village Corapadraka situated in Rohāsīmā-*bhoga* in favour of *Bhaṭṭa* Jejjada of the Kauśika *gotra* and the Kauthuma *śākhā* of the *Chāndoga* (*Sāmveda*). The localities are not identifiable at present.

Even though this is the only record in the entire hoard not explicitly connected with any temple and made to a Brāhmaṇa donee, it must also have been connected with some religious establishment, either the Bāleśvara temple or some other subsidiary shrine or some monastic establishment attached to it, which would explain its inclusion in the hoard. Probably the Brāhmaṇa beneficiary was in charge of some activity like worship connected with a shrine.

The last two records (sets 7 and 8), though undated due to oversight, can be easily brought into close relation with the dated ones by their being associated with the Bāleśvara temple at Śrīpura. If the donation of a village in a particular *bhoga* is of any significance in this matter, set 7 was evidently close in point of time to set 5 as both record gifts of places included in the Cullāṭ(ḍ)asīmā-*bhoga* and thus may have been issued around the forty-eighth regnal year. On the same consideration No. 8 might be connected with No. 2 and may be dated close to the thirty-seventh year of Śivagupta's reign. Of course, one cannot be quite sure on this point.

14. Evidently, she lent her name to the shrine built by her and in this respect this case is comparable, in this particular hoard, to that of Amaradevī. Perhaps it may be too much to try to associate these ladies with the royal family.

III

MALLAR PLATES OF ŚIVAGUPTA, YEAR 57

Recently a copper-plate grant of the Pāṇḍuvaṁśin king Śivagupta was found at the well-known antiquarian town of Mallar in the Bilaspur district of Madhya Pradesh. I got this information from Shri Rahul Kumar Singh who presented a detailed note on the charter at the seminar on the Art of Chhattisgarh.

The record is incised on a set of three plates measuring 14.5 × 21 cm, and the seal attached to the ring holding the plates together has a diameter of 9 cm. The total weight of the plates, seal and the ring is 2.900 kg. The obverse of the first plate is left blank, while the other two plates bear the writing on both sides. All the inscribed sides have eight lines each. The inscription on the seal as well as the initial part of the record is the same as met with in other grants of the king who is described as son of Harṣagupta.

The record is of great importance mainly for two reasons: (*i*) being issued on the *first* twelfth day (*dvādaśī*)[15] of the dark fortnight of the month of Phālguna in the fifty-seventh regnal year,[16] this happens to be the latest record of his reign;[17] and (*ii*) it supplies very valuable information regarding the Bāleśvara temple built by Śivagupta and the Pāśupata sect of Śaivism as will be shown in the sequel.

The inscription records a grant by Śivagupta of the twin villages Pāśipadraka and Kurapadraka[18] situated in the Uṇi-*bhoga*,[19] in lieu of the earlier granted village of Bhāṇḍāgāra-Tulapadraka included in the same *bhoga*, to a renowned Pāśupata teacher for certain charitable acts. We are told that Śivagupta built the temple of Bāleśvara-bhaṭṭāraka and for the maintenance of the penance grove (*tapovana*) attached to it he placed the above-mentioned villages at the disposal of the illustrious revered Bhīmasoma, pupil of the illustrious Tejasoma and grand-pupil of the illustrious Rudrasoma,[20] who

15. There were apparently two *dvādaśīs* in the dark fortnight of Phālguna that year and the first one (*prathama*) was meant.
16. This date is recorded in words at the end of the record. But on the obverse of the first plate the details are given in figures as the twelfth (?) day of the month of Phagguṇa (Phālguna) in the fifty-seventh (?) year (of the king's reign). This would show that the months recorded in the Pāṇḍuvaṁśin records are to be taken as *pūrṇimānta*.
17. The Lodhia plates of the fifty-seventh year were given on the full-moon day of the month of Kārttika (*supra*, 131, text-lines 31-32), whereas the stray plate from Mallar, attributable to him, was issued on the thirtieth day of Māgha in the same year (*ibid.*, 164, text-lines 7-8). The present grant was thus later than the other Mallar charter by twelve days.
18. Literally rendered, the expression would mean "Pāśipadraka together with Kurapadraka", showing that greater importance was attached to Pāśipadraka. In a subsequent line also the village (Pāśipadraka) is said to have been given along with Kurapadraka.
19. The name is spelt subsequently in the same record as Oṇi-*bhoga*.
20. Rudrasoma is styled *guru*.

belonged to the line of teachers hailing from the illustrious Lakulīśa-nātha who himself was born in the Brāhmaṇa family of Somaśarman, was 'the moon for the world' and was initiated with the *mahāvrata*. It is said that sixty-six incarnations of Śiva[21] take place in various *yugas* for the welfare of the world and that Śiva incarnated himself as Lakulīśa[22] in the Kali age. There is also mention of the eight forms of Śiva.[23] The perpetual grant was made to Bhīmasoma to meet the expenses of sacrifices, initiatory rites, preaching and residence of his pupils and grand-pupils (*i.e.* the line of Śaiva ascetics emanating from him) and of the repairs to the temple.

We also get a detailed description of the extent of the gift villages in terms of the *hasta* measure which is explicitly stated to be equal to twenty-four digits (*aṅgulas*). We are told that in the east extending north-south from the half-river (Mahānadī) the land measured 7350 *hastas*, in the south extending north-west 6151 *hastas*, in the west extending south-north 7000 *hastas*, and in the north extending west-east 6350 *hastas*. This sort of detailed measurement is extremely interesting as it is not met with in either the Pāṇḍuvaṁśin records or in any other epigraph included in this volume. In fact, this is the exact measurement of the land from Pāśipadraka to Kurapadraka situated to the south of the river Mahānadī with the temple of Bāleśvara-bhaṭṭāraka situated between them diagonally.

Fortunately for us, the localities mentioned in the record can still be identified easily and convincingly. Thus, Pāśipadraka is now represented by the village of Pāsida on the southern bank of the Mahānadī, Kurapadraka by Kolapadar situated diagonally opposite Pāsida in the south-east, while between these two villages Bāleśvara-bhaṭṭāraka is now known as Bhālesar Pahāḍ. As seen from some earlier records, Bāleśvara temple was located at Śrīpura which was evidently a great centre of the Paśupata sect. Thus the record is of great value for the reconstruction of the socio-religious and economic conditions during the last days of the Pāṇḍuvaṁśin rule in South Kosalā.

IV

MALLAR STONE INSCRIPTION OF ŚIVAGUPTA BĀLĀRJUNA

The red stone slab, bearing this extremely fragmentary inscription, running into twenty-one lines and measuring 32″ × 16″, was obtained by

21. The actual expression *Gahaneśasya mūrttayo Rudrāḥ* used here means that they are in fact Rudras who are exact replicas (*mūrtti*) of Śiva, here called Gahaneśa.
22. The record reads *adhunā Kali-kālam=āsādya śrīmal=Lakulīśanāth=ovatīryya.*
23. For Kālidāsa's reference to the eight bodies of Śiva, see *Abhijñāna—Śākuntala*, I.1. An early Vākāṭaka sculptural representation of Aṣṭamūrti Śiva has been reported from Mandhal in Nagpur district during excavations conducted by the Nagpur University. In it eight forms of the god are represented by eight heads, four on top, two on Shoulders and two on hips.

Pandit Chhedilal Pandey from one Basin Dipra of Mallar around 1970. Broken vertically into three pieces, this is now preserved with Shri Raghunandan Prasad Pandey of the town. Due to the present fragmentary condition of the record only the name Bālārjuna, who donated the villages of Gokṣaragrāma and Vorāpāṭaka to a certain establishment, whose exact nature is yet to be ascertained, can be made out definitely. The record also mentions a saint, named Aghorajyoti, evidently belonging to the Pāśupata sect of Śaivism.[24]

V

SOME MORE INSCRIPTIONS OF ŚIVAGUPTA BĀLĀRJUNA AT SIRPUR

We have included a few inscriptions of Śivagupta Bālārjuna from the Gandharveśvara temple at Sirpur earlier in this volume.[25] A few more inscriptions on stone slabs deposited within the premises of this temple have been mentioned by Hira Lal following some earlier writers, and we may notice them here briefly.

(*i*) This record is engraved on a slab built into the floor at the entrance. It refers to Bālārjuna (Śivagupta) and the gardeners (*mālākāras*) of Praṇavahaṭṭaka, which is evidently the same as Navahaṭṭaka of another inscription from the same temple.[26] The object of this record was undoubtedly to mention offerings of flowers during Bālārjuna's rule by the gardeners of the New Market at Śrīpura to god Śiva who is praised in the beginning of the epigraph.[27]

(*ii*) This inscription is engraved on three sides of a pillar deposited in the temple premises. It is a long record, but much mutilated. In the fourth line on the northern face occurs the name Śivagupta who is said to have obtained the title of Bālārjuna by his skill in the use of arrows by which he killed enemies in war. Śrīpurī, evidently another form of Śrīpura, is mentioned in the fourteenth line, and the poet Sumaṅgala, who was evidently the composer of the record and is known from some other records at Sirpur, in the twentieth line. The eastern face gives the names Śivagupta and Bālārjuna in lines 4 and 5 respectively.[28]

(*iii*) It is incised on the western face of another pillar opposite the above and comprises 51 lines in small letters but is much worn out. It apparently recorded a grant as would follow from the word *grāmo* in line 40 and imprecatory stanzas at the end. The name Bālārjuna can be made out in line 5.[29]

There is another stone inscription of Śivagupta at the Surang Mound at Sirpur which is badly damaged. It refers to the king Śivagupta, and its composer was perhaps Śīlāditya.[30]

xx xx xx xx

24. I owe this information to Shri Singh.
25. *Supra*, 152-153, 160-161.
26. *Supra*, 160-161.
27. Hira Lal, *ICPB*, 98-99.
28. *Ibid.*, 99.
29. *Ibid.*
30. *Archaeological Survey Reports*, XVII, p. 27; Hira Lal, *ICPB*, 111.

COPPER-PLATE GRANTS OF MAHĀBHAVAGUPTA I JANAMEJAYA

Three copper-plate inscriptions of the Somavaṁśin king Mahābhavagupta I Janamejaya have recently come to light and have been procured for the Orrissa State Museum, Bhubaneswar. Some important details about these records supplied by Dr Snigdha Tripathy, Epigraphist, Orissa State Museum, Bhubaneswar, are as follows:

These records have all been found from village Gopalpur under Loisinga Police station in Bolangir District, Orissa. The three sets were issued by Mahābhavagupta I Janamejaya in his first, tenth and twelfth regnal years and purport to record grants in favour of *Bhaṭṭa* Sādhāraṇa, son of *Bhaṭṭa* Śobhana, who is well-known from some other grants of his reign. The first two grants were issued from Suvarṇapura, while the third was given from Mūrasīma-kaṭaka. The grant of the first year of his reign was issued on the occasion of the first anniversary of his coronation (*prathama-rājy-ābhiṣeka-samaye*) and engraved by Saṅgrāma, son of Davara Ojhā. The charter of the tenth year was incised by (another) Saṅgrāma, son of Rayaṇa Ojhā, and that of the twelfth year by Haradāsa, son of Siulla.

INDEX

The following abbreviations have been used:
a—author; *ad*—administrative division; *b*—book or ancient text; *c*—chief; *d*—deity, *de*—demon; *do*—donee; *dyn*—dynasty; *eh*—epic hero; *k*—king; *m*—mountain; *o*—office; *p*—place; *pt*—poet; *q*—queen; *r*—river; *rt*—revenue term; *t*—title. The figures printed in bold refer to the text of inscriptions. When a word is found both in the text and elsewhere on the same page, the one in the text alone has been indexed. (The Index does not take note of the Addenda.)

ERRATA

Page	*Line*	*Read*	*For*
6	8	दानाच्छ्रेयोनुपालनम्	दानाच्छ्यॊनुपालनम्
,,	25	2. 4/5″	2-4/5″
9	11	दानाच्छ्रेयोनुपाल-	दानाच्छ्योनुपाल–
12	10	मातापितृपादानुद्ध्यात	मातापितृपादानुद्धयात
,,	33	Kurāḷa	Kurāla
15	5	तान्येव	तात्येव
,,	22	वर्ष°	वष°
17	14	शरभपुरात्	शदभपुरात्
,,	16	गोप्रद ✕	गोप्रद
,,	32	letter *s*	letters
18	1	°द्दिस्वामिनस्सोमोपरागे	°द्दिस्वामिनस्सोभोपरागे
19	11-13	Kadambapadrullaka	Kadambadrupallaka
,,	30	°दिवस:ₒ	°दिवस:
21	1	°वतिष्ठते	°वतिष्ठत
,,	20	°रान्धकारं	°रान्धकारं°
,,	25	*vṛ*	*vr*
,,	30	*ṇ*	*n*
22	1	राजभि°	राजिभि°
25	7	भोगभागमुपनय-	भोगमागमुपनय
28	33	°म्बुभिर्धौत°	°म्बुभिधौति°
29	6	°सोपनिधि°	°सोपर्निधि°
,,	17	लोका य ✕	लोकाय ✕
30	23	°म्महिमता°	°म्महिमता:
36	5	°सोपनिधि°	°सोपर्निध°
39	17	सेकाम्बुधौतपादयुगलो	सेकाम्बुधौ तपादयुगलो
,,	29	Pandeya: *Oṁ*	Pandeya:
,,	35	*daṇḍa*	*danda*
40	27	°वत्सात्रेय°	°वत्सात्रे°
47	31	°र्म्येतयोराज्ञा°	°र्म्येंतयोराज्ञा°
48	19	ग्रामार्द्धस्याधिका	ग्रामार्द्धंस्याधिका
,,	34	3. 5/8″	3-5/8″
49	29	Delete comma after 'Bazar'	
50	15	°सेकाम्बुधौत°	°सेकाम्बुधौ
,,	16	°पादानुद्ध्यात°	°पादानुद्धयात°
,,	19	°घोरान्धकारं	°धोरान्धकारं
51	19	By oversight	Oversight
,,	19	medial *ṛ*	medial *r*
,,	25	Delete the word 'may'	

Page	*Line*	*Read*	*For*
67	9	standard	Standard
74	5	वत्सेश्वरः	वत्सेवरः
,,	10	देव्यां द्रोणभट्टारिकायामुत्पन्नः	देण्यां द्रोणभट्टारि-कायमुत्पन्नः
,,	11	तुरग	तुग्ग
77	27	*Vatseśvara*	*Vatśesvara*
86	11	2. 3/4″	2-¾″
96	2	seventh	Seventh
,,	15	खड्ग°	खङ्ग°
97	1	खड्गात्क°	खङ्गात्क°
,,	31	धृतायतिर्गुरुरपि	धृतायतिर्गुरुपि
,,	31	शिक्षोद्यमो	शिक्षोधमो
98	12	भूमिर्य्यस्य	भू मिर्य्यास्य
,,	27	सकलमि°	सकलमणि
,,	42	sufficient	suffi-cient
102	23-24	°क्षारवारि°	°क्षाखारि°
103	22	एकत्रि (न्त्रि) विक्रमोपाद्ध्याय	एवत्रिपाद्धया (न्त्रि) विक्रमोपाद्धयाय
104	23	°श्र (म) क्षसा°	°श्र (म) क्षसा°
108	4	°क्षारवारि°	°क्षाखारि°
,,	15	लुब्धो यशसि	लुब्धोयशसि
109	12	द्वय (यं)	द्वय (ठ)
109	12	यद्भूवतामभि (भी)°	यद्भूवताम भि (भी)°
109	15	ब्या (व्या) स°	ब्या (व्या) स°
,,	17	भूर्व्वेष्णवि (वी)	भूर्व्वैष्णवि (वी)
,,	20	तान्येव	तात्येव
113	15	मेङ्किट्टके	मोङ्किट्टके
,,	27	copper	coppes
114	14	दानाच्छ्रेयो°	दानाच्छ्रयो°
119	22	सम्पूज्य	सम्पून्य
120	30	*Madhyāhnarūpebhyo*	*Madhyāhnarupebhyo*
122	35	thirteenth	thirteen
124	22	(शि) व°	(शि) व°
125	20	भूर्व्वेष्णवि (वी)	भूर्व्वैष्णवि (वी)
,,	23	सगरादिभिः	सागरादिभिः
127	4	is only	isonly
130	13-14	भूर्व्वे44 (०र्व्वे)°	भूर्व्वै44 (र्व्वै)°
131	9	(च्छ्रे)	(च्छे)
135	18	भूर्व्वेष्ण (वी)	भूर्व्वैष्ण (वी)
141	19	ङ्गुल्य°	गुङल्य°
,,	19-20	चरणश्चक्रिणः खे धनो°	चरणश्चक्रिण-खेधनो°
,,	22	विलोक्य	विलोभ्य

Page	*Line*	*Read*	*For*
141	24	शाङ्ख्या	शङ्ख्या
,,	24	सजिह्वमिवासिना	सचिह्वमिवासिना
142	16	[ग्रक्षुण्णाः]	[ग्र क्षु ण:]
143	16	भूपैरवदीर्णो हि निमज्जयत्यधः	भूपैरवदीर्णोहिनिमज्जचत्यधः
,,	23	बह्वृचोत्तमाः	बह्वचोत्तमाः
,,	27	द्युत°	द्युत°
148	32	a symbol	asymbol
150	16	पूर्ण्णां नन्नेश्वराख्यो	पूर्ण्णांनन्नेश्वराख्यो
154	17	सिद्धम् [।*][3]	सिद्धम् । [×][3]
,,	17	°रभसोत्पल (त) द°	°रभसोत्पल (त) द्°
,,	19	निर्द्दग्धोप्यत्त्र	निर्द्दग्धोप्यत्र
,,	20	(यम्)	(यम)
,,	25	°चमूचयस्य	°चमूचस्यस्य
155	2	तस्मादभूद्भुवन°	तस्माद् भूद् भुवन°
,,	7	संप्राप्तैर्विषयैश्च यस्य	संप्राप्तैर्व्विर्षयैश्चयस य
,,	17	वृद्धिः	वृद्धिः
,,	23	°तलान्विता	°तल्नान्विता
,,	27	राजति	रात्रति
156	2	°[द] क्षदीक्षाया	°[द] क्षरीक्षाया
,,	3	विधानीयमन्त्रस्य च	विधानीयमन्त्रस्यच
,,	5	°गर्त्तामु°	°गर्त्तामु°
,,	14	सकलकर्म्मं°	सकलकर्म्म°
,,	32	*Śāśvatakośa*	*Sāsvatakośa*
,,	33	Śrīharṣa's	Śriharṣa's
157	20	district names	districtnames
161	6	°तनयः	°तनन्वयः
167	35	a legend	alegend
168	1	यथास्माभिरयं	यथा स्माभिरयं
,,	18	भूर्व्वैष्णवी	भूव्वैष्णवी
169	13	°कोइघोषेण	°कोद्घोषेण
171	20	Koighoṣa	Kaighoṣa
173	12	कौथ (थु) मशाखा°	कौथ (थु) मशारवा°
174	12	°चन्द्रतार [का*] क्र्क°	°चन्द्रतार [का*] क्र्क°
176	1	ग्राषाढ-मासे	ग्राषाढ़-मासे
,,	6	ग्रस्ति	ग्रास्ति
177	33	Khaṇḍakṣetra	Khandakṣetra
180	22	भूर्व्वैष्णवी	भूर्व्वैष्णत्री
184	18	°नचरणनूपु (पु) र°	°नचरणनूपुर (पु) र°
184	18	°पारावत°	°पारावत्त°
,,	22	महिम्नः	महिम्न
,,	25	°ख्यस्तृ°	°रव्यस्तृ°

Page	*Line*	*Read*	*For*
,,	25	(श)–	(वंश)
185	5	(वं।)ह्म–	(ब्रा)ह्म
186	1	भूब्रमिः(मि)त(स्त)स्य	भूमिः (मि) त (स्त) स्य
187	1	फाल्गुनमासद्वि–	फाल्गुनमासाद्वि–
,,	30	Mūrasīman	Mūrasiman
189	18	°रवोद्भ्रान्तमत्तपारावत°	°खोद्भ्रान्त भत्त पारावात°
,,	30	9″	9''
,,	32	1″	1''
,,	37	is somewhat	issomewhat
190	4	भोक्त(क्तु)कामः	भोक्त(क्तु) कामः
,,	10	°जनपदान(न्)	°जनपदान (न)
,,	11	°राजवल्लभादीन(न्)	°राजवल्लभादीन(न)
,,	13	°र्वान(न्)	°र्वान(न)
,,	20	मातापित्रोरात्मनश्च	मातापित्रोत्मनश्च
,,	20	°यशोभिवृद्धये ताम्र(म्र)°	°यशोभिवृद्धयेताम्र(म्र)°
191	8	यः	थः
194	18	°नचरणनूपुररव°	°नचरणनूपुरख°
,,	24	4″	4''
195	26	°*mahimnaḥ*	°*mahimnah*
196	19	स्वर्गर्गा(गा)मिनौ	स्वर्गगा(गा)मिनौ
197	17	सी(शि)क्षाकल्पेतिहास[40]	सी(शि) क्षाल्पेतिहास[40]
,,	19	°न्त्रिणा	°त्रिणा
,,	19	(व्यू)ढं	(व्यु)ढं
200	17	°नचरणनूपुररवत्रस्त°	°नचरणनूपुरखत्रस्त°
,,	18	°विद्वज्जन°	°विद्वजन°
,,	21	°मसमावासित°	°मसमावसित°
201	4	ऋ(ऋ)षिग्रामे व्रा(ब्रा)°	ऋ (ऋ) षिग्रामे (व्रा)(ब्र)°
,,	15	°ग्रामविनिर्गताय	°ग्रामविनिर्गलाय
,,	17	°तारकार्कक्षिति°	°तारकार्कक्षि ति°
202	11	°गृह्णाति यश्य	°गृह्णाति यश्च
,,	9	भूमेरप्यर्द्धमङ्गुलं	भूमेर्प्यर्द्धमङ्गुलं
,,	29	यन्त्राङ्कतः	यात्राङ्कतः
208	17	°नुरोधाच्च	°नुरोधच्च
209	,,	वा[रु*]णैः[35]	वा[रू*]णैः[35]
,,	20	ताङ्घ्रि(ङ्घ्र)	ताङ्घ्रि(ङ्घ्र)
210	1	पृथ्वीशचूडामणिः	पृथ्वीशचूडामिणः
,,	4	वेदवेदाङ्ग°	वदवेदाङ्ग-
,,	6	व्यूढं	व्यूढं
210	9	यत्राङ्के°	यात्राङ्के°
211	46	Gaya	Gya
212	6	rulers	ruler

Page	*Line*	*Read*	*For*
213	23	कोष(स)ल°	कोष(स्)ल°
214	9	चन्द्रतारकाक्षिति°	चन्द्रतारकाशिक्षिति°
,,	13	°व्यमिति	°व्यामिति
,,	20	°म्(ण्णं) भूर्व्वैष्णवी	°मू(ण्णं)मूर्व्वैष्णत्री
221	10	ग्राचन्द्रतारक[48] (का)र्कक्षिति°	ग्राचन्द्रतारक[48](का)र्कशिक्षिति°
222	12	°रप्यर्द्धमङ्गुलं	°रप्यर्द्धमङ्गल
222	22	रामचन्द्रः	रामभन्द्रः
224	23	Kuḍukulokhaṇḍakṣetra	kuḍukul okhaṇḍakṣetra
,,	39	Somavaṁśin	Somavaṁśīn
,,	41	*khaṇḍa-kṣetra*	*khaṇḍa-kṣerta*
228	9	पार्थिवाः	पार्थिवां:
,,	14	°भूवौ(वैं)°	भूवो(वैं)°
230	34	Laskar	Laskar'
232	13	Somavaṁśin	Somavaṁśīn
233	21	प्रणयिनः	प्रणिनः
,,	21	प्रविशङ्कि[9]	प्रविशङ्क°
,,	23	°चयैर्ध्व°	°चर्यैर्ध्व°
234	9	खड्गा°	खड़गा°
,,	,,	°द्विपघटा[14] कुम्भस्थ°	द्विप[14]घटाकुम्भस्थ–
,,	13	°खङ्ग°	°खङ्ग°
235	4	सव्वा(र्व्वा)न्	सव्वा(र्ब्बा)न्
,,	7	सजलस्थ–	सजलस्थ
236	11	भूमेरप्यर्द्धमङ्गुलम्[47]	भूमेरप्यर्द्धङ्गुलम्[47]
238	33	Puri-	Puru-
241	1	गन्धटपाटिमण्डले[7]	°गन्धटपाटिलमण्डले[7]
243	8	सम्ब-	सभ्व-
245	1	*Ṭhakkura*	*Thakkura*
248	20	भूर्व्वैष्णवी	भूर्व्वैष्णवी
249	15	शुक्लपक्षे	शुक्ल्पक्षे
,,	18	°तथागतेनेति	°तथातेनेति
251	20	तन्वतोः	तत्वतोः
,,	25	°न्निर्य्यात°	°न्निर्य्याति°
,,	26	°ध्वान्त°	°ह्वन्ति°
257	23	स्मररसः	स्मरसरसः
258	1	°तेष्याकिलहेष्वपि	तेष्यकिलहेष्वधि
,,	2	°न्तर्व्यथा[:*]	°न्तर्व्यथ[:*]
258	10	°वितान°	°वित्तान°
,,	12	°खङ्ग°	°खङ्ग°
,,	15	शश्वद्द्वार°	शश्वद्द्वार
,,	41	खङ्गी	खङ्गी

Page	*Line*	*Read*	*For*
264	29	सर्वोपरिकरकरादान°	सर्वोपरिकरादान°
270	2	जनितसुरवधू°	जनितसुखधू°
271	19	भूर्व्वेष्णवी	भूर्व्वेष्णवी
276	21	°धर्म्मामृता[वि]°	°धर्म्मामृत[व]°
277	2	°निवेशित°	°निवेशित्त°
283	46	Madhyadeśa denotes	Madhya deśadenotes
285	20	रतिपतेः शस्त्रै°	रतिपतेःशस त्रै°
288	6	गार्ग्ग (र्ग्यं)	मार्ग्ग (र्ग्यं)
,,	26	प्रतिगृह्णाति	प्रतिगह्णति
289	8	(से)तुनृं पाणां	(से)तुर्न पाणां
293	4	the fourth year of the	the
296	17	किसरकेल्लासमावा°	"किसरकेल्लासभाव°
299	4	Kisarakellā	Kisarkella
304	६	°नृपतेर्ल्ल°	°नृपतेर्म्म°
,,	5	°द्विख्यातो	°द्विरव्यातो
305	2	भृत्या°	भत्या°
,,	18	खे	रवे
,,	20	प्रासादोभ्रङ्कशा°	प्रासादोभ्रङ्क°
,,	21	[चारु]	[चारू]
,,	23	कीर्त्ति°	कीर्ति°
,,	26	°देर्वा[स्त्रिलोकी]°	°देर्वा[स्रलोकी]°
,,	27	ब्रं*]ह्मा	ब्रं*] ला
,,	28	ऊर्द्ध्वभ्राजत्कनककलश°	ग्रर्द्धवभ्राजत्ककनककलशो°
309	20	शस्त्रैक°	शस्त्रैक°
	27	14×8:7"	14×8:7;
,,	28	Narayana	Naryana
310	1	नृपति°	नपति°
,,	4	लिहु(च्छ)द्यना	लिहु (च्छ) द्धना
,,	16	विलसन्निस्त्रिंस (श)°	विलसन्निश्रिंस (श)°
,,	27	नरेन्द्रै	नरेन्दै
312	2	साभ्रमधूकप्रभृति°	साभ्रमधूकप्रभृनि°
,,	23	भूमिदः	भूमिडः
,,	25	भूर्व्वेष्णवी	भूर्व्वेष्णवी
,,	29	नस्त्राता	नस्त्राता
,,	31	प्रतिगृह्णाति	प्रतिगह्णति
313	4	वारुणैः	वारूणैः
,,	15	खण्डितै°	खैण्डितै°
,,	17	यस्य वु(बु)द्धिव(ब)लाल्लक्ष्मी°	यस्यवु(बु)द्धिव(ब) लाल्लक्ष्मी°
315	13	*Rāṇī*	*Raṇī*
320	3	सखण्डपालीयः	सखण्डपालनीयः

Page	*Line*	*Read*	*For*
321	9	परदत्तानुपालनात (त्)	पददत्तानुपालनात (त्)
,,	13	गामेकां	गमिकां
321	22	*Kumāra*[52d] **Someśvaradeva**	*Kumārā*[52d] **Someśvaradeva**
328	19	°लक्ष्यते°	°लक्ष्यतें°
330	15	°नुरोधाच्च	°नुरोधच्चि
,,	17	तदा	पदा
,,	23	°त्रयस्तेन	°त्रय-स्तेन
,,	28	तडागानां	तडागनां
331	4	°जीवितश्च	°जीवित्तश्च
337	30	Kahnapura	Kahapura
339	4	पारंपर्यक (क्र) माग–	पारंपर्यक (क्र) भाग–
346	10	Kolleḍā	Kolleda
,,	32	Kolleḍā	Koleḍā
349	37	*vṛkṣaḥ*	*vrkṣaḥ*
350	4	°रु (रू) पश्च	°रु (रु) पश्च
,,	21	वरवौड°	वखौड°
,,	24	मातापित्रो°	मालापित्रो°
,,	25	प्रदत्तोस्माभिः	प्रदत्तोस्याभिः
352	23	Osmanabad	Oosmanabad
354	23	°छद्मना	°छद्धना
355	1	शीता (तां)	शीता (सां)
,,	15	यद्वैरिप्रमदाजनो	यदैरिप्रमदाजनो
356	10	ऋग्वेदीय°	ऋग्वेदीय
,,	22	द्वौ	दौ
,,	23	भूर्वी (वें) ष्णवी	भूर्वी (वैं) ष्णवी
357	9-10	वैरियुवतीरित्रे (?) षु काश्यामहं (हम्)?	वैरियुवती रित्रेषुका श्याहमं
,,	13	श्रीमदुद्द्योत°	श्रीमद्‌ द्योत°
,,	16	°भ्याउ (मु) क्ती (त्की)–	°भ्याउ (मू) क्ती (त्की)–
360	7	भूमेरप्यर्द्धमङगुलं (लम्)	भूमेरप्यर्द्धमङ्गुलं (लम्)
362	21	डक[5a]	डक[5a]

Plates

INSCRIPTIONS OF THE ŚARABHAPURĪYAS

I.I PIPARḌŪLĀ PLATES OF NARENDRA, YR. 3

FIRST PLATE

SECOND PLATE : FIRST SIDE

PL.II

SECOND PLATE : SECOND SIDE

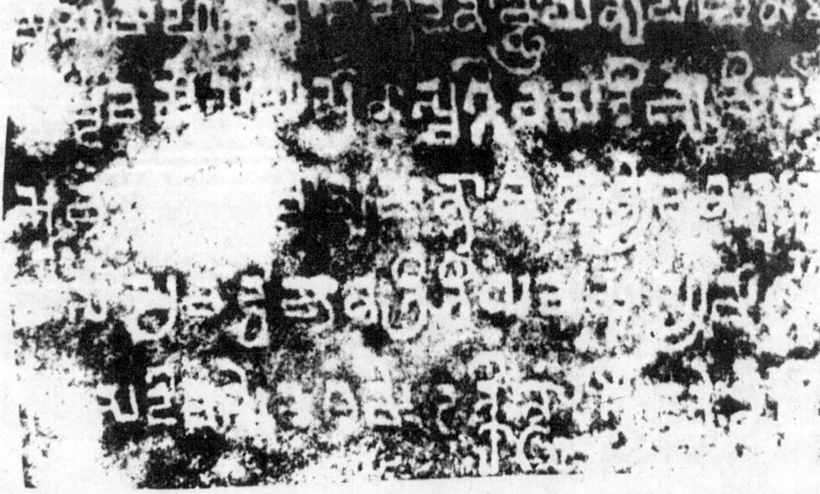

THIRD PLATE

SEAL

I:II. KURUD PLATES OF NARENDRA, YR. 24

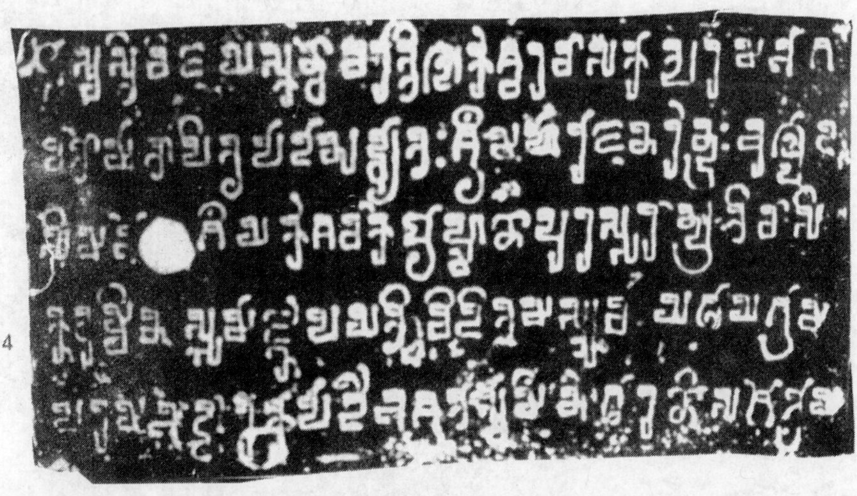

FIRST PLATE

PL.IV

SECOND PLATE : FIRST SIDE

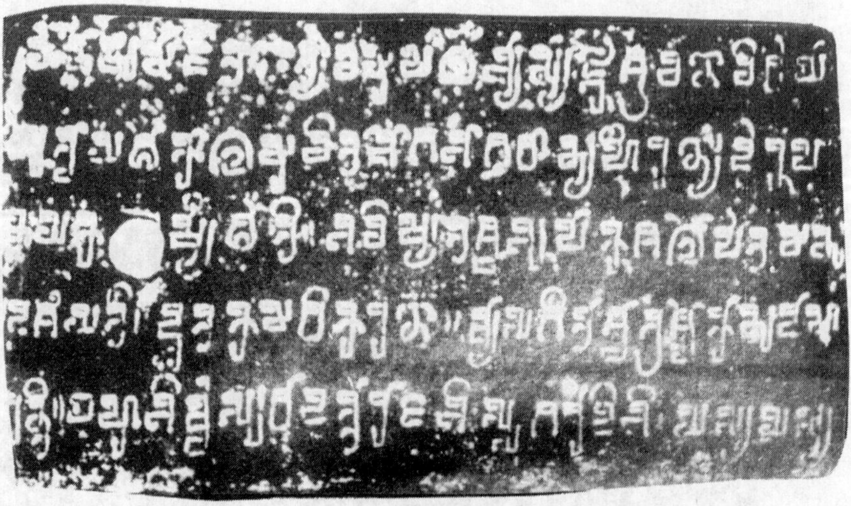

SECOND PLATE : SECOND SIDE

PL.V

THIRD PLATE

SEAL

PL.VI

I:III. RAWAN PLATE OF NARENDRA

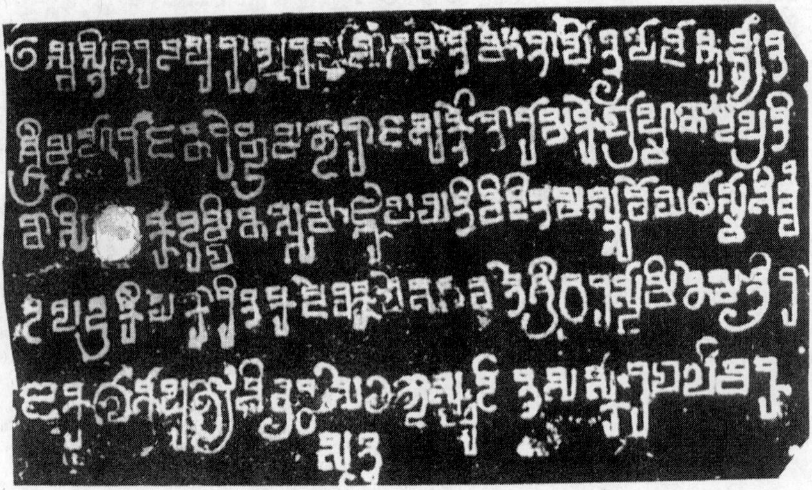

I : IV. AMGURA PLATES OF JAYARAJA, YR. 3

FIRST PLATE

PL.VII

SECOND PLATE : FIRST SIDE

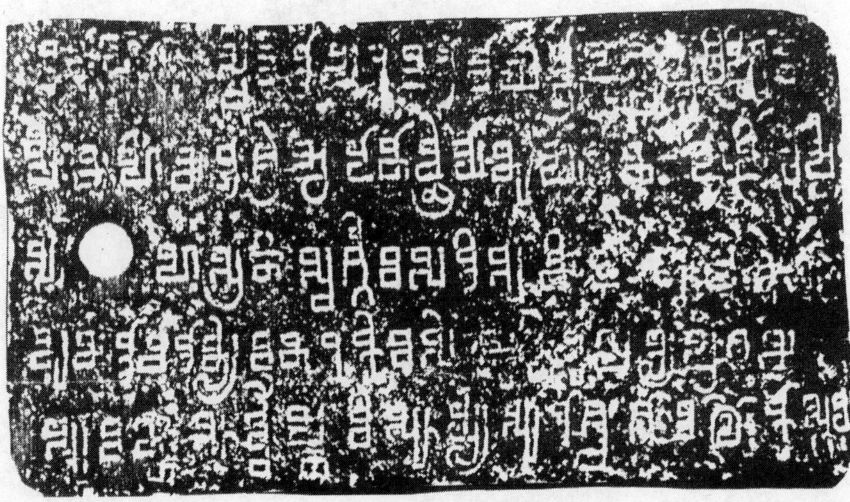

SECOND PLATE : SECOND SIDE

PL.VIII

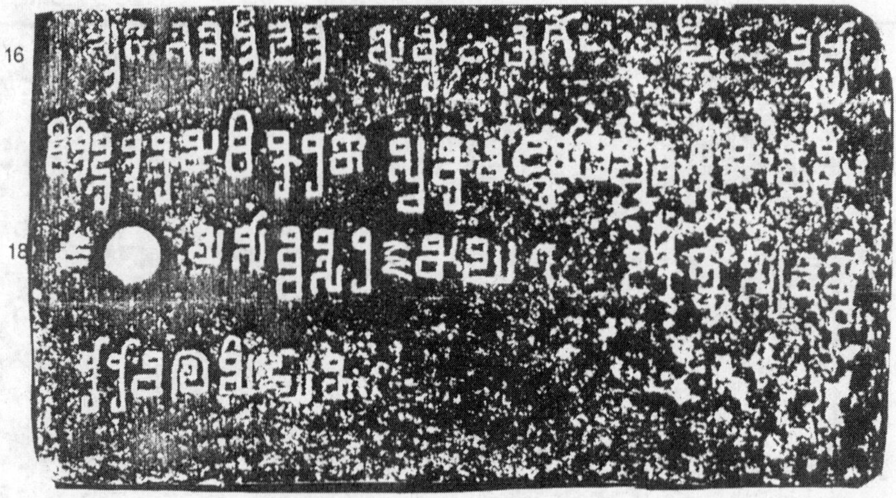

THIRD PLATE

SEAL

I : V. MALLAR PLATES OF JAYA RAJA, YR . 5

FIRST PLATE

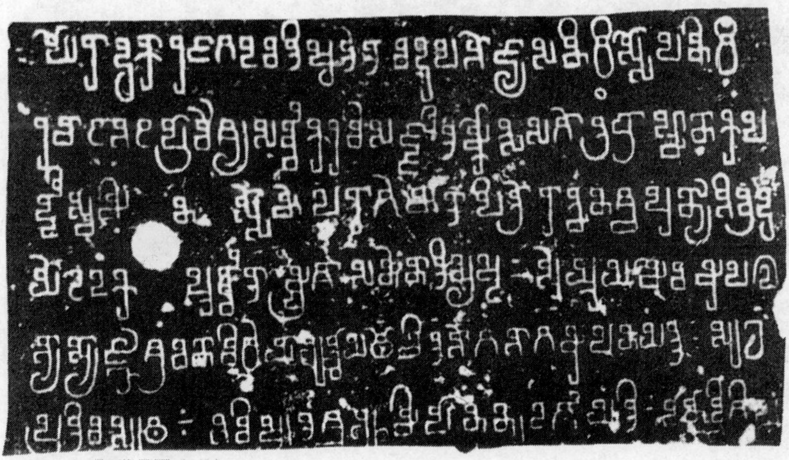

SECOND PLATE : FIRST SIDE

PL.X

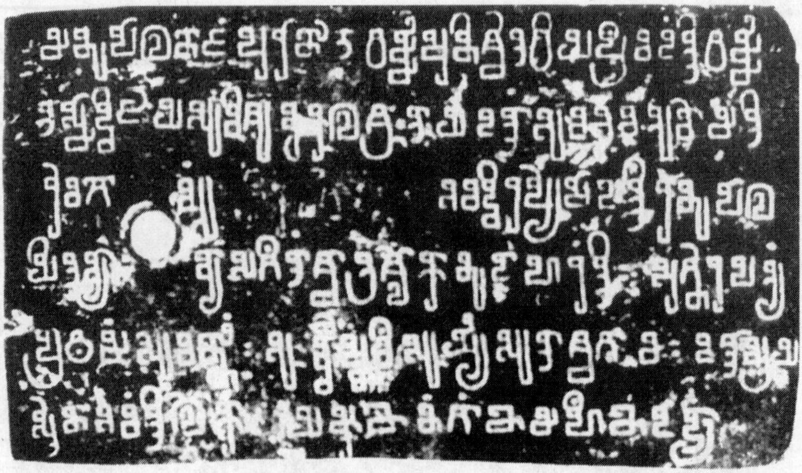

SECOND PLATE : SECOND SIDE

THIRD PLATE

I : VI ARANG PLATES OF JAYARĀJA, YR. 5

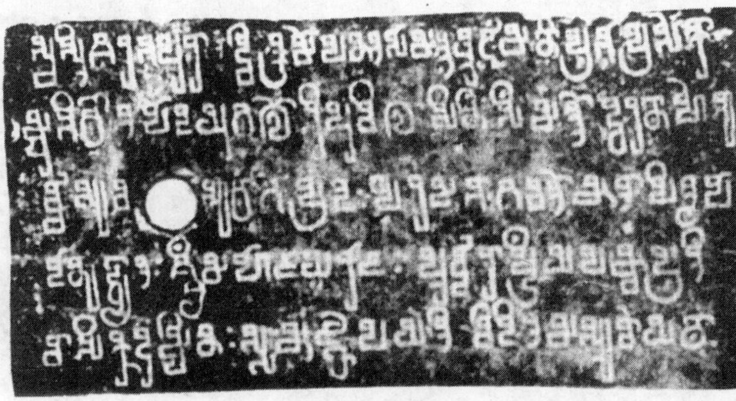

FIRST PLATE

SECOND PLATE : FIRST SIDE

PL.XII

SECOND PLATE : SECOND SIDE

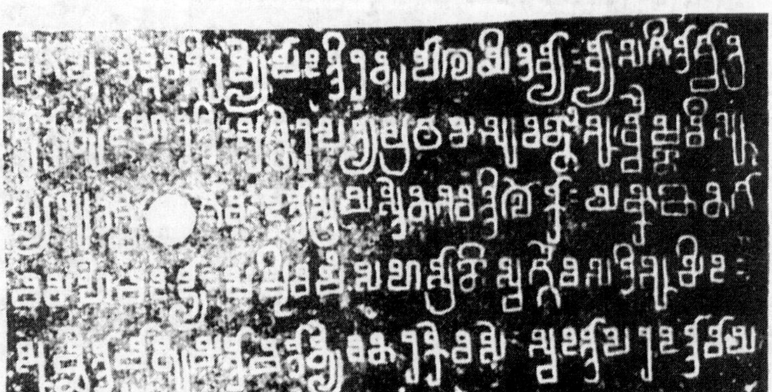

THIRD PLATE : FIRST SIDE

THIRD PLATE : SECOND SIDE

SEAL

PL.XIV

I : VII. MALLAR PLATES OF JAYARĀJA, YR. 9

2

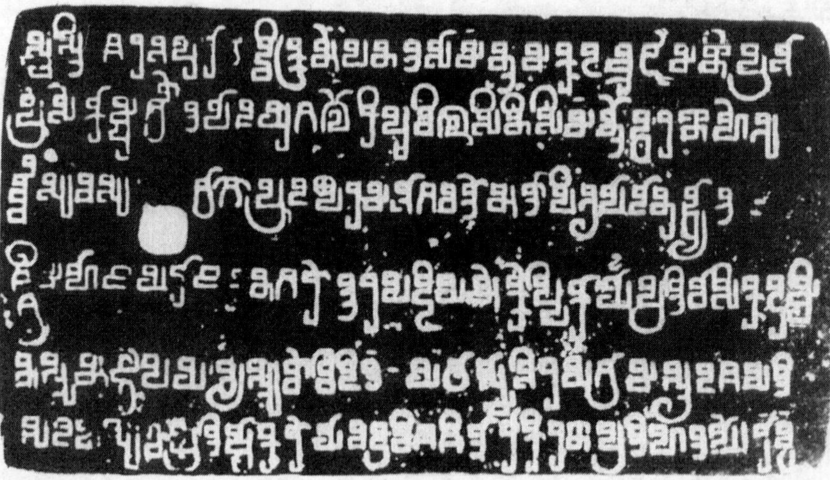

FIRST PLATE

8

12

SECOND PLATE : FIRST SIDE

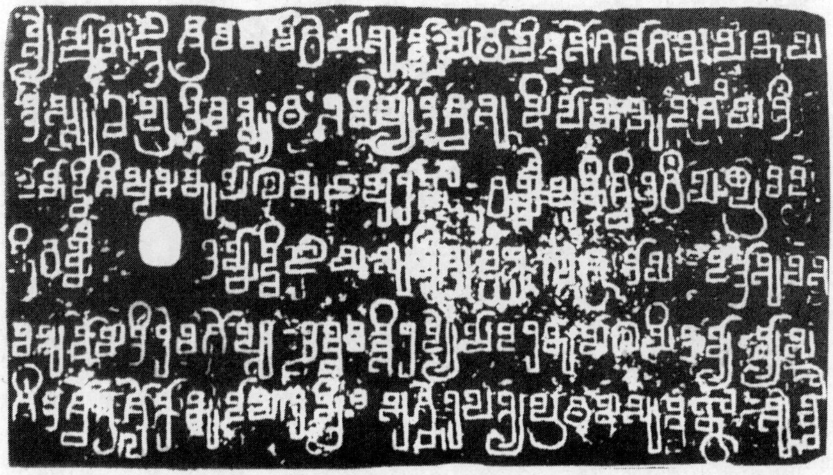

SECOND PLATE : SECOND SIDE

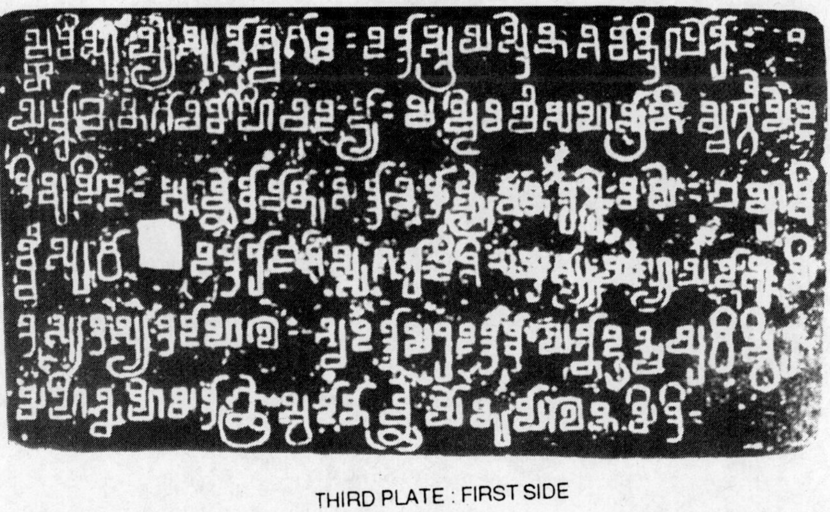

THIRD PLATE : FIRST SIDE

PL.XVI

26

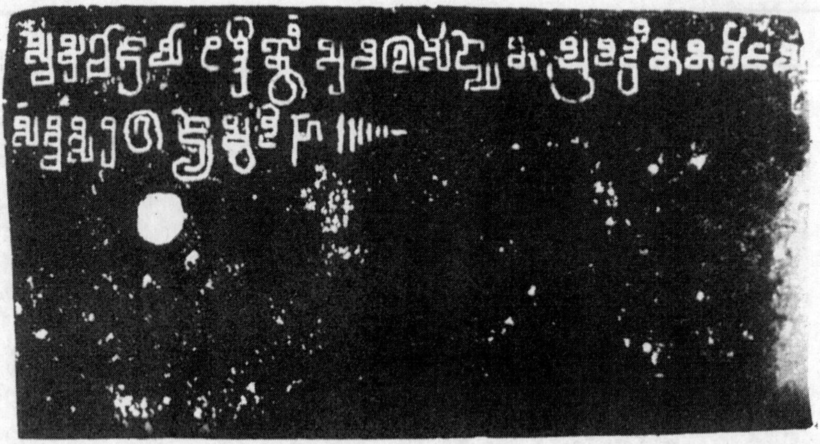

THIRD PLATE : SECOND SIDE

SEAL

I : VIII. NAHNA PLATES OF SUDEVARAJA, YR. 2

FIRST PLATE

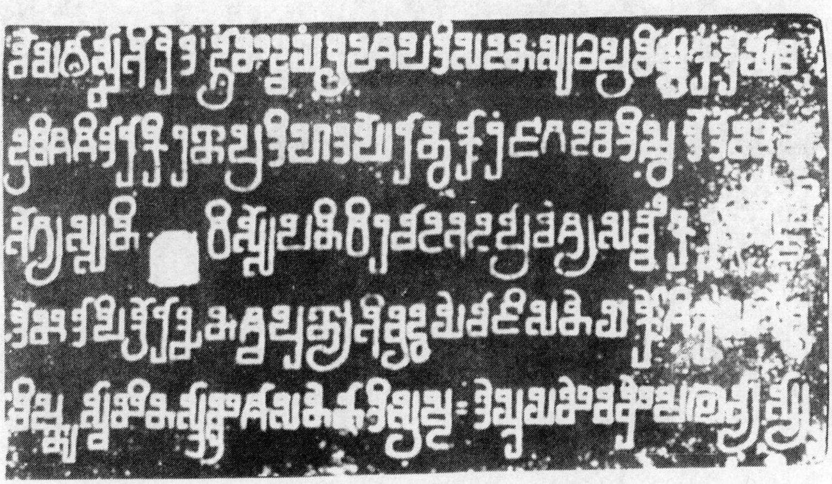

SECOND PLATE : FIRST SIDE

PL.XVIII

SECOND PLATE : SECOND SIDE

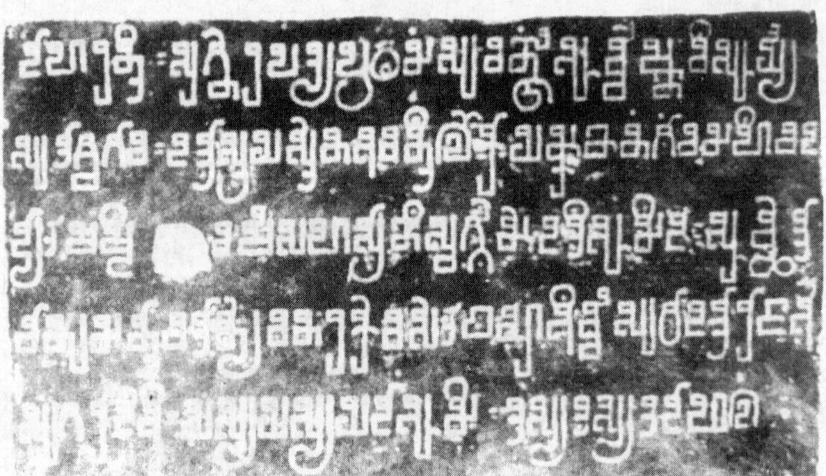

THIRD PLATE : FIRST SIDE

THIRD PLATE : SECOND SIDE

SEAL

PL.XX

I : IX. DHAMATARI PLATES OF SUDEVARĀJA, YR. 3

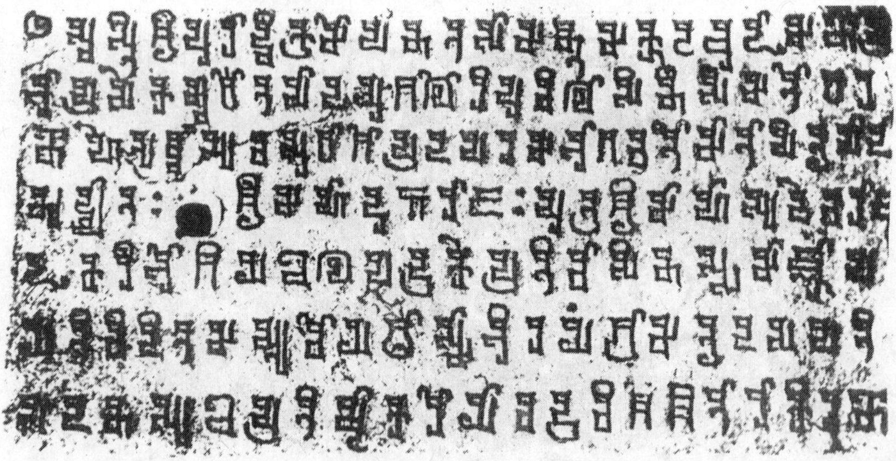

FIRST PLATE

SECOND PLATE : FIRST SIDE

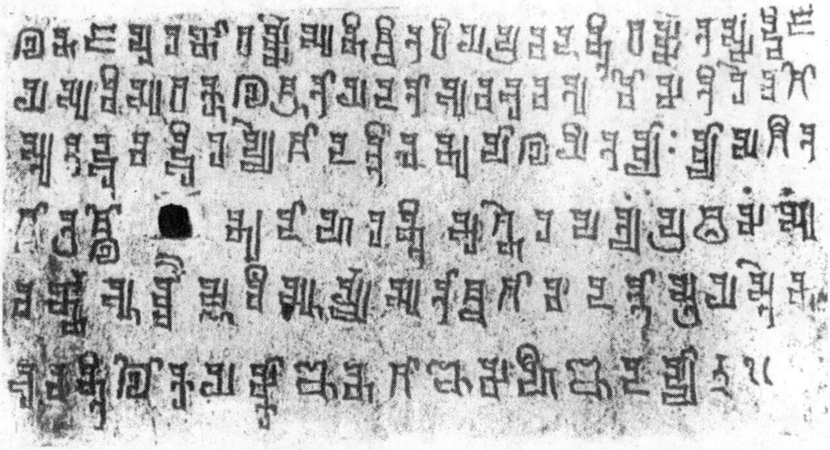

SECOND PLATE : SECOND SIDE

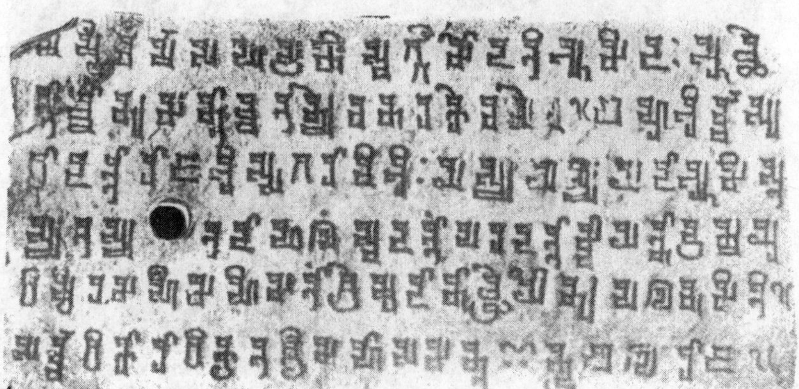

THIRD PLATE : FIRST SIDE

PL.XXII

28

THIRD PLATE : SECOND SIDE

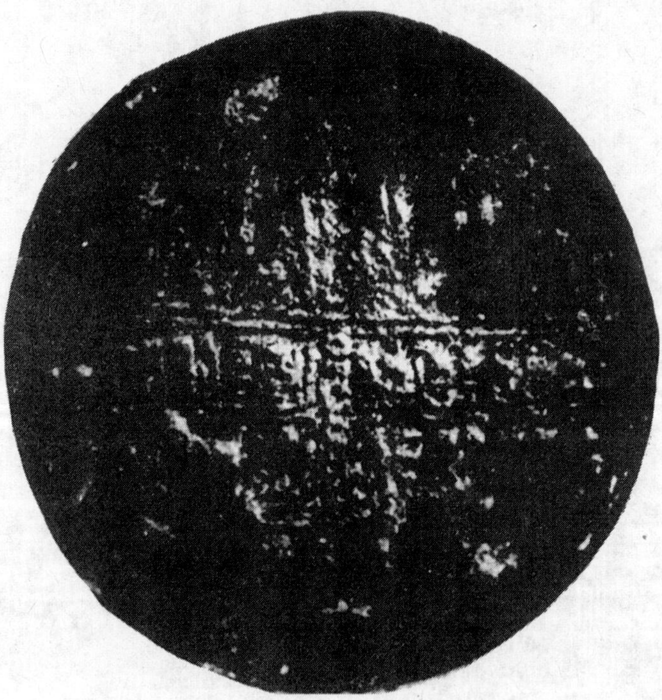

SEAL

I : X SIRPUR PLATES OF SUDEVARĀJA, YR. 7

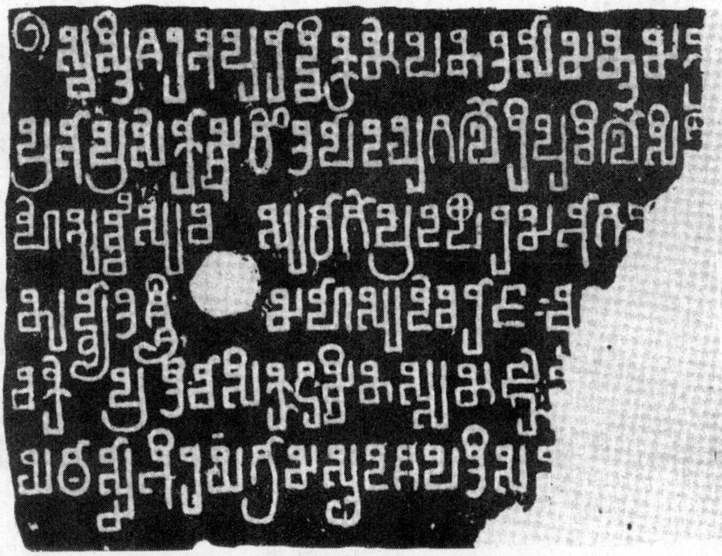

FIRST PLATE

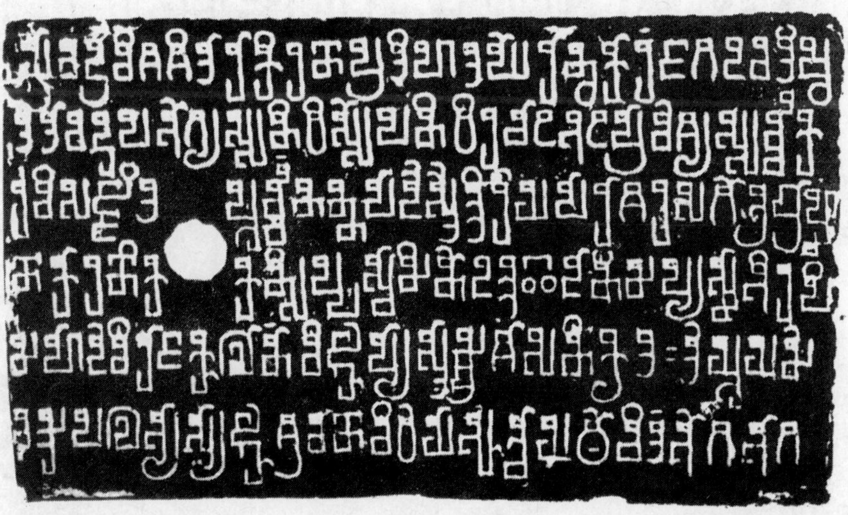

SECOND PLATE : FIRST SIDE

PL.XXIV

SECOND PLATE : SECOND SIDE

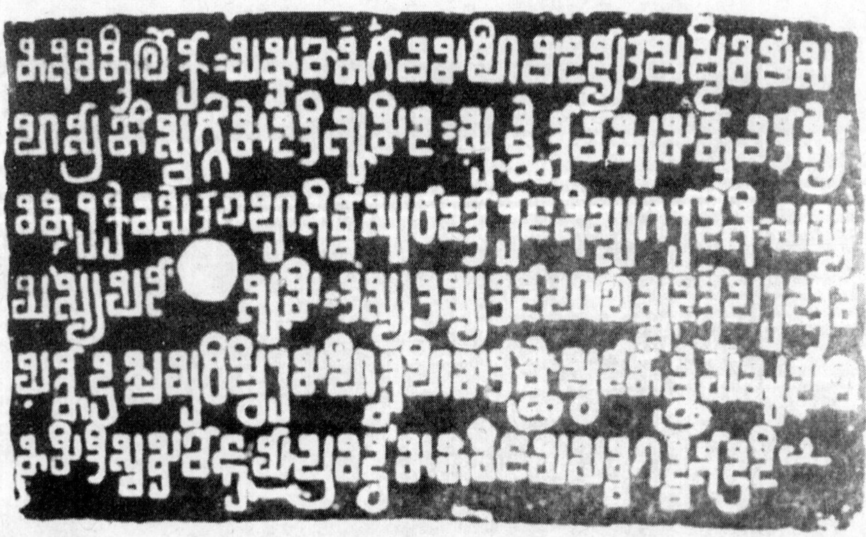

THIRD PLATE : FIRST SIDE

THIRD PLATE : SECOND SIDE

SEAL

PL.XXVI

I : XI. ARANG PLATES OF SUDEVARĀJA, YR. 7

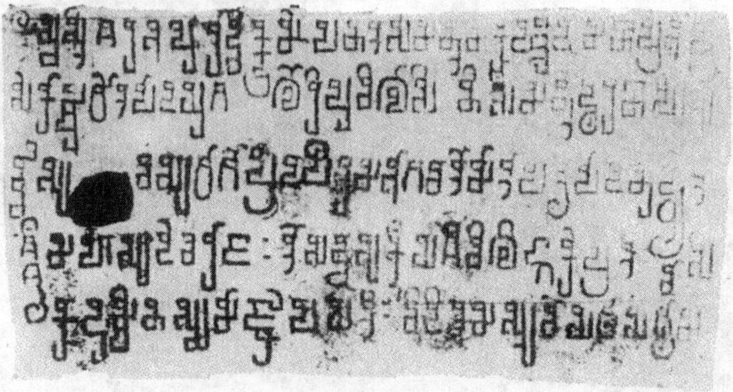

FIRST PLATE

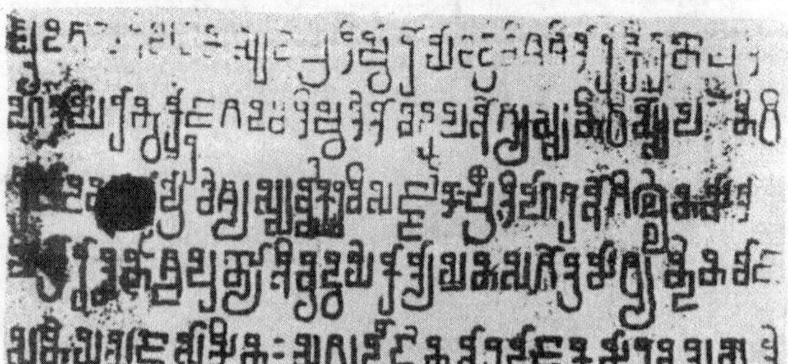

SECOND PLATE : FIRST SIDE

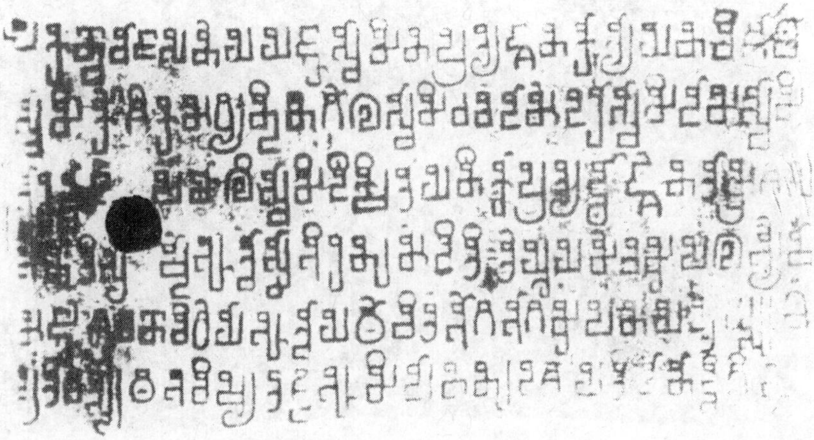

SECOND PLATE : SECOND SIDE

THIRD PLATE : FIRST SIDE

PL.XXVIII

THIRD PLATE : SECOND SIDE

SEAL

I. XII. KAUVATAL PLATES OF SUDEVARĀJA, YR. 7

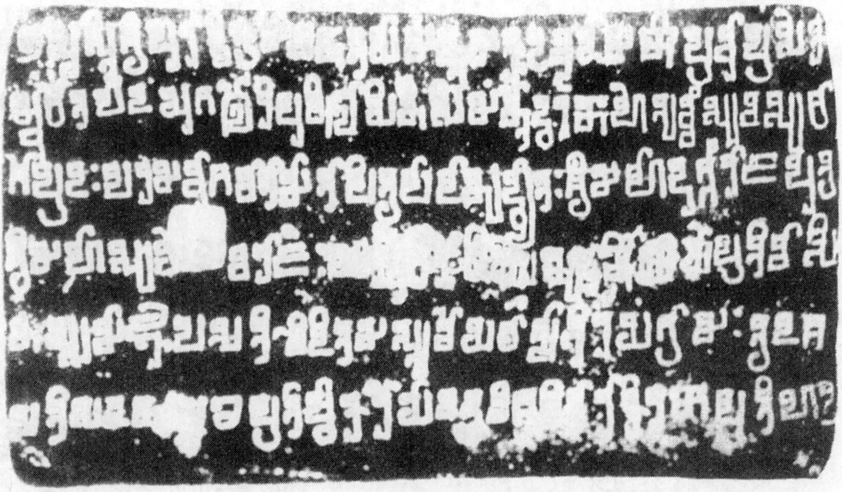

FIRST PLATE

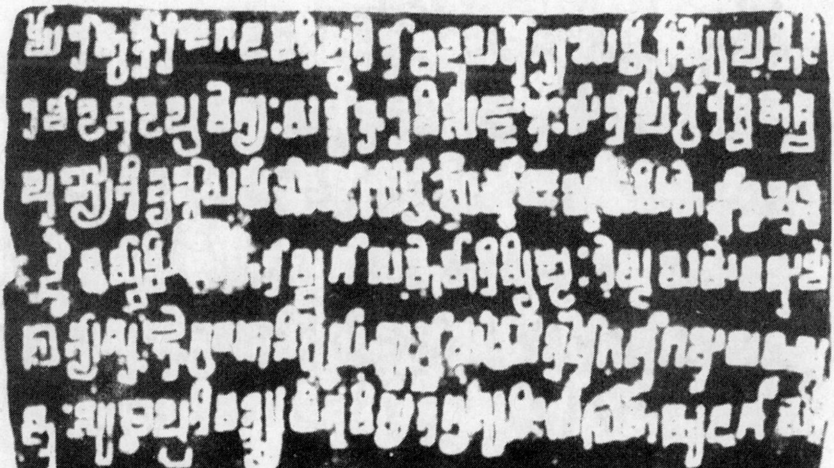

SECOND PLATE : FIRST SIDE

PL.XXX

SECOND PLATE : SECOND SIDE

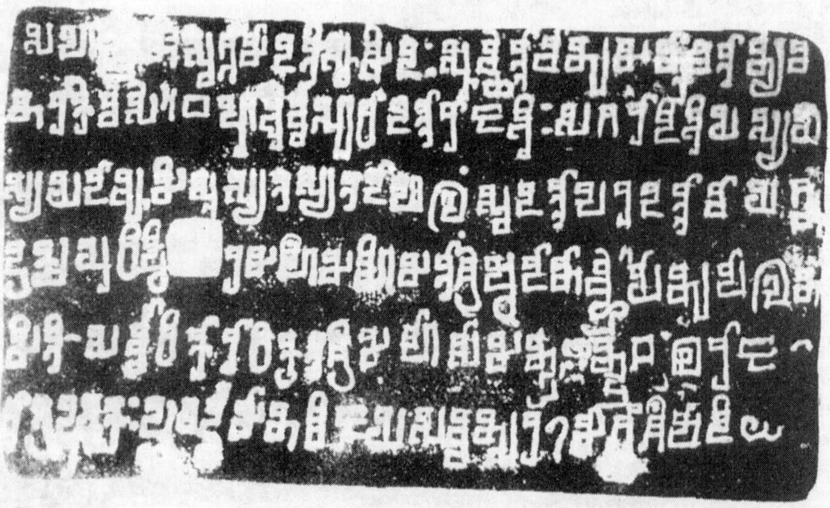

THIRD PLATE : FIRST SIDE

THIRD PLATE : SECOND SIDE

SEAL

PL.XXXII

I. XIII. RAIPUR PLATES OF SUDEVARĀJA, YR. 10

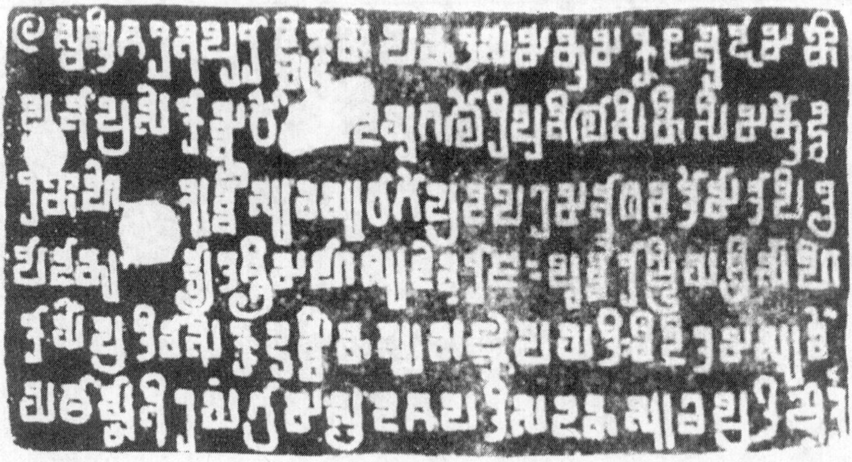

FIRST PLATE

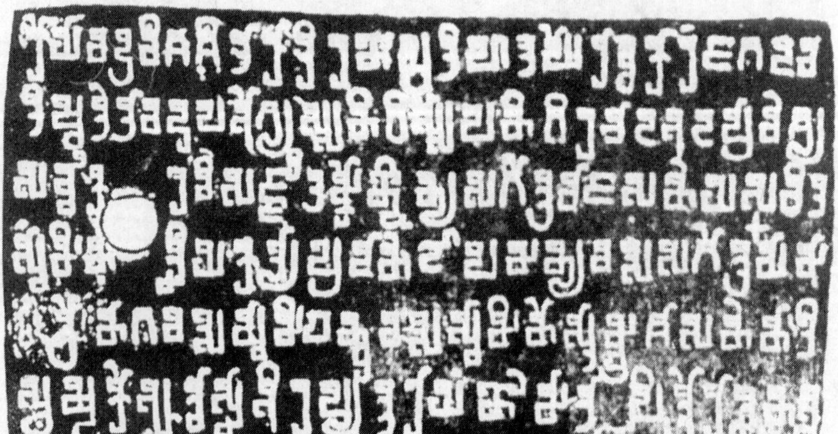

SECOND PLATE : FIRST SIDE

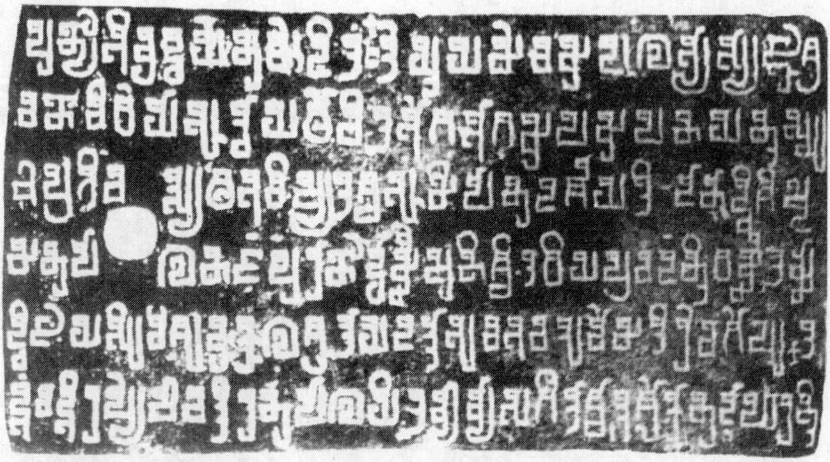

SECOND PLATE : SECOND SIDE

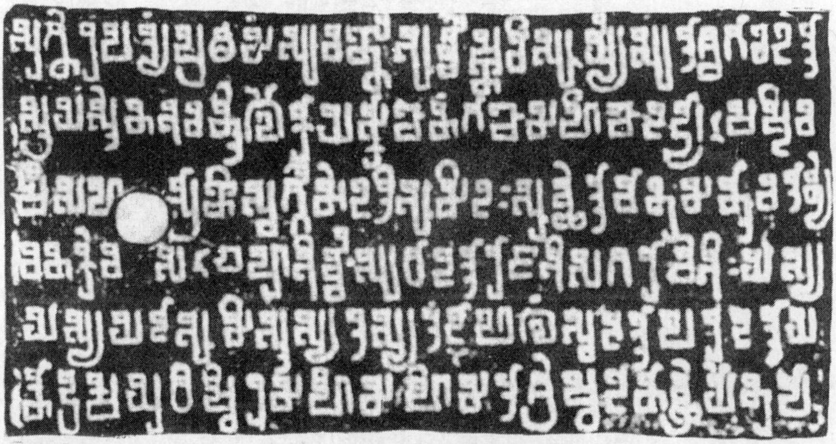

THIRD PLATE : FIRST SIDE

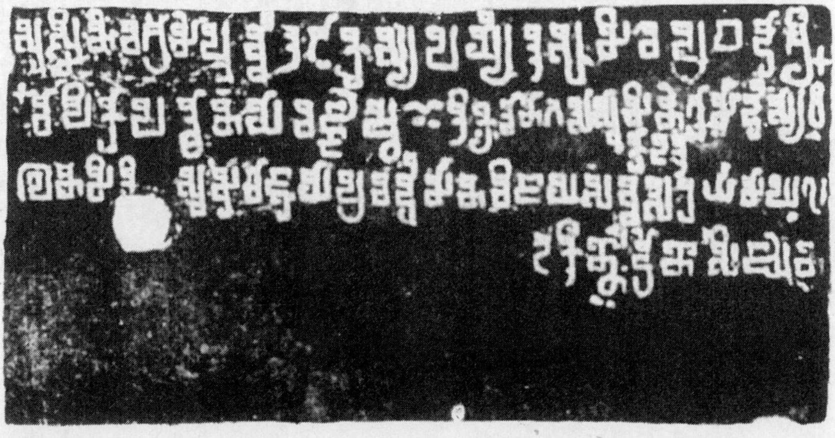

PL.XXXIV

I : XIV. SARANGARH PLATES OF SUDEVARĀJA

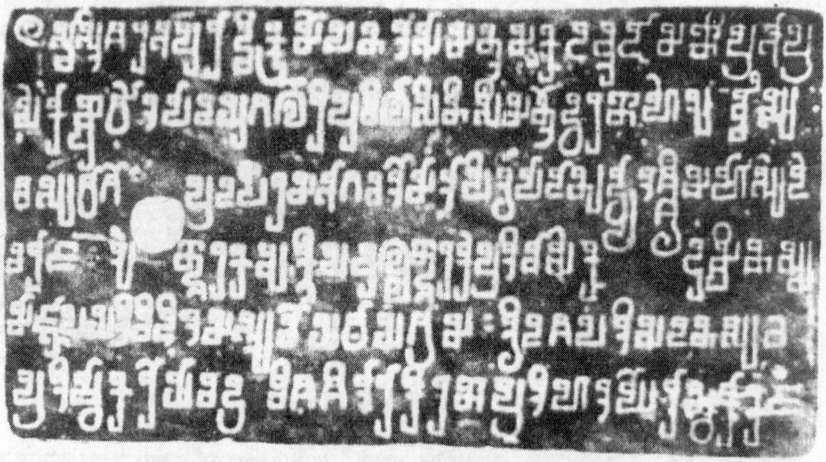

FIRST PLATE

SECOND PLATE : FIRST SIDE

PL.XXXV

SECOND PLATE : SECOND SIDE

I : XV. THAKURDIYA PLATE OF PRAVARARĀJA YR. 3

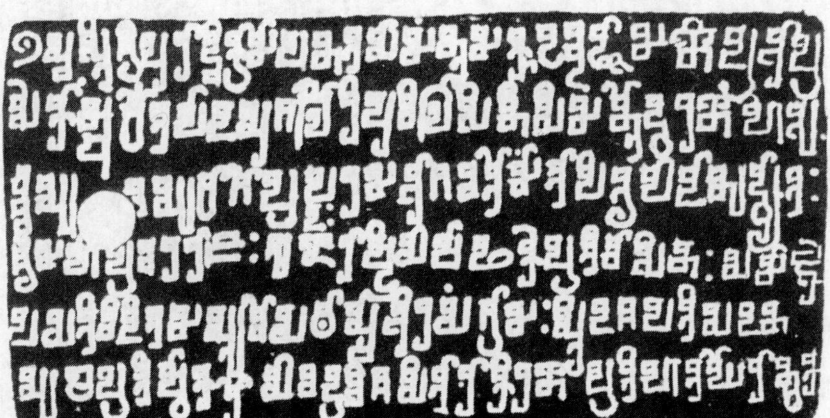

FIRST PLATE

PL.XXXVI

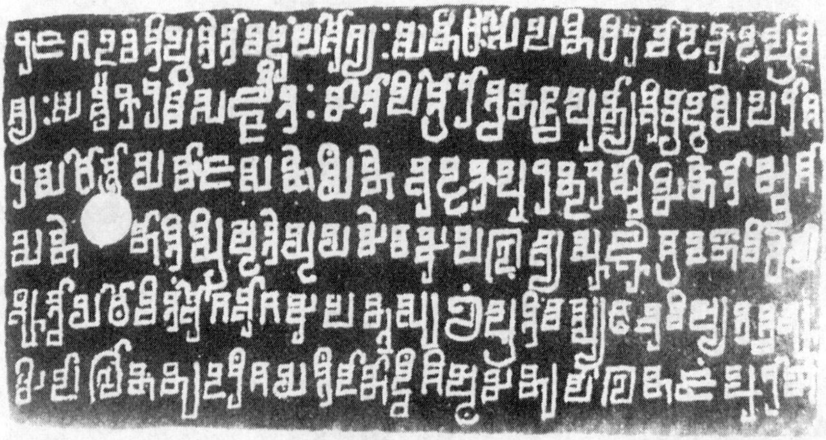

SECOND PLATE : FIRST SIDE

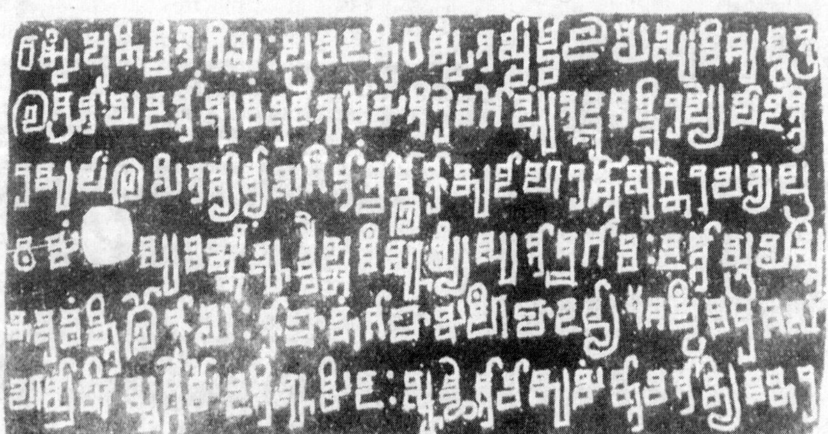

SECOND PLATE : SECOND SIDE

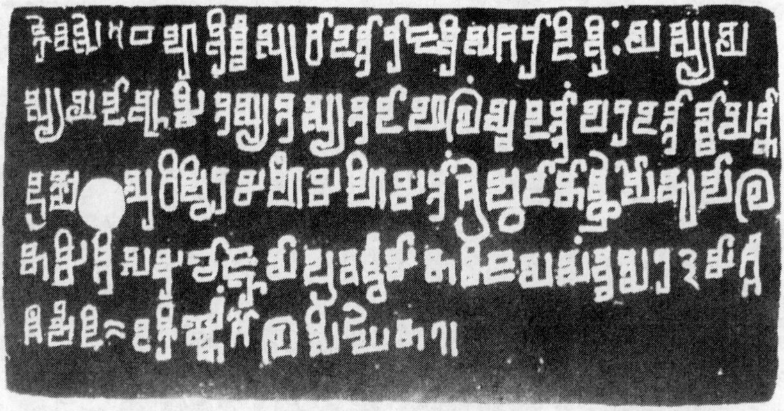

THIRD PLATE : FIRST SIDE

SEAL

PL.XXXVII

I : XVI. MALLAR PLATES OF PRAVARARĀJA, YR. 3

FIRST PLATE

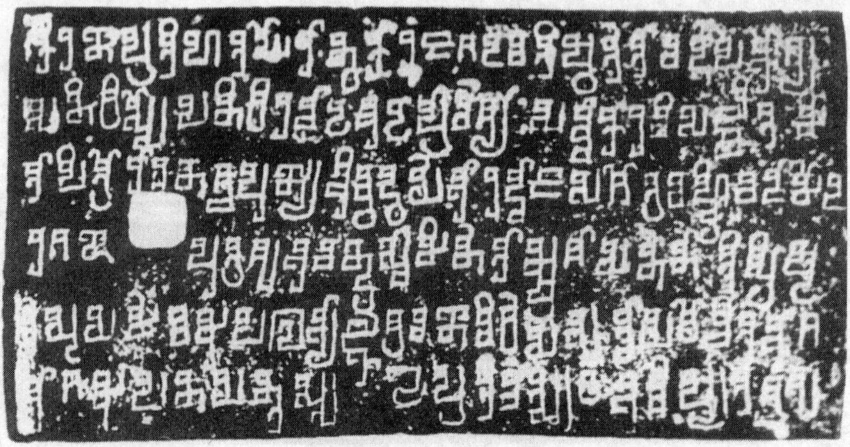

SECOND PLATE : FIRST SIDE

SECOND PLATE : SECOND SIDE

THIRD PLATE : FIRST SIDE

PL.XL

24

THIRD PLATE : SECOND SIDE

SEAL

I : APP. I. A STRAY ŚARABHĀPURĪYA PLATE

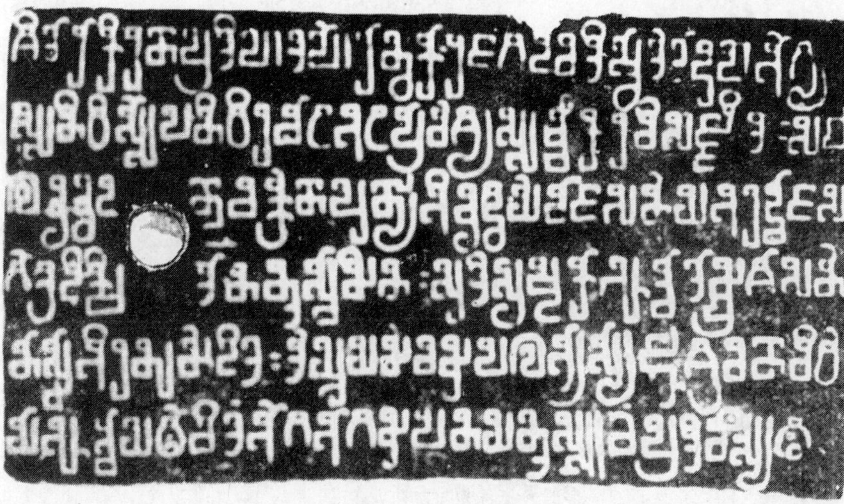

SECOND PLATE : FIRST SIDE

SECOND PLATE : SECOND SIDE

I : APP. II. MALLAR PLATES OF VYĀGHRARĀJA

FIRST PLATE

SECOND PLATE : FIRST SIDE

SECOND PLATE : SECOND SIDE

THIRD PLATE

PL.XLIV

SEAL

II

INSCRIPTIONS OF THE PĀṆḌUVAṀŚINS OF MEKALĀ

II : I BAMHANI PLATES OF UDĪRṆAVAIRA, YR 2

FIRST PLATE

SECOND PLATE : FIRST SIDE

PL.XLVIII

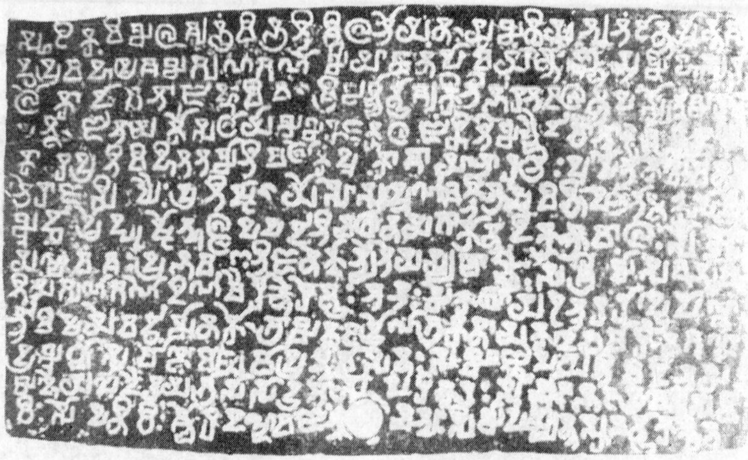

SECOND PLATE : SECOND SIDE

THIRD PLATE

II : II MALLAR PLATES OF ŚŪRABALA UDIRṆAVAIRA YR 8

FIRST PLATE

SECOND PLATE : FIRST SIDE

SECOND PLATE : SECOND SIDE

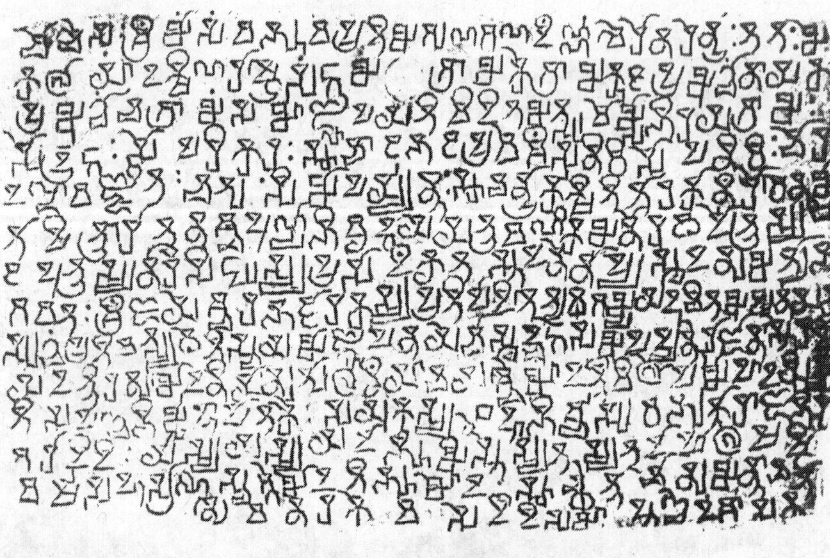

THIRD PLATE : FIRST SIDE

PL.LI

THIRD PLATE : SECOND SIDE

SEAL

PL.LII

II. APP. MALGA PLATES OF SĀMANTA INDRARĀJA

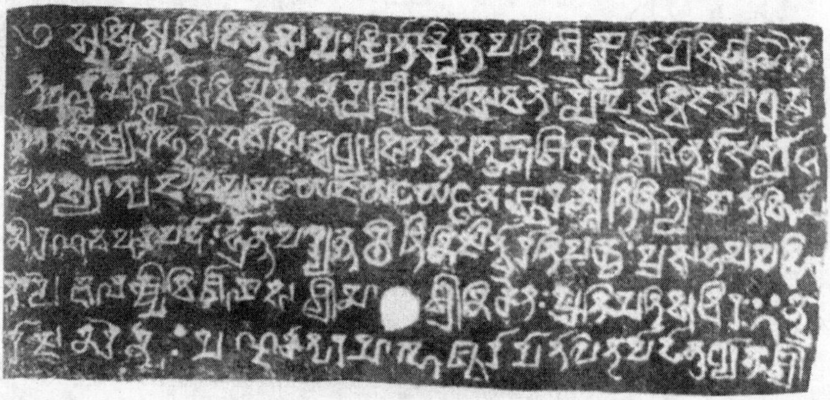

FIRST PLATE

SECOND PLATE : FIRST SIDE

SECOND PLATE : SECOND SIDE

PL.LIV

THIRD PLATE : FIRST SIDE

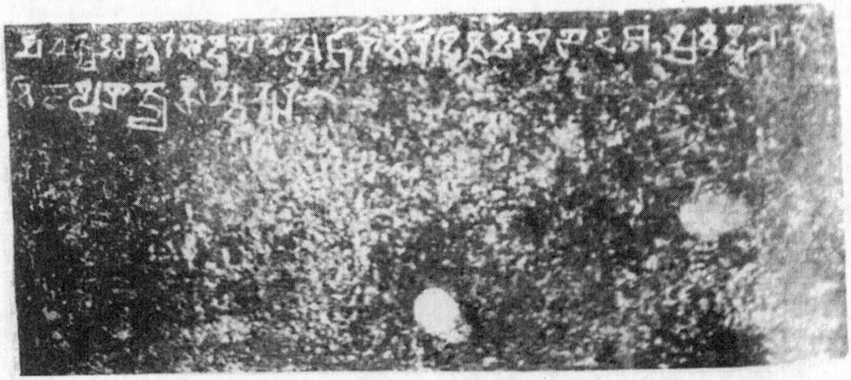

THIRD PLATE : SECOND SIDE

III

INSCRIPTIONS OF THE PĀṆḌUVAṀŚINS OF SOUTH KOSALA

PL. LVII

III : I A RANG STONE INSCRIPTION OF NANNA RAJA

PL.LVIII

III : II. BONDA PLATES OF TIVARADEVA, YR. 5

FIRST PLATE

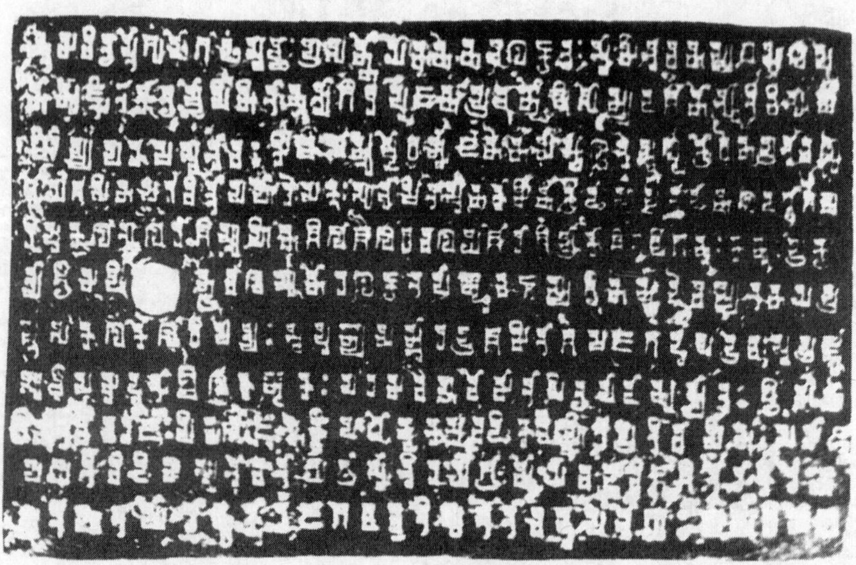

SECOND PLATE : FIRST SIDE

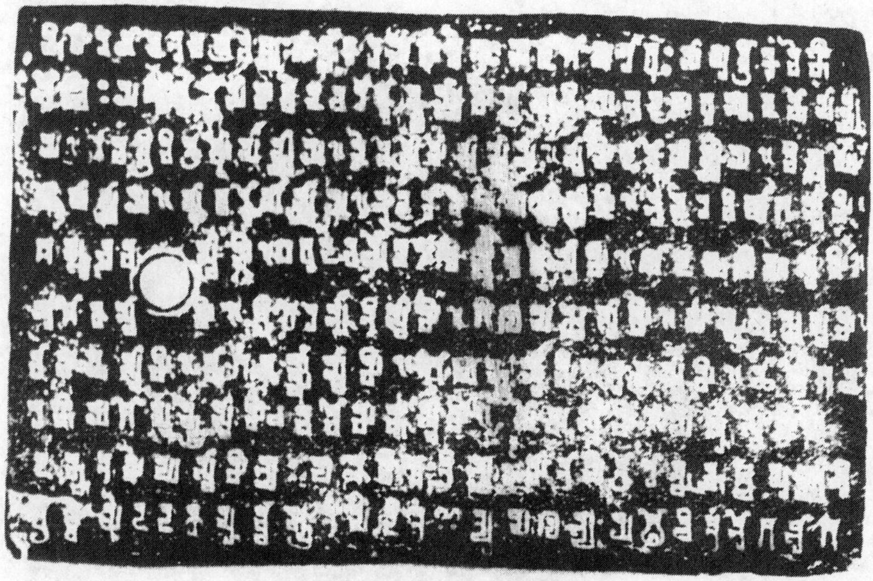

SECOND PLATE : SECOND SIDE

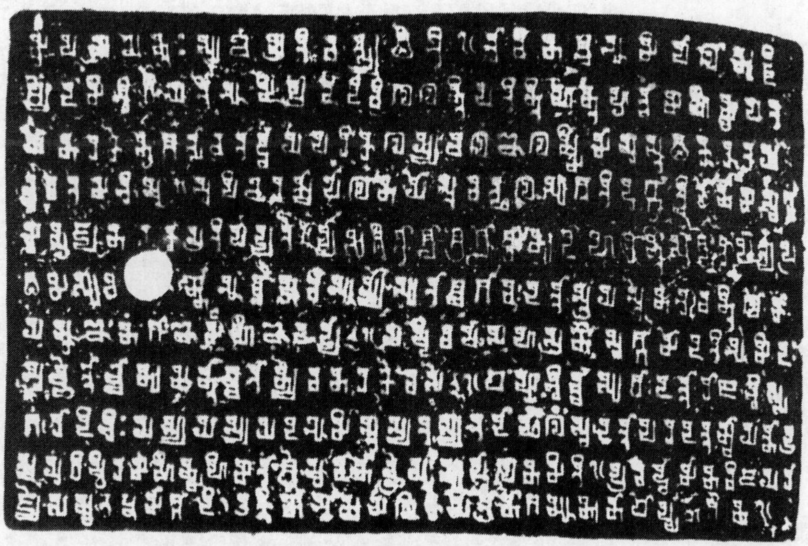

THIRD PLATE

PL.LX

SEAL

III : III. RAJIM PLATES OF TĪVARADEVA, YR. 7

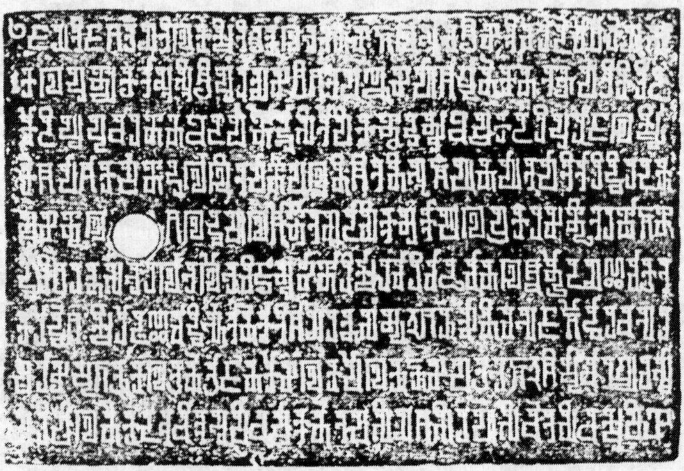

FIRST PLATE

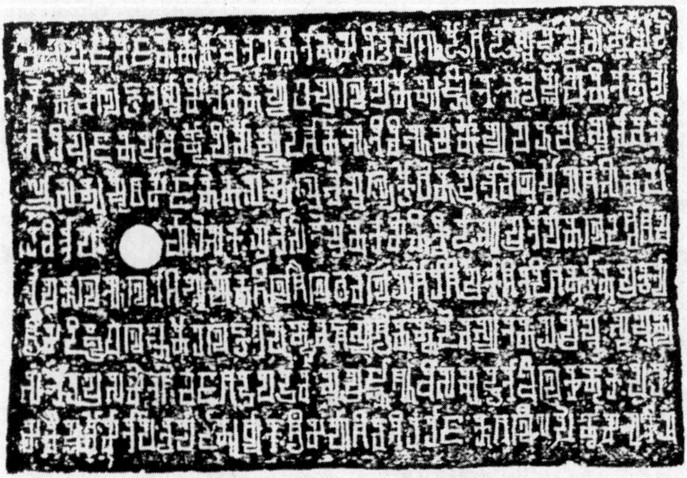

SECOND PLATE : FIRST SIDE

SECOND PLATE : SECOND SIDE

PL.LXII

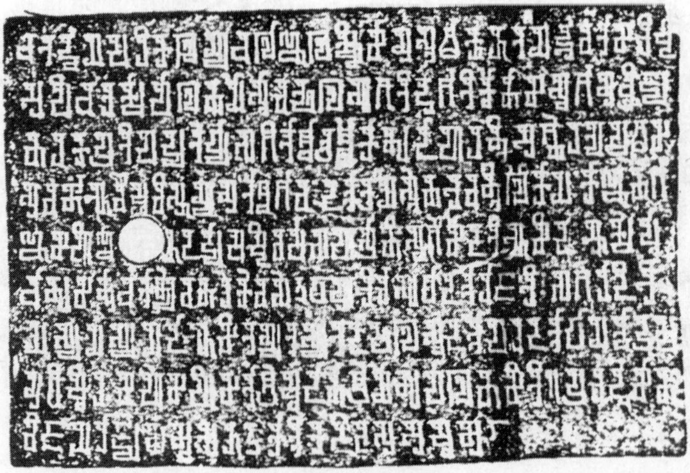

THIRD PLATE

SEAL

III : IV. BALODA PLATES OF TIVARADEVA, YR. 9

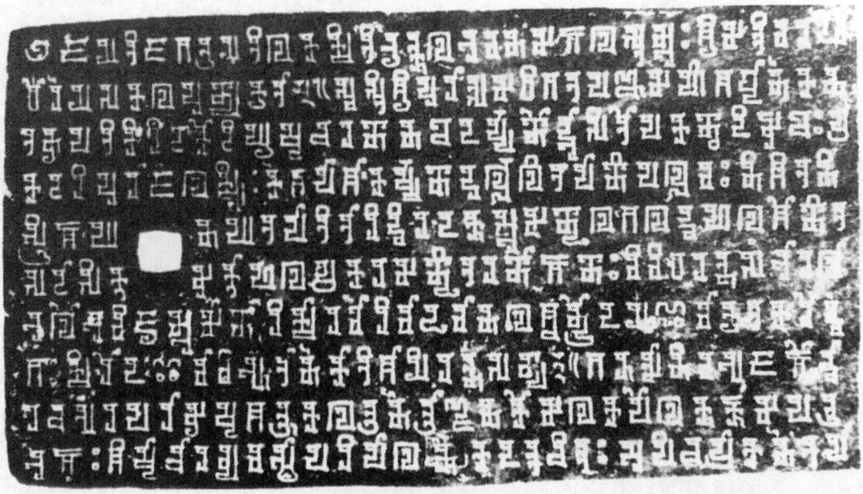

FIRST PLATE

SECOND PLATE : FIRST SIDE

PL.LXIV

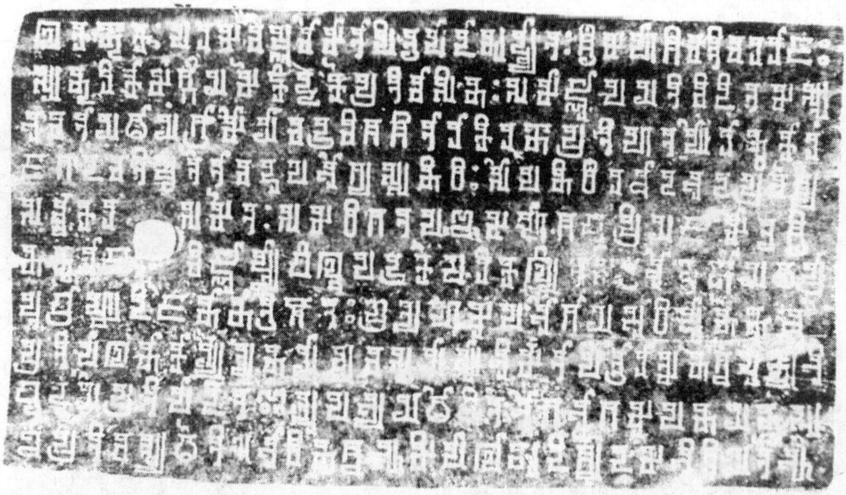

SECOND PLATE : SECOND SIDE

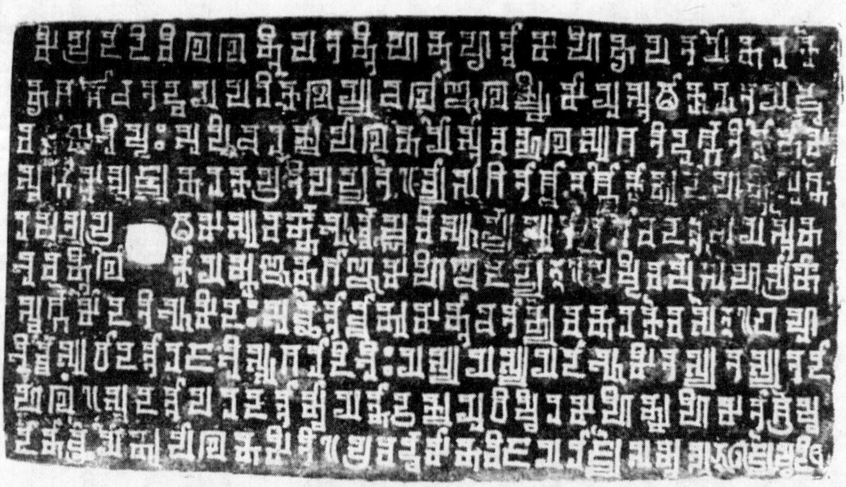

THIRD PLATE : FIRST SIDE

III. V. ADHABHĀRA PLATES OF NANNARĀJA

FIRST PLATE

SECOND PLATE : FIRST SIDE

PL.LXVI

SECOND PLATE : SECOND SIDE

THIRD PLATE

PL.LXVII

III. VI. BARDULA PLATES OF ŚIVAGUPTA, YR. 9

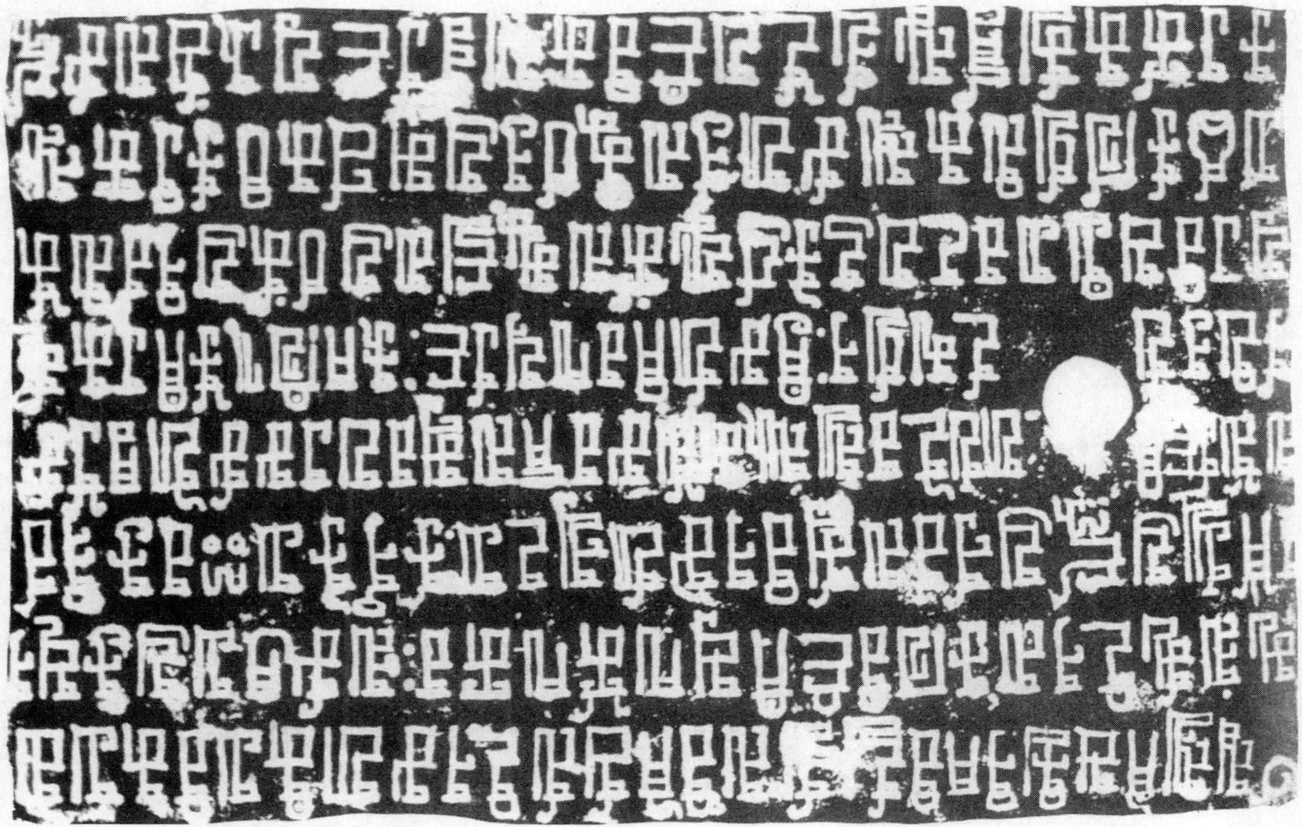

FIRST PLATE

PL.LXVIII

SECOND PLATE : FIRST SIDE

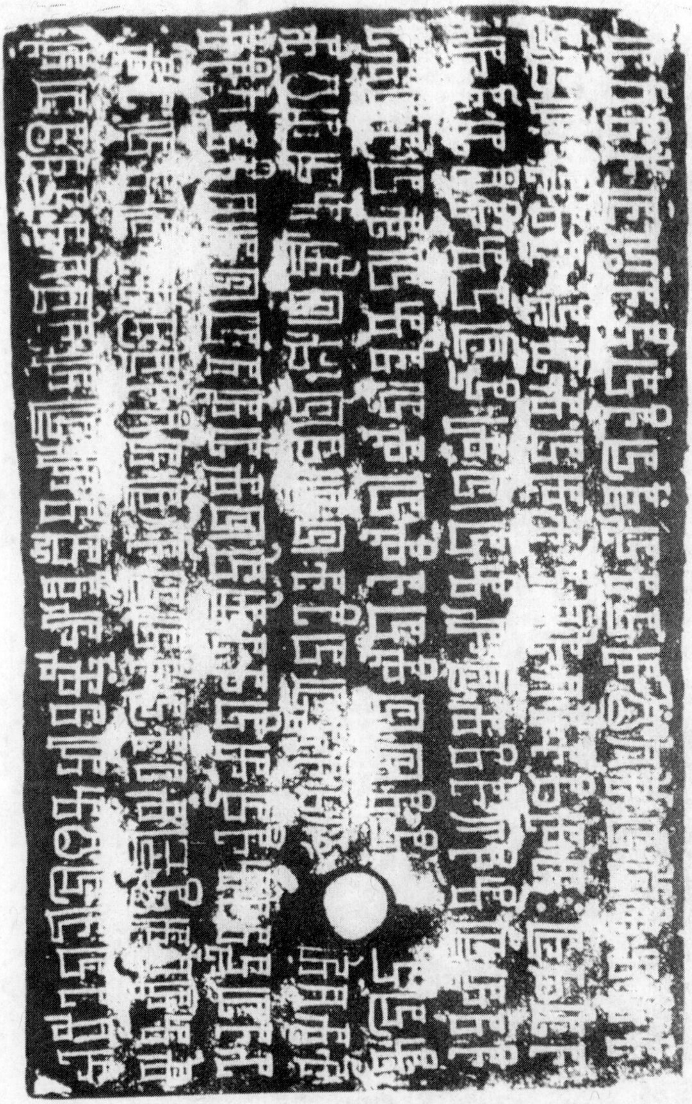

18 20 22 24

SECOND PLATE : SECOND SIDE

PL.LXX

THIRD PLATE

III.VII. BONDA PLATES OF ŚIVAGUPTA, YR. 22

FIRST PLATE

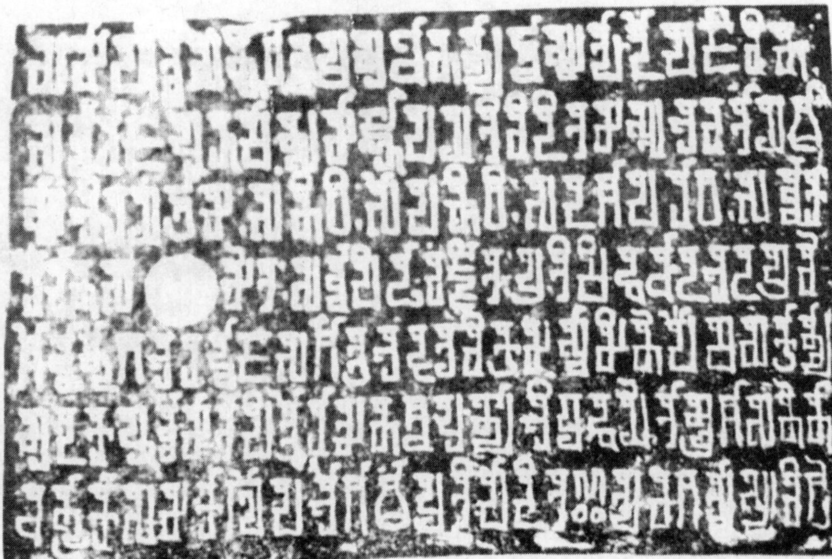

SECOND PLATE : FIRST SIDE

PL.LXXII

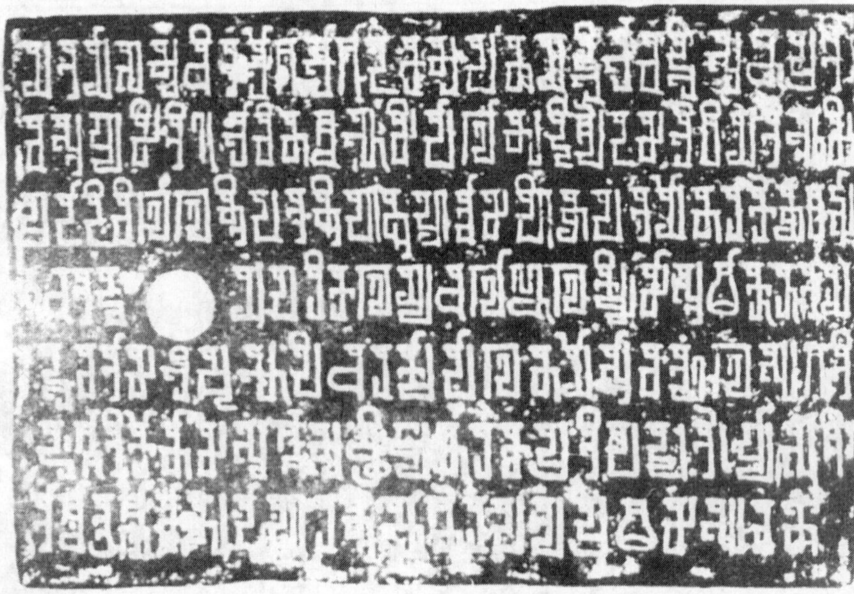

SECOND PLATE : SECOND SIDE

THIRD PLATE : FIRST SIDE

29

THIRD PLATE : SECOND SIDE

SEAL

PL.LXXIV

III : VIII. LODHIA PLATES OF ŚIVAGUPTA, YR. 57

FIRST PLATE

SECOND PLATE : FIRST SIDE

SECOND PLATE : SECOND SIDE

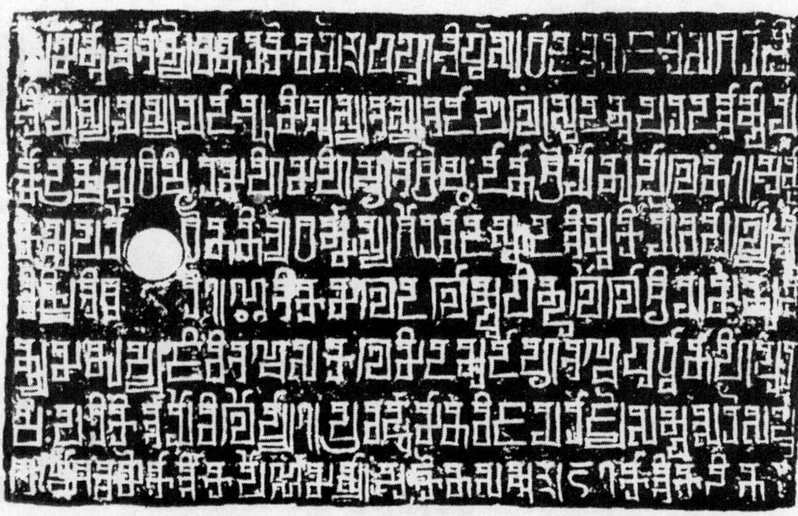

THIRD PLATE

SEAL

III : IX. MALLAR PLATES OF SIVAGUPTA

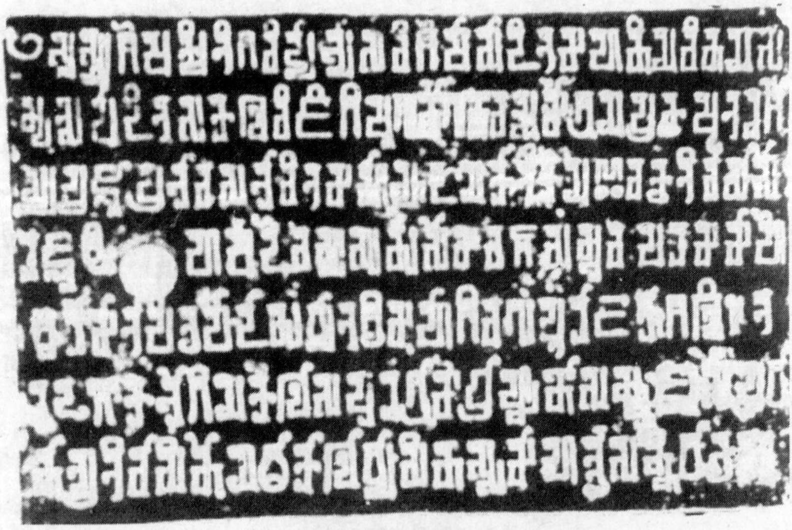

FIRST PLATE

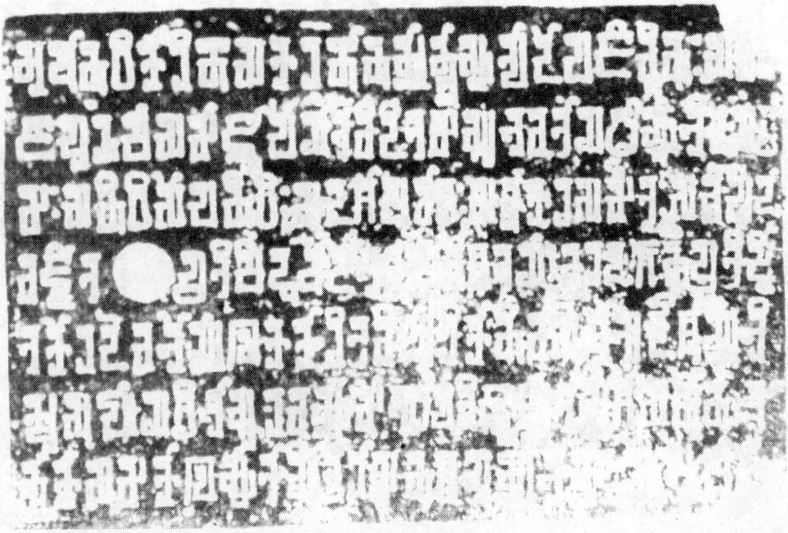

SECOND PLATE : FIRST SIDE

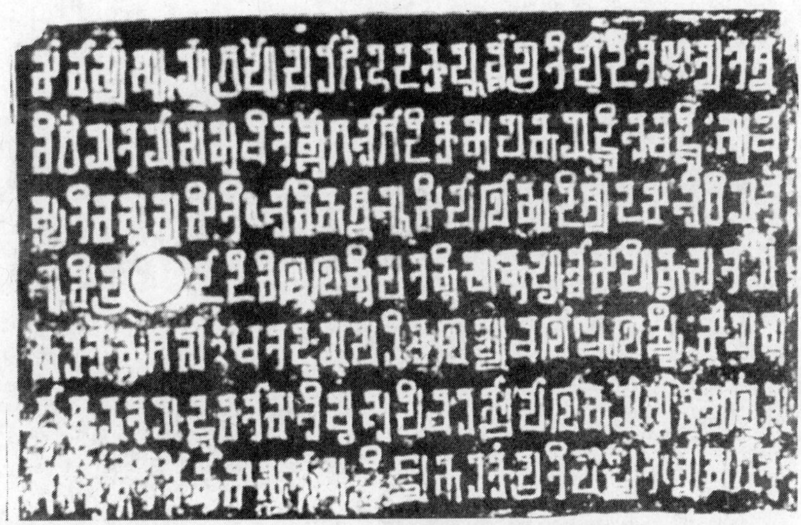

SECOND PLATE : SECOND SIDE

PL.LXXVIII

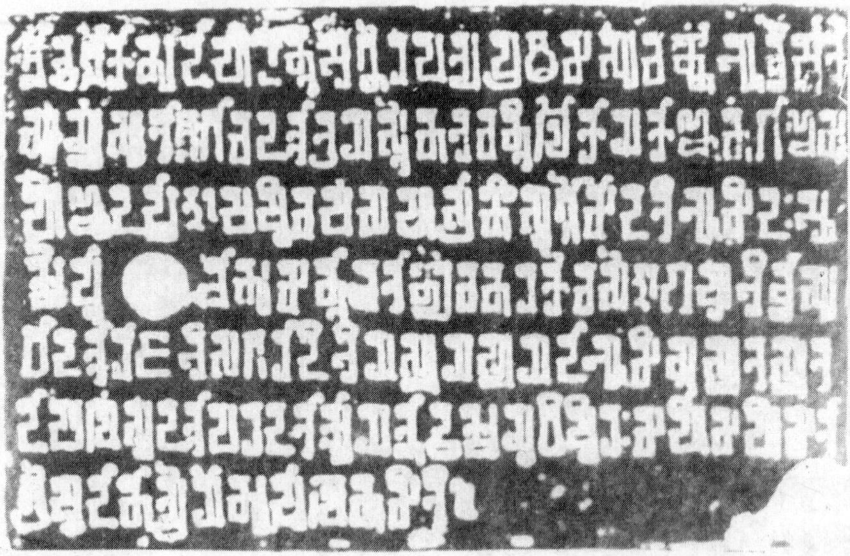

THIRD PLATE

SEAL

III : X. MALLAR PLATES OF ŚIVAGUPTA

FIRST PLATE

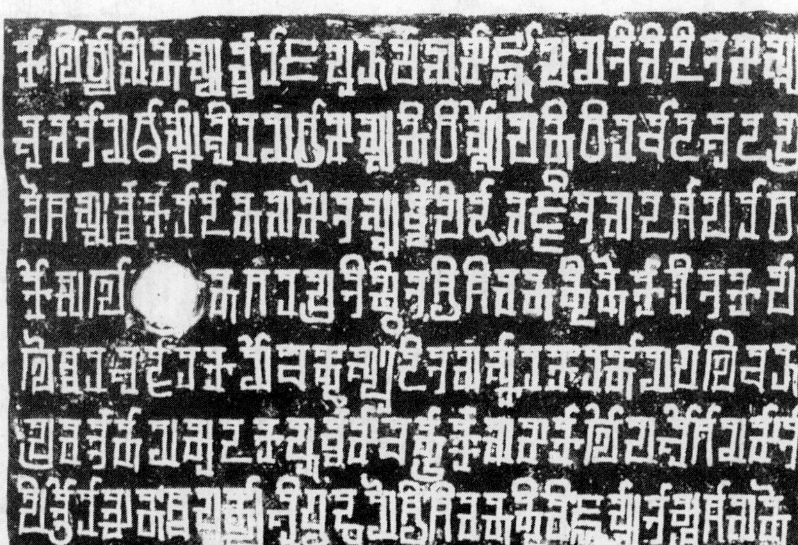

SECOND PLATE : FIRST SIDE

PL.LXXX

SECOND PLATE : SECOND SIDE

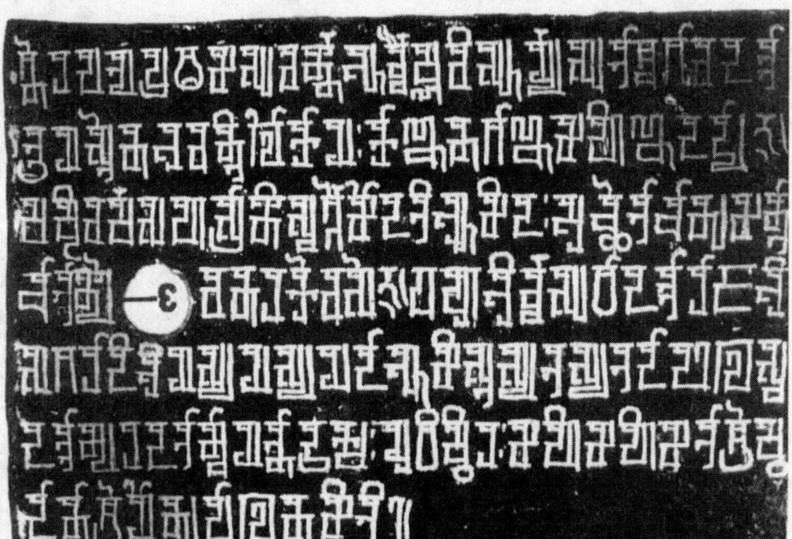

THIRD PLATE

PL.LXXXI

SEAL

III.XI. SIRPUR LAKṢMAṆA TEMPLE INSCRIPTION OF ŚIVAGUPTA

III. XII. SIRPUR STONE SLAB INSCRIPTION OF SIVAGUPTA

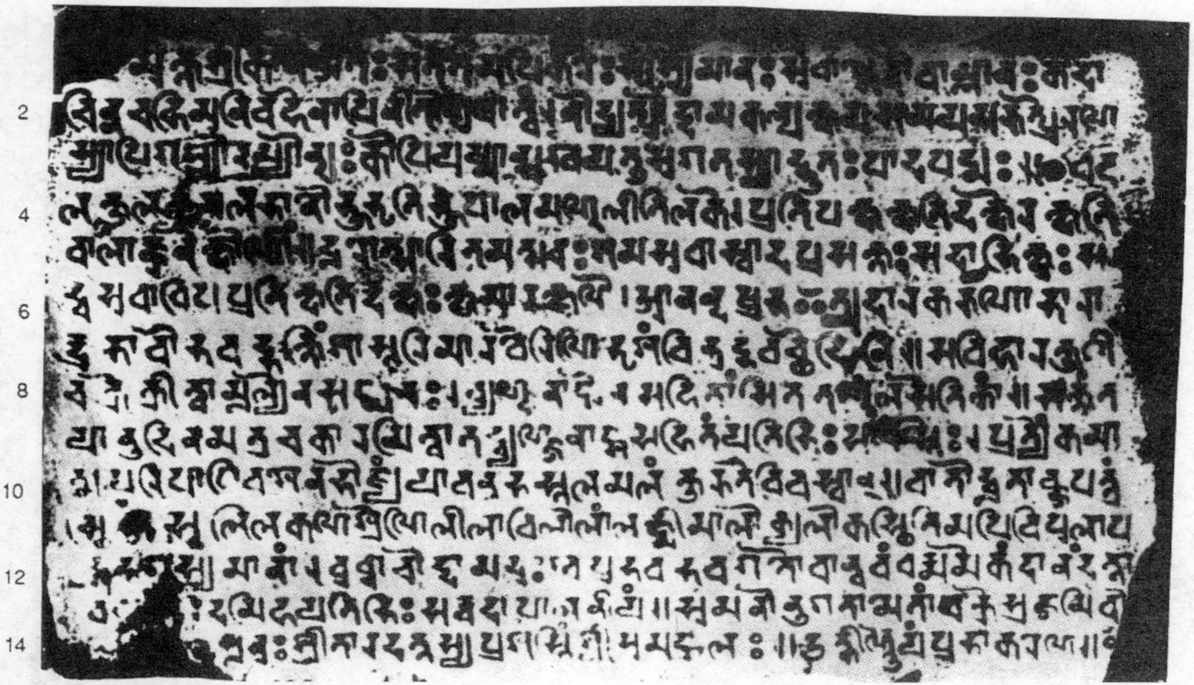

THIRD PLATE

PL.LXXXIV

III: XIII. SIRPUR STONE INSCRIPTION OF ŚIVAGUPTA

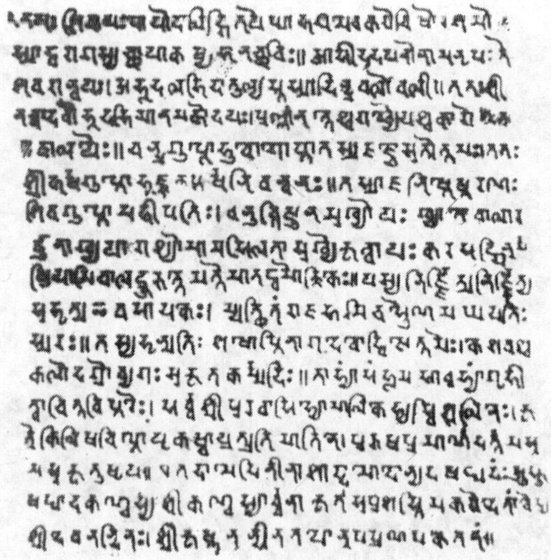

III:XIV. SIRPUR GANDHEŚVARA INSCRIPTION OF ŚIVAGUPTA

III XV SENKAPAT STONE INSCRIPTION OF ŚIVĀGUPTA

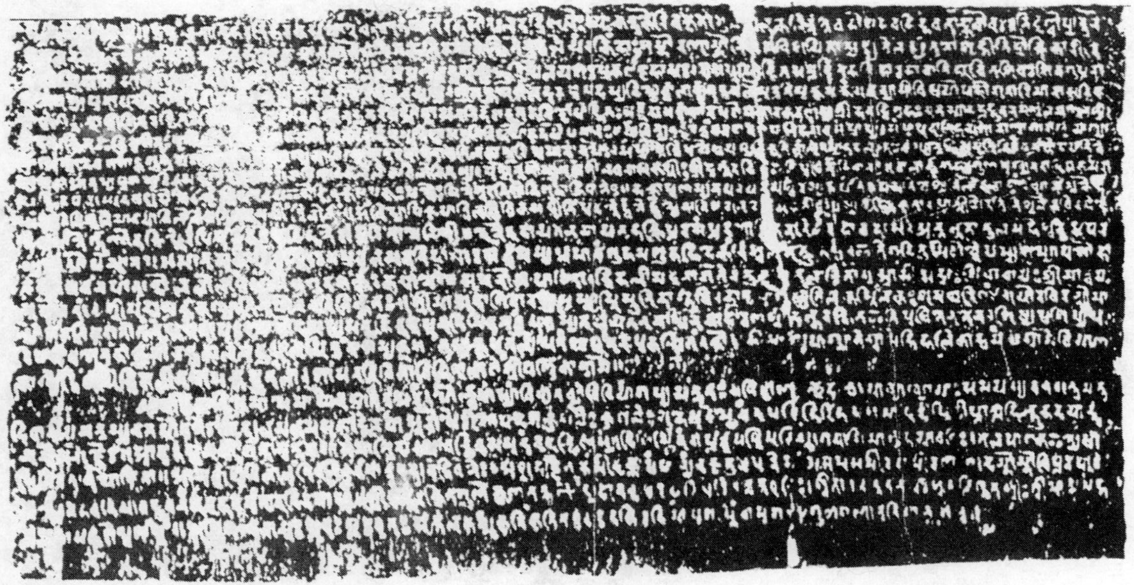

PL LXXXV

PL.LXXXVI

III : APP.I. A FRAGMENTARY SIRPUR GANDHEŚVARA INSCRIPTION

III:APP.II. A STRAY PLATE OF ŚIVAGUPTA YR. 57

IV
INSCRIPTIONS OF THE SOMAVAMŚINS

IV. I. VAKRATENTALI GRANT OF MAHĀBHAVAGUPTA I JANAMEJAYA, YR. 3

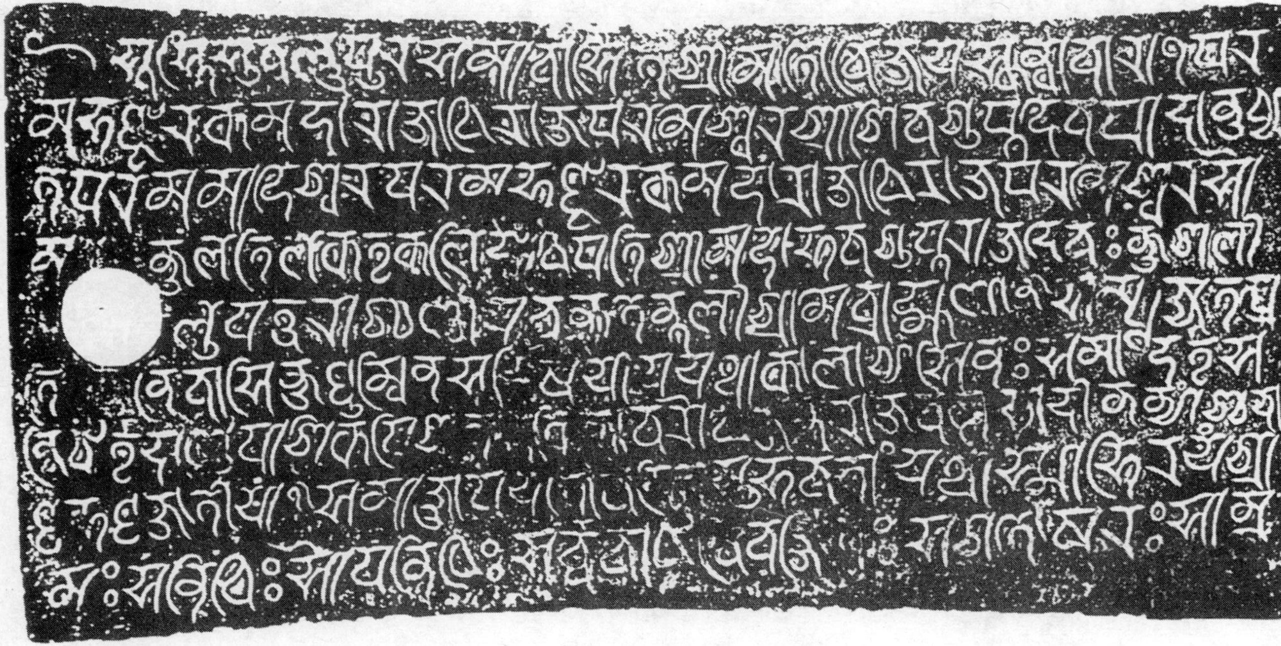

FIRST PLATE

PL.XCII

SECOND PLATE : FIRST SIDE

PL.XCIII

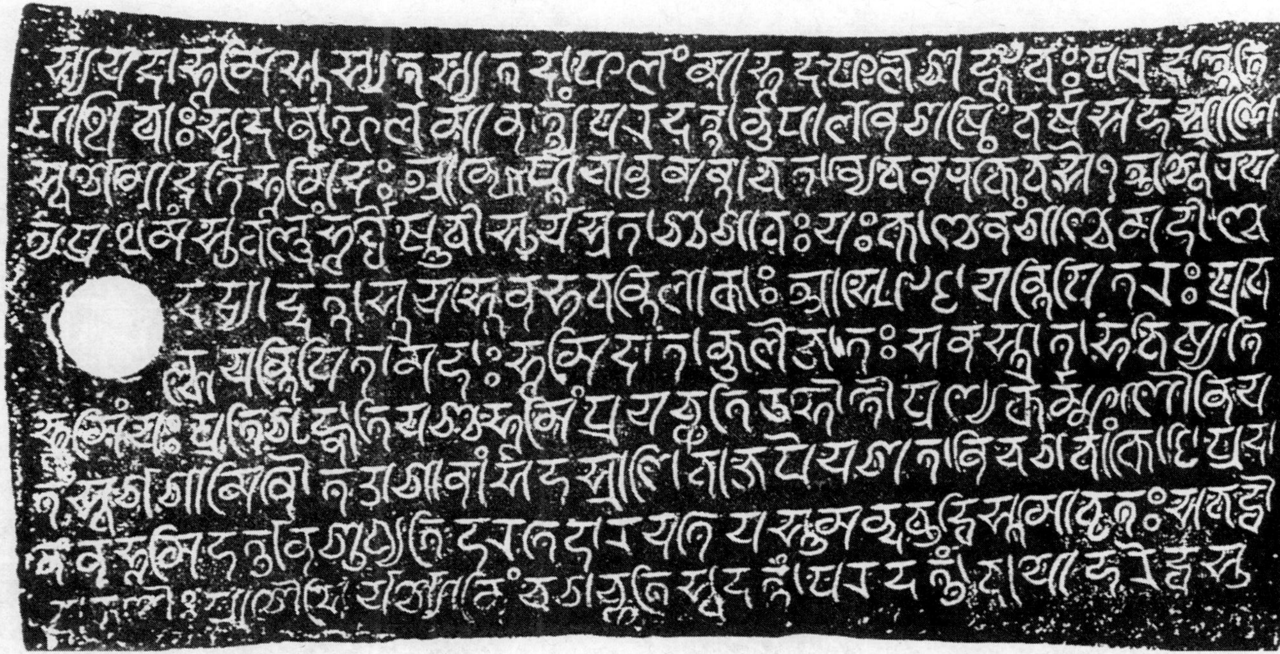

SECOND PLATE : SECOND SIDE

PL.XCIV

THIRD PLATE

IV : II. PATNA PLATES OF MAHĀBHAVAGUPTA I JANAMEJAYA,
YR. 6 (i)

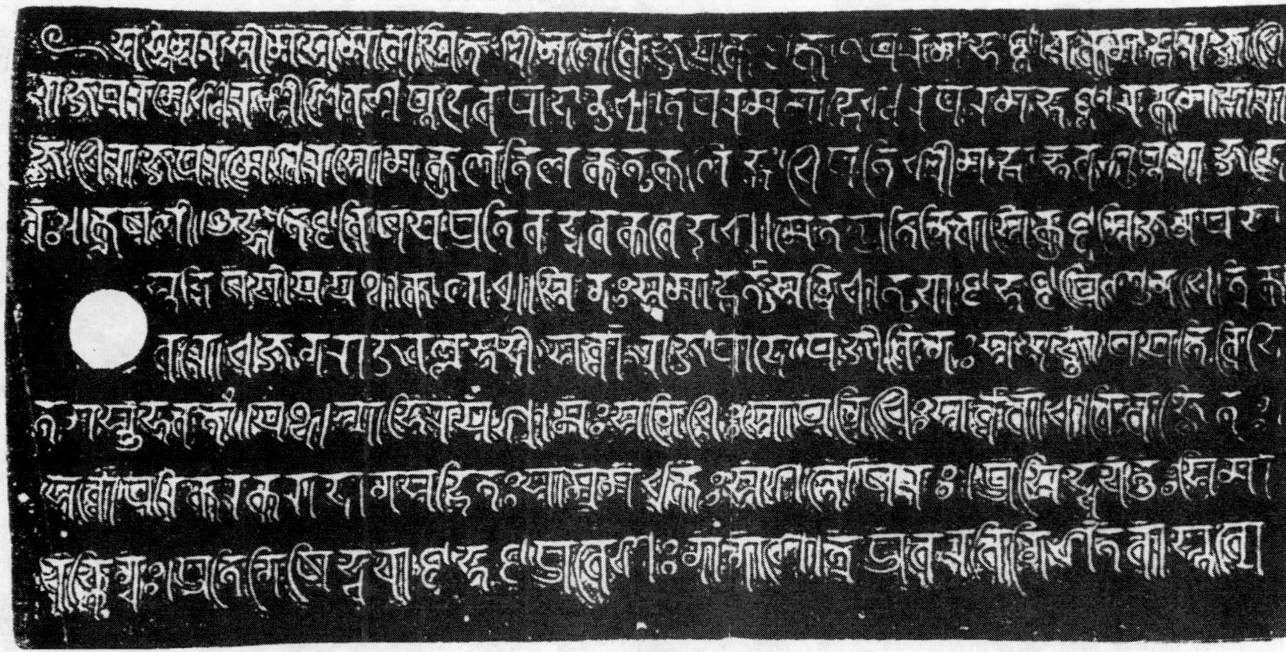

FIRST PLATE

PL. XCVI

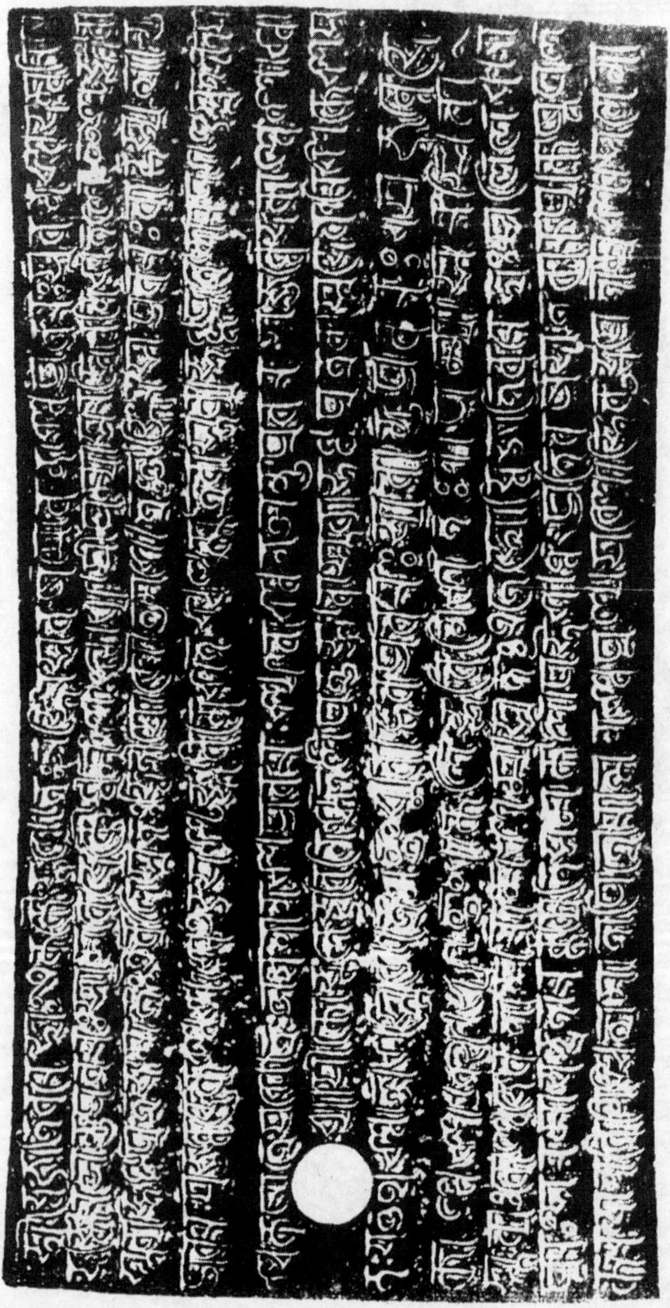

SECOND PLATE : FIRST SIDE

PL.XCVII

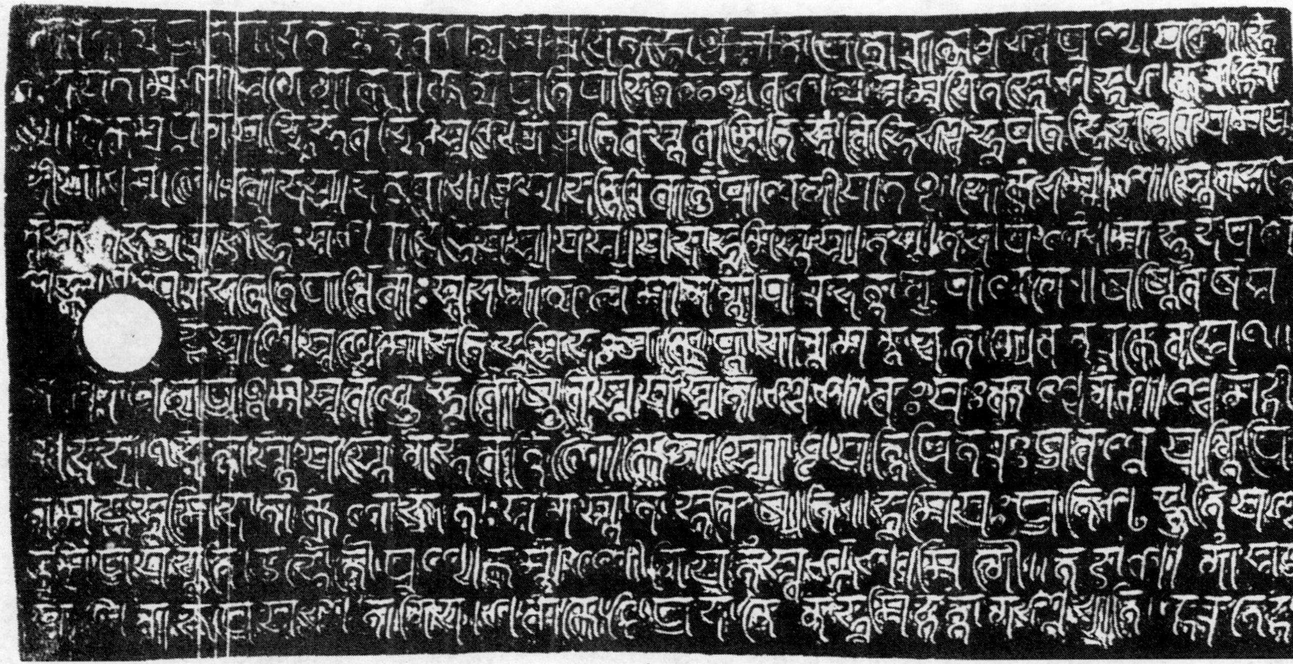

SECOND PLATE : SECOND SIDE

PL.XCVIII

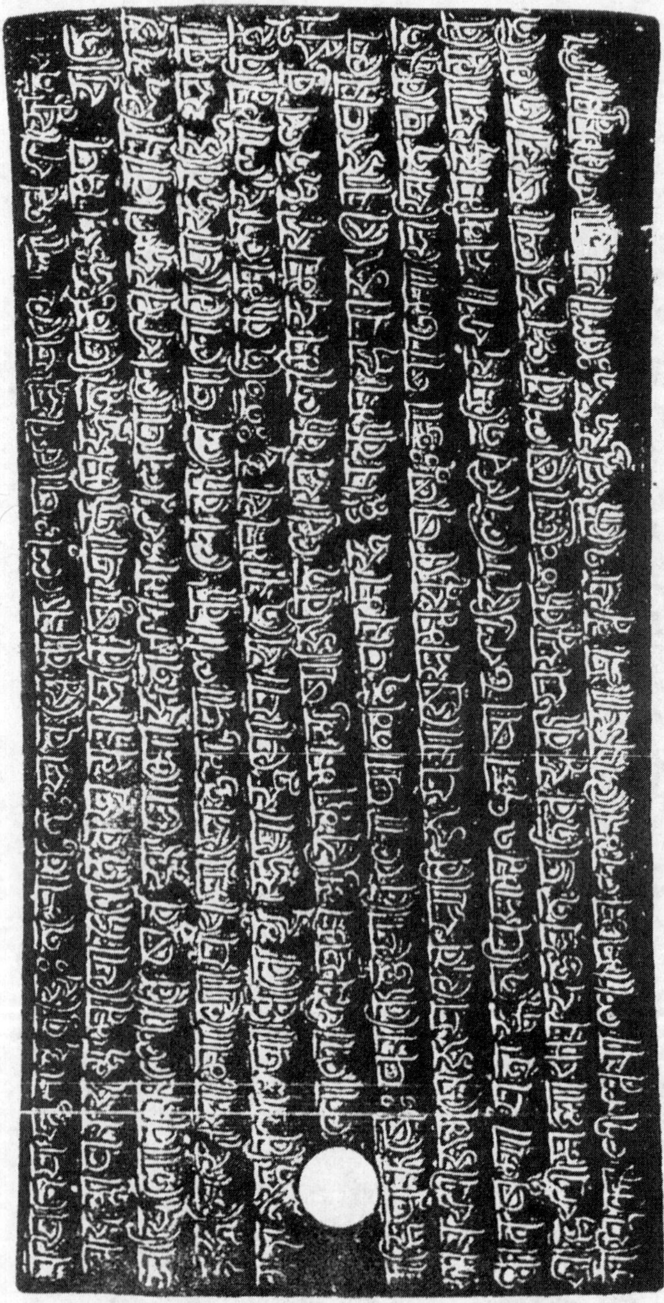

THIRD PLATE : FIRST SIDE

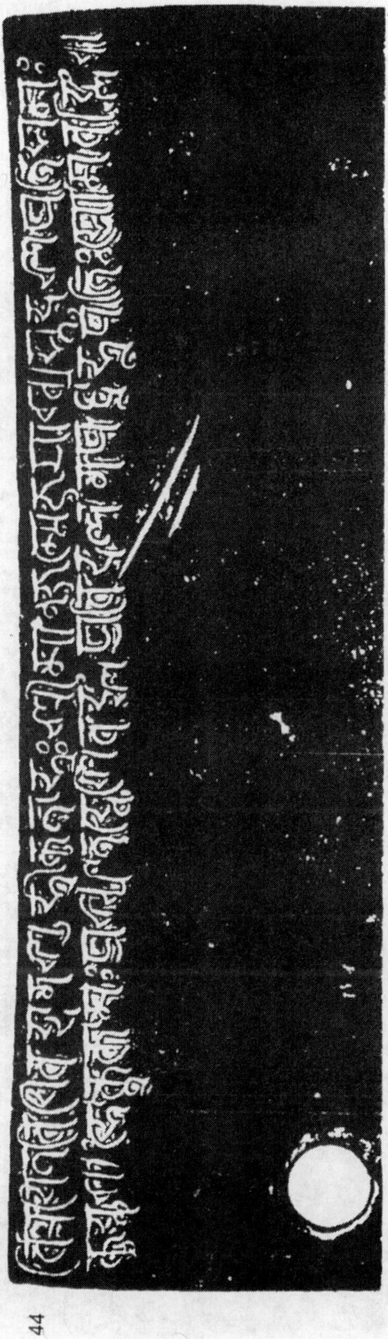

THIRD PLATE : SECOND SIDE

IV : III. PATNA PLATES OF MAHĀBHAVAGUPTA JANAMEJAYA, YR. 6 (ii)

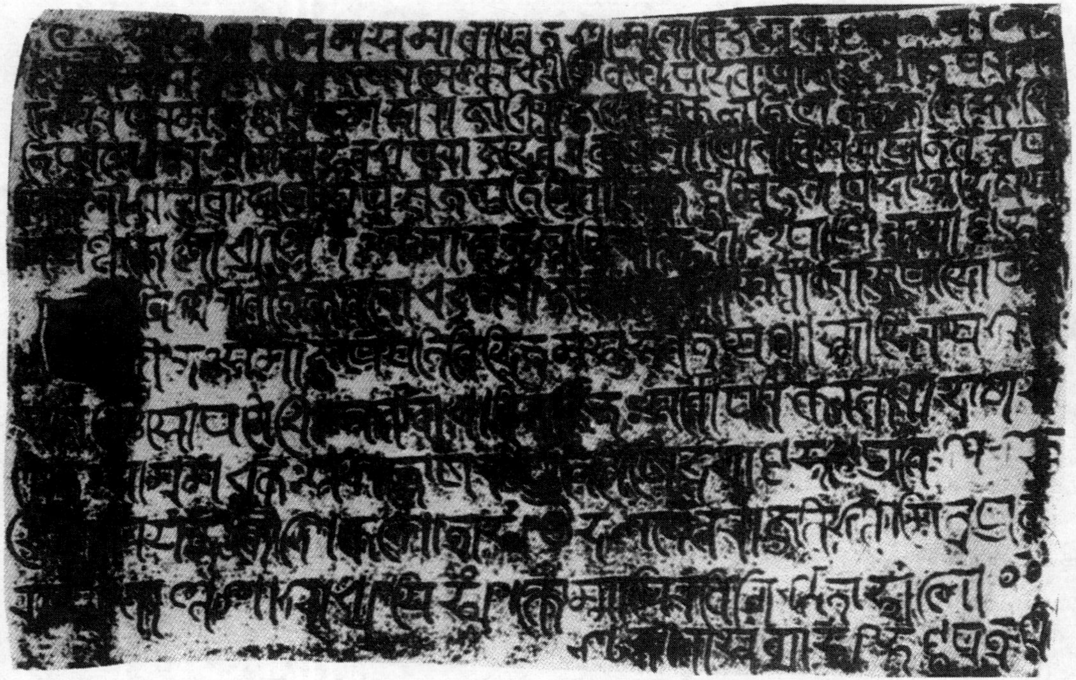

FIRST PLATE

PL.CI

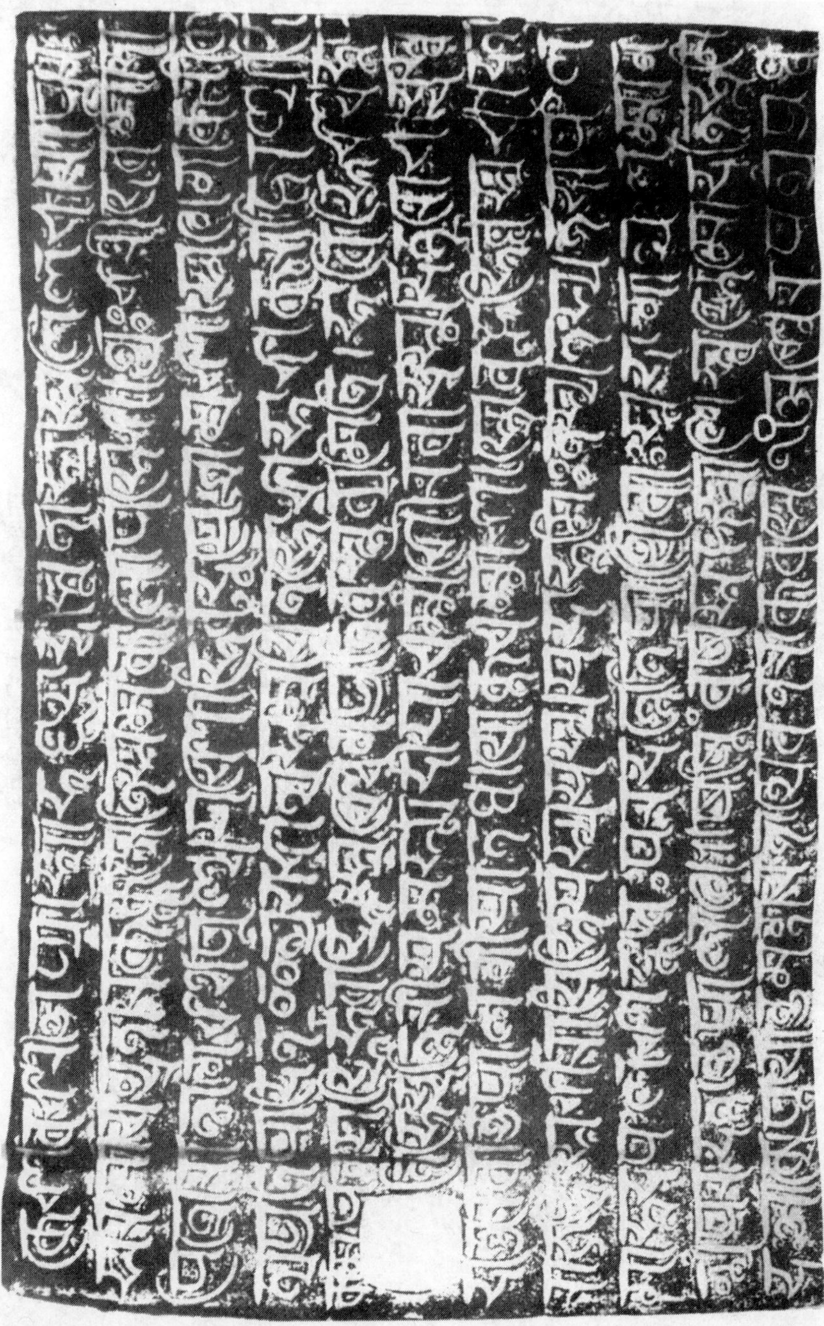

SECOND PLATE : FIRST SIDE

PL.CII

SECOND PLATE : SECOND SIDE

PL.CIII

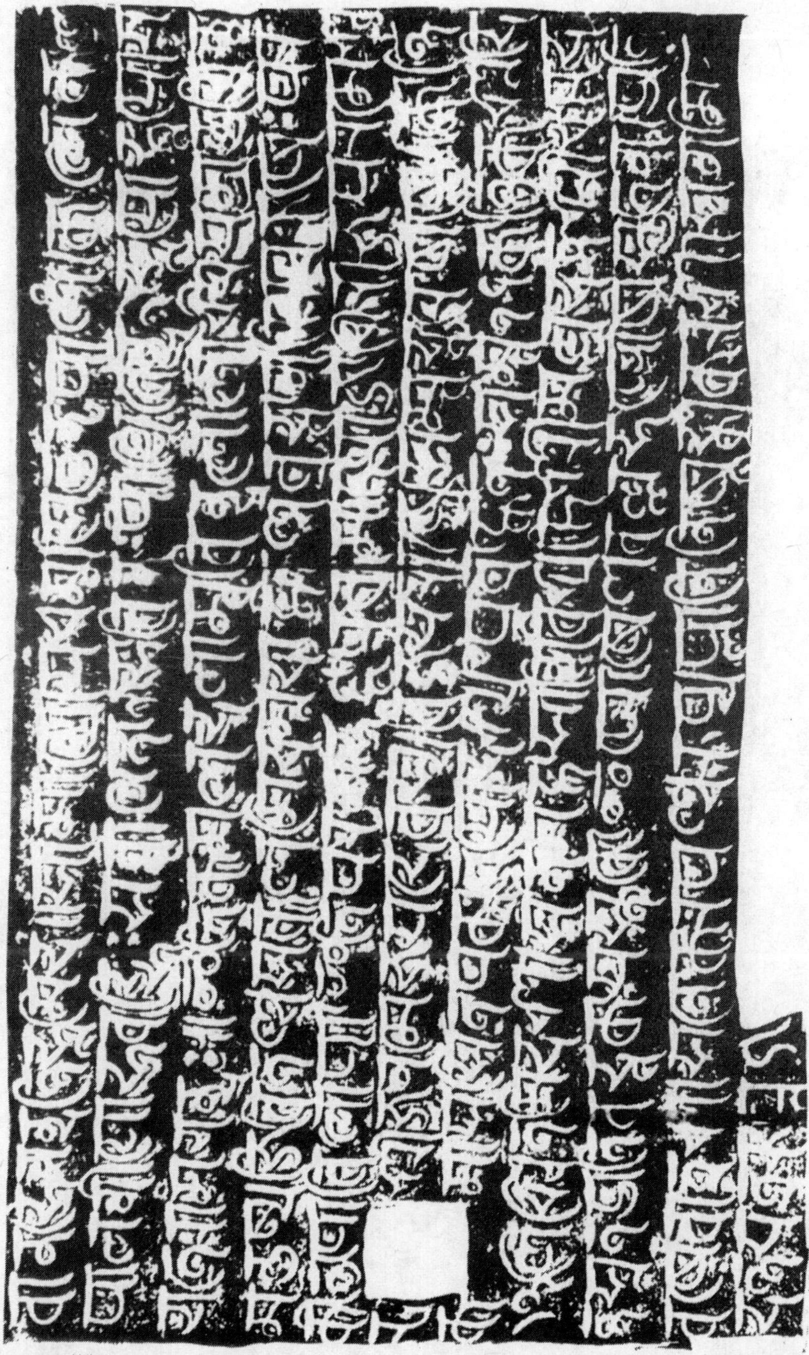

THIRD PLATE

IV : IV. KĀLIBHANĀ PLATES OF MAHĀBHAVAGUPTA I JANAMEJAYA, YR. 6

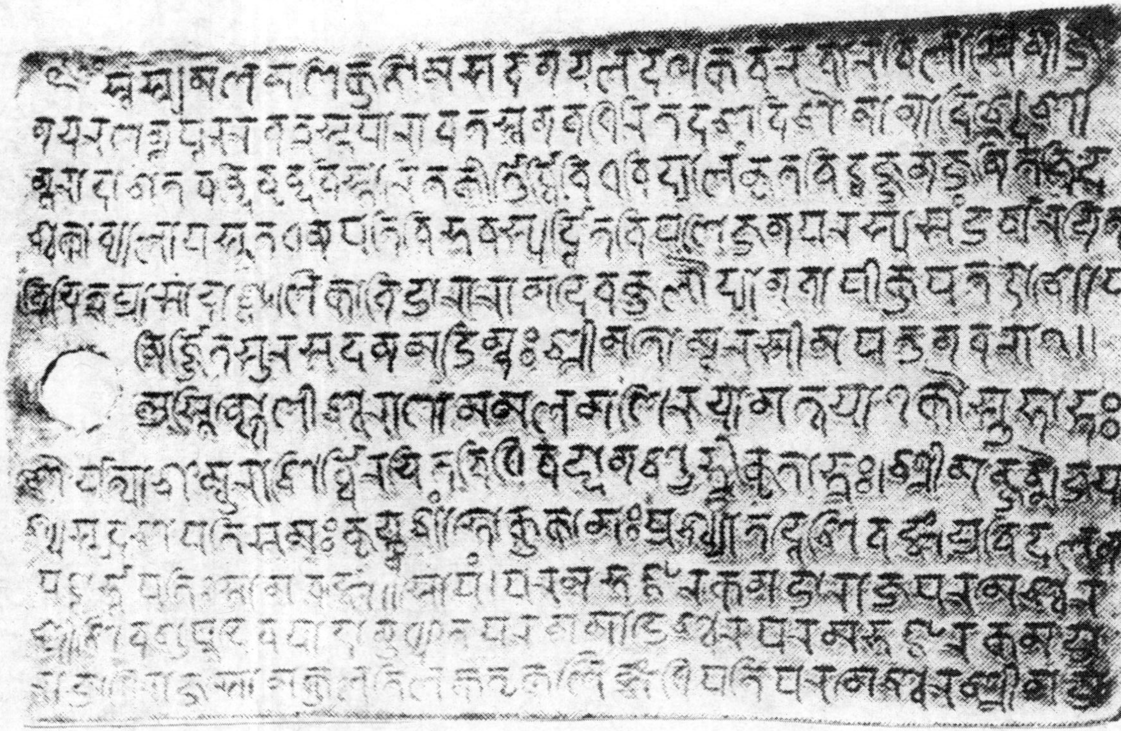

FIRST PLATE

PL.CV

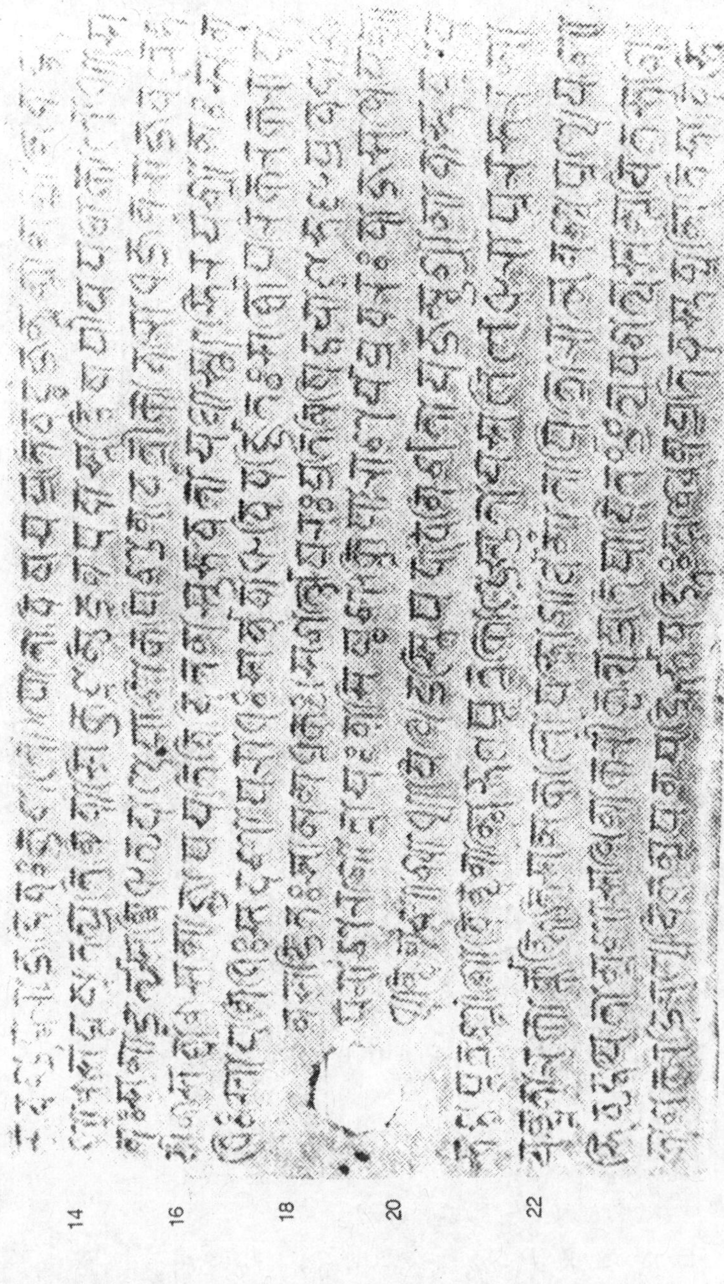

SECOND PLATE : FIRST SIDE

PL.CVI

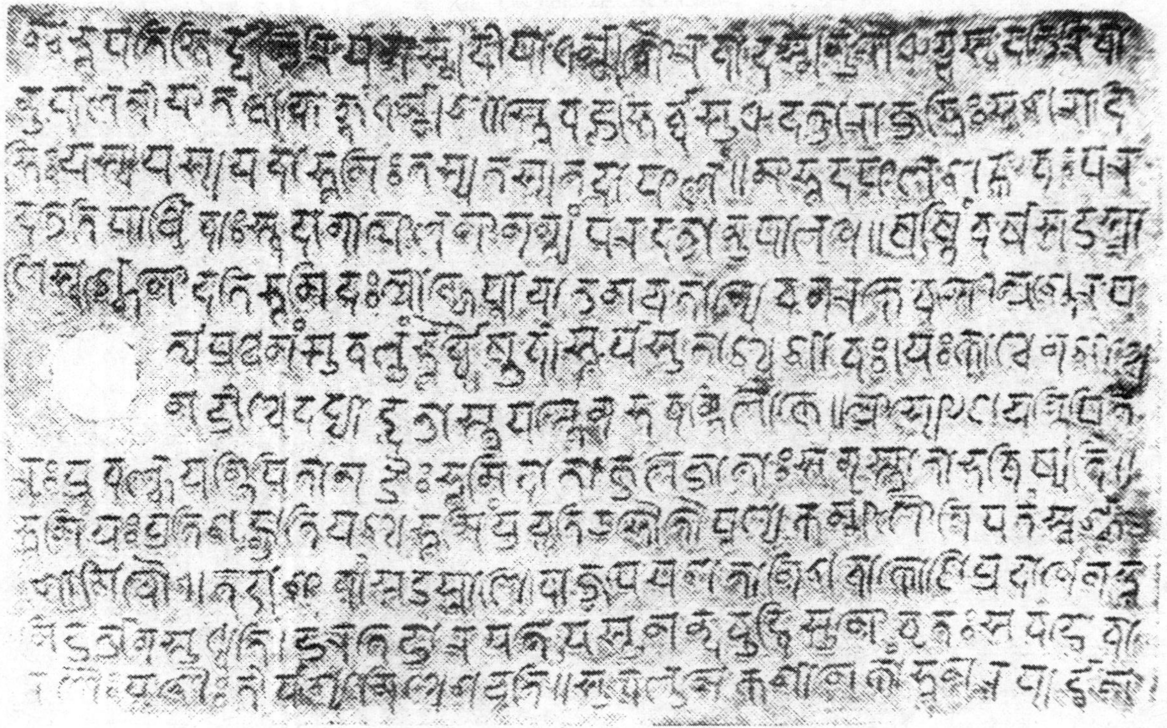

SECOND PLATE : SECOND SIDE

PL.CVII

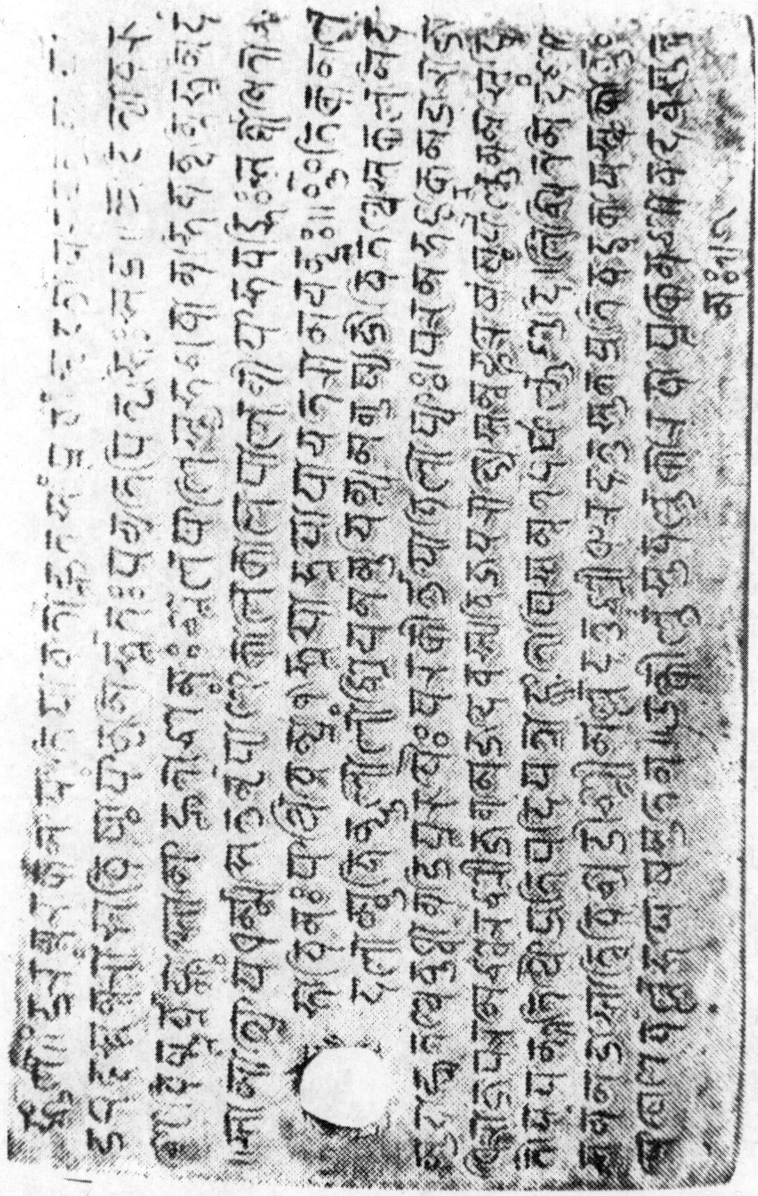

THIRD PLATE

PL.CVIII

IV : V. SATALMA PLATES OF MAHĀBHAVAGUPTA I JANAMEJAYA, YR. 8

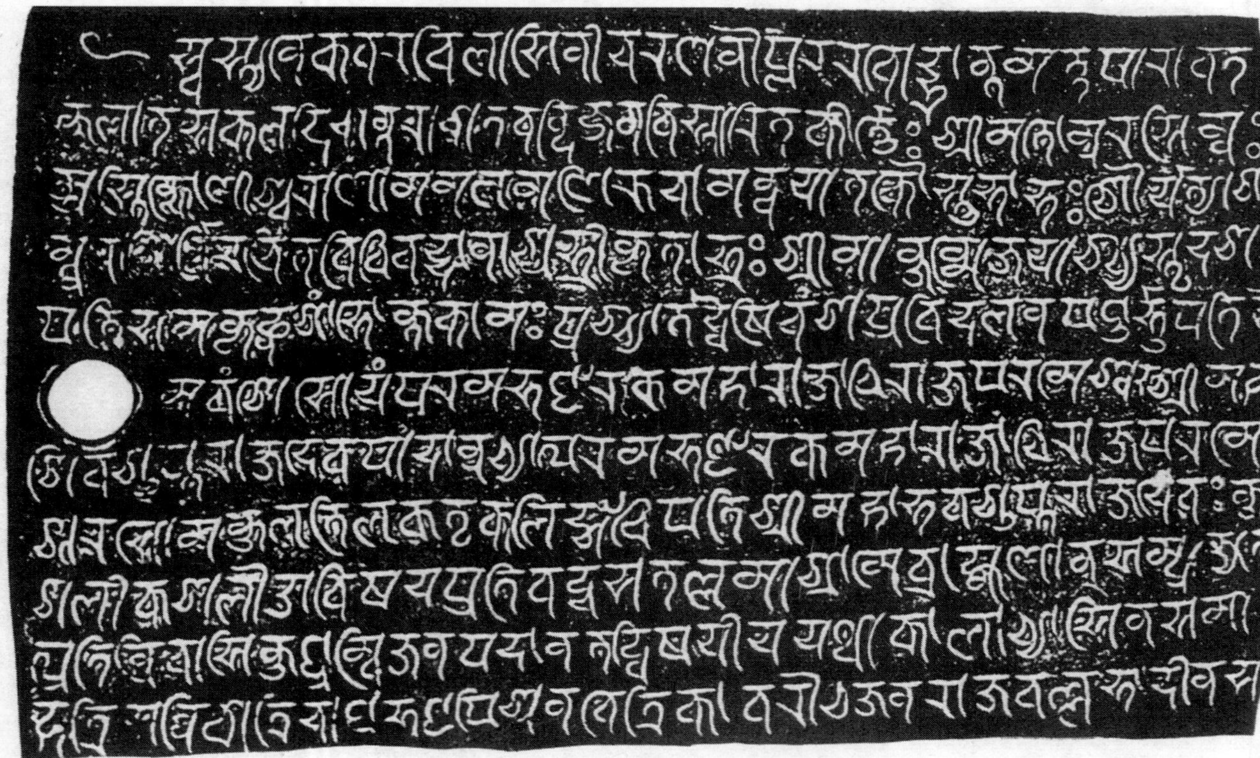

FIRST PLATE

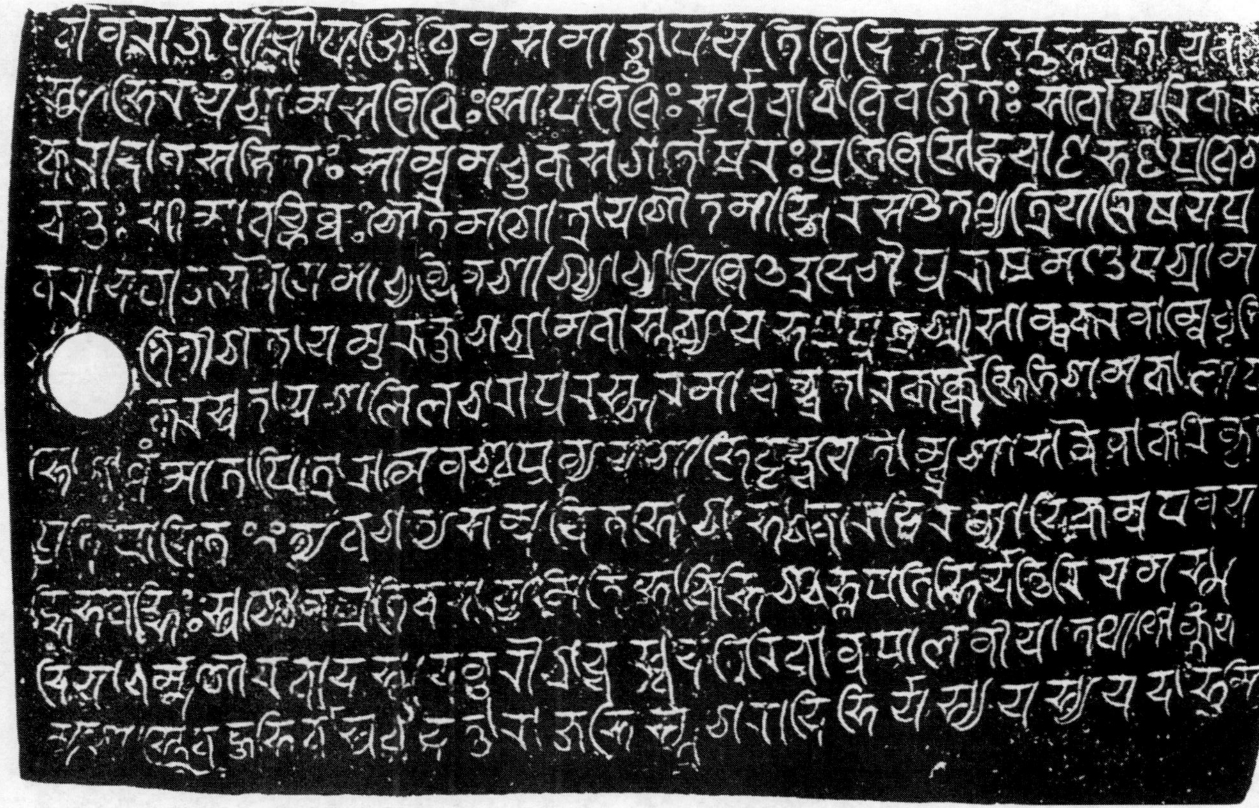

SECOND PLATE : FIRST SIDE

PL.CX

SECOND PLATE : SECOND SIDE

PL.CXI

THIRD PLATE

IV : VI. SONPUR PLATES OF MAHĀBHAVAGUPTA I JANAMEJAYA, YR. 17

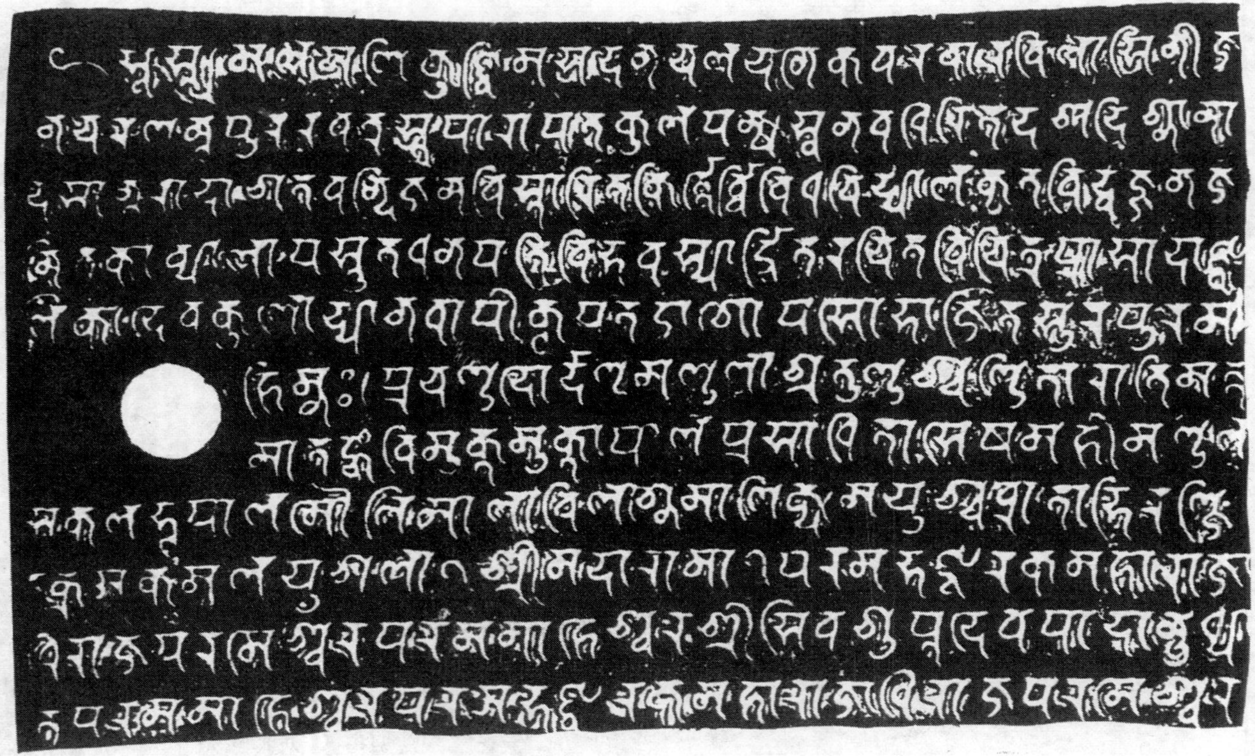

FIRST PLATE

PL.CXIII

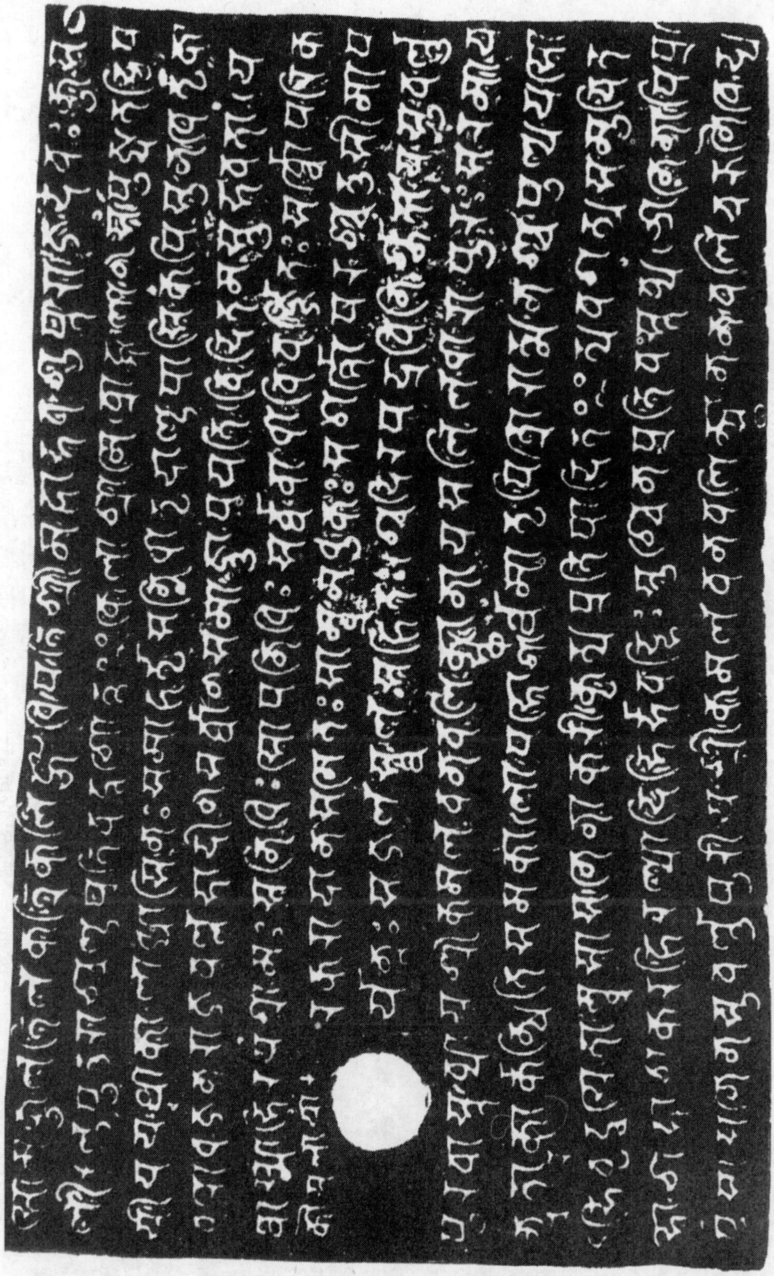

SECOND PLATE : FIRST SIDE

PL.CXIV

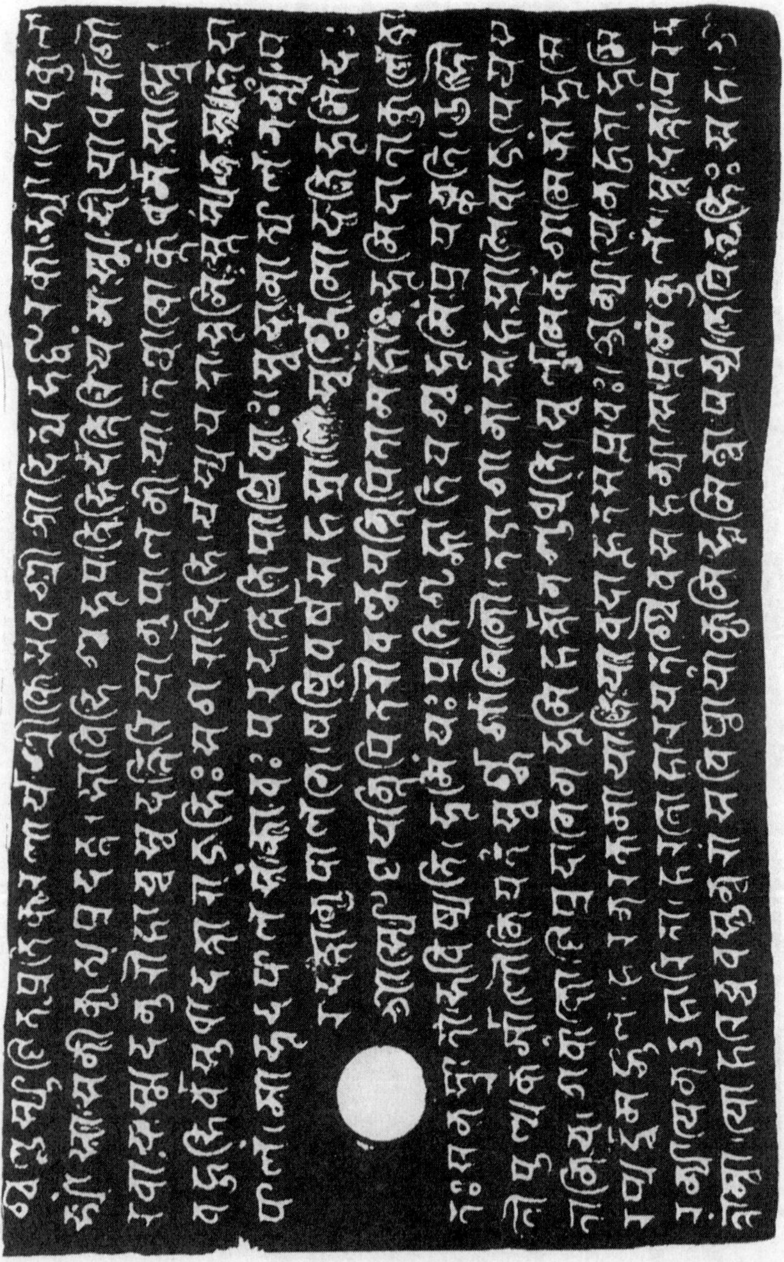

SECOND PLATE : SECOND SIDE

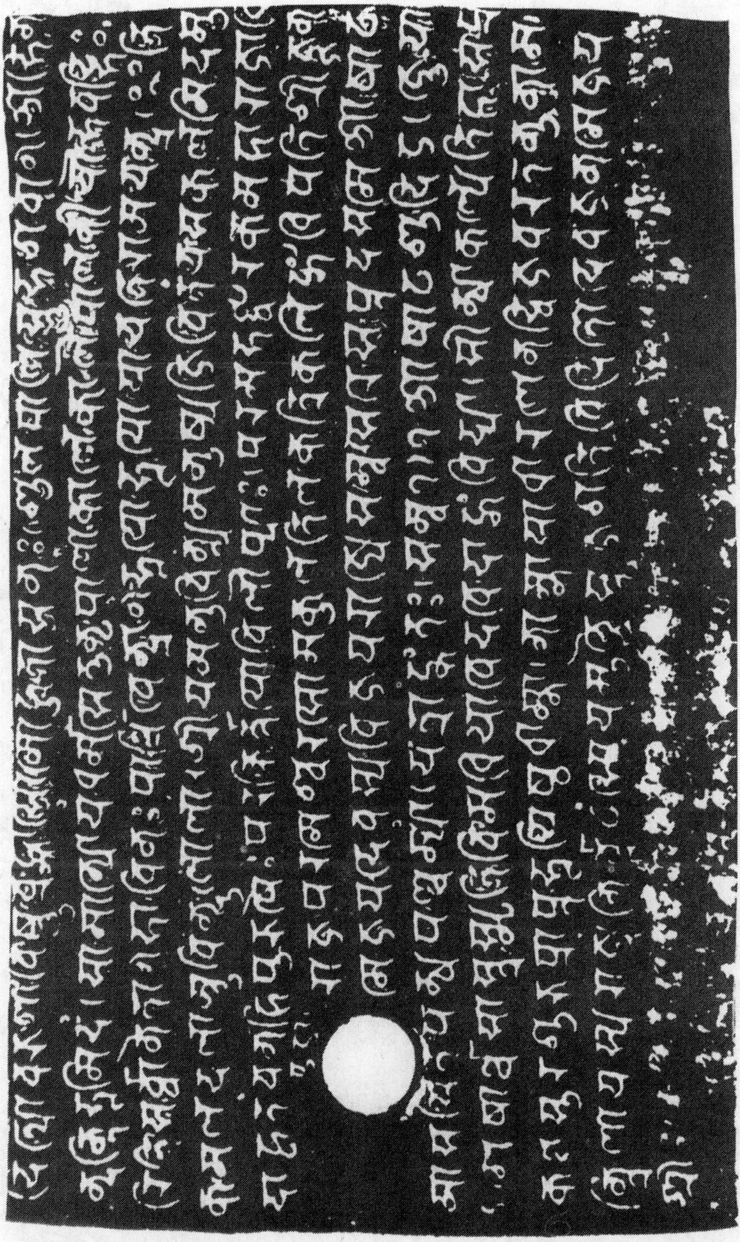

THIRD PLATE : FIRST SIDE

50

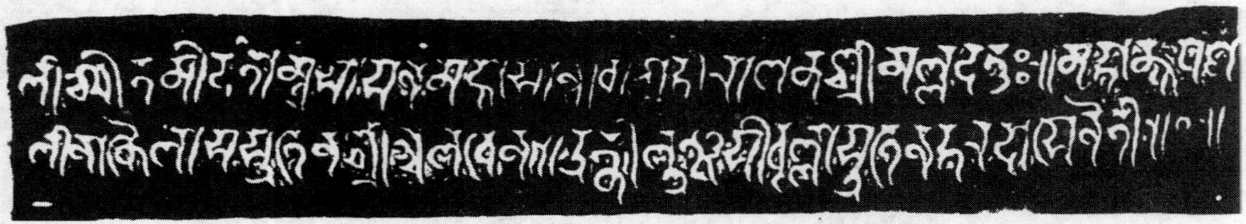

THIRD PLATE : SECOND SIDE

IV : VII. GAINTALA PLATES OF MAHĀBHAVAGUPTA I
JANAMEJAYA, YR. 17

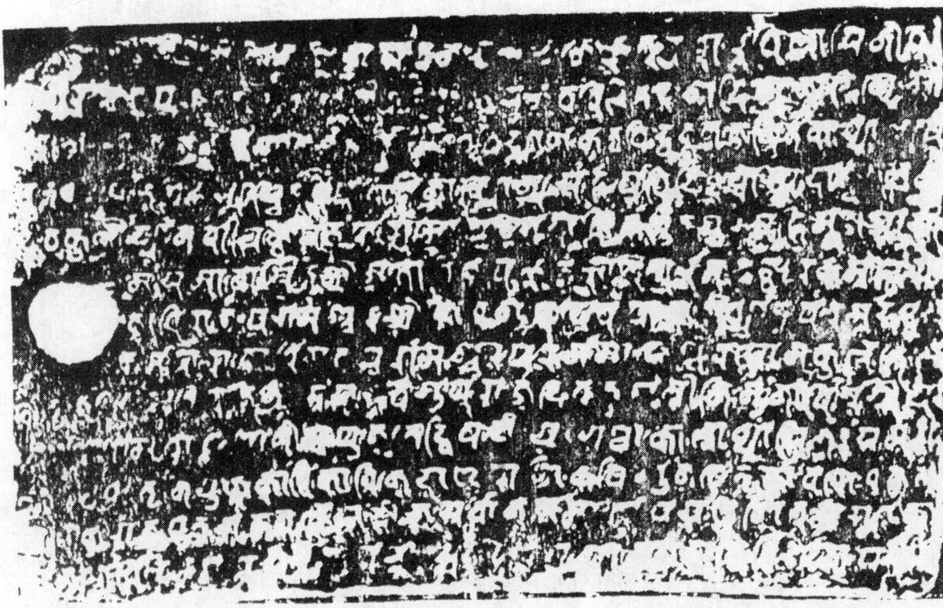

FIRST PLATE

SECOND PLATE : FIRST SIDE

PL.CXVIII

SECOND PLATE : SECOND SIDE

THIRD PLATE

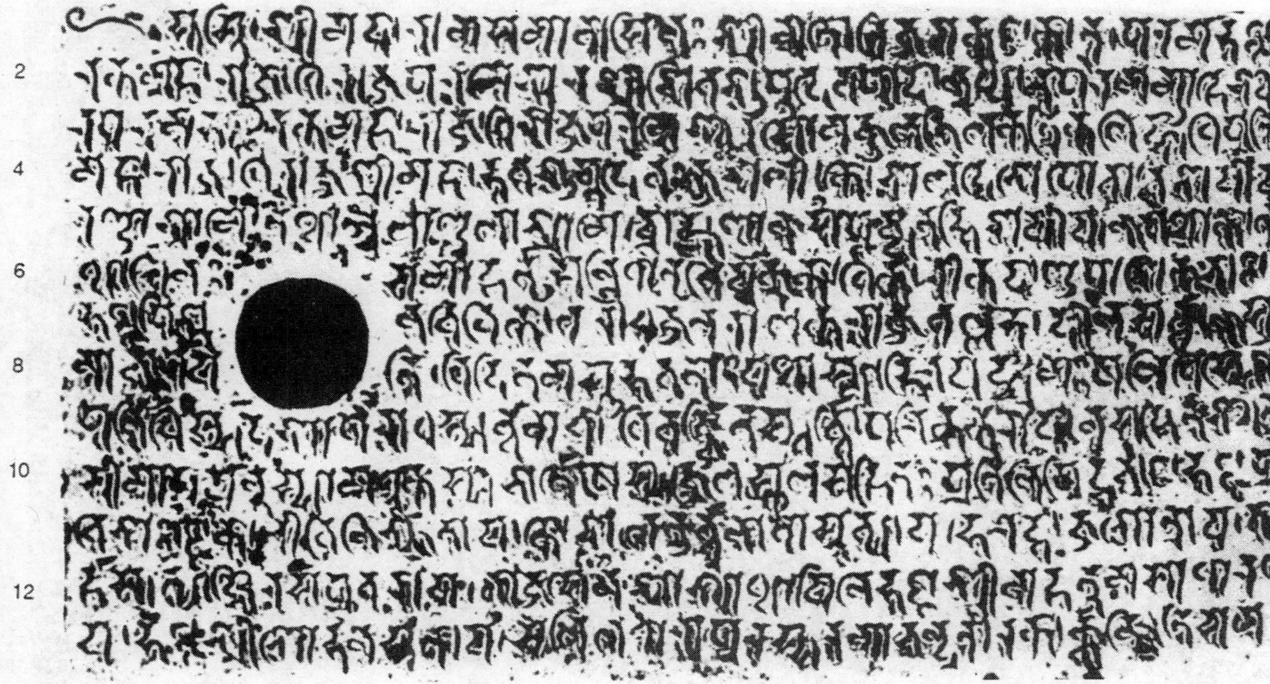

FIRST PLATE

PL.CXX

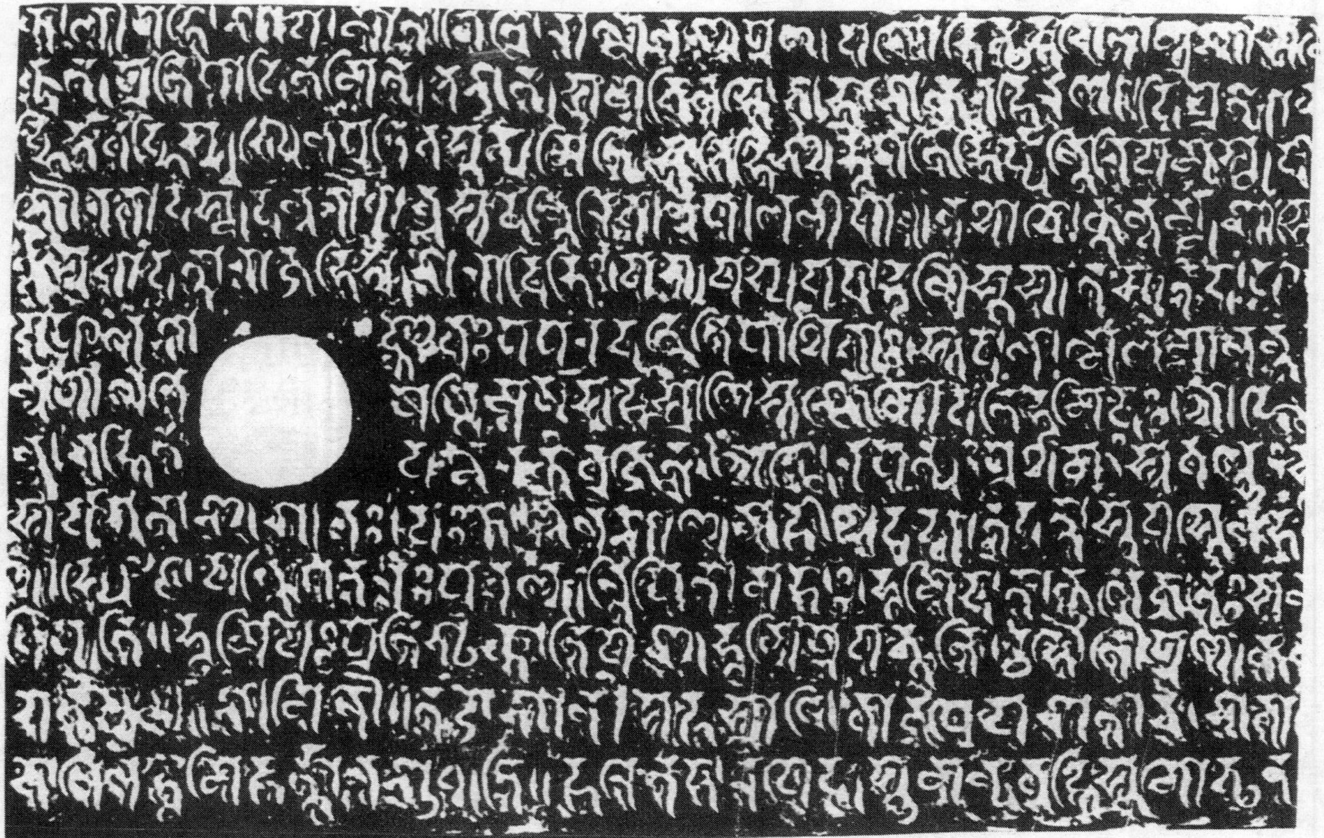

SECOND PLATE : FIRST SIDE

PL.CXXI

SECOND PLATE : SECOND SIDE

PL.CXXII

THIRD PLATE

IV : XI. KALIBHANA PLATES OF MAHĀBHAVAGUPTA
JANAMEJAYA. YR. 34

FIRST PLATE

PL.CXXIV

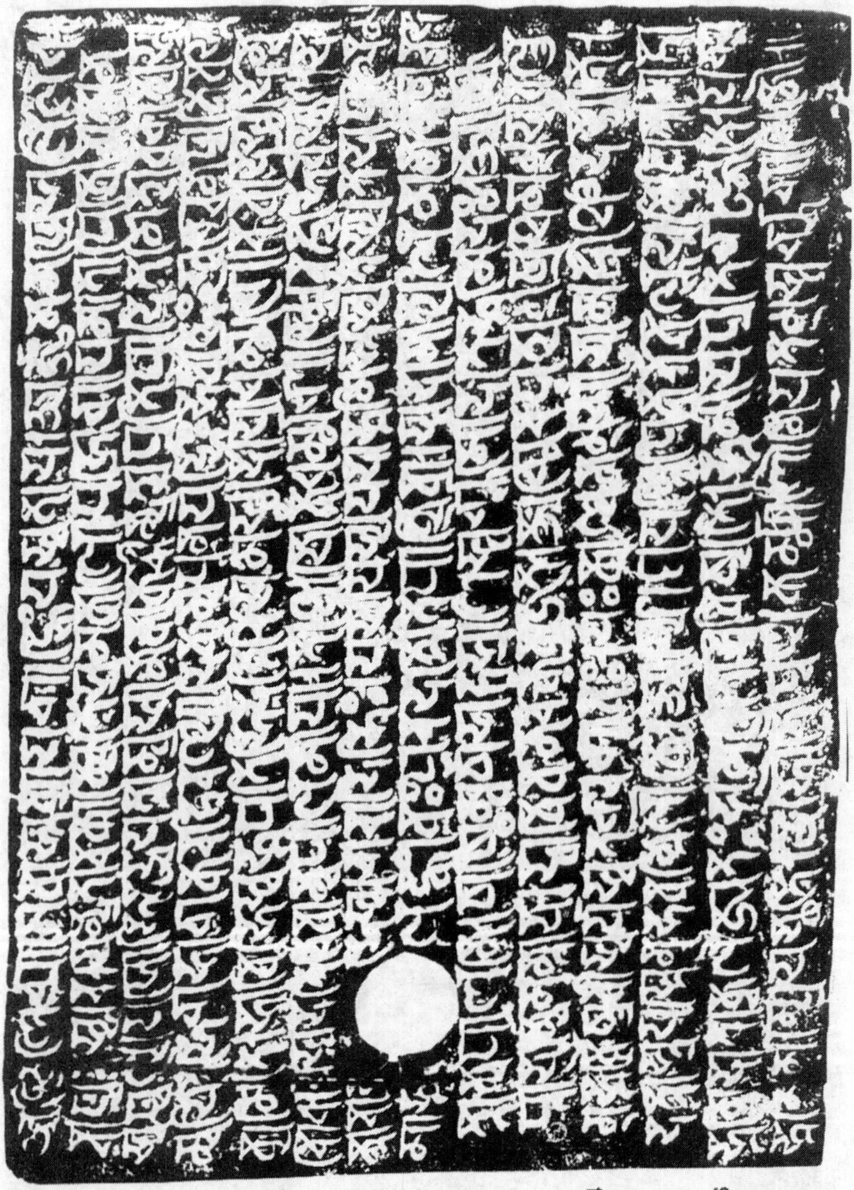

SECOND PLATE : FIRST SIDE

PL.CXXV

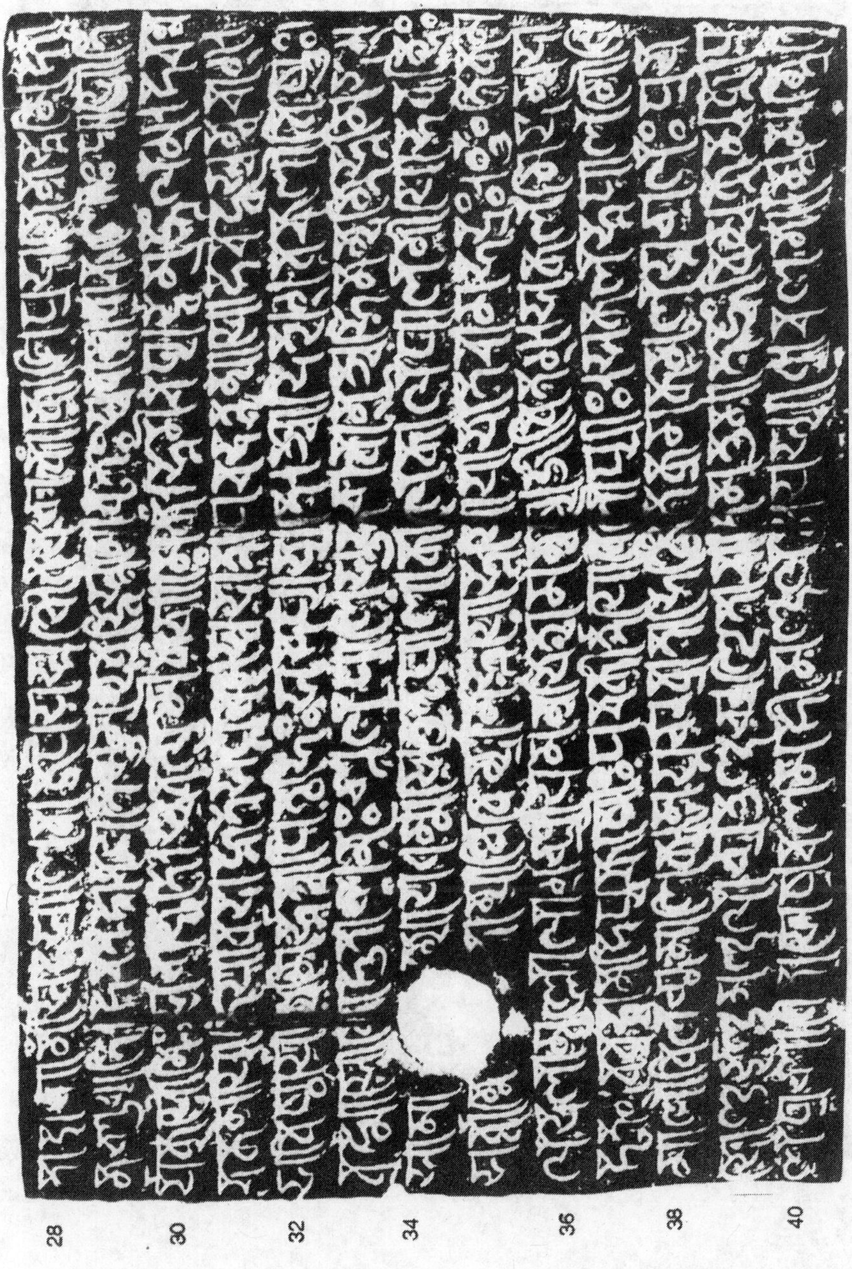

SECOND PLATE : SECOND SIDE

PL.CXXVI

THIRD PLATE

IV : XII. ORISSA STATE MUSEUM PLATES OF MAHĀŚIVAGUPTA I YAYĀTI, YR. 4

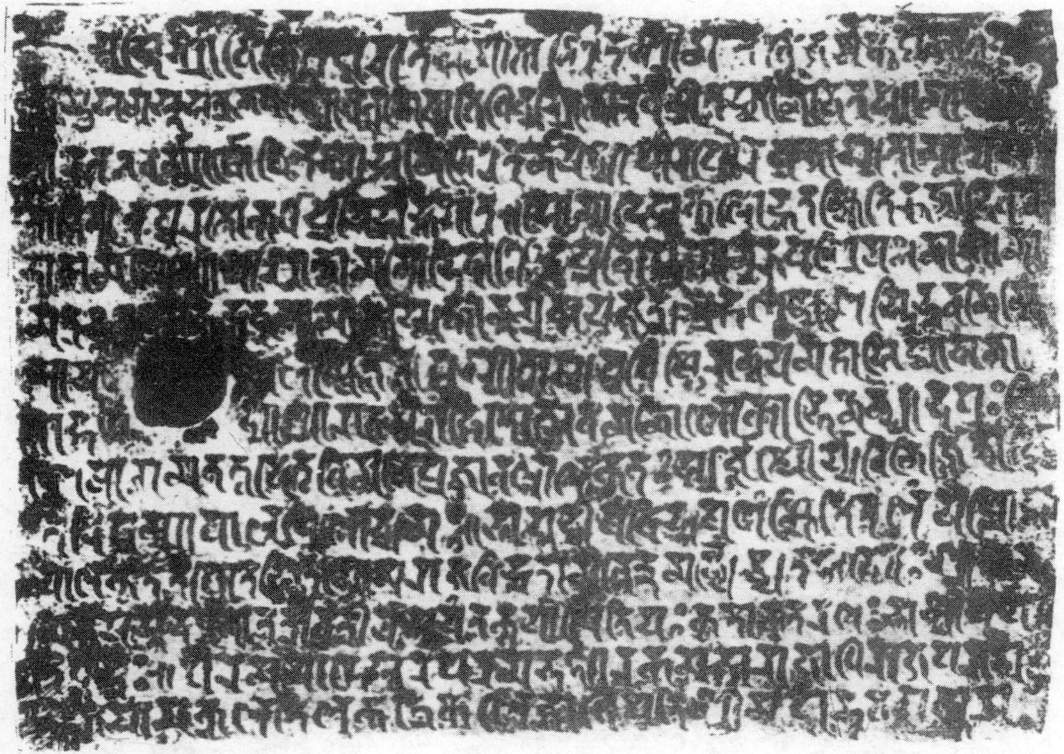

FIRST PLATE

PL.C XXVIII

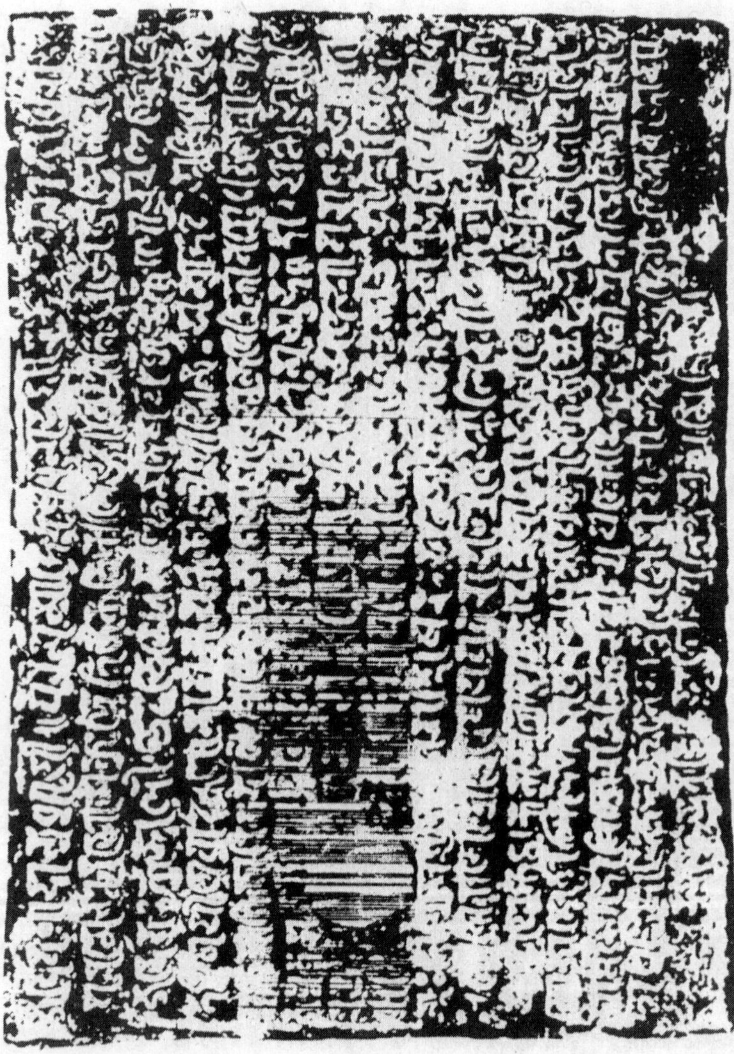

SECOND PLATE : FIRST SIDE

PL.CXXIX

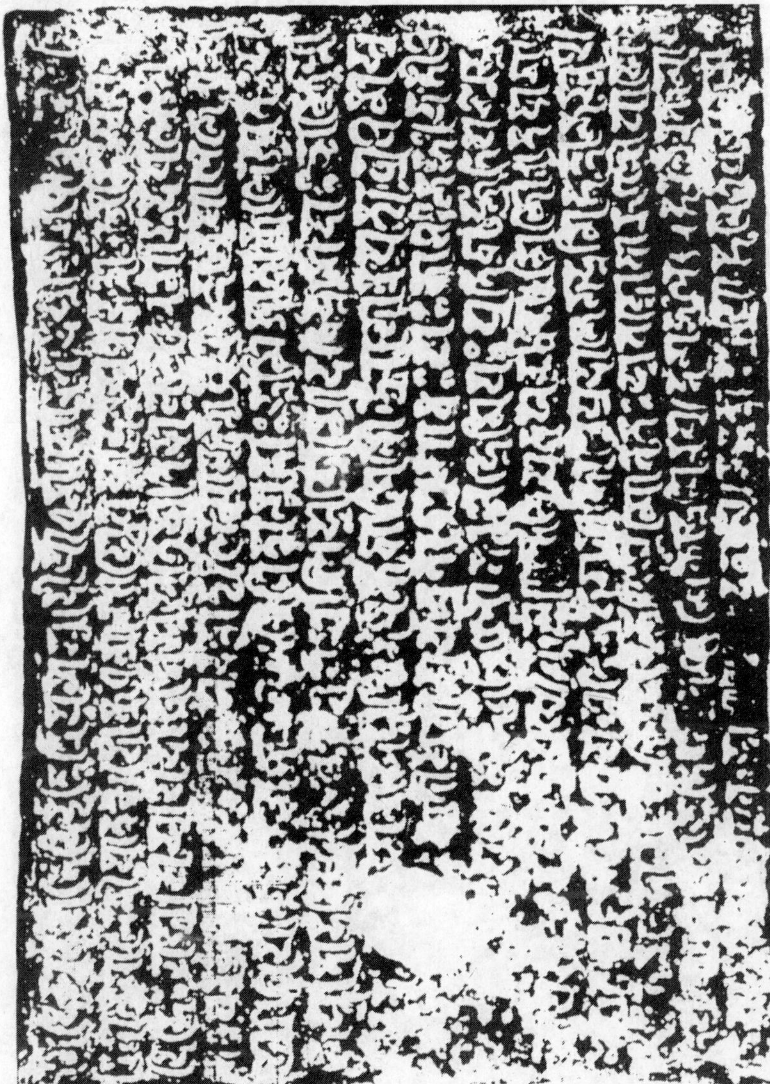

SECOND PLATE : FIRST SIDE

PL.CXXX

THIRD PLATE

IV:XIII. PATNA PLATES OF MAHĀŚIVAGUPTA I YAYĀTI, YR. 8

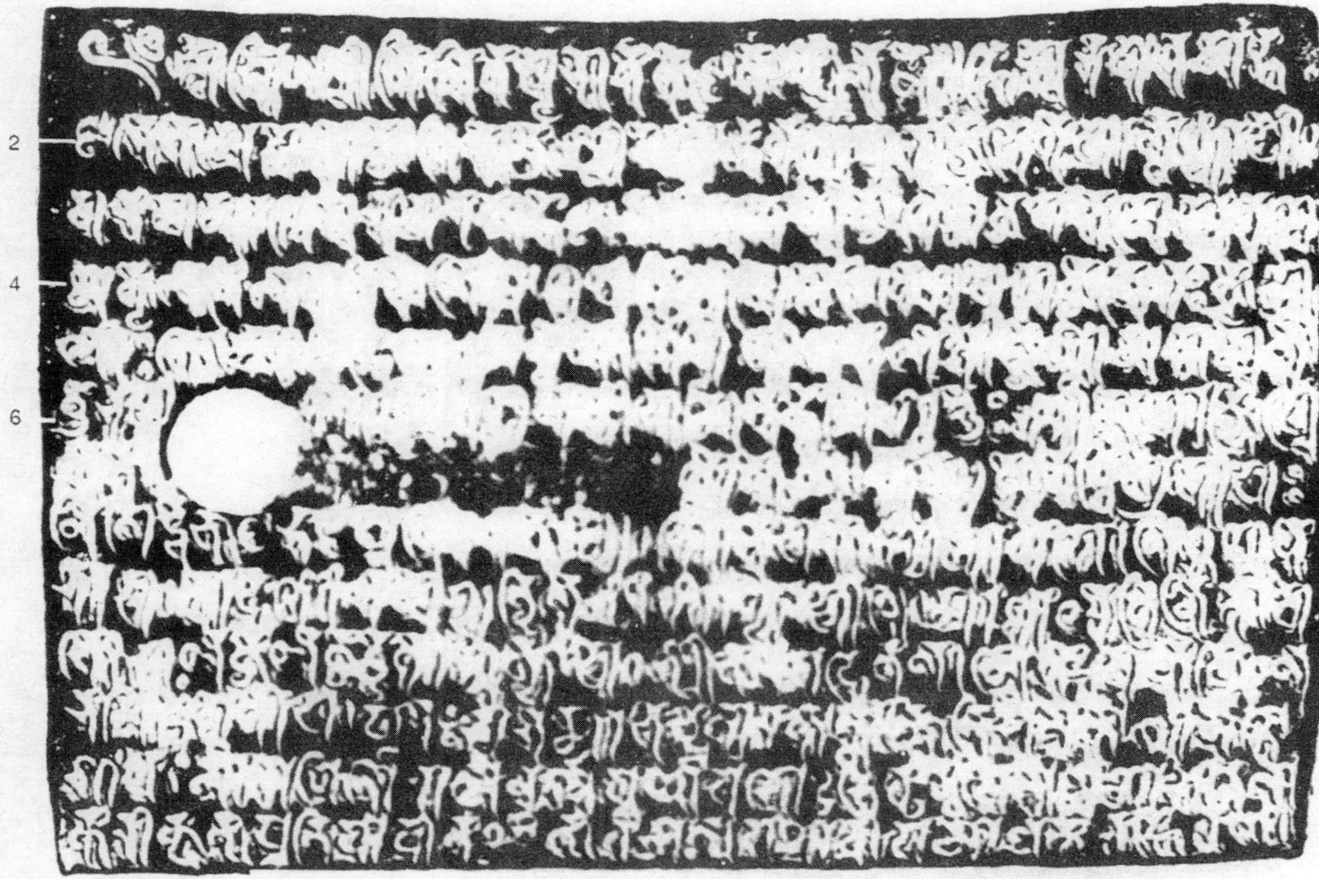

FIRST PLATE

PL.CXXXII

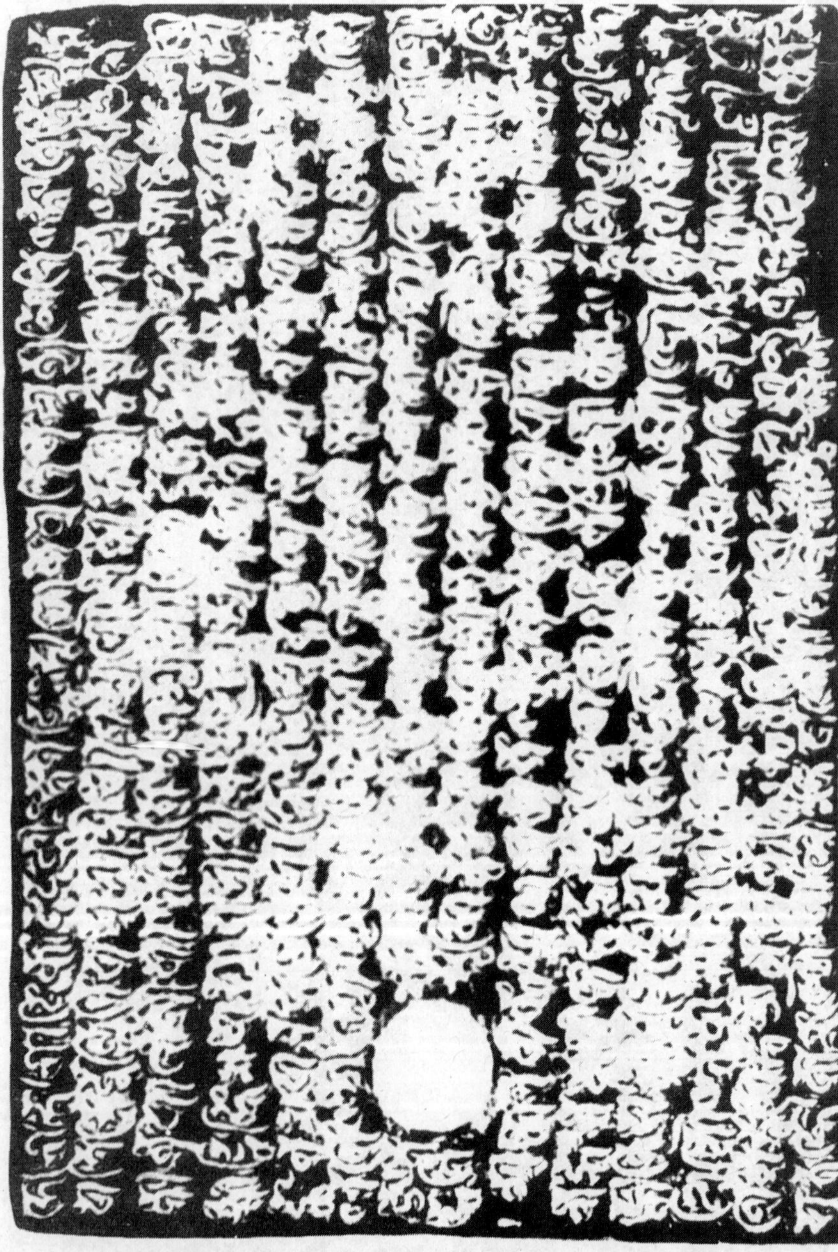

SECOND PLATE : FIRST SIDE

SECOND PLATE : SECOND SIDE

PL.CXXXIV

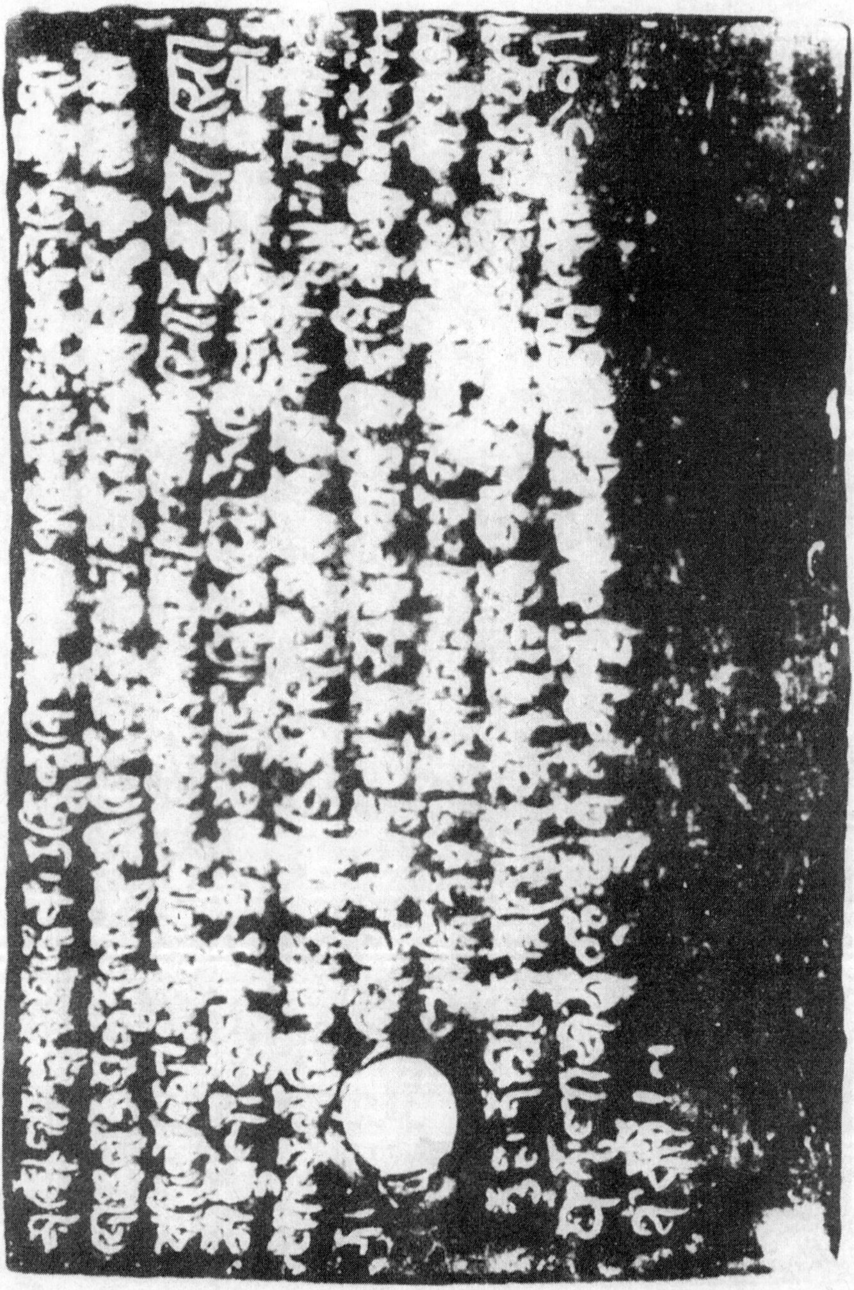

THIRD PLATE

SEAL

IV:XIV. CUTTACK PLATES OF MAHĀŚIVAGUPTA I
YAYĀTI, YR. 9

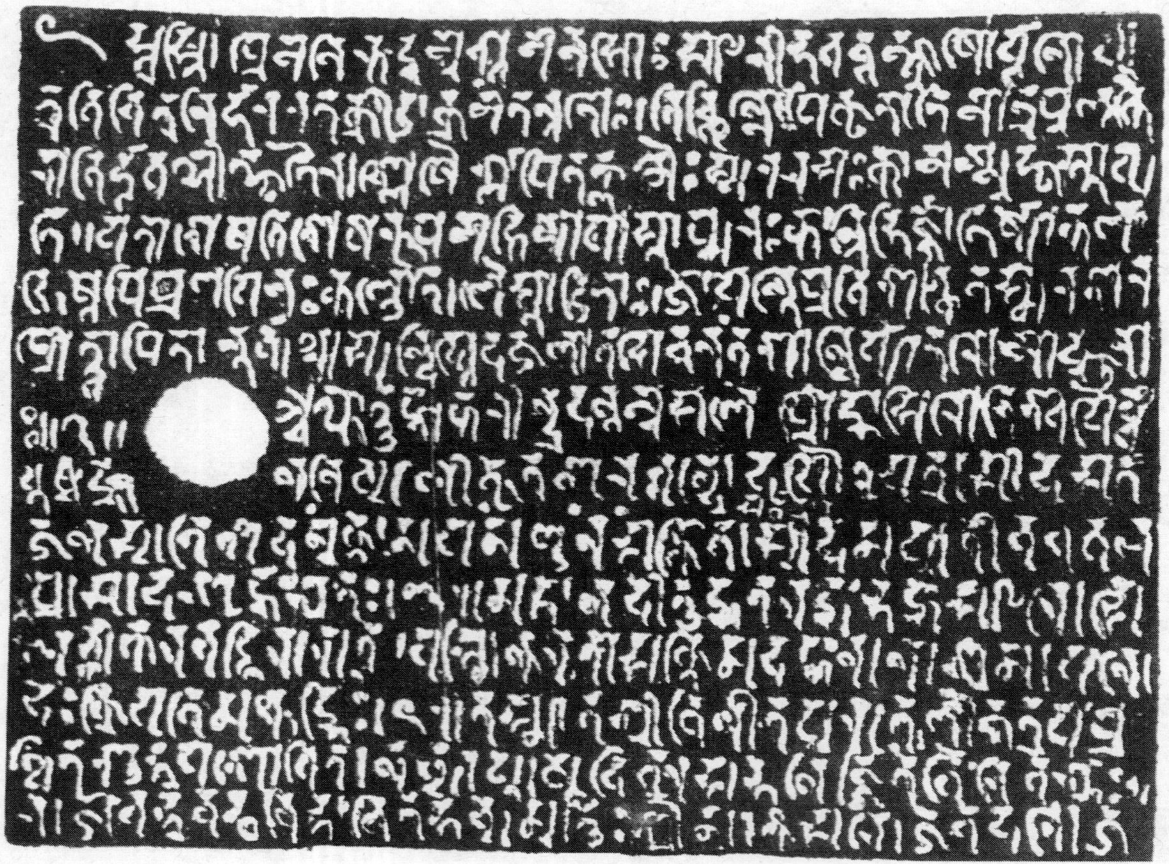

FIRST PLATE

PL.CXXXVII

SECOND PLATE : FIRST SIDE

PL.CXXXVIII

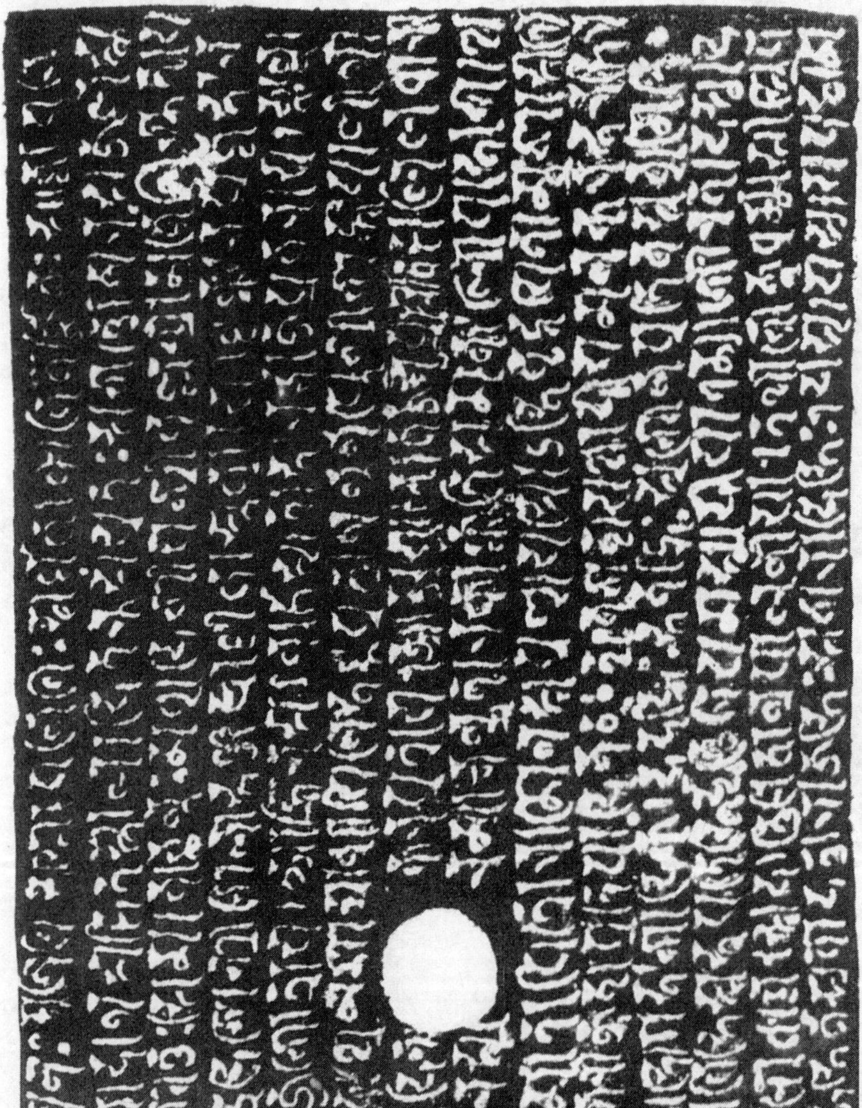

SECOND PLATE : SECOND SIDE

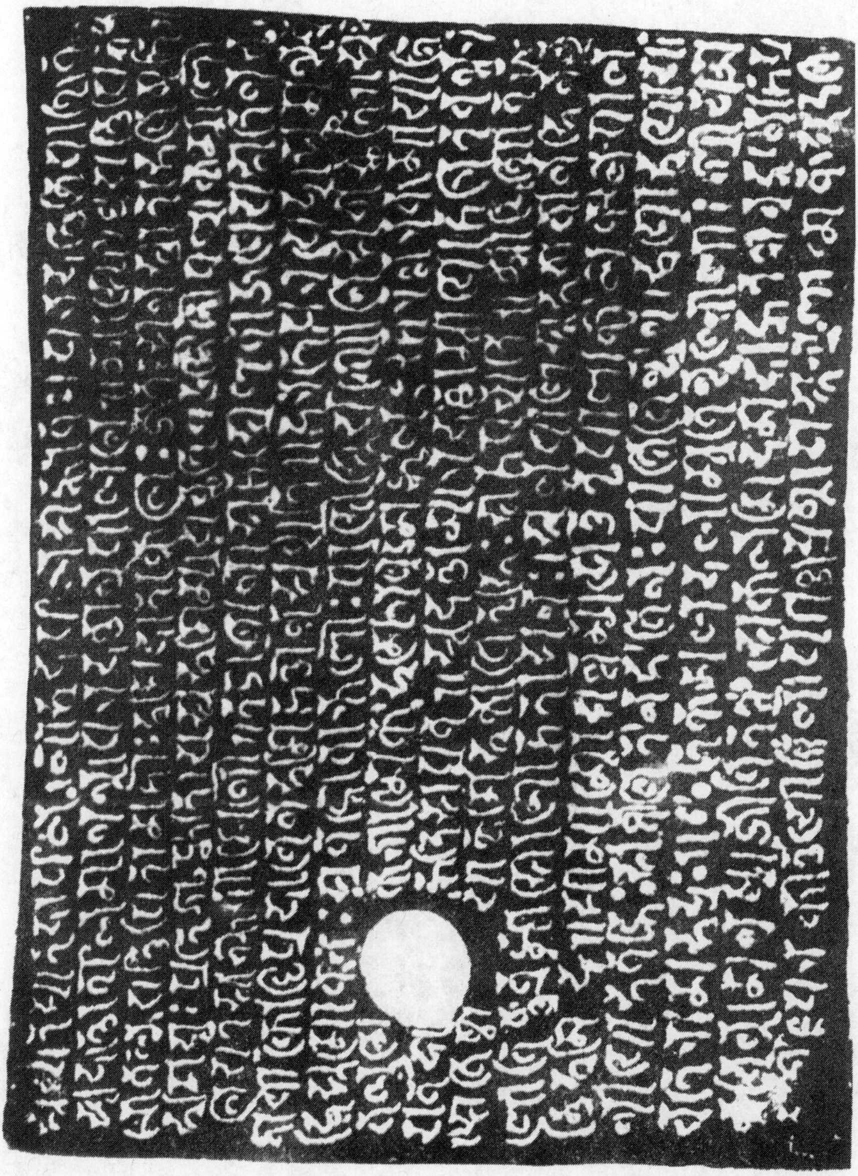

THIRD PLATE : FIRST SIDE

PL.CXL

THIRD PLATE : SECOND SIDE

IV:XV. NIBINNA PLATES OF MAHĀŚIVAGUPTA I
YAYĀTI, YR. 15

FIRST PLATE

PL.CXLII

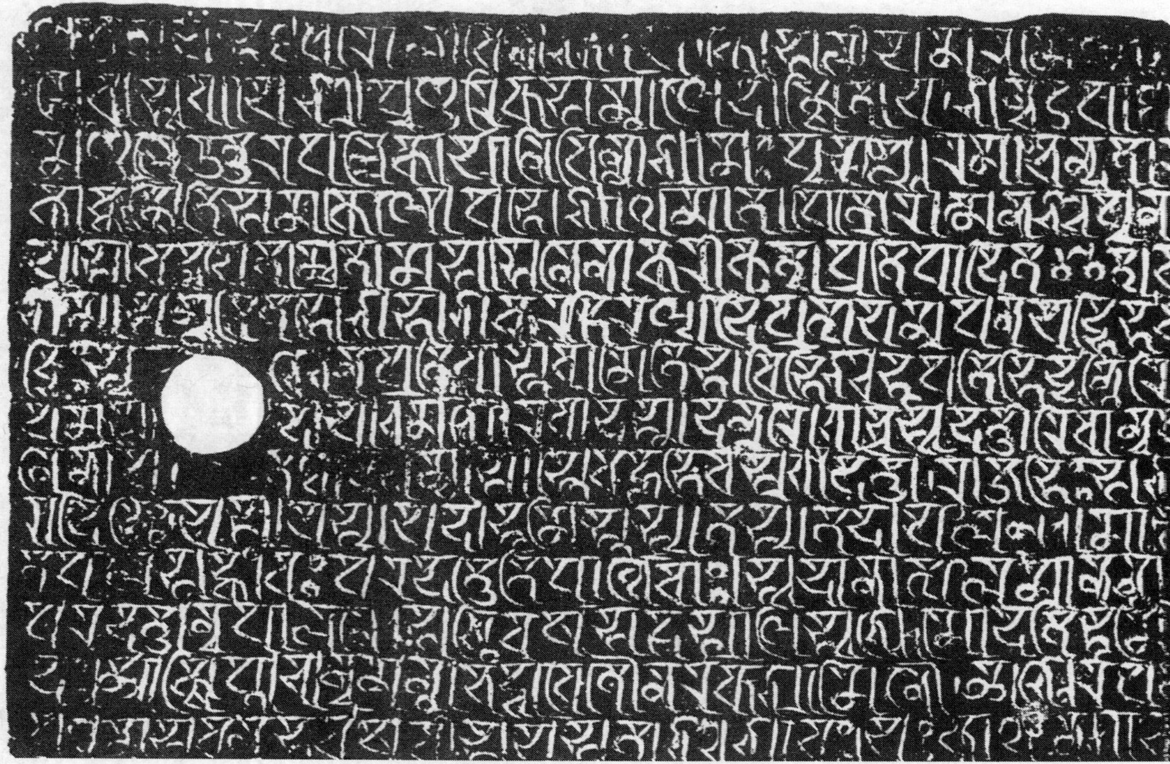

SECOND PLATE : FIRST SIDE

SECOND PLATE : SECOND SIDE

PL.CXLIV

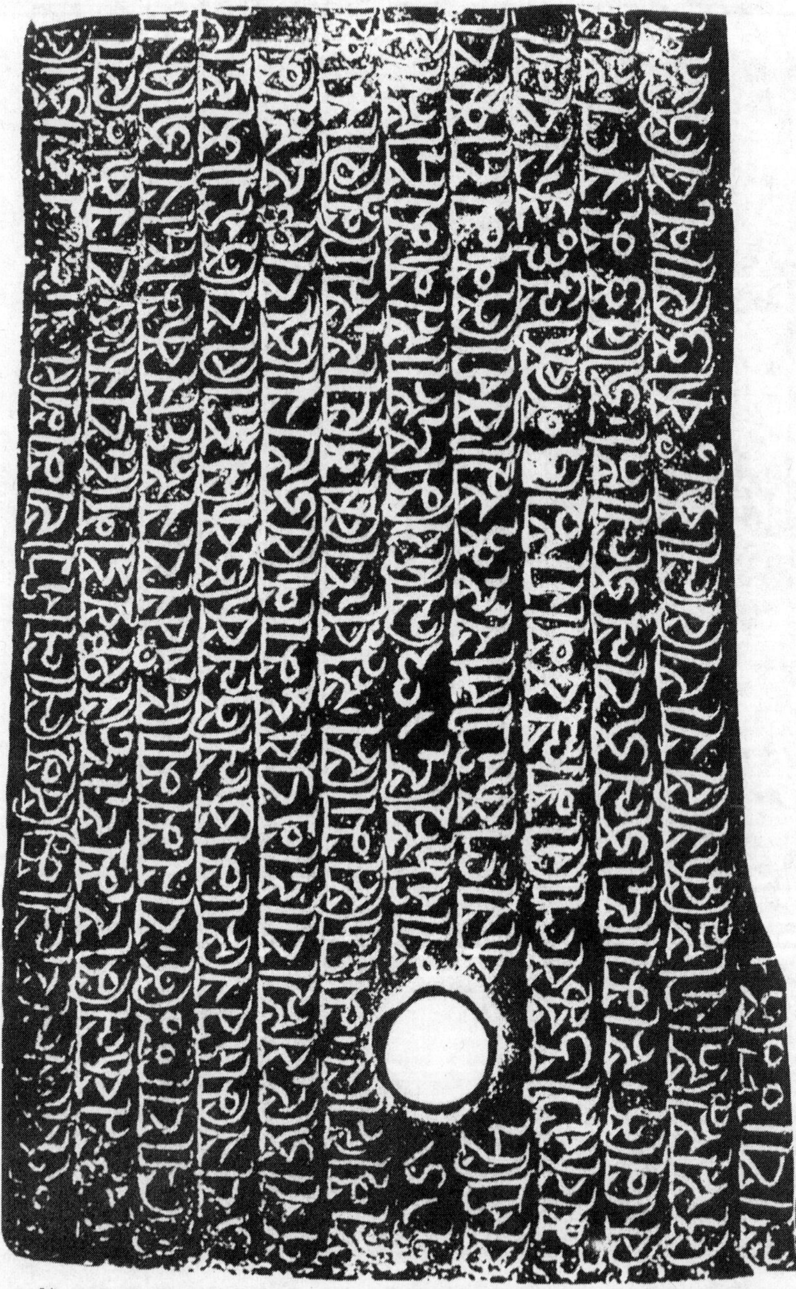

THIRD PLATE

IV:XVI. PĀṬNĀ PLATES OF MAHĀŚIVAGUPTA I YAYĀTI, YR. 24

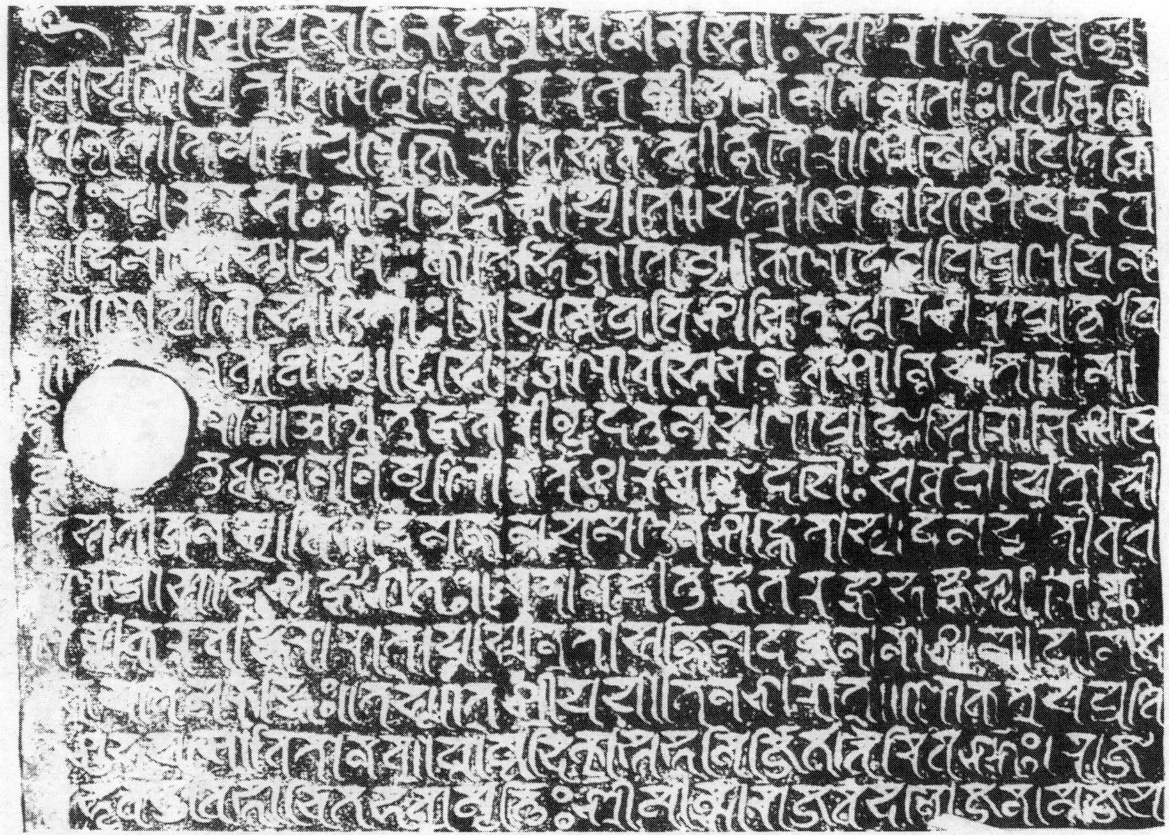

FIRST PLATE

PL.CXLVI

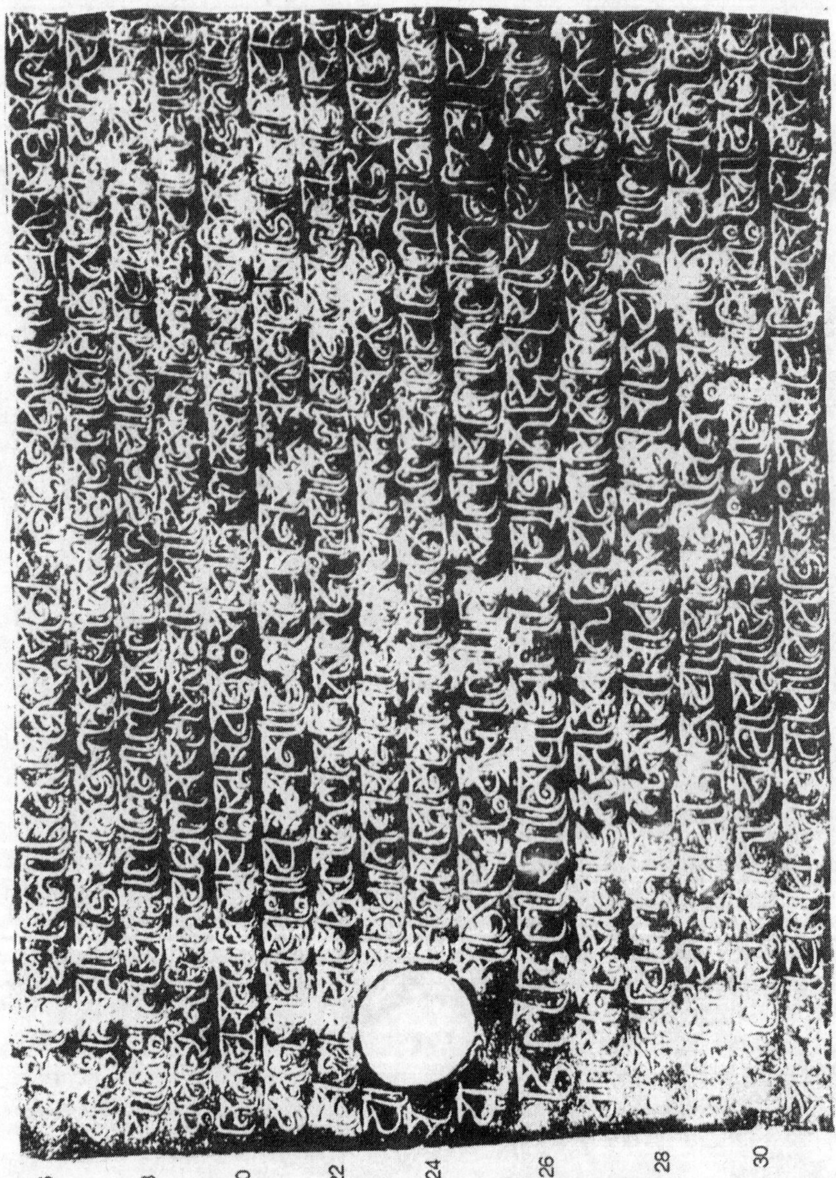

SECOND PLATE : FIRST SIDE

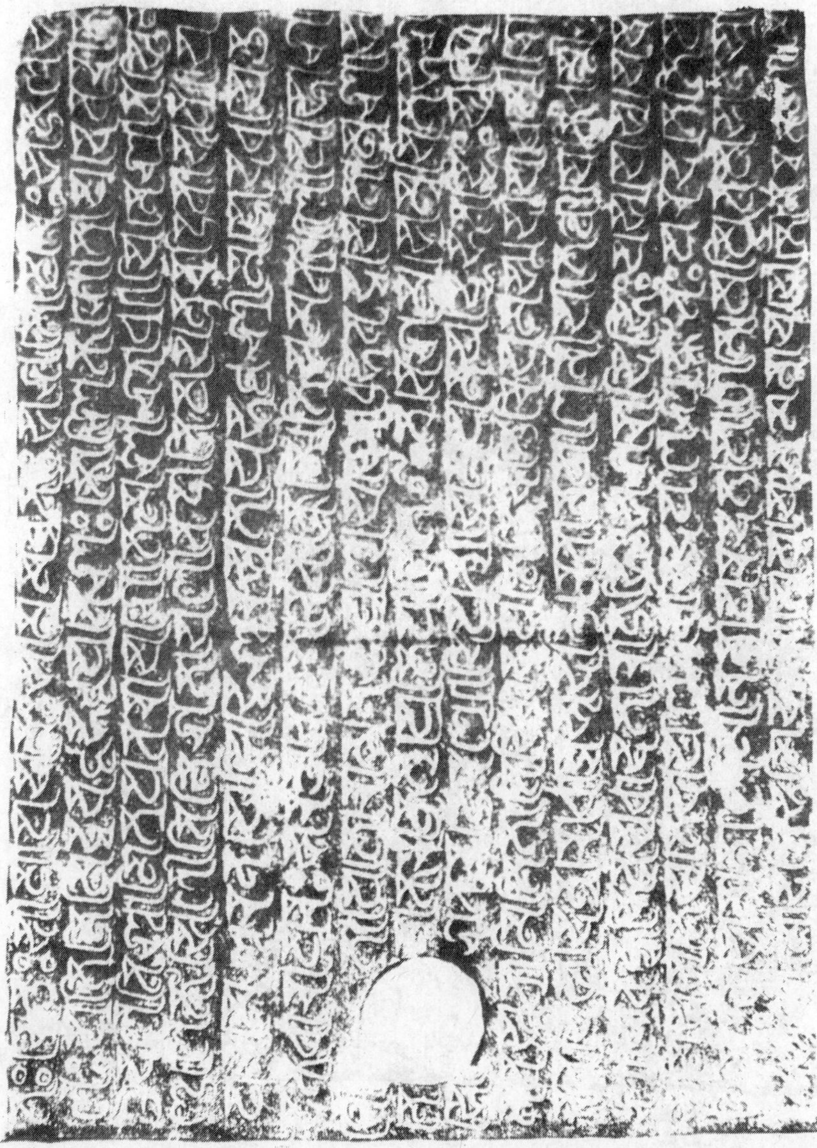

SECOND PLATE : SECOND SIDE

PL.CXLVIII

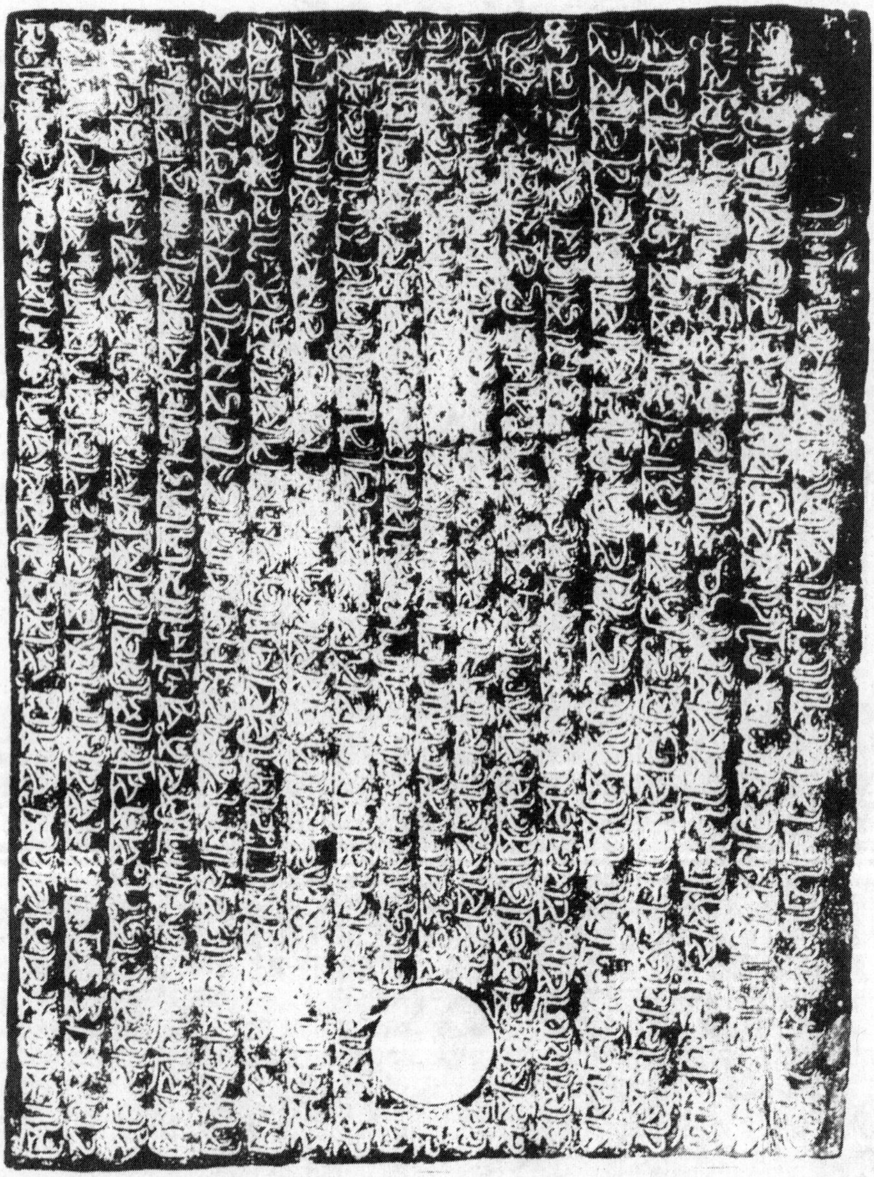

48 50 52 54 56 58 60 62 64

THIRD PLATE

IV:XVII. PATNA PLATES OF MAHĀŚIVAGUPTA I
YAYĀTI, YR. 28

FIRST PLATE

PL.CL

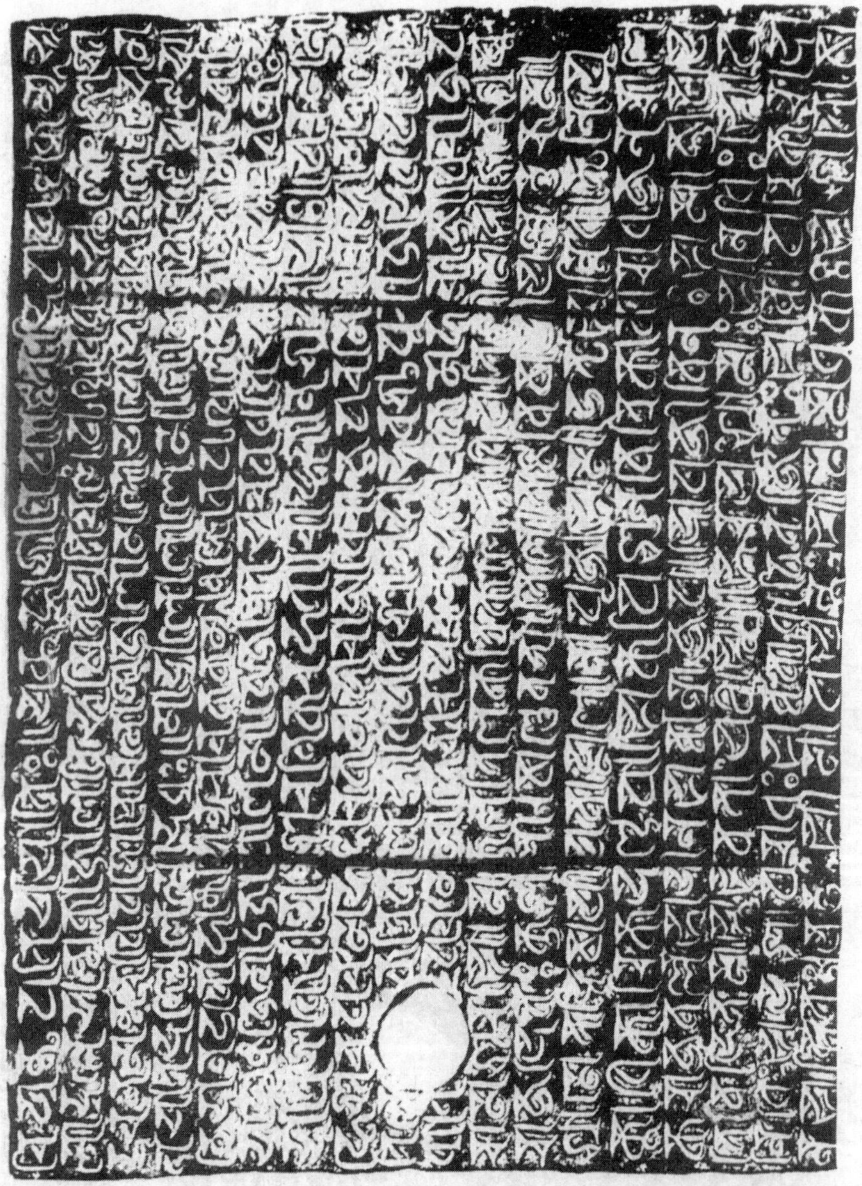

SECOND PLATE : FIRST SIDE

PL.CLI

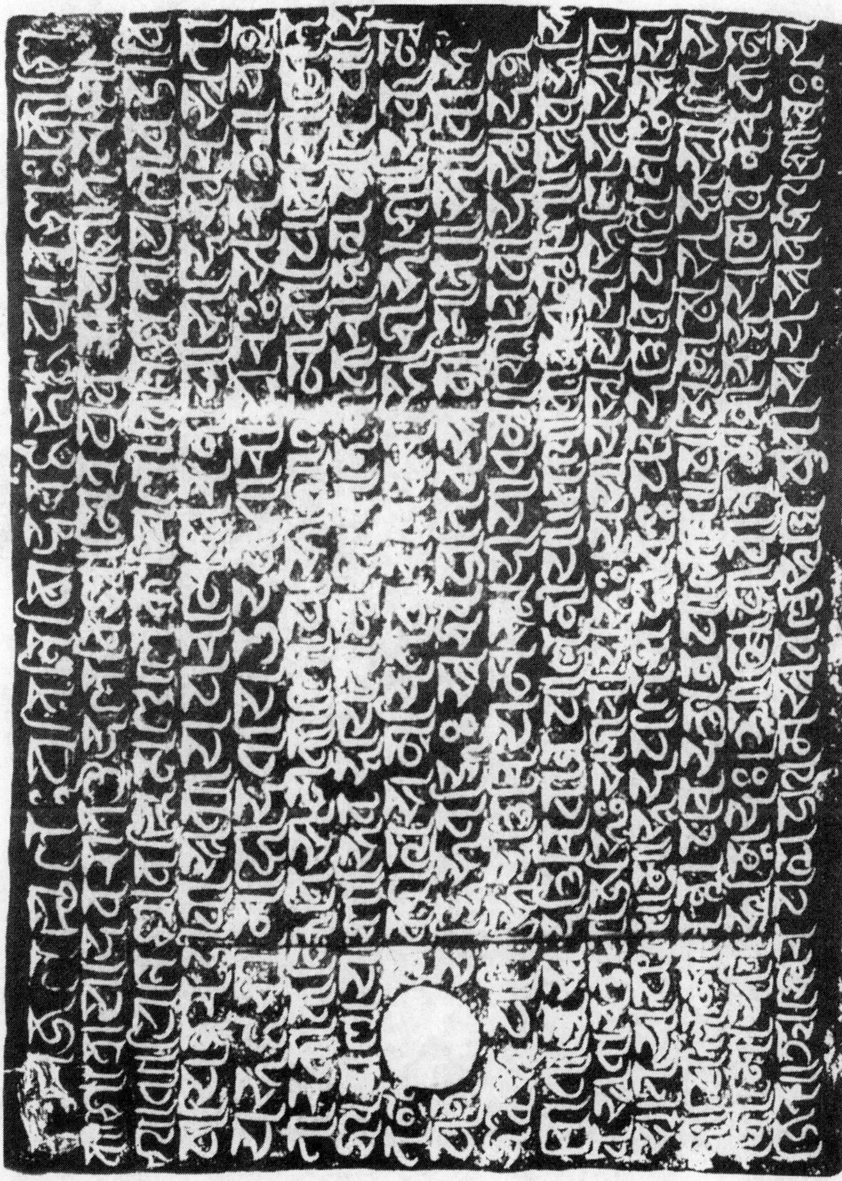

SECOND PLATE : SECOND SIDE

PL.CLII

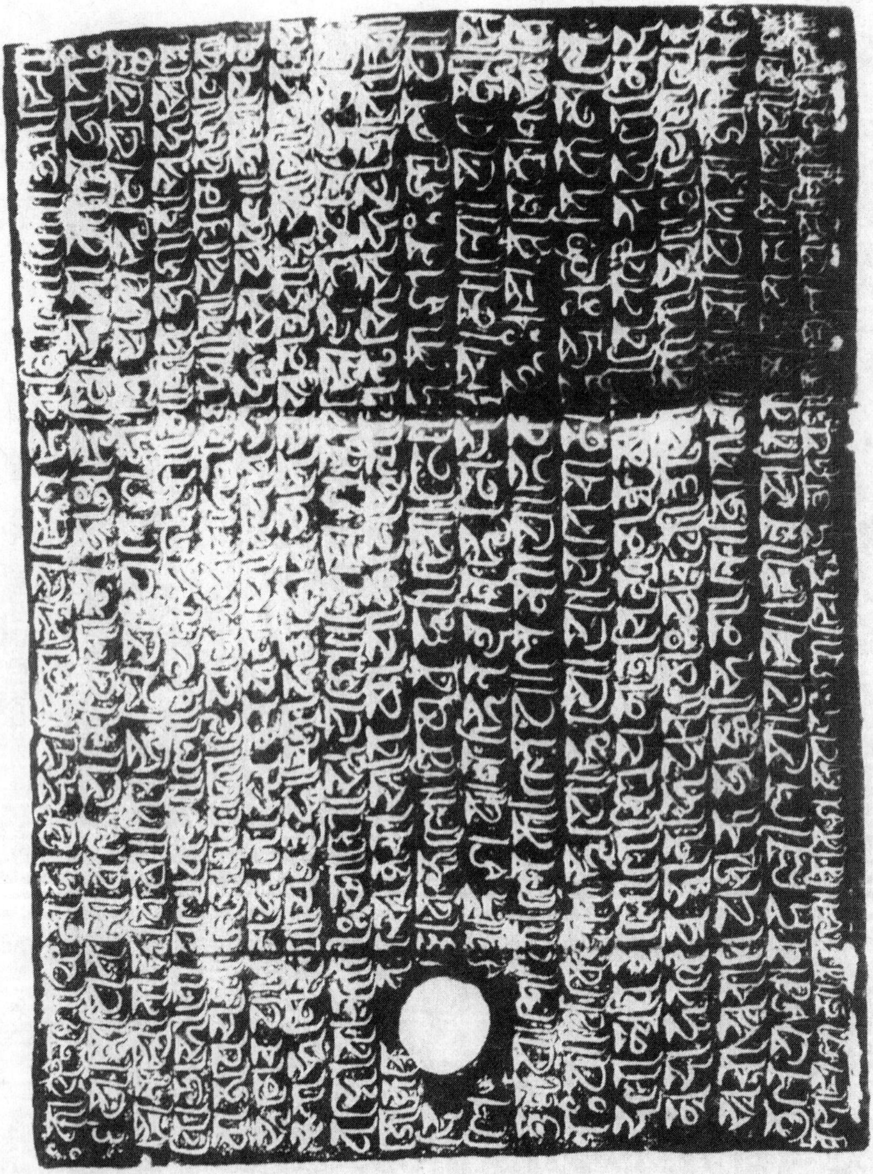

THIRD PLATE : FIRST SIDE

THIRD PLATE : SECOND SIDE

IV : XVIII. CUTTACK PLATES OF MAHĀBHAVAGUPTA II
BHĪMARATHA, YR. 3

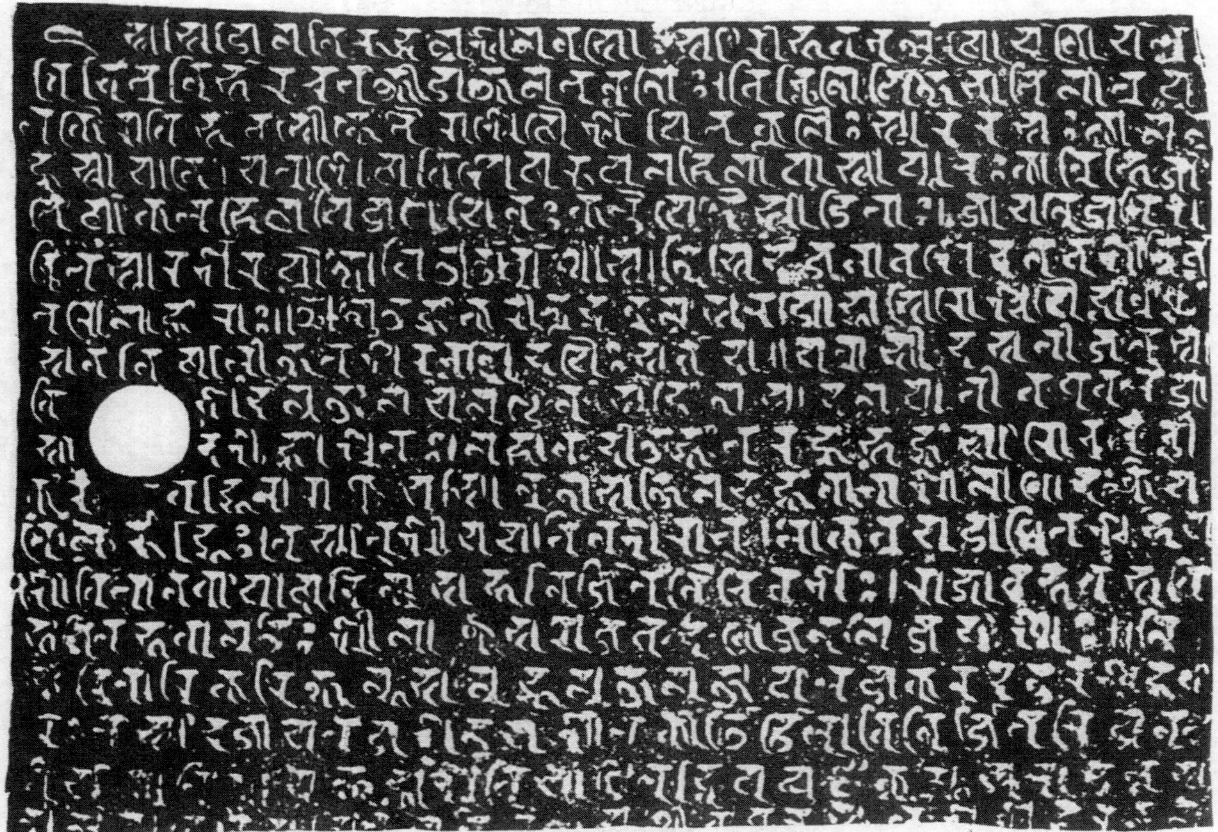

FIRST PLATE

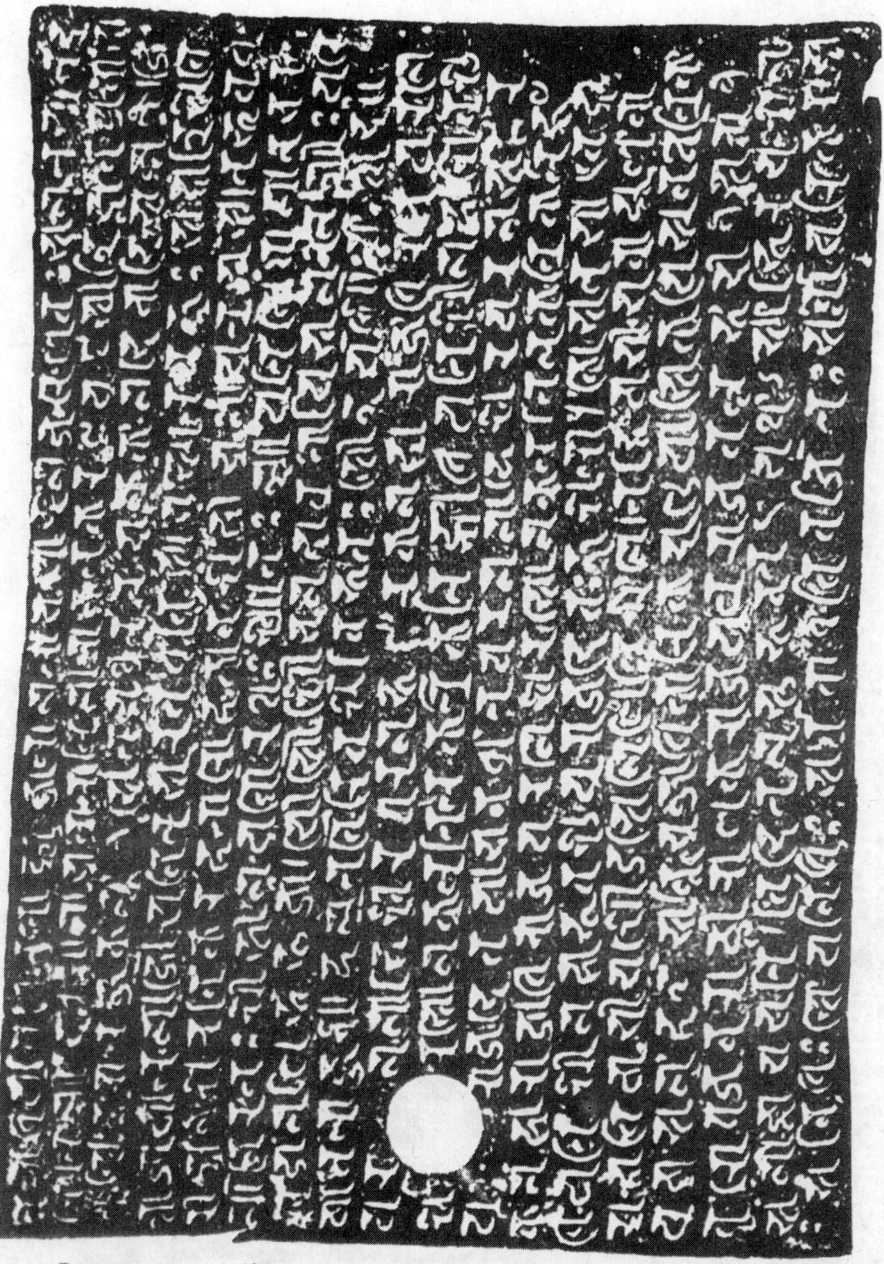

SECOND PLATE : FIRST SIDE

PL.CLVI

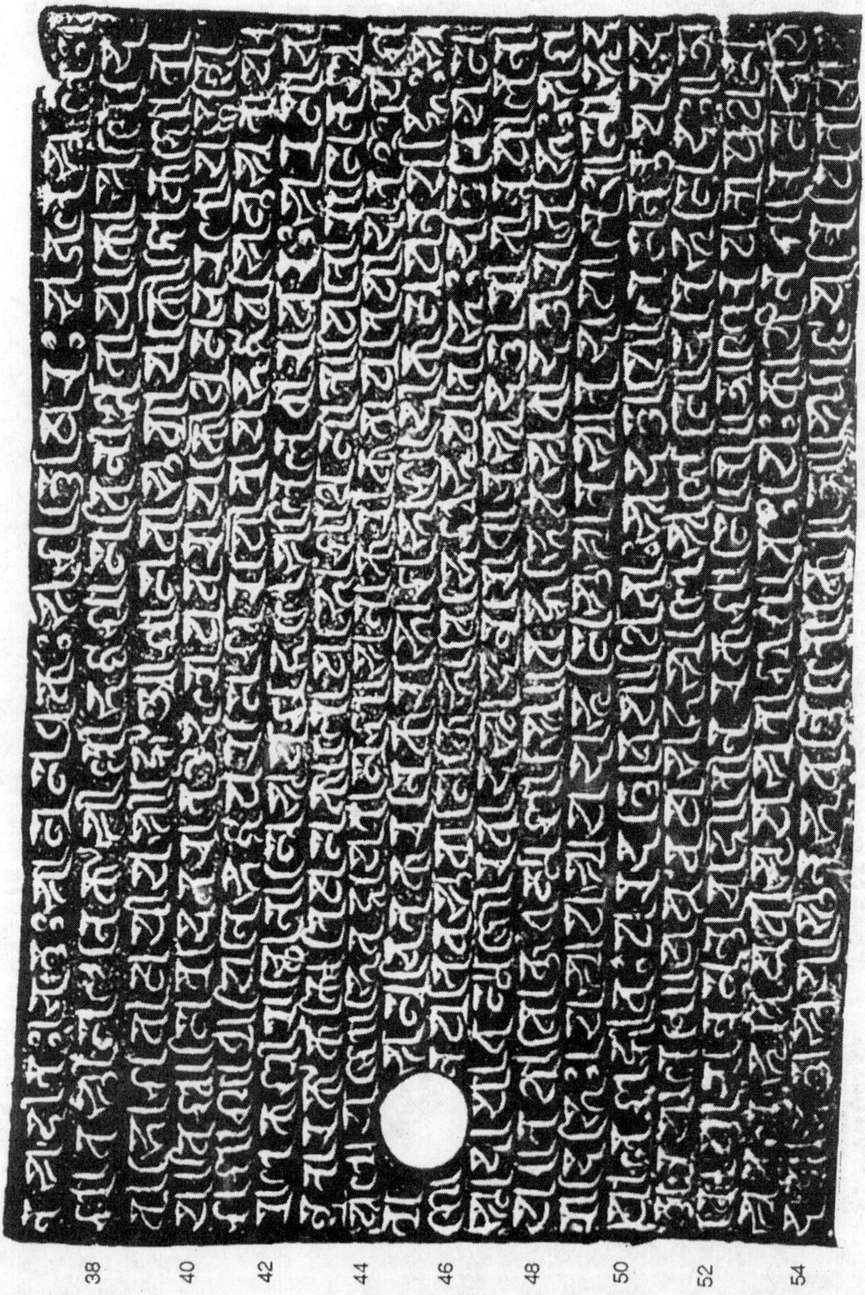

SECOND PLATE : SECOND SIDE

PL.CLVII

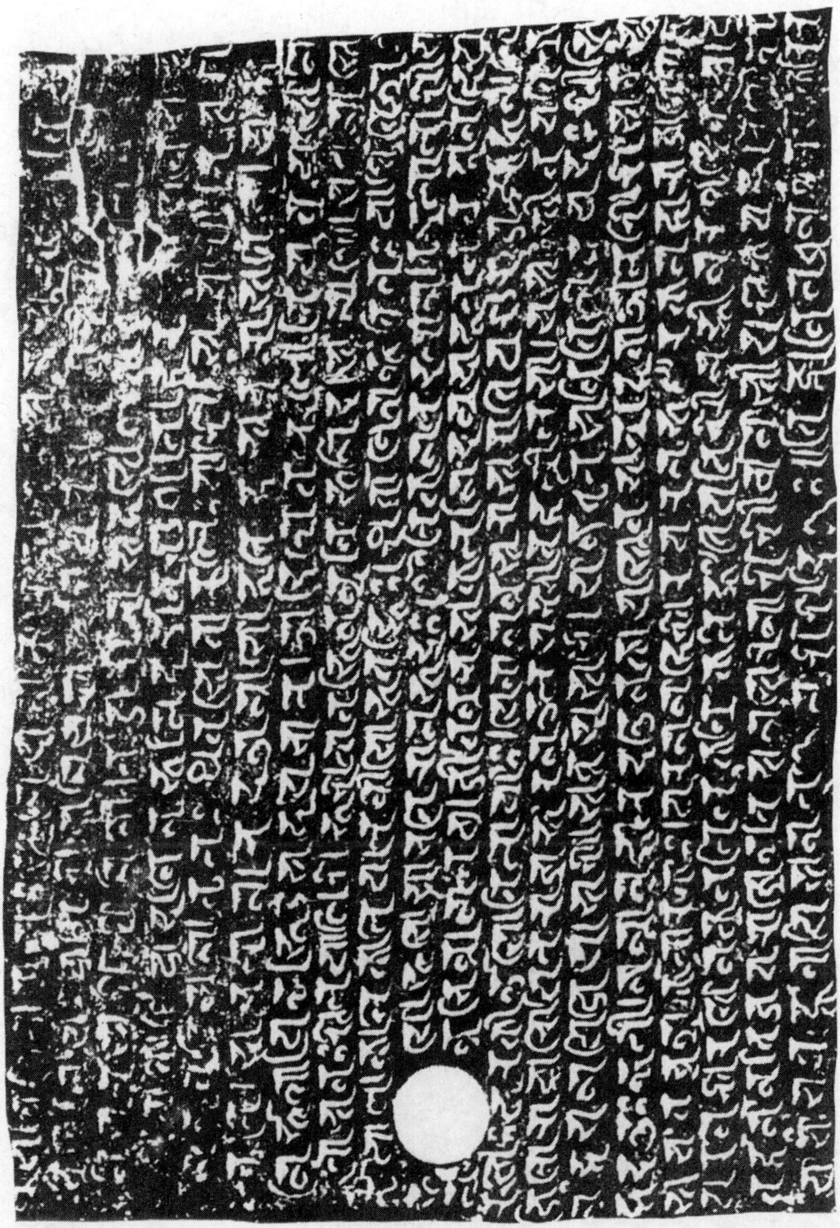

THIRD PLATE

IV : XIX. KUDOPALI PLATES OF MAHĀBHAVAGUPTA II
BHĪMARATHA, YR. 13

FIRST PLATE : FIRST SIDE

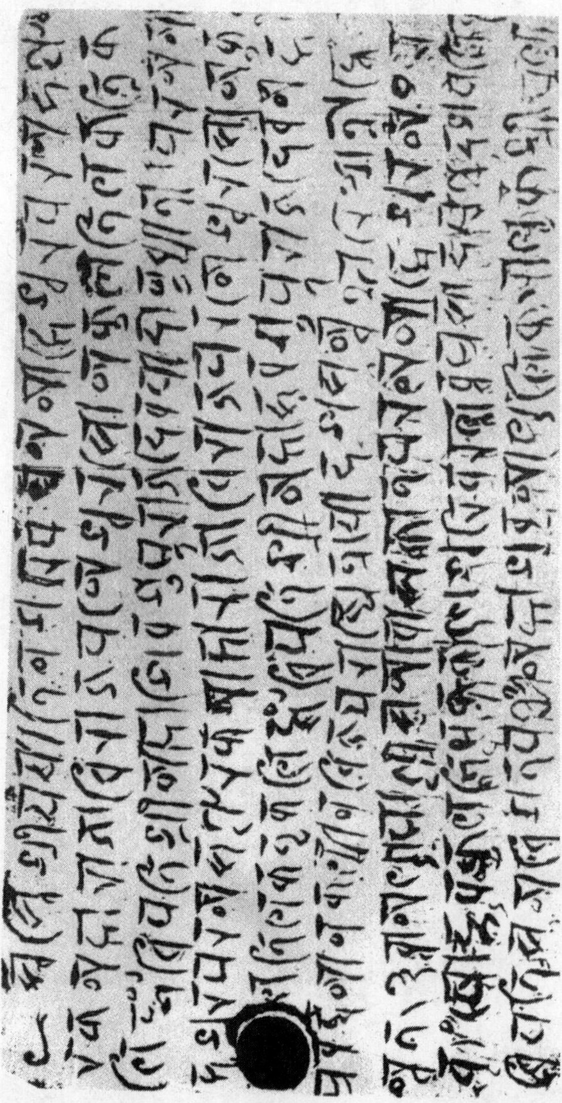

FIRST PLATE : SECOND SIDE

PL.CLX

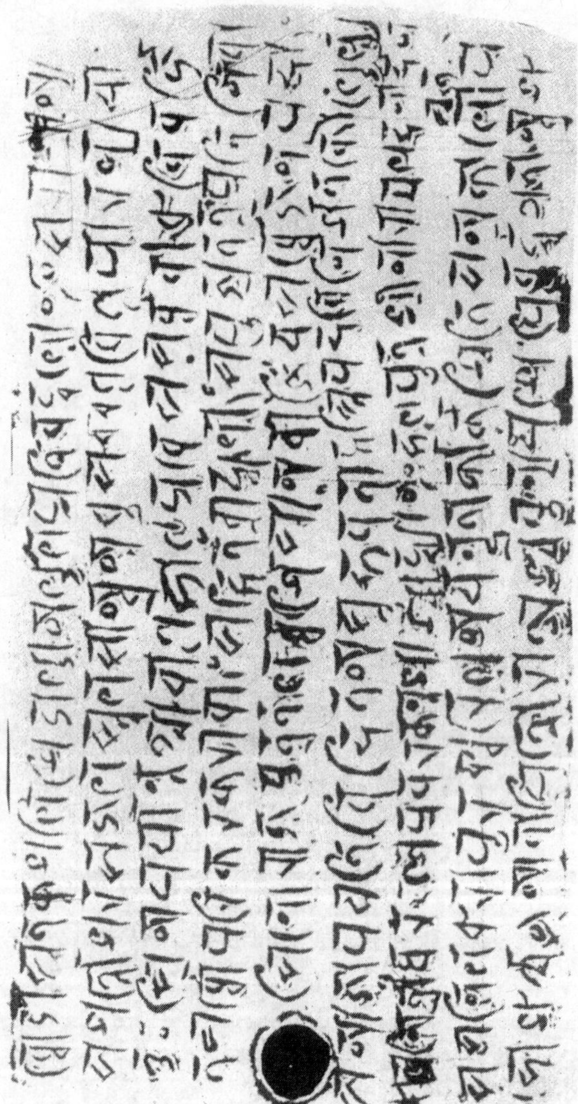

SECOND PLATE : FIRST SIDE

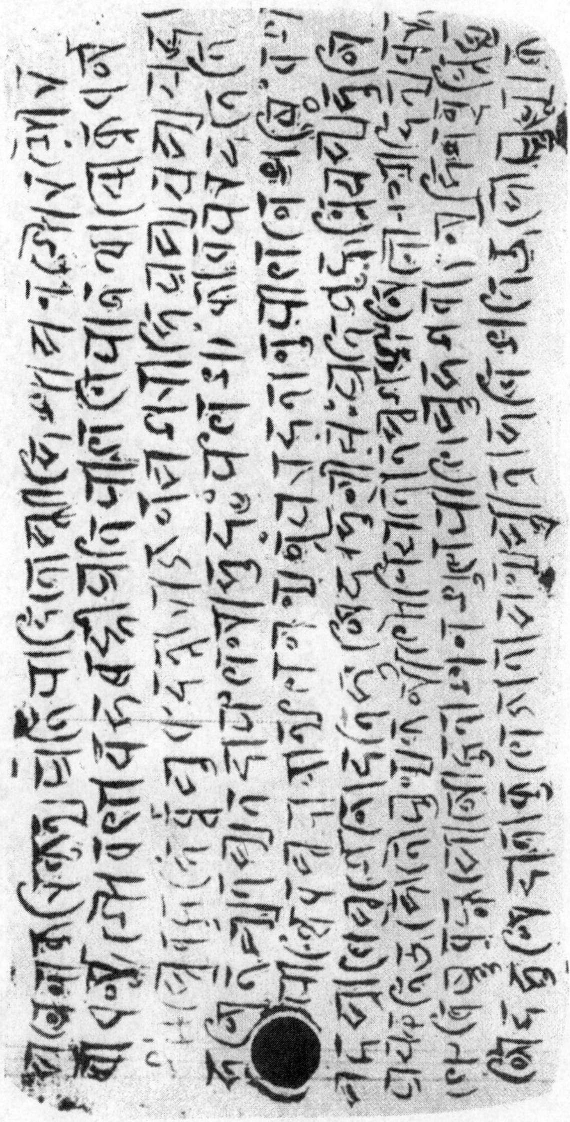

SECOND PLATE : SECOND SIDE

PL.CLXII

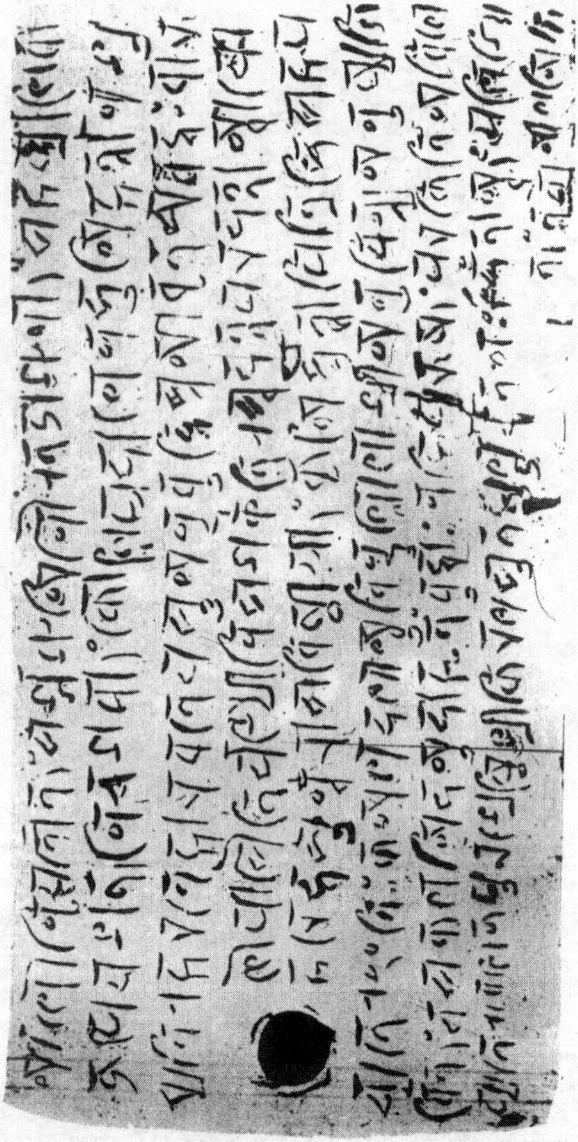

THIRD PLATE

IV : XX. MAHULPARA PLATES OF MAHĀŚIVAGUPTA II
DHARMARATHA, YR. 11

FIRST PLATE

PL. CLXIII

PL.CLXIV

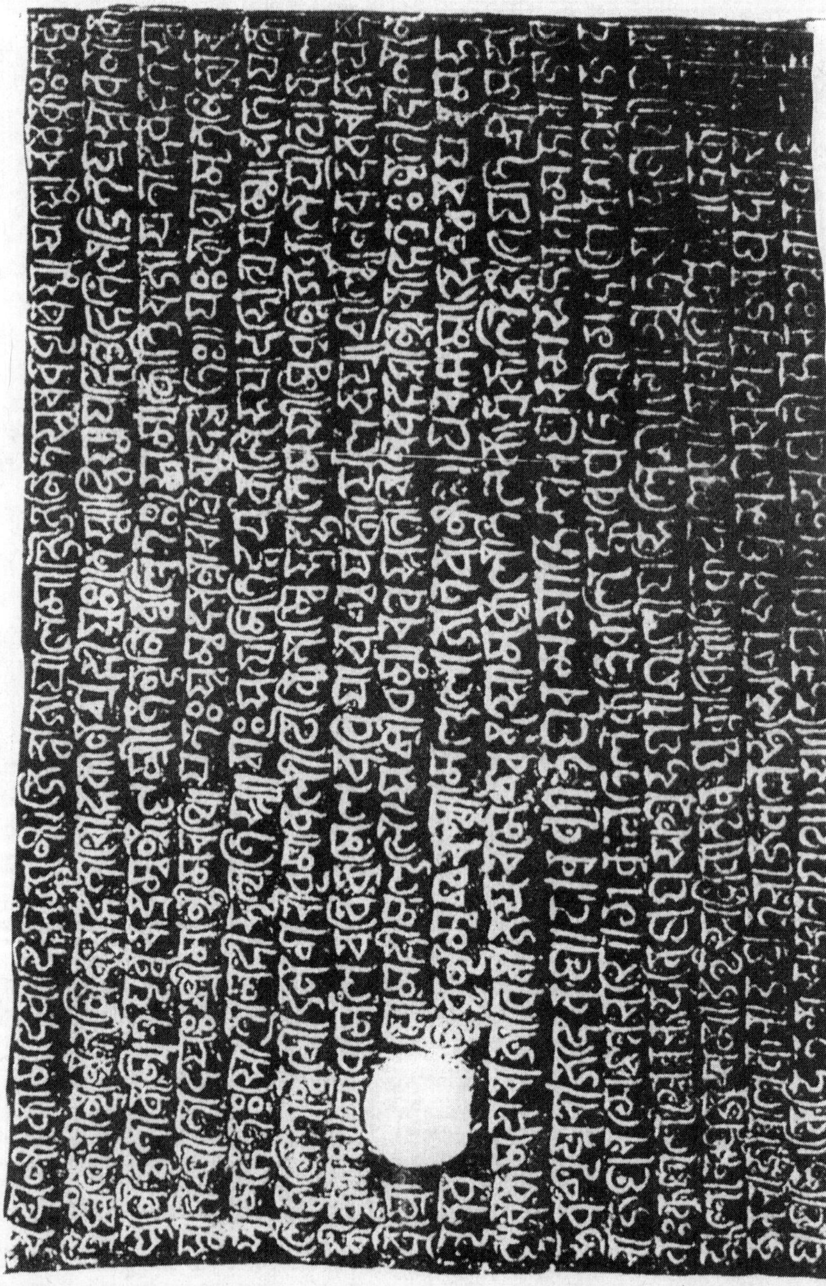

SECOND PLATE : FIRST SIDE

PL.CLXV

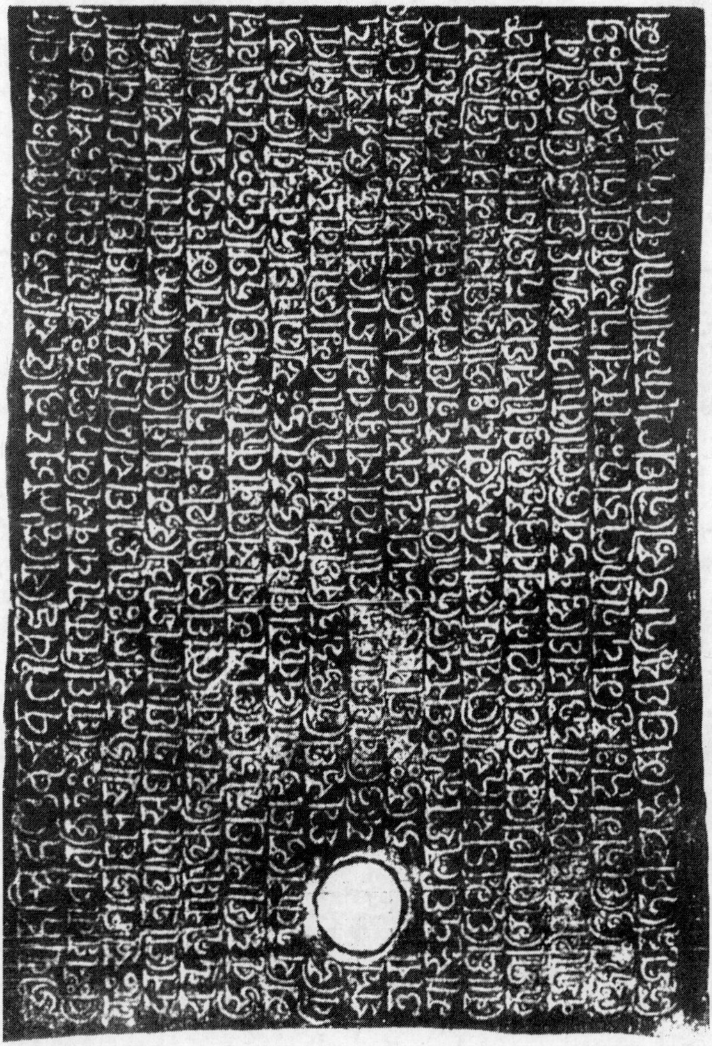

SECOND PLATE : SECOND SIDE

PL.CLXVI

THIRD PLATE

IV:XXI. JATESINGA-DUNGRI PLATES OF MAHĀŚIVAGUPTA III YAYĀTI YR. 3

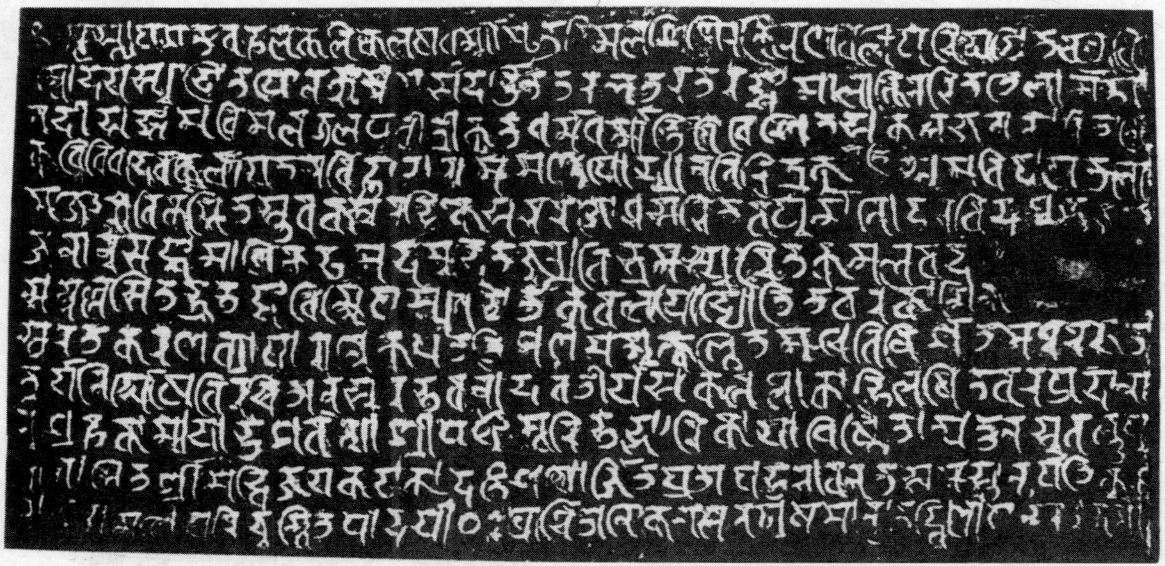

FIRST PLATE

PL.CLXVIII

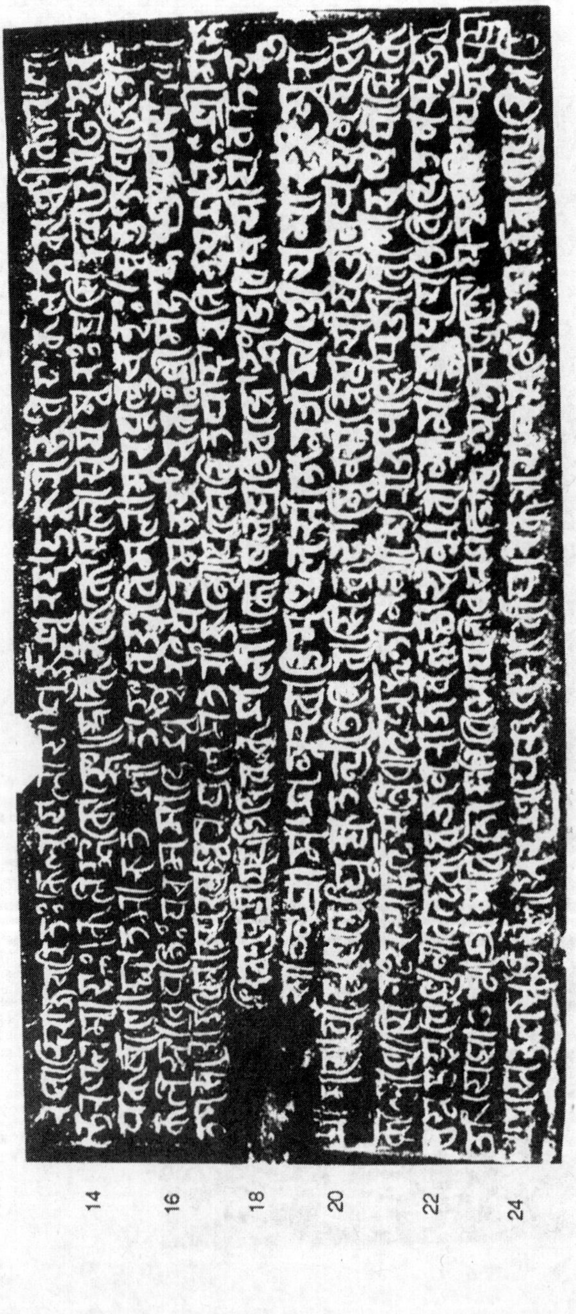

SECOND PLATE : FIRST SIDE

PL.CLXIX

SECOND PLATE : SECOND SIDE

PL.CLXX

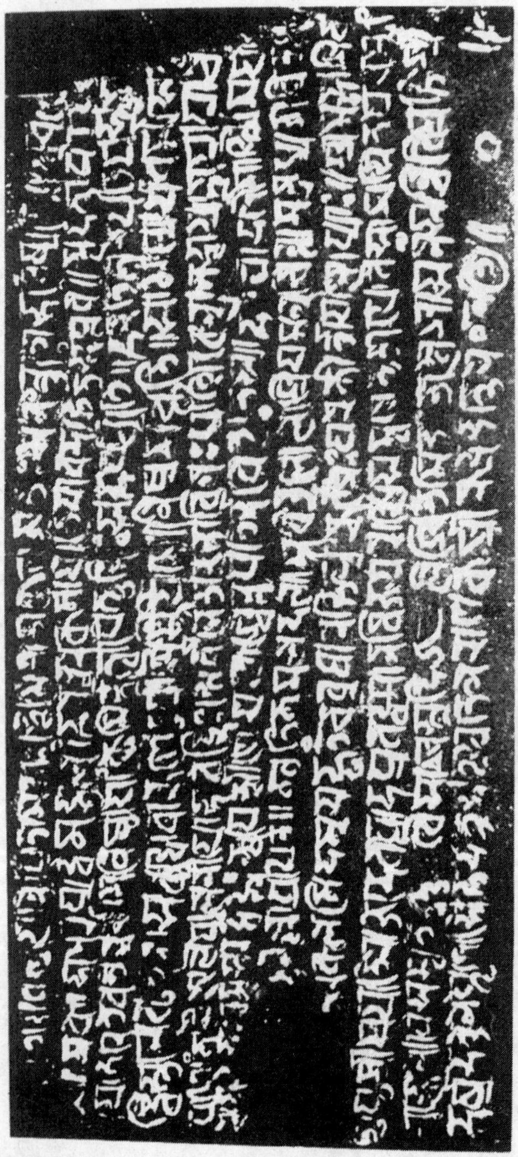

THIRD PLATE

IV : XXIII. LALĀṬENDUKESARI'S CAVE INSCRIPTION OF MAHĀBHAVAGUPTA IV UDDYOTAKESARIN, YR. 5

FIRST PLATE

IV : XXIV. MAHAKOSALA HISTORICAL SOCIETY'S PLATES OF MAHĀBHAVAGUPTA IV UDDYOTAKESARIN, YR. 11

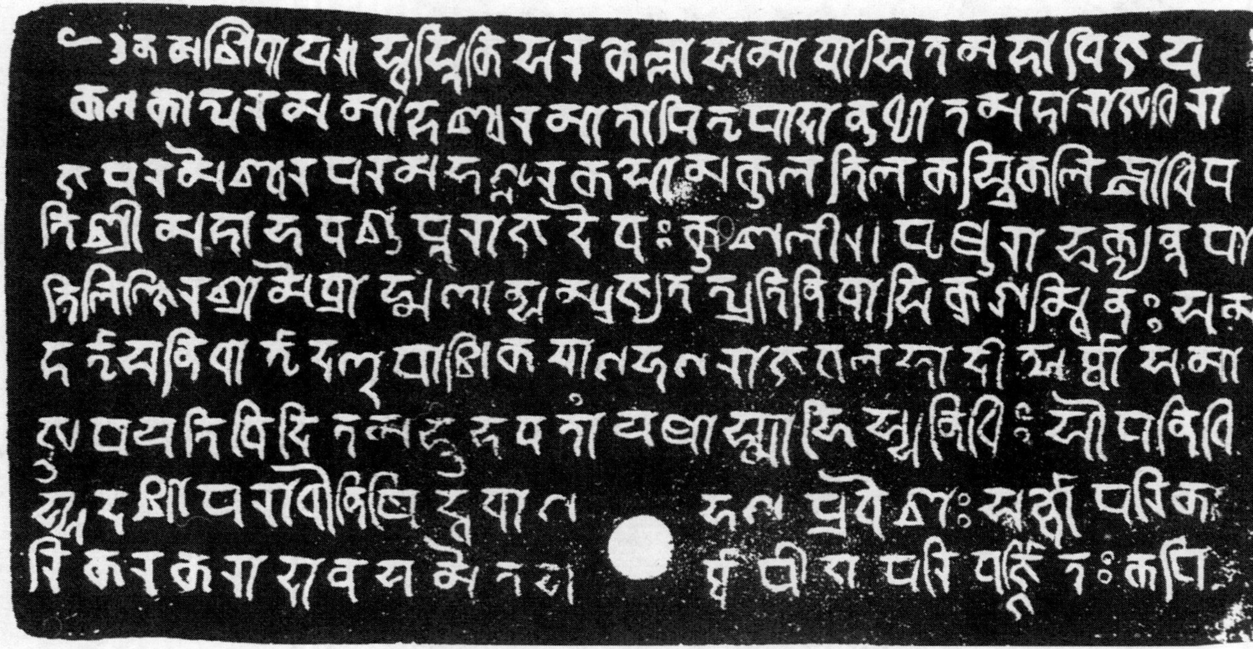

FIRST PLATE

PL.CLXXIII

SECOND PLATE : FIRST SIDE

PL.CLXXIV

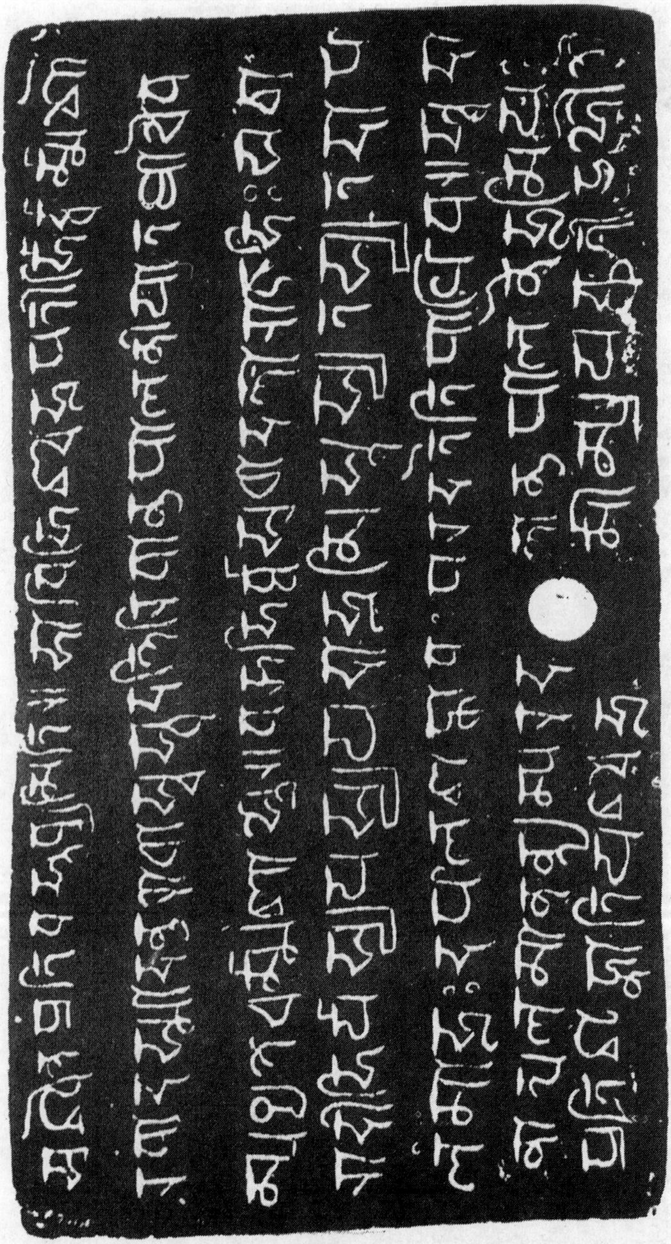

18

20

SECOND PLATE : SECOND SIDE

THIRD PLATE : FIRST SIDE

PL.CLXXVI

36 38

THIRD PLATE : SECOND SIDE

SEAL

IV:XXV. NAVAMUNI CAVE INSCRIPTION OF MAHĀBHAVAGUPTA IV UDDYOTAKESARIN, YR. 18

PL.CLXXVIII

IV : XXVI BRAHMEŚVARA TEMPLE INSCRIPTION OF MAHĀBHAVAGUPTA IV UDDYOTAKESARIN

IV:XXVII RATNAGIRI PLATES OF MAHĀŚIVAGUPTA V.

KARṆA, YR. 6

FIRST PLATE

PL.CLXXX

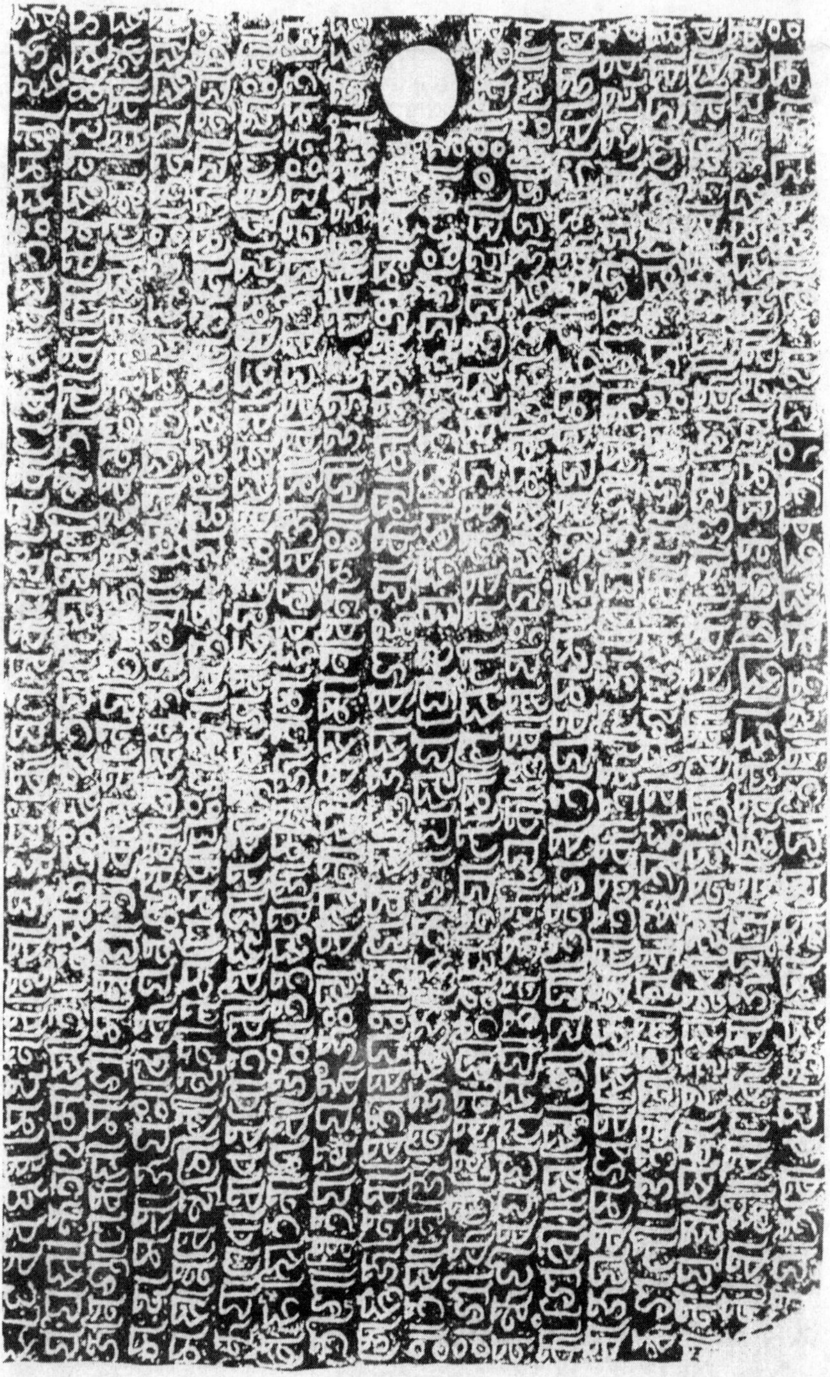

SECOND PLATE : FIRST SIDE

SECOND PLATE : SECOND SIDE

PL.CLXXXII

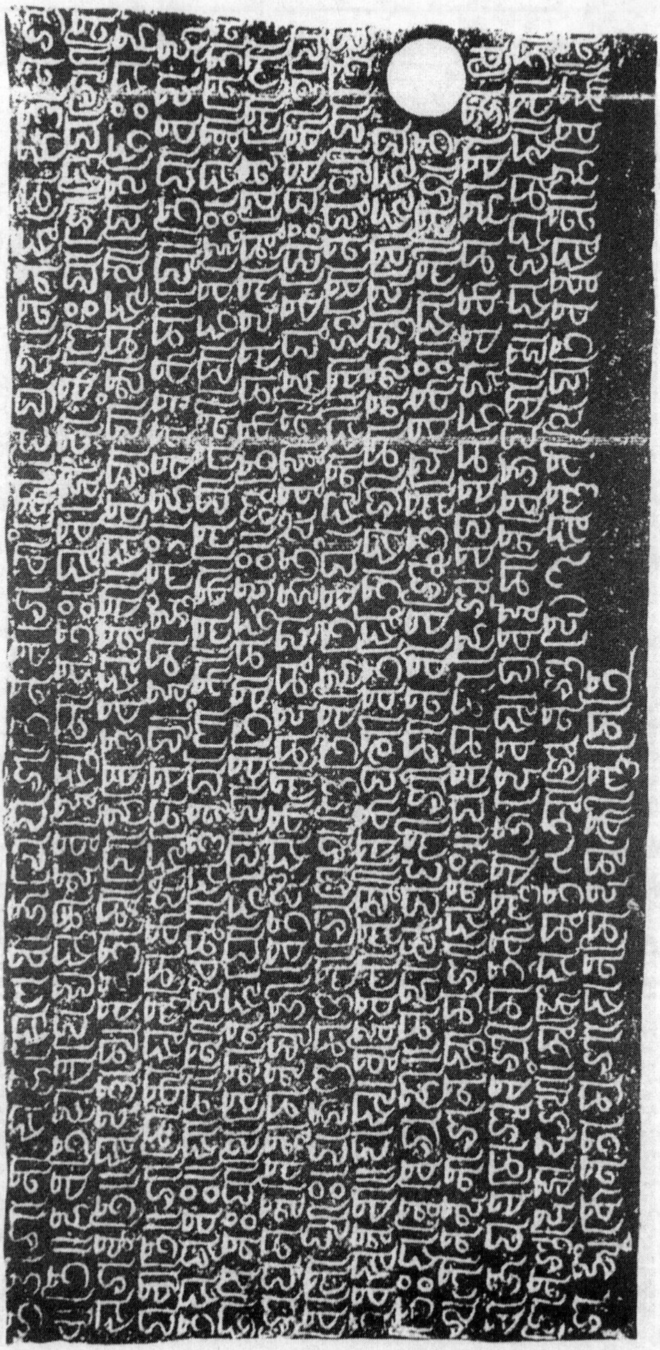

THIRD PLATE

IV:XXVIII KELGA PLATES OF SOMEŚVARADEVA, YR. 1

FIRST PLATE

SECOND PLATE : FIRST SIDE

PL.CLXXXV

SECOND PLATE : SECOND SIDE

PL.CLXXXVI

THIRD PLATE

IV : APP.I. BANPUR PLATES OF INDRARATHA, YR. 6

FIRST PLATE

PL.CLXXXVIII

SECOND PLATE : FIRST SIDE

SECOND PLATE : SECOND SIDE

PL.CXC

THIRD PLATE

IV: APP. II. A STRAY PLATE OF UDDYOTAKESARIN FROM MAHADA

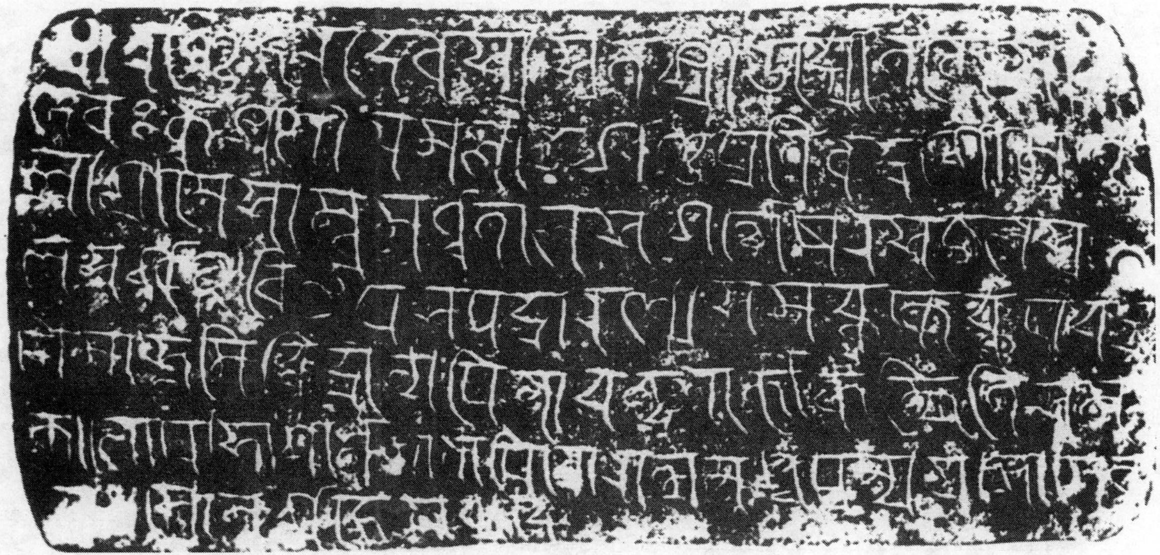

FIRST PLATE

PL.CXCII

SECOND SIDE

APP. IV. A STRAY PLATE OF A SOMAVAMŚIN OR TELUGU-CODA GRANT FROM KELGA

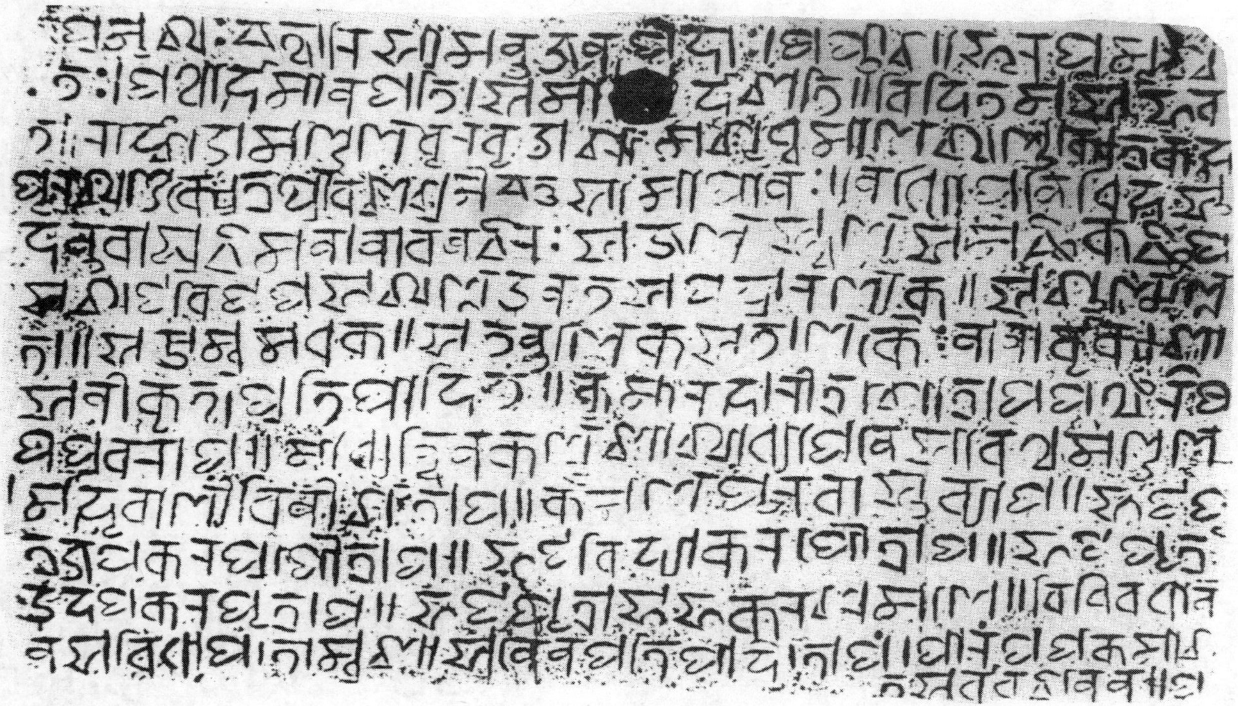

FIRST SIDE

PL.CXCIV

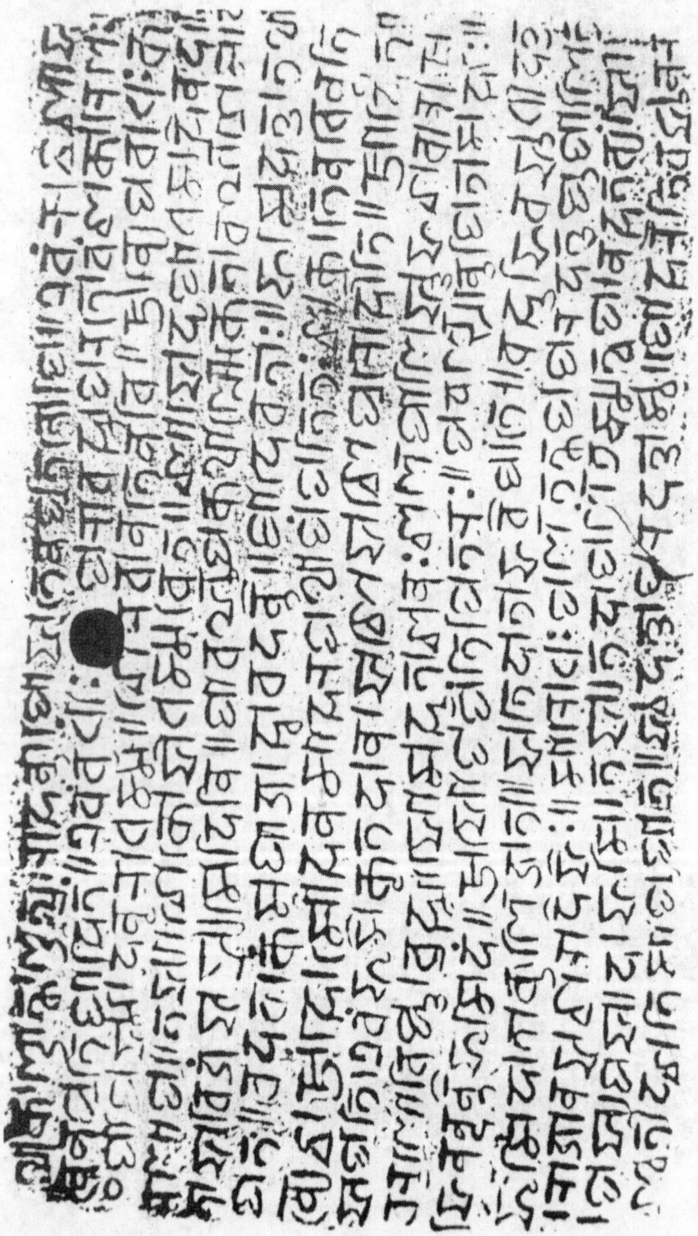

SECOND SIDE

SUPPLEMENTARY INSCRIPTIONS

SUPPL. I. SAMBALPUR UNIVERSITY MUSEUM
PLATES OF MAHĀBHAVAGUPTA I JANAMEJAYA, YR. 23

FIRST PLATE

PL.CXCVIII

SECOND PLATE : FIRST SIDE

SECOND PLATE : SECOND SIDE

PL.CC

THIRD PLATE : FIRST SIDE

THIRD PLATE : SECOND SIDE

SUPPL. II. DEGAON PLATES OF MAHABHAVAGUPTA I JANAMEJAYA

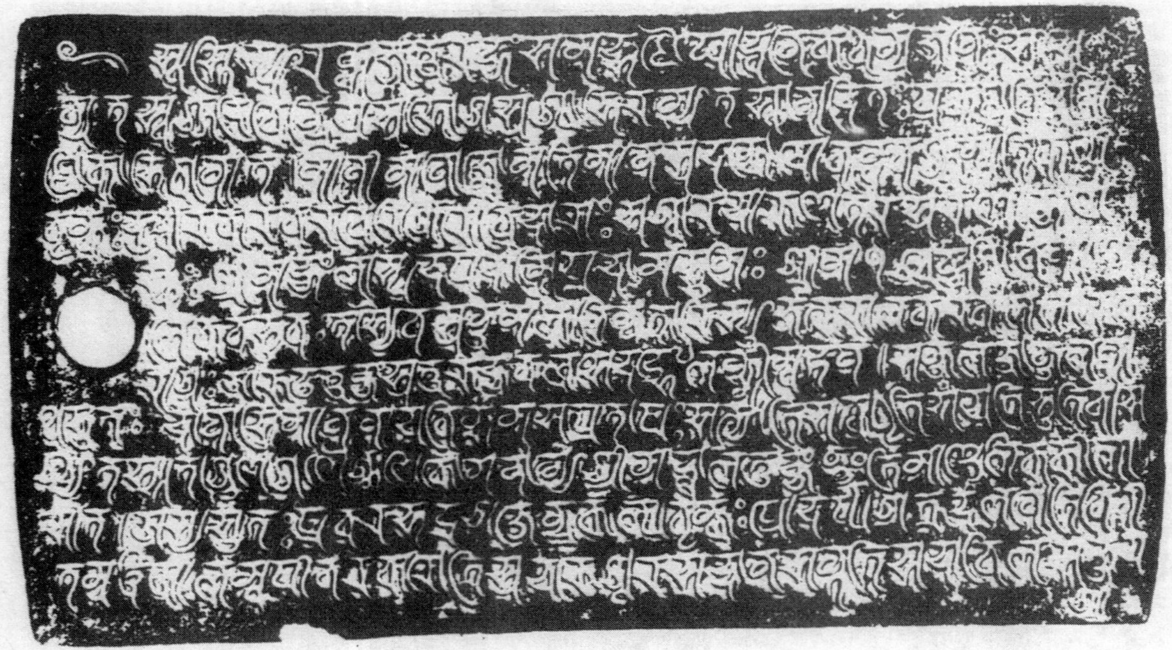

FIRST PLATE

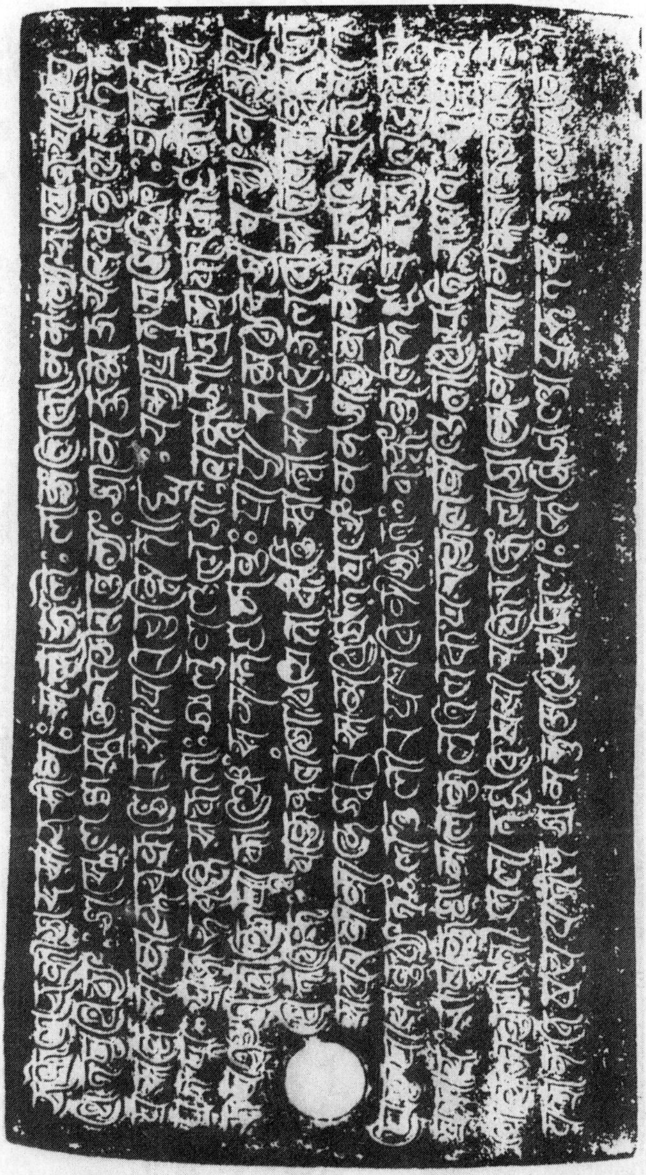

SECOND PLATE : FIRST SIDE

PL.CCIV

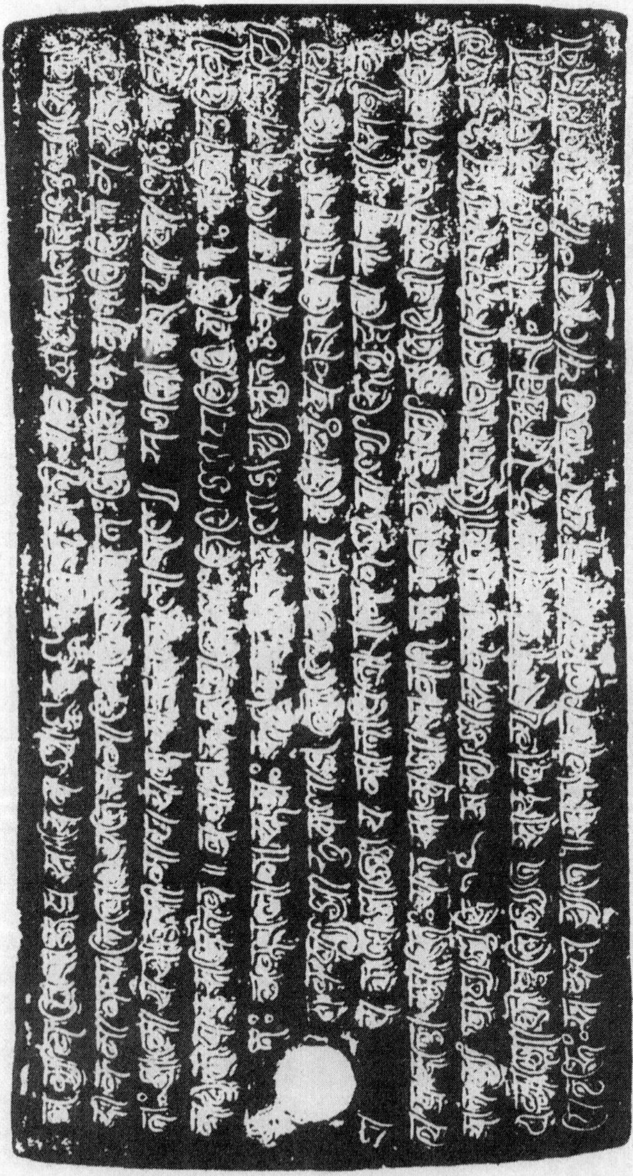

SECOND PLATE : SECOND SIDE

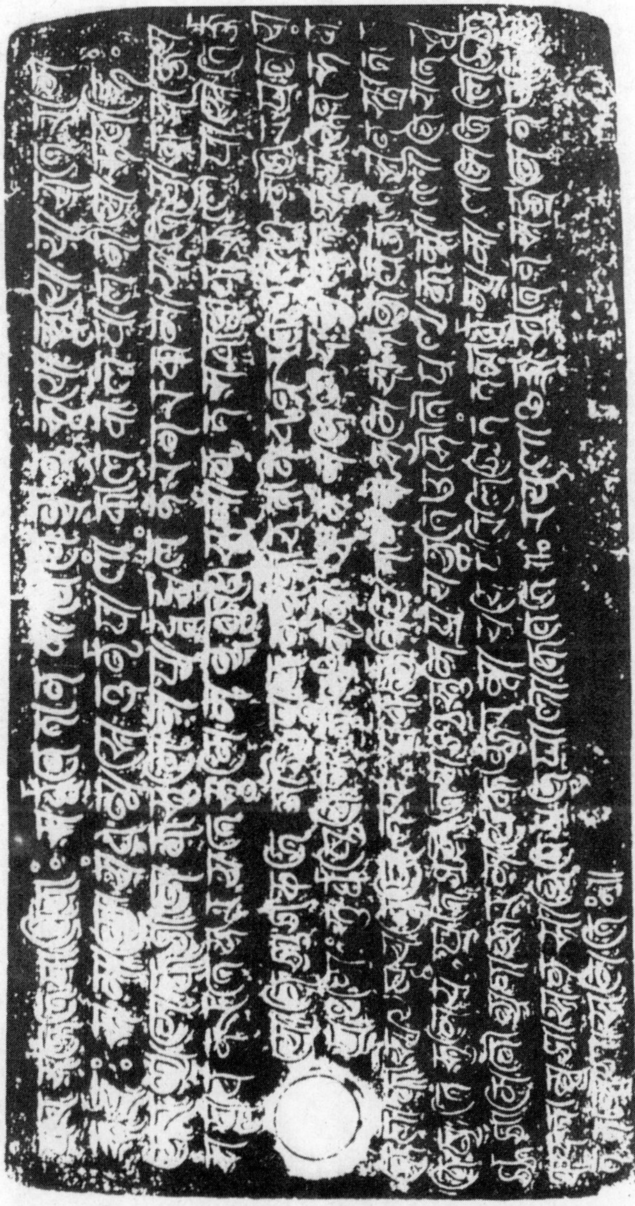

THIRD PLATE

PL.CCVI

SEAL

SUPPL. III SANKHAMERI PLATES OF MAHABHAVAGUPTA IV
UDDYOTAKESARIN, YR. 4

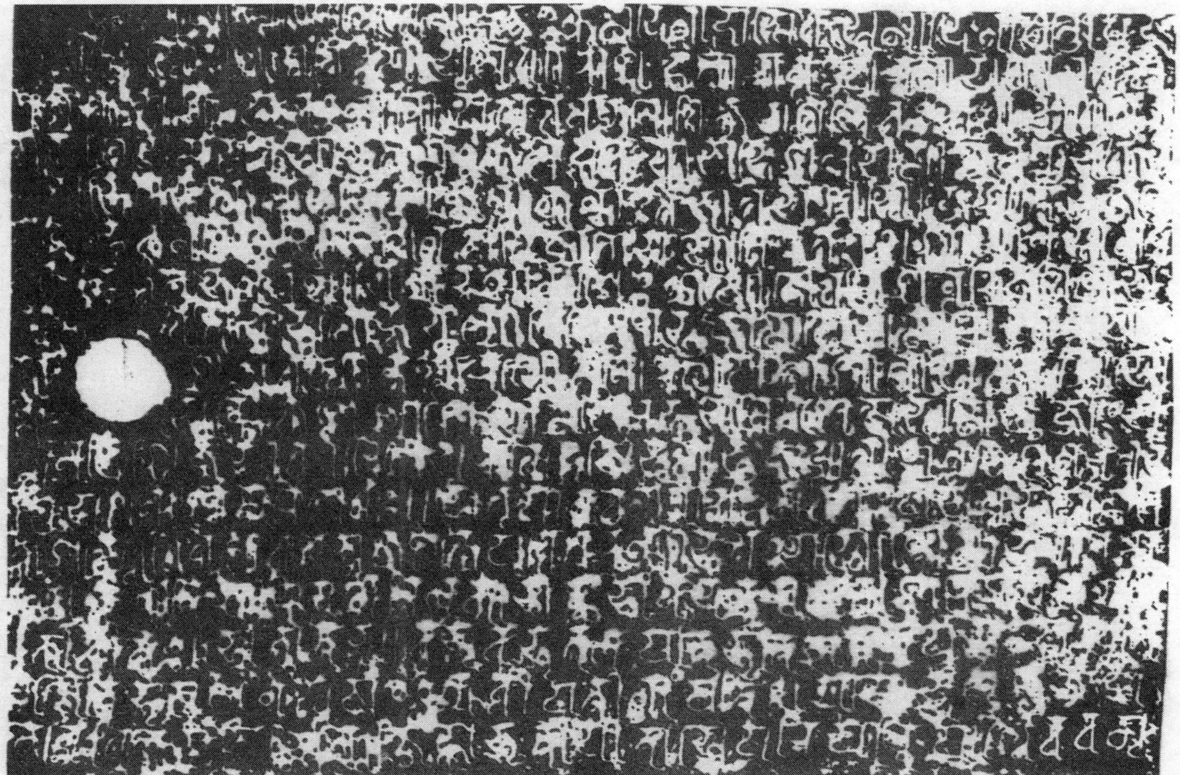

FIRST PLATE

PL.CCVIII

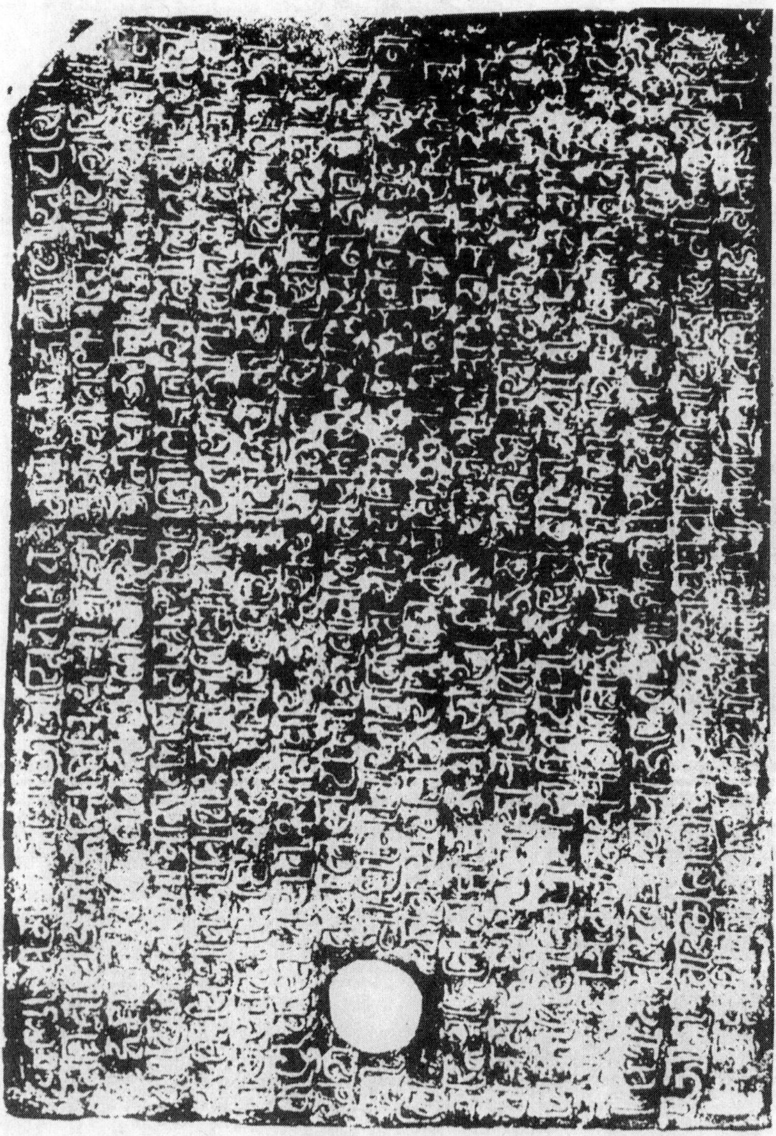

SECOND PLATE : FIRST SIDE

SECOND PLATE : SECOND SIDE

PL.CCX

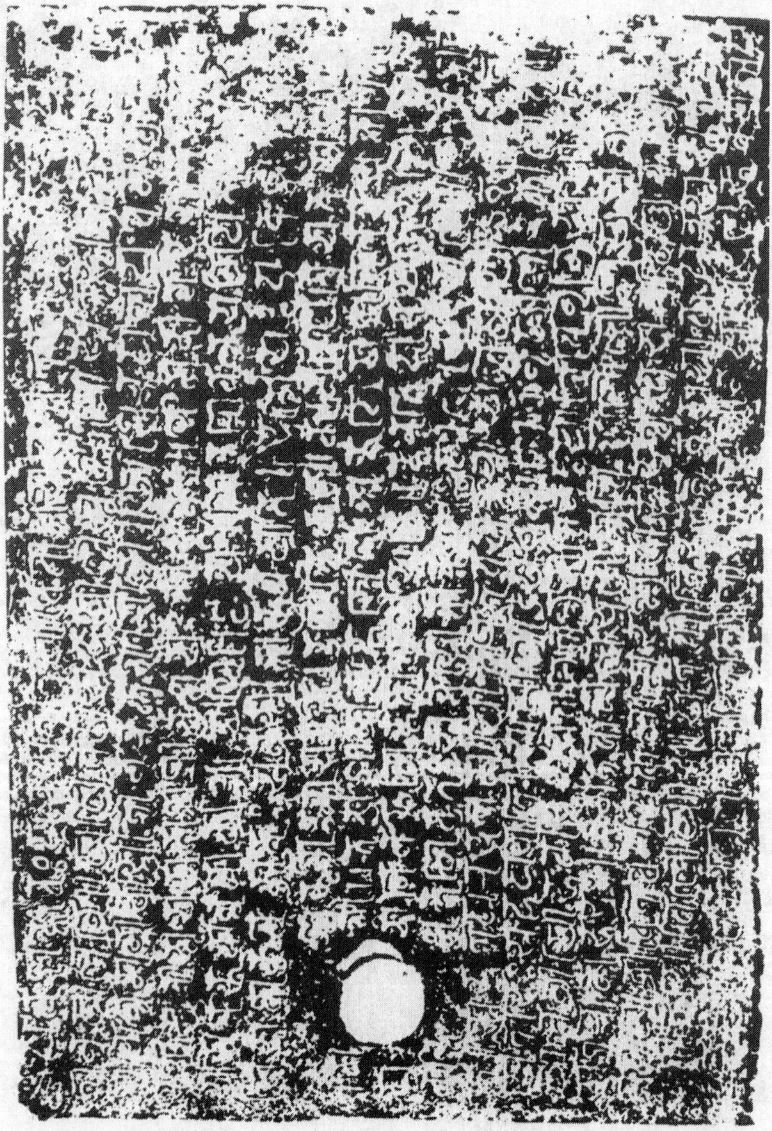

THIRD PLATE : FIRST SIDE

PL.CCXI

THIRD PLATE : SECOND SIDE

PL.CCXII

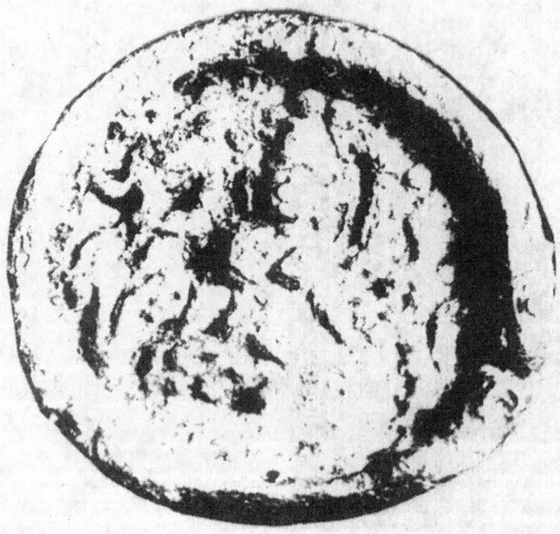

SEAL

SUPPL. IV. NUAPATNA PLATES OF MAHĀŚIVAGUPTA IV
JANAMEJAYA, YR. 5

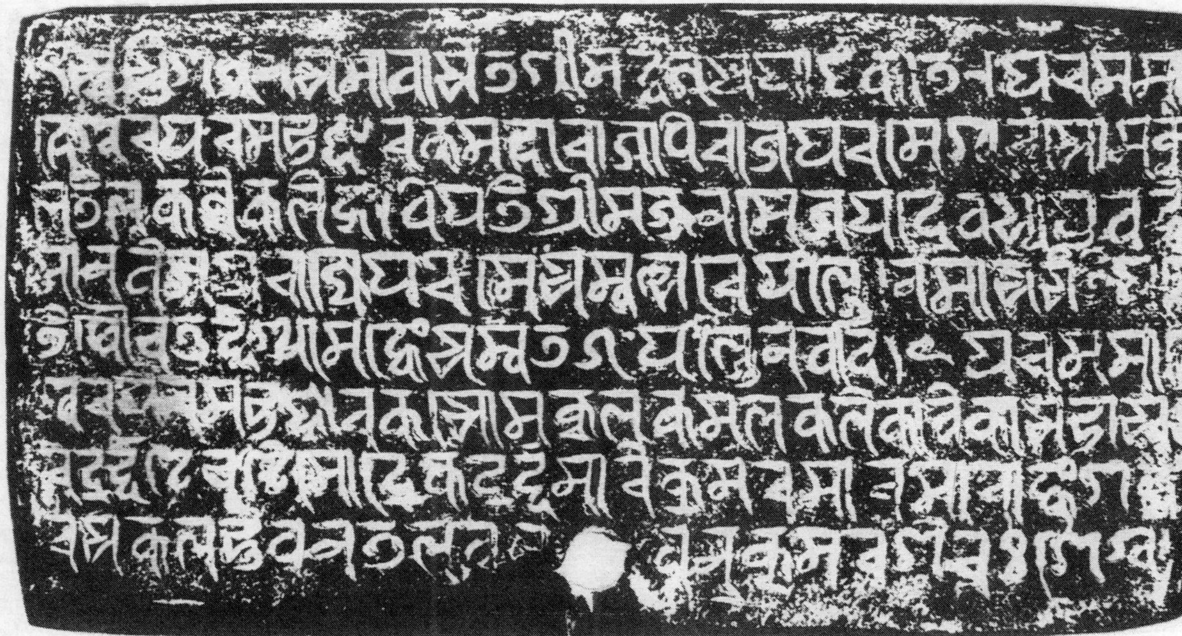

FIRST PLATE

PL.CCXIV

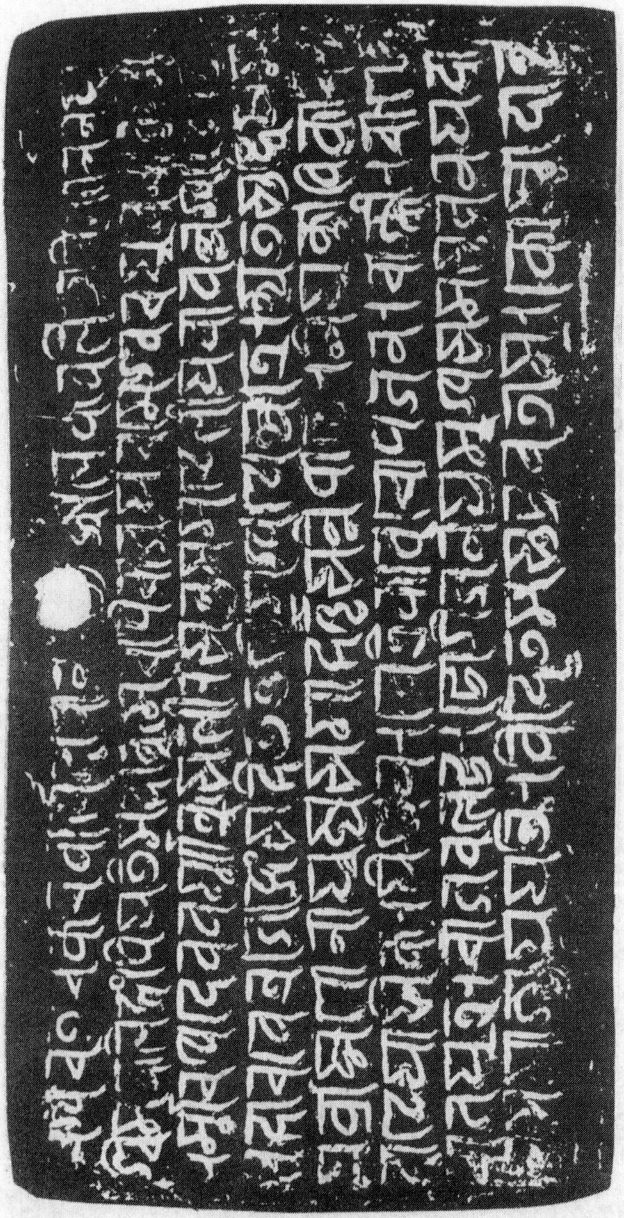

SECOND PLATE : FIRST SIDE

PL.CCXV

SECOND PLATE : SECOND SIDE

PL.CCXVI

THIRD PLATE : FIRST SIDE

THIRD PLATE : SECOND SIDE

SUPPL. V. KAMALPUR PLATES OF MAHĀŚIVAGUPTA V
KARṆA, YR. 4

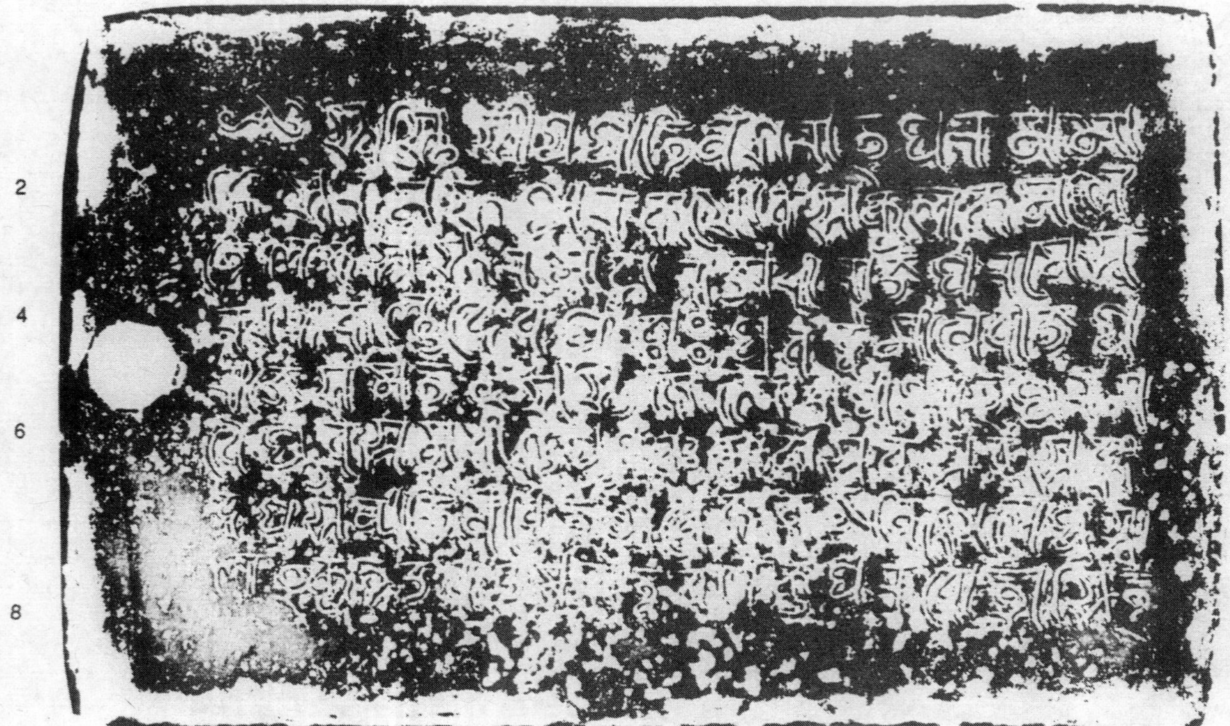

FIRST PLATE

PL.CCXIX

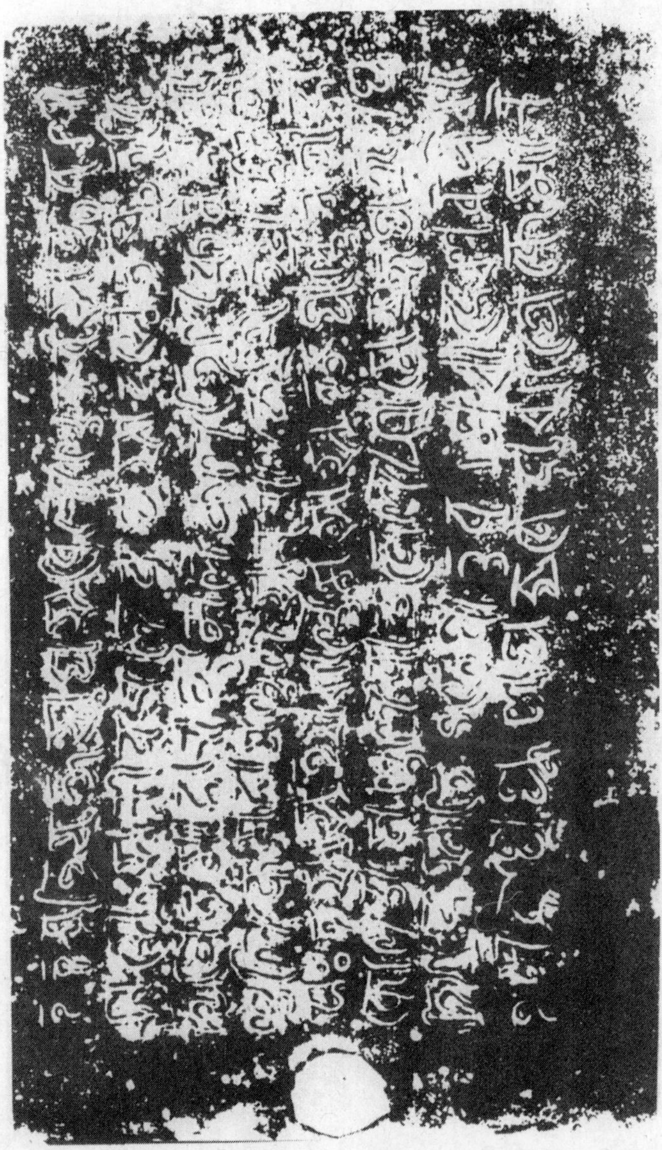

SECOND PLATE : FIRST SIDE

PL.CCXX

18 20 22 24

SECOND PLATE : SECOND SIDE

PL.CCXXI

25 28 30

THIRD PLATE